WORK AND AUTHORITY IN INDUSTRY

A contribution from the research program of the Institute
of Industrial Relations of the University of California, Berkeley.

WORK AND AUTHORITY

Ideologies of Management in the Course

IN INDUSTRY

of Industrialization

by Reinhard Bendix

UNIVERSITY OF CALIFORNIA PRESS
BERKELEY, LOS ANGELES, LONDON

Copyright © 1956 by John Wiley & Sons, Inc.
Chapter 7, "Industrialization, Ideologies, and Social Structure," is copyright © 1959 by the American Sociological Association
Introduction copyright © 1974 by the Regents of the University of California

First California Edition, 1974
California Paperback Edition, 1974

ISBN: 0–520–02628–4 (paper-bound)
       0–520–02473–7 (cloth-bound)
Library of Congress Catalog Card Number: 73–78553

Printed in the United States of America

Foreword

In the relatively brief span of years since Bendix' *Work and Authority in Industry* was first published, the problems to which it is addressed have become of even more compelling interest than they were in 1956. With the emergence of many new nations in Africa, the growing concern over the future of democracy in Latin America, the continuing manifestations of political instability in the Middle East, and the recent attack of Communist China on India, the problems of the underdeveloped parts of the world have increasingly occupied the headlines. And the one thing, above all others, that the underdeveloped countries seem to have in common is an intense aspiration toward industrialization.

The difficulties involved in converting an agrarian population into an efficient industrial work force have come to be widely recognized as a central problem of industrialization. Is a prolonged period of industrial conflict an inevitable accompaniment of the process, as in nineteenth century England? Under what conditions is industrial conflict likely to breed revolution? How does the prognosis differ for those countries that proceed along socialist lines and those that rely heavily on free private enterprise?

That a number of different patterns of labor-management relations may emerge in the developing countries has come to be generally accepted by social scientists, as has the notion that more intensive study of the experience of the industrial nations may provide valuable clues to likely patterns of relationships. But Bendix was one of the first to see that it was not enough to study the rise of the labor movement in the nineteenth century, as so many previous studies had done. Instead, he set out to analyze the various ways in which the entreprencurial class had responded to the challenge of creating, and later managing, an industrial work force in several widely differing types of industrial societies. His scholarly and penetrating re-examination of an aspect of economic history that had been largely taken for granted has now become something of a classic and has been followed by a number of other studies of managerial attitudes and ideologies in both developed and underdeveloped countries. Moreover, his central notion, that the behavior of the capitalist class or the country's "elite" may be even more important than the behavior of the working class in determining the course of events, is now widely accepted.

Bendix' study was one of a group of research projects conducted at the Institute of Industrial Relations as part of the Inter-University Study of the Labor Problem in Economic Development, which was carried on at Harvard, Princeton, the Massachusetts Institute of Technology, the University of Chicago, and the University of California (Berkeley) under a large grant from the Ford Foundation. Several of the scholars who participated in that project, including Bendix, are now members of the Research and Training Group in Comparative Developmental Studies, which was formed in the fall of 1961 under the auspices of the Institute of Industrial Relations, with the assistance of a grant from the Carnegie Corporation. Members of the group include about a dozen distinguished faculty members from the Departments of Anthropology, Business Administration, Economics, History, Political Science, and Sociology, all of whom are engaged in research on the problems of developing societies.

ARTHUR M. ROSS
Director, Institute of Industrial
Relations
University of California

January, 1963

Preface

The social sciences involve controversy and passion because the questions they deal with are of intense concern to many. A social scientist's preface to his work is, therefore, appropriately an implicit plea for understanding and detachment. It is my hope that this book contributes to our understanding, and I have made an effort to achieve detachment. But I want to make it quite clear that this hope and effort stem from an intense concern of my own, which I have in common with most of my readers.

Constitutional guarantees of personal rights and a heightened interest in individual emotions and personal growth developed in Western Europe and in the United States a short hundred and fifty years ago. This emergence of modern individualism coincided with the development of modern industry in the course of which an ever increasing number of individuals became subject to the strict and impersonal discipline of factory or business office. The subordination of the many had not been a central issue of intellectual controversy as long as custom or traditional authority prevailed more or less unchallenged. But the humane aspirations of the Enlightenment tended to challenge the new subordination to an industrial way of life, and the human problems of an industrial civilization became a matter of controversy from its inception. All the themes of that controversy are contained in a famous passage, written by Alexis de Tocqueville.

> When a workman is unceasingly and exclusively engaged in the fabrication of one thing, he ultimately does his work with singular dexterity;

but at the same time he loses the general faculty of applying his mind to the direction of the work. He every day becomes more adroit and less industrious; so that it may be said of him that in proportion as the workman improves, the man is degraded. . . .

In proportion as it becomes more manifest that the productions of manufactures are by so much the cheaper and better as the manufacture is larger and the amount of capital employed more considerable, wealthy and educated men come forward to embark in manufactures, which were heretofore abandoned to poor or ignorant handicraftsmen . . . Thus at the very time at which the science of manufactures lowers the class of workmen, it raises the class of masters. . . .

The manufacturer asks nothing of the workman but his labor; the workman expects nothing from him but his wages. The one contracts no obligation to protect nor the other to defend, and they are not permanently connected either by habit or by duty. The [manufacturing] aristocracy rarely settles in the midst of the manufacturing population which it directs; the object is not to govern that population, but to use it. An aristocracy thus constituted can have no great hold upon those whom it employs; . . . it first impoverishes and debases the men who serve it and then abandons them to be supported by the charity of the public.[1]

As the art of manufacture improves, the artisan recedes; as the masses are lowered, the masters are raised; and no human bond exists between employers and employed. This indictment of industrial civilization was written by a moderate conservative in 1835. It became a major theme in the lifework of Karl Marx. And it has been reiterated throughout the nineteenth and twentieth centuries by writers of radical and of conservative persuasion. The paradox is that these views of industry and of the relation between employers and workers have not been a reflection of experience, but the impassioned outpourings by men of ideas who reacted imaginatively to conditions of factory work with which they were not intimately familiar. The critique of industry tended, therefore, to project the disquiet and dissatisfactions of intellectuals upon a prototype of "the" industrial worker, who either longed for a return to the imagined emotional warmth of the "good old days" or for the creative satisfactions of individual workmanship and collective participation. As in other falsehoods there is a little truth in these perceptions, but it is not enough to outweigh the romantic imagery of the industrial worker as an embodiment of the purely human which has been suppressed by greedy men and by inhuman machinery. This perspective is misleading since it applies to industrial civilization as a whole—the ideal images and the critical judgments which were evoked by the impact of industrialization in its early phase.

[1] Alexis de Tocqueville, *Democracy in America* (New York: Vintage Books, 1954), II, pp. 168–71.

The present work seeks to correct these distortions of the past by looking at the relations between employers and workers with the eyes of those who have sought to defend and advance the development of industry. The division of labor and the impersonality of industrial relations have elicited responses from the leaders of industry and their spokesmen, not only from the critics of industrialization. This book deals with ideologies of management which seek to justify the subordination of large masses of men to the discipline of factory work and to the authority of employers. Such ideas appeal to men of action, and I have taken care to interpret the evolving problems of industrialization from their point of view. Yet sociological analysis also goes beyond the ken of the participants and other aspects of the empirical evidence. It must always make use of questions and concepts which are not themselves derived from the "facts." In this way implications and relationships come into view which the participants either fail to notice or interpret in a manner that itself forms part of the evidence examined in this study. Such a gain in understanding is obtained by the analyst because he is not involved in action himself and he can, therefore, apply alternative perspectives to the experience of those who are.

My choice of industrial relations as the focus of this study is based on a number of reasons. Ideas concerning work, the authority of employers, and the reasons for subordination form the ideological framework in which the day-to-day operations of economic enterprises are conceived. Hence, they reflect and affect the relations into which men enter in order to make a living and in order to produce the material goods and services on which the industrial way of life depends. These ideas touch upon the life of everyman, his freedom and his well-being; that is what makes them important.

Subordination and discipline are indispensable in economic enterprises, but only the critics of industry referred to this central fact, while the various ideologies of management have at best treated it obliquely. In the Western world the spokesmen of industrial advance have been vociferous in their praise of individual effort, but they referred to the need for subordination in economic enterprises only indirectly by defending the right of the successful man to do as he wished with his "own." In Soviet Russia the spokesmen of industrial advance have been equally vociferous in their praise of collective effort and ownership. They have justified the need for subordination in economic enterprises by the claim that it was not what it seemed, that all workers are owners and, hence, subject to their own authority as represented by the dictatorial party. These equivocations have become an issue in a worldwide conflict of ideas in which the freedom of the individual is at stake. But freedom is not a synonym for the absence of subordination, nor can one take the ideological equivocations concerning freedom at their face value. Another purpose of this book is, therefore, to interpret the differences of fact and ideology between a totalitarian and a nontotalitarian form of subordination in economic enterprises.

Large-scale economic enterprises are not only the workaday environment of the many, they do not only pose critical questions concerning the subordination of the worker in the industrial civilizations of the modern world; they are also significant because they are our most effective instruments for getting the work of the world done. Recent contributions to the sociological analysis of industry have tended to emphasize the importance of psychological factors and informal group relations. The present study views industry as more or less planned and more or less efficient organizations for the production of commodities or the provision of services. It explores the historical and social preconditions which make such organizations possible and which affect their characteristic operations.

These considerations also help to explain certain characteristics of the study itself. It will be seen that I do not share the preference of some social scientists for facts which are untarnished by previous scrutiny. Since I deal with the ideas and actions of men who are prominent by virtue of their leadership in economic enterprises, the facts referred to are already well known. But familiar facts are often not fully understood in terms of their implications and consequences. The purpose of the present study is to contribute to a better understanding of what is generally known about work and authority in industry. I have sought to accomplish this by examining the ideologies of management and their social setting in terms of the twin concepts of "social class" and of "bureaucracy."

"Social class" refers to the universal tendency of men who are similarly situated socially and economically to develop common ideas and to engage in collective actions. "Bureaucracy" refers to the universal tendency of men who are employed in hierarchical organizations to obey directives and to identify their own interests and ideas with the organization and with all those persons in it who share this identification. These are rival tendencies of action. The common ideas and actions of a social class arise from the joining of individuals on the basis of their related but more or less different interests; the common ideas and actions of a bureaucracy arise from the authoritative establishment of identical interests among individuals whose ideas and interests differed prior to their appointment. Employers, entrepreneurs, and managers typically act in such a way as to combine these tendencies. To safeguard and advance their interests they will join with others like them in the collective actions of a social class. But within each of their separate economic enterprises they will use their authority to have the workers identify their ideas and interests with the enterprise rather than with each other. Ideologies of management are attempts by leaders of enterprises to justify the privilege of voluntary action and association for themselves, while imposing upon all subordinates the duty of obedience and the obligation to serve their employers to the best of their ability.

I should add that my approach to the study of ideologies and of management has been prompted by my desire to gain a better understanding of the interrelation between ideas and actions. I was dissatisfied with the prevailing tendency to examine this interrelation where it was most elusive rather than where it was obvious. Originally, this tendency stemmed from the Marxist contention that in any historical period all facets of a society's intellectual life form a superstructure which depends ultimately upon changes in the organization of production. This contention was advanced as a striking challenge to the prevailing approach which treated the history of ideas as a self-contained development, in which disembodied thinkers spun their ideas influenced solely by the ideas of others like themselves. Against this perspective it was plausible to emphasize that men of ideas are also men of flesh and blood, whose every intellectual pursuit was related to the society in which they lived. But this plausible emphasis was quickly turned into an overemphasis. It was denied that ideas could undergo a more or less autonomous development, and the search was on for the discovery of ever more elusive societal influences upon intellectual life. Ideas were neglected, on the other hand, if they were explicitly related to social action and thus more or less revealed the promptings of self-interest. Yet such ideas were worthy of serious attention, for they influence our lives and they are not at all self-explanatory, even if they lack aesthetic or philosophic depth. The ideologies of management in particular afford us an opportunity to examine the interrelations between ideas and actions under conditions where these interrelations are more or less apparent rather than a matter of inference.

Studies of ideologies imply a neglect of persons and private beliefs. I shall treat entrepreneurs and managers as "members" of a social group by virtue of their position in economic enterprises and by virtue of the common problems and experiences to which such positions expose them.

And I shall attribute to this group ideologies of management which have been articulated in response to the logic of authority relationships in economic enterprises. While the publicly expressed ideas of a social group frequently reflect a range of views rather than a single, fully developed ideological position, even this range of views will *not* do justice to the diversity of personal beliefs or attitudes of the group members. As I see it, this is not a serious defect, dictated though it is by the questions I have asked and by the nature of the materials available for study. For the attitudes of individuals do not become the public opinion of a group merely by the process of addition. Instead, public opinion is formed through a constant process of formulation and reformulation by which spokesmen identified with a social group seek to articulate what they sense to be its shared understandings. A study of ideologies deals with these formulations and reformulations and hence with those attitudes which have proved strong enough to gain adherents.

REINHARD BENDIX

March, 1956

Contents

Acknowledgments

This book is dedicated to my father, Dr. jur. Ludwig Bendix (1877–1954), under whose guidance I received my initiation to scholarship and intellectual discipline; he first introduced me to the writings of Karl Marx, Wilhelm Dilthey, Georg Simmel, Max Weber, and Karl Mannheim. My debt to him is great for from him I learned the art of asking questions. He read early drafts of some chapters in this book, but he did not live to see the finished manuscript.

This study owes its inception to conversations with my friend and colleague, Lloyd H. Fisher (deceased 1953), Professor of Political Science at the University of California, Berkeley, and Research Director of the Institute of Industrial Relations. Fisher gave to this study all the stimulation and encouragement an author can hope for. His premature death left a conspicuous void in the scholarly community, and it deprived me of his friendship and intellectual counsel halfway through the work which he had helped to initiate.

I am indebted to Clark Kerr, Chancellor of the University of California, Berkeley, and formerly Director of the Institute of Industrial Relations. His encouragement and unfailing interest have accompanied the study throughout, and I am grateful to him for his willingness to write an introduction despite his crowded schedule.

Several colleagues gave me the benefit of their critical appraisal. To Dr. Ernst Richert of the Institut für Politische Wissenschaft, Berlin, I am obliged for his critical reading of Chapter 6; to Mr. William H. Whyte, Jr., of *Fortune* for his suggestions regarding Chapter 5; and to Professor

Wilbert Moore, Princeton University, Professor Seymour M. Lipset and Professor William Peterson, University of California, Berkeley, for their comments and suggestions on the book as a whole.

A number of Graduate Research Assistants at the Institute of Industrial Relations, University of California, Berkeley, worked on various phases of the study under my direction. I should like to express my appreciation to William T. Delany, Julie Eagan, Cesar Grana, Frank H. Howton, and Eugene Powell. A special note of thanks is due to Gaston Rimlinger, who assisted me during the three years that the writing of the book was in progress.

Financial aid from the Interuniversity Study of Labor Problems in Economic Development is gratefully acknowledged. The study was facilitated also through an arrangement with the Institute of Industrial Relations at the University of California, which enabled me to devote a substantial portion of my time to research. During 1953–1954 I received a Fulbright research fellowship which enabled me to make the studies necessary for Chapter 6 of the book, and which made it possible for me to devote an entire year to writing.

The various revisions of the manuscript were typed by Jeanette Podvin of the Institute of Industrial Relations, and I am indebted to her for her unfailing patience and helpfulness.

A word may be added concerning documentation. The facts presented will be familiar to specialists, and references other than direct quotations have been held to a minimum. In Chapters 2 and 3 I have relied upon the literature on English and Russian social history which was readily available to me. Given the scope of what is available, I do not doubt that there are important works which I have missed; in studies of this kind there comes a time also when further citations yield diminishing returns. In Chapters 4, 5, and 6 the materials presented are based on independent investigation, though of course I have made use wherever possible of the work of other scholars. In connection with Chapter 6 I should mention also that I had access to the unpublished materials of the Archiv Friesdorf, Bad Godesberg, Germany, which provided me with indispensable background information on East Germany. I am indebted to Dr. Werner Leimbach, the Director of the Archiv, for his permission to examine these materials.

All translations are my own, unless indicated otherwise.

REINHARD BENDIX

Introduction

Work and Authority in Industry was written in the early 1950's and published in 1956.* Out of print for several years, the book is now republished through the good offices of the University of California Press. This introduction (or should I say postscript?) gives me an opportunity to state in brief the thematic sequence of my work to date. Republication also allows me a personal reassessment of the intellectual choices I have made, and of their moral implications.

In Part I of this introduction, I indicate how I came to write this book and the several thematic levels on which it can be read. Part II puts the study within the framework of Max Weber's typology of domination. Since my emphasis is on the study of long-range trends, I also try to assess how historical changes since

* Published under the auspices of the Institute of Industrial Relations, University of California, Berkeley, the book appeared in hardcover with a Foreword by Professor Authur Ross and an Introduction by then Chancellor Clark Kerr. The American publisher was John Wiley & Sons, Inc. and the English publisher was Chapman & Hall, Ltd. In 1963, the book appeared as a paperback in the Torchbook series of Harper & Row, Publishers. In this paperback-edition Chancellor Kerr's introduction and the original concluding chapter were omitted. This last chapter was replaced by the text of my MacIver lecture, "Industrialization, Ideologies and Social Structure," which had appeared originally in the American Sociological Review, XXIV (October, 1959), pp. 613–623. The present republication replaces all introductory matter, including my own original preface, with this new introduction, but retains the MacIver lecture as the concluding chapter. The book is unchanged in all other respects.

In writing this new introduction I have benefited from the critical comments and suggestions of Professors Gregory Grossman, Kenneth Jowitt, David Riesman, and Guenther Roth.

the 1950's may be seen from the vantage-point of this analysis. Part III deals with a reinterpretation of social protest in the era of industrialization. Part IV comments on the perspectives of *Work and Authority in Industry* and of *Nation-Building and Citizenship* in a more speculative vein along lines of inquiry in which I am engaged currently. And Part V attempts to state what my work has meant to me personally as well as intellectually.

I.

I begin with my M.A. dissertation, *The Rise and Acceptance of German Sociology* (1943) which was never published because it was too long, cumbersome and at crucial points unfinished. But in relation to my later work the thesis had a question worth noting. Written by a German refugee and in the midst of the war Hitler had unleashed, it asked a seemingly esoteric question. Taking sociology *grosso modo* as an attempt to approach social questions in a rational spirit, I wanted to know under what circumstances such an approach had been articulated within the German tradition and had eventually achieved institutional recognition in the universities. I do not think I answered the question. But the circumstantial, institutional, and—yes—irrational foundations of rationality haunt me still. It is a question now being debated with regard to the natural sciences, at long last. For me it was a question that had grown out of a reading of Nietzsche and out of my devotion to my father, a lawyer during the Weimar Republic who had sought to defend the rational core of the law by means of a head-on confrontation with its institutional and psychological value-ambiguities. My father called this complex of questions the "multiple interpretability of facts and legal norms" (*die Mehrdeutigkeit von Tatsachen und Rechtssaetzen*). Since I had learned much from him, it was natural for me to begin my career by investigating an analogous problem.[1]

But in the circumstances of the day esoterica were not enough. I had escaped from the holocaust, but millions of others had perished—victims not merely of personal tyranny but of a structure of authority bent on destruction. Hundreds of thousands had done the direct bidding of one man's commands (millions had followed suit) and in the process they had created a bastion of barbarism in the center of Europe. In this setting, why had government officials become such willing tools in the destruction of civilization? In Germany, officials had made a public display of their impartiality and legal rectitude. Yet under Hitler they had gone beyond mere compliance in their eagerness to follow the dictates of a criminal regime. By contrast, American civil servants at the federal level made

---

[1] A more detailed presentation of my father's work is contained in my introduction to Ludwig Bendix, *Zur Psychologie der Urteilstaetigkeit des Berufsrichters* (Neuwied: Hermann Luchterhand, 1968), pp. 17-66. A shortened English version of that introduction appeared as Reinhard Bendix, "A Memoir of my Father," *Canadian Review of Sociology and Anthropology*, II (1965), pp. 1-18.

few claims and were accorded little public recognition. Yet, despite the traditions of the spoils system and the short period of civil service reforms they appeared, on the whole, to act responsibly under the law. The questions implied in this contrast were too diffuse to fit within the empirical framework required of a Ph.D. dissertation in Sociology. So I divided my work between a broader historical discussion of the conditions of administrative rationality and a narrower, empirical inquiry into the social origins and careers of a sample of higher Federal administrators. Uneasily held together as these two parts of *Higher Civil Servants in American Society* (1949) remained, the study still exemplified that concern with the social conditioning of ideas and with the presuppositions of rationality with which I had begun.

At the same time, I had to recognize the disparity between the expectations of my teachers and peers in sociology and the penchant for a wider historical framework which derived from my German background. The impulse to write *Work and Authority in Industry* arose out of an effort to respond to that disparity. In a seemingly unrelated essay, *Social Science and the Distrust of Reason* (1951), I tried to wrestle with the dilemmas posed by the demand for empirical verification. Having studied at the University of Chicago in the waning years of the "Chicago School of Sociology," I recognized the validity of that demand. But having a penchant for seeing immediate experience in a larger context, I also recognized that this demand had intellectual antecedents and a significance which did not seem apparent to my American colleagues. From the very beginning of modern science exhortations had been voiced against the effects of wishful thinking, against the unwitting influence of our education and converse with others, against the distortions arising from our use of words and from fashionable systems of thought. Basing myself on the seminal work of Hans Barth (*Wahrheit und Ideologie*, 1945), I traced this concern with "idols of the mind" from Bacon to Freud. In the process I re-discovered that in social thought the growth of reason consisted to a considerable extent in an increased understanding of human fallibility. A sisyphean principle of uncertainty seemed to be at work. Our efforts to control bias always remained a step behind our discovery of new sources of bias—at any rate in the social sciences. In view of this historical record, an act of faith was required to continue the effort, a belief that further improvements in our methods would bring the desired control of bias. I thought this a "reasonable faith" and do so still, because no one knows what cannot be known. But it remains an act of faith and one that is peculiarly liable to spurious imitations of the natural sciences.[2]

---

[2] For a further discussion of these points see the essays in Part I of my book, *Embattled Reason* (New York: Oxford University Press, 1970) and the related debate with R. K. Merton in Edward A. Tiryakian, ed., *The Phenomenon of Sociology* (New York: Appleton-Century-Crofts, 1971), pp. 173-201.

At the time, it seemed important to me to go beyond the analysis of a dilemma. My 1951 essay had ended with the demand that methodological and substantive concerns should be balanced. Was this more than pious admonition? The only answer seemed to try and, after five years of work, the result was *Work and Authority in Industry*. There are several levels at which the book can be read, an important point in my view but certainly a drawback from the standpoint of methodological purism.

A study of managerial ideologies commended itself to me because I was dissatisfied with the prevailing tendency to look at ideas and actions where their interrelations were most elusive. (My own study of German sociology was a case in point.) Originally, the Marxist tradition had emphasized that men of ideas are also men of flesh and blood, whose every intellectual pursuit is related to the society in which they live. But this plausible emphasis was soon distorted. Even the most esoteric ideas were made into mere epiphenomena of the "material process of production," mere excrescences of the way in which men make their living. Thus, the relative automony of ideas was denied, even though the development of many scientific fields clearly showed considerable autonomy. (So, indeed, did Marxist theory itself.) At the same time, more mundane ideas were neglected just because they were directly related to social action and revealed the promptings of self-interest. Yet, ideas concerning work, the authority of employers, and the reasons for subordination (in short, ideologies of management) were worthy of serious attention. They are not at all self-explanatory and they affect the relations into which men enter in order to make a living. By reflecting the industrial way of life upon which goods and services depend, these ideas touch the life of every man, his freedom and his well-being. A study of ideas as weapons in the management of organizations could afford a better understanding of the relations between ideas and action. The analysis of organization and ideas had been my two main emphases before and it seemed natural to combine the two in this effort to relate empirical findings to a larger theoretical and historical perspective.

A second and continuing concern was the study of rationality. Large-scale economic enterprises are our most effective instruments for getting the work of the world done. In earlier essays, I had explored the conditions of rationality in bureaucratic organizations and the mutually exclusive assumptions with which they had been studied. Some scholars had looked upon such organizations in terms of their hierarchic efficiency. All authority and knowledge are concentrated at the top while commands are implemented by successively lower echelons in accord with a planned division of labor. To others, this formal model seemed entirely unrealistic. Their studies of psychological factors and informal group relations had sometimes brought them close to the view that planning and organization are futile. As Leo Tolstoy had stated this perspective in *War and Peace*, those who command cannot act, and those who act cannot think. It seemed to me then, as it does still, that the evidence is against both views. Between 1966 and 1973, American car manufacturers recalled approximately forty million cars for the correction of some mechanical error that had been discovered. One can marvel at several things: the sudden evidence that under a new law the error is not merely discovered but announced publicly, and that there is the psychological and organizational capacity to correct errors of such magnitude. Anyone with some memory of earlier conditions will not mistake this statement for a paeon to American efficiency. Why were such errors not discovered earlier? And why was there neither publicity nor correction of faulty designs before Ralph Nader and others forced American manufacturers to mend their ways? The record is mixed. What the "Prussian" approach to organization *as well as* Tolstoy and his modern followers seem to lack is a sense of proportion, an understanding that human achievements are proximate and must be judged by the weight of the evidence.

That sense of proportion is also missing in the third concern which bears on *Work and Authority in Industry*. Subordination to an industrial way of life had challenged the humane aspirations of the Enlightenment from the beginning. In my original preface I quoted an eloquent passage from Tocqueville's *Democracy in America* (1835) which stated the main themes of that indictment. As the art of manufacture improves, the artisan recedes; as the masters are raised, the masses are lowered; and no human bond exists between employers and employed. This indictment of industrial civilization was the *common* theme of conservative *and* radical critics which has been reiterated ever since the end of the eighteenth century. These views of industry and industrial relations were not a reflection of experience. Instead they were the impassioned outpourings of men of ideas who reacted imaginatively to conditions of factory work with which they were not intimately familiar. Their critique of industry tended to project the disquiet of intellectuals upon a prototype of "the" industrial worker, who longed for a return to the imagined emotional warmth of the "good old days" and for the creative satisfactions of individual workmanship and collective participation. There is a little truth in these perceptions, but it is not enough to outweigh the romantic imagery of the industrial worker as an embodiment of the purely human which has been suppressed by greedy men and inhuman machinery. Of course there are greedy men and routine work imposes great psychological burdens. But an anti-industrial imagery based on these truisms is at fault because it fails to think responsibly about the psychological burdens of alternative social structures, including other types of exploitation, greed, and the ravages of poverty.

Thus, the book was prompted in part by an effort to correct past distortions of both, rationality and exploitation. I decided to look at the relations between employers and workers with the eyes of those who promoted the development of industry. Leading entrepreneurs and their spokesmen seek to justify the subordination of men to the discipline of factory work and the authority of employers. Naturally, such ideas appeal to men of action and I take care to interpret the evolving problems of industrialization from their point of view. Yet, sociological analysis also goes beyond the ken of the participants, it always uses questions and concepts which are not themselves derived from their experience. The analyst is not involved in action himself and can, therefore, apply alternative perspectives to the experience of those who are. In this way implications and relationships come into view which the participants (or actors) fail to notice or interpret in a manner that itself forms part of the evidence. As it turned out, this was preeminently the case with justifications of authority.

Subordination and discipline are indispensable in economic enterprises. In the Western world, spokesmen of industrial advance were vociferous in their praise of individual effort and in defending the right of the successful man to manage his property as he saw fit. Ostensibly, these ideas vouchsafed the individualism of a capitalist economy, but in practice they were meaningless without the subordination of the many which gave very little room to the cultivation of individualism. In the Soviet Union, spokesmen of industrial advance were equally vociferous in their praise of collective ownership and effort. And they justified the need for subordination by the claim that all workers are owners and hence subject to their own authority as represented by the dictatorial party. These equivocations have become an issue in a worldwide conflict of ideas in which the freedom of the individual is at stake. Only two things seem certain. The equivocations concerning individual and collective ownership cannot be taken at face value; and individual freedom cannot be synonymous with the absence of subordination. Apparently, there are individualistic and collectivist forms of subordination in economic enterprises. Hence, another purpose of this book is to interpret the differences in fact and ideology between the structures of authority which determine these two types of subordination.

The contrast between individual and collective ownership also involves the distinction between social class and bureaucracy. Class refers to the tendency to develop common ideas and engage in collective action on the part of men who are similarly situated socially and economically. Bureaucracy refers to the tendency of men who are employed in hierarchical organizations to obey directives and identify their own interests with the manipulation of career opportunities in those organizations. These are rival tendencies of actions and ideas, though in practice they are combined in many ways.

Capitalist employers typically join with others like themselves in order to advance their common interests, though this does not preclude conflicts of interest. But within his own enterprise each employer will use his authority to have the workers identify themselves with that enterprise rather than with each other. In this context, ideologies of management are attempts by leaders of enterprises to justify the privilege of voluntary action and association for themselves, while imposing upon all subordinates the duty of obedience and of service to the best of their ability. In the ideal world of laissez-faire employers, the right to combine is theirs alone based on the rights of property-ownership. The worker's right to combine is usurpation, an illegitimate interference with the inalienable rights of property-owners.

The collectivist model starts from opposite assumptions. It does not depend upon the common social and economic experience of individuals to develop common ideas and hence engage in collective actions. Rather, it takes as given that individuals out there in society are divided by all kinds of ideas and interests. When these individuals join the organization, or are coopted by it, they must then leave their divergent interests behind and abide by the obligations which become theirs upon entry. Leaders of such organizations are well aware that the pull of private interest does not cease with entry; the achievement of organizational goals is constantly jeopardized by the individual's efforts (after entry) to manipulate the hierarchic opportunity-structure to his own advantage. Accordingly, ideologies of management typically hypostatize a transcendent collectivity (working class, race, nation, etc.) to which *all* members of the organization are subservient. Rank-differences only indicate that some individuals show greater capacity to serve that collectivity than others. In this perspective, any pursuit of private ends (within the organization but of course also outside it) is a token of disloyalty. This challenge to the superordinate claims of the transcendent collectivity must be corrected. In the ideal world of a collectivist organization, there is no right to combine for private pursuits and indeed no right to privacy at all.[3]

These are the models used in this study, but naturally the real world is more complex and some of this complexity must be left aside. Studies of ideologies imply a neglect of persons and private beliefs. I shall treat entrepreneurs and managers as well as autocratic or party-officials and enterprise directors in terms of their respective organizational positions and by virtue of the common experiences to which such positions expose them. And I shall attribute to such "groups" ideologies of management which have been articulated in response to

[3] Of course, bureaucratic organizations exist under individualist as well as under collectivist auspices. The main difference is the absence of a transcendent collectivity under the former. As Jeremy Bentham put it: "The interest of the community is one of the most general expressions that can occur in the phraseology of morals: no wonder that the meaning of it is often lost. When it has a meaning, it is this. The community is a fictitious *body*, composed of the individual persons who are considered as constituting as it were its *members*. The interest of the community then is—what? The sum of the interests of the several members who compose it." See Jeremy Bentham, "An Introduction to the Principles of Morals and Legislation," in E.A. Burtt, ed., *The English Philosophers from Bacon to Mill* (New York: The Modern Library, 1939), p. 792.

the logic of authority relations in economic enterprises. While such publicly expressed ideologies frequently reflect a range of views rather than a single, fully developed position, even such a range will *not* do justice to the actual diversity of personal beliefs or attitudes. This defect is dictated by the questions I have asked and the materials available for study. It is not, however, too serious a defect for the attitudes of individuals do not become public opinion merely by the process of addition. Instead, public opinion is formed through a constant process of formulation and reformulation by which spokesmen identified as authoritative seek to articulate what they sense to be the shared understandings of the moment. A study of ideologies deals with these formulations and reformulations which reflect (as nearly as we can make out) collective responses to the challenges of changing circumstance.

There are two other aspects that should be noted. It will be seen that I do not share the preference of some social scientists for facts untarnished by previous scrutiny. The present study interprets what is generally known about work and authority in industry, especially in the historical chapters. I have used a comparative framework which almost necessitates that breadth is obtained at the expense of depth. Newer detailed historical studies such as Sidney Pollard's *The Genesis of Modern Management* on Great Britain (1965) or William Blackwell's *The Beginnings of Russian Industrialization* (1968) would call for modifications of detail. But the study is best left to stand as it is and further work in this area can be done by younger scholars who can profit from a comprehensive reassessment of this study along with all the others.

Probably, change itself is a more serious drawback of republishing a study like this after an interval of some twenty years. Chapters five and six deal with American and East German society respectively, and the setting of both societies has been transformed since the mid-fifties. During the same interval, my own work has gained new perspectives. It seems appropriate, therefore, to indicate briefly in what ways historical change and my own intellectual development have modified or developed the outlook presented in this study.

II.

Historical change since the early 1950's has been dramatic. The era of the Cold War between the Soviet Union and the United States has been superseded by a detente. Mounting conflicts between Russia and China have reenforced that detente at the same time that they have led to an initial rapprochement between the U.S. and China. Internally, the Soviet Union has witnessed a period of de-Stalinization following the 20th Party Congress of 1956. Subsequently, efforts were made to stabilize Bolshevik rule in the face of "coexistence" with the capitalist West, of efforts at liberalization and independence in the satellite countries of Eastern Europe, and of increasingly tense relations with China. In this setting, the building of the wall cordoning off East from West Germany in 1961 is the event which most directly affected the conditions analyzed in Chapter 6 of this study.

Changes on the American side may not have been as dramatic, but their potential implications are far-reaching nevertheless. World War II was followed, as World War I had been, by an anti-Communist agitation, culminating in the McCarthy period. The atmosphere of the Cold War permeated all aspects of American society and directly contributed to the decisions that led to the Korean war and the long agony of the engagement in Viet Nam. With the moralism and middle-class participation characteristic of American foreign policy, sentiments in these decades have swung very widely between isolationism, anti-fascism, anti-Communism—and now under Republican auspices a new set of ambivalences about the Chinese and Russians. Moreover, since the end of World War II, the implications of science and technology have become a concern which goes to the heart of the American creed, examined in part in Chapter 5 of this study. Precipitated by the atomic bombs released over Hiroshima and Nagasaki, apprehension remained confined at first to the scientific community and a small cultural elite. Yet these sentiments would not subside with the termination of the war and they have not remained confined to the counter-cultural agitation of the 1960's. Worries relating to technology can undermine the American belief in progress and with it the trust in the capacity of businessmen to advance the economy without damaging the environment.

Though it is not easy to see these changes in perspective, one purpose of *Work and Authority* was to facilitate the long view. Hence the introduction to a new edition may be the proper place for testing whether the perspective developed here can encompass changes which I could not have anticipated in the early 1950's. Along with most of my other writings, my book was inspired by the work of Max Weber, especially his analysis of domination (*Herrschaft*). Since the present study focuses attention on the relations of authority in industry, it is appropriate to put it within the framework Weber has provided.[4]

In his analysis of *Herrschaft*, or domination, Weber relates authority to administrators, the people, types of legitimation and the limitations implicit in each type. All the elements stated below are found in some part of his discussion, but it may be helpful to set them out in a more schematic form than he did.

Weber emphasized that these three types are "ultimate principles" while specific historical cases are bound to be admixtures, often combining elements from each of the three types.[5] In practice it is difficult to keep the general and

---

[4] See my essay "Culture, Social Structure and Social Change," in *Embattled Reason, op. cit.*, esp. pp. 150-164 for a related discussion.

[5] See Max Weber, *Economy and Society* (tr. and ed. by Guenther Roth and Claus Wittich; New York: The Bedminster Press, 1968) III, p. 954.

TYPES OF DOMINATION

	1 Authority	2 Staff	3 People	4 Legitimation*	5 Limitation*
I	Personal (including charismatic)	Confidants, Disciples	Followers	Personal gift (inc. Divine inspiration, destiny, etc.)	Followers demand proof of gift (e.g. miracles)
II	Traditional	Household servants; retainers, vassals, etc.	Subjects	Custom sanctioning (a) ancient usage (b) ruler's prerogative	Traditional rights associated with an established rank- order of society
III	Legal	Bureaucrats	Citizens	Constitution and enacted law; equality under the law	Public reactions (including abstract ideals of natural law)

* Legitimation refers to "claims to legitimacy" on the part of the rulers and limitation to "claims for a quid pro quo" on the part of the ruled. The two claims are antithetical and the outcome of the interaction is uncertain. Terms like "legitimacy" or "social contract" are avoided, because they are too definitive and lend themselves to the fallacy of misplaced concreteness.

the specific in proper balance and Weber is not always helpful on this point. For example, by including administrative structures, he moves his general types of domination close to historical configurations like feudalism, even though the discussion of legitimation remains at a very abstract level. It is more useful to consider this abstract level first by concentrating on the meaning of legitimation (Columns 1, 4, and 5) and then attempt an historical typology proper (see Section IV).

Reading from left to right, I have chosen the phrase "personal authority" to designate the first type. This is an all-encompassing term which includes personal leadership as well as the special case of a leader with charismatic appeal. Both ordinary and charismatic leaders typically assemble confidants or disciples around them who will assist them in their mission. The main point here is that these assistants are tied to their leader by a shared belief in his mission as well as by personal loyalty. Among the people, leaders have a following of true believers and echoes of that commitment reverberate at least to some extent among the population at large. This much is straightforward. The legitimation of authority and its related limits are more complex. Legitimation is always based upon a belief shared by rulers, their "staff" and the people subject to authority. An order founded upon personal authority involves the conviction that a leader possesses

> . . . a certain quality . . . by virtue of which he is set apart from ordinary men and treated as endowed with supernatural, superhuman, or at least specifically exceptional powers or qualities. These [powers or qualities] . . . are regarded as of divine origin or as exemplary, and on the basis of them the individual concerned is treated as a 'leader'.[6]

The circularity of this definition is related to the *interaction* between the leader and his confidants and followers. For the leader's claim to exceptional

[6] *Ibid.*, I, p. 241.

powers or qualities is inevitably modified in practice, however unconditionally he construes the claim in theory. Similarly, the followers are ever seeking for some sign or symbol of those special qualities, however unconditionally they have committed themselves to a duty of obedience in theory. Personal authority emerges through the problematic relations between leaders and followers, which are marked by such opposite and ambivalent imperatives of theory and practice. I found no occasion to use this concept in my study of *Work and Authority*, but Joseph Schumpeter's analysis of entrepreneurial leadership makes plain that the concept has its place in studies of economic development.

Traditional authority is more directly relevant to *Work and Authority*, since the book surveys two centuries of industrialization. Weber's concept was formulated largely from the standpoint of the ruling strata in medieval European society. There, authority was believed in "by virtue of the sanctity of age-old rules" *and* by virtue of the master's traditional status-prerogative which enjoined personal obedience on his subjects and allowed him to use his discretion (to act at pleasure, to bestow his grace). Such authority was exercised directly through household servants and retainers (patrimonialism, family enterprises), and indirectly through vassals who might emerge from the ranks of personal retainers and who remained tied to the ruler through contract and personal loyalty (feudalism, sub-contracting). In this setting, the legitimation of rule also depends upon the interaction between a ruler, those who help him govern the realm, and the subject population. Ordinary people were recognized to be in an inferior position and were excluded from all political participation, but nevertheless custom sanctioned some of their claims. Under traditional authority, rulers and subjects must come to terms with opposite and frequently conflicting imperatives. As rightful incumbents, rulers insist on their time-honored prerogatives, but such insistence may lead to "too many" transgressions of ancient usage and thus jeopardize the claim to legitimacy. In the ideal case, the ruler's prerogative, though sanctioned by tradition, is limited by the usages and rights which are also sanctioned by tradition. Conversely, subjects insist on their traditional rights, but too much insistence verges on disloyalty and treason. It was in this context that the early recruits to an industrial work-force justified rioting by an appeal to their "ancient rights" which were denied them by their employers under the pressures of industrialization.

Thirdly, legal authority. The concept is related directly to individual ownership of property and the entrepreneurship of early industrialization. Under legal authority, all persons are equal before the abstract rules of that authority. That is, each person is the equal of every other solely in his legal capacity, of which the law takes cognizance. The great asset of this approach lies in the fact that every official can exercise the authority of office only on the basis of formally legal commands.

The typical person in authority, the 'superior', is himself subject to an impersonal order by orienting his actions to it in his own dispositions and commands. (This is true not only for persons exercising legal authority who are in the usual sense 'officials,' but, for instance, for the elected president of a state.)[7]

Under a system of rules, appointed officials rather than disciples, servants or retainers are charged with the task of implementation, while the people are no longer followers or subjects, but citizens who possess formal rights of participation. Legitimation of legal authority resides in the constitution which contains the basic authentication of the law-making process and in the laws and regulations which are the product of that process. Formally, all citizens became equal before the law, as voters who have the right to elect representatives and as individuals who possess the same formal rights as everyone else. These formal rights were meaningful symbols of emancipation as long as the laws of the ancient regime protected privileges and the inherited inequalities of the traditional status-order. But when these privileges and inequalities decline, formal equality before the law revealed itself as a claim that benefited those best able to make use of it, and that excluded the vast majority of the disadvantaged. The great liability of this approach lies in the fact that in his civic, economic and social capacities the individual is left to fend for himself. The legitimation of legal authority therefore found its limits wherever public reactions focused on the discrepancies between formal equality and substantive inequality. Chapter 2 of this book analyzes how in England entrepreneurial ideologies were developed to cope with both, the denial of traditional rights and the conflicts between property-interests and the claims of those disadvantaged by industrialization.

After publishing *Work and Authority* in 1956 I studied Max Weber's work more intensively and came to recognize that my own materials had gone beyond those encompassed by his types of domination. The analysis of entrepreneurial ideologies in eighteenth and nineteenth century Russia (Chapter 3) even raised some questions about the appropriateness of "traditional authority". Russian history seemed to allow for little differentiation between "ancient usage" and the "ruler's prerogative" so that there was little room for the development of "traditional rights" which could limit the latter. Weber had discussed this "variant" and had allowed for it by such categories as "patrimonialism" and "Sultanism". But if this permitted the inclusion of the Russian "case" under traditional authority broadly interpreted, the facts of Soviet rule posed more difficult problems of interpretation. I consider these and related problems below (in Section IV), because they relate *Work and Authority* to my recent and current research. At this point, I turn to a reinterpretation of social protest in the era of industrialization.

---

[7] *Ibid.*, I, p. 217.

III.

In this edition, the concluding essay on "Industrialization, Ideologies and Social Structure" replaces the conclusion to the 1956 edition of *Work and Authority* and provides a précis of the work as a whole.[8] But the original version put special emphasis upon the civic position of the work-force and this issue is of continuing interest wherever industrialization is initiated.

> Industrialization in its early phase poses a very general problem. It is accompanied by the creation of a nonagricultural work force which is usually forced to bear the consequences of great social and economic dislocations. These dislocations terminate the traditional subordination of the 'lower classes' in the preindustrial society. Though this development varies considerably with the relative speed and with the social setting of industrialization, its result is that the 'lower classes' are deprived of their recognized, if subordinate, place in society. A major problem facing all societies undergoing industrialization is the civic integration of the newly created industrial work force.[9]

Tocqueville had recognized that in the interval between an accepted system of inequality and a new system of equality "no one knows exactly what he is or what he may be or what he ought to be." In such a setting masters and servants become ill-natured and intractable. The lines that divide right from might have become confused and authority is indistinguishable from oppression. Society is undergoing a revolutionary upheaval in which "the reigns of domestic government dangle between [masters and servants] to be snatched at by one or the other."[10]

At the time, I went on to discuss the role which the English and Russian ruling classes had played in coping with the problem of political mobilization. A comparative study of the "ideologies of management in the course of industrialization" necessarily dealt with the approach of different ruling classes to the disruption of traditional subordination among the people. But subsequently, my interest shifted to the other side of the coin, namely the civic integration of the newly emerging industrial work-force or, failing that, the cumulation of that revolutionary potential which Tocqueville had discerned in the spread of equalitarian ideas.

Then as now, it seemed to me useful to combine Tocqueville's insight with that of Marx, though in a way that was not fully compatible with either. Tocqueville saw that the transition from the old inequality to a new equality

---

[8] This essay is the text of my MacIver lecture, given on the occasion of receiving the MacIver award for this book from the American Sociological Association in 1958. The lecture reassesses the book as a whole, looking back upon it after an interval of two years.

[9] Reinhard Bendix, *Work and Authority in Industry* (New York: John Wiley & Sons, 1956), p. 434.

[10] Alexis de Tocqueville, *Democracy in America* (New York: Vintage Books, 1954), II, p. 195.

generated a revolutionary potential. He did not identify that potential with any particular group, but rather with the disturbance of social relations by equalitarian claims. And he emphasized strongly that the individualism associated with these claims would diminish social solidarity and endlessly multiply individual demands for governmental assistance, thus leading to an unprecedented concentration of governmental power. On the other hand, Marx emphasized the formation of groups under the impact of industrialization and their growth of class-consciousness. Where Tocqueville saw social relations disturbed by equalitarian claims, Marx saw these claims denied by economic exploitation, which was the basis for all other forms of exploitation. Marx also believed that workers protested their lack of social recognition. But he dismissed all claims to traditional rights as "false consciousness" and staked everything upon a revolutionary overthrow which would recreate on a collective level that sense of self in productive work which capitalist exploitation has destroyed.

My own initial conclusion was that

> industrialization tends to create a revolutionary potential as a consequence of the problems engendered in the early phase of industrialization. The resolution of these problems may take a long period of time. Partial resolutions of the problem only lead to partial dissipations of the revolutionary potential . . . . In such cases the unresolved problems of the early phase linger on long after economic enterprises have been well developed. The revolutionary potential of the proletariat will disappear, on the other hand, where this work force is more or less rapidly reincorporated in the national community. . . . Societies differ in this capacity and willingness to accord civic recognition to an 'internal proletariat' (Toynbee).[11]

In this approach I sided with Tocqueville in an emphasis on the civic problem of self-respect arising from the disruption of a traditional order. I also followed him in seeing "revolution" not as an *event* that had occurred once and for all (or would occur again in the future), but as an enduring condition of change (which he attributed to the failure of institution-building in France based on the idea of equality.) At the same time, I sided with Marx in seeing the importance of industrialization, of class-formation and colonialism as the conditions which continually engendered unrest and protest against social and economic injustice. By combining these two perspectives one might be able to bring into one coherent account the possibility of civic integration (as in England), the phenomenon of partial integration (as in Germany and France), the case of Russia where the impact of industrialization and of Western ideas had engendered a cumulation of revolutionary energies, and even the protest movements in colonial countries which had suffered their own long-standing disruption of traditional social orders and won opportunities for independence through the mounting disarray of the colonizing powers.

[11] See *Work and Authority*, p. 437.

Thoughts along these lines suggested themselves through a growing impatience with two prevalent intellectual tendencies, the reductionist elimination of political life and the generalization of "capitalism" as the master-cause of change in the last five hundred years. Some sociologists and political scientists share with classical Marxism the belief that political behavior is explained by the social status of the individuals and groups involved. Certainly, economic interest and social experience often help to make political behavior more intelligible. "But by analyzing the social determinants of political behavior we should not inadvertently explain away the very facts of political life."[12] In this respect Tocqueville saw farther than Marx although he had none of Marx's theoretical grasp. Tocqueville recognized the give and take of human interaction as the foundation of institutions. Accordingly, he gave full attention to the sentiments and opinions of people, which Marx tended to dismiss as "false consciousness" that would be "eliminated" by the historical movement. Marx was too ready to extrapolate from observed tendencies of early industrialization—no doubt out of a desire (based on philosophical constructions) to locate an historical force for a final solution of human ills. But if there are no final solutions (and Marx was inconsistent in implying that there were), then one is forced to be more patient with the proximate solutions that are available through more or less enduring institutional structures.

At the same time, it does not make good sense to attribute all changes of the last four or five centuries to "capitalism". "Old societies" have been disrupted more or less coercively as European commercialism and Christian missionary activity, the emergence and demonstration effects of industrial economies, and finally the ideals of the French revolution have had successive repercussions in all parts of the world. This revolutionary process began with the first empires built by Portugal and Spain in the late fifteenth century, a process which Marx aptly described as "primitive accumulation." With the decolonization of most African and Asian societies that process is entering its final phase only now. So conceived, the main locus of this protracted revolutionizing process is shifted away from the conflicts endemic to "capitalism" and towards conflicts which have arisen wherever commerce, industry, scientific and technical discoveries as well as general ideals have overturned established social relations and political structures. "Capitalism" is merely one of several sources of disruption, among other things because the ideal of equality has religious roots that antedate modern economic developments. In this way, attention can be focused on a revolutionary process since the sixteenth century in which peasant uprisings and workers' protests are of a piece with nationalist movements and the vanguard-role of intellectuals. These protean movements are noteworthy less for their group- or class-characteristics than as varied reactions to having

---

[12] Reinhard Bendix and Seymour M. Lipset, "Political Sociology," *Current Sociology,* VI (1957), p. 85.

lost one's place in an established order of things and hence of seeking, often desperately, for a new basis of personal and collective self-respect. Such sentiments are not defined solely by a person's relations to the work-process and the use of his faculties in that process. They are defined, rather, by the network of his interactions with significant others in which a man's occupational role is an important source of identity, but only one of many.

With these modifications it becomes possible to encompass two movements of thought and action—the quest for citizenship and nationalism—which did not have a place either in Tocqueville's scheme or in Marx's. In *Nation-Building and Citizenship* (1946) I followed the interpretation of citizenship which T.H. Marshall developed for England. Marshall had distinguished between civil, political and social rights. Civil rights refer to the principal concerns of the French revolution: liberty of person, freedom of speech, thought and faith, the right to own property and conclude valid contracts, and the right to justice. Political rights involve the franchise and an access to public office unrestricted by particularistic legal disabilities (such as titles, birth, inheritance, etc.). In turn, social rights refer to minimum-standards of security and welfare as well as to minimum-opportunities of education.[13] Marshall analyzed the development of these rights in successive stages of English history from the eighteenth to the twentieth centuries. My own treatment examined the right of association (a civil right), the right to an elementary education (a social right), the franchise and secret balloting (political rights) on a comparative basis for several Western-European countries.[14] Some of these rights were granted only in response to cumulative political pressure, others resulted from preventive governmental reforms. And some rights were indistinguishable from duties: the right to an elementary education also involves the duty to attend school, and under social security the rights to benefits are inseparable from the obligation to register and make contributory payments. Thus, the extension of the rights of citizenship is a complex process which belies the simplified image of rights granted solely in response to protests against the denial of rights.

It seems possible to combine these perspectives with an analysis of nationalism though as yet I have done little to explore this possibility. The extension of citizenship always involves claims for participation and/or benefits. Implicitly at least, these claims are demands for recognition by the society at large. Those previously excluded claim a right to be heard and those who suffer deprivation claim a right to a minimum level of existence which alone would make their participation possible. Such claims are typically addressed to the ruling institutions of society, thus reflecting an aspiration to

---

[13] See T. H. Marshall, *Class, Citizenship and Social Development* (Garden City: Doubleday & Co., 1964), pp. 71-72.
[14] Reinhard Bendix, *Nation-Building and Citizenship* (New York: John Wiley & Sons, 1964), pp. 80-101.

belong to the national society as a going concern. Fundamentally, this is a nationalist motivation which has prompted labor movements to identify themselves with "their country" at crucial points in the history of working classes in industrial societies. Only where this drive to achieve recognition is frustrated for too long, i.e. where "the nation" does not hold out the promise of civic integration, there demands will arise for a restructuring of society so that a proper recognition or integration can be achieved. So conceived, the freedom or independence movements in colonial countries are of a piece with the agitation of peasants and workers in the colonizing countries, for in both cases it is a quest for civic recognition or for a society in which such recognition becomes possible.

IV.

These perspectives on social protest and nationalism during the nineteenth century have suggested lines of inquiry with which I am concerned today. I shall indicate how *Work and Authority* together with its sequel *Nation-Building* provide a framework of interpretation for my current studies.

Agitation for extension of the rights of citizenship presupposes the existence of a nation-state, i.e. an institutional structure in which major functions of governmental authority are centralized while all adult citizens are *individual* bearers of rights and duties. Broadly speaking, the movements of social protest and nationalism seem to fall into two phases. In their early stages they call forth passionate commitment to high ideals which are typically articulated by intellectuals. The intensity of commitment and articulation is concomitant with the generalization of a grievance, be it foreign occupation, economic exploitation, or the denial of political and social rights.[15] But passionate commitment moves on to other goals once independence is won, exploitation alleviated, or the previous denial of rights terminated by appropriate constitutional or legal changes. As long as the right to vote was restricted, those who were denied that right felt that exclusion branded them as second-class citizens. But once full citizenship is achieved, the right to vote appears as a matter of course and the satisfactions derived from its exercise seem minimal. When the right to vote is taken for granted, nothing can quite recapture that passionate fellow-feeling which had united those who had joined in the movement to extend the suffrage. In much the same way, nationalist movements are capable of arousing paroxysms of fraternal enthusiasm. But once the nation-state is established, this sense of community becomes for many a matter of routine and consensus at the national level acquires an impersonal quality which does not satisfy the craving

[15] Georg Simmel developed this observation in his discussion of "the negative character of collective behavior" in Kurt Wolff, ed., *The Sociology of Georg Simmel* (Glencoe: The Free Press, 1950), pp. 396-401.

for fraternity.[16] This is one reason why the issue of alienation has accompanied the whole development of the nation-state since its inception in the eighteenth century.

Another reason for the persistence of this issue is the decline of solidarity in secondary groups. Tocqueville was among the most discerning in emphasizing that the centralization of government was accompanied by the decline of estate-society with its hierarchy of ranks and hence by the social isolation of the individual citizen. And he related the two by showing that this social isolation would prompt the individual in his need to turn to the government for help and hence enhance its centralization of power still further.

> As in periods of equality no man is compelled to lend his assistance to his fellow men, and none has any right to expect much support from them, everyone is at once independent and powerless. These two conditions, which must never be either separately considered or confounded together, inspire the citizen of a democratic country with very contrary propensities. His independence fills him with self-reliance and pride among his equals; his debility makes him feel from time to time the want of some outward assistance, which he cannot expect from any of them, because they are all impotent and unsympathizing.

And in a footnote to this passage Tocqueville analyzes the mechanism involved somewhat further:

> It frequently happens that the members of the community promote the influence of the central power without intending to . . . There is always a multitude of men engaged in difficult or novel undertakings, which they follow by themselves without shackling themselves to their fellows. Such persons will admit, as a general principle, that the public authority ought not to interfere in private concerns; but, by an exception to that rule, each of them craves its assistance in the particular concern on which he is engaged and seeks to draw upon the influence of the government for his own benefit, although he would restrict it on all other occasions. If a large number of men applies this particular exception to a great variety of different purposes, the sphere of the central power extends itself imperceptibly in all directions, although everyone wishes it to be circumscribed.[17]

From the perspective of the 1830s, Tocqueville perceived individualism in this literal fashion, but in other contexts he emphasized the principle of voluntary association, especially among Americans in contrast to Frenchmen. His prescription was that men must cultivate the "art of associating together" where the equality of conditions is increased, i.e. where a man is no longer "*compelled* to lend his assistance to his fellow men" and no longer has "any

---

[16] For these people the personal commitment to the nation recaptures some of its former intensity only in national emergencies or in confrontations with other cultures. For others, of course, patriotism remains an important part of their conventional creed but even then it becomes a sentiment for special occasions, not the all-consuming passion of a nationalist movement. See my *Nation-Building and Citizenship, op. cit.*, pp. 136-38.

[17] Tocqueville, *Democracy in America, op. cit.*, II, pp. 311-12.

right to expect much support from them."[18] The individual suffers from social isolation where he is no longer obliged to belong to those "mutual aid" associations of an estate society which protected his rights only if he fulfilled his duties. No association based on a coalescence of interests or on ethnic and religious affiliation can recapture the intense reciprocity of rights and duties that was peculiar to these corporate jurisdictions.

But there is a lacuna in Tocqueville's approach. He failed to see that men would associate together not just for the "vast multitude of lesser undertakings" performed every day, but specifically for the purpose of enlisting governmental assistance in the advancement of their major economic interests. That is to say, he *did not connect* the two tendencies he observed: the growth of voluntary associations and the "craving for governmental assistance." When these two tendencies are combined (as is characteristic of the advanced industrial societies in the West), one can discern *historical types* of authority that should be distinguished as clearly as may be from Weber's *ideal types* (or universal principles) discussed previously (in section II).

In making this point I tread on uncertain ground, because terminology in this field is undeveloped, the tendencies referred to point to the future as well as the past, and the distinction between historical and ideal types is difficult to handle properly. The last point requires special emphasis. Naturally, Weber drew on his own background in proposing his tripartite typology. "Charisma" or the "gift of grace" derives from the Christian tradition; "tradition" evokes connotations of European feudalism; and "legality" is a specifically Occidental phenomenon. But in reaching for a higher level of abstraction, Weber's intention was clearly to divest these terms of as much of their historical peculiarity as possible and still retain a vocabulary that could be understood. Certainly, personal (including charismatic) authority occurs outside the Christian context. Traditional authority is not confined to the usages of European feudalism (Weber himself enumerated a three-fold classification of feudalisms with seven sub-types). And legal authority or the adjudication of disputes in accordance with rules acknowledged as binding prior to the dispute can be found in all parts of the world. Until a more comprehensive and less culture-bound terminology becomes available, it will be well to retain this one, aware of its limitations and of the fact that such universal principles are programs of research rather than ready-to-use labels which are somehow self-explanatory.

Weber himself was aware that the *political foundations* of legal authority were changing in his life-time and they have changed further since his day. To bring these changes into focus it is best to treat *legal domination* as an aspect of the nation-state and then subdivide it in terms of transformations of the

---

[18] *Ibid.*, II, pp. 114–118 where Tocqueville discusses the "use which Americans make of public associations in civic life."

political structure.[19] The nation-state has reached its full development only since the French revolution. It is best to define the state in terms of this modern type

> ... but at the same time in terms which abstract from the values of the present day, since these are particularly subject to change. The primary formal characteristic of the modern state are as follows: It possesses an administrative and legal order subject to change by legislation, to which the organized activities of the administrative staff, which are also controlled by regulations, are oriented. This system of order claims binding authority, not only over the members of the state, the citizens, most of whom have obtained membership by birth, but also to a very large extent over all action taking place in the area of its jurisdiction. It is thus a compulsory organization with a territorial basis. Furthermore, today, the use of force is regarded as legitimate only so far as it is either permitted by the state or prescribed by it ... The claim of the modern state to monopolize the use of force is as essential to it as its character of compulsory jurisdiction and of continuous operation.[20]

In this classification, Weber's ideal type of legal domination is subdivided into two, roughly successive phases and thus brought closer to the historical configurations as we know them. (The second phase is subdivided further under b_1 and b_2 because these subordinate types exist concurrently and the distinction between them is a matter of emphasis in different sectors of modern Western societies.)

This schema of legal domination as an *historical* type can be elaborated, depending on different purposes of analysis and on further developments. The terms used are non-technical, but "representation," "referendum," and "plebiscite" require a special comment. ("Pillarization" is explained below.) As used here, representation refers to delegates (or agents) who participate in public decision-making on behalf of a constituency of voters, interest-groups, etc. Referendum refers to the direct vote on a public issue by all qualified voters. In practice, both principles become attenuated. Delegates interpose their judgment of what is best for their constituency, their own political survival, and the community at large, except when they are bound by an imperative mandate. And referenda on public issues are often supplemented or replaced by plebiscites, i.e. by appeals to consent through acclamation or by the tacit assumption that such acclamation is forthcoming or will not be withheld.

---

[19] In what follows, I confine myself to a discussion of legal and plebiscitarian authority as political sub-types of the nation-state. It is awkward to use the term "legal authority" both in a universal and a historical sense, but I try to make the difference clear by the addition of qualifying adjectives and in the commentary below. Weber was well aware of the need for such sub-classification and although some of his phrases like "patrimonial bureaucracy" are rather *ad hoc*, he also made more systematic attempts. For his sub-classification of traditional and charismatic authority cf. Weber, *Economy and Society, op. cit.*, III, pp. 1070-73, 1159-63.

[20] See Weber, *Economy and Society, op. cit.*, I, p. 56.

A. LEGAL TYPES OF DOMINATION IN NATION-STATES

	1 *Ratification of Authority*	2 *Politics*	3 *Staff*	4 *People*	5 *Legitimation*	6 *Limitation*
a.	Traditional-legal (emphasis on representation as a prerogative)	Notables as the natural leaders of the community	Bureaucrats often recruited from privileged strata	First and Second-class citizens	Enacted law; lower-class status retains legal liabilities	Public reactions under close surveillance
b₁	Legal (emphasis on balance between representation, referendum, and plebiscite)	Mass parties organize the electorate; at the same time the representation of "organized interests" develops	Bureaucrats (recruited under formal merit system)	Citizens organized for mass participation in election campaigns *minus* the unaffiliated	Constitution and enacted law; formal equality before the law	Public reactions ranging from individual complaints to mass demonstrations; appeals range from private interests to abstract ideals of natural law
b₂	Pluralist (emphasis on mixture of representation, referendum and plebiscite, but with more stress on representation)	Mass parties organize the electorate; at the same time "pillarization" based on interest- and affinity-groups plays an increased role in public decision-making	Bureaucrats // Group representatives	Citizens organized segmentally *minus* the unorganized	Constitution and enacted law; wide-spread consultation with organized interests; co-optation of private organizations for quasi-public functions	Same as under b₁, but special importance of organized interests in decision-making, e.g., "veto-groups" (Riesman).

The three concepts remain distinct in that representation always interposes an interpreting agent between public sentiments and governmental decision-making, referenda always provide the public with a choice, while plebiscites always involve the direct acclamation of a public act by the people at large. As an ideal type, legal domination presupposes *some* balance between the representation of interests, choice by referenda, and rule by acclamation. Thus, under traditional-legal authority, representation by notables claims to speak in the best interest of the people. Under legal authority, the interposition of judgments by designated representatives is balanced at several levels by opportunities for the direct expression of public sentiment. And under pluralist authority, decision-making by representatives (if not in legislatures, then through interest-groups) gains at the expense of plebiscitary participation. Still, for legal domination to endure some balance is needed if decision-making is to combine informed judgments with the direct impact of public demands.[21]

The changes of legal domination (from a to b_1 and b_2) are relatively uncomplicated, at least in outline. During the French Revolution, the debates in the constitutional assembly made clear that equality before the law did not mean equality of political participation. Despite some moves towards universal suffrage, the franchise remained tied to property ownership as it did throughout the nineteenth century in most Western countries. (The United States is an exception in this respect.) Also, balloting was public rather than secret for varying lengths of time so that in practice voting was greatly affected by the wishes of notables who dominated the community, both socially and economically. In practice, politics remained the preserve of an elite, public officials were often recruited from the higher social strata, and only those who were in a position to participate actively in public affairs could be considered first-class citizens.

Much of this changed with the extension of the franchise and the introduction of the secret ballot. Political parties developed in response to the need for organizing the people in periodic election campaigns. As a consequence, political participation spread beyond the circle of notables. Some could combine a public career with their type of work (especially lawyers); others managed to live "off" politics rather than "for" it, as Weber put the distinction between plebeian and aristocratic politicians. And where active politics recruited men from many social strata, the demand for equal access to public employment rose apace. Thus, civil service reform is directly related to the demand for equal opportunity that arose with widespread political participation. If no invidious distinctions were to be made concerning the right to vote, then no rationale

---

[21] For the distinction between the representative and the plebiscitarian principle I am indebted to Ernst Fraenkel, *Die Repraesentative und die Plebiszitaere Komponente im Demokratischen Verfassungsstaat* (Heft 219-220 of Recht und Staat; Tuebingen: J.C.B. Mohr, 1958), passim. The use of this distinction is my own.

remained concerning exclusion from public service—except educational qualifications related to the performance of duties in office. But as indicated earlier, the extension of the franchise (and of access to public office) made these political rights appear less attractive than they had been as long as they were denied. And the work of political parties to mobilize the public for mass-participation found its limits in the lack of interest among those who remain unaffiliated despite efforts to organize them.

In the advanced industrial societies of the West the politics of mass-parties continues to the present and I see no reason to anticipate changes in this respect. Indeed, there is evidence that some communist parties (such as those of France and Italy) seek to accommodate themselves in the interest of becoming acceptable partners in coalition governments. But within this framework of mass-politics another tendency is discernible which Dutch sociologists have called *verzuiling*, or pillarization.

> The phenomenon of *verzuiling* is by no means confined to politics. Each denominational bloc has set up a whole array of organizations encompassing practically every sphere of social life. Schools and universities, radio and television corporations, trade unions, health and welfare agencies, sport associations, and so on, all fit into the *zuilen* system. . . .
>
> The final aim of the confessional blocs can perhaps be described best as 'segmented integration': they aspire to participate in all national decision-making and to benefit fully from all national facilities while at the same time maintaining internal unity and cohesion.[22]

This segmentation of the public has developed nowhere as far as it has in Holland, but elements of this process are discernible in many societies. Early on, the German Social Democratic Party responded to its ostracism under Bismarck by a proliferation of associations which allowed the individual member to pass from the cradle to the grave under party-sponsorship. Wherever the Catholic Church or fundamentalist Protestant denominations have retained their hold on the faithful, they have developed similar affiliated organizations. Likewise, political parties, trade unions, business firms and others have frequently sponsored organizations providing a mixture of sociability, services and benefits to which members of employees (and their families) have exclusive access. At still other levels, organizations farm out their own work to other organizations, whether business firms hire organizations to manufacture parts, do accounting and public relations, etc., or governments contract for public work to be carried out by what one writer has called "quasi non-governmental organizations."

In tendencies of this kind, Tocqueville's two principles of individualism and voluntary association appear to be joined. Associations are formed (by in-

---

[22] Johan Goudsblom, *Dutch Society* (New York: Random House, 1967), pp. 32, 124.

dividuals or organizations) on the basis of common interests or common affinities to provide services, obtain benefits and participate in decision-making processes. But Tocqueville's individualism has been left behind by a development through which the representatives of organized interests come to work in close symbiosis with each other and with government officials.[23] For some sections of the public this development has gone so far that the segmental organization of citizens (in interest-or affinity-groups) is on a par with, or even exceeds, the importance of political parties. Political parties attain their peak activity during election years, interest organizations operate on a continuous basis. But the non-voter may also be the non-joiner, thus compounding the disabilities of those who are left behind in an organizationally managed society. The question for the future is how in such a society common public interests can be made to prevail over the purposes of "organized interests." Nineteenth-century liberalism and socialism assumed that technological advance and increased productivity would resolve short-run conflicts between individual and public interests. Probably, this assumption was always doubtful, but in the twentieth century it has become quite unrealistic. And where the repercussions of technological advance and increased productivity are deleterious or may become so, a system of legal authority based on individualistic premises may be severely strained.[24]

It should be apparent that these considerations apply to American managerial ideologies (Chapter 5). As noted earlier, the use of atomic bombs to end World War II and the subsequent counter-cultural agitation of the 1960s raised apprehensions which affected the American belief in progress and with it the trust in technology and business. Managers and their spokesmen have responded to these circumstances by yet another change of vocabulary, indicating their awareness of environmental issues and further elaborating upon the social and psychological attributes of men in an organizational context.[25] Authority relations in industrial enterprises are based upon the ownership and management of private property. Hence, a study of changes in American managerial ideologies fits into the on-going development of legal authority on which I have commented.

Let us now turn to the plebiscitarian type of domination in nation-states,

---

[23] A comprehensive, comparative survey of this material is contained in Joseph Kaiser, *Die Repraesentation organisierter Interessen* (Berlin: Duncker & Humblot, 1956), passim.
[24] Note the convergence on this question between a conservative and a Social-Democratic spokesman in Irving Kristol, "Capitalism, Socialism, and Nihilism," *The Public Interest*, No. 31 (Spring, 1973), pp. 3-16 and Richard Löwenthal, "Mit dem Sozialismus überleben," *Die Zeit* (April 20, 1973), pp. 3-5.
[25] For an analysis of American managerial ideologies since the "human relations" movement of the 1930's cf. Alexander Bergmann, *The Evolution of Managerial Attitudes towards Organizational and Environmental Responsibilities* (Ph.D. Dissertation, School of Business Administration, University of California, Berkeley, 1973).

specifically Communist dictatorships.[26] As in other *historical* types, these systems combine charismatic, traditional and legal elements, and over time their configuration is subject to structural changes without losing its distinctive characteristics. But this historical type is clearly outside Weber's tripartite division and one may well ask whether the old terminology of charisma, tradition, and legality is applicable at all, or more specifically whether any admixture of these terms would fit the plebiscitarian case. Weber did not live to witness such one-party dictatorships, but his terms are surprisingly suitable. In the case of the Soviet Union, Lenin was clearly a charismatic leader and the preservation of his body continues to this day as a symbolic authentication of the regime. Annually, the great event of the 1917 revolution is celebrated in ceremonies of rededication, and citations from the classic writings of Marx, Engels and Lenin remain a symbol of ideological purity. Such facts are too familiar to require elaboration. With the passage of time, the power of such symbolic persuasion has probably diminished and recent or current rulers are "routinized" heirs to a revolutionary inspiration. Yet from that inspiration they retain the claim to be the unquestioned fountainhead of political (and spiritual) truth. As rulers of a large empire, their every utterance is not to be challenged, while those below are made responsible for the implementation of the "party-line." Thus, plebiscitarian regimes are founded upon the *principle* of absolute commands, on the one side, and absolute responsibility for their implementation, on the other. But as always, practice differs from principle: depending on circumstances and strategies commands may not be pressed to the limit just as subordinate organizations may get away with a good deal of evasion. In Weber's tripartite division, the staff most characteristically charged with the impersonal implementation of specific commands is a bureaucracy, while only disciples of a charismatic leader dedicate themselves to follow him in his mission. Under modern conditions, plebiscitarian regimes tend to combine features from both the charismatic and the legal complex. The rulers of such regimes give specific directives as if they were in legal authority, but make each of these directives absolute as if they held charismatic authority. Under legal authority, theirs would be the ultimate responsibility. But by making their commands absolute, they evade that responsibility and shift the blame for failure on to the executive agencies. In turn, these agencies are organized bureaucratically while being called upon to show the loyal dedication of charismatic disciples. And when called to account, such agencies can try to evade their (bureaucratic) responsibility by pointing to the absolute commands which they have merely obeyed. There are seeds of danger in all exercise of

[26] My formulation is confined to the Soviet case, which alone is relevant to the discussion in Chapter 6 below. I recognize that eventually it is necessary to find formulations abstract enough to apply to other single-party systems as well, but I have not attempted this here.

authority. But today we know that on occasion in this particular combination the different dangers of charisma and of bureaucracy have been compounded and escalated at a disastrous cost to all humanity.

Still, the application of Weber's categories is not enough. A schematic representation may be helpful again in order to interpret plebiscitarian domination as an historical type.

Plebiscitarian authority embodies the historic mission of a transcendent collectivity. It cannot be bound either by the inspirations of personal authority, the benevolent authoritarianism of traditional authority. or the rule-bound dictates of science and "rational planning," although all these elements may play a role. The ideal type of a plebiscitarian regime depends on the principle that all decision-making is concentrated at the apex of the single party and all responsibility for failure is attributed to the echelons of party and government below that apex. Only such concentration can ensure that the true vanguard of the people (as interpreted by the leading cadre of that vanguard) will fulfill the historic mission of the world-proletariat. The party-leadership alone interprets the mandate of the people while the elected representatives provide the leadership with the "evidence" of public acclamation.

Where such regimes are established, they typically duplicate the established hierarchy of government officials by a second hierarchy of party-cadres. The relations between these two hierarchies fluctuate with changing policies, as I note below. Here the main point is that party-cadres are typically charged with intervening in the ordinary conduct of affairs on an emergency basis. They are employed to implement commands emanating from the decision-making center of the party which has the prerogative of overruling other centers of decision-making on an ad hoc basis. This double hierarchy of authority develops systematically what are, one suspects, incipient tendencies in all types of authority; namely, the effort to supervise subordinates by agents especially designated for the purpose. At any rate, a single-party authority exists only when these "agents" are centrally organized themselves, at the beck and call of the central leadership. At the top, decision-making is monopolized on behalf of the people conceived as a more or less undifferentiated whole. "The people" are contrasted sharply with an ever-present collective enemy whose identity varies with the party-line, but whose omnipresence is a mainstay of the simulated combat-conditions with which the civil order is imbued ideologically. As a matter of principle, everyone is equally liable to be mobilized so that privacy or diminished effort are literally interpreted as treason, i.e., as evidence of having gone over to the omnipresent internal enemy. In this sense, plebiscitarian rule finds "limits" only in passive resistance, and since any failure is presumptive evidence of disloyalty, passive resistance is suspected widely indeed. But such regimes must also get the work done. And in the absence of more direct sources of information changes of party-line are

B. PLEBISCITARIAN TYPES OF DOMINATION IN NATION-STATES

	1 Ratification of Authority	2 Politics	3 Staff	4 People	5 Legitimation	6 Limitation
a.	Plebiscitarian (mixture of representation and plebiscite but representation becomes nominal and plebiscite decisive)	Single-Party Dictatorship with subordinate bureaucratic interest constellations (e.g. military, secret service, heavy industry etc at central as well as regional levels)	Party-Cadres // Bureaucrats	"The People" (Workers, Peasants and Intelligents) *minus* their enemies (defined by class, race, or party-line)	Vanguard-party "representing the people" and their historic movement (based on principle of equal liability to mobilization)	Emigration, withdrawal from participation, and cumulative reactions to shifts of party line
b.	Same as under a.	Single-Party Dictatorship symbiotic with bureaucratic interest constellations (e.g. military, secret service heavy industry, etc. at central as well as regional levels)	Same as under a. but party and bureaucratic personnel have become technically proficient	Same as under a.	Same as under a. but reinforced by successful industrialization, nationalist appeals, and promises of peace and equality	Same as under a. but higher levels of education add new dimensions ranging from clandestine critiques (*Samizdat*) to evaluations of official policies based on the expertise of bureaucratic interest constellations at central as well as regional levels

prompted by evidence that bottlenecks have developed from the implementation of previous directives. Frequent changes of party-line (each being asserted with equal vehemence) are bound to produce cumulative reactions among the people subjected to such conditions.

Much of this remains true of Communist regimes today. Nevertheless, conditions have changed in the period of de-Stalinization (since the 20th Party Congress of 1956) and in East Germany especially since the building of the wall in 1961. An analysis appropriate at an earlier time is no longer valid empirically and my schematic presentation tentatively suggests the directions in which change has taken place. In East Germany, that change has been dramatic. Since the end of World War II, the country had lost approximately one sixth of its population by emigration to West Germany. Clearly, a regime facing such a drain of its manpower was in jeopardy and could be expected to maximize pressure upon its people. Until the building of the wall in 1961, East Germany was reputed as the most "Stalinist" country of Eastern Europe and some of that reputation lingers on even today. No other country (except North Korea) faces the "capitalist enemy" quite so directly and such agreements as have been reached between the two Germanies in 1972 were in part the result of Russian pressure upon the German Democratic Republic (GRD). The relaxation of dictatorial measures has remained quite limited (as it has in the Soviet Union in the post-Stalin period), but some relaxation clearly has occurred. An empirical examination of this change is beyond the scope of this introduction, but it is legitimate to ask in what way changes of this kind may be accommodated within the ideal type of plebiscitarian domination.

In fact, a parallel question applies to all ideal types of domination. Under personal authority, a leader's demand for complete personal devotion (based on his exceptional qualities and his sense of mission) is always at odds with his followers' hope for some sign of his gift and its special powers. Under traditional authority, the ruler's prerogative based on ancient usage is always at odds with his subjects' claims to traditional rights, also based on ancient usage. Under legal authority, laws and directives broadly derived from the constitution are always at odds with some public reactions based on particular interests and/or abstract notions of justice. Also, commands and public reactions are pressed home with varying intensity depending upon circumstances. Such tensions are managed from case to case without nullifying the broad applicability of the type of authority in question.

These considerations also apply to plebiscitarian types of domination. Here, too, it is claims against expectations, because all authority relations are bilateral and only unrelenting coercion borders on the unilateral.[27] The single party

---

[27] I say "borders" because even coercion is a human act with the torturer seeking in some way to elicit signs of affection (though not necessarily in relation to his victim) and the tortured seeking in some way to relieve their agony by some token of a *quid pro quo* for their suffering. But these extremities of the human condition need not be considered here.

proclaims itself the vanguard of "the people," a transcendent collectivity which only the party itself knows how to interpret. Though the people are differentiated in many respects, party-ideology represents them symbolically as a unit with an historic mission. This mission demands the participation of everyone. As discussed in Chapter 6, the party-cadres are a principal instrument of such public mobilization. But conditions fluctuate even when this structure remains intact. Concretely, after the wall was built, the constant jeopardy of mass-defection ceased and the GDR regime undertook a massive drive to catch up with modern technology.[28] Under these new conditions, how does a single-party authority restructure and/or relax its mobilization drives without relinquishing either its complete control over the party-apparatus or its ability to resume maximum pressure when the party-line calls for such pressure? Also, how is this restructuring and/or relaxation handled when "the people" find their situation literally inescapable (as in the Soviet Union), while successful technological change offers increasing opportunities to the technical cadres? At the time Chapter 6 was written, these and related questions had not presented themselves, but for specialists on countries in the Soviet orbit they rank high on their agenda today.

All authority-relations have in common that those in command cannot fully control those who obey. To be effective, authority depends on the assumption that subordinates will follow instructions in terms of the spirit rather than the letter of the rules. Two things are implied here: that the subordinate will adopt the behavior alternatives selected for him, and that he will give his "good will" to carrying out his orders. As this formulation suggests, "good will" involves judgment and initiative. If these are withheld by a "withdrawal of efficiency" (Veblen), a slavish clinging to the letter of the rules, or active sabotage, then the subordinate uses his judgment for purposes of his own.[29] The analysis of

---

[28] Of course, the psychological impact of West German prosperity on the East German population remained a threat and other threats like the Hungarian uprising and the short-lived Dubcek regime in Czechoslovakia probably had the effect of keeping the degree of relaxation quite limited. Since this book was written, other studies and especially Peter Ludz, *Parteielite im Wandel* (Köln: Westdeutscher Verlag, 1968), passim, with its analysis of a "consultative-authoritarian" regime, have examined the relevant development.

[29] My formulation is indebted to Herbert Simon, *Administrative Behavior* (New York: The Macmillan Co., 1959), p. 125 and passim, who has replaced Chester Barnard's "zone of indifference" by the more appropriate "zone of acceptance," which is defined as "a general rule which permits the communicated decision of another to guide his [the subordinate's] own choices. . . without deliberation on his own part on the expediency of those premises." To this it is necessary to add a "zone of judgment" pertaining to the execution of the accepted directive. In *Work and Authority*, I call this phenomenon the worker's (or subordinate's) "strategy of independence". My use of the term "good will" is derived from the "work according to rule" strike of English postal workers in 1962 which a union official explained by saying: "What we are doing is merely withdrawing our good will." See *Time Magazine* (January 19, 1962), p. 22.

Chapter 6 bears on this problem because it shows the social isolation of the party activists and the tremendous pressure to which they were subjected by the regime. Party-cadres were told that the word "impossible" is banished from the language, that "what was correct yesterday is already outdated and incorrect today." In other words, they were made to realize that advancement depends upon compliance and maximum performance, and in case of doubt compliance was rated higher. By simulating combat-conditions in peace-time, the regime concentrated all power at the top and pushed all responsibility downwards. Under these conditions it was only natural if party activists clung to the letter of their rules, even at the risk of alienating others and failing to perform as expected. For the alternative was to be suspected of disloyalty or treason. This condition is analyzed in Chapter 6 and remains an aspect of single-party rule. But this condition also produced mindless agitation, empty conformity, the failure of any feedback-information that could be of use to the regime, and hence the necessity to shift the party-line repeatedly in response to the cumulative inefficiencies produced by overconformity to the previous dispensation. In the post-Stalin period efforts have, therefore, been made to come to terms with these drawbacks of single-party authority—albeit in a way that will preserve the integrity of the regime as presently constituted. Typically, party-cadres have been instructed to develop initiative, to combat empty conformity by showing true leadership-qualities, etc. At the highest levels it may also have taken the form of new accommodations between the Politbureau and the elites of various executive bureaucracies such as the military, heavy industry, the secret service, and so on. The analysis of these changes goes well beyond the scope of the present study but is not, I believe, incompatible with its results.[30] Probably, these regimes cannot return to their Stalinist past. It is certainly the case that new personnel techniques in the party are efforts to cope with the mounting disutilities of the earlier methods, the rising articulation of critical judgments in high quarters and, in relations with "the public", the increasing social distance between the party and the people. But these measures to shore up single-party authority are not indications of its dissolution. For the time being, one can only hazard the guess that a transformed type of plebiscitarian domination (b) is in the making and we simply do not know how far this transformation can be developed within the plebiscitarian framework.

V.

In this introduction to *Work and Authority in Industry* I have attempted to provide a framework—both personal and intellectual—in which that study elaborates upon the structures of authority in more empirical detail. But this

---

[30] I am indebted to my colleague Professor Kenneth Jowitt for alerting me to these developments in the field of East European studies.

elaboration assumes the existence of the nation-state and that assumption is of limited applicability.

> Today we face a world in which the expansion of European ideas and institutions has placed the task of nation-building on the agenda of most countries, whether or not they are ready to tackle the job... We may well face a period in history in which fragments of nation-building—like the quest for a national culture, the unification of language, the detribalization of a population, the assimilation of ethnic communities, the formalization of laws, the elimination of corruption, the maintenance of order, the demilitarization of quasi-autonomous groups, and a thousand other issues—are tackled piecemeal and without immediate prospect of a definitive outcome. In that perspective the dominant experience of our generation appears to be that the unanticipated repercussions of European expansion were effective enough to undermine or destroy existing social frameworks, but often not nearly effective enough to provide viable, structural alternatives.[31]

It is probably idle for now to develop speculative typologies for the structures of authority that may emerge from this world-wide travail. Much of our knowledge in these matters is retrospective, as Hegel knew: "The owl of Minerva spreads its wings only with the falling of the dusk." However, it is not idle to state in what spirit our study of these problems should proceed.

Social theories are trial presentations of the world, not subject to decisive tests of verification. To me it has always seemed that idle curiosity and scientific advance were insufficient grounds of choice for the social theorist. Neither the productivity of his quest for knowledge nor its benefits are sufficient for the kind of self-absorbed preoccupation which has often proved so productive in the natural sciences. At the same time it is obvious that many choices have been made for us. We are all unwitting legatees of a development which witnessed the expansion of Western civilization around the world. Neither contrition nor slashing indictments of our own tradition can undo the effects of that expansion or be persuasive to its victims and their heirs. At the same time and inevitably, we continue to utilize the intellectual framework which itself was shaped by that expansion and remains an important reservoir of analytic tools even for the people on the peripheries, in countries that are "old societies and new states." This is the context in which we can perform a service when we re-examine our conceptual apparatus with the idea of making it more generally applicable.

To this end it may be helpful if I conclude this introduction in a more personal vein. Comparative historical studies, conceived in a sociological perspective, have become my main scholarly preoccupation. My German background gave an impetus in this direction, as I indicated earlier. The experience of teaching at American universities provided another incentive.

---

[31] Bendix, *Nation-Building and Citizenship*, *op. cit.*, pp. 300-301. There are also signs that in the established nation-states new questions arise, as supranational organizations both public and private involve citizens in more than one framework of allegiance.

From my days of teaching in the College at the University of Chicago in the 1940s I was impressed by the mounting distance between teachers and students, as specialization and technical expertise became the dominant focus of the social sciences. Only a small minority of our students would become professional social scientists and even many of these were likely to be teachers rather than researchers. The vast majority would become white-collar workers of some kind and what did we have to offer them? Indeed, what would be the outlook of social scientists proper, if they knew more and more about less and less, to use that hackneyed phrase? Certainly, such disparagement makes a travesty of the enormous effort with which dedicated men and women have sought to advance valid and reliable knowledge in the social sciences and I want no part of the anti-intellectualism that has been manifest so often. But every intellectual stance exacts its price in missed alternatives. And where so many colleagues were engaged in advancing specialization, there was room for some of us to go in another direction.

I have given an account of my successive efforts in bringing together what others have studied separately and in greater detail. But synthetic analyses can be no more random than specialized inquiries and these efforts have had to be guided by leading questions in turn. Why have I been so concerned with structures of authority? The answer goes back to the shattering experience with which I began. I was seventeen years of age when Hitler's conquest of power destroyed the ordered world in which I grew up. Since then much scholarly work has taught us how precarious and ill-constructed that world had been, but for me this knowledge does not efface the abstract significance of that experience. No social order is possible without authority, but authority can be used for good or ill. This is the root metaphor on which my attention has been riveted ever since.

In examining some of the problems suggested by that metaphor I have been guided by several related considerations. Under favorable conditions authority may be benign, but it cannot function without inequality. The division is deep between the few who exercise authority and the many who acquiesce, between the "elite" and the "masses". Nevertheless, there are limits to what authority can do: the enormity of Hitler's power impressed me no more than the abyss of his defeat. For however extreme coercion becomes and however unilateral power-relations seem to be between the few and the many, there is always interaction. I remembered Georg Simmel's example from some ancient text that at the building of the pyramids ten thousand slaves under the whip would voice their protest by murmuring in unison. Reflections of this kind give an inkling of the perplexities of action. Authority entails inescapable hazards not only because it is bound up with inequality, but because it must steer a course between being too forceful and not being forceful enough, between the arrogance of power and the failure of nerve. And at the level of social action, the same perspective can be applied to the relations between ideas and interests. As Otto Hintze has written,

> Everywhere the first impulse to social action is given as a rule by political and economic interests. But ideal interests lend wings to these real interests, give them a spiritual meaning, and serve to justify them. Man does not live by bread alone. He wants to have a good conscience as he pursues his life-interests. And in pursuing them he develops his capacities to the highest extent only if in so doing he serves a higher rather than a purely egoistic purpose. Interests without such 'spiritual wings' are lame; but on the other hand, ideas can win out in history only if and insofar as they are associated with real interests.[32]

This Weberian notion of conflicting imperatives has many ramifications.

In the context of authority it means a never-ending tension between rule-observance and individual interests. There can be no legal order without rules and hence there must be functionaries (judges, officials, policemen) who insist that the rules be followed. But rules are general, they do not take account of specific circumstances, and they work many hardships upon the lives of individuals. In his scholarly work, my father had maintained that because of this discrepancy lawyers must exhaust to the full the legal possibilities of defense, if the individual is to be protected against the necessary rigidities of rule-making. Something like this is also manifest in the relations between politics and social structure. There are a thousand constraints arising from the givens of geography, resources, the legacies of history and the social organization of economic life. All these impose an impersonal structure of limits and opportunities upon society. But active men also endeavor to shape and reshape their lives closer to their heart's desire. Subject to constraints though it is, politics is a part of that reshaping and represents a chance of freedom in a sea of necessities. Much the same may be said of culture. The accident of birth places everyone into contexts that are not of his making. Only through the formation of habits will he become a functioning adult and, for good or ill, habits impose indispensable rigidities that derive in part from what our culture takes for granted. But as John Dewey pointed out, habits facilitate as well as limit; under favorable conditions they allow us to explore the possibilities of action by enabling us to take so much for granted. And like individuals, cultures can achieve their high points of creativity only because so much culturally conditioned behavior is routine.

The recognition of such conflicting imperatives has formed a constant background of my work; I see it as an indispensable attribute of scholarship in the social sciences. Each intellectual construction has its vision and its blindness. Each cultural and historical situation has its achievements and the costs bound up with those achievements. And to the extent that one can use this

---

[32] Otto Hintze, "Kalvinismus und Staatsraeson in Brandenburg zu Beginn des 17ten Jahrhunderts," *Historische Zeitschrift*, vol. 144 (1931), p. 232.

insight properly, attention to both perspectives is an important methodological tool. But this type of rationalism has a moral dimension which should be made explicit. The ancient Greeks taught that the wise man faces up to the eternal mutability of fortunes. In good times and bad, he should be mindful of the opposite extremity of the human condition. This stoic view of our predicament is difficult to accept for legatees of the Enlightenment. Even the sceptics among us believe in the possibilities of reason, though a century of wars and revolutions and the growing complexities of civilization have cast a shadow over the earlier confidence. In a world of conflict and uncertainty we are perhaps learning to live with proximate solutions. But hope continues that knowledge can contribute its share to help make such solutions viable rather than inconclusive.

CHAPTER 1

Industrialization, Management, and Ideological Appeals

> *The strongest is never strong enough to be always master, unless he transforms his strength into right, and obedience into duty.*—J.-J. Rousseau, *Social Contract.*

a. Major Themes

This study deals with the role of ideas in the management of economic enterprises. Wherever enterprises are set up, a few command and many obey. The few, however, have seldom been satisfied to command without a higher justification even when they abjured all interest in ideas, and the many have seldom been docile enough not to provoke such justifications. This study deals with the ideas and interests of the few who have managed the work force of industrial and business enterprises since the Industrial Revolution. It is particularly concerned with ideas which pertain to the relations between workers and employers or their agents. Such ideas have been expressed by employers, financiers, public-relations men, personnel specialists, general managers, engineers, economists, political theorists, psychologists, government officials, policemen, political agitators, and many, many others. All these men have had in common a direct concern with the problems of industrial organization, whether or not they have worked in some managerial capacity themselves.

Industrialization has been defended in terms of the claim that the few will lead as well as benefit the many. It has been attacked in terms of the assertion that both the exploiting few and the exploited many are made to suffer, body and soul. The most rapidly advancing industrialized nations, the United States and Soviet Russia, are heir to these conflicting ideological antecedents. Since this conflict is the point of departure for the present study, it is appropriate to formulate at the beginning the common core of the two entrepreneurial or managerial ideologies which have been used in the advance of industrialization.[1]

In the West industrialization has been defended by ideological appeals which justified the exercise of authority in economic enterprises. Qualities of excellence were attributed to employers or managers which made them appear worthy of the position they occupied. More or less elaborate theories were used in order to explain that excellence and to relate it to a larger view of the world. The exercise of authority would also be justified in terms of the "naturally" subordinate position of the

[1] I shall use the phrase "ideologies of management" as the generic designation. All ideas which are espoused by or for those who exercise authority in economic enterprises, and which seek to explain and justify that authority, are subsumed under this phrase. "Entrepreneurial ideologies" will refer to such ideas in the early phase of industrialization and "managerial ideologies" will refer to the analogous ideas in modern industries. The term "industrialization" is used to refer to the process by which large numbers of employees are concentrated in single enterprises and become dependent upon the directing and coordinating activities of entrepreneurs and managers. (By "large numbers" I refer to any number of employees in excess of that which still permits a face-to-face relationship between employer and employee.) The terms "industrial enterprise" and "economic enterprise" will be used as interchangeable synonyms with the understanding that reference is made to all income-producing enterprises in which large numbers of employees work under managerial direction. No effort is made to distinguish between owners, employers, entrepreneurs, managers, or leaders of economic enterprises; these terms are used interchangeably to refer to all those engaged in coordinating and directing the work of employees in economic enterprises. However, the leaders of enterprises during the early phase of industrialization will on occasion be distinguished from the leaders of modern industry; in such cases the terms: "entrepreneur" and "manager" will be used.

many who obey. To this a further reference to the social order was usually added, holding out a promise to the many who with proper exertion might better themselves or even advance to positions of authority. These ideas appear to lack humane appeal. A creed which expounds the identity of virtue and success will strengthen the conviction of those who are convinced already. And the related admonition to the "poor" to exert themselves as their "betters" have, will be reassuring to those who have arrived. Such appeals express the interests of a group of men, whose power and social position are more or less secure by virtue of their successful leadership of economic enterprises. But it is probable that these ideas have also had a strong appeal for those who spend their daily life under the authority of the very employers whose achievements are celebrated. Indeed that authority has been defended on the ground that each man is free to enjoy what he can acquire on his own, and the promise of freedom based on exertion has excited the human imagination. But this position has also been attacked on the ground that the few are rewarded while the many are deprived, that the promise of freedom is spurious as long as it implies the risk of starvation as well as each man's dependence upon an irrational market and an inhuman machine. Still, the ideological defense of industrialization has helped to structure our image of the social world—within the orbit of Anglo-American civilization. The following study examines this ideological defense, first at the inception of industrialization, and then in its contemporary setting.

In Soviet Russia industrialization has been advanced by ideologies of management, which originated as a critique of industry. That critique pointed to two disastrous consequences which society must avoid or undo. Through their pursuit of gain men had been alienated from their fellows; the relations among them had come to depend upon the cash-nexus. And through the division of labor industrialism had subjected the individual producer to the degrading domination of the machine, depriving him of the satisfaction which the craftsman enjoyed. To undo these consequences it was necessary to afford all men the opportunity of doing their work as participants in a common undertaking. Accordingly, the commands of managers and the obedience of workers should receive their justification from the subordination of both groups to a body which represented managers and workers so that each man would obey policies he had helped to formulate. Hence, the exercise of authority by the few and the subordination of the many would be justified by the service each group rendered to the achievement of goals determined for it. And the relations between employers and workers would be regulated in conformity with an authoritative determination of the role of each.

If the Western spokesmen of industry can be identified by the expression of material interests, their opponents in Russia may be identified by the assertion that their interests are identical with the higher interests of mankind. Communism has owed its strength to the articulation of grievances against the industrial way of life. The belief that the pursuit of gain alienates men from their fellows, that the rich are depraved and the poor are deprived, constitutes a potent appeal to the dissatisfactions of the many and facilitates identification with humanity. Yet this attack has been incorporated in a managerial ideology, which combines these negative appeals with the ideal of collective ownership and planning. Karl Marx had capped his attack upon capitalism with the proposal to restore "real" freedom. Men "should consciously regulate production in accordance with a settled plan" so that they would carry on their work with the means of production in common.[2] All should own and plan as well as work, so that all might be free. These ideas have been defended on the ground that men can find personal fulfillment only when they own their tools and consciously direct their own activity. They have been attacked on the ground that such personal participation in collective ownership and planning is nominal only, that the promise of personal fulfillment is spurious as long as each must carry on his work in accordance with dictates and in the absence of privacy. This, then, is the other ideology which this study examines, again at the inception of industrialization and in its contemporary setting. For we are confronted with the paradox that the ideas with which the effects of industry were condemned have been incorporated in ideologies of management which today prevail within the orbit of Russian civilization.

I propose to examine the major entrepreneurial ideologies in the early phases of industrialization in England and in Russia (Chapters 2 and 3). Subsequently, I shall examine the major managerial ideologies which have evolved in the recent industrial history of the United States and which are used currently in the Soviet Zone of East Germany (Chapters 5 and 6). The link between my consideration of "then" and "now" is formed by a chapter on the bureaucratization of industry (Chapter 4).

During the early phase of industrialization a new way of life is in the making and an old way of life is on the defensive. In this respect I shall compare England and Russia during the eighteenth and nineteenth centuries. For those who initiate the development of industry must

2 See Karl Marx, *Capital* (New York: Modern Library, Inc., 1936), pp. 92–93.

overcome the opposition of many groups, and the ideas they advance concerning the relations between employers and workers will appear as part of the whole effort to gain acceptance for, and to facilitate, the development of industry.

While the initiation of industry involves everywhere a break with the past, it also involves quite dissimilar patterns of developments. In taking my cue from the present division of the world into East and West, I have chosen two such patterns of industrialization. These may be distinguished in the sense that English industrialization resulted principally from the struggle of a rising entrepreneurial class, while in Russia the interaction among social classes which was connected with industrialization was continually subject to autocratic intervention and bureaucratic controls.

This contrast between a society in which those who govern industry form a more or less autonomous social class, and a society in which entrepreneurs are subordinate to governmental controls, has endured till the present day; but the internal organization of economic enterprise has undergone profound changes, which have consisted, broadly speaking, in the multiplication of technical and administrative tasks as well as in the lengthening of the rank-order of authority in industrial organizations. As a result the tasks of management have increased in number and complexity, and the ideas concerning the relations between employers and workers have become a part of the effort to solve these managerial tasks more successfully. Accordingly, the outline of this study may be represented by the following schematic representation:

	Entrepreneurs and managers form an autonomous class	Entrepreneurs and managers are subordinate to government control
Entrepreneurial ideologies at the inception of industry	England	Russia
Managerial ideologies in large-scale economic enterprises	United States	East Germany

It will be useful to state the major themes of this study by giving an over-all description of the comparisons and contrasts implicit in this scheme.

I. At the inception of industry entrepreneurial ideologies are similar in certain respects. The problems of industrial organization and labor management will appear as part of the whole effort to gain acceptance for, and thereby to facilitate, the development of industry. During this early phase, employers and their agents have little experience with these problems; the consideration of management as a technical problem does not belong, therefore, to this early phase. Rather the practices and ideologies of management may be understood as a part of the effort to promote industry in a relatively hostile environment. The ideas which are used to justify the exercise of authority in industry are employed primarily to justify the entrepreneurs before the public at large. That public consists typically of two major social groups, a politically dominant aristocracy and a newly recruited industrial work force. Spokesmen for these groups often oppose industry with the same arguments, but their reasons for these arguments differ significantly. For members of a ruling aristocracy industrialization constitutes a threat to their political dominance as well as to their way of life. For members of a newly recruited industrial work force industrialization constitutes a threat to their established way of life and hence provides an opportunity to make invidious contrasts between that way of life and the new opportunities, demands, and deprivations laid upon them. Hence, the entrepreneurial ideologies during the initial phases of industrialization are primarily justifications of industry and of the leaders of industry which are called forth by this opposition of antagonistic social groups. Therefore, a good bit more is involved than the analysis of ideological trends. It is necessary to identify who the early entrepreneurs were and what their relationship was to the "ruling classes" in the society in which industrialization was initiated. Relations between these entrepreneurs and their workers are strongly affected by the traditional master-servant relationships. It is necessary to characterize the latter before analyzing how the practices and ideologies of industrial management are differentiated from them and developed further. Moreover, the industrial entrepreneurs, the workers in their enterprises, and the ruling social groups are engaged in social and political interaction in their respective efforts to come to terms with the industrial way of life. Each group seeks to do so in a manner it regards as advantageous (or less disadvantageous) to itself. It is necessary to characterize this interaction in order to understand the terms of the controversy in which the ideological weapons are fashioned by those who initiate the development of industry.

II. At the inception of industry entrepreneurial ideologies differ in certain respects. Such differences arise from the historical legacies and the social structures of the countries under consideration. The early phase of industrialization in England was characterized by a rising entrepreneurial class, which fought for social recognition and political power at the same time that it developed its enterprises, and recruited and disciplined an industrial work force. In Russia this early phase was characterized by the governmental promotion of enterprises and by the dependence of many, mutually antagonistic groups upon the government in terms of administrative and police measures which would aid their economic activities as well as the recruitment and disciplining of the work force.

In the West, the ideas which have been used to advance industrialization have reflected and affected the actions of entrepreneurs and managers of industry. These leaders of enterprise developed or made use of ideas which enhanced their social cohesion and active unity as a social class. Such cohesion and unity arise from the common interests of similarly situated individuals. These individuals may be combined in an organization or they may be divided by conflicting interests; they may exert great power when some issue unites them for the time being. But their unity or diversity in thought and action are never wholly integrated by a hierarchical organization. Social classes are groups of individuals whose common interests in the social and economic order now and again give rise to unifying ideas and united actions but whose cohesion is more or less unstable. This lack of stability is reflected in the development of entrepreneurial ideologies, which have been reformulated in response to changing industrial and social environments. Such reformulations or changes may be considered as more or less flexible adaptations to changing conditions by men of action whose underlying purpose remained the advance of practical interests and the increase of material gain. Ideological adaptations of this kind cannot be considered simply as an outgrowth of self-interest, for a man must judge what is to his interest, and many factors other than interest may influence his judgment. In nineteenth-century England entrepreneurs and managers of industry were on the whole free to pursue their interests as they saw them. And the strategies of argument with which they and their spokesmen advanced and defended entrepreneurial activities were strongly affected by the historical legacies which permitted men of substance to formulate and pursue their interests in common.

These considerations do *not* apply to the industrialization of Russia, however. The ideas and actions of entrepreneurs and managers who advanced industrialization in eighteenth- and nineteenth-century Russia were subjected to the more or less thorough control of a governmental bureaucracy and to the principle of Tsarist supremacy. This characteristic of Russian civilization may be called an "external bureaucratization" of industry, which should be distinguished from the "factory legislation" which is familiar to us from the industrial history of England and of other countries. For "factory legislation" was typically concerned with stipulating the conditions under which the interaction between employers and workers would take place independently. Such legislation laid down what employers cannot do and what workers can do; it typically expressed an effort to balance the strength of the two parties by legislative means. But the external bureaucratization of Russian industry attempted to do more than this. It stipulated the rights and duties of both parties not only by prohibiting certain actions, but also by ordering what should be done. And in addition the government superimposed on the authority relationship between employers and workers incentives and controls of its own. The purpose was to enhance the authority of managers over workers and the control of the state over managers, as well as to increase the obedience and productivity of the workers.

III. The development of the industrial way of life has transformed this initial setting of entrepreneurial activity in Russia as well as in the countries of Western civilization. One principal difference between then and now is that today the industrial way of life has become accepted (in the countries under consideration), and that the ideologies pertaining to industrial organization and labor management are no longer directly involved in the struggle for or against industrialization. To be sure, the attempt to justify industry before the public at large remains; the leaders of industrial enterprises and their spokesmen still find it necessary to justify their activities and defend them against their critics. This continued defense, however, has become a matter of public relations, concerned with propagandizing the achievements of technology and production which are generally accepted.

A second principal difference between then and now consists in the change from entrepreneurial to managerial ideologies. The ideologies of those who lead the large-scale enterprises of modern industry have come to serve new ends, which have resulted from a process of internal bureaucratization. The increase in the tasks of industrial management was relatively slow in making itself felt. For a long time these tasks remained in the hands of subordinate employees or contractors, who in turn relied upon the traditional relationships between masters and servants. As we shall see, there has existed, roughly speaking, an inverse relation between the diminishing strength of these traditions and the increasing division of labor in the technical and administrative organization of industrial enterprises. This increasing size and complexity of industry have transformed the authority relationship between managers and workers, and hence the internal organization of industry.

The internal bureaucratization of economic enterprises has had significant consequences. The few who command must control but cannot superintend the execution of their directives. They are bound to delegate more authority as the size of enterprises and the number of persons in positions of some responsibility increase. The delegation of authority has its counterpart in the technical and administrative specialization of those who execute as well as of those who control the implementation of directives. For specialization implies that those lower down in the hierarchy of command know more in a limited field than those who are above them. Of course, it is often said that the more highly placed have the more general view in addition to their greater authority. It should be noted, however, that their subordinates tend to acquire power even without authority to the extent that their *expertise* removes them from the effective control of their superiors. The tasks of management have increased in the sense that the increasing discretion of subordinates has had to be matched by strategies of organizational arrangements, material incentives, and ideological appeals if the ends of management were to be realized. In this respect the managerial ideologies of today are distinguished from the entrepreneurial ideologies of the past in that managerial ideologies are thought to aid employers or their agents in controlling and directing the activities of workers.

In the early phase of industrialization there was no difference between appeals to the workers (if the employers took the trouble to make such appeals) and the effort to win public acceptance for the economic activities with which the employers were identified. Entrepreneurial ideologies reflected the interaction among social classes brought about by industrialization. In modern industry management has had to concern itself, ideologically as well as practically, with industrial organization and labor management as major problems over and above the technical, financial, and marketing aspects of the enterprise. Hence, ideological appeals have become a tool of industrial management and may be distinguished fairly well from the important, but separate, task of developing the public relations between the enterprise and the community. Managerial ideologies are a response to the problems of coordination and direction in large-scale enterprises, and in this respect they are comparable, whatever may be the legacies and social structures of the countries under consideration. The difference between entrepreneurs and managers in early nineteenth-century Russia and in the Russia of today is every bit as great as parallel differences are in England or the United States.

IV. Two interpretations divide the contemporary world. While these interpretations have undergone a certain development, each of them is characterized by central tendencies which have persisted. These tendencies may be analyzed in the context of entrepreneurial and managerial practice and ideology. Throughout the industrialization of the West industrial leadership has been presented as the achievement of individuals. In Russia and in the countries within her orbit that leadership has been presented as the achievement of those who represent the nation (the Tsar or the party). In the West the exercise of authority in industry has rarely been denied. At most it has been attenuated, in the sense either that such authority was said to be accessible to all who qualified or that it could not be exercised effectively without benefit for the many. In the East the exercise of authority in industry is interpreted in a much more complex way, because it is said to represent the supreme authority of the state. And since that supreme authority is interpreted as the authentic voice of the people, various institutions and ideologies see to it that the exercise of authority by the industrial manager is not so much checked, as counterbalanced, supervised, and, if need be, corrected. Such supervision, counterbalancing, and correction are held to be compatible with the absolute authority of the manager within the enterprise; they are merely made necessary by the "more absolute" authority of the Tsar or the party. And in Soviet Russia the managers of industry (and those whose orders they obey) represent their appeals to the workers as expressing the interests and demands of the workers themselves.

In these general respects there has existed a difference in the historical legacies of the two worlds, which has endured regardless of the profound changes which have occurred during the last two centuries. Today, this difference may be observed especially in the authority relationship between managers and workers. As the delegation of authority and technical specialization have become more important for the successful functioning of modern enterprises, management has had either to rely upon, or to make sure of, the good faith of its employees. Certainly, detailed controls are needed even where good faith exists. But the effectiveness of managerial controls depends either upon a substratum of mutual trust or upon the institution of additional controls where that trust does not exist. In the one case superiors have, or act as if they had, confidence in the compliance and work habits of their subordinates, while the latter follow directives with a modicum of spontaneous good faith. As a result, controls upon the execution of directives need not greatly exceed those which are indispensable for technical and administrative efficiency. In the other case superiors lack this confidence in the sense that they do not expect subordinates to follow directives or to exert themselves much beyond what is necessary to escape deprivations or penalties. As a result, there will be a persistent tendency to impose further controls in order to check up on the execution of directives and to prevent, if possible, the workers' "withdrawal of efficiency" (Veblen). Admittedly, these are extreme alternatives, but they point to certain central tendencies in the management of industry which are an outgrowth of historical legacies in Anglo-American and in Russian civilization.

The consequences of this difference for the managerial practices and ideologies in modern industry are far-reaching, for there exists a pervasive, even though superficial, contradiction between managerial appeals and political traditions. In the West, and especially in the United States, authority in industry is justified explicitly on the ground that the man who already enjoys the good things in life has earned them and is entitled to the privileges which they confer. Hence, the employer's authority as well as his earnings and privileges are the rewards of past and present exertions. For the people at large such rewards are promises held out for the future and little effort is made to disguise the heavy burden of labor. Most attempts to increase the *present* satisfactions of work consist rather in promises of future rewards and in benefits and appeals which have the character of additional incentives offered by the employer. Not one but all goals are offered to the individual as grounds for increasing his exertions: getting ahead and not falling behind, personal satisfaction and shining before others, more work and more leisure, individual accomplishment and teamwork, material possessions and spiritual values. The list of homilies is endless and all-embracing, and it is addressed to the masses of people who must find what comfort they can out of their single-handed efforts to reach these distant goals. In terms of ideology little is done to spare them their frustrations or to equivocate about the privilege and power of the few. Yet this rather basic division between the few and the many occurs in societies in which the masses of the people enjoy a nearly unparalleled extension of personal freedom, not only in the formal political sense but also in the sense of material well-being.

In Soviet Russia, success is regarded as a collective accomplishment, in which managers as well as workers have the right and the duty to participate, but which is attributed primarily to the leadership of the party. Authority in industry is justified explicitly on the ground that the men who exercise it act under orders and are responsible for the highest achievements. The good things in life may be enjoyed by all in proportion to their contribution to society. And it is asserted either that the people are already better off or that they must tighten their belts because of capitalist encirclement. Most attempts to increase *present* satisfactions of work consist in promises of participation in collective achievements of the future or in benefits and appeals which have the character of distinctions received in return for a service to the nation. Only one goal is offered to the individual as the ground for increasing his exertion: that he perform his work out of loyalty to the cause. All the people are said to work for themselves (rather than for an exploiter), because they own the means of production and hence work for their own society, in which power is exercised by the best representatives of the working class. As the individual's right of citizenship imposes on him the duty to do military service, so in Soviet Russia the rights of citizenship impose on everyone the duty of labor. Hence, increases in productivity are rewarded as courage is in battle: by material benefits and honorific distinctions. Everything is done to make every individual a full participant in the crusade to increase production and prepare for the coming struggle with the enemy. And all distinctions of material and honorific rewards are made to serve the solidarity of a society organized on the model of a combat unit. Thus, the nation is put on the basis of a continuous, military emergency, wherein the masses bear the brunt of a nearly unparalleled extinction of privacy and personal freedom, not only in the formal political sense but also in terms of an absence of material well-being.

The following study explores in some detail the problems and major themes which have been described briefly in the preceding remarks. It will be helpful, however, if certain general considerations are added at this point with regard to the analysis of entrepreneurial ideologies and their social setting during the early phase of industrialization, in England and in Russia during the eighteenth and nineteenth centuries. (The parallel considerations which have guided the analysis of managerial ideologies in modern industry, in the United States and in a Soviet satellite, are contained in Chapter 4, in which the major transformation of economic enterprises between "then" and "now" is discussed under the heading "The Bureaucratization of Economic Enterprises.")

b. Industrialization and Entrepreneurial Ideologies in Sociological Perspective

All economic enterprises have in common a basic social relation between the employers who exercise authority and the workers who obey. And all ideologies of management have in common the effort to interpret the exercise of authority in a favorable light. At this most general level it is largely a matter of finding arguments in support of two related contentions. One of these refers to those in authority who are alternately shown not to rule at all, or to rule only in the interest of large numbers. The other refers to the many who obey orders, and who are alternately shown to obey only when they consent to do so, or because such obedience provides them with the greatest opportunities of advancement. Apparently, such ideologies interpret the facts of authority and obedience so as to neutralize or eliminate the conflict between the few and the many in the interest of a more effective exercise of authority. To do this, the exercise of authority is either denied altogether on the ground that the few merely order what the many want; or it is justified with the assertion that the few have qualities of excellence which enable them to realize the interests of the many. This is the common theme which makes ideologies of management comparable despite the different patterns of industrialization and despite the variety of specific interpretations.

The most general contrast between the civilizations of Russia and the West has to do with the extent to which social relations are free from, or are affected by, political decisions and governmental controls. In the context of this study I am concerned with two interrelated aspects of industrialization which underlie the formulation of ideologies of management. Employers or their agents exercise authority over their workers, and this shared position and function may give rise to common interests and actions. An individual entrepreneur, for example, may join other entrepreneurs, in order to formulate the interests that are common to the group and to implement these common aspirations by appropriate collective action. But the act of joining with others and the formulation of common aspirations and their implementation through collective action are not necessarily a by-product of the fact that industrialists are by and large men who have a social position and economic interests in common.[3] The unity of thought and action among

---

[3] This distinction between the social and economic conditions of a social class and the collective actions by the united members of that class is important and has been neglected. In his introduction to *Das Kapital* Marx pointed out that he did not attribute the evils committed by the class of capitalists to capitalists as

employers is necessarily provisional, depending as it does upon their several practical interests. And the ideologies of management which are formulated on this basis are likely to reflect whatever diversity of practical interests exists among the members of this social class.[4]

These statements apply by and large to the industrial history of England and the United States as well as of other countries of western Europe. They do not apply, however, to the industrialization of Russia, for they presuppose that employers are free to exercise authority over their workers and to join together in order to pursue their common interests. To some extent such freedom existed in Russia as well, but the distinctive feature of the Russian development is that the employers' exercise of authority and their collective actions and ideas have been subordinated throughout to the principle of governmental supremacy. While actual administrative intervention in industrial relations has been sporadic, the important point is that the relations between employers and workers have been interpreted throughout as affecting the public interest. Ideologies of management have been formulated, therefore, in the course of interaction between employers and government officials.

There is a significant difference between men who pursue their economic interests and officials who do their appointed task. The unity of thought and action among these two groups arises either on the basis of shared interests or on the basis of authoritative directives. Social classes become effective agents of collective action to the extent that shared social and economic characteristics give rise to organizational cohesion. Bureaucracies become effective agents of collective action to the extent that their hierarchical organizations give rise to shared social and eco-

individuals. Yet the polemical style of the literature which Marx initiated quickly obscured this distinction between individual members of a class and the class as an acting group, and hence the distinction between the economic interests of individuals and their readiness to participate in collective action. Cf. Reinhard Bendix and S. M. Lipset, "Karl Marx' Theory of Social Classes," in Reinhard Bendix and S. M. Lipset, eds., *Class, Status and Power* (Glencoe: The Free Press, 1953), pp. 26–35.

[4] It is awkward but unavoidable to speak of "members" of a social class. Strictly speaking, individuals merely share certain social and economic characteristics, and those who do are therefore "members" of a class only in the classificatory sense; but such individuals may also join to act in common and only then are they members without quotation marks. Since most references to social class, however, relate the shared characteristics of individuals to their capacity and actual readiness for collective action, it is not possible to keep the two meanings verbally separated.

nomic characteristics among the officials. And if officials are called upon to superintend the pursuit of practical interests by employers, then the organization of industry and the management of labor become subordinate to the maintenance and advancement of superordinated administrative hierarchies.[5] These distinctions are frequently blurred in practice, since the officials may support industry for political reasons; but even where the interests of employers and officials coincide, the rival principles of organization remain.[6] And these rival principles are reflected in the different ideologies of management which have developed in Russian and in Anglo-American civilization.

These different ideologies of management are examined in the next two chapters. The attempt is made to trace the development of authority relationships in economic enterprises and of entrepreneurial ideologies in England and in Russia. It will be useful to the reader if the major outlines of these developments are made explicit at the outset.

England. Industrialization in England was initiated by a rising class of entrepreneurs. The formation of a social class may be analyzed in terms of the position its members occupy in the society, and in terms of the ideas by which they achieve a measure of self-identification or class consciousness. In late eighteenth-century England the position of the entrepreneurial class was circumscribed by the activities of its members in the promotion of economic enterprises. While the social origin and the education of the early entrepreneurs will be discussed, major emphasis will be placed upon the development of class consciousness. The

---

[5] This subordination of economic actions to political considerations did not remain confined to Tsarist Russia. It is equally prominent in Lenin's theory of the labor movement. His essay "What is to be done?" contains the most important modern formulation of the conflict between group action based upon political as against economic principles. Its major thesis is that workers by themselves develop "only a trade-union consciousness," a term which stands for their concern with an improvement of wages and working conditions. But these economic interests of the workers are, according to Lenin, not "historical" interests of their class. The workers must rather be educated to recognize these class interests and the historic mission which they imply. And the educators of the working class must be a band of professional revolutionaries, whose intellectual comprehension of history and whose organizational discipline will place them in the vanguard of the labor movement.

[6] Karl Wittfogel has criticized Marx for his failure to consider the role of bureaucracy, but Wittfogel himself fails to make any distinction between a "ruling class" and a "ruling bureaucracy." This distinction is likely to be obscured whenever all political actions and organizations are treated as by-products of "basic" economic changes. Cf. Karl Wittfogel, "The Ruling Bureaucracy of Oriental Despotism," *The Review of Politics,* Vol. XV (1953), pp, 350–59.

early entrepreneurs were welded into a social class, in part because they were caught up in an emerging mass excitement concerning the promise of technology. Moreover, their class consciousness grew because they resented the prevailing aristocratic prejudices against people who engaged in commerce and industry. The opposition of ruling groups in English society to the rising entrepreneurs was an important stimulus to the formation of this social class, for this opposition was strong enough to be experienced as a frustration but not strong enough to suppress the development of collective actions and ideas.

The growth of economic enterprise in the late eighteenth century stimulated the demand for labor. The dislocations associated with this increased demand made the place of the laborer in English society problematic. The traditional life of the worker was disrupted despite his strong reluctance to leave his accustomed work and residence and despite his aversion to factory discipline. Moreover, his poverty was made to appear not as a burden, but as a sign of idleness and sin at a time when his employers became rich, when his own standard of living rose somewhat, and when ideas concerning personal rights became widely known. In this way industrialization coincided with institutional and ideological changes which caused the worker to become aware of his position as a second-class citizen. The traditional subordination of the "lower classes" had always been attributed to forces beyond human control; now, the worker was held personally responsible for the poverty from which he suffered. Thus, the disruption of a traditional way of life coincided with the denial that the worker had a legitimate place in society, for a poverty which resulted from defects of character rather than from inscrutable forces tended to stigmatize the worker and undermine his self-respect.

In England this social isolation of the emerging working class was opposed in many ways. The prevailing view of the English aristocracy was to assert that the "higher classes" were obliged to think for, and to protect, the "poor" while the latter had to be submissive, depending entirely upon their "betters." This view was put into practice in a good many industrial enterprises; aristocratic owners, members of dissenting sects, and entrepreneurs in areas of labor scarcity were among those who managed their work force in the traditional manner. Also, management by subcontractors and foremen encouraged the retention of traditional relations between employers and workers, though this relation could be tyrannical as well as benevolent. Even where traditional practices were abandoned, the belief in them was frequently retained.

Indeed, the assertion that the "higher classes" are responsible and that the "lower classes" may depend upon them, became a matter of conscious agitation. Evangelical preaching reflected preconceptions with which portions of the ruling groups sought to meet the challenge of industrialization. As the rising entrepreneurial class broke with traditionalism ideologically, evangelism increased its efforts to inculcate morality in masses of the people. And although the immediate effect of the evangelical movement was to facilitate the subordination and improve the work habits of the people, its long-run significance was that it succeeded along with the Methodist revival in overcoming the worker's social isolation and restoring his self-respect.

Ideologically, there was considerable tension between evangelical preaching and the beliefs of the early entrepreneurs. The masses of the people were said to be immoral, their distress the result of indolence and sin. No educational or institutional device would improve their evil habits; only hunger could accomplish that. Meanwhile arguments were adduced to show that the rich could do nothing to relieve the distress of the poor. And the laws of nature and of nature's God were employed to show that the poor must help themselves. All the means for their relief, namely moral conduct and the postponement of marriage, were within their power and within their power alone. Eventually, this demand for a reform of the habits of the poor was implemented in a manner which seemed to give to the equation of poverty with immorality the sanction of a public institution. Yet shortly thereafter, in conjunction with the demand for free trade, an entrepreneurial ideology was developed which appealed to the worker as a member of the community, which praised his independence where his insubordination had been condemned, and which preached a gospel of work and hope in lieu of the earlier gospel of work and despair. The English entrepreneurial class had found an ideological basis, on which it could exercise its authority within economic enterprises without condemning the workers to a position of social isolation.

Russia. Industrialization in Russia was initiated by an autocratic ruler, whose centralized power precluded the existence of autonomous social groups. Prior to the eighteenth century the duties of each group had been legally defined: the peasants were bound to the land, and the government exacted specific services from townspeople and landowners. The development of urban centers and of industrial production was greatly retarded. The governmental promotion of economic growth reflected these legacies. Enterprises were set up with state funds. Labor was made available through forced recruitment. The bulk of the products was sold to the government, and management was entrusted to employers who were duty-bound to serve the state and whose "rights" merely consisted in privileges designed to facilitate that service. Under Peter the Great the landed aristocracy stood in a similar relationship to the state. Consequently, conflicts of interest between social groups, such as that between the aristocracy and middle-class employers, consisted in the competition for privileges from the Tsar.

During the eighteenth century the relations among the several social groups changed significantly. After the death of Peter the Great (1725), the obligations of the landed aristocracy were gradually reduced while its privileges were increased. This changing position of the aristocracy had several significant repercussions. The privileges previously granted to merchants and manufacturers were withdrawn. Productive activities increased on the landed estates, as aristocrats were more frequently exempted from military or administrative services and as they encouraged their peasant serfs to engage in trade and production. The greatly improved position of the aristocracy was not, however, a token of its increasing power in the state. Rather, the Tsars, and especially Catherine II, utilized the privileges granted to the aristocracy as a means of keeping it out of power. And the power of the Tsar was strengthened by the growing antagonism among aristocrats, middle-class employers, and the working masses.

This intensification of class differences became especially manifest in the relations among the Tsar, the aristocracy, and the serfs. The privileges of the aristocracy were increased along with the exploitation of the peasantry; but in a predominantly agricultural country income was primarily derived from the work of the peasants, so that the revenue of the state as well as the wealth of the aristocracy depended upon it. Hence, Tsarist officials and aristocratic landowners made competing claims upon the peasantry. In the relations between the landowners and the peasantry this development led to a "moral estrangement between the classes." The increasing exploitation of the peasants was made possible by increased privileges, which had been granted to the aristocracy at a time when that aristocracy was generally exempted from the military or administrative services which had justified its privileges previously. The relations between the Tsar and the peasantry were also transformed, but in a different way. The Tsars retained ultimate authority over the peasant serfs; yet in their efforts to satisfy the aristocracy without giving it power, they increased the landowners' authority over the serfs. Hence, the Tsars' claim to ultimate authority contrasted with their inability and unwillingness to control the landowners' exercise of power over the serfs. In the unavailing but persistent attempts to make their lot more tolerable, the peasant serfs utilized this situation by appealing to the Tsar for relief from their exploiters, and rumors of the Tsar's real intentions were used to justify sporadic rebellions. By such actions the peasants unwittingly upheld the ultimate authority of the Tsars even when the latter failed to do so themselves.

Though primarily related to agriculture, this setting determined the relations between employers and workers and the development of entrepreneurial ideologies in all forms of economic enterprises. Peasants and workers were regarded as beasts of burden, whose complete subordination was essential to the established social order, and whose labor was regarded as a token of their submission. No other moral demand was made upon them, since the authority relations between masters and serfs were modeled after the authority relations between the Tsar and his subjects. In practice this approach led to many difficulties. Tsarist control over labor relations in economic enterprises gave all possible support to the owners and aided them in the exploitation of the serfs. Yet the authorities repeatedly asserted the Tsar's benevolent protection of all his subjects. When the exploitation of workers and peasants by the landowners finally provoked rebellions, the government frequently took over the operation of the enterprise to safeguard order and secure the supplies to the government.

In the case of middle-class employers, moreover, the government sought to achieve the same ends by administrative regulation and police inspection. And its regulation of the so-called possessional enterprises vacillated between an official support of the employer's control over the work force and occasional attempts to control the actions of the employers as well. The Tsarist regime overwhelmingly favored the employers in its effort to uphold the social order. Yet, the regime could never undo the basic principle of its own authority, in accordance with which the Tsar superintended *all* relations among social groups in Russian society. Hence, workers continued to look to the government for protection against their employers, just as the latter looked to the government for support against their workers.

The more rapid development of economic enterprises during the second half of the nineteenth century did not change these relationships, though it made them increasingly tenuous. In the past the government had been very reluctant to interfere with the landowner's power over his serfs; but the emancipation of the serfs in 1861 necessitated more rather than less governmental control of landowners and peasants. Similarly, the growth of economic enterprises from the 1840's on was accompanied by a "hands-off" policy: the Tsarist government lent its support to the authority of the employer and intervened only when disturbances among workers became unmanageable. Yet some Tsarist officials and some employers continued to advocate more regulations. And the prevailing system of taxation and police registration made some governmental regulation of the employers and the workers necessary in any case: it perpetuated the rural residence of industrial workers which resulted in high labor turnover and in a division of control over the work force between the employers and the government. Hence, employers *and* workers continued to look to the government for intervention on their behalf, despite the "hands-off" policy. When such intervention became necessary toward the end of the nineteenth century, Tsarist officials sought to control the relations between employers and workers by prescribing the actions of both groups and, in addition, by seeking to control the workers from within their own ranks.[7] This superimposition of governmental controls, however, implied that every protest against employers was a protest against the government. When the government failed to act in its proclaimed role as a defender of the workers' interests, economic grievances became transformed into a revolution against the prevailing social order.

This brief synopsis of the English and the Russian development may be formulated in more general terms. Where industrialization is the work of a rising entrepreneurial class, that class is likely to seek social recognition from the ruling groups at the same time that its ideas and economic activities challenge the traditions of the ruling groups at many points. These activities lead to the creation of a nonagricultural work force under conditions of great economic distress. While poverty is not a new experience for this rising working class, factory discipline and the disruption of a traditional way of life are. By their ideological appeals the new entrepreneurs may aggravate that new experience by making the workers personally responsible for the distress which industrialization imposes upon them. This social isolation of the workers, which results from the activities of the rising entrepreneurial class, is resisted by the workers and the older ruling groups. Both tend to combat it by clinging fast to the practices and to the ideal images of the preindustrial society. By so doing the older ruling groups seek, in effect, to restore

---

[7] This conception of governmental authority, which supplements the stipulation and enforcement of rules with attempts to organize compliance with the rules from within the ranks of labor or of management, has become the model after which the practices and ideologies of labor management have been fashioned in Soviet Russia.

the working class to an accepted position within society. The workers' quest for an accepted if subordinate place in the new society may take the form of radical demands, but these often derive their strength from an insistence upon traditional rights. The nature of these traditional ideas and practices helps to determine whether and in what manner the "reincorporation" of the workers in the new industrial society is achieved. In England the precepts of evangelism and the Methodist revival among the workers were instrumental both in serving the interests of the entrepreneurs and in aiding this reintegration of the workers. And when a new entrepreneurial ideology was formulated, shortly after the ideological break with traditionalism was complete, the new ideology further contributed to this reintegration. For it is significant that in England the workers adopted many middle-class values in the process of attaining for themselves a recognized position within the industrial society.

When industrialization occurs in a country with a centralized, autocratic regime, then an entrepreneurial class will seek recognition for its economic activities from the government, especially in the form of privileges that will facilitate these activities. Competition with the ruling social groups may be keen, but it is not likely to challenge the principal buttress of this social order: that the government is the ultimate arbiter of conflicting claims by virtue of its control over the distribution of privileges. Essentially the same point applies to the position of the peasants and workers. The government continues to proclaim itself the ultimate authority and the guardian of the people. The peasants and workers continue to act upon this view in seeking redress for their grievances against their masters. Hence, in theory, the subordinate but accepted position of peasants and workers in Russian society remained unchanged, but the emancipation of the serfs and the increased mobility incident to a rising industrial work force altered that subordinate position in fact. The people continued to call upon the government to protect them against exploitation and to grant them the rights which had been withheld in the past, while the government continued to claim ultimate authority but failed to act accordingly. In the end the people rebelled against the Tsar's failure to fulfill his acknowledged obligation to the people, as they interpreted it. That is, they sensed and eventually rebelled against their social isolation from the society after the emancipation of the serfs and industrialization in the second half of the nineteenth century had partly terminated their old subordination, and after the government had opened up and then withdrawn previously unknown opportunities of social recognition.

PART ONE

CHAPTER **2**

Entrepreneurial Ideologies in the Early Phase of Industrialization: The Case of England

> . . . *this most bourgeois of all nations is apparently aiming ultimately at the possession of a bourgeois aristocracy and a bourgeois proletariat as well as a bourgeoisie.*—Engels in a letter to Marx dated October 7, 1858.

a. The Early Entrepreneurs

During the late eighteenth and early nineteenth centuries industrial entrepreneurs in England were struggling for recognition in a relatively hostile environment.[1]   They stood in need of ideas as weapons, in Mr.

---

[1] Industrialization may result from the initiative of *many* social groups: government officials, dissenting religious groups, aristocratic landowners, craftsmen turned into small entrepreneurs, and many others.   In England it was bound up— more perhaps than in any other country—with the economic activities of a large and heterogeneous middle class.   Because of this diversity of origin the term

Lerner's phrase, even though they had little use for ideas as such. In common with other rising social groups, they were engaged in a fight for public recognition of their economic activities and for acceptance of their own position in society. They had to overcome widespread resistance against industry, rooted in the habits of the people and in the ideas of their leaders. Specifically, they had to overcome the resistance of merchants, craftsmen, manufacturers, and others, whose outlook and whose personal security were identified with the old methods of production. They had to overcome also the resistance of groups whose vested claims to political preferment were at stake.

Several considerations may help us to see the early entrepreneurs as they saw themselves. To begin with, many of them came from a modest family background, though probably not as many as is usually assumed.[2]

"entrepreneurial class" is employed here; it refers to the economic function rather than to the social composition of the pioneers of industrialization. In the words of Joseph Schumpeter, "The function of entrepreneurs is to reform or revolutionize the pattern of production by exploiting an invention, or, more generally, an untried technological possibility for producing a new commodity or producing an old one in a new way, by opening up a new source of supply of materials or a new outlet for products, by reorganizing an industry, and so on. . . . To undertake such new things is difficult and constitutes a distinct economic function, first, because they lie outside of the routine tasks which everybody understands and, secondly, because the environment resists in many ways. . . ." See Joseph Schumpeter, *Capitalism, Socialism, and Democracy* (New York: Harper and Brothers, 1950), p. 132. I should add that I am not concerned here with the further implications of Schumpeter's theory. To define an entrepreneurial class in terms of its function, however, is less ambiguous for the beginning phase of industrialization than for later periods.

[2] There is a factual basis for the common opinion that *most* of the early manufacturers came from working-class or lower-middle-class families. Since the major developments of industry in the second half of the eighteenth century occurred in the textile industry and since capital requirements in that industry were very modest at that time, it is probable that a large proportion of the early cotton manufacturers in particular did come from families of workers, craftsmen, and peasants. It is also probable that workers and craftsmen who belonged to one of the dissenting sects had been able to rise through family cohesion and ascetic conduct until they were for the most part middle-class traders. Thus Raistrick has shown that of 250 Quaker bridegrooms in 1680 about three-fifths were craftsmen and one-fifth merchants, whereas these proportions were almost reversed by 1780. See Arthur Raistrick, *Quakers in Science and Industry* (New York: Philosophical Library, 1950), pp. 30–32. But what was true of the cotton industry and of dissenting sects was not by that token true of the entire manufacturing industry. Cf. Paul Mantoux, *The Industrial Revolution in the Eighteenth Century* (New York: Harcourt, Brace and Company, 1927), pp. 376–98, who stresses the diversity of social origin but leaves the impression that a majority of the manufacturers came from families of craftsmen and yeomen.

It should be remembered that the polemics of the period tended to exaggerate the low social origin of the early entrepreneurs. William Cobbett's description of the "new rich" (in 1827) is worth recalling:

> . . . this hatred to the cause of public liberty is, I am sorry to say it, but too common amongst merchants, great manufacturers, and great farmers; especially those who have *risen suddenly* from the dunghill to the chariot. If we look a little more closely into the influence of riches . . . we shall be less surprised at this apparently unnatural feeling in men who were, but the other day, merely journeymen and labourers themselves. . . . Such men are always seeking to cause their origin to be forgotten. . . . Their chief aim is to trample into the very ground all who are beneath them in point of pecuniary circumstances, in order that they may have as few equals as possible, and that there may be *as wide a distance as possible between them and their labourers*.[3]

That is, Cobbett not only emphasized the humble social origin of the early entrepreneurs. He also attributed to their sudden rise the cruel treatment of those beneath them as well as the endeavor to increase the distance between the lower social classes and themselves. There is considerable insight in this description of class prejudice among the *nouveaux riches,* as there often is in a partisan argument. It is quite possible that the extraordinary effort which was required of the craftsman or yeoman in developing his business made him ruthless in the treatment of his workers. But it is probable also, and it sheds a different light upon Cobbett's virulent words, that such men were equally ruthless with themselves.

It is misleading, however, to assume that a majority of the most prominent entrepreneurs were self-made men in this sense. In a survey of 132 industrialists, selected for their prominence in manufacturing during the period 1750–1850, it was found that about one-third came from families of workers and small-scale farmers, whereas two-thirds came from families already established in business.[4] In the decades after 1760 there was a frequent rise *and* fall of new entrepreneurs. There were also many cases in which the families of new entrepreneurs consolidated their economic position or in which already established families succeeded in maintaining and enlarging their enterprises. Moreover, neither the established families nor the second generation of the new manufacturers were self-made in the same sense as the early in-

---

[3] G. D. H. Cole and Margaret Cole, eds., *The Opinions of William Cobbett* (London: The Cobbett Publishing Company, 1944), pp. 86–87.

[4] Of the 132 families, 21 were taken from Mantoux, *op. cit.,* 21 from *Fortunes Made in Business* (London: S. Low, Marston, Searle, and Rivington, 1884–87), Vols. I and II, and the rest from the *Dictionary of National Biography.*

dustrial pioneers. Hence, to speak as if a large majority of the early entrepreneurs had suddenly risen "from the dunghill to the chariot" was intentionally misleading. A number of interpretations by the historians of specific industries confirm this evaluation.

The early manufacturers in the English woolen and worsted industry were recruited "mainly from the class of merchants who were already responsible for the finishing processes, and now turned manufacturers taking over from the clothier all earlier processes." [5] T. S. Ashton, the historian of the iron and steel industries, states that "most of the successful men in industry entered it from the secondary metal trades—successful craftsmen seeking control over the sources of their raw material—or from the merchanting of iron and steel wares." [6] This is not to deny that, as Gaskell remarked, "men who did establish themselves were raised by their own efforts—commencing in a very humble way, and pushing their advance by a series of unceasing exertions, having a very limited capital to begin with, or even none at all save that of their own labor." [7] But the early entrepreneurs did not have their origin primarily, as Gaskell and many others maintained, "in the rank of mere operatives, or . . . of yeomen." [8] It is probable rather that this was more true of some industries than of others, and it is unlikely that it was ever true of any industry for a long period of time.[9]

The same considerations apply, *mutatis mutandis,* to the lack of education among the early entrepreneurs and to the initial disinclination of the manufacturers to have their children acquire an education.

[5] E. Lipson, *The History of the Woolen and Worsted Industries* (London: A. and C. Black, Ltd., 1921), p. 176.

[6] T. S. Ashton, *Iron and Steel in the Industrial Revolution* (Manchester: Manchester University Press, 1951), pp. 209–10.

[7] P. Gaskell, *The Manufacturing Population of England* (London: Baldwin and Cradock, 1833), p. 45.

[8] *Ibid.,* p. 52.

[9] Although cotton-spinning was an industry in which many prominent manufacturers originally rose from modest family backgrounds, S. J. Chapman notes that by 1830 the larger factory owners had become a self-recruited group. See his *Lancashire Cotton Industry* (Manchester: Manchester University Press, 1904), pp. 216–17. Chapman's conclusion refers, however, to the large owners. Throughout the nineteenth century there were a large number of small owners as well, and a study of these small owners in 1912 indicates that 63 per cent of the sample had entered the industry during their lifetime. The two facts are clearly not incompatible. For the latter study see S. J. Chapman and F. J. Marquis, "The Recruiting of the Employing Classes from the Ranks of Wage-Earners in the Cotton Industry," *Journal of the Royal Statistical Society,* Vol. 75 (February, 1912), p. 296.

Robert Owen has described the early textile manufacturers (1790–1800) as "plodding men of business, with little knowledge and limited ideas, except in their own immediate circle of occupation." [10]   Gaskell refers to men in the same industry as having "very limited general information—men who saw and knew little of anything beyond the demand for their twist or cloth. . . . The sprinkling of men of more refined habits amongst the early successful cotton manufacturers was extremely scanty." [11]   Such observations applied primarily to an industry in which men of determination could establish themselves regardless of the unfavorable circumstances of their early life.   In other industries, such as iron and coal, capital was needed in order to make a start, and access to these industries was restricted by and large to the members of families which were at least moderately well-to-do.   Many of these families, however, had at first little taste for education in the public schools or universities which were dominated by the landed aristocracy. And when they did send their sons to the universities for the sake of obtaining social recognition, they were probably aware of the fact that these sons would not follow a business career themselves.[12]   There was then a conspicuous lack of education among the early industrialists; but lack of formal education is not synonymous with the depravity of manners which Gaskell and others attributed so generally to the early industrialists.[13]   It is probable that extreme cruelty and exploitation (judged by the standards of the late eighteenth century rather than by present-day standards) were greatest in the small shops, while they were mitigated in the larger factories.   Thus, the size of the enterprise, rather than the "education" of its owner, tended to be related to the crudest excesses of conduct on the part of the employers.[14]   And the fact that many of the early manufacturers were members of dissenting sects,

[10] M. Beer, ed., *Life of Robert Owen* (New York: Alfred A. Knopf, Inc., 1920), p. 50.

[11] Gaskell, *op. cit.*, pp. 53–54.

[12] None of the 5 per cent of Cambridge students, who indicated that their fathers were businessmen between 1800–1849, went into business careers themselves.   See H. Jenkins and D. C. Jones, "Social Class of Cambridge University Alumni of the Eighteenth and Nineteenth Centuries," *British Journal of Sociology*, Vol. I (June, 1950), p. 99.

[13] This judgment was not confined to Tories like Gaskell and Cobbett.   *The Poor Man's Advocate*, published by John Doherty, expressed similar views; while it deplored the crude manners of the older generation of manufacturers, it was even more contemptuous of their "younger fry" who had been taught at great expense.   Quoted in Chapman, *Lancashire Cotton Industry*, pp. 216–17.

[14] Cf. B. L. Hutchins and A. Harrison, *A History of Factory Legislation* (London: P. S. King and Son, 1911), pp. 19–21.

whose ideas concerning economic conduct were exceedingly strict, re-enforces this interpretation.

Two other characteristics of the early entrepreneurs need to be re-called: their apotheosis of technology and their fight for social recognition. During the second half of the eighteenth century, interest in technical inventions became unusually intensive. For a hundred years prior to 1760, the number of patents issued during each decade had reached 102 only once, and had otherwise fluctuated between a low of 22 (1700–1709) and a high of 92 (1750–1759). During the following thirty-year period (1760–1789), the average number of patents issued increased from 205 in the 1760's to 294 in the 1770's and 477 in the 1780's.[15] This veritable outburst of inventive activity was accompanied by much popular excitement. Poems were written to celebrate the wonders of patented inventions. Magazines were founded for the purpose of describing unusual phenomena of nature and of human design. The *Gentleman's Magazine* adopted as its policy that "the discovery of every new invention and the improvements in every useful art" would be announced in its pages. The editors of another journal, the *Museum Rusticum et Commerciale,* declared that its reports of "new and valuable discoveries" had been reprinted in almost every newspaper or magazine in the kingdom.[16] Other types of evidence, which Professor Bowden has assembled, point to the same intensification of interest. Various semitechnical dictionaries and encyclopedias were published during this period. Particular inventions, like balloon-flying, caught the imagination of many people for a time, only to give way to other fads. Many fanciful mechanical devices were advanced together with others, which proved to be useful in the immediate future. A number of individuals became well-known mechanics and inventors, though their low social origin often restricted their reputation to their native region. Others, however, became nationally known owing to their social prominence as well as to their mechanical aptitude.[17] Writers

[15] These figures are given in Witt Bowden, *Industrial Society in England Towards the End of the Eighteenth Century* (New York: The Macmillan Company, 1925), p. 12. The interest in "art" or innovation was, of course, older than these dates suggest. Cf. the discussion of this earlier literature in E. A. J. Johnson, *Predecessors of Adam Smith* (New York: Prentice-Hall, Inc., 1937), pp. 264–77, as well as the detailed study of E. G. Jacob, *Daniel Defoe, Essay on Projects* (Vol. 8 of *Koelner Anglistische Arbeiten;* Leipzig: Bernhard Tauchnitz, 1929), especially pp. 35–58, 84–126.

[16] See Bowden, *op. cit.,* pp. 15–16.

[17] The participation of the aristocracy in economic activities during the eighteenth century is analyzed in S. D. Stirk, *Die Aristokratie und die industrielle*

during this period asserted that it was more honorable to seek out "new inventions and discoveries" than to devote one's time to literature and the "polite arts." [18] And most important of all, societies were organized for the expressed purpose of encouraging inventions.

Foremost among these organizations was the Society for the Encouragement of Arts, Manufacture, and Commerce, established in London in 1754. The preamble of the plan for the establishment of this Society reads as follows:

> Whereas, the riches, honor, strength, and prosperity of a nation depend in a great measure on knowledge and improvement of useful arts, manufactures, etc., several of the nobility and gentry of this kingdom, being fully sensible that due encouragements and rewards are greatly conducive to excite a spirit of emulation and industry, have resolved to form themselves into a society. . . . The intent and purpose of this society is to encourage ingenuity and industry by bestowing premiums.[19]

The activities of the Society were broadly conceived, including as they did the promotion of the liberal arts as well as agriculture, manufactures, mechanics, chemistry, dyeing, and mineralogy. But in interpreting these purposes, the Society was guided by the belief that "on the improvement of mechanical engines the advancement of the manufactures, and ultimately the arts and commerce of the kingdom, must in a very material manner depend."

The Society acted on this belief to the extent of spending a total of over £28,000 for premiums and medals from 1754 to 1782.[20] In addition to such rewards the Society also initiated and supervised experiments. Above all, its aim was to

> . . . encourage with its rewards those inventors who were in need of financial assistance; and by means of rewards, public honors, and emphasis on the national welfare it sought to increase the number of those who were willing to allow public use of their inventions, thus foregoing private recompense legally permissible in the form of the monopolistic patent. Rewards were never granted for patented inventions; and all machines and models for which premiums or medals were awarded, as well as others donated to the society, became the property of the society, and through it, of the public. For its aim was not merely the promoting of "inventions, discoveries, and improvements," but "the laying open any such to the public." It was stated that "the society have from their institution invari-

Entwicklung Englands (Vol. XV of *Sprache und Kultur der Germanisch-Romanischen Voelker;* Breslau: Hans Priebatsch, 1933), pp. 40–69.

[18] Bowden, *op. cit.*, p. 25.
[19] Quoted in Bowden, *op. cit.*, p. 40.
[20] *Ibid.*, pp. 41–42.

ably endeavored, by every means in their power, to bring forward to public use and notice, all such machines as have a tendency to promote that end." [21]

These activities and declarations of the Society of Arts, as it was called, were symptomatic of the widespread enthusiasm for technology and manufacture. Many similar organizations sprang up in England, dedicated to the same ends. Various public bodies would give cash donations to promote their work. And it is another index of the popularity of these activities that the *Transactions* of the Society of Arts had to be reprinted repeatedly. This enthusiasm for technology was widespread primarily among the merchants, manufacturers, craftsmen, and yeomen of the time, although the Society of Arts was sponsored by members of the aristocracy. The universities did not encourage this interest at all, which led Adam Smith to denounce them without reservation.

> The improvements which in modern times have been made in several different branches of philosophy [i.e., knowledge] have not, the greater part of them, been made in universities, though some no doubt have. The greater part of universities have not even been very forward to adopt those improvements after they were made; and several of those learned societies have chosen to remain for a long time the sanctuaries in which exploded systems and obsolete prejudices found shelter and protection, after they had been hunted out of every other corner of the world.[22]

And in the same context Smith emphasized that the universities were the ideal place in which the young *could* be prepared for the "real business of the world." But this was not the case, in fact. Instead of reforming the universities, it became more and more the custom, according to Smith, to send young men abroad, where they dissipated their best years. "Nothing but the discredit into which the universities are allowing themselves to fall could ever have brought into repute so very absurd a practice as that of travelling at this early period of life." [23]

These observations of Adam Smith suggest that the faith in progress by technology was not merely a fashionable opinion, but the ideology of a social movement. The very enthusiasm for mechanical contrivances, the preoccupation with what Smith called "the real business of the world," were regarded with undisguised contempt by the landed aristocracy of England. It is true that some prominent members of the English aristocracy were concerning themselves with innovations on their

---

[21] *Ibid.*, pp. 42–43.

[22] Adam Smith, *The Wealth of Nations* (Edinburgh: Adam and Charles Black, 1863), p. 347.

[23] *Ibid.*

own estates, and manufacturers were increasingly able to enter the ranks of the aristocracy. But the contempt for the trader concerned with material things continued to be strong enough to provoke intense resentment, though it was not strong enough to interfere effectively with trade and industry. Hence, it provided the early entrepreneurs with the impetus of a frustration great enough to stimulate a social movement.

Spokesmen for the early entrepreneurs left no doubt that they found the aristocratic contempt for commerce and industry provoking in the extreme, though many of them were, nevertheless, eager to be accepted in the ranks of the aristocracy. Perhaps the most telling document in this respect is Daniel Defoe's *Tour Thro' the Whole Island of Great Britain,* published in 1727. Defoe was a self-conscious member of the middle class. In reporting on his travels through England he repeatedly observed that communities which formerly had been in the exclusive possession of some noble family had now passed into the hands of prosperous merchants. In writing about Essex, to cite but one example, Defoe states:

> It is observable, that in this part of the Country, there are several very considerable Estates purchas'd, and now enjoy'd by Citizens of *London,* Merchants, and Tradesmen, as Mr. *Western* an Iron Merchant, near *Kelvedon,* Mr. *Cresnor,* a Wholesale Grocer, who was, a little before he died, nam'd for Sheriff at *Earls Coln* . . . and several others.
>
> I mention this to observe how the present encrease of Wealth in the City of *London* spreads itself into the Country, and plants Families and Fortunes, who in another Age will equal the Families of the Ancient Gentry, who perhaps were bought out.[24]

Defoe did not confine himself to such observations. Self-conscious tradesman that he was, he described and extolled the virtues of commerce throughout his life. And he left his readers in no doubt that these merchants were men whose merit equaled that of the nobility:

> . . . it would be worth the while for those Gentlemen, who talk so much of their antient Family Merit . . . to look into the Roll of our Gentry, and enquire what is become of the Estates of those prodigious Numbers of lost and extinct Families, which now even the Heralds themselves can hardly find; let them tell us if those Estates are not now purchased by Tradesmen and Citizens, or the Posterity of such; and whether those Tradesmen's Posterity do not now fill up the Vacancies, the Gaps, the Chasmes in the great Roll or List of Families, as well of the Gentry, as of the Nobility themselves. . . .

[24] Daniel Defoe, *A Tour Thro' the Whole Island of Great Britain* (London: Peter Davies, 1927), Vol. I, p. 15.

Trade, in a word, raises antient Families when sunk and decay'd: And plants new Families, where the old ones are lost and extinct.[25]

Variations on the same themes continued throughout the eighteenth century. The great inventor and manufacturer, James Watt, wrote in 1787 that "our landed gentlemen reckon us poor mechanics no better than slaves who cultivate their vineyards." Another manufacturer wrote that "the proud and bigoted landowners look down with contempt on the merchant or manufacturer." And yet another writer condemned

> . . . the aristocratic prejudices and the envious contempt of neighboring peers and country gentlemen, proud of their rank and ancient family, who even in these days occasionally disgrace themselves by looking down on the man raised by merit and industry from obscurity to eminence.[26]

A Manchester clergyman, the Reverend Thomas Bancroft, put these sentiments in rhyme (1777):

> Is it then, ye vain lordlings! ye treat us with scorn,
> Because titles and birth your own fortunes adorn?
> What worth to yourselves from high birth can accrue?
> Are your ancestors' glories entailed upon you? . . .
> But peace—'tis presumption—too much would demean 'em
> To hold converse with upstarts, a vulgus profanem.
> Their blood in pure currents thro' ages conveyed
> It were impious to taint with the contact of trade.[27]

By the 1830's and 1840's the same arguments were still a major theme of public debate, except that by that time the contest involved much more than invidious arguments between the representatives of the manufacturers and of the aristocracy. On both sides appeals against the other were used to enlist the support of the workers in factory and field. As Morley has stated:

> The Tories were taunted with the condition of the labourers in the fields, and they retorted by tales of the condition of the operatives in factories. The manufacturers rejoined by asking, if they were so anxious to benefit the workman, why they did not, by repealing the Corn Law, cheapen his bread. The landlords and the millowners each reproached the other with exercising the virtues of humanity at other people's expense.[28]

---

[25] Daniel Defoe, A Plan of the English Commerce (Oxford: Basil Blackwell, 1928), pp. 62–63. Originally published in 1728.

[26] Bowden, op. cit., p. 155.

[27] Ibid., 156–57.

[28] John Morley, The Life of Richard Cobden (London, Chapman and Hall, 1881), Vol. I, p. 301.

This self-conscious resentment of a rising class of manufacturers and merchants was both a consequence and a further cause of the opposition and apprehension in the ranks of the aristocracy. Though it was true that men of wealth were often elevated to the nobility in one way or another,[29] staunch defenders of the hereditary aristocracy considered this process an adulteration. *Bailey's Dictionary* of 1707, for example, defined a gentleman as "a man who has received his nobility from his ancestors, not from the munificence of a Prince or a state." [30] Others insisted on the vital difference between the man who had entered the aristocracy because of his wealth, and the man who belonged to it by virtue of his birth. As Samuel Johnson stated,

> . . . riches do not gain hearty respect; they only procure external attention. A very rich man, from low beginnings, may buy his election in a borough; but a man of family will be preferred. People will prefer a man for whose father their fathers have voted, though they should get no more money, or even less. That shows that the respect for family is not merely fanciful, but has an actual operation. If gentlemen of family would allow the rich upstarts to spend their money profusely, which they are ready enough to do, and not vie with them in expense, the upstarts would soon be at an end, and the gentlemen would remain; but if the gentlemen will vie in expense with the upstarts, which is very foolish, they must be ruined.[31]

Boswell's *Life of Johnson* was published in 1791, before the major agitation for electoral reform had even started, and at a time when many manufacturers were strongly disinclined to concern themselves with political matters at all.[32] Three-quarters of a century later, over thirty years after the Reform Bill of 1832, and after the "middle classes" had acquired considerable representation in the House of Commons, Walter Bagehot still drew the same sharp distinction between the "new men" and the old aristocracy:

> In number the landed gentry in the House far surpass any other class. They have, too, a more intimate connexion with one another; they were educated at the same school; knew one another's family name from boyhood; form a society; are the same kind of men; marry the same kind of women. The merchants and manufacturers in Parliament are a motley race—one educated here, another there, a third not educated at all; some

[29] Examples are given in Ashton, *op. cit.*, pp. 217–18, and in Stirk, *op. cit.*, pp. 70–98.

[30] Stirk, *op. cit.*, p. 70.

[31] James Boswell, *The Life of Samuel Johnson* (New York: Modern Library, Inc., 1952), p. 182.

[32] Cf. Bowden, *op. cit.*, pp. 160–64, for documentation on this point.

are of the second generation of traders, who consider self-made men intruders upon an hereditary place; others are self-made, and regard the men of inherited wealth, which they did not make and do not augment, as beings of neither mind nor place, inferior to themselves because they have no brains, and inferior to Lords because they have no rank. Traders have no bond of union, no habits of intercourse; their wives, if they care for society, want to see the wives not of other such men, but "better people," as they say—the wives of men certainly with land, and, if heaven help, with the titles.[33]

It is true that a number of the families of early industrialists did not participate in this "infiltration" of the aristocracy. Many of the early iron masters came from Quaker families and members of these families intermarried repeatedly with other Quaker families in the iron industry. In this manner they reinvested their earnings in the industry and maintained for a considerable period of time an ascetic pattern of conduct which was in keeping with their religious convictions. Similar practices are reported for other industries.[34] Still, by 1844, a French observer, Leon Faucher, found that the textile manufacturers in Manchester were living in detached villas amidst suburban gardens and parks. Puritan ideas and ideals were weakening and Independents, Baptists, and, to a lesser extent, Quakers had exchanged the plain meeting-houses of the late eighteenth century for chapels built in pseudo-Gothic architecture. According to Faucher, only the Methodists continued to adhere to the standards of austerity.[35] Thus, the rising families of industrialists gradually developed a bourgeois standard of life, even if they did not enter the ranks of the aristocracy. But this did not mean that members of the dissenting sects were any more content with the lack of social recognition than the new aristocrats among their fellow-industrialists. The point is that the early entrepreneurs were not merely defending their social and economic position; they saw themselves as attacking a bastion of unwarranted privi-

[33] Walter Bagehot, *The English Constitution* (New York: D. Appleton and Co., 1907), pp. 231–32. The book was originally published in 1867.

[34] Ashton, *op. cit.,* pp. 212–17. See also Isabel Grubb, *Quakerism and Industry before 1800* (London: Williams and Norgate, 1930), pp. 93–132, 145–81.

[35] L. J. Faucher, *Manchester in 1844* (London: Simpkin, Marshall and Company, 1844), pp. 25–26. Another index of the same trend is the increasing number of domestic servants after 1840, when a proper number of servants became part of the bourgeois standard of life. See Charles Booth, "Occupations of the People of the United Kingdom, 1801–1881," *Journal of the Royal Statistical Society,* Vol. 49 (1886), pp. 314–35, and Roy Lewis and Angus Maude, *The English Middle Classes* (New York: Alfred A. Knopf, Inc., 1950), pp. 303–9.

lege. Theirs was not a belief which required justification in their own eyes; their actions and their success were justification in themselves which was denied a deserved social recognition.

The preceding discussion has pointed up three interrelated considerations, which bear on the role of ideologies in industrialization. The early industrialists as a group were primarily of middle-class or lower middle-class background. They were inspired, especially toward the latter part of the eighteenth century, by a growing enthusiasm for the promise of technology. As men of commerce and industry they felt provoked by the disdain of the ruling aristocracy, especially as the success of their economic undertakings strengthened their self-confidence and intensified their resentment at the lack of social recognition.[36] As a rising social class, the early industrialists were oriented toward the aristocracy, but in their everyday work they were concerned primarily with the problem of labor.

b. The Traditionalism of Labor

The industrialization of England during the late eighteenth and early nineteenth centuries coincided with a rapid increase in population. During the first half of the eighteenth century the population had increased from 5.85 millions to 6.25 millions, or about 6.8 per cent. During the second half of the century, the population increased from 6.25 million to 8.89 million, or an increase of 42.2 per cent. And in the ensuing half-century (1801–1851), the population increased from 8.89 millions to 17.92 millions, or a little more than 100 per cent.[37] This staggering increase of the population was due to natural increase rather than migration, since it is probable that "the emigrants from Great Britain were at least as numerous as the immigrants from Ireland and foreign countries."[38] Along with this growth of the population

---

[36] The strength of resentment against discrimination by the aristocracy should not be underestimated. In his analysis of the ancien régime Alexis de Tocqueville observed that the French Revolution was not primarily due to the oppression by church and nobility, which could no longer be tolerated. It was rather due to the fact that there was a beginning of prosperity among peasants and middle classes alike, which made them resent the burdens imposed on them, especially when the nobility ceased to do those things which had justified these burdens in the past. See Alexis de Tocqueville, *The Old Regime and the Revolution* (New York: Harper and Brothers, 1856), pp. 38–49.

[37] These figures are cited in Guy Chapman, *Culture and Survival* (London: Jonathan Cape, 1940), p. 34.

[38] Arthur Redford, *Labour Migration in England, 1800–50* (London: Longmans, Green and Company, 1926), p. 15.

went a rapid increase in the size of urban areas. The population of Manchester, to cite but one example, rose from 90,000 in 1801 to 237,000 in 1831 and to 400,000 in 1851.[39] During this period of rapid population growth from about 1760 to the middle of the nineteenth century, England experienced the social and economic transformation of the Industrial Revolution.

In the course of this transformation the rising entrepreneurial class was confronted with labor problems of very great complexity. In the case of the early enterprises, especially those of the textile industry, location depended upon the availability of water power; hence many of these enterprises were located on streams in remote country districts where labor was scarce. After steam power was introduced, industrial location depended more upon accessibility to transport and markets in the growing industrial towns, whose resident labor supply was often insufficient. In either case it was frequently necessary to recruit a part or all of the work force from outside the local area. Such recruitment was impeded by the general lack of transportation facilities at the time. In addition to the sheer difficulty of moving about there existed a strong reluctance on the part of peasants and artisans to offer their services at all, even if they were hardpressed economically and even when industrial location was not an obstacle. As a result transients rather than established inhabitants manned the early factories and early factory records disclose a rapid turnover of the work force.[40] Even the expanding opportunities of rising industrial centers did not readily overcome the widespread resistance to factory employment. Many of the early factories had to rely for their labor supply upon the natural increase of the resident population and upon the large number of immigrants from Ireland, for the movement to the cities was characterized by a tardy and lagging "process of short-distance migration from the surrounding country." [41]

The reasons for this resistance to factory employment are generally familiar. To many, poverty at home appeared preferable to the risks of life elsewhere. A customary way of life in which needs were limited often prompted men to respond to economic pressure by limiting consumption rather than by seeking better opportunities in other localities. And the attraction of economic opportunities was diminished under conditions where more work would be done when wages were

[39] J. L. and Barbara Hammond, *The Bleak Age* (West Drayton: Penguin Books, 1947), p. 34.

[40] Redford, *op. cit.*, pp. 18–21.

[41] *Ibid.*, p. 158.

low and less when they were high.   Indeed, many of the early entrepreneurs insisted that the cost of provisions be kept high, for in their
opinion the people would increase their exertions only under such
pressure.[42]   Thus, despite the growth of population the mobilization
of labor was impeded by a customary way of life, in which work was
subordinated to social rather than to economic considerations.   Redford
has described this traditionalism with regard to its deterrent effects on
migration.

> The workers in a decaying branch of industry do not decide in a body
> that their occupation is gone, and that they must seek a livelihood else-
> where.   They feel an ever-increasing difficulty in maintaining their cus-
> tomary standard of living, and a few of the more enterprising men may
> migrate to some rising centre of their own industry.   The great majority,
> however, cling to their old homes; in slack seasons they seek the nearest
> work available, returning to their original occupations at every revival
> of trade.   Even when the last breath of specialized trade has deserted an
> industrial town, most of the population may be retained inertly, offering
> through their low standard of living a temptation to the introduction of
> new industries dependent on low-grade labor.

And what is true of an industrial population is even more true of an
agricultural population, as Redford emphasizes, for the latter is able to
weather economic depressions by a greater reliance upon growing its
own food.[43]

The same complex of circumstances and traditional attitudes which
made peasants and artisans reluctant to offer their services also made
them willing to see their children employed in the factories.   The rapid
increase of the population after 1760 was due primarily to a decline of
infant mortality.   While this is readily explained by reference to the
elementary measures of sanitation which were introduced during this
period, the reasons for the continuation of an exceptionally high birth
rate are not self-evident, as T. H. Marshall has emphasized.[44]   As
long as infant mortality is high, large numbers of children are usually
desired to preserve the continuity of the family as a social and productive unit.   But once infant mortality declines sharply, the continuation of a high birth rate is not entirely explained by such factors as
religious scruples, the relative ignorance of contraceptive or abortive
methods, the relative incapacity to foresee the relation between family

---

[42] Chapman, *Culture and Survival*, pp. 86–89, where observations to this effect
are cited from a number of sources, including the secretary of a trade-union.

[43] Redford, *op. cit.*, p. 157.

[44] T. H. Marshall, "The Population Problem during the Industrial Revolution,"
Economic Journal (*Supplement*), Vol. I (1929), p. 435.

size and family resources, or the relative unwillingness to postpone marriage. In part, the high birth rate must be explained by the traditional conception of children, who were regarded as economic assets because they contributed their share of work to the household of the peasant and the artisan. And this idea was encouraged further, when the rapid growth of the textile industry during the latter half of the eighteenth century provided additional opportunities for the employment of children at the same time that infant mortality declined.[45] Hence, workers accepted the employment of children (and of women), since they were accustomed to the idea that all members of the family contribute to its income, and the widespread practice of child labor was an added stimulus for an exceptionally high birth rate. A Commission of Inquiry which investigated the evasion of previous factory legislation in 1833 reported that parents exhibited a strong interest in misrepresenting the age of their children so that they would not be barred from employment under the existing laws.[46] Thus, while many adults were reluctant to offer their services to the early entrepreneurs and thereby impeded the supply of labor, the interest of many parents to see their children employed tended to have an opposite effect.

It may be added that this aspect of traditionalism should guard us against nostalgic or romantic interpretations. It is certainly a mistake to suppose that in a society guided by adherence to tradition the worker is spiritually or economically secure, while in an industrial society he is a mere commodity buffeted about by the impersonal forces of the market. Such an image mistakes the prevalence of face-to-face contacts in the preindustrial community for a prevalence of warm and satisfying relationships. It forgets that intimate personal contacts can be every bit as unbearable as the impersonality of the market place. It mistakes the absence of a marketing economy of firms for an absence of interest in economic gain. And it fails to perceive that workers in a preindustrial society often "prefer" their traditional way of life, not because they oppose change as such, but because every proposed alternative creates more problems than it solves, socially and economically speaking. It is well to remember, therefore, that the restraints of custom often coincided with poverty, cruel exploitation, exposure to

[45] Chapman, *Culture and Survival*, pp. 61–66. ". . . the employment of children was not originally exploitation by the capitalist: capitalist exploitation was, in fact, an extension to the factory and to other concentrated industries of a form of training in work, which is natural to all primitive economies."

[46] The overseers and masters either connived with them or, at any rate, had no special reason for vigilance. See Maurice W. Thomas, *The Early Factory Legislation* (Leigh-on-Sea: Thomas Bank Publishing Company, 1948), p. 59.

calamities of nature, and to the vicissitudes of economic life which could be every bit as painful as those accompanying industrialization. Under the pressure of economic distress parents could exploit their own children just as much as many employers did in the course of industrialization, and it is an open question certainly whether an exploitation reinforced by ties of personal sentiment is more benign than exploitation untouched by human sympathy.

Still, the fact remains that the creation of a nonagricultural work force in eighteenth-century England inevitably involved a major break with "everyday routine as an inviolable norm of conduct" [47] and this break accounts not only for the inelasticity of the labor supply, but also for the widespread inability or unwillingness of adults to adapt themselves to the "new discipline" of the factory. Several students of the period have pointed to the contrast between the work habits indispensable in a factory and the work habits characteristic of the peasant household or the household workshops of the putting-out system. For the peasant, work varied with the season, involving long hours during the summer months and short hours during the winter. Moreover, many peasants were also occupied in the putting-out system (also called the domestic industries) just as many workers in these industries had at least small strips of land which they cultivated. And the routine of their work entailed an unwitting adaptation to a variety of tasks and to an irregularity of performance which were incompatible with the specialization and machine-driven regularity of factory work. Irregularity was not a synonym of indolence, as so many contemporary writers contended. It resulted rather from the alternation between frenzied work and frenzied recreation, which was especially characteristic of the household industries, since these depended on the fluctuations of the market. Such customs as "St. Mondays," when the workers would relax in the alehouses from their last paroxysms of labor, resulted from this direct impact of the market on the household production of the individual worker. We have the testimony of Francis Place, who explains the irregularity of work habits by speaking of the "sickening aversion" which at times steals over the workingman after laboring for 16 or 18 hours a day and which compels him to indulge in idleness and liquor.[48]

[47] This is Max Weber's definition of traditionalism. See H. H. Gerth and C. Wright Mills, eds., *From Max Weber: Essays in Sociology* (New York: Oxford University Press, 1946), p. 296.

[48] Quoted in Dorothy George, *England in Transition* (London: Penguin Books, 1953), pp. 60–61.

But this adaptation to the conditions of the putting-out system proved to be unsuited for factory production with its emphasis on speed, regularity, and attention. The contrast between the old habits and the new discipline was aggravated, moreover, by the conflicting preoccupations on both sides. The workers unconsciously prized the breathing spells which a capricious market made possible. And the employers were anxious over their investment in a precarious industry; they prized the opportunities for quick gains and they in turn habitually accepted long hours and unremitting toil as a matter of course. The discipline which the employers imposed was intensified by this reciprocal reinforcement of conflicting practices and habits. Workers who had been their own masters even though they labored 14 hours or more, were now subjected to penalties which reflected not only their inexperience with the requirements and hazards of factory work but also the employer's anxious endeavor to control their every move.[49] Under these conditions it is not surprising that employers frequently hired women and children, whom they could discipline more readily than the men. And given their own acceptance of child labor, it is not surprising that the men and women of the working class in early nineteenth-century England became aroused over the extreme exploitation of their children only when the work of children appeared to supplant rather than supplement the work of adults. As Mr. Guy Chapman has pointed out, the Ten-Hours Movement of the 1830's, which was ostensibly aimed at reducing the hours of child labor, received its initial impetus from the desire to reduce unemployment among adult workers.[50]

[49] In one spinning factory the doors were locked during working hours; it was prohibited to drink water despite the prevailing heat; and fines were imposed on such misdemeanors as leaving a window open, being dirty, washing oneself, whistling, putting the light out too soon or not soon enough, being found in the wrong place, and so on. See J. L. Hammond and Barbara Hammond, *The Town Labourer* (London: Longmans, Green and Company, 1925), pp. 19–20.

[50] Chapman, *Culture and Survival*, Chapter 3. This coincides with the interpretation of the Commission of Inquiry of 1833, which reported that its work was obstructed by a ten-hour agitation which was least of all concerned with the fate of the children, the ostensible object of the inquiry. The spokesmen of the workers who favored the ten-hour movement, opposed the exclusive Parliamentary concern with reducing the hours of child labor, because they assumed that a *general* limitation of the working day would lead to a rise of prices and of wages by reducing output, and hence to increased employment for those who were now unemployed. To reduce the hours of work for children would merely reduce the already small income of their families. See Thomas, *op. cit.,* pp. 50, 52. Of course, this is not to deny that the reformers derived their most powerful propagandistic weapons from the agitation against child labor.

It is necessary to understand the full implications of this unemployment of adult men which appeared to result from the employment of children. Families which had traditionally assumed that their children were an economic asset, were suddenly confronted with the manifest evidence that they were an economic liability. If parents had tolerated the suffering of their children because children had always worked and the special deprivations in the factories "merely" added to the age-old burdens of the poor, they were now aroused by the threat that the widespread use of child labor would make their own labor superfluous. Ordinary men think about society by personifying the forces of good and evil as writers do in a tragedy. And when the children seemed to replace their fathers at their places of work, they may well have appeared to their parents as an unwitting instrument of destruction, by which the manufacturers were robbing workers of their manhood and their self-respect.

Indeed, this psychological impact of unemployment, which appeared to be due to child labor, was only the latest evidence for the cumulative social isolation of labor, which seemed to add insult to the injuries inflicted by factory discipline, abject poverty, and the other deprivations attending the rapid development of industry. This isolation or alienation of the working class differed significantly from the low regard in which Puritanism had held the masses of the poor. Neither poverty nor low social esteem were new experiences. While poverty was held to be both inescapable and indispensable throughout the eighteenth century, it is significant that the mercantilist writers of this period believed the laborers of the nation to be one of the most important bulwarks of her prosperity.[51] And this idea was used by the workers and their spokesmen who made an emphatic distinction between the *idle* and the *industrious* poor, and who stressed the major contribution which the latter made to the welfare of the nation. But as industrialization advanced, it undermined this claim to recognition, this emphasis on the self-respect of the worker, who shunned the sin of indolence even as he accepted the burden of poverty. There were many reasons for the growing sense of degradation which resulted.

Toward the end of the eighteenth century the burden of pauperism had risen at an alarming rate,[52] and efforts to cope with the problem

---

[51] See Edgar Furniss, *The Position of the Laborer in a System of Nationalism* (Boston: Houghton Mifflin Company, 1920), pp. 5–74.

[52] Annual expenditures for the relief of destitution by local authorities rose from 2 millions sterling in 1784 to 4 millions in 1803 to 6½ million in 1813 and to almost 8 million in 1818. See Sidney and Beatrice Webb, *English Poor*

increasingly took the form of establishing workhouses, in which the Parish poor would be kept and employed. Given the fact that the Parish authorities would seek to minimize their financial burdens and to discourage the poor from seeking relief, conditions of life and work in these establishments quickly became notorious. And in the absence of a ready and adaptable supply of labor, recruiting agents for the employers scoured the countryside for workhouse labor until the 1830's and even later.[53] The cruelties of this traffic in work slaves have become proverbial, but they were perhaps not as important as our modern sensibilities tend to make them. The sensibilities of the workers themselves were outraged rather by the increasing symbolic identity between the workhouse and the factory, between the harsh penalties imposed for destitution and the deprivations of the workaday life.

After 1760 and especially during the years from 1790 to 1813 production and the cost of living rose, while real wages declined.[54] The resulting experience of extreme distress in the midst of growing wealth was aggravated by the system of poor relief, which over the preceding two-hundred-year period had created settled expectations among peasants, workers, and employers. Those in distress regarded Parish relief as a right rather than as charity, while employers accepted the availability of relief as justification for lowering wages. Since the financial burden of the system fell upon the local rate-payers, settlement legislation had sought to equalize this burden by making relief contingent upon legal residence. But this system only increased the workers' reluctance to move and hence to take advantage of opportunities elsewhere, since leaving the Parish meant abandoning the last safeguard which Parish relief afforded. By the same token the Parish authorities would trade in workers as they might in cattle, for the fewer paupers the village had to support, the lower would be the rates paid for Parish relief.[55] And as the Parishes sought to lighten their burdens by "workhouse relief" while the employers used the system of poor relief to re-

Law History: Part II—The Last Hundred Years (London: Longmans, Green and Company, 1929), pp. 1–2.

[53] Redford, op. cit., pp. 21–23.

[54] Webbs, op. cit., pp. 4–7, and W. W. Rostow, British Economy of the Nineteenth Century (Oxford: At the Clarendon Press, 1948), pp. 13–14. Rostow analyzes the reasons for this discrepancy, which were in part connected with the Continental blockade and the Napoleonic wars.

[55] For documentation on both points cf. J. L. and Barbara Hammond, The Village Labourer (London: Longmans, Green and Company, 1932), pp. 54, 55, 88–94, and passim.

cruit pauper labor at lower wages, the distinction between work and punishment for poverty became blurred.

The resulting experience of degradation was intensified further by the Speenhamland system of poor relief which was introduced in 1795. Karl Polanyi has shown how this system became a major source of alienation for the workers.

> Under Elizabethan Law the poor were forced to work at whatever wages they could get and only those who could obtain no work were entitled to relief. . . . Under Speenhamland Law a man was relieved even if he was in employment, as long as his wages amounted to less than the family income granted to him by the scale. Hence, no laborer had any material interest in satisfying his employer, his income being the same whatever wages he earned . . . [and] the employer could obtain labor at almost any wages; however little he paid, the subsidy from the rates brought the workers' income up to scale. Within a few years, the productivity of labor began to sink to that of pauper labor, thus providing an added reason for employers not to raise wages above the scale. For once the intensity of labor, the care and efficiency with which it was performed, dropped below a definite level, it became indistinguishable from "boondoggling," or the semblance of work maintained for the sake of appearance.[56]

The measure was popular with everyone: parents did not need to care for their children, wages and poor rates could be reduced as long as each was supplemented by the other, and laborers were safe from extreme want whatever the conditions of trade. Many workers came to look upon relief as a "legal compensation for their loss in wages." [57] But the consequence was that laborers would earn the same starvation wages, no matter how hard they worked and regardless of the conditions of trade. For both the Parish authorities and the employers could screw down the rates *and* the wages actually paid out because the other would make up whatever was needed in order to provide the minimum provided by law. As a result labor lost its market value, since employers could lower wages without endangering the subsistence of their employees. And the idea of poor relief lost what little meaning had been left, since the rates were paid as a wage supplement, which was not their purpose, or the rate payment was evaded by confining the recipient in a workhouse and by exploiting his destitution. Henceforth workers were publicly stigmatized as paupers, whether they

[56] Karl Polanyi, *The Great Transformation* (New York: Rinehart and Company, 1944), p. 79.

[57] Cf. Mark Hovell, *The Chartist Movement* (Manchester: Manchester University Press, 1918), pp. 80–85. See also Hammonds, *The Village Labourer*, pp. 142–82.

worked or not, since they were "on relief" in either case. It is not surprising that their self-respect vanished as the distinction between work and relief, between factory and workhouse, between diligence and indolence, disappeared.

Until of late years, there was, amongst the poor, a horror of becoming chargeable to the parish. . . . Never to have been chargeable was a subject of proud exultation. . . . But this feeling is now extinguished; the barrier, the shame, has been broken down. . . .

. . . instead of priding himself upon his little possessions, instead of decking out his children to the best advantage, instead of laying up in store the trifling surplus produce of the harvest month, the labourer now, in but too many instances, takes care to spend all as fast as he gets it, makes himself as poor as he can, and uses all the art that he is master of to cause it to be believed, that he is still more miserable than he really is.[58]

These consequences of the Speenhamland system did not go unnoticed at the time. But widespread recognition was not synonymous with an understanding of the problem. When reform came forty years later with the Poor Law of 1834, it was only to reaffirm once again the outcast position of the working class. To be sure, Parliament had a long-standing tradition of noninterference in matters of local administration. But the point is that during the period of the French Revolution and the Napoleonic Wars this tradition was reinforced by the acute fear that changes in the long-established system of poor relief would arouse the people still further. Moreover, thoroughgoing reform could be accomplished only by combating the rapidly increasing demoralization of the working class. Yet to do so might increase the people's sense of outrage, which was politically dangerous.[59] Such measures would have presupposed that parliamentarians as well as leading groups of entrepreneurs had acquired an understanding of the workers' sense of degradation. The early industrialists, who were themselves engaged in a struggle for social recognition, proved to be incapable of such insight. And the leaders of the Established Church and of Parliament who by a mixture of negligence and intent deprived an estimated 4 million workers of seats in church, and whose acts of enclosure gradually deprived the common people of all means of recreation, likewise failed to understand the demoralized pauperism of the workers which in part had resulted from their own actions.[60]

[58] Statement of William Cobbett in the *Political Register*, July, 1808. See Coles, eds., *Opinions of Cobbett*, pp. 123–24.

[59] Webbs, *op. cit.*, pp. 32–34.

[60] The estimate on the shortage of seating capacity in the churches is contained in Robert F. Wearmouth, *Methodism and the Working-Class Movements*

Certainly there were those who clearly perceived that the common people had been ostracized from the society whose wealth they helped to create.   In December, 1832, William Cobbett declared:

> I have always stood firmly up in defense, not only of the rights, but of the *character* of the common people, who, of late years, have been looked upon by both the political factions, and by all the hordes that live upon the taxes, as not being of the same flesh and blood with themselves. . . . Beginning about fifty years ago, the industrious part of the community, particularly those who create every useful thing by their labour, have been spoken of by every one possessing the power to oppress them in any degree, in just the same manner as we speak of the animals which compose the *stock upon a farm*.[61]

And when Cobbett added that this had not been the manner in which the forefathers of the common people had been treated, he struck a responsive chord in a majority of the peasants and craftsmen and workers in the domestic industries whose way of life had been revolutionized by industrialization.   The rise of industry had not aroused the people's social and political awareness when it brought poverty and destitution, the abuses of poor relief, the exploitation of children, or even the new and intensely hated discipline of the factory.   These were either age-old evils or, at any rate, evils which were now added to the age-old burdens of the poor.   When these burdens became intolerable, the people resisted; but violence did not express a dominant emotion. It was shunned by the leaders of social protest.   And even the workers who engaged in it, attacked only the immediate and most visible causes of their oppression.[62]

The fact is that the common people were aroused to political awareness by the prevailing denial of their rightful place in society, and men

of England, 1800–1850 (London: The Epworth Press, 1937), p. 18.   The effect of enclosures on the elimination of playgrounds and parks is described in Hammonds, *The Bleak Age*, p. 128.   The shortage of seats in church was due to the fact that church buildings did not increase in proportion to the population.

[61] Cobbett's *Political Register*, Vol. LXXVIII (December, 1832), col. 709.

[62] Perhaps the most remarkable feature of English social history during this period is the orderliness of popular violence.   Darvall concludes his comprehensive survey of violent actions with the observation that the aims of the rioters were limited and local, as difficult to suppress as they were incapable of furnishing the basis of a revolutionary movement.   Frank O. Darvall, *Popular Disturbances and Public Order in Regency England* (London: Oxford University Press, 1934), pp. 314–15.   E. J. Hobsbawn has reanalyzed the available evidence to show that machine-breaking and other acts of violence were a form of collective bargaining at a time when "combinations" of workers were prohibited by law.   See his "The Machine Breakers," *Past and Present*, Vol. I (February, 1952), pp. 57–70.

like Cobbett, Oastler, Bamford, Lovett, and others appealed successfully to this sense of righteous injury over the arbitrary and unjust destruction of an established tradition.[63] The social and political ostracism
of the common people was denounced not only by reformers, but also
by conservatives, who were attacking the aspirations and policies of the
rising entrepreneurial class. Disraeli, for example, in commenting on
the Chartist petition of 1839, declared that "the real cause of this . . .
movement . . . was an apprehension on the part of the people that
their civil rights were invaded. Civil rights partook in some degree
of an economical, and in some degree certainly of a political character."
But this movement was neither one nor the other, according to Disraeli, for economic causes lead to tumult but not to organized national
movements, and political rights were of so abstract a character that
they could never be the origin of a great national movement. But the
invasion of civil rights might be the spring of this great movement,
because civil rights "conduced to the comfort, the security, and the
happiness of the subject, and at the same time were invested with a
degree of sentiment, which mere economical [or political] considerations
did not involve." [64]

Disraeli used this argument to attack the destruction of the constitution by those who had introduced the Reform Bill of 1832 and the
New Poor Law of 1834. But an insight is not invalid because it is
partisan, and Disraeli's interpretation was in some measure confirmed
by the fact that the great national movement of Chartism on which
he commented was accompanied by an almost equally extensive religious revival. The Great National Petition for the Charter of 1839
was endorsed by 2,283,000 persons, and a new petition in 1842 was
signed by 3,317,702. If this is interpreted as an index of increased
radicalism, it is worth noting that during the period from 1801 to 1851
the number of Methodist meeting houses increased 14 times, and their
seating capacity increased from 165,000 to 2,194,298, the latter figure
representing one-eighth of the total population in 1851.[65] While it is
true that propaganda for reform received some impetus from Methodist

[63] See, for example, Coles, eds., *op. cit.,* p. 207; Cecil Driver, *Tory Radical,
The Life of Richard Oastler* (New York: Oxford University Press, 1946), pp.
128–29; Hammonds, *The Town Labourer,* pp. 306–8; Hammonds, *The Bleak Age,*
pp. 176–77.

[64] Speech by Disraeli on July 12, 1839, in *Hansard's Parliamentary Debates,*
Vol. XLIX (1839), columns 246–47.

[65] These figures are given in Wearmouth, *op. cit.,* p. 17.

preachers, the dominant tone of Methodism was conservative. Yet, this religious revival had a strong affinity with Chartist radicalism in the sense that both enlisted the active participation of the common people and thereby satisfied their inarticulate quest for social recognition.[66]

Industrialization threatened and frequently destroyed the traditionalism of labor. In protesting against this disruption of their way of life large masses of English peasants and workers were aroused to concerted action by an endeavor to reclaim their lost position in society. Under the pressure of great suffering the leaders of the various working-class movements tended to embellish the traditional position of the people with nostalgic references to the "good old days." The contrast with present hardships and the emotional failings of memory inevitably gave a romantic glow to the harsh realities of the past. But this appeal to hallowed traditions only serves to emphasize that the workers' social protest against the effects of industry consciously relied upon images of traditionalism while the forceful creation of a nonagricultural work force gradually undermined the practices which these images idealized. As J. L. Hammond pointed out:

A study of the working class literature of the time, or of the different popular movements . . . gives the impression of a discontent which is a revolt of the imagination. It is not merely the discontent of men who find themselves poor in a world where some people are rich. There was nothing novel in that inequality. It is the revolt of men and women who find for the first time that their poverty had a sting. And why does this feeling arise now? . . . The real passion of the working class revolt of this time was partly inspired by the envy of wealth, but ultimately in the main by a hostility to a view of life which outraged the poor man's self-respect and gave to his higher wants no place at all in its values.[67]

c. Traditionalism and the Management of Labor

It is an intriguing though superficial paradox that the traditionalism which interfered with the mobilization and adaptation of labor also frequently facilitated the management of labor. The workers' widespread reluctance to change a customary way of life could also be to the advantage of an employer if the relations between them were stabilized by family ties and reciprocal loyalties. This was typically the

[66] Evidence for this interpretation is contained in *ibid.*, pp. 21–22, and Robert F. Wearmouth, *Some Working-Class Movements of the Nineteenth Century* (London: The Epworth Press, 1948), pp. 32–33, and *passim*.

[67] J. L. Hammond, "The Industrial Revolution and Discontent," *The Economic History Review*, Vol. II (1930), pp. 227–28.

case, wherever the traditions of the aristocracy, of religious sects, or of craftsmanship remained in force. In such cases we have to do not with the reluctance of the peasant or artisan who would not move or adapt himself to factory discipline but with the related adherence of an employer and his men to a traditional conception of authority. Such relationships were governed by assumptions and routines, which were largely taken for granted even when they were honored in the breach. According to the "theory of dependence":

> . . . the lot of the poor, in all things which affect them collectively, should be regulated *for* them, not *by* them. They should not be required or encouraged to think for themselves, or give to their own reflection or forecast an influential voice in the determination of their destiny. It is the duty of the higher classes to think for them, and to take the responsibility of their lot, as the commander and officers of an army take that of the soldiers composing it. This function the higher classes should prepare themselves to perform conscientiously, and their whole demeanor should impress the poor with a reliance on it, in order that, while yielding passive and active obedience to the rules prescribed for them, they may resign themselves in all other respects to a trustful *insouciance,* and repose under the shadow of their protectors. The relation between rich and poor should be only partially authoritative; it should be amiable, moral, and sentimental; affectionate tutelage on the one side, respectful and grateful deference on the other. The rich should be *in loco parentis* to the poor, guiding and restraining them like children. Of spontaneous action on their part there should be no need. They should be called on for nothing but to do their day's work, and to be moral and religious. Their morality and religion should be provided for them by their superiors, who should see them properly taught it, and should do all that is necessary to insure their being, in return for labor and attachment, properly fed, clothed, housed, spiritually edified, and innocently amused.[68]

This is an image of society which appeals to our sympathies, as Mill pointed out, because by generalizing upon the "conduct and character of here and there an individual" it idealizes the "good times of our forefathers." Mill emphasized that his was an accurate description of feelings, not of a society, which had existed in the past. Such feelings arose from man's preference for a society held together by strong personal attachments and disinterested self-devotion rather than by pecuniary interests and bought services.[69] This invidious contrast between personal attachments and bought services was used by conservative and radical critics who railed at the rising class of industrial-

[68] John Stuart Mill, *Principles of Political Economy* (Boston: Charles C. Little and James Brown, 1848), Vol. II, pp. 319–20.
[69] *Ibid.,* pp. 320–21.

ists, only to find them wanting. For example, the Tory Greville referred to the Duke of Rutland as a man who spent his whole life in a round of pleasures, "as selfish a man as any of his class." Yet the duke would devote his time and effort to the welfare of the people on his estate from a sense of duty and of inclination. And the Radical Roebuck praised the rural gentry for their "sincere desire to fulfill their duties to the poor." [70] Such idealizations corresponded to the "conduct and character of here and there an individual," as Mill emphasized.

But it would be misleading to assume that the sense of obligation was merely a symbol which was used to praise the "good old days" and to show that the early industrialists were self-centered barbarians. There was more "reality in the conception" than Mill was willing to grant. The feelings to which he referred and the idealizations to which they gave rise constituted a century-old tradition which affected large numbers of people *to some extent,* even if it molded the character of only a few.

The traditional attitude that the poor were children, who must be obedient but who require protection against the vicissitudes of life, was in the minds of some industrialists and of many workers as well as in the minds of the aristocracy. It was natural for the peasants and artisans whose way of life had been revolutionized by the coming of industry to regard their fathers' or grandfathers' relationship to their employers in a nostalgic light. And this idealization of a personalized relationship between master and servant was shared by some of the early industrialists, especially those who were active members in one of the dissenting sects. The historian G. M. Trevelyan has given a description of the father of John Bright, the famous propagandist of the Anti-Corn Law League, which gives a very vivid impression of these attitudes and practices.

Although Greenbank mill at Rochdale was only ten miles from Manchester, in some respects it was worlds away. In the smaller manufacturing towns of Lancashire and Yorkshire, many masters were still relatively poor, still preserved the simple habits of life and expenditure and the old ways of mixing on more or less intimate terms with their men that had marked the manufacturers of former generations. When John Bright at the age of fifteen began to "help in the warehouse," he was entering a society democratic in its atmosphere and singularly free from social distinctions. The "cash-nexus" was far from being the only bond between his father, Jacob Bright, and the hands in the mill, which stood . . . at the door

[70] See O. F. Christie, *The Transition from Aristocracy* (London: Seeley, Service and Company, 1927), pp. 21–22.

of his own modest dwelling. Jacob Bright knew each of his employees, and much about their families. So good a Friend could not fail to take thought, after the manner of his sect, for the human beings with whom he came in daily contact. He was often consulted by his people as to their private affairs, and in their quarrels and difficulties was welcomed as a judge in Israel. He was constantly helping their households in those bad times, out of his private means. When anyone married, he increased their wages. The children employed in the factory were never allowed to be beaten: the leathern strap, hung up in so many mills in the bad days before the factory acts, had never been seen at Greenbank. He had the children taught out of his own funds, and finally built them a school. "On winter nights with a large lantern in his hand, and wrapped up warmly in a thick overcoat, he would stand at his mill gates, giving directions to the respective men to superintend the children on their way home." He was "owd Jacob" with his men, many of whom continued through life to call his sons plain "John" and "Thomas" when speaking to them.[71]

Jacob Bright was a Quaker, whose adherence to the traditional outlook was probably conscientious and heartfelt. But ideal-typical as this case may be, it highlights the essential features of a relation between masters and men which was retained, albeit in varying degrees, by many employers well into the nineteenth century.

One reason for this retention was that the traditional attitude of employers was not necessarily synonymous with a mere adherence to customary practices and to the "amiable, moral, and sentimental" relation between rich and poor. It was in fact quite compatible with calculating methods of labor management. The work of Robert Owen is sometimes cited as an anticipation of modern methods of labor management, at a time when most employers were treating their workers as impersonally as all other factors of production.[72] Yet, Owen's personnel practices in the organization of his factories were developed in keeping with a painstakingly elaborated model of the traditional relationship between master and servant. He regarded his workers with "affectionate tutelage" and he thought of himself as their trustee.

> My intention was not to be a mere manager of cotton mills, as such mills were at this time generally managed; but to introduce principles in the conduct of the people, which I had successfully commenced with the workpeople in Mr. Drinkwater's factory; and to change the conditions

[71] G. M. Trevelyan, *The Life of John Bright* (London: Constable and Company, 1913), p. 17. Jacob Bright opened his mill in Greenbank in 1809.

[72] See, for example, the interpretation in L. Urwick and E. F. L. Brech, *The Making of Scientific Management* (London: Management Publications Trust, 1949), Vol. II, pp. 40–59.

of the people, who, I saw, were surrounded by circumstances having an injurious influence upon the character of the entire population of New Lanark.[73]

There is no need to go into the details of Owen's management at New Lanark, but it may be helpful to examine one of its aspects. This shows clearly that Owen's traditional conception of the master-servant relationship, in which the master thought for the servant and protected him against the hazards of life as well as against his own weaknesses, was quite compatible with the strictest organization of the work force.

> . . . that which I found to be the most efficient check upon inferior conduct was the contrivance of a silent monitor for each one employed in the establishment. This consisted of a four-sided piece of wood, about two inches long and one broad, each side coloured—one side black, another blue, the third yellow, and the fourth white, tapered at the top, and finished with wire eyes, to hang upon a hook with either side to the front. One of these was suspended in a conspicuous place near to each of the persons employed, and the colour at the front told the conduct of the individual during the preceding day, to four degrees of comparison. Bad, denoted by black and No. 4; indifferent by blue, and No. 3; good by yellow, and No. 2; and excellent by white and No. 1. Then books of character were provided, for each department, in which the name of each one employed in it was inserted in the front of succeeding columns, which sufficed to mark by the number the daily conduct, day by day, for two months; and these books were changed six times a year, and were preserved; by which arrangement I had the conduct of each registered to four degrees of comparison during every day of the week, Sundays excepted, for every year they remained in my employment.[74]

When this system of discipline is considered together with Owen's statement that for the first eight years he was continually occupied in "training the people, improving the village and machinery," it becomes apparent that he had more in common with the traditional conception of an aristocratic master of men than with the personnel manager in a modern factory.

Although Owen gave to his version of traditionalism a unique personal touch by turning the practice of "affectionate tutelage" into a social philosophy, his approach to the management of labor was neither unprecedented, nor was it unique in his own time. For example, there was considerable similarity between Owen's managerial policies and those of the Crowley Ironworks, which were started in 1682.[75]

---

[73] Beer, ed., *Life of Owen*, p. 78.
[74] *Ibid.*, p. 111.
[75] See Ashton, *op. cit.*, pp. 194–98, and *passim*.

And in his own lifetime Owen's work apparently influenced a number of other manufacturers, who like him combined an active if domineering concern for the welfare of their workers with the enforcement of the strictest discipline over them. One of these men, William Brown of Dundee, referred in his writings to "Marshall, Haddon, Leys, Owen" as "the brightest examples in the spinning profession," and from this praise and Brown's own policies it may be inferred that these manufacturers had adopted somewhat similar practices of labor management.[76] There is no better summary of these practices than that of Owen himself:

> My time, from early to late, and my mind, were continually occupied in devising measures and directing their execution, to improve the condition of the people, and to advance at the same time the works and the machinery as a manufacturing establishment.[77]

It is apparent that a strict enforcement of discipline and a very efficient organization of production were quite compatible with relations between employer and workers that were partly "authoritative" and partly "amiable, moral, and sentimental" (Mill). But the traditional approach emphasized the arbitrary will of the master, whose judgment of what was good for his workers was absolute, whose interest, convenience, and petty selfishness frequently prevailed. It required not only a humane regard for the workers but an iron self-discipline and sense for business organization if the despotism implied in the traditional approach was to be benevolent rather than tyrannical. Such qualities were inevitably confined to a few men and it is necessary to recognize that paternalistic benevolence and ruthless oppression of the workers often made use of exactly the same managerial devices.

> Oldknow provided facilities for a number of his workpeople and tenants to keep cattle. He also kept a herd of milking cows to supply the needs of his factory workers and deducted the amount of their purchases from their wages. . . . For the purpose of supplying the factory hands and tenants with meat, bullocks were reared, and some of these were used for draught, a practice then dying out.[78]

These practices of Oldknow do not seem to have been used for the purpose of lowering real wages, but for the purpose of lightening the

[76] See the brief analysis of labor relations in Dennis Chapman, "William Brown of Dundee, 1791–1864: Management in a Scottish Flax Mill," *Explorations in Entrepreneurial History*, Vol. IV (February, 1952), especially pp. 131–34.

[77] Beer, ed., *Life of Owen*, p. 112.

[78] George Unwin, Arthur Hulme, and George Taylor, *Samuel Oldknow and the Arkwrights* (Manchester: Manchester University Press, 1924), p. 205.

burden of the workers, especially during periods when trade was slack. They were analogous to the infamous truck system, however, in which part of the wages were paid in kind; thus, the employer could make additional profits by raising the price of the goods given to the workers in partial payment of wages or sold to them on credit. Cruel exploitation as well as genuine efforts to see to the feeding, clothing, and housing of the workers often occurred side by side. And the traditional theory of dependence, which had motivated the genuine efforts, would be used to justify cruel exploitation as well.

There is another aspect of these traditional practices of the early industrialists which one has to bear in mind. In his detailed analysis of *An Eighteenth-Century Industrialist* T. S. Ashton remarks that by the end of that century the apprenticeship system had lost much of its original justification as a system of technical training and had become instead a system of obtaining cheap, juvenile labor.

> In the metal trades of most parts of England the custom had grown up for workmen, no less than for employers, to take apprentices; and there are some indications that this was so in the case of wage-earners employed by Stubs in Warrington. It seems likely, however, that before a workman entered into an indenture with a youth, he had first to obtain the authority of his employer, and it is possible that some control was exercised over the conditions of work and pay of apprentices so bound. For when, in 1804, one of Stubs' file-forgers, Thomas Swindon, engaged a boy to serve him for three years, the contract was witnessed by John Stubs and Joseph Wood, the one a partner and the other a traveller for the firm. Whatever may have been the evils of apprenticeship to employers those of apprenticeship to workmen far outweighed them. Peter Stubs and his sons were men of sensibility and humanity; and at a later stage in the history of the concern, when the harmful effects of the practice had become patent, they insisted that all apprentices should be bound to them directly and not to their employees—though elsewhere, in the file-making industry, workmen-bound apprenticeship appears to have increased, rather than to have declined, as time went on.[79]

Again it is clear that this system was easily abused, and arbitrary abuse far outweighed the occasional acts of benevolence which after all were equally arbitrary. The case is of interest, moreover, because it indicates that the worst abuses were often practiced by the small master and that the early industrialist was often able to treat his workers benevolently by comparison, or at any rate claim that he would, but that it was out of his hands to do so.

[79] T. S. Ashton, *An Eighteenth Century Industrialist: Peter Stubs of Warrington, 1756–1806* (Manchester: Manchester University Press, 1939), pp. 28–29.

Indeed, this claim was not as hypocritical as is often supposed, for the merchants or manufacturers frequently did not deal with their workers directly, but through various middlemen. During the period of transition which extended well into the nineteenth century, the recruitment and the management of labor were often left in the hands of masters, foremen, subcontractors, and others, for reasons of technology and of organization. This delegation of all control over the workers to a variety of middlemen was not confined to the putting-out system, but prevailed in many industries in which the workers had already been gathered under one "roof." For example, G. C. Allen has shown that a system of subcontracting existed in many of the metal industries of the West Midland for most of the nineteenth century. He describes the labor management of a smelting mill in the following terms:

> The upper part of the blast furnace was in charge of a subcontractor, called a *"bridge-stocker"* who kept horses, employed a gang of men, women and boys (termed "fillers"), and whose duty it was to supply the furnace with the necessary materials. He was paid so much a ton on the produce of the furnace, and he made his own arrangements with his underhands. The *"stock taker"* was the subcontractor in charge of the lower part of the furnace, and his men prepared the sand and looked after the casting and weighing of the pigs. The number employed at each furnace naturally varied according to its size and mechanical equipment; but usually there were about 12 men on each shift at the furnace, and from 10 to 20 more who were engaged in carrying materials. The typical ironworks, with three blast-furnaces, thus employed 100 to 130 persons. The units, consisting of single cold-blast furnaces, were much smaller; while the large ironmasters with several groups of furnaces, must have had 300 to 400 men.[80]

It was obviously up to these subcontractors to deal with their "underhands," whom they recruited, employed, trained, supervised, disciplined, paid, and fired. This system seems to have been common, aside from iron-making and cutlery, in engineering, building, textiles, pin-manufactures, clothing, match-industry, boot and shoe industry, printing, paper, mining, and transportation.[81]

[80] G. C. Allen, *The Industrial Development of Birmingham and the Black Country* (London: George Allen and Unwin, 1929), p. 146.

[81] The extent of this system can only be suggested by such a list. The following sources contain details on each of the industries listed. Building: J. H. Clapham, *An Economic History of Modern Britain* (Cambridge: The University Press, 1926), Vol. I, pp. 177–78. Textiles: Chapman, *Lancashire Cotton Industry*, pp. 48, 61–62, and G. H. Tupling, *Economic History of Rossendale* (Manchester: Manchester University Press, 1927), pp. 206–7. Pin Manufacture: T. S. Ashton, "The Records of a Pin Manufactory," *Economica*, Vol. V (1925), pp.

The fact that "middlemen" rather than merchants and manufacturers controlled the workers in many industries and for a considerable period of time may account in some measure for the complete neglect of all humane considerations which was so notorious a feature of early nineteenth-century industry. Contemporary writers had some reason to attribute the worst forms of exploitation to the subcontractors and to the small entrepreneurs, who had but recently been workers themselves. To be sure, they frequently omitted to add that the merchants and manufacturers were responsible for this exploitation, even if they had no direct relationship with the workers. For these entrepreneurs would drive as hard a bargain as they could with the "middlemen," who in turn were forced to exploit their "underhands" in order to survive economically. However the burden of responsibility may be apportioned, it is clear that the belief in an authoritative but amiable relationship between masters and men was modified though not abandoned, as the actual management of labor fell into the hands of people who had neither the wealth nor the leisure which in the past had made paternal benevolence a relatively easy virtue to practice.

It would be wrong, therefore, to attribute the gradual abandonment of traditional practices to the system of subcontracting and to the abuses of exploitation which accompanied it. Even the extreme pressures of early industrialization did not destroy a traditionalism which subcontractors and workers took for granted despite all the exploitation and hypocrisy which often coincided with it. It should also be recognized that these ideas and practices had been part and parcel of the relation between master craftsmen and their apprentices. Hard work, accuracy, close attention to detail, the importance of tools and of materials, and of high standards of workmanship had been emphasized by master craftsmen and this was of great aid in the development of industry. These traditional practices and ideas were of special importance in view

281–92. Clothing, Match Industry, Boot and Shoe Industry, Printing, and Paper: David F. Schloss, *Methods of Industrial Remuneration* (London: Williams and Norgate, 1898), pp. 197–203. Coal Mining: T. S. Ashton, *The Coal Industry of the Eighteenth Century* (Manchester: Manchester University Press, 1929), pp. 100–47, and G. C. Allen, *op. cit.,* pp. 144, 164. Tin and Copper Mining: Charles Babbage, *Economy of Machinery and Manufactures* (London: John Murray, 1846), pp. 252–53. Slate Quarries: Schloss, *op. cit.,* pp. 182–84. Dock Workers: J. F. Rees, *A Social and Industrial History of England* (London: Methuen and Company, Ltd., 1920), pp. 137–38. Railroads: Clapham, *op. cit.,* pp. 407–12. It should be added that subcontracting still persists today among longshoremen, building-trade workers, and others.

of the resistance of many workers to the unfamiliar demands of factory discipline. For the subcontractors, whose middleman role often depended upon their technical skills, could manage the work force of the early enterprises more or less on the basis of the existing and cumulative traditions of the master-apprentice relationship. And it is probable that English industrialization would have been greatly retarded, if these traditions had not remained intact long after entrepreneurs and their spokesmen had begun to attack this and all other aspects of traditionalism in economic life. To say, as Mill did, that the theory of dependence corresponded to feelings but not to actions is to ignore not only the retention of traditionalism among employers, but also the long-persisting adherence by subcontractors and foremen to personalized relations with their "underhands." Hearings before an investigating committee of the Charity Organization Society of London, held in 1908, give a vivid picture of traditional practices of labor management among these "middlemen."

Personal acquaintance and influence counted for much, when subcontractors or foremen of the old type recruited their employees. As one witness explained:

> You trust the foreman to find you men, and he generally finds those he knows, and they would be those in the district that he lives in.
> We have a great objection to giving work to anyone we do not know, because we have to train him. Each of us has his fad, I suppose, and we do not often give a man we do not know a job unless we are very much pushed. . . .[82]

Yet the foreman may not always know enough men personally; hence, he is likely to ask the workers already employed to bring with them men whom they in turn know personally. Also, sources of information other than personal acquaintance were used in the recruitment of labor, and these illustrate further the traditional ties which characterize this form of labor management.

> In 99 per cent of the cases, I should think, the foreman takes on the men. . . . Sometimes a letter of introduction is brought. Sometimes a clergyman of one or other of the parishes writes a letter, or sometimes a Borough Councellor writes a letter. . . . There is another way in which the increase of our staff is brought about, and that is by the sons of those who are already in our employ. We have a father in our employ for a good many years, and when his sons come along he is in most cases

[82] Charity Organization Society, London: Special Committee on Unskilled Labor, *Report and Minutes of Evidence* (1908), pp. 96–97, Questions 134 and 138.

anxious that they should obtain employment with us as he has done, and he speaks to his foreman. That is how they get put on.[83]

Personal relations and personal arbitrariness prevailed under these conditions of labor management. All the decisions concerning wages, hours, discipline, and generally the organization of production were enmeshed in a web of personal loyalties. This would often have the result that the subcontractor or foreman could count on his workers to an extent which made him quite independent from the firm with which he himself had a contract. One foreman in the building industry testified:

> . . . of my own particular gang 50 per cent would go wherever I went. Q. They follow a particular foreman? —Yes, they follow the foreman, not the firm. Q. The personal link is with the foreman not the firm. —Yes, with the foreman. Q. If you went to another firm, they would come to your job? —Yes. They are not engaged by the firm at all.[84]

Yet this close tie by no means reduced the arbitrariness with which subcontractors and old-type foremen exercised their authority. Craftsmen might have weekly contracts at best, while unskilled hands were employed by the hour or by the day. And although the skilled workers were "the last to be fired, and the first to be hired," all workers were watched closely and dismissed instantly, if they did not prove themselves.

> The foreman of each trade is held partially responsible, not only for the number of men but quality. . . . Should a casual hand be taken on, he is questioned as to his capabilities before starting. Very seldom would a laborer think of asking for employment in any other section but that which he was accustomed to. He can be judged in a few hours, and then if he is not satisfactory, one hour's notice finishes him.[85]

In this system the subcontractor or foreman relied for the most part upon his "own fellows who are really known hands" in order to get his job done, and their economic survival often depended upon the solidarity of such a work group as a whole.

Personalized relations between employers and workers were not confined, of course, to subcontractors and their "hands." Initially, such relations existed even in enterprises in which work operations were

[83] *Ibid.,* p. 169, Q. 865.

[84] *Ibid.,* p. 98.

[85] *Ibid.,* p. 109. In another part of the testimony a "casual hand" is defined as "one that is not known." The phrase need not have reference to unskilled workers, though the chances are that skilled workers are well known, partly because they may not have been as mobile as unskilled workers.

concentrated and organized in accordance with an over-all production schedule. In such enterprises management depended upon a personal relationship between an employer and his workers, and hence upon the accidents of personal knowledge as well as upon the well-understood but unformulated relationship of trust which existed traditionally between a master and his men. While this pattern of labor management continued to prevail in some industries throughout the nineteenth century, it came to be superseded generally by an impersonal management of labor which depended upon the formulation of the conditions of employment and upon elaborate controls which verified the workers' compliance with these conditions. An early example of this transition has been analyzed by Erich Roll in his study of the Boulton and Watt Factory in the years 1775–1806. Originally the relations between employers and workers were characterized by a quasi-familial paternalism patterned after the relation between the master-craftsman and his apprentices. In his speech at the opening of the Soho Foundry Matthew Boulton expressed his attitude toward "his" workers in this manner:

> As the Smith cannot do without his Striker, so neither can the Master do without his Workmen. Let each perform his part well and do their duty in that state to which it hath pleased God to call them, and this they will find to be the true rational ground of equality.[86]

Boulton maintained a personal relationship with his workers, knew their names and their families, and relied upon this relationship to ensure the discipline and work performance needed in his enterprise. Roll indicates that Boulton adhered to these principles, however impatient he was privately with the demands made by the workers. But in 1796, when Boulton gave the speech quoted above, the firm was already in the hands of a new management.

These men of a new generation of industrialists were less inclined to regard their workers as persons who were familiar, even if socially inferior. Moreover, they did not believe that their work performance could be controlled on this personal basis. Rather they tended to regard the workers as factors of production, *whose cost could be calculated*.

> In the same way as in any well-organized factory of today, the purpose of keeping statistical records at Soho was mainly for the detection of waste and lack of efficiency. When new methods of wage payment were devised, recourse was had to the elaborate time-sheets for different

[86] Erich Roll, *An Early Experiment in Industrial Organization, Being a History of the Firm of Boulton and Watt, 1775–1805* (London: Longmans, Green and Company, 1930), pp. 221–22.

shops. Thus these time-sheets fulfilled four objects: they supplied a basis for ascertaining the workers' wages for the job; they were used in the calculation of the costs of engines; they could serve as the starting-point for changes in the methods of production, such as speeding-up and greater application of machinery; and lastly, they were used, as already mentioned, in the computation of new wage-rates. . . .

In general, it may be stated that all the different aspects of the great changes at Soho were strictly co-ordinated and were, consciously or unconsciously, parts of a general and very elaborate plan of the new business organization. . . .

[On the other hand] the objection of great expense could not have weighed heavily at Soho. Two bookkeepers, one cashier, who sometimes acted for the other Soho businesses as well, and a limited number of clerks were employed. Their salaries were not very high, and since regular hours for the office staff do not seem to have existed, the expense of keeping up the new system [of maintaining time-sheets] must have been negligible compared with its results.[87]

It is probable, though the evidence is not conclusive, that this system was introduced when the firm passed from the original founders into the hands of the younger generation. It should be remembered, however, that this firm was exceptional in the degree to which its methods of cost accounting and internal factory administration had developed. A change which took place in a generation in the case of one famous factory has occurred throughout English industry over a period of a century and more.

Traditionalism in economic life was an obstacle to the new economic undertakings, not because it was more humane, but because its rhythm of work and leisure, the inviolability of an accustomed life routine, interfered at every point with the "new discipline" of the factory.[88] Though it is true that the carry-over of the traditional relationship between master and apprentice facilitated the management of labor wherever the system of subcontracting was in use, it is also true that this carry-over readily turned from an aid into a barrier wherever labor management was put on an impersonal, systematic basis, as in the case of the Boulton and Watt factory. The mobilization of labor was not enough; it was necessary for workers to adapt themselves to the conditions of factory production. And wherever their reluctance to do so was not or could not be evaded by the employment of women and children, it presented a formidable obstacle to the success of the early enterprises. Con-

---

[87] *Ibid.*, pp. 250–51.
[88] Hammonds, *The Town Labourer*, pp. 17–36, and Chapman, *Culture and Survival*, pp. 58–60.

temporary observers were well aware of this problem, though in expressing themselves on it they were of necessity less impartial than we can afford to be. The following statement of Andrew Ure is much to the point:

> The main difficulty did not, to my apprehension, lie so much in the invention of a proper self-acting mechanism for drawing out and twisting cotton into a continuous thread, as in the distribution of the different members of the apparatus into one cooperative body, in impelling each organ with its appropriate delicacy and speed, and above all, in training human beings to renounce their desultory habits of work, and to identify themselves with the unvarying regularity of the complex automaton. To devise and administer a successful code of factory discipline, suited to the necessities of factory diligence, was the Herculean enterprise, the noble achievement of Arkwright. Even at the present day, when the system is perfectly organized, and its labour lightened to the utmost, it is found nearly impossible to convert persons past the age of puberty, whether drawn from rural or from handicraft occupations, into useful factory hands.

And in commenting on the reasons for the failure of John Wyatt, who had made the essential inventions already in the 1730's, and for the success of Richard Arkwright, Ure states:

> It required, in fact, a man of a Napoleon nerve and ambition to subdue the refractory tempers of work-people accustomed to irregular paroxysms of diligence, and to urge on his multifarious and intricate constructions in the face of prejudice, passion, and envy.[89]

It is fair to say then that the redistribution and the adaptation of a rapidly increasing working population presented the early industrialists with formidable society-wide problems, for whose solution they had no precedent.

In their attempts to solve these problems and enhance their own interests the rising entrepreneurial class was ruthless in its exploitation of men, women, and children. The members and spokesmen of this class have, indeed, become notorious for the callousness with which they justified this exploitation. But while these facts are undisputed, their interpretation is not, for our assessment of the early English entrepreneurs hinges upon an implicit comparison. Cruel as their exploitation was, it should not be judged by modern standards, or even by the standards of contemporary critics who were advancing the cause of social and political reform. It should be judged rather in terms of the

---

[89] Andrew Ure, *The Philosophy of Manufactures* (London: H. G. Bohn, 1861), pp. 15–16. This work was published originally in 1835.

exploitation which was a common occurrence in English society long before the Industrial Revolution, and in these terms the early entrepreneurs lose a measure of their inhumanity. None of the emphasis I have placed upon the continued adherence to traditional beliefs and practices should be interpreted to imply that the personalized relationship of tutelage and deference between employers and workers was *necessarily* benevolent. In fact, a personalized exploitation can be every bit as cruel as an impersonal one. And there is every reason to accept Mill's judicious statement that in its positive sense the theory of dependence was exemplified only here and there in the conduct and in the character of an individual.

The exploitation, which was an accepted fact of life, had been justified by the traditional claims to authority which Mill stated so succinctly. And this belief in the dependence of the poor and the responsibility of the rich continued to be expressed well into the nineteenth century. Underneath this "verbal hold" of traditional beliefs the ideas of the laissez faire doctrine were gaining ground steadily. But it is necessary to recognize that the basic assumptions of the theory of dependence were taken for granted by large sections of the aristocracy and the middle class, long after many traditional practices had been abandoned. Only this retention of traditional beliefs can explain that the doctrines of laissez faire had a profoundly disturbing effect on the prevailing class-ideologies at the end of the eighteenth century.

d. Traditionalism and the Ideology of Class Relations

During the late eighteenth and early nineteenth century the mobilization and adaptation of labor were seriously handicapped by the retention of a traditional way of life among the common people of England. On the other hand, the retention of the traditional master-servant relationship tended to facilitate labor management, wherever the early enterprises could take advantage of these partly amiable and partly authoritative ties in order to cut down labor turnover and increase efficiency. The rising entrepreneurial class, however, was also confronted with a widespread acceptance of traditional modes of thought among the opinion leaders of London society and of the ruling political groups. And this ideology of traditionalism was more or less incompatible with the ideological legitimation developed by the entrepreneurs and their spokesmen.

The traditional ideology of class relations in seventeenth- and eighteenth-century England is revealed most clearly in the debates over the position of the laboring poor in society. There were certain ideas which were widely accepted. The number of laborers in a country was regarded as an index of its wealth. Each laborer had the right to be employed and the duty to work hard. Poverty was useful, because it enforced the "duty to labor" and it was also inescapable, since wages could never for long rise above the level of subsistence.[90] But while poverty and the dependence of laborers were accepted facts, there were rising problems of vagrancy, of drunkenness and begging, of labor scarcity when trade was good, and of an increasing burden of poor relief. And the efforts to cope with these problems led to a marked shift in the prevailing opinions concerning the position of labor in society.

During the seventeenth century most of the tracts dealing with the problem of poverty were written in years when the price of bread was high.[91] That is, poverty was attributed to the high price of food and hence to the want of trade and money, over which the individual had no control. Widespread distress was believed to result from the economic circumstances of the nation, not from the depravity of the laboring poor. The measures suggested for relief consisted primarily of schemes whereby the poor and the vagrants could be employed for the benefit of the nation.[92] Until the end of the seventeenth century poverty was regarded as a misfortune due to adverse circumstances, which the "higher classes" were obliged to alleviate. Hence, ideally, the customary harshness toward the laboring poor was attenuated both by the emotionalism of tutelage and of deference. The poor were children, they must be disciplined, they must be guided, and on occasion they might be indulged.

Charity as well as the character of the poor, however, came to be reinterpreted toward the end of the seventeenth century. The poor were children still, but they were no longer to be indulged. It is significant in this connection that during the eighteenth century a majority o the pamphlets dealing with the problem of poverty were written during

[90] E. A. J. Johnson, *op. cit.*, pp. 247–56, 281–97. See also Furniss, *op. cit* *passim.*

[91] Dorothy Marshall, *The English Poor in the Eighteenth Century* (London George Routledge and Sons, 1926), pp. 20–21. "Out of 22 pamphlets dealin with the poor, 18 were written in years when the price of corn was high, an only 4 when it was low."

[92] Several writers maintained that it was "our duty to God and Nature" provide for and employ the poor, even if such employment would not result in material benefit to the nation. This is clearly an example of undiluted trac tionalism. Cf. the discussion of seventeenth-century writers in *ibid.*, pp. 18–3

years when bread was cheap.[93]   Poverty had come to be regarded as the result of indolence, not of circumstances: laborers remained poor *despite* the cheap price of provisions.   In 1704 Daniel Defoe had written:

> . . . the reason why so many pretend to want work is that they can live so well with the pretence of wanting work, they would be mad to leave it and work in earnest; and I affirm of my own knowledge, when I have wanted a man for labouring work and offer'd 9s per week to strouling fellows at my door, they have frequently told me to my face, they could get more abegging, and I once set a lusty fellow in the stocks for making the experiment.[94]

There were several reasons why the opinion that poverty resulted from vice, not from misfortune, was reiterated throughout the eighteenth century.   The increase in trade during the eighteenth century prompted an increase in the demand for labor, but merchants and manufacturers were hampered by a relative scarcity of labor despite the increase in population.   As we have seen, workers were reluctant to disrupt their accustomed way of life, especially when the low price of corn enabled them to maintain this way of life with less work rather than more.   Finally, the settlement laws interfered with, and the system of Parish relief discouraged, the mobility of the worker, even if he were willing.   It is in this setting of the employers' unsatisfied demand for labor, the workers' reluctance to offer their services, and the institutional obstacles to labor mobility, that eighteenth-century writers asserted the depravity of the laboring poor.   As Dorothy Marshall has observed, "Nothing would be more exasperating to a man who needed hands than the sight of vagrants begging in every street, while he had to pay money, which he wanted as capital for the expansion of his own business, toward the relief of persons whose labour he could well employ." [95]   Under such circumstances it was no longer a question of establishing workhouses so that the poor would be employed.   Instead, it had become a question of reforming the character of the poor under conditions of the strictest discipline.[96]

---

[93] Cf. *ibid.,* pp. 32–33.   "Throughout the eighteenth century the greater number of pamphlets written about the poor were published in years when corn was cheap, as if that, rather than the scarcity of provisions, was apt to cause a crisis in the affairs of the working class."

[94] Daniel Defoe, "Giving Alms No Charity," in J. R. McCulloch, ed., *A Select Collection of Scarce and Valuable Economic Tracts* (London: 1859), p. 40. Cf. the survey of similar opinions in Furniss, *op. cit.,* pp. 117–56.

[95] Dorothy Marshall, *op. cit.,* p. 33.

[96] There were proposals other than reform through workhouse discipline which did not become as widely accepted at the time.   Some writers urged that the

Noteworthy as this shift in emphasis was between the seventeenth and the eighteenth centuries, it remained in fact within the framework of traditional beliefs. To regard poverty as a result of indolence and insubordination was as old as the idea that the poor must be instructed in the virtues of industry, humility, and thrift. In the past it had been believed that poverty was a punishment sufficient in itself; the instruction of the poor had taken the form of sermons, and relief consisted in giving alms or finding them employment. But towards the end of the eighteenth century many came to believe that the rich should regulate the lot of the poor in a thoroughgoing fashion by reforming their habits rather than by finding them employment. Poverty was still regarded as an inescapable lot, but an increasing number of pamphleteers and philanthropists were abandoning the mercantilist belief, according to which, in the words of Arthur Young, "everyone but an idiot knows that the lower classes must be kept poor, or they will never be industrious." [97]

This belief in the utility of poverty was questioned by those who observed that poverty did *not* make the poor industrious. Something needed to be done to reform the indolence and dissolute habits of the people. The dilemma was clearly expressed by Daniel Defoe who asserted that there was more than enough work for all, but that begging had become a form of employment. Hence, begging had to be made undesirable. Yet this could not be done as long as the people gave their alms not only to the weak and to the handicapped (the "impotent poor") but to the able-bodied as well. To do so was not charity but an encouragement of beggars and vagrants. Defoe even anticipated the later doctrines of laissez faire when he criticized the prevailing laws of poor relief for being based on the mistaken assumption that it is "our business to find them work, and to employ them rather than to oblige them to find themselves work, and go about it." [98] Nothing came of this suggestion; the whole weight of eighteenth-century opinion was against the idea that the problem of poverty might be solved by letting the poor shift for themselves. For Defoe's suggestion implied that the poor should be self-dependent in an age when everyone was agreed that the rich should govern and the poor should be subordinate. Indeed,

poor should be employed in separate enterprises, established for the purpose. Others already anticipated the later view of the laissez faire economists by demanding that the poor should be forced, if need be, to find work for themselves. It is indicative of the persistence of traditionalist conceptions that the latter view did not become popular, despite the fact that it was urged by such well-known writers as Defoe, Locke, and Dunning.

[97] Quoted in Furniss, *op. cit.*, p. 118.

[98] Defoe, "Giving Alms No Charity," *op. cit.*, pp. 36–41.

the growing pauperism of the period with its attendant evils of vagrancy and begging was believed to call for an ever more complete subordination of the poor as well as for their re-education.

Many devout people in the early eighteenth century proceeded to develop schemes which would inculcate the Christian duty to labor in all able-bodied poor. Societies for the reformation of manners were organized to prosecute vice, indolence, and intemperance.[99] And the Society for Promoting Christian Knowledge coordinated the efforts to set up charity schools for educating the children of the poor. If it was the purpose of the former to "pluck up the weeds" of immorality and to "prepare the ground," the purpose of the charity schools was to "sow the good seed." [100] In keeping with this general purpose, the function of the charity schools, according to the historian of this movement, was: "The children were to be rescued from idleness and vagrancy, washed and combed, and instructed in their duties by the catechism, that they might become good men and women and useful servants." [101] To this end the children were to be taught humility and submission to superiors. The clothes issued to them were to be of the coarsest kind. Care was taken that these children were clearly distinguished from children of the better rank. No gaiety of color and no ornamentation was allowed, lest children of the poor take pleasure in them. Prayers and hymns were taught whose major purpose was to inculcate duty and obedience. The spirit of the charity schools was clearly expressed in a sermon by the Bishop of Norwich (in 1755):

> There must be drudges of labor (hewers of wood and drawers of water, the Scriptures call them) as well as Counsellors to direct, and Rulers to preside. . . . To which of these classes we belong, especially the more inferior ones, our birth determines. . . . These poor children are born to be daily laborers, for the most part to earn their bread by the sweat of their brows. It is evident then that if such children are, by charity, brought up in a manner that is only proper to qualify them for a rank to which they ought not to aspire, such a child would be injurious to the Community.[102]

The bishop, it should be noted, expressed these sentiments as a protagonist of the charity schools, not as an opponent.

[99] See Garnet V. Portus, *Caritas Anglicana* (London: A. R. Mowbray and Company, 1912), *passim*.

[100] This contemporary estimate of Dr. Josiah Woodward (1701) is quoted in M. G. Jones, *The Charity School Movement* (Cambridge: Cambridge University Press, 1938), p. 36.

[101] *Ibid.*, p. 74.

[102] Quoted in *ibid.*, pp. 74–75.

This single-minded insistence upon the subordination of the poor and upon an "education" which prepared the children for their low rank in society, indicates none of the "amiable, moral, and sentimental" relationship to which John Stuart Mill had referred. *This* theory of dependence emphasized instead a hard-headed belief in the unalterable rank-order of society. The feelings of obligation and deference which Mill characterized had had a medieval origin,[103] but by the eighteenth century they had been superseded by a formalized insistence upon differences of rank from which all amiable sentiment had evaporated, leaving only an austere demand for moral conduct.[104]

The ideological importance of this austerity is well illustrated by the fact that even the unquestioning insistence on the subordination of the poor did not save the charity schools from vigorous attack. To be sure, the attack upon the schools, as well as their defense, was interwoven with the party strife of the period. Opponents claimed that the schools were being abused by the High Church party which favored a Jacobite restoration, while defenders denied this. But these political aspects of the controversy need not concern us, since the arguments on both sides exemplify the characteristic approach of leading spokesmen to the problem of the poor. One of the most outstanding attacks on the charity schools was made by Bernard Mandeville, who claimed that poverty was the only means to ensure an adequate supply of labor for the hard and dirty work of the world. Therefore, the education of children in the charity schools diverted them from the performance of their duty. These children only needed to attend church on Sundays; this would leave them free to work during the week. To divert children from useful labor is a wrong way to qualify them for it when they are grown up.[105] This attack was given considerable support. Special apprehension was expressed at the literary quality of the curriculum, con-

---

[103] To understand them in their original setting one would have to go back to a time when attitudes toward authority were profoundly emotional, buttressed by unquestioned sanctions, when all persons in authority stood in *loco parentis,* and when the exercise of rule as well as the expressions of deference by inferiors were couched in words and acts of dramatic intensity. Examples are cited in Sylvia L. Thrupp, *The Merchant Class of Medieval London, 1300–1500* (Chicago: University of Chicago Press, 1948), pp. 16–27.

[104] Exceptions to this statement were found in the master-servant relationships of some aristocratic families, among members of dissenting sects, and in very attenuated form among craftsmen. Cf. section b of this chapter.

[105] Bernard Mandeville, "Essay on Charity and Charity Schools," in F. B. Kaye, ed., *The Fable of the Bees* (Oxford: At the Clarendon Press, 1929), Vol. I, pp. 253–322.

sisting as it did of the three R's, because there was danger that the poor would develop such skills as to qualify them for superior posts.[106]

Subsequently, the Society for Promoting Christian Knowledge proceeded to safeguard the schools against what its spokesmen undoubtedly regarded as a justified criticism. No advocate of the charity schools regarded the education offered by them as anything more than a device to reform manners, promote religion, and ensure discipline. Hence, the immediate response to the attack by Mandeville and others was to introduce some kind of industrial work into the curriculum of the schools. For a time this addition to instruction in the catechism was widely adopted.[107] There appeared to be many advantages in setting the children in the schools to work at some productive task. The school trustees saw some of the costs of subscription reduced by the earnings of the children; parents approved if their children earned, however little; and the public demands for the employment rather than the instruction of the children were satisfied, at least in part. Yet, this innovation was short-lived. To employ the children in some productive labor involved additional expenditures for raw materials. The efforts to reduce these as well as the regular costs of the school made it necessary to find a market for the defective products of the children. These as well as other difficulties were sufficient to prevent the success of a scheme, which everyone favored.

This setback of the charity-school movement was only temporary. Great as the danger appeared to be that the children would be educated to aspire above their station, and that education would divert them from their duty to labor, the need for education remained. Indeed this need increased with the rapid growth of population and the mounting difficulties encountered in the mobilization and adaptation of labor toward the end of the eighteenth century. For the problem of pauperism was aggravated at a time when the French Revolution greatly intensified the fear of popular unrest and the endeavors to buttress the complete subordination of the poor. The fact that in the eighteenth century poverty did not prevent vagrancy and begging even if work was available, together with the continued assumption of the "higher classes" that they were responsible for governing the poor, led to other schemes for reforming the manners of the poor. Among these the introduction of Sunday schools was of major importance. Although the numbers involved cannot be verified, it is apparent that the new Sunday school proved to

---

[106] A comment to this effect by Dr. Isaac Watts, who was a warm defender of the schools, is quoted in Jones, *op. cit.,* p. 88.

[107] *Ibid.,* pp. 88–96.

be more successful than the older charity schools. Robert Raikes estimated in 1787 that a quarter of a million children were attending Sunday schools, and the Sunday School Society reported a decade later that the number of schools affiliated with it had increased from 201 in 1787 to 1,086 in 1797.[108] By 1833 the number of children attending Sunday schools had increased to a million and a half.[109]

The curriculum in the Sunday schools was the same as that of the charity schools. Both had for their objective to reform manners, to inculcate discipline, and to promote religion, and such instruction was readily adapted to the requirements of labor management.

Instruction. There is one kind of dishonesty which is often practiced without thought by workmen, and that is wasting the time for which they are paid and the materials belonging to the Trade or Manufacture they work at. Of the same nature with this is the crime of many household servants who take every opportunity of being idle and who make no scruple of wasting provisions or giving them away without leave; nay too often they go farther and pilfer tea and sugar, and other things which they suppose will not be missed, but they should remember that nothing is hid from the eye of God and that the Day of Judgment will come when they will be called to account for all their bad actions.

Questions. Is it honest for workmen to waste and destroy the materials and implements which they make use of? (Ans. No.) Who do these things belong to? (Ans. Their master.) Whose eyes see you when your master is not by? (Ans. God's.) . . . Who sees people when they are pilfering tea and sugar and such things? (Ans. God.) Does God approve of such actions? (Ans. No.) What will God do to thieves of all kinds? (Ans. Punish them.) . . . What do masters and mistresses pay their servants for? (Ans. Their time and labor.) Suppose a man, a woman, a boy, or girl, loiters away any of the hours they have agreed to work in, what do they do? (Ans. They rob their master or mistress.) Is it not just the same as taking money out of their pocket? (Ans. Yes.) Is it not much better to be able to say when you take wages, *I earned this fairly and honestly?* (Ans. Yes, etc.) [110]

Such instruction should be interpreted in terms of contemporary traditions. The common people of England had been bred to a sense of subordination long before charity schools and Sunday schools made it an explicit object of instruction. Though there was the "demoralization"

[108] Jones, *op. cit.*, p. 153.

[109] See H. F. Mathews, *Methodism and the Education of the People* (London: The Epworth Press, 1949), p. 35.

[110] Sarah Trimmer, *The Economy of Charity* (London: Johnson and Rivington, 1801), Vol. I, pp. 332–33. A few of the questions were apparently omitted in this work. They have been inserted from a quotation in Jones, *op. cit.*, p. 78, which is taken from another work by Mrs. Trimmer.

and "insubordination" of vagrancy and of the dependence upon poor relief, as well as outbursts of violence, there was also the abhorrence of "going on the rates" and the austere probity of Methodist class-meetings which point to respect for the rank-order of society. And it should be remembered that religious evangelism was the only cultivated language of ideas with which illiterate peasants and workers were familiar. The fact is that this education had a widespread effect on the behavior of the common people of England.[111]

But such education did not simply "reflect" the interests of the early entrepreneurs. Evangelical preaching among the poor, as well as the charity-school movement, had developed many decades before the accelerated development of industry from 1760 on.[112] Also, the evangelical movement manifested an invigorated belief in the responsibility and in the ability of the "higher classes" to guide and reform the masses of the people. The whole idea that the acknowledged depravity of the poor must be combated by sermons and education as well as penalized by poverty and distress, implied the traditional belief that the fate of the poor, both in this world and in the next, depended upon the actions of their "betters." An essential part of evangelical preaching since the seventeenth century had been the doctrine that the poor should work hard, obey their superiors, and be satisfied with the station to which God had called them. As industry developed, such teaching was increasingly used to justify every exploitation by employers and every failure of Parliament to enact reforms, and it was used also to explain away all the evils of starvation and child labor, of accidents and of ill health.[113] But this utilization of evangelical preaching in the interests of entrepreneurs obscures the fact that *all* acts of charity implied a Christian duty of the "higher classes" to care for the poor, an obligation which the entrepreneurs were eager to deny. Even an education which

---

[111] See the evidence cited in M. J. Quinlan, *Victorian Prelude* (New York: Columbia University Press, 1941), pp. 160–78. Of course, the Sunday schools were only one of many factors which account for this change. But the change itself is emphasized by Francis Place, whose testimony is cited by Quinlan from the unpublished manuscripts, and in whose judgment one can place considerable confidence. See also Mathews, *op. cit.*, pp. 71–108. Professor Asher Tropp's forthcoming work on English education during the nineteenth century will contain a detailed examination of this problem.

[112] The work of Hannah More at the end of the eighteenth century was paralleled, for example, by the work of Robert Nelson at the beginning. Cf. Jones, *op. cit.*, pp. 11–12.

[113] See Hammonds, *The Town Labourer*, pp. 221–46, where this aspect of the evangelical movement is treated with dramatic effect.

taught the people to be subordinate and industrious, reinforced the accepted, traditional belief that the rich must govern the people and that the people should depend upon them. Employers did not find it easy to object to such instruction, since it upheld religious piety and served to secure the subservience of the people, and hence facilitate the management of labor. Yet, this very usefulness of evangelism obscured the conflict of interest between the traditional conceptions of the master-servant relationship and the imperatives of the new industrial order.

Sarah Trimmer has been cited as one of the most active protagonists of Sunday schools for the children of the poor. Her book *The Economy of Charity* was addressed to ladies of society "with a particular view to the cultivation of religious principles among the lower orders of people." [114] Mrs. Trimmer was not a critic of industry or of society. England, as she saw it, was peopled with a vast mass of brutalized poor, deprived of all decency and all religion. Her mission was to make inroads upon this ocean of depravity in the name of the Lord. The rich who neglected their Christian duties were as guilty in her eyes as the poor who were insubordinate to God and man. The weight of contemporary opinion certainly prompted Mrs. Trimmer to concentrate her attention on the sins of the poor, and on the measures designed to save the poor. But despite her evangelical zeal she was quite sensitive to, and critical of, the changes in the relation between employer and worker, which were occurring at that time and which were gradually undermining the idea that the rich are obliged to relieve the poor. In her work she quoted with approval a sermon of the Rev. John Hewlett which is of interest here because it spells out how active members of this evangelical movement conceived of the relation between "higher" and "lower" classes. The poor looked up to the middle classes for instruction, employment, protection, and relief. The Rev. Hewlett, therefore, admonished the merchants and farmers to be mindful of the fact that their present and their future wealth was derived from the labor of the poor. Hence, they should respect the usefulness of humble folk and be particularly kind toward them in their misfortunes, remembering always that "what are trifling losses and calamities to some may be attended with almost irretrievable ruin to others." The sermon then enumerates the various conditions of distress in which the rich should be ready to relieve the poor. But the Rev. Hewlett went on to emphasize that even under ordinary circumstances the middle classes should be models of conduct in their general behavior to the poor, showing pity and courtesy and avoiding all unnecessary harshness. Indeed, the

[114] This phrase is taken from the subtitle of the work.

pressure of the times was such that all the resources of the law and of Christian and brotherly love were needed to relieve the wants of the poor, correct their morals, improve their conduct, and better their condition.

> It is a misfortune that the relation between the master and the servant, and between the employer and the employed, is often distant and remote. There is frequently but little personal intercourse of kindness between them. Everything that tends to raise or sink the poor man, everything that may be kindly meant to increase his comforts, or that may have the effect of aggravating his distress, reaches him through the medium of under agents; sometimes with the disadvantage of the good being diminished, and the evil encreased. This is productive of much depravity among our poor brethren, while it encreases their difficulties. It makes them, as it were, an *insulated body* in society. . . .[115]

It was this insulation of the poor which led to their depravity. And the Rev. Hewlett concluded by stating that communication with the "middle classes" was essential if the poor were to learn self-respect, improve their manners, and become "wiser and more provident in managing their little store."

But the evangelical reformers found the "higher classes" wanting in their manners, as well as in their charity toward the poor. Mrs. Trimmer quotes with approval a report of the *Society for Bettering the Conditions of the Poor,* in which it is stated that the idleness of the poor is a common theme of declamation, "particularly among those, *who are very little employed themselves."* The drunkenness with which the poor are charged is called "an odious and pernicious vice, not confined . . . to any particular class of men." [116]   And although Mrs. Trimmer's book was primarily concerned with the instruction of the poor in the virtues of subordination and of industry, it also contained a strongly worded condemnation of the manufacturers.

> It may be said that in many Parishes there are large Manufactories which employ all the Children, and that in these places *Schools of Industry* cannot be necessary; my opinion is totally different. These Manufactories certainly might be rendered very beneficial to Parishes at large, as well as to poor families; but it too frequently happens that a sacrifice of health and morals is made in them to pecuniary advantages. The Children are crowded together in close apartments, without any regard for their improvement, excepting in one particular branch of the

[115] Rev. John Hewlett, "Observations on the Duty and Influence of the Middle Classes of Society, on the Condition of the Poor," quoted in Trimmer, *op. cit.,* Vol. II, pp. 298–300.
[116] *Ibid.,* p. 292. My italics.

Manufactory, for which probably their size will disqualify them after a few years, when they must give place to smaller children, and turn into the world unacquainted with any art, by which they may gain a future livelihood, and if they are females, ignorant even of the use of the needle, so necessary to be known by every wife and mother in the lower ranks of life.

I cannot indeed think of little children, who work in Manufactories, without the utmost commiseration. It is impossible, surely, to view those countenances, in which, according to their time of life, the roses of health should bloom, pale and sodden—those limbs which should be straight, robust, and active, stinted in their growth, or distorted by sitting in one continued posture; or to hear those tongues uttering oaths, and other profane language, which should be taught the words of piety and virtue.[117]

The same critical approach to the "higher classes" and the employers recurs in the writings of Hannah More. Her conversion from the life of high society to a life of charitable labors among the poor was prompted by the idea that

> . . . reformation must begin with the great, or it will never be effectual. Their example is the fountain whence the vulgar draw their habits, actions, and characters. To expect to reform the poor, while the opulent are corrupt, is to throw odours into the stream while the springs are poisoned.[118]

Similarly, the diary which contains a "Narrative of the Charitable Labours of Hannah and Martha More," refers time and again to the hardheartedness of the rich farmers, to their depravity in thought and action. One farmer assured the sisters More that religious instruction of the children would be the ruin of agriculture. In another case an "avaricious employer" had deceived them and they found that the children in one school of industry did not earn as much as they had been led to expect. The sisters encountered a "great lady" who offered a glass of gin to every person who stayed away from Sunday school. While the More sisters also cited contrary examples, even some of these contained a moral criticism of the rich. There is a reference to the gentleman at Congresbury, who—"bursting with his wealth and consequence, and purple with his daily bottle of port"—was so impressed by the performance of the children as to promise them twopence apiece as a reward. Martha More calls this "a piece of generosity unknown

[117] *Ibid.*, Vol. I, pp. 198–200.

[118] Quoted from Hannah More, *Thoughts on the Importance of the Manners of the Great* (1788), in Annett M. B. Meakin, *Hannah More* (London: Smith, Elder and Company, 1911), p. 257. See also Quinlan, *Victorian Prelude*, pp. 51–67.

in the family before." [119]   The sisters were thoroughly aware of the fact that the "higher classes" opposed their efforts to give the children of the poor a rudimentary education.   It was only after "irresistible flatteries" and after being told that this education of the poor would secure their orchards from being robbed, their game from being stolen, and might even lower the poor rates—that these "rich savages" and "petty tyrants" gave their occasional consent.[120]   Thus, even though the whole effort of the More sisters could serve in effect as an apologia for the emerging industrial order, it was at the same time a reaffirmation of the traditional view that the poor should trust themselves to be guided and governed by the rich.

In the past the use of evangelism in defending the rising industrial order may have been overemphasized, while the conflict between evangelism and the ideologies of the entrepreneurial class was neglected. But it is certainly true that the evangelists were primarily concerned with ensuring the industrious and moral habits, and the subordination of the people, and that their moral uplift of the "higher classes" remained for the most part a pious admonition which was easily dismissed.   As a result there was conflict as well as agreement between the prevailing beliefs of traditionalism and the emergence of the new entreprenurial class.   The conflict was primarily ideological, for evangelism strongly urged that the "higher classes" assume the responsibility of guiding the poor, and that the people be taught to depend upon their "superiors." Eventually, the entrepreneurs and their spokesmen came to reject this appeal by resolutely denying their own responsibility for the people, by claiming that they were *unable* to reform the habits of the poor, and by demanding that the people must depend exclusively upon their own efforts.   Yet, this ideological conflict was difficult to perceive, and the ideological emancipation of the entrepreneurial class was perhaps held back, because evangelism apparently promoted the material interests of the rising entrepreneurs.   While the intense moralism of evangelical preaching asserted a tutelage over the poor which the entrepreneurs

[119] These examples are taken from Arthur Roberts, ed., *Mendip Annals, or A Narrative of the Charitable Labours of Hannah and Martha More* (London: James Nisbet and Company, 1859), pp. 24, 60, 70–71, and *passim*.   The Hammonds have quoted this document, especially Hannah More's speech to the starving women of Shipham in 1801, as evidence of the unfeeling partisanship of evangelical reformers on behalf of the owners.   They fail to mention that these owners were, nevertheless, frequently opposed to the work of the More sisters.

[120] For a description of their experience cf. Hannah More's letter to Wilberforce in *ibid.*, p. 17.

were eager to deny, it also inculcated a spirit of discipline and subordination which was much to their advantage. And this advantage made it difficult to see that it might be even more advantageous to have industrial discipline result, not from preaching with its implicit obligations, but from want and misery. The ideological break with traditionalism was, in fact, accomplished along these lines. But the traditional beliefs of evangelism did *not* disappear even after their assumptions had been challenged effectively. Instead, evangelism continued in full strength right along with the developing formulation of an entrepreneurial ideology, and the two gradually blended in the moral strictures of the Victorian Age. I stated earlier that the radicalism of Chartist agitation among workers should be considered together with the conservatism of the Methodist revival, and I suggest here that the entrepreneurial denial of responsibility and the demand for the "self-dependence" of the people should be considered together with the traditional beliefs of evangelism. This religious revival among the workers and the persistence of evangelical preaching among the ruling groups had the great effect of overcoming the civic isolation of the rising industrial work force of which Disraeli had spoken.

e. The Ideological Break with Traditionalism

Most eighteenth-century writers believed that a large population of workers was important for the nation's wealth, though only if it was properly employed. These writers emphasized the workers' duty to labor, the utility of poverty because it would enforce this duty, the idea that wages could never rise above the subsistence level, the great depravity of the poor, and finally the Christian virtues such as humility, industry, and piety, which were appropriate to a subordinate social position. All of these ideas presupposed the traditional theory of dependence. Toward the end of the eighteenth century, however, two new ideas were introduced which were clearly exemplified in the everyday practice of employers, but which were, nevertheless, startling when stated as matters of principle. One was that the people must depend upon themselves. The other was that the "higher classes" are not and, in fact, cannot be responsible for the employment of the people or for the relief of the poor.

The idea that the people must depend upon themselves was formulated largely in response to the experience with the Poor Laws and with the problems of rural labor. In his *Dissertation on the Poor Laws* the Rev. Joseph Townsend wrote in 1786 that the distress of the poor appeared to mount as the money collected for their relief increased. Like others before him, Townsend observed the perplexing fact that "poverty and wretchedness have increased in exact proportion to the efforts . . . made for the subsistence of the poor," while distress is at a minimum "where the least provision has been made for the supply" of the poor.[121] Though Townsend's observation was hardly new, his conclusions were. Unlike the "higher ranks," the "poor" were not prompted to exert themselves by pride, honor, and ambition. Only the experience of hunger would "goad them on to labour." Yet the Poor Laws provided that "they shall never hunger." While it was true that these laws also provided that they should be compelled to work, the trouble associated with these legal provisions made them worse than useless. On the other hand,

> Hunger is not only a peaceable, silent and unremitted pressure, but, as the most natural motive to industry and labour, it calls forth the most powerful exertions; and, when satisfied by the free bounty of another, lays a lasting and sure foundation for good will and gratitude. The slave must be compelled to work; *but the freeman should be left to his own judgement and discretion;* should be protected in the full enjoyment of his own, be it much or little; and punished when he invades his neighbor's property. By recurring to these basic motives which influence the slave, and trusting only to compulsion, all the benefits of free service, both to the servant and to the master must be lost.[122]

This doctrine of self-dependence was a new departure. Throughout the century the poor had been taught their duty to labor and to be satisfied with the station to which God had called them. Throughout the century they had been condemned for their indolence and dissipation. But it had never been suggested before that the people should be left to their own judgment and discretion. Probably, Townsend did not perceive the implications of his statement. By neglecting the distinction between workers and paupers he took it for granted that all laboring people would have to respond to the "silent, unremitted pressure" of hunger. Hence, their judgment and discretion would be entirely absorbed in the effort to stay alive. Like previous writers he assumed also that the wages of labor could never rise above the level of subsistence. Consequently, hunger must be permitted to do its work; it

---

[121] Rev. Joseph Townsend, *A Dissertation on the Poor Laws by a Well-Wisher of Mankind* in McCulloch, ed., *op. cit.,* p. 400. In the years immediately preceding the publication of Townsend's pamphlet, the total annual expenditure for poor relief had risen from 1.5 to a little over 2 million pounds. See Gilbert Slater, *Poverty and the State* (New York: Richard R. Smith, 1930), pp. 77–82.

[122] Townsend, *op. cit.,* p. 404. My italics.

was the precise condition which would compel laborers to relieve their dire want. To mitigate this pressure through legal provisions would only cause them to reduce their exertions, for it would allow them to fall back upon a last safeguard against starvation.[123] The logic of the argument was that the worker's need to live had no bearing on the matter. If, in fact, hunger was the only motive of labor, then every worker would see to it that he survived, and his continued distress merely indicated that as yet he was not trying hard enough.

> . . . labor is a commodity, and, as such, an article of trade. . . . When any commodity is carried to market, it is not the necessity of the vendor, but the necessity of the purchaser, that raises the price. . . . *The impossibility of subsistence of the man who carries his labor to a market is totally beside the question,* in this way of viewing it. The only question is, What is it worth to the buyer? [124]

To be sure, Burke, like Townsend, allowed that charity was a "direct and obligatory duty upon all Christians, next in order after the payment of debts." But it was a duty left to private discretion. And it was utterly mistaken to believe that it was within the competence of the government or of the rich "to supply to the poor those necessaries which it has pleased the Divine Providence for a while to withhold from them." [125]

This reference to Divine Providence involved a great deal more than the self-centered hypocrisy of a man who chose to defend the status quo by attributing the cruelties surrounding him to the inscrutable wisdom of God. Received opinion had held that the rich were responsible and the poor should depend upon them. The mere assertion that the poor must go hungry before they will work would not have challenged this opinion, for the "utility of poverty" was an old idea. But Townsend and Burke went a step further when they demanded that nothing be done to mitigate that hunger. In this view the "higher classes" could not help the poor except by employing them in so far as this was in their

---

[123] It is worth recalling the contemporary setting of this approach which makes it at least more intelligible, if not more humane. The fact is that under the Poor Laws a minimum subsistence was guaranteed, and that the reciprocal supplementation of poor rates and wages demoralized the workers. Also, it should be noted that hunger was, in fact, a major stimulus to exertion, when peasants and artisans would suffer considerable deprivation rather than offer their services for factory employment.

[124] Edmund Burke, "Thoughts and Details on Scarcity," in *Works* (Boston: Little, Brown Company, 1869), Vol. V, p. 142. My italics. This essay was first published in 1795.

[125] *Ibid.,* pp. 146, 156–57.

own interest. This denial that the "higher classes" could be responsible for the poor, required a strong justification in an age when conservative opinion took it for granted that the highest ranks of society stood at the pinnacle of power as well as of privilege. By referring to the absolute power of Divine Providence, Burke accounted alike for the distresses of the poor, for the inability of the rich to relieve them, and for the absence of any conflict between the interests of workers and employers. No action of the employer could be detrimental to the worker, since it was in the employer's interest to keep his workers in good condition.

> . . . their interests are always the same, and it is absolutely impossible that their free contracts can be onerous to either party. It is the interest of the farmer that his work should be done with effect and celerity; and that cannot be, unless the laborer is . . . found with such necessaries of animal life . . . as may keep the body in full force, and the mind gay and cheerful. . . .
> On the other hand, if the farmer ceases to profit of the laborer, and that his capital is not continually manured and fructified, it is impossible that he should continue that abundant nutriment and clothing and lodging proper for the protection of the instruments he employs.
> It is therefore the first and fundamental interest of the laborer, that the farmer should have a full incoming profit on the product of his labor. The proposition is self-evident; and nothing but the malignity, perverseness, and ill-governed passions of mankind, and particularly the envy they bear to each other's prosperity, could prevent their seeing and acknowledging it, with thankfulness to the benign and wise Disposer of all things, who obliges men, whether they will or not, in pursuing their own selfish interests, to connect the general good with their own individual success. . . .[126]

These statements illustrate Burke's straightforward denial of responsibility on behalf of the "higher classes." It is hunger which compels the worker to offer his services on the market, and it is the "necessity of the purchaser" which determines his wage. Once employed, the anticipation of hunger should induce the worker to perform his labor willingly and conscientiously. Yet, hunger is not really in prospect for the obedient servant. The interest of the employer in maximizing his profit means that he will offer employment and good wages to all good servants who "need not be afraid of wanting work." Only the "most brutish, the most obstinate, and the most perverse" would suffer hunger till they had learnt to reform their conduct.[127]

These views did not agree with the ideological implications of the evangelical revival. In keeping with his interest in the conservative

[126] *Ibid.*, pp. 139–41.   [127] Townsend, *op. cit.*, pp. 407–8.

function of religion, Burke admonished the poor to be satisfied with their station in life. But unlike the evangelicals he did not remind the "higher classes" of their Christian duty to excel in their manners and their piety. He claimed instead that the rich would enhance the "general good" by pursuing their selfish interests, "whether they will or not." Where Hannah More denounced the farmers of her acquaintance as "rich savages," Burke was quick to point out that it was important to safeguard the "freedom" of the rich in their private acts of charity.[128] Burke was not concerned with religion for the rich. Instead, he declared his trust in the "wise Disposer of all things" who had the general good arise from selfish interests rather than from virtue and piety, a view which helped to undermine the traditional "theory of dependence," according to which the rich had the duty to think for the poor and regulate their lot.

It is certainly paradoxical that a self-conscious defender of the established order like Edmund Burke should have contributed inadvertently to its destruction. The reason for it may be sought more in the conflicting circumstances of his time than in the illogic of his position. For the ruling aristocracy with which he identified himself frequently vacillated between a mere insistence upon superior rank which required no justification and the more or less halfhearted attempts to legitimate that rank by piety and charitable labors. Though wealth and complacency had strengthened the first view during the eighteenth century, the upheavals of the French Revolution provoked an emphasis on the second. By attacking the idea that the rich were responsible and that the poor should depend upon them, Burke made himself the spokesman of an aristocracy whose complacent acceptance of superiority and whose unwitting rejection of all social obligations he identified with the status quo. Yet, he did so just at a time when the French Revolution had challenged that complacency and that rejection. Consequently, anxiety concerning popular unrest was at its height, and nothing was more likely to provoke that unrest than the assertion that the poor must go hungry and that the rich could do no wrong. Of course, in their conduct the "higher classes" had adhered to such beliefs for the better part of the century. But before Burke no one had *formu-*

---

[128] See M. G. Jones, *Hannah More, 1745–1833* (Cambridge: Cambridge University Press, 1952), p. 135, where Burke's contempt for the poor is contrasted with Hannah More's affection and humanity. This ambivalence explains the great popularity of Hannah More's trenchant attacks upon the manners and irreligion of the ruling aristocracy, even in the circles of that aristocracy. Cf. *ibid.,* pp. 103–21.

lated the implications of such conduct and made them into a principle of the social order. Unwittingly, Burke weakened the case he sought to defend, by discarding the conventional hypocrisies of aristocratic rule.

From the viewpoint of the early entrepreneurs Burke's position was manifestly advantageous, but it had also certain weaknesses. At the end of the eighteenth century, his justification of the "higher classes" could only refer to the ruling aristocracy, not to the conduct of merchants and manufacturers. To a social group which was attacking the position of the aristocracy, it could hardly be satisfactory to be told that the economic interests of that aristocracy were identical with the common good. Also, the early entrepreneurs could not readily adopt Burke's denial that the "higher classes" were obliged to employ and relieve the poor. Such a denial was risky perhaps, but not unprecedented, for a ruling aristocracy whose dominance was as yet unchallenged. It was unconvincing if employed on behalf of merchants and manufacturers who were often held in contempt and whose claim to recognition as a "higher class" was yet to be established. Convenient as many of Burke's arguments proved to be, they had to be adapted from the defense of a ruling aristocracy to the strategies of a rising social class.

It is improbable of course that the early entrepreneurs were explicitly concerned with such problems or difficulties. Nevertheless, the fact that the ideological break with traditionalism was first undertaken on behalf of the ruling aristocracy reveals the points of weakness at which ideological defenses were likely to be built. There were two principal problems. How could the "higher classes" deny their responsibility for the poor and at the same time justify their power and authority over them? How could the poor be taught self-dependence without developing in them a dangerous independence? A comprehensive answer to these questions which was in keeping with the interests of the early entrepreneurs was contained in Thomas R. Malthus' *Essay on Population,* first published in 1798. This essay proved that the "higher classes" were unable to relieve the poor and that the poor must reform their habits if they were to escape starvation.

The basic thesis of the essay was the principle of population:

> We will suppose the means of subsistence in any country just equal to the easy support of its inhabitants. The constant effort towards population, which is found to act even in the most vicious societies, increases the number of people before the means of subsistence are increased. . . . The poor consequently must live much worse, and many of them be reduced to severe distress. . . . During this season of distress, the discouragement

to marriage and the difficulty of rearing a family are so great that population is at a stand. In the meantime the cheapness of labour, the plenty of labourers, and the necessity of an increased industry amongst them, encourage cultivators to employ more labour upon their land. . . . The situation of the labourer being then again tolerably comfortable, the restraints to population are in some degree loosened; and the same retrograde and progressive movements with respect to happiness are repeated.[129]

It was a law of nature that population always tended to increase faster than subsistence. There were only two ways in which population could be brought into line with the available food suply: through the positive checks of vice and misery or through the preventive check of strict moral conduct and the postponement of marriage. The "higher classes" could not alter this law of nature; and they could alleviate the condition of the poor only by educating them in the exercise of moral restraint. If they attempted to do more, as for example in the system of the Poor Laws, they would merely aggravate the misery of the poor. For such relief would induce them to increase their families beyond the limit of the available supply of food.

Many of Malthus' ideas had been expressed before. That poverty was inescapable, and indeed a necessary stimulus to labor, was accepted doctrine throughout the eighteenth century. That the Poor Laws were inadvertently increasing indolence and improvidence had been said by many, though official acceptance of this view had to wait until the 1830's. That the "higher classes" were not, and could not be, responsible for the poor had been urged by Townsend and Burke, among others.[130] But Malthus added more than systematization to these and other anticipations of his view. By resting his argument upon a basic limitation of nature he reformulated the relations between the classes. In his judgment only a knowledge of the principle of population would enable the "higher classes" to meet their responsibilities effectively and enable the "lower classes" to mitigate their distress to the extent that this was within the power of man.

The responsibility of the "higher classes" was very strictly circumscribed by a basic law of nature. Unlike Burke, Malthus did not take the position that the self-interest of the rich was identical with the com-

---

[129] T. R. Malthus, *First Essay on Population, 1798* (Reprinted for the Royal Economic Society; London: The Macmillan Company, 1926), pp. 29–31.

[130] Many of Malthus' more specific doctrines were also expressed before 1798, but usually in an incidental manner. A survey of pre-Malthusian opinions is contained in Kenneth Smith, *The Malthusian Controversy* (London: Routledge and Kegan Paul, 1951), pp. 3–32.

mon good.   Instead he attributed their inability to protect the poor to a
condition of nature.   Hence, what appeared as a merely arbitrary identification of class-interest with Divine Providence in Burke was transformed by Malthus into an apparently conscientious concern with the
responsibility of the "higher classes."   A proper delineation of this
responsibility depended upon a knowledge of the principle of population.

> Among the higher and middle classes of society, the effect of this
> knowledge will, I hope, be to direct without relaxing their efforts in bet-
> tering the condition of the poor; to show them what they can and what
> they cannot do; and that, although much may be done by advice and
> instruction, by encouraging habits of prudence and cleanliness, by dis-
> criminate charity, and by any mode of bettering the present condition of
> the poor which is followed by an increase of the preventive check, yet
> that, without this last effect, all the former effects would be futile. . . .
> This knowledge, by tending to prevent the rich from destroying the good
> effects of their own exertion and wasting their efforts in a direction where
> success is unattainable, would confine their attention to the proper ob-
> jects, and thus enable them to do more good.[131]

Malthus deplored the miseries visited upon the poor, although he
thought them well-nigh inevitable.   Where Burke had still believed that
the farmers would employ the people as much as the market allowed
and thus minimize poverty as a consequence of self-interest, Malthus
took the view that, owing to the pressure of population, poverty could
be minimized only by the moral restraint of the poor.   As a consequence,
he rested his eloquent plea for a system of national education on the
need for instructing the "lower classes" in the principle of population.
Only education would enable the poor to escape from as much misery
as they could.   And since there was no other way to mitigate the inevitable miseries which were the lot of man, Malthus believed all
arguments against the education of the people to be illiberal and feeble.
In his judgment, the "higher classes" had no warrant for withholding
from the poor the only means of raising themselves above the level of
acute distress.[132]

[131] T. R. Malthus, *An Essay on the Principle of Population* (2nd ed., Everyman's Library; New York: E. P. Dutton and Company, Inc., 1933), Vol. II, p. 259.

[132] Cf. the discussion of education in Malthus, *Essay (2nd ed.)*, Vol. II, pp. 210–
15.   It should be remembered that Malthus' unqualified advocacy of education
for the poor was still a matter of controversy, for it always entailed a recurrence
of Mandeville's argument that education made the poor unfit to labor.   The
controversy over whether writing should be taught to Sunday school children
is a case in point.   See Mathews, *Methodism and the Education of the People*,
pp. 64–68.

It is clear that Malthus was, if anything, even more pessimistic than Burke concerning the ability of the rich to protect the poor. In fact, founding the relation between the classes upon a law of nature (rather than selfishness endorsed by Providence), Malthus placed the major responsibility for poverty upon the poor. In one sense, this was a mere reformulation of the Calvinistic distinction between the elect and the damned. But it was made to rest, not on the Divine predestination of man's fate, but upon the divinely ordained pressure of population in the face of which man must prove himself by the exercise of moral restraint. Malthus had concluded his *First Essay* with two chapters on theology. In these he argued that the Creator stood revealed in His creation. A certain time of trial was needed even by Him, in order that, as Malthus put it, beings will be formed "with those exalted qualities of mind which will fit them for His high purpose." If we consider man "as he really is, inert, sluggish, and averse from labour, unless compelled by necessity . . . we may pronounce, with certainty, that the world would not have been peopled, but for the superiority of the power of population to the means of subsistence." [133] This was the hidden purpose in the tendency of population to exceed its subsistence and nothing should be done to defeat that purpose. Consequently, the desire for marriage should not be discouraged though men were duty-bound to curb their passions and defer marriage until they could support a family. While Malthus enjoined a strictly moral conduct before marriage, he was also emphatic in opposing "any artificial and unnatural modes of checking population [after marriage], both on account of their immorality and their tendency to remove a necessary stimulus to industry." [134] The urge to marry and the unrestricted growth of the population after marriage were regarded by Malthus as a divinely ordained law of nature, compliance with which had peopled the world and had forced men to exert themselves.

But population growth was not only indispensable for the welfare of man, it was also the inevitable cause of his unhappiness. Owing to man's lack of foresight, population had been limited time and again by the positive check of vice and misery. Hence, the only way to increase man's happiness—to check the excess of population over food supply, to act morally and yet to avoid wars, starvation, and disease—was to increase man's foresight. Malthus regarded the exercise of moral

[133] Malthus, *First Essay*, pp. 352, 363–64.
[134] Quoted from Malthus' reply to James Grahame in D. V. Glass, "Malthus and the Limitation of Population Growth," in D. V. Glass, ed., *Introduction to Malthus* (London: Watts and Company, 1953), p. 29.

restraint—the postponement of marriage—as the principal solution to this problem. And that solution, be it noted, was entirely up to the "lower classes" of society, who at best could only be aided by the educational efforts of the "higher classes."

Malthus' views concerning the exercise of moral restraint embodied a new conception of the relation between rich and poor. While his theory made it inevitable that the passions of man were more powerful than his reason (for else the excess of population would have been checked long ago), there was considerable room for improvement. To be sure, some sections of the population were beyond the reach of education: the positive checks of vice and misery were "confined chiefly to the lowest orders of society." [135] But powerful as the impulses of passion were, "they are generally to some degree modified by reason," [136] among those who do *not* live under conditions of hopeless indigence.

> . . . poverty itself, which appears to be the great spur to industry, when it has once passed certain limits, almost ceases to operate. The indigence which is hopeless destroys all vigorous exertion, and confines the efforts to what is sufficient for bare existence. It is the hope of bettering our condition, and the fear of want, rather than want itself, that is the best stimulus to industry; and its most constant and best directed efforts will almost invariably be found among a class of people above the class of the wretchedly poor.[137]

Hence, the struggle against misery and vice, and against poverty itself, the encouragement of habits of industry, the efforts to minimize the pressure of population against subsistence, indeed the whole of man's quest for happiness was made to depend—in Malthus' way of viewing things—upon the exercise of moral restraint among the "lower classes."

In the past, almost everything that had been done for the poor had tended to obscure the true cause of their poverty and had, therefore, prevented their practicing moral restraint as the only means of bettering their condition. And the people themselves had attributed their miserable distress to all manner of causes: to the insufficiency of wages, the inadequacy of Parish relief, the avarice of the rich, the unjust institutions of society, and even the dispensations of providence. In searching for objects of accusation, the people would never think of accusing themselves, "on whom, in fact, the principal blame lies, except so far as they have been deceived by the higher classes of society." It was, therefore,

135 Malthus, *First Essay,* pp. 63–73.
136 Malthus, *Essay (2nd ed.).* Vol. II, p. 169.
137 *Ibid.,* Vol. II, p. 143.

necessary clearly to explain to the people the "true and permanent cause of poverty," and it did not seem "entirely visionary" to Malthus that such education would have "some, and perhaps not an inconsiderable, influence on their conduct." [138]   Though it was important to teach the principle of population to the "higher classes,"

> among the poor themselves, its effects would be still more important. That the principal and most permanent cause of poverty has little or no *direct* relation to forms of government, or the unequal division of property; and that, as the rich do not in reality possess the *power* of finding employment and maintenance for the poor, the poor cannot, in the nature of things, possess the *right* to demand them; are important truths flowing from the principle of population, which, when explained, would by no means be above the most ordinary comprehensions.[139]

Accordingly, knowledge of the principle of population would foster a spirit of patience and contentment among the poor, as well as teach them that they alone had the power to reduce poverty through the exercise of moral restraint. The people must shoulder the burden of their distress, for they alone are responsible for it.

Malthus' attack upon the traditional theory of dependence had great effect as a defense of the rising industrial order. He challenged the vulgarized Puritan assumption that the poor were incapable of virtue. He challenged also the eighteenth-century belief that poverty was inescapable and depravity was its cause. He denied the responsibility of the "higher classes," but he did more than declare, as Burke had, that their self-interest would promote the common good. He affirmed that the common people should be left to their "judgment and discretion," but he did more than declare, as Townsend had, that hunger was the "most natural motive to industry and labor." In his principle of population, Malthus combined elements from all these views, but in so doing he reformulated the relations between the classes. With regard to the "higher classes," he merely contended that they could do little to help the poor except through education; still, he emphasized that they should do what they could, and also that they could do wrong. The thrust of his argument, however, concerned the "lower classes." Poverty was their lot; it was as inescapable as the excess of human passion

---

[138] *Ibid.,* Vol. II, pp. 169–70. This deception of the "higher classes" refers to the population doctrines of the eighteenth century, according to which all increases in the number of people were regarded as conducive to the wealth of the country.

[139] *Ibid.,* Vol. II, pp. 259–60. See also the chapter "Of the Only Effectual Means of Improving the Condition of the Poor," *ibid.,* pp. 168–73.

over reason. Yet, to some degree human reason could have "not an inconsiderable influence upon conduct."

In this view the differences between the classes were put down to the exercise of foresight or prudence. Indeed, virtues and vices, diligence and indolence, success and failure, and all the intangible emotions of men were made to depend upon this calculation of a man's resources. No virtue of a poor man could henceforth exempt him from condemnation. The fact of poverty showed that a man had married when he should have stayed single, just as the fact of success demonstrated that a man had exercised proper foresight. Malthus removed vice and virtue from the vague realm of religious feeling and exhortation. He made the use of reason, i.e., the calculation of chances with regard to supporting a family, the touchstone of virtue and of a man's fate in the world.

The implications of this view were as convenient and flattering to the rich as they were outrageous to the poor. Landlords and manufacturers could use the principle of population to explain their own inaction, their unbending opposition to all proposed reforms, and the inevitability of misery among the poor. All the evils attending the process of industrialization could be put down to a law of nature and of God and the same law tended to prove that economic success was evidence of foresight and moral restraint. It showed furthermore that all poverty and distress was both the responsibility and the fault of the common people, a view which "seemed to be intentionally adding the burden of misery and vice to their already unfortunate lot." [140]

It is not surprising that these arguments evoked feelings of outrage among the common people and their spokesmen, accustomed though many of them were to the disabilities of their subordinate position. Malthus had acknowledged that the "wretchedly poor" would never be able to exercise moral restraint; moreover neither piety nor virtue could aid those above this level of bare survival, for it appeared as if poverty could only be held at bay by an indefinite postponement or prevention of family life. In this interpretation the people had been condemned to a life, from which all passion and sentiment had to be barred if they would save themselves from semistarvation. Indeed, the desire for sexual gratification and for the familial continuity of life,

---

[140] James A. Field, "The Malthusian Controversy in England," *Essays in Population* (Chicago: University of Chicago Press, 1931), p. 30 and *passim*. This essay covers the same material as Smith, *op. cit.*, pp. 47–206, namely, the controversial literature initiated by Malthus. Both studies are valuable.

which were a vital buttress to their self-respect, were now made expendable, a price to be paid for the sake of money-making.[141] Sexual gratification as a reward of wealth and sexual deprivation as the added punishment of poverty: these were the alternatives which Malthus' doctrine seemed to pose for those most directly affected by it.[142]

These uses and abuses of the Malthusian doctrine, together with the plethora of intellectual controversy which it evoked, tend to obscure its significance for the changing managerial ideologies of the period. One might say that under the guise of unwittingly defending the interest of a rising entrepreneurial class and outraging the poor Malthus had prepared the emancipation of the English working class. To be sure, this was an implication of his approach which neither he nor any of his contemporaries perceived. It was obscured by the obvious manner in which the failure of the poor to exercise moral restraint was used to defend every vested interest and indeed attribute to common laborers all responsibility for the consequences of that exploitation, from which they and their women and children suffered. But this total reversal of the traditional theory of dependence, this complete exemption of the "higher classes" and this equally complete insistence upon the self-dependence of the people, had eventual repercussions which were foreshadowed in Malthus' own argument. Lack of foresight made it impossible for man to exercise moral restraint.

> But though this want of foresight, which is fostered by ignorance and despotism, tends thus rather to encourage the procreation of children, it is absolutely fatal to the industry which is to support them. Industry cannot exist without foresight and security. . . .[143]

In urging the exercise of foresight and moral restraint upon the common people, Malthus inadvertently encouraged in them precisely those qualities which on his own showing had led to economic success among the "higher classes." Such a doctrine had important equalitarian implications in an age when it was regarded as dangerous to "let the poor know that the rich had faults," and as monstrous for the "higher classes" to be told that their hearts were as sinful as those of the "com-

---

[141] These conclusions are largely based on my reading of the implications of William Cobbett's diatribes. A convenient survey of Cobbett's arguments against Malthus is contained in Herman Ausubel, "William Cobbett and Malthusianism." *Journal of the History of Ideas,* Vol. XIII (April, 1952), pp. 250–56.

[142] Such a doctrine certainly helped to make workers "an insulated body in society." (Rev. Hewlett, as quoted in Trimmer, *op. cit.*)

[143] Malthus, *Essay (2nd ed.),* Vol. II, p. 143.

mon wretches that crawl on the earth." [144]   Like the evangelicals, but
with less religious fervor and more emphasis on the rational planning
of life, Malthus was saying that the poor could be virtuous.   Virtue or
moral restraint was to Malthus an outgrowth of knowledge, not of
religious devotion.   And while knowledge could be acquired with the
help of the "higher classes," the exercise of moral restraint depended
entirely upon the poor.   Unlike the evangelicals Malthus emphasized
the essential self-dependence of the common people.[145]

f. The Denial of Responsibility, the Claims to Authority, and the Demand for Self-Dependence

Malthus' synthesis of ideas is of interest in the present context because it contained the basic tenets of an emerging entrepreneurial ideology.   The denial of responsibility on the part of the "higher classes"
and the demand for self-dependence on the part of the "poor" became
the basic orientation of Parliamentary efforts to solve the problems of
poor relief.   It is true that manufacturers and their spokesmen were not
directly concerned with these questions which related primarily to
problems of rural administration, but these men became involved with
the new conception of class relations which the Malthusian doctrine
contained.   Their daily solution of managerial problems, their efforts to
defend themselves against public attacks, and their strong opposition
to governmental regulation led them to disclaim all responsibility for
the great distress created by rapid industrialization, and to justify their
power in terms of their contribution to the wealth of the nation.

Common interests had led English entrepreneurs at an early time to
form organizations which would advance their interests,[146] but such

[144] This first was a critical comment in 1813 on Hannah More's *Cheap Reposi-
tory Tracts,* in which the vices of the rich as well as the vices of the poor were
illustrated for the "vulgar."   Quoted in Jones, *Hannah More, 1745–1833,* p. 148.
The second comment is that of an aristocratic lady on the dangers of Methodism
quoted in B. N. Schilling, *Conservative England and the Case against Voltaire*
(New York: Columbia University Press, 1950), p. 128.

[145] In *The Great Transformation* Karl Polanyi has emphasized that the erection
of a free labor market in the 1830's destroyed all existing safeguards which had
protected workers in the past.   It should be added, however, that most proponents of laissez faire were educational reformers, who rejected the traditional
view according to which education would lead to insubordination.   Inadequate as
this education was to begin with, it became eventually an essential substitute for
the safeguards which made the protection of labor synonymous with its subordination.

[146] See, for example, the organization of the General Chamber of Manufacturers in Manchester in the 1770's, which is discussed in Bowden, *op. cit.,*
pp. 175–81.

awareness of common interests on specific issues was not identical with the development of an ideology. The formulation of an ideology is typically a matter of slow growth, combining as it must the interests and ideas of many individuals before an effective intellectual systematization can take place, which must then be applied in turn to enhance on-going activities. In the present case an entrepreneurial ideology also developed slowly, because it had to win acceptance in opposition to habits of thought which were widely taken for granted, however little they were applied in practice. Though Malthus' work contained the major tenets of an entrepreneurial ideology, the ground for its acceptance was prepared by the manner in which the early entrepreneurs "solved" the problems of labor management with which they were confronted. Since the major ideological issue involved the responsibility of the "higher classes" for the relief and employment of the poor, it is important to see what the denial of such responsibility meant in practical terms. A contemporary observer has described how the managerial practices of the time inadvertently led to the excessive length of the working day:

> The duration of labour is the opprobriousness rather of our manufacturing system than of individuals. The masters with whom I have conversed are men of humanity, and willing, I believe, to adopt any practical proposal to amend the health and improve the state of their work-people. But they are scarcely conscious of the extent of the mischief. We underrate evils to which we are accustomed. The diminution of the intervals of work has been a gradual encroachment. Formerly an hour was allowed for dinner; but one great manufacturer, pressed by his engagements, wished his work-people to return five minutes earlier. This abridgment was promptly adopted at other mills. Five minutes led to ten. It was found also that breakfast and drinking (afternoon meal) might be taken while the people were at work. Time was thus saved; more work was done; and the manufactured article could be offered at a less price. If one house offered it at a lower rate, all other houses, to compete in the market, were obliged to use similar means. Thus what was at first partial and temporary has become general and permanent. And the unfortunate artizans, working before in excess, have now to carry labour to a still greater and more destructive extent . . . so established are the hours of work that no individual master can, without loss, liberate his people at an earlier period. A legislative enactment is the only remedy for this.[147]

Yet, all suggested legislation was opposed by the manufacturers for precisely the same reasons that led to the lengthening of the working day. Each proposed method of reform was bound to vary in its effect

---

[147] Dr. Turner Thackrah, "Effects of Trades on Health" (1831), quoted in Hutchins and Harrison, *op. cit.*, pp. 35–36.

upon different enterprises, depending upon the particular conditions of each, and, consequently, arguments were readily found for opposing all legislative regulation on the ground of inequity or impracticality.[148] And as the agitation for reform through legislative regulation continued, employers would alternately attempt to show that conditions were not bad at all, that they were much worse in some other industry than in their own, and that the government had the duty, not to regulate them, but to protect their property as well as their right to do with their own as they saw fit.

What stands out in this reaction of the early entrepreneurs (and many of their fellows since then) is their utter unconcern with ideas of any kind, and their complete preoccupation with the affairs of the moment. If ideology is defined as the attempt to interpret the actions of the moment so that they appear to exemplify a more or less consistent orientation (if not a larger purpose), then it is clear that the most fundamental contrast to ideology is a single-minded attention to expediency. In their numerous protests against Commissions of inquiry, factory inspectors, new legislative proposals, or anything else that threatened to interfere with their pursuit of the main chance, the entrepreneurs and their spokesmen used stock arguments: the proposal (any proposal) would not work; the evil complained of was not there or was the fault of others; and, in any case, all interference was unjust and would kill the goose that laid the golden eggs. Yet, even the most resolute rejection of all concern with ideas or principles of justification has the paradoxical result of becoming involved in the formulation of ideologies.

There are essentially two reasons for this. One is that actions themselves, however expedient and consciously unprincipled they may be, add up to a pattern of conduct which can be defined in abstract terms, largely because circumstances as well as existing ideologies limit the range of available choices. The pressure of circumstances tends to force some pattern of consistency upon expediency itself. The early entrepreneurs who solved their labor problem by the employment and exploitation of women and children on a large scale, and who rejected

---

[148] Cf. the comment in the report of 1833 quoted in Thomas, *op. cit.,* p. 56. The manufacturers held such views with unbending tenacity. Their opposition to all factory legislation was such that it took twenty-five years of legislative deliberation to restrict children of nine to a sixty-nine-hour week, and that only in the cotton mills. See Hutchins and Harrison, *op. cit.,* p. 21. See also Thomas, *op. cit.,* pp. 20–21, 32, 41–42, 70–74, 82–85, 115–33, for descriptions of employers' reactions to legislation.

all criticism with any argument that seemed serviceable at the moment, thereby took a position which could be formulated in ideological terms. For their practices implied a resolute rejection of the traditional theory of dependence, according to which "it is the duty of the higher classes to think for [the poor] and to take the responsibility for their lot." The early entrepreneurs rejected this traditional conception by their actions alone. But if they would not be bothered with the arguments of less intensely practical men, they were still unable to prevent these others from demanding that the pursuit of gain make some sense beyond that of lining their pockets. Hence, the numberless adjustments to the advantages of the moment were formulated eventually into a more or less consistent orientation. And this was done by men of ideas, members of a heterogeneous intelligentsia, who identified their attempts to make sense out of what they observed in society with a reasoned justification of the early entrepreneurs. That is the second reason why the expedient actions of a prominent social group cannot long escape involvement with ideas.

In the past, responsibility for the poor had been the justification of authority over them. Now that the entrepreneurs denied this responsibility by their everyday actions, and in the face of constant agitation for reform, it became necessary to spell out the particular advantages derived from the development of industry, which made all criticism absurd and demonstrated the singular beneficence of the manufacturers. This is the spirit of Dr. Andrew Ure's *Philosophy of Manufactures.* Ure agreed with the view that workers were, in Malthus' phrase, "inert, sluggish, and averse from labour." He attributed the enmity of workers toward the capitalist to the fact that the latter "animated their otherwise torpid talents." [149] Workers should rejoice at the success of their employers and commend themselves by regularity and skill. In this way they could advance their condition to that of managers, giving thereby the gratifying example of "skillful workmen becoming opulent proprietors." [150] Ure's emphasis, however, was on the indolence of workers and the employer's heavy task rather than on the promise of success. In addition, Ure's defense of the manufacturing system was concerned with three major issues. He wanted to show that child labor was not the cruel and inhuman outrage it was said to be. He stated that any combination of workers was the product of agitators who incited to violence and crime, and who interfered with the freedom of workers

[149] Ure, *op. cit.,* p. 279.
[150] *Ibid.,* pp. 279–80.

to offer their services to the employers. And he emphasized the fact, again and again, that manufacturers created employment opportunities, eased human labor through the use of machinery compared with the hand labor of the domestic industries,[151] and that they raised the wages of labor.

Rhapsodic as Ure's praise of machinery was, it had, nevertheless, a strikingly apologetic undertone. Ure's arguments concerning child labor are a case in point. The passage is famous in which Ure describes his visit to Manchester factories, where children were never beaten or out of humor, where they seemed to him always cheerful and alert, "taking pleasure in the light play of their muscles—enjoying the mobility natural to their age." He found it exhilarating and delightful to observe the nimbleness with which the children pieced the broken ends, and the leisure ("after a few seconds' exercise of their tiny fingers,") in which they "amused themselves in any attitude they chose." [152] These statements have been cited frequently as evidence of the unfeeling brutality of the early manufacturers. But there was another side to Ure's argument. He maintained that the manufacturers were both "innocent and unconscious" of the existence of exploitation.[153] He did not deny that the children were exploited cruelly, not even with reference to the cotton industry of which he was a special champion. For all his panegyric on the beauties of child labor he repeatedly pointed out that the mill-owners had nothing to do with the employment of children. And when they did, this could only accrue to the children's benefit.

The real exploiters of the children, Ure maintained, were those workers who employed them as helpers.[154] In many instances parents employed their own children. In saying this he also asserted that this exploitation was checked, as far as lay in the power of the mill-owner, both by the direct supervision of the spinners, and indirectly by inspecting the quality of the yarn. If found defective, deductions would be made from the wages paid, and since defects would result from an over-working of the children, this was automatically checked. Ure further

---

[151] *Ibid.,* p. 8. "The constant aim and effect of scientific improvement in manufactures is philanthropic, as they tend to relieve the workmen either from the niceties of adjustment which exhaust his mind and fatigue his eyes, or from painful repetition of efforts which distort or wear out his frame."

[152] *Ibid.,* p. 301.

[153] *Ibid.,* p. 300.

[154] According to Ure, the introduction of machinery would put an end to the cruel exploitation of children, such as the "fearful despotism" of the wool-slubbers over their young helpers. *Ibid.,* pp. 8–9.

quoted from the testimony given before a Factory Commission in which it was stated that the spinners, not the master, beat the children. The master prohibited the employment of children under age, and he did not allow the beating of children, or was ignorant of it, when it occurred.[155]

> The operatives, blinded by envy, and misled by phantoms of gain, need, in fact, defense against their self-defamation. I am certain that the general accusation of cruelty is groundless in respect even to this class of individuals. They dare not be cruel, from fear of the just resentment of the very masters whom they falsely charge with cruelty. That particular instances of ill-usage of children do occur sometimes in factories, as in families and schools, is undoubtedly true; and they will happen wherever the depraved nature of men is not renovated by the Christian spirit; but they are exceedingly rare. It would be a gross exaggeration to say they equal in amount one-tenth of the hardships which children have to endure in pin manufactories and many agricultural employments.[156]

This passage reveals the gist of Ure's argument on behalf of industry, and the cotton mills in particular. It ran typically as follows: the evils of which manufacturers are accused do not exist in the majority of cases; when they exist, they are usually the fault of subcontractors or skilled workers who act against the explicit instructions of the owner; and in any case the hardships complained of are not "one-tenth" as bad in cotton-spinning as they are in other types of employment. And indeed, they are never as bad in manufacturing of any type as they are in the home industries, for it is the beneficent result of machinery that the workers of the home industries are relieved of their inhuman drudgery.[157]

In this defense of the manufacturers Ure did not make any reference to the Malthusian doctrine, and his references to population were confined to a survey of the labor force employed in the textile mills. Nevertheless, the two authors are related in the sense that Malthus' intellectual systematization and Ure's practical orientation toward the problems faced by the cotton manufacturers contained the same basic tenets. Both authors denied that the "higher classes" could take the responsibility of finding employment for the common people or of safeguarding them against extreme poverty and hunger. But where Malthus had demanded a generation earlier that the "higher classes" teach the people moral restraint as "the only effectual means of improving the

---

[155] *Ibid.,* pp. 303–4.
[156] *Ibid.,* pp. 303–4.
[157] *Ibid.,* pp. 333–39.

condition of the poor," [158] Ure maintained that the manufacturers were successfully meeting their obligations by the employment of men, women, and children.

Ure used the reports of the Poor Law Commissioners to make an invidious comparison between the conditions of rural and industrial workers.

> From the documents published by this unexceptionable tribunal, it appears that, but for the renovating influence of its manufacturers, England would have been overrun ere now with the most ignorant and depraved race of men to be met with in any civilized region of the globe. It is, in fact, in the factory districts alone that the demoralizing agency of pauperism has been effectually resisted, and a noble spirit of industry, enterprise, and intelligence called forth. What a contrast is there at this day between the torpor and brutality which pervade very many of the farming parishes, as delineated in the official reports, and the beneficent activity which animates all the cotton-factory towns, villages, and hamlets.[159]

It was, according to Ure, a "singular effrontery in the feudal legislators" to accuse the manufacturers as the "main authors of the national corruption" and to impose upon them responsibility for the education of the juvenile operatives.[160]   Such would have been unnecessary if the children of agricultural laborers had been educated in the first place. Instead, the "uneducated state of the lower orders" constituted a "dark den of incendiarism and misrule in the farming districts" [161] and the same danger would have to be anticipated in the manufacturing districts in view of the concentrations of peoples which afforded "every facility of secret cabal and co-operative union among the work-people . . . and ample means of inflaming their passions. . . ." [162]

But Ure apprehended no such result, because everything had already been done by the manufacturers and their workers to produce an "abundant increase of intelligence and moral sentiments." [163]   In support of this sweeping contention Ure cited the influence of Sunday schools; he quoted with approval the statement that the advocates of general education were hearing no more of the danger of educating the lowest classes; he made reference to the model factories of David Dale at New Lanark without troubling to mention that these had been organized in this manner by that notorious radical, Robert Owen.   He referred to the model of Prussian education, which unlike its English

---

[158] Malthus, *Essay (2nd ed.)*, Vol. II, pp. 168–73.
[159] Ure, *op. cit.*, p. 354.
[160] *Ibid.*, p. 405.
[161] *Ibid.*, p. 404.
[162] *Ibid.*, p. 407.
[163] *Ibid.*, p. 408.

counterpart had combined popular instruction with the inculcation of moral and religious principles such that *hopeless* poverty "appeared in man, serene, contented, lofty, [and] graceful." And he discoursed upon the Gospel truth "Godliness is great gain" by contending that the moral discipline or the dissolute manners of the mill-owners or managers would produce a like conduct in their workers and that the organization of the moral machinery on sound principles was "as much for the advantage as it is the duty of every factory proprietor." [164] According to Ure, the whole evil bent of human nature was successfully corrected among the laboring people by the social benevolence of the manufacturers, and by the "two most glorious features" of his time: the vast circulation of Scriptures and the increase of Sunday schools.[165]

It is apparent that Ure's approach was less academic than that of Malthus. In keeping with the antagonism between entrepreneurs and the landed gentry Ure made his case by invidious comparisons between rural distress, immorality, and turbulence on the one side, and the intelligence and morality of the work people in the manufacturing districts on the other. Ure used the argument of Burke, that Divine Providence obliged employers to connect their self-interest with the general good, or the argument of Malthus that moral and religious education of the people was the only means to mitigate their distress. But the accent of his appeal was upon the claim that the manufacturers already fulfilled their responsibility. He vigorously denounced the "ill-educated state of the higher orders" which had been a "prolific parent of a never-ceasing round of political and legislative blunders, under the consequences of which no people less energetic than the middle classes of Great Britain could have upheld their heads." [166] These middle classes were right in opposing such ill-considered governmental regulation because the manufacturers were already solving all social problems by their "wise and liberal policy." [167] Ure mentioned the licentious life of owners and managers only to point out that such dissolute manners conflicted with their most immediate economic interests.

In the face of rising agitation against the manufacturers, this was a bold position to take. To argue in the midst of notorious deprivations that the entrepreneurs were already doing all that could be done was likely to be convincing only to those who believed it already. The argument was supported not primarily by a denial that exploitation

---

[164] *Ibid.*, pp. 406, 410, 412–13, 415–18, and 425–27.
[165] *Ibid.*, p. 428.
[166] *Ibid.*, p. 404.
[167] *Ibid.*, pp. 405–8, and *passim*.

was cruel and widespread, but by the assertion that others, the rural gentry or the hardpressed craftsmen, were responsible for it. Presumably, this strategy of argument facilitated the solidarity of manufacturers who could unite most readily by opposition against common enemies. But in his eagerness to deny all accusations, and to argue against trade unions and legislative interference by constant references to the social benevolence of the manufacturers, Ure made the latter into a "higher class" which regulated the lot of the laboring people. That is, he abandoned, albeit unwittingly, the contention of Malthus that the poor could and should be self-dependent. And although he favored education for the people, as Malthus had, he reverted to the evangelicals in his insistence upon religious instruction as a means of safeguarding the subordination of the workers. As a man closely associated with the practical problems encountered by the manufacturers, Ure saw only the need for discipline and obedience. The renewed demand for the self-dependence of the people, and especially its practical implementation, arose instead in connection with the debates concerning the "management of the poor."

These debates of the Poor Laws, which had taken place since at least the beginning of the eighteenth century, were brought to a head in the work of the Poor Law Commission of 1832 and in the Poor Law Amendment Act of 1834. These legislative deliberations and enactments made the theory of self-dependence for the first time the center of widespread public attention, and eventually implemented the Malthusian view that poverty was the fault of the poor, not the responsibility of the rich. Of course, manufacturers utilized these arguments, as Ure had done, when they found them convenient. But the poor with whom the Poor Laws were concerned were primarily the laborers of the rural parishes, and the rich whose responsibility was denied were primarily the farmers who employed them.[168] The problems which were now considered for the first time in a systematic and authoritative manner have been summarized in the classic study on this subject:

> The decisive element was undoubtedly a recognition of the bad behaviour induced alike among employers and employed by the various devices for maintaining the able-bodied, wholly or partially, out of the Poor Rate. When, under the Allowance system, the farmers and manufacturers became aware that they could reduce wages indefinitely, and the manual workers felt secure of subsistence without the need for exert-

---

[168] See Karl Polanyi, *Origins of our Time* (London: Victor Gollancz, 1945), pp. 286–92. The note to which I refer was added to the English edition of *The Great Transformation*.

ing themselves to retain any particular employment, the standard of skill and conduct of all concerned rapidly declined. To single out the dull-witted employer and the lazy workman for special grants out of public funds, to the detriment of the keen organizer and the zealous worker, was obviously bad psychology as well as bad economics. When adding to the number of children automatically increased the family income, young persons hastened to get married, as it was, indeed, intended they should do by the Justices of the Peace who adopted the Speenhamland Scale. Even worse in its moral effects was the "parish pay" given for illegitimate children, combined with the hideous blackmail of reputed fathers which inevitably arose from the bastardy provisions of the old Poor Law. . . . The Elizabethan Poor Law had become, by the beginning of the nineteenth century, a systematic provision, not so much for the unfortunate as for the less competent and the less provident, whom the humanity or carelessness of the Justices and the Overseers had combined specially to endow out of public funds.[169]

These conditions gave a ready popularity to the Malthusian doctrine. When young men married early and when many children were regarded as an economic asset, it was reasonable to argue for the exercise of moral restraint, or to attribute to improvidence the prevalence of poverty and the burden of the poor rates. To a certain extent these evils of the system were acknowledged even by William Cobbett, perhaps the most vigorous opponent of Malthus and of the Poor Law reformers.

But if the evils were widely acknowledged, their remedy was a subject of embittered controversy. Relief was not to be denied, but it would be available to the poor only under conditions of "wholesome restraint" (Chadwick). This policy would force the poor to exercise foresight. It was true, of course, as Francis Place had pointed out in 1822, that the employers of farm labor were as demoralized as the workers.[170] But the whole burden of the Malthusian argument was to place upon the worker himself the responsibility for his own welfare. Thus, the criticism which had been directed at the Poor Laws was in effect directed at the poor. There is no more reasoned statement of this approach than that of Nassau Senior in his letter to Lord Althorp.

> The great fault of a Labour-rate is that it destroys the distinction between pauperism and independence. . . . It is only by keeping these things separated, . . . and by making relief in all cases less agreeable than wages, that any thing deserving the name of improvement can be

[169] Sidney and Beatrice Webb, *English Poor Law History,* pp. 14–15.
[170] Francis Place, *Illustrations and Proofs of the Principle of Population* (London: Longman, Hurst, Rees, Orme, and Brown, 1822), pp. 167–71.

hoped for. But under the Labour-rate system, relief and wages are utterly confounded. All the wages partake of relief, and all the relief partakes of wages. The labourer is employed not because he is a good workman, but because he is a parishioner. He receives a certain sum not because that sum is the value of his services, but because it is what the vestry has ordered to be paid. Good conduct, diligence, skill, all become valueless. Can it be supposed that they will be preserved? We deplore the misconception of the poor in thinking that wages are not a matter of contract but of right; that any diminution of their comforts . . . is an evil to be remedied not by themselves, but by the magistrate—not an error, or even a misfortune, but an injustice.[171]

The solution to the problem, which the Commissioners proposed under the guidance of Nassau Senior, was the famous principle of "less eligibility." All relief to able-bodied persons and their families would be administered in a "well-regulated workhouse." And it would be available only upon application and under conditions which made all relief "less eligible" than "independent poverty."

This solution of poor relief applied primarily to the agricultural laborers; but sanctioned as it was by government authority, it became symbolic for the relations between the classes in the new industrial order. The New Poor Law of 1834 combined two principal tenets. It enjoined the poor to be self-dependent and bear principal responsibility for their own well-being. And it denied that the employers or the government had an obligation to relieve the poor beyond preventing starvation under workhouse conditions which were made deliberately undesirable. In 1832 Nassau Senior had written that

> The present system [of the Poor Laws] gives the labourer . . . a sort of independence. He need not study to please his master, he need not bestir himself to seek work, he need not put any restraint on his temper, he need not ask relief as a favour, he need not fear that his idleness, or drunkenness, will injure his family; he has, in short, all a slave's security for subsistence without his liabilities to punishment.[172]

The management of the workhouses was to remedy these evils by an exacting discipline. But in the eyes of the critics this discipline of the workhouse, which was designed for the indolent, became symbolic of

[171] Quoted in Marian Bowley, *Nassau Senior and Classical Economics* (London: Allen and Unwin, 1937), pp. 290–91. I should add that Senior, Chadwick, and other Poor Law reformers were critical of Malthus, whose pessimism was incompatible with their interest in reform. But this criticism does not preclude a close affinity between Malthus' emphasis on moral restraint and the reformer's distinction between pauperism and independence.

[172] *Ibid.*, pp. 291–92.

the regard in which the higher classes held the masses of the laboring poor.[173]

Of course, this was a "misinterpretation." The proponents of reform did not intend an abolition of the responsibility for relief. They did not intend to punish poverty: they only maintained that the workhouse was needed as a deterrent in order to eliminate pauperism as distinguished from poverty.[174] Moreover, the New Poor Law of 1834 did not abolish "outdoor relief," except to the able-bodied. The sick or the aged or the mentally deficient were to be cared for outside the workhouse; and if they had to be cared for in an institution, this was to be done in separate houses especially designed for this purpose.[175] Finally, men like Senior, Chadwick, and others, were ardent supporters of educational reforms, housing measures, public health legislation, which certainly made them less unregenerate advocates of laissez faire in the face of pressing social problems than their reputation would indicate.[176] Nor was it the fault of the reformers if in practice the workhouse turned out to be a veritable hell while outdoor relief to the disabled was shrouded in obscurity. The facts appear to be that paupers of all types were crowded together although the law had explicitly prescribed separate establishments for different types of indigents.[177]

But the intentions of the reformers, the plausible explanations of administrative failure and the welter of controversial opinions on all sides of the question, while interesting in themselves, do not elucidate

[173] Cf. Senior's letter to Lord Lansdown cited in Bowley, *op. cit.*, pp. 324–25.

[174] See Webbs, *English Poor Law History*, pp. 154–64. Cf. also Hammonds, *The Town Labourer*, pp. 60–94.

[175] Webbs, *English Poor Law History*, pp. 56–61, 142–53.

[176] See, for example, the detailed analysis of Senior's opinions concerning the legitimate scope of government in Bowley, *op. cit.*, pp. 237–81. Also, S. E. Finer, *The Life and Times of Edwin Chadwick* (London: Methuen and Company, 1952).

[177] The reasons for this departure from the declared purpose of the law are complex. It was partly the result of administrative difficulties which had not been anticipated. In part it stemmed from the influence of Sir George Nicholls, one of the Poor Law Commissioners. Moreover, as the Webbs point out, the distinction between the institutional treatment of the infirm and the workhouse as a test of destitution was not understood. Compounding these and other difficulties, however, was the undoubted callousness and indifference of local administrators, of whom an unusual measure of judgment would have been required, if they were to distinguish between the able-bodied paupers, whom they were instructed to treat harshly, and all others, whom they might have treated otherwise. The whole matter is analyzed in Webbs, *English Poor Law History*, pp. 121–42.

the major point at issue in the present context. The salient fact is that the system of poor relief which had led to untold abuses through the deliberate or unwitting connivance of entrepreneurs, farmers, Parish authorities, and others, as well as through the gradual demoralization of the laborers themselves, was now to be reformed solely by means of disciplines imposed upon the last. The workhouse system of pauper relief implemented the Malthusian doctrine not by the admonition to exercise moral restraint, nor by means of education, nor yet by exposing the poor to the impersonal pressure of misery and hunger, but by making indolence and lack of foresight an object of punishment in a "well-regulated work-house." Where Malthus had believed that famine and disease would be the penalty for a lack of moral restraint, and where Ure thought that proper instruction would make the laborers content with their lot, Senior, Chadwick, and their colleagues proposed to enforce virtue and self-dependence by governmentally administered penalties.

The contrast between Ure and Senior is instructive. Both men formulated a consistent approach to the problems of the rising industrial order, and both men sought to solve these problems in terms of an affirmative attitude toward the society of their day. Both men were attacking resolutely the remaining legacies of the traditional theory of dependence. But Ure was intimately familiar with the technical and managerial problems of factory production, and his effort to facilitate the manufacturer's task by formulating a "philosophy of manufactures" consisted in rejecting the idea of responsibility and in claiming that the entrepreneurs' actions fully justified their exercise of power. His whole attention was focussed upon the manufacturer's claim to authority against the threatened interference of government, and this orientation accentuated the need for the subordination of the laboring people. The actions of the ruling aristocracy and of the rising class of entrepreneurs exemplified the idea that the "rich" could not protect the poor and were doing all they could in any case. But while this prepared the ground for Ure's hymns of praise, it also helped to relegate Malthus' demand for the independence of the poor to the realm of pious admonitions. To recognize the compatibility between this demand for independence and the security of the established order required a thoroughly intellectual approach to the problem, such as the Benthamite school provided. This was the approach of Nassau Senior and his colleagues. Yet, this decisive break with the legacies of traditionalism, in practice as well as in theory, posed problems in turn.

The New Poor Law attributed pauperism to individual improvidence at a time when the dislocations of a rapid industrial development were placing an ever mounting burden of deprivations upon the "poor," while the champions of that development proclaimed all problems solved by the social benevolence of the manufacturers. Even though the reformers did not identify pauperism with poverty, it is not surprising that manufacturers would use this invidious identification to justify their own actions, just as workers and their spokesmen used it to attack their alienation from the society. Long hours, poor health conditions, cruel exploitation of children, low wages, and all similar conditions could be explained or justified, if need be, if the source of all misery was the improvidence of the laboring people, as the New Poor Law seemed to imply. Though not intended for this purpose, the "well-managed work-house" appeared to give added justification to the manufacturers' exercise of iron discipline in their enterprises. And under these conditions it appeared as if the spokesmen for the industrial order made their claim to authority by attributing the responsibility for economic progress to the manufacturers and the responsibility for all distress and poverty to the people at large. For while Ure defended the manufacturers by blaming the landed gentry and the workers in the domestic industries, Senior sought to reform English Poor Law administration by blaming the rural paupers. And as controversy and passion blurred all distinctions, these two disparate, though related, approaches seemed to blend into one justification of industrial society which exonerated the entrepreneurs and placed the burden of guilt upon those who suffered most.

g. The Formulation of an Entrepreneurial Ideology

The weakness of Ure's philosophy of manufactures arose from his failure to make an untrammeled assertion of moral leadership. It was a more or less evasive answer to the accusations of critics; and it was so much concerned with denouncing the infamy of combinations among workers that it widened the existing gulf between manufacturers and their employees despite its endorsement of religious education for the workers. Also, the blending of Ure's defense with the arguments of the Poor Law reformers helped to link the manufacturer's claim to authority with a renewed emphasis upon the improvidence of the common people. As a result the defense of the industrial order was still bound up by the 1830's with the belief that poverty was inevitable and that its burdens could be made lighter or heavier solely by the exercise of foresight. After a process of industrialization extending over two generations, the spokesmen for the new order still did not promise a living for all.

But ideologies do not develop in isolation. By the time of the New Poor Law, political agitation among the English working class had challenged the civic alienation which that enactment symbolized. In 1826 the laws had been abolished which had prevented workers from combining in order to bargain with their employers. Large masses of people had engaged in political agitation for the Reform Act of 1832, and subsequently for the demands incorporated in the Charter. In other words, the urban workers of England had acquired qualities of independence by the 1830's, which would have to be channelized by the entrepreneurial class, if the latter was to substantiate its claim to leadership and authority. The spirit which animated the working classes at that time was vividly described by John Stuart Mill in 1848.

> Of the working men, at least in the more advanced countries of Europe, it may be pronounced certain that the patriarchal or paternal system of government is one to which they will not again be subject. That question was decided, when they were taught to read, and allowed access to newspapers and political tracts; when dissenting preachers were suffered to go among them, and appeal to their faculties and feelings in opposition to the creeds professed and countenanced by their superiors; when they were brought together in numbers, to work socially under the same roof; when railways enabled them to shift from place to place, and change their patrons and employers as easily as their coats; when they were encouraged to seek a share in the government, by means of the electoral franchise. The working classes have taken their interests into their own hands, and are perpetually showing that they think the interests of their employers not identical with their own, but opposite to them. Some among the higher classes flatter themselves that these tendencies may be counteracted by moral and religious education; but they have let the time go by for giving an education which can serve their purpose. The principles of the Reformation have reached as low down in society as reading and writing, and the poor will not much longer accept morals and religion of other people's prescribing.[178]

The ideological appeals of the Anti-Corn Law League must be appraised as a response to this transformation of the working classes. The major purpose of this organization was the repeal of the Corn Laws and the establishment of the principle of free trade. But in pursuing these ends the leaders of the League became the spokesmen for the people as a whole at the same time that they were the avowed representatives of industry. This was a new departure in the development

[178] Mill, *Principles of Political Economy*, pp. 322–23.

of entrepreneurial ideology. Before, the poor had been condemned to economic destitution, a celibate life, or "voluntary" confinement in a well-managed workhouse, while the spokesmen of manufacturers had denied the miseries of industrialization or had blamed them on others. Now, industrialists came to the fore to assert that they were the champions of the people. The claim to authority on the basis of a denunciation of the poor, or on the basis of a mere denial of well-publicized abuses, had changed into an assumption of moral leadership. By claiming that they represented the people at large, spokesmen of the industrialists could make a moral claim to leadership. Their efforts to advance the wealth of the nation were now declared to benefit employers and workers alike.[179] And this new emphasis on the interest of all, together with a de-emphasis on the invidious denunciations of the people, became the credo of an entrepreneurial class, which had become animated by a positive sense of mission. By its appeals the Anti-Corn Law League sought to obtain leadership over the increasingly restive working class, on the one hand, and to wrest leadership from the politically entrenched, landholding aristocracy, on the other.

This agitation of the League involved an intensive political activation of men who had been preoccupied exclusively with the pursuit of their economic interests. The life-careers of Richard Cobden and John Bright, the two foremost champions of the League, illustrate this growing political involvement of merchants and manufacturers. Both men were successful in business before they entered political life. Cobden was born in 1804, the son of an old family of yeomen, who entered his uncle's warehouse as a clerk at the age of fifteen, and became an independent businessman at the age of twenty-four. Bright came from a family of devout Quakers, his father the owner of a cotton factory which passed into the hands of the sons. Bright was born in 1811, worked in his father's factory from adolescence on, and directed its affairs until his political activities forced him to leave them in the hands of his brother. Both men belonged to a new generation of manufacturers, conscious both of their contribution to the national wealth and of their political impotence despite the Reform Bill of 1832. They inherited the economic achievements of the early generation of industrialists without needing to endorse the brutality of early industrialization and, indeed, without being absorbed, as their predecessors

---

[179] The accent from Burke to Dr. Ure had been different. According to the harmony-of-interest theory, no amount of profits and exploitation could be detrimental to the poor, since any curtailment of either would reduce the ability of employers to provide jobs.

had been, in the pursuit of business affairs to a degree that excluded all extraneous consideration.

Much of this is reflected in Bright's early and very active participation in the politics, and especially the church politics, of his community. It is also reflected in Cobden's abounding energy and wide interests, both as a businessman and as a political philosopher. Having traveled widely as a young man, Cobden came back to England with a view of her future which stood in marked contrast both to the pessimism of the Malthusian doctrine and to the apologetics of Dr. Ure. A great population had gathered in the new centers of industry, and it had become necessary to adapt the government to the changing and improving condition of the English people. Cobden recognized that the industrial transformation of England and the Western world had become inevitable. But while industry was here to stay, Cobden did not conclude that anything done by the manufacturers to promote industry was sufficient justification in itself. Instead, he recognized that evils existed, and he did not take it for granted that the entrepreneurial class was unable to cope with them.[180] To a new generation of industrialists it was no longer as self-evident as it had been to Malthus and his followers, that the evils of industrialization were as inevitable as a law of nature and that their remedy was solely a matter of moral conduct on the part of the poor.

Cobden and Bright were outstanding individuals whose political involvement and breadth of vision certainly differed from that of the average manufacturer. But the ideas which animated their exceptional activities elicited a response which indicates that their vision came to be shared by large numbers of people.

In an age when political meetings were rare events, and serious politicians seldom spoke outside "the House" except officially from the hustings— Cobden and his lieutenants addressed immense meetings night after night over a series of years. Once a month or oftener, from March 1843 until the Corn Law fell in 1846, a London opera house was packed from floor to ceiling, from the back of the pit to the back of the stage, with an audience that was never once bored and never once lukewarm; and in the twelve weeks between December 1842 and the end of the following

---

[180] ". . . the factory system, which sprang from the discoveries of machinery, has been adopted by all the civilized nations of the world, and it is in vain for us to think of discountenancing its application to the necessities of this country; it only remains for us to mitigate, as far as possible, the evils that are perhaps not inseparably connected with this novel social element." Quoted from Cobden's first pamphlet (1835–36) in John Morley, *The Life of Richard Cobden*, I, pp. 96–97.

February, one hundred and thirty-six smaller meetings were held in London alone; in the provinces, each big city had a mass meeting nearly every month, and each market town at least once a year. In an age when political literature was limited in quantity, and perfunctory and personal in such arguments as it advanced, the League, in 1843 alone, distributed nine million carefully argued tracts, by means of a staff of eight hundred persons. In an age when finance and government were regarded as mysteries reserved for a few political families and their protégés, the League lecturers taught political economy, with its application to the year's budget, to vast audiences of merchants, clerks, and working men. All this and much more besides in the way of monster petitions, demonstrations, industrial exhibitions, was paid for by a series of League "funds," rising from £5,000 and £10,000 in earlier years to £50,000 in 1842–43, £100,000 in 1843–44, and £250,000 in 1845–46.[181]

What was the nature of the appeal which commanded such ample resources and organizing talent, and which apparently appealed to large numbers of entrepreneurs and of workers?

The agitation of the League was getting under way in 1838. At that time Cobden admitted that most of them "entered upon this struggle with the belief that we had some distinct class interest in the question, and that we should carry it . . . against the will and consent of other portions of the community." [182] But even then the question had been raised how the interests of the manufacturers were related to those of other groups in the community. And in 1841 Cobden reminded the House of Commons that it was the condition of the nation, not the interests of a class, or the abstract doctrines of the economist, that cried for relief.[183] The same enlargement of perspective was true of others in the League. The testimony of Archibald Prentice, a member of its executive council, is of interest in this connection:

> I will not assert the unmixed benevolence of all who gave their money and their labor to the movement. If I did, I should be claiming what they did not claim for themselves. They did not sound a trumpet and proclaim for themselves, as others did, the "poor man's friends." What they said was that their interests and the interests of the community were identical. What they asked of the working man was to help them for his own benefit—for his own rescue from starvation.[184]

181 Trevelyan, *Life of John Bright*, pp. 90–91.
182 Morley, *op. cit.*, Vol. I, p. 141.
183 *Ibid.*, p. 178.
184 Archibald Prentice, *History of the Anti-Corn-Law League* (London: W. F. G. Cash, 1853), I, pp. 94–95. Cf. also the report of a speech by a manufacturer of calico on pp. 352–53, and Bright's maiden speech in the House in 1843: "The rich here are attended to; the poor are too frequently neglected." And in ad-

Thus, the merchants and industrialists, who were active in the League, could come to terms with the unaccustomed role of national leadership. Until the passage of the New Poor Law it had been a common opinion that poverty was a self-inflicted evil of the lower classes. Now, the fight against the Corn Laws made it possible to take the side of the lower classes and attribute their poverty to the evils of trade restriction and the political predominance of the "clodpole aristocracy," as Cobden put it.

Bright, Cobden, and the other speakers of the League did not leave any doubt that their struggle for free trade was a class struggle of the rising middle classes against the entrenched power of the landholding aristocracy. In a speech at Covent Garden Opera House in 1845 John Bright had stated this view in unmistakable terms: "I believe this to be a movement of the commercial and industrial classes against the Lords and great proprietors of the soil. . . ." In making his case Bright referred to the multitudes who "have died of hunger in the United Kingdom since we first asked the Government to repeal the Corn Laws," and he charged the great and powerful with heavy guilt for having sacrificed those who suffer mutely and die in silence. He did not hesitate to liken the agitation against the Corn Laws with the struggle of the people against Charles I two centuries earlier, calling upon public opinion to resist the "giant wrong" perpetrated by the aristocracy as their forefathers had resisted a "despotic and treacherous monarch." [185] Bright's view of the Anti-Corn Law agitation was naturally reciprocated by the landholding aristocracy. In 1842 Cobden wrote to his brother that "nothing seems to be considered so decided a stigma as to brand a man as a mill-owner." [186] And Trevelyan reports that in 1866, twenty-three years after Bright's entry into the House of Commons, "London Society was outraged and bewildered beyond expression because Lord Russell was known to have invited him to dinner." [187]

dressing himself to Sir Robert Peel he stated: "I should be glad to see the Right Hon. Baronet not the Minister of the Queen merely, but the Minister of the people also. . . . I should be glad to see him bearing in mind the source from which he has sprung, the source of his power and wealth, as it is the source of much of the power and wealth and greatness of this Empire." Trevelyan, *Life of John Bright*, pp. 117–18. Peel came from a family of cotton manufacturers and Bright was obviously branding him as a "traitor" to his class.

[185] Trevelyan, *op. cit.*, pp. 141–42.

[186] Morley, *op. cit.*, Vol. I, p. 227. Cf. also Christie, *Transition from Aristocracy*, pp. 152–54 and *passim*, for examples of social discrimination against Cobden and Bright.

[187] Trevelyan, *op. cit.*, p. 116.

Arguments of the middle class against the aristocracy had been common enough for almost a century and a half. The agitation of the Anti-Corn Law League, however, linked this anti-aristocratic tradition with a direct appeal to the working class to support this cause in their own interest. Andrew Ure's *Philosophy of Manufactures* had extolled the subordination of the working class, but only six years after its publication Cobden pointed out in the House of Commons that the family of a nobleman paid a "bread tax" of about one half-penny on every £100 of its income, while the "bread tax" paid by the family of a worker amounted to 20 per cent of its combined earnings.[188] And whereas the New Poor Law of 1834 had seemed to attribute pauperism to the poor, Cobden observed in 1841 that starvation was stalking through the manufacturing districts and he attributed murder to the Legislature as long as it taxed the people's bread.[189] When Cobden was approached in the following year for a contribution to a fund for church buildings, he refused on the ground that all his resources went into the fight against the Corn Laws. Thus, while other spokesmen upheld religious instruction as the buttress of sobriety and subordination, this foremost spokesman of the manufacturing interests declared that the feeding of the hungry was the only means of raising the morality of the working classes. For Cobden it was in strict harmony with Christian principles to fight against the Corn Laws rather than build churches.[190]

Such statements and actions embodied a new view of the relations between the classes, involving as it did an appeal by the employers for the political support of the workers. In one of his first campaign speeches John Bright stated this case with his customary candor (1843):

> I am a workingman as much as you. My father was as poor as any man in this crowd. He was of your own body, entirely. He boasts not—nor do I—of birth, nor of great family distinctions. What he has made, he has made by his own industry and successful commerce. What I have comes from him, and from my own exertions. . . . I come before you as a friend of my own class and order; as one of the people; as one who would, on all occasions, be the firm defender of your rights, and the asserter of all those privileges to which you are justly entitled. . . . It is on these grounds that I solicit your suffrage. . . .

And after pointing out that workers had a vital interest in the abolition of the Corn Laws, for themselves and their children, Bright pointed to

---

[188] Morley, *op. cit.*, Vol. I, p. 178.   See also Trevelyan, *op. cit.*, pp. 94–95.
[189] Morley, *op. cit.*, Vol. I, pp. 186–87.   [190] *Ibid.*, p. 233.

the consequences which were sure to follow if these laws were not abolished by the time their children had become adults.

> Trade will then have become still more crippled; the supply of food still more diminished; the taxation of the country still further increased. The great lords, and other people, will have become still more powerful, unless the freemen and electors of Durham and of other places stand to their guns, and resolve that, whatever may come of Queen, or Lords, or Commons, or Church, or anybody—great and powerful and noble though they be—the working classes will stand by the working classes; and will no longer lay themselves down in the dust to be trampled upon by the iron heel of monopoly, and have their very lives squeezed out of them by evils such as I have described.[191]

Owing to his leadership of the Anti-Corn Law League, Bright was one of the most vocal spokesmen of the entrepreneurial class. By appealing to the workers of England for support in his agitation against the Corn Laws, Bright treated them as self-dependent men. This view had been expressed half a century earlier by the Rev. Joseph Townsend. But in the interval between 1786 and 1834 it had been caught up in the agitation over the Poor Laws, and under the influence of the Malthusian doctrine it had been used as an instrument to beat the poor, not to lead them.[192] Now, the propagandists for the Anti-Corn Law League went all over the country proclaiming that the workers of England had a citizen's right to protest against a law which served the narrow self-interest of the aristocracy while it held them down in a condition of semistarvation. Yet, by the 1840's the workers to whom Bright, Cobden, and others appealed had developed a political awareness of their own. The agitation against the Corn Laws had to compete with the appeals for civil rights embodied in the Chartist movement.[193] But while it was necessary to differentiate the agitation of the League from the Chartist movement, this could not be pushed too far.[194] The

[191] Trevelyan, *op. cit.,* pp. 113–14.

[192] See the comprehensive summary in Kenneth Smith, *The Malthusian Controversy,* pp. 290–305.

[193] In an open-air meeting at Rochdale in 1839 the audience to which Bright had proposed a resolution condemning the Corn Laws voted to amend it by calling the Corn Law injurious but stressing that the people must have their political rights first. See Trevelyan, *op. cit.,* pp. 30–31. This did not deter Bright from continuing his appeal to the working classes, but Cobden was obviously less inclined to do so. Cf. Morley, *op. cit.,* Vol. I, pp. 248–49.

[194] Trevelyan, *op. cit.,* p. 184, cites a letter from Bright to his wife, written in 1848: "The Government seems to make a great uproar about the Chartists. . . . The aristocracy want to frighten the middle classes from the pursuit of Reform,

ends of the Anti-Corn Law League could only be attained by arousing public opinion and rallying voters and nonvoters alike behind this movement of the middle class against the politically powerful aristocracy.

Nevertheless, the propagandists of the League had to safeguard their middle-class agitation against becoming a vehicle for a more radical, political movement. Bright, Cobden, and others vigorously opposed factory legislation. While he acknowledged the need for a limitation of the working day, especially for children, Cobden opposed the idea of legislative reforms. In his opinion such restrictions should result from the "resolute demands and independent action of the workers themselves." Yet he also opposed with all his might the "combinations" of workers, which were "founded upon principles of brutal tyranny and monopoly." [195] Thus, spokesmen for the League would oppose the political and trade-union agitation of the workers at the same time that they solicited the support of the workers for the struggle against the aristocracy. For example, Archibald Prentice reminded the workers in 1838 of the "ceaseless labor and the enormous expense" which had been incurred in the struggle against Combination Laws, the truck system, the New Poor Law and for the Ten-Hour Law, cooperative societies, and so on. All this had taken place while the Corn Laws were "grinding down the reward of their labor . . . and raising the price of their food." Prentice declared that the workers would be in a much better position if they had resolutely joined in "one combined and energetic effort against the land-owners' monopoly," a suggestion which Chartist leaders countered with the accusation that the League sought to divert the workers from their political objectives. Prentice answered this with the assertion that the two campaigns were not in conflict. He would not advise anyone to abandon agitation for the Charter; but he pleaded with the workers to lend a helping hand in the "agitation for the repeal of practical grievances." [196] Clearly, there was considerable ambivalence in this appeal to the workers. The members of the League differed among themselves concerning the extent to which they would acquiesce in the demands of the Chartist movement.

and to do this they and their emissaries stimulate a portion of the least wise of the people to menace and violence, to damage the cause of Reform, and for a time they succeed."

[195] Morley, *op. cit.*, Vol. I, pp. 298–99, 464–68. Cf. also Bright's opposition to the ten-hour law in Trevelyan, *op. cit.*, pp. 155, 157–58.

[196] Prentice, *op. cit.*, pp. 57–58, 329.

But as long as the landholding aristocracy was the major opponent, the spokesmen of the League could not divorce their own agitation from this uneasy involvement with the working class.

The Corn Laws were repealed in 1846, the repeal to take effect three years later. G. M. Trevelyan has pointed out that after the repeal, the members of the upper middle class became unfitted for further efforts in Radicalism. Once their rebellion against the landlords had succeeded, they were gradually giving way to "churchmanship in religion and Conservatism in politics." [197] Much the same conclusion was reached by Cobden in a letter to Bright, written in 1851, in which he advised his friend that he should not deceive himself, "the same men will not fight the battle of Parliamentary Reform" who fought the battle of the Anti-Corn Law League.[198] Cobden had differed from Bright with regard to the franchise for some time past, maintaining that it should be extended only on the basis of a property qualification. On many occasions Cobden stated that he had never referred to the "superior judgment of the working classes," but that he desired to attack the "citadel of privilege . . . with the help of the propertied classes in the middle ranks of society, and by raising up a portion of the working-class to become members of a propertied order." [199] Bright's estimate of the people was more generous, and he proceeded to fight for their enfranchisement after the repeal of the Corn Laws.[200] The struggle for the franchise was eventually successful. But the merchants and entrepreneurs who had been active in the Anti-Corn Law League did not believe in universal suffrage, and Bright's leadership of this movement did not reflect their opinions. To ascertain these, we must turn away from colorful, liberal champions like John Bright and consider, instead, the drab successors of Andrew Ure.

[197] Trevelyan, *op. cit.*, p. 177.
[198] Morley, *op. cit.*, Vol. II, pp. 94–95.
[199] Morley, *op. cit.*, Vol. I, pp. 401–2, and Vol. II, p. 53.
[200] Bright did not believe that the victory of free trade had established the political supremacy of the middle class, hence the support of the people was still needed. Also he stated that the trade-union movement would become revolutionary if the wage earners were "condemned to remain a separate and suspected order in our social system," a view which coincided with that of Disraeli; though the two men differed basically in their political orientation. Bright also predicted that industrial war would go from bad to worse so long as "the class receiving wages is shut out from the questions and the interests which occupy the minds and engage the energies of the employing class." See Trevelyan, *op. cit.*, pp. 279–80.

The work of Samuel Smiles is relevant here, because the ideas which animated it became immensely popular.[201] Smiles formulated the new creed of the entrepreneurial class: that the successful man of business had worked hard and had done well, and that the means by which he had become successful were within reach of everyone. A series of volumes was devoted to biographical accounts of successful merchants, engineers, manufacturers, inventors, and others, and the chronological details of each man's career were interspersed by moral homilies, in which the virtues of the hero were described and upheld as models to be emulated by all. Another series of books, eloquently entitled *Self-Help, Character, Thrift, Duty,* contained didactic essays on the old-fashioned virtues and the corresponding vices, each of which was abundantly illustrated by biographical and other documentation.

The circumstances under which Smiles developed an interest in writing and teaching along these lines are recounted in the introduction to his book on *Self-Help, with Illustrations of Character, Conduct, and Perseverance.* He tells us there that in about 1844 several young men "of the humblest rank" met together in a town in Northern England for the purpose of improving themselves by exchanging knowledge with each other. With the winter approaching, it was decided to rent a hall for their meetings, in which "those who knew a little taught those who knew less—improving themselves while they improved the others." Among the subjects which were taken up were reading, writing, arithmetic, geography, and "even" mathematics, chemistry, and some of the modern languages.[202] Eventually, these young men decided to invite lecturers, among them Samuel Smiles.

> He [Smiles] could not fail to be touched by the admirable self-helping spirit which they had displayed; and, though entertaining but slight faith in popular lecturing, he felt that a few words of encouragement, honestly and sincerely uttered, might not be without some good effect. And in this spirit he addressed them on more than one occasion, citing examples of what other men had done, as illustrations of what each might, in a greater or less degree, do for himself; and pointing out that their happiness and well-being as individuals in after-life must necessarily depend mainly upon

[201] See Asa Briggs, "Samuel Smiles and the Gospel of Work," *The Cambridge Journal,* Vol. II (June, 1949), p. 553 for figures on the sales of Smiles's books. See also Asa Briggs, *Victorian People* (London: Odhams Press, Ltd., 1954) for a fuller discussion of Smiles. This work also contains a perceptive appraisal of John Bright and other representative figures in mid-nineteenth-century England.

[202] See Samuel Smiles, *Self-Help* (Chicago: Belford, Clarke and Company, 1881), pp. ix–x. The book was published originally in 1859.

themselves—upon their diligent self-culture, self-discipline, and self-control—and, above all, on that honest and upright performance of individual duty which is the glory of manly character.[203]

As Smiles observed in the same preface, this counsel was as old as the Proverbs of Solomon. But in the past, biblical passages extolling the honor and dignity of hard work had been cited in order to teach the poor diligence and resignation. Only the agitation of the Anti-Corn Law League had broken with this traditional subordination when it sought to rally politically restive workers in support of the middle-class challenge of the Corn Laws and of aristocratic supremacy. The repeal of the Corn Laws led to retrenchment in politics, but it did not lead back to the belief in the subordination of the working class. The appeal for the people's support against the Corn Laws had nullified that belief, and Smiles's message of virtue and success for the humble became the new positive appeal, which expressed the optimism of the entrepreneurial class and which appeared as a viable alternative to the agitation for the franchise.

Three generations earlier, Townsend and Burke had maintained that the poor should be self-dependent, that poverty was self-inflicted, that the higher classes should do nothing to mitigate their hunger, for this would merely encourage idle men and prevent them from exerting themselves. In writing this they partly reflected the mercantilist belief in the utility of poverty as a stimulus to hard work. They also reflected the emerging idea that the higher classes should be prevented from interfering with the laws of the market, which were the laws of nature. From the 1850's on, this doctrine was finally abandoned. Instead, Smiles stated his belief, and reiterated it constantly, that the poor need not remain dependent and impoverished. The higher classes had demonstrated by their own success that it was possible for each to "secure his independence." To be sure, Smiles continued the old theme that the workers were idle and dissolute.[204] But he did this so that a knowledge of idleness, thoughtlessness, vanity, vice, and intemperance would "induce men to employ their means for worthy purposes." At considerable length and in wearying detail he recounted the many ways in which even the most humble could aspire to higher things, by hard work, attention to detail, and systematic savings. In a characteristic chapter entitled "Little Things" Smiles celebrated the small things, the unimportant events of daily life, as the foundation stones of home, hap-

---

[203] *Ibid.*, pp. x–xi.
[204] Cf., for example, *Thrift* (London: John Murray, 1875), pp. 30–64.

piness and fortune, including seven different calculations of the monetary benefits accruing from saving a penny a day.[205]

Smiles preached a gospel not merely of work, but of hope. He demonstrated the humble origin of industrialists. He explained their success in terms of qualities, which did not depend on individual talent as much as on the systematic cultivation of will power.[206] He founded the industrialists' claim to authority and leadership on a creed which attributed their success to qualities readily accessible to the poor. In fact, he enjoined upon the higher classes the task of doing all that lay in their power to instill these qualities in their workers. Smiles deplored the prevailing want of sympathy between masters and men. Of course, he still propounded the old view that charity often tended to increase the vices of the poor by the very act of relieving their poverty. Yet, he did not leave charity or generosity to the caprice of the rich man, as Burke had done. Instead, Smiles attacked the character of the rich man of business, and in his discussion of charity he analyzed his vices.

> The love of gold threatens to drive everything before it. The pursuit of money has become the settled custom of the country. Many are so absorbed by it that every other kind of well-being is either lost sight of or altogether undervalued. And then the lovers of money think to recover their moral tone by bestowing charity. Mountains of gold weigh heavily upon the heart and soul. The man who can withstand the weight of riches, and still be diligent, industrious, and strong in mind and heart, must be made of strong stuff. For, people who are rich are almost invariably disposed to be idle, luxurious, and self-indulgent.[207]

Masters and men should draw nearer to one another. Above all there should be less pomp and triumph on the part of the rich and more concern for the welfare of the public. These rich men, Smiles maintained, go on toiling; they scrape together money by fair means and foul; they have already more than they can enjoy; they lack education; they have no taste for books; sometimes they cannot write their own names. The vast majority of them are of "no moral or social account." [208] Smiles did not take for granted what men like Townsend,

<hr />

[205] *Ibid.*, pp. 159–78.

[206] In his volume on *Thrift* Smiles speaks at one point of the fact that the successful men are not great because they are rich, but rich because they are great (pp. 189–90). But the greatness he extols is a greatness of perseverance, not of innate superiority.

[207] *Ibid.*, p. 290.

[208] *Ibid.*, pp. 291–94. The author appends to this diatribe a disquisition on the emotional poverty of the rich and the opportunities for happiness among the poor which is a curious amalgamation of self-serving argument and accurate

Burke, Malthus, and Ure had accepted as a matter of course. To him, economic success was not by itself evidence of virtue. In fact, he observed that often such virtue was present only in the first generation of an entrepreneurial family, while the children dissipated the fortune which had been amassed, and the third generation had to begin all over again. And he conjures up the dreadful image of the rich man grown old, who dies a lonely death amidst his useless wealth.[209]

It is against this background of moral strictures that we must assess Smiles's conception of the relation between the "higher" and "lower" classes. By taking a forthright stand against the immorality of the rich as well as the poor, he could advance the claim to authority and leadership on the part of the entrepreneurial class. He formulated an ideology which avoided the political risks involved in the extension of the suffrage but did not abandon the claim to moral leadership which had animated the agitation of the Anti-Corn Law League.

Smiles's conception of the relation between employers and workers is a case in point. To the former he commended an active promotion of thrift, prudence, and sobriety among their employees.

> If masters fully understood the immense amount of influence which they possess, they would extend their sympathy and confidence to their workmen, which would cost them so very little, and profit them so very much. We know of no instance where an employer has displayed a concern for the social well-being and improvement of his workmen, in which he has not been repaid by their increased respect and zeal on his behalf.

He then mentions how employers can accommodate their workers by making wage payments convenient to them, and he continues:

> But masters can do more than this. They can actively aid their workmen in the formation of prudent habits, by establishing savings banks for men and women, and penny banks for boys and girls; by encouraging the formation of provident clubs and building societies, of provision and clothing clubs, and in many other ways. They might also distribute among them, without any officious interference, good counsel as to the manner in which they might make the best use of their wages. Many large employers have already accomplished much practical good, by encouraging the formation of provident institutions, in which they have never failed to secure the respect, and generally the cooperation, of their workmen.[210]

observation. Themes which have recurred time and again are here touched upon, such as the anxiety, indigestion, and insomnia of the rich, and the importance of work and self-denial to the pursuit of happiness. See pp. 297–301.

[209] *Ibid.,* pp. 292–95.

[210] *Ibid.,* pp. 179–80. In another place Smiles discusses the Christian forms of charity which he endorses, in the following terms: "The societies for improving

This passage clearly reflects a major shift in entrepreneurial ideology since Malthus' *Essay on Population*. Economic success is no longer synonymous with virtue triumphant. The rich have a great opportunity for influencing the working class, and they have therefore the social responsibility for doing all they can. Malthus, it will be remembered, had denied both the power and the responsibility of the higher classes. And he had consequently confined their activities to the task of educating the poor in the knowledge of the principle of population. Smiles did not rule out the education of the poor by the rich, but his proposal had more tact. Education of the poor was only one of many charitable activities, and Smiles demanded that the rich must be educated as well. All this is reflected in his characterization of the working class itself.

> The working man is now more of a citizen than he ever was before. He is a recognized power, and has been admitted within the pale of the constitution. For him mechanics' institutes, newspapers, benefit societies, and all the modern agencies of civilization, exist in abundance. He is admitted to the domain of intellect; and, from time to time, great thinkers, artists, engineers, philosophers, and poets rise up from his order, to proclaim that intellect is of no rank, and nobility of no exclusive order. The influences of civilization are rousing society to its depths; and daily evidences are furnished of the rise of the industrious classes to a position of social power. Discontent may, and does, exhibit itself; but discontent is only the necessary condition of improvement; for a man will not be stimulated to rise up into a higher condition unless he be first made dissatisfied with the lower condition out of which he has to rise. To be satisfied is to repose; while to be rationally dissatisfied is to contrive, to work, and to act, with an eye to future advancement.[211]

That Smiles could think of dissatisfaction among workers in positive terms at all is perhaps the clearest indication of how much entrepreneurial ideologies had changed since the beginning of the nineteenth century.

We do not know how accurately Smiles reflected the opinions of those for whom he wished to speak, though the popularity of his writ-

the dwellings of the industrious classes, for building baths and washhouses, for establishing workmen's, seamen's, and servants' homes, for cultivating habits of providence and frugality amongst the working classes, and for extending the advantages of knowledge amongst the people, are important agencies of this kind. These, instead of sapping the foundations of self-reliance, are really and truly helping the people to help themselves, and are deserving of every approbation and encouragement. They tend to elevate the condition of the mass; they are embodiments of philanthropy in its highest form; and are calculated to bear good fruit through all time." *Ibid.*, p. 305.

[211] *Ibid.*, p. 55.

ings suggests that he was quite close to the mark. Every old theme of the last three generations could be associated with the doctrine of self-help by the poor and moral leadership by the rich. The work of W. R. Greg is a striking case in point. Greg was a somewhat unsuccessful manufacturer, who published several books of the same general character as Smiles. One of these books, entitled *Mistaken Aims and Attainable Ideals,* is of special interest here. It contains all the themes of entrepreneurial ideology during the nineteenth century, and it illustrates thereby how Smiles's appeal could be combined with more traditional ideas. According to Greg, workers are misguided and intemperate;[212] charity would only increase those evils;[213] the poor have no right to charity;[214] the belief of workers that they have a right to employment is absurd;[215] high taxes, rapid population increase, and trade restrictions are the causes of destitution;[216] workers deliberately impoverish themselves by going on strike and by bringing paupers into the world;[217] the misery of the poor which comes from their improvidence, idleness, dissipation, and early marriages should be left to do its necessary work;[218] and so on. Yet, Greg imitated Smiles as readily as he did all of Smiles's predecessors. The wealth of the manufacturer is the result of patient savings from moderate profits; in fact, people are unaware of the extent to which saving is within the power of the factory operative.[219] No amount of legislative assistance and no degree of benevolence on the part of the employers are really capable of aiding the worker. It is up to the worker himself to exercise foresight and frugality which are the "appointed purchase-money" of his comfort and independence.[220] Greg professed to be as much concerned with popular suffering as any leader of the working class, to have as bright and hopeful a vision of the workers' future as any socialist.[221] Workers did "well to be angry" with the conditions of struggle and wretchedness in which "intelligent beings should not consent to live,"[222] but, according to Greg, the remedy was for "our artisans and skilled laborers in every line to become capitalists,"[223] and not to be diverted from the true cause of their suffering by organizing trade-unions or by other schemes which are either irrelevant or pernicious.[224]

[212] W. R. Greg, *Mistaken Aims and Attainable Ideals* (London: Trubner and Company, 1876), pp. iv, v.

[213] *Ibid.,* pp. 86–87.

[214] *Ibid.,* pp. 93–94.

[215] *Ibid.,* pp. 96–97.

[216] *Ibid.,* p. 99.

[217] *Ibid.,* pp. 101–2.

[218] *Ibid.,* p. 103.

[219] *Ibid.,* pp. 132–33.

[220] *Ibid.,* pp. 139–40.

[221] *Ibid.,* pp. 227–28.

[222] *Ibid.,* pp. 256–57.

[223] *Ibid.,* p. 268.

[224] *Ibid.,* pp. 257–58, 270–71, 283–89.

Greg's work illustrates the manner in which Smiles's optimistic tenet of self-help as the cure of poverty available to all could be embedded in a web of the old sayings which were part of an earlier and gloomier doctrine. The viability of ideologies seems to depend upon such fusion with old ideas. The emergence of a class-conscious, entrepreneurial ideology, from Townsend's pamphlet in 1786 to the Poor Law reform of 1834, had had to overcome the traditional ideas of the master-servant relationship. In so doing this ideology advanced a gloomy and divisive doctrine which seemed to relegate the people to a life of self-inflicted deprivation. But while Smiles, Greg, and others retained the principal tenets of this ideology, they managed to turn its pessimistic message into an optimistic creed, valid for rich and poor alike.

It might appear as if this new entrepreneurial ideology could be of little avail by the time it became popular during the 1860's and 1870's. For the workers of England had already won major victories. Trade-unions flourished, suffrage was gradually extended. The individual independence of the worker which Malthus and Senior wanted to enforce, which Ure decried, and which Cobden and Bright wanted to lead, had by then changed from a demand of the employers and their spokesmen into a political force which the doctrine of self-help could not undo. For the workers had used their independence to build organizations of their own, which could oppose the employer with commensurate power as the individual could not. The workers had helped themselves in their own way, and the doctrine of self-help appeared to them as a means of undermining the solidarity within their ranks.

Yet this ideology had major significance in the development of English industrial society. For the optimistic appeal of self-help meant that a new formula had been found on the basis of which employers and workers were conceived as members of the same community. Evangelism had continued the traditional belief in the responsibility of the rich and the dependence of the poor, a belief which affirmed the deep division between classes but which also asserted their interdependence. Now, the doctrine of self-help proclaimed that employers and workers were alike in self-dependence, and that regardless of class each man's success was a proof of himself and a contribution to the common wealth. There was evangelical zeal in this appeal of employers to the drive and ambition of the people. By bidding the people to seek success as they did themselves, the employers manifested their abiding belief in the existence of a moral community regardless of class, for they proposed to measure the worth of each man by the same standard. This inadvertent but enduring implication of the entrepreneurial ideology has been obscured by the conventional interpretations which see in "self-help" little more than an ill-disguised assertion of selfishness. The significance of this implication will become more apparent by considering the contrasting case of Russian industrialization.

CHAPTER 3

Entrepreneurial Ideologies in Eighteenth- and Nineteenth-Century Russia

It is a shallow view of Russian history which sees Bolshevism as an alien excrescence grafted on the Russian body politic by a handful of power-lusting conspirators without roots in the past. The triumph of the Bolshevik Revolution was in no sense inevitable, but Bolshevism as a movement was an indigenous, authoritarian response to the environment of Tsarist absolutism which nurtured it. Autocracy generates its own authoritarian antibodies and endows them with its own peculiar contours.
—Merle Fainsod, *How Russia is Ruled.*

a. Preconditions of Industrialization in the West and in Russia

I have used the term "industrialization" to refer to the increasing number of single enterprises in which relatively large numbers of employees are concentrated and in which their productive activities depend upon the directing and coordinating activities of entrepreneurs and managers. This meaning of the term is reasonably unequivocal as long as it is restricted to economic developments since the eighteenth century. While industrialization took place both in western Europe and in

Russia from the eighteenth century on, it did so as a result of divergent historical legacies.

Alexis de Tocqueville commented upon this divergence over a century ago when he remarked that Russia and the United States were two great nations which had grown up unnoticed, but seemed marked out "to sway the destinies of half the globe." The adversary of the Russian, he wrote, is man, not nature; civilization, not the wilderness. And the tool the Russian uses in this struggle against man and civilization is the sword, not the plowshare; the authority of one, not the interest and unguided exertions of the many. De Tocqueville's observation is an apt motto to guide a study of ideologies and industrialization in Russia, for the freedom of the West and the servitude of Russia have a special meaning in the economic history of both.

Among the preconditions of industrialization in the West, one of the most important has been the relative independence of economic activities from governmental regulations. This independence was enhanced when commercial as well as legal transactions became increasingly secure against arbitrary interference by the king or by members of the landed aristocracy. Such increasing security involved a century-long process, in which the earlier identification of the national government with the interests of the royal household and the identification of judicial and administrative functions with the prerogatives of the aristocracy were very gradually abandoned. This process of disentanglement began in the early Middle Ages with the separation of one after another government office from the corresponding office in the royal household. And it eventuated in the establishment of a professional civil service and a professional judiciary during the eighteenth and nineteenth centuries with the result that the performance of administrative and judicial functions was separated from their earlier identification with the privileged position of aristocratic families. The end result of this process was the development of the "state as a service-rendering organization for the protection of rights and enforcement of duties." [1]

This over-all change in the functioning of government was initiated and driven forward by the existence within western European societies of a landed aristocracy and of relatively autonomous municipalities, whose prerogatives and local power enabled them in the long run to limit the centralization of royal power and authority. That limitation of central power stemmed from the fact that in western Europe the

---

[1] Ernest Barker, *The Development of Public Services in Western Europe* (London: Oxford University Press, 1944), p. 6 and *passim,* where the development since 1660 is traced on a comparative basis.

kings obtained military and administrative services from their subjects by grants of land, of charters, and of other privileges which involved a limited delegation of administrative and judicial authority. The landed aristocracy or the municipalities would frequently use such authority to increase their local autonomy as well as to render the service for which the reward and the authority had been granted. But such centripetal tendencies were partly checked time and again by the king (especially in France and England) who would make new grants of land and authority to families, who were, or could be made, more dependent upon the central power than the older aristocratic families. Thus, demands for autonomy and efforts to centralize authority were made simultaneously and with varying results in the several countries of western Europe. Frequently, the power of the king increased, but many advances toward a more centralized power were obtained at the price of new delegations of authority.[2] And this balancing of conflicting tendencies prepared the ground for the growing independence of economic activities from governmental regulations and for the compatability of this independence with the economic interests of the king and the aristocracy.

In Russia, such preconditions of industrialization never existed. Instead, industrialization was initiated during the seventeenth century on the basis of extensive privileges and subsidies which the Tsar granted to foreign merchants and native entrepreneurs. At the beginning of the eighteenth century these initial developments were considerably bolstered by the attempts of Peter the Great to make the country economically independent within his lifetime. The dependence of economic enterprises upon subvention and protection by the government was bound up inextricably with the dependence of class relations upon the authority of the Tsar. This determining influence of the government on all aspects of social and economic life had not existed in Kievan Russia (878–1237), when the relations among dukes, boyars (landed aristocracy), and cities had been broadly analogous to those of the West. But the early development of Russian civilization was destroyed by the Mongol conquest (1237–1240) and the subsequent Mongol supremacy which lasted until 1452. Thus, a government based on conquest by a foreign power was superimposed upon the indigenous groups of Russian society which were competing with each other for ascendancy. The pre-eminent position of the Russian Tsar originated

[2] For details see Otto Hintze, "Weltgeschichtliche Bedingungen der Repraesentativverfassung," *Historische Zeitschrift*, Vol. CXLIII (1931), pp. 1–47.

in the course of the struggle for emancipation from Mongol domination.

The process of emancipation accounts both for the centralization of Tsarist authority and for the absence or weakness of countervailing forces. The system of universal taxation and conscription established by the Mongol rulers (except in the case of the church) facilitated the centralization of power. Eventually the Grand Duchy of Moscow achieved ascendancy over all rival princes, and it is noteworthy that the rule of primogeniture (inheritance by the oldest son) was adopted by the Moscovite dukes, while all other princes and boyars adhered to the rule of equal division among all sons in keeping with Russian private law.[3] While it was more or less fortuitous that the Grand Duke of Moscow achieved this ascendance, the weakness of countervailing forces was a direct outcome of Mongol rule and as such an important precondition of the Russian economic development.

The Mongol invasion in the mid-thirteenth century had destroyed a large number of flourishing cities and had caused the dispersion of Russian craftsmen in the Mongol Empire. Industrial production in the cities was disrupted for a century, and as a consequence production by skilled craftsmen was developed on the estates of princes, boyars, and monasteries. The same development also increased the political and administrative importance of the landed estates, and as a consequence boyar landownership increased under Mongol rule. The growing wealth and influence of the boyar class, however, did *not* lead to political power which could challenge the ruling princes. One reason was that the authority of each prince depended on the khan's patent; hence, the princes could ask for Mongol protection against internal opposition.[4] On the other hand, the boyars had very great freedom, for they could leave the service of one prince and enter that of another without forfeiting their estates. Conceivably, this freedom was also bolstered by the Mongol rulers, for it helped to keep the Russian princes in check by perpetuating the division among them. And the princes could not challenge boyar freedom without risking internecine strife which would

[3] Vernadsky calls this a first sign that "reasons of state" prevailed over private interests and prevailing tradition, which presumably was both a cause and a consequence of Muscovite ascendance. He states also that the first signs of increased power led to a rapid joining of forces under Moscow leadership at a time when Mongol power declined and was less able than before to rekindle the persistent divisions among the Russian rulers. See George Vernadsky, *The Mongols and Russia* (Vol. III of *A History of Russia;* New Haven: Yale University Press, 1953), pp. 351–54 and *passim*. The following summary of early Russian social history is based on this work and the work of V. I. Kluchevsky.

[4] *Ibid.,* p. 347.

weaken the opposition to the Mongols.[5] Thus, the landed aristocracy obtained wealth and independence as a by-product of Mongol supremacy; but in the absence of legal or constitutional safeguards this independence was lost in the struggle for emancipation from Mongol rule. Beginning at the end of the fourteenth century, the boyars were increasingly compelled to do administrative and military services for only one prince, and the terror agaist the boyars under Ivan IV (the *oprichnina* of 1565)[6] abolished their remaining freedoms with regard to the nature and extent of their service obligation. Hence, the political weakness of the Russian aristocracy as well as the dispersion of craft production on their estates was an outcome of Mongol rule.

The eventual subordination of all social classes to the Moscovite rulers was due also to the precarious position of the rising state for almost three centuries *after* the overthrow of Mongol rule.

> In the southeast and south Muscovy was still threatened by the Tatars; in the west the struggle for power between Moscow and Lithuania (after 1569, between Moscow and Poland) continued to flare up at almost regular intervals; in the northwest . . . the Moscow government had to take over the task . . . of containing the pressure of the Livonian Knights and of Sweden. . . . When Moscow defied the authority of the khan of the Golden Horde, there still remained several Tatar succession states, and the Tatars continued to raid the southern and eastern provinces of Muscovy almost yearly, looting and seizing thousands of captives. Thus the drain on Russian resources increased rather than decreased after the emancipation of the grand duke of Moscow from Mongol rule. There were no natural boundaries in the steppes between Muscovy and the Tatars, and the Moscow government had to keep the whole frontier constantly guarded. . . . The process continued throughout the 17th and 18th centuries, ending, in the south, with the annexation of the Crimea in 1783.[7]

If this continued threat to Russian territories helps to explain the dependence of all social classes upon the central authority of the Tsars, it explains also the increasing importance of the servitor aristocracy as the instrument of Tsarist power.[8]

---

[5] Hence, interprincely treaties guaranteeing this freedom were concluded until the fourteenth and fifteenth centuries, though the tendency to deny this right of the boyars began under Muscovite leadership in the fourteenth century. See *ibid.*, pp. 346–47.

[6] So-called after the name of the bodyguard of Ivan IV.

[7] Vernadsky, *op. cit.*, pp. 389–90.

[8] It should be added that the rise of the servitor aristocracy and the decline of boyar independence went hand in hand. In the process of this amalgamation the boyar families sought to preserve their superior social position. The respective positions and obligations of different ranks of the aristocracy were regulated

This aristocracy had its origin in the administration of the household and the domains of the Grand Duke of Moscow. As these domains expanded during the Mongol period, the duke frequently rewarded his officials by permitting them to "feed themselves" (*kormlenie* or tax-farming system) from the area they administered. The people could petition the duke for relief from the abuses of these officials, and the duke saw to their rotation in office in order to prevent their entrenchment.[9] In western Europe the same device had frequently led to the increasing independence of such a service aristocracy, for extensive domains and backward transportation as well as the countervailing power of the landed aristocracy impeded the effectiveness of central control.[10] In Russia, the Grand Dukes of Moscow and the Tsars were able to forestall such a development, because Mongol supremacy and the threat to the frontiers after the overthrow of the Mongols increased the dependence of these courtiers or *dvoriane* upon the power of their master.[11] Thus, the Muscovite Tsars retained their control of the rising servitor aristocracy. They were able to build up their military strength by temporary grants of land, which were made proportionate to the military service rendered (military fief or *pomestie* system). Also, the Tsars retained their ownership of the land by redistributing it among their officials. And the lands reverted to the Tsar at the death of each

in a place order (*mestnichestvo*) early in the sixteenth century. The leading families were made members of the Duma (assembly of counselors), the boyars and servitor princes forming the first rank and the principal military leaders (*okolnichi*) the second rank; by the middle of the sixteenth century the Tsar created a third rank of the Duma to which members of the rising servitor aristocracy (*dvoriane*) could be appointed.

[9] The several offices involved are discussed in *ibid.*, pp. 359–64. Two of these, the head of all the duke's servitors and courtiers (*dvorski*) and the head of his military forces (quartermaster general or *okolnichi*) are of special importance, the latter particularly in connection with the decline of the city militia. The Russian terms for nobleman and nobility or aristocracy (*dvorianin* and *dvorianstvo*) referred originally to the courtiers of the Grand Duke, who were obligated to serve him for a time or for life, in contrast to the boyars upon whom this obligation was enforced by degrees in the fifteenth and sixteenth centuries.

[10] See Otto Hintze, "Die Entstehung der modernen Staatsministerien," *Historische Zeitschrift*, Vol. C (1908), pp. 53–111, and *Der Beamtenstand*, Vol. III of *Vorträge der Gehe-Stiftung* (Dresden, 1911).

[11] The same dependence is indicated by the so-called servitor-princes, descendants of the house of Rurik who came to cede or sell their sovereign rights to the Grand Duke of Moscow during the fourteenth and fifteenth centuries. Apparently, these princes held domains in the borderland areas, e.g., between Russia and Lithuania and also in East Russia, and were thus threatened by powers from both sides. See *Vernadsky, op. cit.*, p. 368.

courtier, while his family was allowed to retain only enough land to maintain itself. It is apparent that the success of the Tsars depended upon the availability of land, and, hence, on their ability to acquire land in their struggle with the nomads, with rival principalities, with the boyars, the cities, and the church. There existed, then, a reciprocal reinforcement between the Tsar's control over the servitor aristocracy (*dvorianstvo*) and his ability to conquer new territories and to subjugate previously independent groups.

The parallel rise to power of the Tsar and of the servitor aristocracy led to the complete subjugation of the peasantry and of the townspeople, and this subjugation was of major significance for the subsequent industrial development. During the sixteenth century, the use of land grants for building up the Tsar's military forces had become extensive; but as more land became available for cultivation, more opportunities arose for the peasants to move to the new land, especially in the areas adjacent to the shifting frontiers. Frequently, peasants would leave the estates in central Russia despite their indebtedness which nominally bound them to the land. As masses of peasants fled toward the outlying areas, the supply of labor in central Russia became scarce, while many *pomeshchiks* in the sparsely settled regions were glad to permit escaping peasants to settle on their land. Toward the end of the sixteenth century penalties for escaping peasants and for those who took them in illegally were increasing in severity until in 1649, largely at the insistence of the servitor aristocracy, the peasants were bound to the land in perpetuity. Since this enserfment of the peasants had been preceded by the enforcement of an obligation to serve the Tsar on all members of the aristocracy, the end result of these developments was a social structure in which all noblemen served the Tsar, were rewarded with land, and, from 1649 on, were granted the right to exploit a servile and immobilized peasantry; but the peasants retained their obligation to the Tsar, even under these conditions. During the eighteenth century their duties were assessed on the basis of a periodic census, while the collection of taxes from the peasants was made a duty of the aristocracy. In this manner the Tsars established firm supremacy over both classes. The consequences of this relationship for the later Russian development will be discussed below.

In view of the central significance of urban centers for the economic development of the West, special importance may be attached to the slow growth of the Russian cities generally, and especially to the subjugation of the townspeople in the seventeenth century which paralleled that of the peasants. Reference has been made to the destruction of many cities during the Mongol conquest, to the dispersion of craftsmen, and to the disruption of trade. In addition, the rule of the Mongols undermined the freedom of the cities. In Kievan Russia the major cities had been free of taxation by a ruler, they had furnished their own militia, and they had been governed by a city assembly (*veche*). The Mongol rulers imposed taxation and conscription on the Russian cities (with the exception of Novgorod and Pskov), and they enlisted the cooperation of the Russian princes and boyars in suppressing urban agitation. While the cities cooperated with the princes in the effort to overthrow Mongol rule, the princes, and especially the Grand Duke of Moscow, maintained their leadership over the cities and continued their opposition to the city assembly. After the overthrow of Mongol rule, the Grand Dukes continued the Mongol system of requiring the townspeople to pay taxes and to supply labor, and they virtually abolished the city assembly. In 1478 and 1510 Novgorod and Pskov, which had retained their independence under the Mongols, were annexed to Moscow under the same conditions. Thus, the cities lost their independence through the Mongol conquest, and they failed to regain it when Mongol rule declined.

During the sixteenth and seventeenth centuries, the Russian cities remained weak, not only politically, but also economically, since they retained a distinctly rural character. Townspeople carried on a considerable amount of agricultural production, while handicraft production was frequently located in villages throughout the countryside. To be sure, there were craftsmen in the towns also, but a high proportion of them were bakers, butchers, tailors, and shoemakers, whose work was closely related to agriculture. On the other hand, there was only a small number of craftsmen in the towns who were engaged in manufacturing for sale on the market. Hence, the great bulk of the existing trade was in agricultural products, and in commodities, such as iron and salt, which could not be produced in households. Most of this trade was carried on over relatively short distances, though there was also some interregional trade between northern and central Russia.

As Henri Pirenne has shown, one of the important factors accounting for the growth of the cities in western Europe was the development of trade, and especially of foreign trade. Cities grew in size and numbers as their handicraft production and trade flourished, but in the Russian cities of the sixteenth and seventeenth centuries the techniques of production were quite primitive compared with those used in the urban centers of western Europe or the Orient. In her foreign trade Russia was in the position of a colony, since she sold her raw materials, or semifinished products such as hides and furs, in exchange for the manufactured goods from abroad. This position was clearly unfavorable to the expansion of her handicraft production and to a more rapid development of urban life. Not being able to compete abroad, Russian handicraft production remained primarily confined to the local market.[12] Indeed, a great deal of active trading was carried on in the Russian cities despite their predominantly rural character. For example, Kluchevsky has stated that the cities of the central and northern regions had a large trading population during the sixteenth century; but the point is that people from all ranks of Russian society, from the Tsar himself down to the humblest peasant, were engaged in trade. Since most of them dealt in extremely small quantities, such trading did not constitute the beginnings of a rapid urban development. Instead, its prevalence was a sign of economic weakness.[13] All of these facts point to the economic backwardness of the Russian cities, and this retardation may be attributed in good measure to the development of an aristocracy whose title to the land was contingent upon their performance of military service. For the *pomestie* system diverted a majority of this aristocracy from the towns to the country, which deprived the urban craftsmen of their best customers and further encouraged the development of handicraft production on the estates.[14]

The marked backwardness of the Russian cities was also due to certain administrative measures of the Múscovite rulers. In their efforts to control and exploit the politically restive urban populations the Tsars increased the social and economic differentiation between wealthy and poor citizens. Thus, the top layer of the merchants of Moscow was exempt from all obligations to pay taxes or to furnish labor services. In return for these privileges the leading families had to assist the Tsar in financial administration and especially in the collection of taxes. The middle and lower classes of the urban population were obliged, on the

[12] It should be added that a good deal of this international trade was in the hands of foreign merchants, who had no interest in, and did little to encourage, the development of Russian production. Nevertheless, foreign trade acquired some significance in the cities along the northern and the Volga trade routes, even though transportation was primitive and the activities of foreign merchants were restricted as well as facilitated by the Tsar and his officials. Since this extension of foreign trade was based on raw materials, however, it did little to further the development of cities.

[13] Cf. Joseph Kulischer, *Russische Wirtschaftsgeschichte* (Jena: Gustav Fischer, 1925), Vol. I, pp. 283–86, 329–31.

[14] V. O. Kluchevsky, *A History of Russia* (New York: E. P. Dutton and Company, 1912), Vol. II, pp. 144–45.

other hand, to pay taxes.[15] In this way the burden of taxes was imposed on the masses of urban residents, while those best able to pay were not only exempt from taxation but charged with the responsibility for tax collection. Under these circumstances it is not surprising that many urban craftsmen made use of the pledge system (*zaklad*), whereby a free individual could place himself into voluntary dependence to another man as security for a loan or in return for service. This system was distinct from slavery because it could be terminated by agreement; and it proved attractive to many because state taxes were higher than the dues which the peasants on the estates had to pay. Hence, many of the poor residents either left the towns for the rural villages or they pledged their services and their shops to members of the aristocracy or of the church hierarchy. Thus, artisans and traders who were "pledged" in this manner came to compete with residents who were liable to the state tax. The latter regarded this system as a great misfortune, while the landed aristocracy and the monasteries benefited from the system since it furnished them with a ready supply of skilled workers. Kluchevsky states that many cities of the Muscovite state came to be ringed with suburbs in which artisans and traders who were exempted from the state tax had settled as "pledged" servants of boyars, officials, and church dignitaries.[16] This system of voluntary bondage obviously militated against the growth of towns, because it undermined their tax base, both by the competition between tax-exempt and tax-liable residents, and by the migration of the "pledged" artisans to the estates, where they contributed to the growth of rural trade and handicraft production.[17] Voluntary bondage also undermined the tendencies toward a corporate organization of artisans in the cities, which might have furthered handicraft production as the guilds did in the cities of western Europe.

The tax-paying townspeople protested vigorously against this system of "self-pledging" and its consequences for their cities. This together with the desire to maximize state revenue led in 1649 to the enactment of new regulations "concerning the People of Towns" (Chapter 19 of the *Ulozhenie*). Self-pledging was declared illegal, tax-free suburban

[15] Vernadsky, *op. cit.*, pp. 373–74. Fines imposed for offenses against the honor of the leading merchants (*gosti*) and of the townspeople illustrate the difference between them. Offenses against the *gosti* were fined 50 rubles, those against *townspeople* 1 ruble.

[16] Kluchevsky, *op. cit.*, Vol. III, pp. 147–49, 161–66.

[17] See also Peter I. Lyashchenko, *History of the National Economy of Russia* (New York: The Macmillan Company, 1949), pp. 209–14.

areas were incorporated and taxed, and urban dwellers were attached to their place of residence as well as to their tax obligation under threat of severe penalties, including capital punishment. It is apparent that the artisans prized exemption from taxes more than they dreaded bondage; for when the Code of 1649 decreed that "unto no man shall any Christian man sell himself," the artisans of Moscow rose in rebellion against this deprivation of their "rights." As Kluchevsky observed:

> . . . personal freedom had become obligatory, and was supported by the *knut*. But a right whereof the enjoyment is compulsory also becomes an impost. . . . Consequently, the Ulozhenie did not abolish personal bondage in the name of freedom: it converted personal freedom [i.e., including the freedom to enter bondage] into bondage in the name of the interests of the state.[18]

Henceforth. urban craftsmen were forced to live in the cities and to pay the urban taxes regardless of their continued poverty. It cannot be surprising that this "obligatory freedom" discouraged personal or corporate initiative. Artisans were now bound to the town which had a corporate obligation to the Tsar in return for a corporate privilege to engage in trade and industry.

The preceding discussion has described some of the historical legacies which have had a major effect on Russia's industrial history. These legacies have had to do with the highly centralized power of the Tsar and the correlative absence of autonomous groups which might have challenged the Tsar. As a result, the economic development of Russia depended primarily upon the initiative of the Tsar and his officials, who would introduce changes in the methods of production and distribution. The power of the Tsar as well as the absence of autonomous groups also affected the urban development of Russia. Cities were centers of administration and trade rather than of production; they suffered from the prolonged dependence on, and competition with, privileged foreign merchants, from the heavy burden of taxation imposed on commerce and finally from the growth of competitive industries and trade outside the urban tax districts. By the middle of the seventeenth century, all peasants and townspeople had been immobilized by law.

By that time, however, the limitation of Tsarist autocracy had become visible also. The increasing power of the servitor aristocracy could be held in check as long as the threat to the frontiers continued; but in times of peace and at the death of a Tsar the hidden conflicts within the ranks of the aristocracy and between the aristocracy and the Tsar would

[18] Kluchevsky, *op. cit.,* Vol. III, pp. 148–49.

come out into the open. The rivalries between the boyar families and
the servitor aristocracy came to a head during the so-called Time of
Troubles (1605–1613), when a long series of struggles occurred over
the right of succession to the throne. In the long run, this rivalry
ended with the ascendancy of the new aristocracy, but this led in turn
to greater conflicts of interest between the Tsar and "his" servitors. To
be sure, the personal supremacy of the Tsar was not challenged, resting
as it did upon the legacies of centralization which originated in the overthrow of Mongol rule. But questions of legitimate succession to the
throne arose frequently during the seventeenth and eighteenth centuries,
and in this respect the new servitor aristocracy came to play an ever
more decisive role, largely by virtue of the guard regiments stationed
in Moscow. As a consequence, industrialization in Russia was initiated
at a time when the exercise of supreme power depended in part upon
the shifting balance of forces between the landed aristocracy and the
Tsar.

b. Social Classes and Economic Change in Eighteenth-Century Russia

The early industrialization of Russia should not be considered in
terms of Western analogies, since the preconditions of her industrialization differed greatly from those of the West. There were parallels, of
course. In Russia as well as in the West the early entrepreneurs came
from diverse social backgrounds. Also, mercantilist policies had much
in common in eastern and western Europe. But in England a class of
entrepreneurs came into its own by opposing corporate restrictions of
trade and industry as well as governmental regulations, and such a class
also emerged in France and Germany, though more gradually. On the
other hand, in Russia an entrepreneurial class did not develop until the
later part of the nineteenth century. Moreover, although in many other
countries industrialization depended at its beginning upon governmental
support and supervision, in Russia this dependence lasted for a period
of two hundred years and indeed has increased rather than diminished.
Hence, Russia's economic growth has been related to dynastic policies,
which have had a direct impact upon the relations among the various
social classes engaged in the development of her economic enterprises.

1. The work of Peter the Great

Peter the Great (1689–1725) greatly accelerated the Russian industrial development. Prior to the end of the seventeenth century, industrial production had developed to some extent in mining and metallurgy.

At the beginning of Peter's reign, some manufacturing enterprises existed in the form of governmental grants to members of the landed aristocracy, who sold to the government the products of their estates, such as salt, potash, weapons, etc. In addition, there was a fair amount of handicraft production in the villages as well as in the towns. The large-scale requirements of the Tsar, his government, and the army were met by wholesale merchants (*gosti*) who were appointed servants of the Tsar and who procured the needed quantities through imports and the "putting-out" system. At the beginning of the eighteenth century, Russia was a predominantly agricultural country with a total population of some 13 million people, of whom about 300,000 or 2.3 per cent were residents of "urban" areas in 1722. And in 1725, at the end of Peter's reign, there existed according to one count 233 manufactories which were owned by the state or by private individuals.[19]

The economic development depended almost entirely upon governmental initiative. In the past this initiative had consisted primarily in the large-scale trading activities undertaken by or on behalf of the government, and in the special privileges extended to private traders or manufacturers. This governmental promotion of economic activities was intensified in order to meet the needs of Russia's military establishment, for during Peter's reign of thirty-six years Russia was at peace for a little less than two years. Military requirements do not explain all of Peter's policies, however, since he also promoted economic enterprises which had no immediate military significance. The fact is that, in keeping with Russia's autocratic tradition and with his own extraordinary energy and vision, Peter made a single-handed attempt to advance the prosperity of his country, since increased wealth would make it militarily strong and furnish the state with added means to promote the economy still further.[20] Like his predecessors Peter invited or hired foreign craftsmen and manufacturers whom he attracted by grants of various privileges. He dispatched Russian citizens to foreign countries to learn a trade or a science, though these sons of the aristocracy were so lacking in elementary education and so xenophobic in outlook

[19] See M. Tugan-Baranowski, *Geschichte der russischen Fabrik* (Berlin: Emil Felber, 1900), pp. 11–12. According to Lyashchenko, no accurate enumeration is available of the number of enterprises in the eighteenth century, though all observers agree that this number increased substantially during the reign of Peter the Great. Cf. Lyashchenko, *op. cit.,* pp. 302–4.

[20] The literature on Peter's economic policies is discussed critically in Wassily Leontief, "Peter der Grosse, seine Wirtschaftspolitik und sein angeblicher Merkantilismus," *Jahrbücher für Geschichte Osteuropas,* Vol. II (1937), pp. 234–71.

that this effort was wasted to a considerable extent. He established factories, built canals, founded cities, promoted the translation of useful books, adopted a new calendar, prescribed Western clothing—and indeed engaged in an almost single-handed propaganda campaign to establish commerce and industry as an honorable occupation and to defame those who regarded such pursuits as beneath their social position.

Peter used the government to implement his industrial policies. While he founded several state enterprises, these were soon found to be unprofitable and turned over to private entrepreneurs under favorable conditions. Members of the aristocracy were encouraged to provide industrial training for their sons (other than the heir); manufacturers and their most important aides were exempted from military service. Above all, specific facilities were provided for enterprises such as mines, iron works, manufactories of weapons, of linen, and of sailcloth. The state treasury would advance capital without interest to groups of merchants; the government would build factories and rent them to private individuals under favorable conditions; new factories were declared tax-exempt for the first few years of their operation. In cases in which entrepreneurs obtained capital on their own, the government would furnish them with tools and facilitate the supply of raw materials. Manufacturers also obtained such privileges as separate adjudication, special housing facilities, and others. Moreover, the sale of all their products was guaranteed in advance, either through outright purchase by the government, through high tariffs, occasionally through the prohibition of imports, or through a grant of monopoly by the government.

Privileged as these enterprises were, they were perpetually plagued by a scarcity of labor (as well as by other obstacles). In the case of state enterprises it was relatively easy to transfer the workers to the new private owners. Otherwise labor had to be obtained from among beggars, vagrants, prostitutes, women convicted of some crime, minor children of soldiers, and peasant serfs who had escaped from private estates or state holdings. The last group formed the major contingent of the industrial labor force in the early eighteenth century, and an edict of 1722 expressly legalized this violation of the law. Still, labor continued to be scarce, and the complaints of entrepreneurs as well as the need of the state for deliveries were so urgent as to lead in the end to a system of forced labor. An edict of 1721 gave manufacturers the right, previously restricted to the aristocracy, to purchase whole villages which henceforth would be attached permanently to the "possessional factory." Another edict of 1736 determined that the manufacturers had to pay compensation for escaped serfs and their families to their original owners, i.e., in the case of trained workers. And even the workers who had been free wage-earners were now placed in bondage.[21]

This many-sided promotion of economic enterprises together with large-scale undertakings in shipbuilding, canal construction, production of military supplies, as well as the mounting expenditures for military campaigns required a large and ever increasing state revenue. In the 1724 budget quoted by Kluchevsky, military expenditures alone amounted to 5,796,493 rubles. State revenue for the same year consisted of about 4½ million rubles from the tax imposed on all male citizens regardless of age (the "souls-tax") and a little over 4 million rubles (or 45 per cent) from customs, excise, and industrial tolls. Thus, the military budget constituted 67 per cent of the estimated and 75 per cent of the actually realized revenue. It should be added that the 1724 budget involved three times the estimated revenue of 1710, but that the deficit had increased in the same period from 13 to 18 per cent. That these burdens produced a mounting incubus upon the economic activities of the entire Russian population is perhaps best conveyed by the fact that Peter, in his desperate need for new sources of revenue, offered prizes for suggestions on this score, and a veritable flood of new taxes resulted. Thus, in 1704 alone new taxes had been introduced:

> . . . upon land, upon weights and measures, upon agricultural teams, upon varieties of headdress, upon boots, upon peasant souls, upon stage drivers' earnings, upon sowings, upon reapings, upon horse and cattle hide-tannings, upon bees, upon bathhouses, upon mills, upon taverns, upon rents, upon market stands, upon timber fellings, upon ice cuttings, upon graves, upon fountains, upon stove pipes, upon marine arrivals and departures, upon ships, upon firewood, upon sales of provisions, upon watermelons, upon cucumbers, and upon (to quote from a list of the day) "nuts and other small ingatherings." [22]

Added to these was a tax on religious dissenters, who were tolerated but not for nothing, while during the following year Peter imposed a tax on beards prorated in accordance with the social status of the wearer.

This all-out effort to increase state revenue as well as Peter's endeavor to activate the country's entire economic resources placed an enormous work load upon the officials of the government. And all

---

[21] Tugan-Baranowski, *op. cit.*, pp. 28–29. The text of the edict of 1721 is reprinted in Valentin Gitermann, *Geschichte Russlands* (Zürich: Büchergilde Gutenberg, 1945), Vol. II, pp. 124–25.

[22] Kluchevsky, *op. cit.*, Vol. IV, p. 132. The data on the 1724 budget are taken from the same volume, pp. 144–45.

leading members of this bureaucracy were members of the servitor aristocracy who received grants of land in exchange for their administrative and military services. During his reign Peter bolstered the position of this aristocracy at the same time that he made a concerted attack upon the old boyar families, their social and economic position as well as their whole way of life. In his edict of 1714 Peter had made all land hereditary, a measure which eliminated remaining distinctions between boyars and servitors with regard to their title to the land. By an edict of 1718, as well as by subsequent edicts, Peter also transformed the previous system of taxation which had been based on a homestead assessment.[23] Henceforth, taxation was to be based upon a periodic census of all male persons, and the aristocratic landowners (*pomeshchiki*), who themselves were exempt from taxation, were made responsible for the collection of this souls-tax. In 1722, Peter established a new Table of Ranks, which favored the servitor aristocracy by abolishing the distinctions between its members and the boyars, which the old rank order (*mestnichestvo*) had emphasized. Peter's demands on the aristocracy had much the same effect; the compulsory shaving of beards, the prescription of German clothing, and the use of corporal punishment regardless of rank eliminated the prerogatives and the distinctiveness of the old aristocratic families. Finally, the guard regiments of Moscow were recruited exclusively from among the members of the servitor aristocracy, a practice which signalized the ascendancy of this class as well as the mutual dependence of the Tsar's power and the social position of his servitors. A report of 1737 stated that at the end of the seventeenth century some 18,000 families of landowners had belonged to the old aristocracy, while by the end of Peter's reign (1725) the servitor aristocracy was made up of some 500,000 families.[24] Thus Peter's centralized promotion of Russia's economic growth was accompanied by the rise to power of a new aristocracy as well as by the improved economic position of middle-class entrepreneurs.

The ample privileges extended to these groups, however, were not expected to provide a sufficient inducement. If privileges were lavished on individuals to further the policies of the government, failure to implement these was subject to dire penalties. In line with the autocratic tradition Peter repeatedly expressed the belief that men would act only under coercion. His industrial policy was based on the principle that

[23] See *ibid.*, pp. 106–7, 137–38. Kluchevsky points out that under this system taxes were evaded by wholesale flights of peasants and by a reduction of acreage under cultivation.

[24] *Ibid.*, Vol. IV, p. 82.

everyone, regardless of rank, was duty-bound to put his person, his labor and skill, as well as his property at the disposal of the government. Military service became a universal obligation, and corporal punishment a universal liability. Exemption in these respects was itself a special privilege which the Tsar would grant to individuals on condition that they render some special service. Peter would impose penalties as readily as he granted privileges or imposed taxes. In one edict he obliged every member of the aristocracy to learn reading, writing, arithmetic, and geometry before beginning his military service at the age of fifteen, or else suffer the penalty of not being permitted to marry. In another edict he simply threatened everyone who failed to render the required service with capital punishment or complete loss of all rights and property.[25]

> Indeed, there was not an offence against the law, from presentation of an inopportune petition for a permit to fell an oak tree or a "masthead" spruce of more than the statutory height to the failure of a *dvorianin* to attend an annual inspection, or to a mercantile transaction in Russian cloth, for which he did not ordain, variously, confiscation of property, loss of civil rights, the *knut,* the galleys, or the gallows—either, that is to say, political extinction or physical death.[26]

Such penalties were applied with ruthless cruelty, but they were threatened more often than they were implemented. And it may be, as Kluchevsky observes, that this use of the verbal goad eventually lost its stimulating force. For the penalties were as unpredictable as the privileges, and thus imposed on all social groups not only the universal obligation to serve the state but also the same insecurity concerning their rights. This monopolization of all initiative in the hands of the Tsar and the suppression of all group action which was independent of the central power made the struggle between social classes and especially between the landed aristocracy and the merchant manufacturers into a fight for privileges and exemptions granted by the Tsar.

That struggle antedated the eighteenth century. With regard to the self-pledge system the aristocracy had taken the side of the urban craftsmen and traders who had escaped the tax burden of the cities by entering the services of a landowner. And during the eighteenth century a similar conflict occurred over the regulation of the "possessional factories." Peter the Great had made the ascription of peasant serfs— and often of whole villages—a part of the transaction by which middle-class entrepreneurs were granted the ownership of enterprises which

[25] Gitermann, *op. cit.,* Vol. II, pp. 124–25.
[26] Kluchevsky, *op. cit.,* Vol. IV, p. 224.

the government had built. The constant complaints of these entrepreneurs during the first half of the eighteenth century concerning the scarcity of labor make it obvious that some such measure was necessary in order to ensure to these enterprises the labor supply on which their operation depended. It is also obvious, however, that this method involved an infringement upon the exclusive rights of the aristocracy to own serfs. Moreover, in order to facilitate the labor supply of his factories Peter issued various exceptions to the rule that escaped serfs had to be returned to their owners. The need of the government for the products of these manufactories was so great that these and other privileges were extended to middle-class entrepreneurs despite the strong opposition of the ever more powerful aristocracy, on the condition, of course, that the former actually performed the service expected of them.[27]

2. Aristocratic privileges and economic enterprises on landed estates

This conflict between the landed aristocracy and the middle-class entrepreneurs remained latent as long as Peter was alive, but after his death in 1725 the legitimate successor to the Tsarist throne was in doubt, and this further strengthened the already powerful servitor aristocracy.[28] As long as Peter was alive he had been relentless in exacting services in exchange for the privileges he granted, from the aristocracy as well as from other social groups. This pressure subsided when Peter died, and, as a consequence, the services required of the aristocracy were rapidly diminished. Peter's insistence on the military service of every member of the aristocracy had led to the prolonged absence of these landlords from their estates and hence to enormous abuses by local officials, which seriously threatened the revenue of the state. Only two years after Peter's death, two-thirds of the landlords were exempted from military service so that they could return to their estates. Under

---

[27] Thus, the edict of 1736 decreed the permanent enserfment of all skilled factory workers together with their families, who were employed by the factories at the time the edict was issued. The employers, however, were obliged to compensate the former owners of these workers. See Tugan-Baranowski, *op. cit.*, p. 29.

[28] In his edict of 1722 Peter had declared that succession to the throne should be at the discretion of the Tsar, but then he had failed to name a successor. While this policy was undoubtedly meant to express the Tsar's supreme and arbitrary power, it also precluded any *principle* of legitimacy and hence opened the way to repeated struggles over the succession. During the eighteenth century, these struggles were fought by competing factions within the aristocracy with the guard regiments in Moscow playing an especially important role.

Peter members of the aristocracy had been obliged to enter military service as common soldiers, a manifestation of Peter's belief that men of all ranks had the identical obligation to serve the state. Six years after his death a cadet corps was formed in which aristocrats would receive their training as army officers. In 1736, their obligation to do military service was cut down to twenty-five years; and the same edict permitted the fathers of two or more eligible sons to keep one of them at home to help with the management of the estate. During subsequent years a series of similar measures gradually diminished one after another of the aristocracy's many obligations to perform military and civilian services for the state, and there is no need here to recount these in detail. It has to be added only that this development was consummated by the Manifesto of Peter III in 1762, which bestowed full freedom from service upon the aristocracy.[29]

This diminution of the obligation to serve the state had an important bearing on the social and economic development of eighteenth-century Russia. After Peter's death the aristocracy was "largely brought back from the milieu of the regiment and the metropolis to the milieu of the rural manor." [30] At this point I shall consider the changing position of the aristocracy in terms of its impact upon the middle-class entrepreneurs. That impact consisted in a more or less constant attack by spokesmen of the aristocracy on the privileges which Peter the Great had extended to urban merchants and craftsmen. And it consisted, furthermore, in the development of trade and of manufacturing enterprises on the landed estates of the aristocracy.

Following the reign of Peter the Great the spokesmen of the aristocracy protested repeatedly against the manner in which middle-class entrepreneurs "abused" their privileges. Some complaints were simply made on the ground that these entrepreneurs were not entitled to the purchase of land and of serfs. Others would specify that these merchant manufacturers should sell the villages which had been ascribed to their factories, and that they should only be permitted to employ free laborers. Others yet stated that these entrepreneurs wasted their time in luxury and idleness; they should be deprived of the land and the

---

[29] To be sure, the Manifesto contained numerous reservations. The government retained the right to summon members of the aristocracy to perform services when the need arose. But this as well as other remaining obligations was no longer imperative in the old sense, for in cases of noncompliance the aristocracy was threatened only with the Tsar's "grievous displeasure" and not with the dire penalties of Peter's reign. See Kluchevsky, *op. cit.*, Vol. IV, pp. 338–39.

[30] *Ibid.*, Vol. IV, p. 317.

villages unless they produced goods which compared in quality with those of foreigners. There were complaints also that the peasants were oppressed by these middle-class employers. These employers should be subject to lawsuits in the ordinary courts instead of the special court of the Commission of Manufacturers, since the latter made it difficult for the landowners to retrieve their absconding peasants.[31] The attack upon the possessional manufacturers, many of whom had been wealthy merchants, was not confined to members of the aristocracy. The small merchants protested also, since they had not received similar privileges from the government. Thus, the inhabitants of Moscow protested against the added burdens imposed on them by virtue of the exemptions granted to the manufacturers. Other town residents added pleas against the exemptions granted to workers in the possessional factories.[32] Of the many attacks on the privileged merchant manufacturers and their "possessional" factories, those coming from the landed aristocracy were the most important, however.

In the years after Peter's death the privileges which had been granted previously, were gradually withdrawn. In 1746 merchants were forbidden to possess serfs, with or without land. In 1758 all individuals liable to pay state taxes were forbidden to own land, which meant that the ownership of land became once more an exclusive prerogative of the servitor aristocracy. Finally, the edict of Peter III in 1762 prohibited the purchase of serfs for employment in factories and other enterprises. Moreover, this edict, in which the aristocracy was exempted from its obligation to serve the state, did nothing to exempt the merchants and manufacturers, who continued to pay a head tax, to serve the state in the administration of its monopolies (salt, liquor, paper, etc.) and in such other matters as billeting soldiers, furnishing transportation and postal services, and so on. Subsequent legislation abolished still other privileges which had been extended to the merchant manufacturers by Peter the Great, such as the Commission of Manufacturers and separate

---

[31] Tugan-Baranowski, *op. cit.,* pp. 36–37. These complaints were aired before the investigating commission instituted by Peter III in 1762; but they expressed grievances of long standing.

[32] "They live in their own houses, are free of dues and billeting from the police. Hence, all of the burdens fall upon the remaining merchants, on those of modest or scanty means; hence, the merchant class decays. Yet, the manufacturers are wealthiest, and therefore they should be on an equal footing with the other merchants with reference to dues and service obligations. . . . The manufacturers should be forced to repay what has been paid for them in previous years." This quotation is taken from the petition of the residents of Yaroslavly as cited in Tugan-Baranowski, *op. cit.,* pp. 38–39.

courts for manufacturers (in 1779).[33] This cancellation of privileges was no doubt grating psychologically; but the new restrictions imposed upon the economic activities of middle-class merchants and manufacturers were not prohibitive, apparently. The scarcity of free labor was not as acute in the second half of the century as it had been in the first. In 1767, 17,823 or 39 per cent of all workers in industrial production were free while the remainder consisted of serfs and "possessional" workers. By 1804 the number of free industrial workers had increased to 45,600 (or 47 per cent).[34]

Under these circumstances it was relatively unimportant that the merchant manufacturers were now forbidden to acquire serfs and employ them in the manufactories. Moreover, figures on foreign trade for the period 1742–1762 indicate that despite these greater restrictions the prosperity of middle-class merchants and manufacturers increased.[35] But the economic activities of the middle class were threatened all the same, because they were faced with increasing competition arising from the productive activities on the landed estates. The aristocracy was certainly a parasitic leisure class, which used its steadily increasing privileges to exploit land and serf labor more effectively. It is necessary, however, to balance this view by calling attention to a small, but important group of aristocratic entrepreneurs, as well as to the existence of peasant serfs, who engaged in trade and production. The commercial and productive activities of peasant serfs on the landed estates contributed significantly to the economic growth of the country in the late eighteenth and early nineteenth centuries.

Several economic enterprises had been established by members of the aristocracy already during the seventeenth century. Thus, the Boyar Morosov developed mines and iron works as well as the production of potash, while the Stroganov family became prominent on the basis of its extensive salt mines, iron works, and trade in furs.[36] In the first part

---

[33] Tugan-Baranowski, *op. cit.*, pp. 49–50, and Georg Sacke, "Adel und Bürgertum in der Regierungszeit Katharinas II von Russland," *Revue Belge de Philologie et d'Histoire*, Vol. XVII (1938), p. 818.

[34] See A. G. Rashin, *Formirovanie Promishlenovo Proletariata v Rossii* (Moscow, 1940), pp. 14, 56.

[35] During this period the value of Russian exports increased from 4.5 to 12.7 million rubles. Cf. Sacke, "Adel und Bürgertum . . . ," p. 820.

[36] Josef Kulischer, "Die kapitalistischen Unternehmer in Russland in den Anfangsstadien des Kapitalismus," *Archiv für Sozialwissenschaft*, Vol. LXV (1931), pp. 313–16. The author lists a number of other aristocrats, who engaged in various enterprises on the basis of state aid and who, when these enterprises failed, obtained, nevertheless, large sums of money out of their resale to the treasury.

of the eighteenth century industrial production on the landed estates was concerned primarily with state enterprises such as iron works, state forests, and silk works which were in most cases initiated by the government and then turned over together with ascribed villages to a prominent landowner.[37] Such transfers of state enterprises to members of the aristocracy were of a piece with the large grants of land which were given to favorites of the Tsarist court. The management of these enterprises and estates was a secondary consideration as far as a majority of the aristocratic beneficiaries was concerned. As long as they obtained the largest possible income from their holdings, they would leave the management of enterprises and estates to their agents.

The economic enterprises on these landed estates did not remain confined, however, to those which the government had built and transferred to the ownership of an aristocrat. During the second half of the eighteenth century, the aristocracy received very extensive grants of land along with its other increasing privileges, and on these expanding estates some members of the aristocracy began to develop manufacturing enterprises of their own. These estate manufactories were largely concerned with the production of cloth, and the available statistical information clearly reflects this increasing interest of landowners in manufacturing.

TABLE 1. Number and Per Cent of Workers in Industrial Production in Russia in the Years 1767, 1804, and 1825 *

		Number of Workers			In Per Cent of Total		
Year	Total Number of Workers	Posses-sional Workers	Estate Peasants (serfs)	Free	Posses-sional Workers	Estate Peasants (serfs)	Free
1767	45,464	21,855	5,786	17,823	48.1	12.7	39.2
1804	95,200	30,200	19,400	45,600	31.7	20.4	47.9
1825	210,600	29,400	66,700	114,500	14.0	31.6	54.4

* Data taken from A. G. Rashin, *op. cit.*, pp. 14, 56.

Table 1 shows a striking increase in the number and proportion of estate peasants who were engaged in industrial production; but these figures do not indicate the full extent of this development, since aristocrats were also granted state enterprises in which "possessional" workers might be employed. The importance of the estate factories is also evi-

[37] It was probably of little or no concern to Peter the Great, whether such "possessional" enterprises were turned over to aristocrats or middle-class merchants; but there was a natural division between them which depended upon the urban or rural location of the enterprise.

dent from a survey of factories in 1773. Of the 305 factories for which data were sufficient, 57 belonged to members of the aristocracy, but these accounted for almost one-third of total production. Another survey for the year 1809 revealed that of the 98 cloth manufacturers who sold their total output to the government, only 12 belonged to the merchant class, while 74 belonged to the aristocracy, and the remainder to foreigners.[38] Thus, toward the end of the eighteenth century, a considerable number of factories were estate enterprises belonging to the aristocracy, and among these were many of the largest enterprises in the rapidly expanding textile industry. The participation of merchants in the development of economic enterprises, which Peter the Great had encouraged, was challenged by portions of the landholding aristocracy, especially after 1762. It may be added that this entrepreneurial activity among members of the aristocracy declined markedly only in the 1840's.[39]

The number of aristocrats who took an active interest in developing economic enterprises on their estates remained limited throughout. It is, therefore, important to recognize that the leisure-class aristocracy, which had no such interests, also became involved in the development of commercial and industrial enterprises, though this involvement was indirect. The social standing of this class depended upon its wealth and hence upon the productivity of its estates and of the serfs working on these estates. During the period in which compulsory military service had required the absence from their estates, many members of the aristocracy had found it convenient to have the lands cultivated by the serfs in return for a rent (*obrok*) rather than organize the cultivation of the land on the basis of serf labor (*barshchina*). And this system of *obrok* was not abandoned after the aristocracy achieved exemption from state service. Many landowners preferred to remain in the towns, close to the military authorities and hence safe from the frequent peasant uprisings, and the *obrok* system enabled absentee landowners to increase the rent at will.[40] While the serfs could also be exploited under the *barshchina* system, commutation of services into money payments

[38] Tugan-Baranowski, *op. cit.*, pp. 35–36.

[39] Lyashchenko, *op. cit.*, pp. 294–96.

[40] Kluchevsky, *op. cit.*, Vol. V, pp. 78–80. Data for 1777 and later indicate that many members of the aristocracy resided in the towns rather than on their estates. Such urban residence was not by itself an aspect of the *obrok* system. The *barshchina* system could be used in a similar way, because landowners would have their estates managed by agents, and they would increase their income by increasing the work duty of their serfs. In the later eighteenth century this went often so far that landowners would supply their serfs with food, since the demands for

appeared to be more advantageous from the standpoint of a leisure aristocracy, which was interested in maximizing its income and minimizing its managerial responsibilities, especially in areas where agricultural productivity was low and the demand for manufactured products high.

In the second half of the eighteenth century, *obrok* was paid by 35 per cent to 65 per cent of the serfs in the Moscow region and by 65 per cent to 100 per cent in the northeastern territories.[41] In order to pay the tithe the serfs were often impelled to increase their income, and there is evidence of a rapid growth in the domestic industry (*kustar*) and the commercial activities of peasant serfs. This increase of trade and production in the villages was more independent of the control by urban merchants than it had been previously; hence, peasants were competing once again with the economic development of urban areas. Contemporary observers remarked that peasants were abandoning agriculture in order to take up trade or handicraft production with the result that the cultivated acreage and grain reserves were reduced and the cost of living rose. Some peasants were growing rich and many agricultural villages were acquiring "the aspect of towns inhabited by handicraft peasants." [42] A number of peasants had learned new production techniques in the "possessional" factories. They could apply them now in their household industries, for the increasing number of free laborers and the prohibition of the purchase of serfs by middle-class entrepreneurs made it possible for the peasant serfs to work for themselves or for other peasant serfs who became merchants.[43]

labor service prevented the serfs from raising their own food supply. Cf. also the observation of a peasant in A. N. Radishchev, *Reise von Petersburg nach Moskau* (1790) (Leipzig: Historia Verlag Paul Schraepler, 1922), pp. 14–16, that things could be still worse, for they were at least permitted to work for themselves at night.

[41] Lyashchenko, *op. cit.*, p. 275. See also Henry Rosovsky, "The Serf Entrepreneur in Russia," *Explorations in Entrepreneurial History*, Vol. VI (May, 1954), pp. 209–11.

[42] Quoted in Lyashchenko, *op. cit.*, p. 272.

[43] This does not mean that the peasant industry was an outgrowth of the "possessional" factories as Tugan-Baranowski has maintained. See Kulischer, "Die kapitalistischen Unternehmer . . . ," p. 338. In fact, this entrepreneurial activity of the peasants had had a considerable history, especially since the seventeenth century when peasants became prominent traders on the estates of the rising servitor aristocracy, as Kulischer has suggested. The legal prohibitions of commercial activities by the peasants seem to have been ineffective, though they were frequently repeated at the insistence of city merchants. It is undisputed, however, that peasants became more active in trade and industrial production during the second half of the eighteenth century.

Information concerning the commercial and productive activities of the peasants is available on the basis of the discussions in the "legislative" commission of 1767, which had been initiated by Catherine the Great. State peasants as well as manorial peasants had at times considerable capital at their disposal; they would buy and sell in the cities, travel to Siberia, and return with consignments of merchandise. Likewise, they engaged in the sale of foreign products, in trade with oriental peoples, and in export to western Europe. Sums of 50,000 rubles are mentioned which were at the disposal of the peasants. Whole villages engaged in trade rather than in agriculture. And some cases were cited, in which peasants refused to sell their agricultural produce to urban merchants in order to damage them and help the merchants among their fellow serfs.[44]

All of these peasant traders were serfs and none of them could have engaged in such extensive economic activities unless they had been actively supported by their aristocratic masters. From the support of the self-pledge system before 1649 to this encouragement of the peasant traders in the eighteenth century, the aristocracy had an obvious interest in sponsoring activities which increased its wealth. If peasants got into difficulties, their masters would bail them out. Aristocrats would use their influence to secure for their peasant traders good positions on the market place. And in view of the legal disabilities of serfs, their lords would advance money to them, collect their debts, and give them permission to trade in the name of their masters. As a result, urban magistrates were often reluctant to confiscate the goods of the peasants, even where this trade was illegal, because such action might entail litigation with a member of the aristocracy.[45] It is of major interest in

---

[44] Other evidence obtained in this inquiry points to some interesting consequences of this peasant trade. A southern deputy maintained that the trading class was weak and inefficient in his area, so much so that at the last census many cities were found which contained no merchants at all, for even those who were merchants did not engage in trade. As a consequence, many people traded directly without the aid of merchants, or they relied on itinerant Cossacks who were engaged in trade. The deputy declared that the peasants should not be forbidden to engage in trade, which was the proposal under discussion, for they would often have to wait a whole year to sell their produce, if trading was made an exclusive right of the merchants. Other reports indicated that similar conditions prevailed in the north, and that peasants were engaged in trade despite all prohibitions to the contrary.

[45] The preceding discussion is a summary of Kulischer. "Die kapitalistischen Unternehmer . . . ," pp. 328–35. The position of these peasant traders in their home villages was often made desirable, even though spokesmen of the aristocracy

this connection that this growing trade and industry of peasant serfs was defended vigorously by spokesmen of the landed aristocracy. In the meetings of an investigating commission under Catherine II aristocratic representatives from many different districts spoke up in favor of protecting the economic activities of the peasants against the attacks of the merchants. Some of these spokesmen even advocated greater freedom for the commercial transactions of the serf—surely an unexpected attitude among the aristocratic landowners of eighteenth-century Russia.[46]

In the light of these facts it is understandable that the merchant manufacturers were not only concerned with the opposition of the aristocracy, but even more with the competition of the peasants. For example, the merchants of Vorotynsk complained that the peasants in their district travel around, buy up the flax, and work it up in their homes. Should this not be prohibited? A similar complaint was voiced by the residents of Kostroma, who stated that the peasants bought large quantities of linen in the villages and then sent these to the ports. Again, there were complaints that the peasants possess oil and leather manufactories. One petition read as follows:

> Many of our neighbors, residents of the village of Norsk, as well as of other villages, buy up iron, manufacture nails at home, and, after large quantities of nails have been purchased from their neighbors, they are sent to Petersburg or Moscow. When we became aware of this damage which was being done to us by the peasants, we decided to have the peasants arrested in order to initiate a court-investigation . . . , since these peasants have shipped a not inconsiderable quantity of previously purchased nails, and of other goods, to Petersburg.[47]

frequently exaggerated the advantages of this patriarchal relationship. There is no doubt though that the landowners had an interest in encouraging their serfs, albeit capriciously and in order to exploit them more effectively later. A summary of the legal disabilities of the serfs at the end of the eighteenth century makes it clear, moreover, that without some encouragement from thir owners the serfs could have done literally nothing. Cf. J. Engelmann, *Die Leibeigenschaft* (Leipzig: Duncker and Humblot, 1884), pp. 152–56.

[46] Of course, there were also contrary opinions. A staunch conservative like Count Shcherbatov came to deplore the growth of trade and industry among the peasants. He said that they engaged in these economic activities in response to the increasing tax burdens imposed on them by their owners as well as by the state; but he maintained that the peasants had been satisfied though poor as long as they cultivated the land, whereas now they had grown rich while agriculture was falling into decay. Cf. the references in Tugan-Baranowski, *op. cit.*, p. 54, n. 5.

[47] Quoted in Tugan-Baranowski, *op. cit.*, p. 46.

The authorities, however, disallowed this petition and returned the goods to the peasants, despite the protest of the petitioners. Similar complaints were lodged by the merchants of many communities. And the whole situation was aptly summarized in one petition which stated that the peasants themselves had become merchants, who by their competition made the existence of a real merchant class impossible.[48]

3. Economic growth and autocratic rule

The preceding survey of trade and production makes it clear that the economic growth of eighteenth-century Russia depended to a considerable extent upon economic activities on the estates of the landed aristocracy. No accurate statistics are available for this period, especially none which would compare the number of enterprises owned by landowners and merchant manufacturers respectively, but there is no doubt that the development of manufacturing was considerable. According to one count, the number of state and private manufactories increased from 233 at the end of Peter's reign (1725) to 984 at the accession of Catherine II (1762) and to 3,161 in the year of her death (1796).[49] Another count indicates that the "number of enterprises" was 498 in 1767 and 2,399 in 1804.[50] The reason for such discrepancies is that the meaning of "enterprise" was not standardized, and Lyashchenko has suggested that the increases of area and population are a more reliable index of growth. Thus, the area of the Russian market increased from 687,000 to 913,000 squares miles during the eighteenth century, while the total population increased from 13 to 29 million people.[51] Still another index of economic growth for the second half of the eighteenth century is the number of workers employed in industrial production, which increased from 45,000 in 1767 to 95,000 in 1804.[52] These figures appear to include only workers in manufacturing enterprises. In addition, there were 99,330 ascribed "male souls" in the mountain works of the Treasury, according to the Census of 1762, while another 43,187 ascribed "souls" worked in privately owned mountain works. By the time of the fifth Census, in 1794–1796, the

[48] *Ibid.,* pp. 45–46.
[49] Tugan-Baranowski, *op. cit.,* pp. 11–12, 49–50.
[50] See Rashin, *op. cit.,* pp. 14, 23.
[51] Lyashchenko, *op. cit.,* p. 271. The urban population of Russia increased from 300,000 or 2.3 per cent in 1722 to 1,300,000 or 3.6 per cent in 1796. See *ibid.,* p. 273. Cf. also the maps included in this volume, which show the geographic location of industries in the eighteenth century.
[52] Cf. p. 138 above, where the source of these figures is cited.

number of ascribed workers in the mountain works of the Treasury had risen to 241,253 and of those in privately owned mountain works to 70,965. At that time, the number of workers in manufacturing enterprises was 80,000. Thus, the total industrial work force increased from 190,000 in 1762 to 390,000 in 1796,[53] while during the same period the value of Russian exports increased from 20.3 to 109.5 million rubles.[54]

This significant expansion of industry and commerce should be considered in conjunction with the increasing involvement of the aristocracy in the promotion of economic activities and with the related changes in the political sphere. Earlier in the eighteenth century the landed aristocracy had been unanimous in opposing the privileges extended to middle-class manufacturers. This opposition, however, was gradually abandoned by *some* prominent members of the aristocracy, who advocated policies of benefit to commerce and industry as a whole. Thus, as early as 1745, a number of aristocratic spokesmen advocated policies which would encourage the development of trade in the Black Sea area, and in the 1750's negotiations with several countries were carried forward for the purpose of facilitating trade by Russian merchants. Similarly, internal tariffs were removed at that time and this benefited trade and industry regardless of social class. In a legislative commission of 1754 members of the aristocracy discussed measures designed to increase the prestige and the rights of merchants, and they even advocated the appointment of an advisory council in which the representatives of the merchants would be on an equal footing with those of the aristocracy.[55]

During the 1760's these "liberal" tendencies within the aristocracy came to a head in the proposals of two brothers, Peter and Nikita Panin. One was a prominent general, the other a Russian diplomat, who became the tutor of Paul, the son and heir apparent of Peter III and the later Catherine the Great. While the Panins were spokesmen

---

[53] See James Mavor, *An Economic History of Russia* (New York: E. P. Dutton and Company, Inc., 1914), Vol. I, pp. 441, 493. These "mountain works" were stone quarries, mines of coal and iron ore, state forests, and other enterprises in which raw materials were procured. Manufacturing activities, such as smithies, however, were often connected with these enterprises.

[54] Cited in Sacke, "Adel und Bürgertum . . . ," p. 848.

[55] The advocacy of commercial interests by prominent members of the aristocracy was plausible enough, since a number of the leading statesmen had a direct financial interest in certain commercial enterprises. Others, however, were simply becoming aware of the benefits to be derived from the promotion of trade. Cf. the discussion in Sacke, *op. cit.*, pp. 820–27.

of the aristocracy, who never questioned the institution of serfdom, they were at the same time critics of the class they represented. They wanted to see the power of the aristocracy curbed: they opposed the sale of serfs as recruits and the breakup of peasant families when they were sold. They advocated that the duties imposed on the serfs be legally regulated, and that they be granted certain rights of ownership. And they proposed that members of the landed aristocracy be permitted to sell their estates to members of other classes. This critical appraisal of the aristocracy was combined with a strong advocacy of commerce. Nikita Panin proposed the creation of a commission whose principal task would be the elaboration of plans for the development of trade. And he followed this with a plan for constitutional reform. In this plan Panin criticized the predominance of favorites at the Tsarist court of Elizabeth, and he proposed the establishment of an advisory council with whose aid the Tsar could put the legislative and administrative process of the government upon an orderly basis.[56] At the time when these proposals were made, other spokesmen of the aristocracy opposed the remaining privileges of the "possessional manufacturers" in the strongest terms, and sought to enlarge the political as well as the social privileges of the landowners still further.[57]

It is clear then, that in the second half of the eighteenth century liberal as well as conservative spokesmen of the aristocracy were advocating measures which, though conflicting in purpose, would have curbed the autocratic power of the Tsar. Their proposals envisaged that elected representatives of middle-class merchants and aristocratic landowners, or of the latter class alone, would have a recognized advisory function on all legislative and administrative questions. But the ascendancy of the aristocracy coincided with a gradually increasing division of interests within its own ranks; and the more rapid economic development in the later eighteenth century only increased this division by encouraging a preoccupation with commercial interests in one segment of the aristocracy. It was this division of interests as well as the continual struggle between the old-line aristocracy and the rising

[56] Georg Sacke, *Die gesetzgebende Kommission Katharinas II* (Beiheft 2 of *Jahrbücher für Geschichte Osteuropas;* Breslau: Verlag Priebatschs Buchhandlung, 1940), pp. 40–45. It may be added that Panin combined his proposal with a critique of the Senate (*Duma*), in which the traditional spokesmen of the aristocracy had expressed demands which Panin characterized as lacking in respect for the authority of the Tsar. Presumably, Panin was attempting to win Tsarist favor for his proposal by this criticism, though the proposal itself reflected a genuine division of opinion within the aristocracy.

[57] See Sacke, "Adel und Bürgertum . . ." *op. cit.,* p. 825.

middle class of merchants and manufacturers, which enabled Catherine II to reassert the centralized, autocratic power of the Tsar, which Peter the Great had exercised, and which his more or less weak successors had not fully utilized. This reassertion meant that neither the increasing economic activities in the urban areas and on the landed estates nor the complete exemption of the aristocracy from compulsory service to the state was made the basis for an exercise of political power.

The short reign of Peter III and the *coup d'état* in 1762 may be regarded as a turning point in Russian social history, in this respect. The landed aristocracy had reached the pinnacle of its "political" power by that time, since more often than not it had been successful in its running, though tacit, struggle with the Tsarist bureaucracy. The edict of 1762 reflected this success, for Peter III granted more than full freedom from the obligation to serve the state. *He was also prepared to grant the aristocracy a major voice in legislative and administrative matters.* This political ascendancy of the aristocracy was short-lived, however. After a reign of a few months, Peter III was murdered and his wife, Catherine, was placed upon the Tsarist throne by leaders of the aristocracy and the guard regiments of the capital. In preceding decades such struggles over the succession had signified the political ascendancy of the aristocracy; the new incumbents of the throne would reward their supporters among the aristocracy. Catherine, however, was able to retain the initiative of autocratic power by fully meeting all wishes of the aristocracy with regard to its powers over the serfs and in terms of economic concessions at the same time that she withheld her recognition of the political role which Peter III had been prepared to accept. Immediately after the *coup d'état* of 1762 Catherine confirmed the landowners' absolute power over their serfs, and reminded the latter of their duty to absolute obedience. In 1765 she granted landowners the right to condemn their serfs to forced labor. In 1766 she confirmed the landowners' right to send disobedient peasants to Siberia. And in 1767 she denied the peasants the right to petition against their masters, especially to petition the Empress personally, on pain of lifelong imprisonment.

This unprecedented extension of the aristocracy's legal power over the serfs was coupled with various material concessions by which Catherine managed to obtain the support of other sections of the aristocracy as well as of the urban merchants and manufacturers. During the thirty-five years of her reign, she granted state lands and state peasants to the landed aristocracy with the result that she increased the serf population by 800,000.[58]   In various measures Catherine gave her support to the social pre-eminence of the aristocracy.   She confirmed its exclusive prerogative to the ownership of land and of serfs.   A program of land surveys was instituted which was of great economic benefit to the land-owners.   Catherine's concessions to the landowners were paralleled, however, by a systematic policy of encouraging middle-class merchants and manufacturers.   Internal customs barriers were removed, favorable export- and import-regulations were instituted, the government under-took to improve the system of transportation and to facilitate credit, and Russia's foreign policy was designed to strengthen her foreign trade. Catherine also extended to well-to-do merchants many of the privileges which in 1762 had been confirmed as the exclusive prerogative of the aristocracy.[59]   Obviously, such measures helped to increase the existing antagonism between urban merchants and the landed aristocracy, and hence furthered Catherine's interest in a precarious balance of power between the classes.

After Catherine's accession to the throne, the greatest danger to her power was to be expected from the landed aristocracy which had just obtained its greatest privileges under Peter III.   While Catherine con-firmed these privileges immediately, she also declared that they were still insufficient.   And instead of giving her confirmation in final, legal form, she appointed a commission to investigate the prerogatives of the aristocracy with the ostensible purpose of improving upon Peter III's edict.   The work of this commission came to nothing, and Cather-ine was even able to delay the formal confirmation of the existing exemptions (from service, from taxes, and from corporal punishment) until 1785.   The purpose of that delay, however, was not to curtail the social and economic pre-eminence of the aristocracy, but to in-crease its dependence upon the power of the Tsar.   And the fact that her successor, Paul I, granted 600,000 state peasants to the landowners during his four-year reign certainly indicates that such grants of privi-

---

[58] Lyashchenko, op. cit., pp. 273–74.   The peasants on the so-called "black lands" of the state were bound to the land like other peasant serfs; but the state peasants were only obliged to pay the state tax, while the peasants on private or church lands were obliged to render labor services as well.   Although the state tax was higher than the manorial dues of the peasant serfs, the state peasants had been exempt from personal service; but this exemption disappeared, when they were ascribed to private owners.

[59] Among these were abolition of compulsory state service, of corporal pun-ishment, of the souls-tax; further privileges consisted in the establishment of separate jurisdiction, in the facilitation of acquiring land and title, and in other measures.   See Sacke, "Adel und Bürgertum . . ." pp. 827 ff., and 845–49.

leges continued to be used as a means of ensuring the supremacy of the Tsar over the aristocracy.[60] It is true that from time to time the aristocracy was able to exact concessions from the Tsars (e.g., the fall of Speransky, 1812, under Alexander I), but it was never able to curb their autocratic exercise of power. The members of the aristocracy remainded divided in terms of economic interests, in terms of their competition for position and privilege at the Tsarist court, and in terms of their conflict with government officials. The Tsars, on the other hand, could command a central corps of government officials entirely dependent upon them. And this control, together with the lavish distribution of benefits, enabled the rulers to give the aristocracy wealth and prestige but to preserve their own political supremacy.[61]

This pattern of Tsarist rule was highlighted by Catherine's token endorsement of liberal ideas and institutions, which she utilized to reject the aristocracy's pretensions to a share of political power. By calling for the "election" of a legislative commission in 1767, she appeared to satisfy the highest expectations of all those who longed for a limitation of autocratic power; but this "election" was so manipulated that the landed aristocracy, which might oppose the Empress, was represented by 160 delegates, while the cities which would support her were represented by 207. Moreover, there were 78 representatives of the free peasantry and 28 high government officials, all of whom were entirely subservient to Catherine. Hence, the commission was stacked in favor of the groups who had benefited most under Catherine's reign. And the procedures of the commission were so arranged that these reliable representatives as well as her personal agents managed to have the commission as a whole offer to Catherine the title "Catherine the Great" and "Mother of the fatherland," thereby legitimizing her questionable claim to the throne.[62] It was on this basis that Catherine II succeeded

---

[60] Cf. the discussion of Catherine's policies with regard to the prerogatives of the aristocracy in Georg Sacke, "Katharina II im Kampf um Thron und Selbstherrschaft," *Archiv für Kulturgeschichte,* Vol. XIII (1932), pp. 191–96. The figure on the number of peasants ascribed to private owners under Paul I is given in Lyashchenko, *op. cit.,* p. 274. After the emancipation of 1861, extensive grants of land served the same purpose. See Anatole Leroy-Beaulieu, *The Empire of the Tsars* (New York: G. P. Putnam's Sons, 1894), Vol. II, p. 104.

[61] See the interpretation of Alexander von Schelting, *Russland und Europa im Russischen Geschichtsdenken* (Bern: A. Francke, 1948), pp. 274–79, and Max Weber, *Wirtschaft und Gesellschaft* (Tübingen: J. C. B. Mohr, 1925), Vol. II, pp. 719 ff.

[62] Detailed proof for this interpretation is contained in Sacke's work *Die gesetzgebende Kommission Katharinas II,* cited above. As Sacke shows con-

in curbing the supremacy of the landed aristocracy only five years after its rise to a pinnacle of apparent power (in the edict of 1762). And while her subsequent policies clearly favored the development of commerce and industry, her successful manipulation of the "legislative" commission of 1767 forestalled the development of any representative institutions. As a consequence, Russia's economic growth continued to depend for the most part upon the initiative and the close supervision of government officials, and upon the privileges within the gift of the Tsar as an autocratic ruler.

At this point I shall summarize the interrelations between economic growth and the development of social classes which I have discussed in this section. The commercial and industrial development of eighteenth-century Russia resulted from the efforts of many social groups, which were dependent throughout upon the directing impulse of the Tsar. Peter the Great and Catherine II not only aided the enterprises of merchants and landowners by their internal and imperialist policies; they also took active steps in setting up new enterprises and in furthering their development by the full use of governmental power. Both native and foreign merchants individually benefited from these measures to a considerable extent, even if the efficiency of their enterprises and the Russian economy as a whole suffered. As a consequence, the number and the social prestige of middle-class manufacturers increased significantly during the eighteenth century, a development which was curtailed but not checked by the withdrawal of special privileges and the ascendancy of the landholding aristocracy. Although the majority of the aristocracy was a leisure class primarily concerned with safeguarding and enhancing its social and political dominance, an influential minority promoted economic enterprises on their estates or at least facilitated the economic activities of their peasant serfs. This economic development on the estates of the aristocracy certainly impeded the growth of a class of middle-class entrepreneurs; but it also helped to promote policies designed to aid commerce and industry, and under Catherine II it led indirectly to a considerable improvement in the social position of these entrepreneurs.

vincingly, the legislative work of the commission was little more than a smoke screen. In this respect a most convincing detail is the fact that two days after the offer of the title by the commission, Catherine decreed that the government officials, who were members of the commission, should return to their regular work, which should not be disrupted. Apparently, their regular attendance in the meetings of the commission was no longer needed. *Ibid.*, pp. 144–45.

The most striking result of the Russian development was the intensification of class differences. The paradox is that in England the growth of economic enterprises led to the gradual mitigation of these differences despite vigorous and protracted struggles among the social classes, while in Russia these differences deepened, although struggles among the classes were manipulated or suppressed by an autocratic ruler. The point is that the Tsars, and especially Peter the Great and Catherine II, utilized the latent conflict among the social classes to strengthen their own position and to facilitate the execution of autocratic decisions by willing government officials. They accomplished their purpose, but at the price of deepening the existing divisions within Russian society. I shall now turn to a consideration of the Tsar in relation to the aristocracy and the serfs, for it is in the light of these relations that we can understand the legacies of servitude which shaped the emerging relationship between masters and serfs and between employers and workers in economic enterprises.

c. The Tsar, the Aristocracy, and the Serfs

The interrelation between social classes and the economic growth of eighteenth-century Russia presents a certain paradox. In terms of its social position, its increased wealth, its enhanced authority in local government and its power over the serfs, the aristocracy had a record of increasing influence. Yet, this ability to obtain concessions did not effectively challenge Tsarist autocracy; and the complete control of the serfs by their masters did not undermine the idea that the Tsar possessed ultimate authority over all his subjects. Indeed, the development of the eighteenth century ended under Catherine II with the complete political impotence of the aristocracy, as well as with an unprecedented expansion of its prerogatives. It is true that the aristocracy frequently played a decisive role in the struggles over the succession to the Tsarist throne. Yet, these forces were never able to accomplish more than a momentary curb on the autocratic exercise of power. Once the new Tsar had been recognized as the "legitimate" successor, he was again the supreme ruler, who would grant the aristocracy many privileges, but never the privilege of having a recognized voice in policy decisions.

The coexistence of Tsarist supremacy and aristocratic prerogative had special significance for the relations between landowners and their serfs, and indirectly also for the relations between employers and workers in manufacturing enterprises. The privileges, the social standing, and the local authority of the aristocracy remained dependent throughout upon arbitrary gifts from the Tsar, whether or not these gifts carried with them the obligation to serve the state. The Tsar's ability to use such arbitrary gifts as a major instrument of exercising power rested, on the one hand, upon appointments in the army and the central bureaucracy, and upon the exploitation of the peasantry, on the other. Leading officials were personal favorites of the Tsar, and as such the major beneficiaries of the regime. Appointments and promotions were entirely dependent upon the Tsar and his immediate entourage, a circumstance which enhanced their central power as well as the competition for favors among members of the aristocracy. This use of appointments as a means of exercising power is familiar, but it can hardly explain why members of the aristocracy who were already recipients of many privileges should vie with one another in their efforts to receive government appointments and to enhance their position in court society, especially after they had been exempted from the compulsory obligation to serve the state. The reason is that the successors of Peter the Great made the established rank-order of society dependent upon the rank-order of government offices and thus structured the life of the aristocracy from the court and the capital down to every center of provincial and local government. And the increasing leisure as well as the importation from western Europe of polite manners and literary culture added to this bureaucratic hierarchy an elaborate social life which became a principal preoccupation of the landed aristocracy.[63] And since successful participation in this social life depended upon great wealth, it should be added that appointments to important positions in the army and the government provided numerous opportunities for illicit aggrandizement.[64]

[63] This "Westernization" of aristocratic social life was both a continuation of, and a reaction against, Peter's reforms. Contemporary observers like Pososhkov described the "withdrawal of efficiency" (Veblen) with which the aristocracy met Peter's incessant demands for service and his efforts to promote the application of Western technical skills. After his death, the influence of Western ideas increased greatly, but in social manners and literary culture rather than in the technical arts. The aristocratic aversion to Peter's demand for technical training is described in George V. Plekhanov, *History of Russian Social Thought* (Vol. 16 of Translation into English of Foreign Social Science Monographs; New York: Columbia University, mimeographed, 1938), pp. 1–48. The introduction of social and literary culture during the eighteenth century is described in Emile Haumant, *La culture française en Russie* (Paris: Librairie Hachette, 1913), pp. 43–53, 69–118. See also Kluchevsky's summary statement in *op. cit.*, Vol. V, pp. 117–19.

[64] Cf. the analysis of corruption in Leroy-Beaulieu, *op. cit.*, Vol. II, pp. 97 ff., where it is shown to function as a substitute for representation.

This development of an aristocratic leisure class, as well as the ability of the Tsars to satisfy the demands of this class in a manner which ensured its political impotence, rested entirely upon an ever-increasing exploitation of the peasantry. Two numerical indexes of that exploitation may be cited. According to Lyashchenko, the total Russian population increased from 13 to 19 million between 1722 and 1762, and from 19 to 36 million between 1762 and 1796. In these same years the number of serfs increased from 4.4 (1724) to 7.6 and to 20 million persons.[65] Hence, the increase in the number of serfs greatly exceeded the increase of the population as a whole (163 per cent against 89 per cent from 1762 to 1796), a fact which is explained in large part by the grants of state lands and of state peasants to favored members of the aristocracy. The increasing exploitation of the peasantry is also indicated by the rise in average *obrok* payments, especially since the 1760's.

TABLE 2.   AVERAGE "OBROK" PAYMENTS PER PERSON (ANNUALLY) *

1760's	1–2	rubles
1770's	2–3	"
1780's	4	"
1790's	5	"
1810's	10–14	"

* Lyashchenko, *op. cit.*, pp. 315–16. From 1760 to 1790 *barshchina* obligations appear to have doubled. *Ibid.*, p. 314.

This rapid increase in the obligations of the peasantry along with the increase of its commercial and industrial activities reflected the growing pressure which arose from the competing claims of landowners and Tsarist officials.

Both looked upon the mass of peasant producers as the major source of income or revenue. Hence, every good harvest, every improvement, every expansion of peasant trade and production redounded to the benefit of the aristocracy and the government, unless the peasants managed to conceal their success. Moreover, landowners and officials made competing claims upon the earnings of the peasants. Tsarist officials had succeeded in raising the *obrok* to be paid by state peasants from 40 kopeks in 1718 to 3 rubles in 1783, a seven-fold increase. But they were not able to raise the souls-tax of the serfs on the landed estates of the aristocracy by more than 1½ times, since the landowners col-

[65] Lyashchenko, *op. cit.*, p. 273. The figure of 4.4 million serfs in 1724 is taken from Kluchevsky's analysis of the budget for that year. See Kluchevsky, *op. cit.*, Vol. IV, pp. 144–45.

lected this tax as well as their own dues and were able to increase their own take at the expense of the state.[66] Thus, while the landowners and the government officials were equally interested in exploiting the peasantry, the two groups had partly conflicting interests. This conflict of interests tended to intensify the pressure on the peasantry still further, and thus led to important consequences for the relations among the Tsar, the masters, and the serfs.

At the end of Peter's reign an official reported bad harvests and famine. He stated that the collection of the souls-tax had led to a wholesale pauperization of the peasants with the result that many of them fled the land. In the years 1719–1727, an official estimate had put the number of runaway peasants at 200,000, a figure which, in Kluchevsky's words, stood at a certain official distance from the facts. But such reports were disregarded since the landowners as well as the Tsarist officials were equally interested in increasing their immediate income and, hence, in perpetuating the conditions which produced pauperization and provoked mass migration.[67] Landowners were, moreover, the local administrators of the Tsarist government; and in view of their high social position and of the prevailing conception of serfs as beasts of burden, the government would seek to combat tax evasions and peasant flights by making the landowners responsible for the eradication of evils which their own abuse of the peasants had created. When the situation became worse rather than better, the Tsarist government would seek to check the abuses of the landowners by sending government officials or military units in order to interfere with the administration of local affairs.[68] While Tsarist officials were of course predisposed in favor of the landowners, and thoroughly averse from interfering with them, the government could not remain passive when its tax base and its recruitment of soldiers were in jeopardy. As a consequence, Tsarist policies vacillated throughout the century between the over-all tendency of granting further powers to the aristocracy and occasional efforts to check the resulting abuses by bureaucratic or military interference.

[66] Kluchevsky, *op. cit.*, Vol. V, pp. 88–89.

[67] The reminder may be useful at this point that the vast areas on Russia's inland frontiers were still subject to sporadic invasions during the eighteenth century, and that opportunities for escaping peasants increased with the distance from the centers of effective administrative and military control.

[68] See Kluchevsky, *op. cit.*, Vol. V, pp. 44–59, who describes the process by which provincial administration became divided between officials responsible to the central government and the local administrators responsible to the local landed aristocracy. Also Leroy-Beaulieu, *op. cit.*, Vol. II, pp. 89–91.

Time and again, officials of the government expressed their concern over the harshness of the landowners and the need to relieve the peasants of their overwhelming burdens. For example, a report for 1724 indicated that during the preceding year the collections of the souls-tax had fallen short by 18 per cent or some 850,000 rubles, because

> . . . nowhere can souls-tax moneys be collected in full, by reason of the leanness of the peasantry, and of the mischances of the harvest, and of needs to subtract sums which have twice or thrice been inscribed in the tax books, and of abscondings not pursuable, and of seizings of men for recruits, and of the case that many persons are grown old, or halt or blind, or are orphaned babes . . . or sons of soldiers with no land. . . .[69]

This report reflects the repercussions of bad administration, the inequity of a head tax imposed on all alike regardless of circumstances, and the manner in which the recruitment of soldiers interfered with the collection of taxes. Other measures reflected specifically the abuses of the landowners, and the weakness of the government in combating these admitted evils. For example, an edict of Catherine I accused the landowners of raiding the countryside like wolves; but the same edict charged them with the responsibility of collecting the souls-tax and of supervising the administration of municipalities. In a *règlement* of 1730 the landowners were instructed to forward the taxes bi-annually to the local government official, on pain of having a regiment sent to their estates to punish those responsible for the delay. Thus, the landowners were made liable, in principle, for the payment of the souls-tax, although they were of course exempted from the tax themselves. Sometimes, the government would interfere with the landowners to protect the peasants. For example, after a couple of bad harvests in 1733–1734, the government charged the landowners with the responsibility of feeding the peasants in times of scarcity and of advancing them seed corn. Nevertheless, starving peasants flocked to the cities in search of charity, and the government threatened the landowners with "torture and ruin" if they did not comply. There is ample evidence that such threats were without avail in many cases, even when the interests of the government were directly involved. In an edict of 1752, for instance, the government annulled tax arrears of 2.5 million rubles but admonished the local administrators and especially certain outstanding representatives of the aristocracy to improve their collection of the tax. Apparently this admonition had little effect, because eight years later the same dignitaries were officially accused of "diverse irregularities

---

[69] Quoted in Kluchevsky, *op. cit.*, Vol. IV, p. 143.

and illegalities." Even the immediate needs of the government for military supplies were neglected as a result of widespread local corruption; for example, vehicles for the standing army of 100,000 men were manufactured, but somehow failed to reach the supply depot.[70]

These illustrations make it clear that the conflicts between the Tsarist government and the landholding aristocracy were frequently resolved in favor of the latter. And indeed the rights and privileges of the aristocracy were increased again and again throughout the century. Aside from conferring upon landowners inalienable proprietary rights over their estates (1731), the government gradually extended their rights over the peasantry. While these laws often merely legalized established practices, such a legalization was significant ideologically because the government sanctioned a complete enslavement of the peasants at a time when it allowed ever more exemptions from state service to their lords. Hence, the customary legitimation that the ownership of serfs constituted a privilege in return for the military and civilian services which the aristocracy rendered was now being undermined by government edict. The general effect of this development was "to bring about both a juridical differentiation and a sharp moral estrangement between the hereditary *dvorianstvo* and the other social classes." [71]

A major reason for this extension of privileges was that Tsarist government sought to ensure its revenue by increasing the power of the landowners. In a sense, the serfs were owned jointly by the landowners and the state with the understanding that the landowners would collect the taxes from the serfs. Both the revenue of the state and the social and economic position of the aristocracy depended upon the productivity of the serfs. It was, therefore, logical that the government would sanction every abuse of power over the serfs on the widely accepted assumption that more exploitation would produce more income. The members of the aristocracy, however, did not concern themselves in most cases with the development of agricultural production or of rural industry. In view of their increasing preoccupation with advancing their position in the intertwined rank-orders of government and social life, the landowners would frequently view their estates not in terms of exploiting the land with the help of their serfs, but in terms of exploiting the serfs with the help of the land. And the extension of their power

---

[70] *Ibid.*, Vol. IV, pp. 324–29.

[71] *Ibid.*, Vol. IV, p. 338. The legal changes which document this extension of privileges and the simultaneous elimination of duties are summarized in *ibid.*, p. 334 and *passim*.

over the serfs certainly accentuated this view. Thus, when the Russian aristocracy was exempted from the compulsory obligation to serve the state, it did not become a class of rural proprietors. It became, instead, a class of masters who would use the power of the state to maximize their exploitation of serfs and on that basis advance their social and bureaucratic position.

It is now pertinent to turn from this discussion of the relations among the Tsars, their officials, and the landed aristocracy to a consideration of the peasantry. In the course of the seventeenth century, a tradition of universal subservience to the Tsar had been established, as the development of an aristocracy of service was paralleled by the gradual enserfment of the peasantry. The subservience of all persons to the Tsar's unlimited authority implied, however, that the Tsar would also act as a court of last appeal, who would hear grievances and prevent injustice. Documents from the seventeenth century indicate that the peasants acted upon this belief in the Tsar as the supreme arbiter, when they addressed to him petitions in which they sought to obtain relief from the oppression of their masters. And an outspoken defender of Tsarist authority like the early eighteenth-century writer Pososhkov expressed the same view, when he stated that the Tsar was the true lord of all the people, and that the landowners had the peasant serfs "in their keeping . . . for a season only." [72] This ultimate authority of the Tsar over the peasantry has been of major significance in the social history of Russia, even though it was obscured time and again by the indefinite extension of the landowners' power over their serfs. The basic pattern of the relations between employers and workers in Tsarist Russia (and in a modified sense even in Soviet Russia and her satellites) was shaped by this supremacy of the Tsars.

This sweeping assertion presents another paradox. The history of eighteenth-century Russia is very largely a history of administrative failure with regard to the peasantry. In edict after edict the Tsars sought to deal with the fact that large numbers of peasant serfs would escape the burdens of taxation and personal oppression by leaving "their" land. Yet neither the edicts nor the cruel punishments could

[72] Cf. the text of a petition addressed to the Tsar by the peasants of Count Shyedakov, in 1625, reprinted in Valentin Gitermann, *op. cit.*, Vol. I, pp. 472–73. In this petition the count's exploitation of his peasants (e.g., his demand of two *obrok* payments) is linked repeatedly with his immoral conduct, and the cringing but sly appeal is made to the Tsar as the benevolent father of his people. Pososhkov's statement is quoted in Kluchevsky, *op. cit.*, Vol. IV, p. 103.

cope with these symptoms, let alone with their underlying causes.[73]
This persistent failure of the government is well illustrated by repeated
modifications of the law, according to which escaped serfs must be
returned to their owners. Time and again, the authorities found it
expedient to leave serfs on the land where they had settled after their
flight, for to return them would create a new shortage of labor as well
as add to the mobility which the government sought to prevent. And
the steadily increasing prerogatives over the peasantry, which the Tsars
granted to the aristocracy, were both another way of dealing with the
peasant problem and a tacit acknowledgement of failure on the part of
the Tsarist government itself. If it is somewhat paradoxical that the
Tsars retained the political initiative despite the ever increasing prerogatives granted to the aristocracy, it is at least equally puzzling that they
retained the ultimate authority over the peasants despite their apparent
inability to exercise that authority.

This problem may be most readily understood in connection with the
rule of Peter the Great. I have already mentioned the enormous
pressure which Peter's efforts to develop the country placed upon all
ranks of society. These efforts involved not only a staggering increase
of obligations of every kind, but also a peremptory and seemingly meaningless interference with established traditions. The underlying temper
of Peter's reforms was the totalitarian assumption that everything he
ordered was possible. On that assumption it became logical to issue
orders without regard to the feasibility of their execution, and then to
inflict extraordinary punishments upon those held responsible for failure. While there was a minority to whom Peter appeared as the father
leading his children out of darkness,

> . . . many people of an indifferent or an obdurate cast of mind could
> not but recoil from the methods and the conditions inevitably connected
> with an activity which sought attainment of its ends rather through
> authoritative might than through spiritual influence . . . and governed
> the State mostly from the post-chaise and the stagehouse, and thought
> always of affairs, and never of persons, and felt too assured of its power
> to be capable of indulgence toward passive resistance.[74]

Thus, Peter aroused hostility and a multitude of simmering grievances,
which were widespread among the masses of the people as well as among
the aristocracy. And the manner in which this tacit opposition was

[73] Leroy-Beaulieu analyzes the bureaucracy and shows how it supported the
supreme power of the Tsar, but made his rule ineffective. See *op. cit.*, Vol. II,
pp. 109 ff.

[74] Kluchevsky, *op. cit.*, Vol. IV, p. 227.

expressed, during Peter's reign as well as after his death, reveals how the relations among the Tsar, the masters, and the serfs were popularly conceived.

Peter had certainly departed from the accustomed role of the Tsar. His predecessors had been aloof from the people; only the officials of the government were visible to them; hence, blame was attached to these officials, not to the Tsar himself. But Peter destroyed this aspect of Tsarist authority. He was in direct contact with his people; he discarded the ritual and paraphernalia of the court; he was famous for his craftmanship and his eagerness to work with his hands; and he was infamous for his German dress, his war on beards and Russian costume, and his liking for coarse manners and amusements. No Tsar before Peter had ever done such things as he: acting on occasion as the personal executioner of rebels, sending his wife to a convent, drinking with foreigners, melting down church bells to make cannon. Kluchevsky cites some of the gossip which was overheard by police officials.[75] Peasants were heard to say that there had not been a single day of prosperity since "God sent us this Tsar for a ruler." The village was overburdened by taxes and other obligations, so that no one could gain respite from these impositions. There was doubt whether Peter was a Russian at all.

> "A fine Tsar this!" the Moscow police reported a peasant as saying, "A Tsar born of a German outcast, and abandoned as a foundling! Aye, for before the Tsaritsa had left childbed she did say unto him: 'No son of mine art thou. Thou art a changeling.' And for yourselves can ye see that always he doth wear German clothing! Known unto all men is it that he is one come of the Germans."

It was asserted that this Tsar was the anti-Christ, for he had compelled people to shave their beards (or pay a tax) and to wear German clothing. It was well known that he disregarded fast days, and he had even changed the sacred calendar.

Contemporary experience with totalitarian regimes has sensitized us to the significance of gossip and rumor. They are weapons in the political struggle, when all politics are suppressed. To be sure, the legends concerning Peter as usurper and anti-Christ simply reflected the popular resentment of the burdens he had imposed and of the ruthlessness with which he had violated cherished traditions. These rumors also implied that a Tsar who did such outrageous things could not be the "rightful" Tsar. The people cast Peter in the image of the usurper

[75] *Ibid.,* Vol. IV, pp. 234–36.

and anti-Christ, because that would explain an arbitrary and oppressive regime whose purposes they could not understand. In a world out of joint it was imperative to find a symbol which made such profound disorder meaningful, even if this did nothing to make suffering more tolerable. But such expressions of popular hostility show also that the peasants accepted the ultimate authority of the Tsar as their judge and father. If they questioned the Tsar's claim to the throne when he failed to act as their protector, that response still reflected the official justification of Tsarist authority. Indeed, their use of the official view was their only political weapon. And the peasants' belief in the Tsar as the father of his people may well be one reason why the autocratic power of the Tsars remained unchallenged even as the Tsars became unable and unwilling to exercise that authority against the will of the aristocracy.

The open rebellion of peasants and Cossacks under the leadership of Pugachev in 1773–1774 is a case in point. Pugachev represented himself as Peter III, who had merely been in hiding, and who had now reappeared to lead his people to liberation. The immediate reason for impersonating Peter III may have been that under Catherine II the oppression of the peasants had increased precipitously. And since Peter III had been overthrown by favorites of the Empress, the people associated their desires with his name. At any rate, following his reign in 1762, there were no less than five persons who represented themselves as Peter III and it may be added that during the seventeenth and eighteenth centuries several dozen such pretenders to the throne had appeared. Apparently, the people felt that their revolt against oppression was legitimate and they could express that feeling best by finding, or if need be by inventing, a pretender who would become the new and the just Tsar. If it seemed reasonable to suspect the legitimacy of the incumbent Tsar because he had tolerated the oppression of his people, it was just as reasonable to justify a revolt against him on the ground that a successor had appeared among the people, whose claim was legitimate because he opposed oppression.

One cannot assume that the followers of such supposed Tsars, who were very numerous in many instances, thoroughly believed in the genuine character of the pretender's claim. Such ideas of pretenders to the Throne are accepted where dissatisfaction and oppression are rife. Each rumor of the appearance of a pretended ruler or of his pretended relative is welcomed by the masses with satisfaction, because they attach to it the hope that the position of the people will be improved. Many of these rumors have no basis in fact whatever. Where no one was found to play the role of the pretender, the phantom of such a pretender was invented and this also produced the desired effect. Thus, there was no one among the followers of the famous brigand Stenka Rasin, who really assumed the role of the former Patriarch Nikon, but it was sufficient that one pointed to the boat on which the patriarch was said to be, in order to arouse the imagination of the people.[76]

Thus, the peasants followed pretenders like Pugachev because they desired some show of legitimacy, and their quest for liberation probably made them disregard whatever lingering doubts they had.

Although these popular uprisings were unsuccessful, they had considerable political significance. The Tsars whom the pretenders sought to impersonate were frequently figures who had met with violent death in the palace revolutions of the eighteenth century. In the eyes of the people such figures symbolized opposition to the ruling regime. And by identifying their protest with the defeated side in the repeated struggles over succession, as well as by the circulation of rumors, the peasants participated in the political life of the nation. Pugachev's rebellion of 1773–1774 was of special significance in this respect, because it expressed the mass excitement which had resulted from the Act of 1762. Since by this edict Peter III had liberated the aristocracy from its compulsory obligation to serve the state, he had also aroused the expectation that another decree would order the emancipation of the peasants. To be sure, these expectations were frequently denounced by spokesmen of the Tsarist government; but in the face of mounting oppression at the hands of landowners, whose privileges were increased as their duties declined, "false" rumors of emancipation became an important weapon in the struggle of the peasants against their masters.

When men are subjected to the crushing burdens of a tyrannical regime, they will attempt to maintain their self-respect and keep alive their hope for a better future. Under the conditions of eighteenth-century Russia these two drives tended to be mutually exclusive. The self-respect of the peasants was identified with an insistence on their legitimate rights.[77] But these rights had been abrogated with every

[76] Alexander Bruckner, "Zur Naturgeschichte der Prätendenten," in *Beiträge zur Kulturgeschichte Russlands im 17. Jahrhundert* (Leipzig: B. Elischer, 1887), p. 30. Cf. also Mavor, *op. cit.,* Vol. II, pp. 43–44.

[77] It may be of interest to add that according to Vernadsky "the peasants of all categories were still personally free in the Mongol period. Moreover, the East Russian peasant of this period was not a mere tenant on somebody else's land but had his own right—the 'toiler's right' (*trudovoe pravo*)—on the piece of land he actually tilled. . . . Nobody could legally remove him from his farm, and his rights on it were recognized by the courts—as long as he continued to work on the land and pay his taxes." See Vernadsky, *op. cit.,* p. 376. No doubt, the peasants embellished this right and made it appear to be more recent than it was.

further increase in the privileges of the aristocracy, so that hope for a better future found less and less support in reality. Hence, the peasants would seek to maintain through hope and fantasy what was denied them by the Tsar. Their rights were abrogated illegitimately. The Tsar would do justice, but his officials abused their authority. Edicts of the government were either forged or would soon be replaced by more favorable actions. And when the highest authority confirmed all the wrongs which had been done them, the peasants concluded that the Tsar was in the hands of evil advisors, or else that he was not the "rightful" Tsar. There was an unwitting purposiveness in this spread of rumors by which the peasants would "defend" themselves under conditions that allowed no defense.

> If that which they expected did not happen immediately, they soon began to exhibit symptoms of disorder. For example, when they learned that Peter III had forbidden the purchase of peasants for the factories, the previously purchased peasants understood that this meant freedom for them, and forthwith began to act upon this belief. So also when the peasants of the Church were transferred to the State, and when the nobility were released from compulsory service, the peasants thought that freedom for them must ensue. When this result did not follow, they regarded themselves as being defrauded by the proprietors of the benefits which had been conferred upon them by the Tsar. In general, they refused to believe that ukases were genuine unless the ukases gave them what they wanted. If an alleged ukase met their views, they customarily regarded it as genuine, in spite of evidence to the contrary. Peasants and Cossacks alike were thus peculiarly exposed to deception by false ukases and by impostors. It may be that this and other peasant traits were the natural consequences of habitual oppression . . . (which) predisposed peasant and Cossack alike to look always for some benefit from above—to hope always for some ukase of the Tsar which would by a stroke of the pen alter all conditions of their life. The peasants were indeed always in an attitude of expectancy that a Messiah would arise among them and by a mere announcement prevent oppression and bestow upon them economical prosperity.[78]

In this manner the masses of peasants helped to perpetuate the belief in Tsarist autocracy; for despite the Tsars' frequent inability to implement that belief by controlling the local authority of landowners, the peasants continued to seek relief from oppression by petitioning the Tsar.

[78] Mavor, op. cit., Vol. II, p. 25. The use of rumors by the politically impotent is a very widespread phenomenon. Exact parallels to the Russian experience may be found in J. Ziekursch, Hundert Jahre Schlesischer Agrargeschichte (Breslau: Ferdinand Hirt, 1915), pp. 211, 241 ff., 315, 372.

In this respect the peasants and their masters "agreed." For the aristocracy also helped to support the ultimate authority of the Tsar by competing for ever more privileges from the Tsar rather than by employing its considerable prerogatives in a quest for political power. And it is important to recognize that on occasion even the inarticulate response of the peasants had its political effects. In her efforts to win support for her reign, Catherine II had made a propaganda tour of the provinces prior to the "election" of the "legislative" commission of 1767. On this tour she had accepted hundreds of petitions; but after the commission was assembled, she denied the peasants the right to address to her petitions against their masters. Henceforth, they should be submitted to the delegates in the commission. When the commission was discontinued, this abrogation of the right to petition the Empress remained as a concession to the aristocracy. But Catherine II continued to receive them, nevertheless, for she could not abandon the claim to be the protector of her subjects, even though she had no intention of interfering with the landowners' power over their serfs.[79] Under these circumstances Tsarist autocracy continued as an ideology which all social groups accepted and sought to utilize for their own advantage.

d. The Ideologies of the Masters

In eighteenth-century Russia the Tsars retained their autocratic supremacy despite the increasing authority of the landed aristocracy and despite its absolute power over the serfs. By using the premises of autocratic rule for its own ends, the popular protest of the masses had a similar political effect. I shall turn now to a consideration of the ideologies which emerged from these social and political relations among the Tsar, the aristocracy, and the serfs, and which had a direct effect upon the relations between employers and workers. These considerations will carry us well into the nineteenth century, for the class relations and ideologies which had come to prevail during the eighteenth century remained relatively unaffected by the political developments up to the emancipation of the serfs in 1861.

Toward the end of the eighteenth century, different types of economic enterprises existed side by side. Enterprises of the state were either managed by officials of the government or leased to private entrepreneurs. Manufacturing enterprises and the so-called mountain works were located on the landed estates of the aristocracy. And commercial or industrial enterprises were in the hands of foreign or native merchants

---

[79] See Sacke, *Die Gesetzgebende Kommission Katharinas II*, pp. 98–99, 117–19.

and manufacturers. The agents and owners who managed these enterprises exercised their power over the serfs and the free laborers on the assumption that nothing but ill will and laziness could be expected of them. Work, they believed, was the result of fear, and punishments must be cruel and frequent, or else fear, and hence the stimulus to labor, would diminish. Of course, there were exceptions; wherever the exercise of power over subordinates is absolute and arbitrary, it can be benevolent as well as tyrannical. And it may be that the chances for benevolence were greater among those managers whose wealth and social position were very secure, and consequently relieved them of all pressures which in others would aggravate their exercise of power. Among the landowners the chances for a benevolent treatment of the peasant serfs increased also, wherever such treatment would enhance the commercial and productive enterprises among the serfs and hence accrue to the benefit of the masters. Such due allowances should certainly be made, but they merely take account of individual idiosyncrasies. The chances for moral conduct in the mass are probably greatest when they are favored by the general conditions of a social order, and such conditions did not exist in eighteenth- and nineteenth-century Russia.

Several documents illustrate the prevailing ideologies of the masters. In 1717 Peter the Great ordered the translation of a German manual entitled *The True Mirror of Youth or Instructions in Etiquette*. Along with illuminating instructions on how to behave in public, the young nobleman was advised how he should treat his servants. He should converse in a foreign language so as to distinguish himself from "various numskulls" and to prevent servants from understanding what he said. He should not speak with servants more than was necessary. And he should not trust them, for they distort what they hear and they divulge secrets.

> He who keeps good discipline in his household is served well and respectfully, for the slaves are by nature impolite, stubborn, and shameless. Therefore, it is necessary to break their spirit and to humiliate them.[80]

These instructions referred originally to the treatment of domestic servants. But the Russian translation referred instead to "slaves." Its popularity suggests that the Russian readers perceived little or no difference between unruly domestic "slaves" and the mass of peasant serfs. The whole approach implied a sense of rank-order, which was

[80] Quoted in Plekhanov, *op. cit.*, p. 21. See also pp. 18–22 and Kluchevsky, *op. cit.*, Vol. IV, pp. 259–60.

expressed with classic simplicity over a hundred years later in the address of an aristocratic landowner to his peasants.

> I am your master, and my master is the Emperor. The Emperor can issue his commands to me, and I must obey him; but he issues no commands to you. I am the Emperor upon my estate; I am your God in this world, and I have to answer for you to the God above.[81]

The implications of this ideology for the relations between the employer and his workmen are revealed in a report by John Perry, an English engineer who had been engaged by Peter the Great to act as supervisor of canal construction and of other projects. Perry observed that peasant serfs who were skilled craftsmen would anxiously hide their ability at all times. It was apparent that they anticipated an even more intensified exploitation by their masters, if their ability became known. In Perry's judgment, the major obstacle to improvement was the practice of demanding work without wages.

> . . . this being the custom of Russia, when I have made my utmost application for the encouragement of some few persons who have been really ingenious, that they might have but a copeck a day reward allow'd them to animate the rest, I have received for answer, particularly by my lord Apraxin . . . that there was no such precedent for the giving of money out of the Czar's treasure for men to do their duty for which they were sent; but in the place of it they had batoags that grew in Russia, and if they did not do their work, when requir'd, they must be beaten to it.[82]

A similar attitude is revealed by a set of instructions which a landowner, Count P. A. Rumiantsev, gave to his estate steward in 1751. The Count was a military man who conceived of the household order on his estate after the manner of a commander in the army. Serfs were to receive the most severe penalties for every misdemeanor. Petty theft, for example, was to be punished by loss of property, flagellation with whips, and consignment to the army, penalties which the legal code reserved for such crimes as brigandage or arson. For insulting a master the serfs were to be beaten with rods until the insulted person was satisfied, aside from a fine of two rubles to the master.[83] General practices such as the trade in serfs and the frequent disregard of court jurisdiction in

---

[81] Cited in Baron von Haxthausen, *The Russian Empire, Its People, Institutions, and Resources* (London: Chapman and Hall, 1856), Vol. I, p. 335.

[82] John Perry, "The State of Russia," in Peter Putnam, ed., *Seven Britons in Imperial Russia* (Princeton: Princeton University Press, 1952), p. 61. Apraxin was an admiral in the Russian navy under Peter the Great.

[83] See Kluchevsky, *op. cit.*, Vol. V, pp. 82–83, where this and other examples are cited.

criminal cases or special evils such as the breakup of peasant families went unchecked.

Such absolute power of the masters over their serfs was interpreted as a principle of government which supported the established social order. Consequently, proposed reforms concerning the serfs were persistently rejected on the ground that nothing should be done to interfere with the power of the landowners. According to one critic, a grant of rights to the peasants would only mean that the landowners might violate the law, a contingency that could be avoided, obviously, if no rights were granted.[84] Even masters who had committed crimes against their serfs, like murder or rape, were immune from prosecution, though such crimes were legally prohibited. The law forbade the serfs to enter complaints against their masters, and the police officials, who were ordered to uphold the law, would not proceed against members of the aristocracy. It is significant that the serfs had only one right which limited the power of their masters, and that right was a duty. The serfs were obliged to bring complaints against their masters in case the latter had committed crimes against the state.[85] Hence, the subjugation of the serfs was limited by the interests of the state. Yet, many actions of the masters interfered with these interests, even if they did not constitute crimes against the state. And the simultaneous effort of the Tsars to safeguard these interests *and* to support the pre-eminent position of the aristocracy led to an ambivalent approach to the governmental control of labor relations.

A Senate investigation of privately owned mountain works under Catherine II illustrates the dilemma.[86] According to an official memorandum, the major task was to bring the peasants "into the usual slavish obedience." Where disturbances continued, a manifesto of the Empress was to be read to the peasants, according to which "those who oppose our authority resist God." Such declarations and the presence of military forces were frequently insufficient, however, and the ideology of leading Tsarist officials is revealed in their "solution" of the recurrent

---

[84] See Engelmann, *op. cit.*, pp. 134–51.

[85] *Ibid.*, pp. 155–56. It is in keeping with the character of autocratic rule that the one right of the serfs was officially regarded as a duty, while the "rights" of the aristocracy were, in fact, privileges inasmuch as they were subject to an arbitrary revocation by the Tsar.

[86] Like others, this investigation, in 1762, was initiated as a result of local uprisings and numerous petitions. Of course, the distinction between petitions and uprisings often depended on how officials chose to regard the petitions submitted to them.

difficulties in the mountain works. In her Manifesto Catherine II revealed herself as the protector of all her subjects.

> Our just and merciful intention is to correct the simple and those who have fallen into error, to defend those against whom offences have been committed, and to avoid direct aggression against the peasants by administering the works to their advantage, paying them according to their labor, or allowing them to go from the works as may be found more advantageous for their own welfare and for the safety of the works.

In her instructions, however, the Empress directed Prince Vyazemsky to punish the peasants for their insubordination, and then to inquire into their grievances. If owners or their managers were found to be at fault, then these individuals should be punished also. Punishment of individuals in the highest ranks was reserved for the Empress. Moreover, the instructions added the observation that owners or managers should not be punished except in the most extreme cases, because otherwise the peasants might become too proud. And if their offenses were relatively minor, then punishment should be administered in secret, so that "the simple people might not be given a motive to step out of servility." [87] Apparently, the need of the government to correct the abuses of the owners was checked at every point by the fear that the "insolence of the peasants" would gain the upper hand.

Since the government was unable and unwilling to penalize highly placed persons, it tended to avoid the issue by entrusting the management of mountain works to its own officials. In the period from 1762 to 1796 the number of serfs in the mountain works of the Treasury increased almost three times, while in the privately owned works it increased only by a little more than one-half.[88] The reason for this discrepancy was that the government found itself unable to transfer these works to private ownership despite the fact that whole villages would be ascribed to the new owner and all necessary equipment would be furnished as well. Apparently, the aristocratic landowners who were

---

[87] Quotations from the Manifesto and the instructions in Mavor, op. cit., I, pp. 454–55. It may be added that some managers and clerks of the mountain works were actually punished, though superior officials were not. Vyazemsky was also reluctant to find those responsible for the deaths of peasants from beating. Cf. ibid., Vol. I, p. 461. The investigation of Prince Vyazemsky was greeted by the peasants in the expectation that finally the Empress herself had decided to right all wrongs. When their previous condition was confirmed by the highest authority instead, the peasants became ready to join Pugachev. See ibid., pp. 464–65.

[88] The figures are respectively: from 99,000 to 241,000 and from 43,000 to 71,000. See Mavor, op. cit., Vol. I, pp. 441, 493, cited on p. 144, n. 53.

so favored either shunned the obligation to make payments and deliveries to the government or they failed to meet these obligations through the inefficiency of their agents. Thus, when Count Shuvalov died, two of his mountain works owed the Treasury 600,000 rubles, and the government resumed operation in an attempt to obtain partial payment of the arrears which had accumulated.[89] The need of the government to receive deliveries from these enterprises, however, was only one of the reasons why most of them remained under the management of officials.

An equally important reason was the fact that the treatment of the ascribed workers deteriorated seriously when these mountain works were transferred from the Treasury into the hands of private owners. Such transfers were accompanied by drastic reduction in wages, by the employment of artisans who had been exempt from such service, by the prohibition of work outside the enterprise which had been permitted before by payment in kind rather than money, by arbitrary removal over great distances, and many others.[90] Of course, the government officials who managed the mountain works of the Treasury probably were as inefficient and corrupt as the agents of private owners. And government officials as well as private agents conceived of the peasant serfs as chattels to be exploited for the benefit of the owner, whether he was the Tsar or a private landlord. The difference between these two groups was therefore by no means clear-cut, but it was significant nonetheless. The private owner of a mine or his agent could be single-minded in the exploitation of his serfs, because he could always count upon the aid of the military authorities to protect life and property against uprisings of the peasant serfs. Government officials, however, were responsible themselves for the success or failure of their management. Their somewhat greater leniency may have been due, therefore, to the recognition that the brutal treatment of serfs led time and again to disturbances the government was called upon to suppress.

If the government continued for the most part to have its own officials manage the mountain works because it could not control the actions of the landed aristocracy, the same reasoning did not apply to the enterprises of merchants and manufacturers. The supervision of these

---

[89] And this action led in turn to disturbances among the peasants, who claimed that an edict of the government had limited their period of service, and that they were consequently free to leave. Of course, no such edict existed, but the resumption of government operations sufficed for rumors to start. See *ibid.*, Vol. I, pp. 473–74.

[90] *Ibid.*, Vol. I, p. 495. Other examples are given on the following pages.

"possessional factories" may be contrasted, therefore, with the virtual absence of supervision with regard to the aristocratic owners of mountain works. Owners of "possessional" enterprises were not permitted to dissolve them, or to sell the ascribed workers without also selling the enterprise, or to transfer these workers to a different enterprise, or to change the organization of production, or to limit output. No change of ownership was permitted without prior authorization by the government. The workers who had been ascribed to the enterprise were to be paid a "sufficient" wage, though the government granted the owners the right to determine the wage rate and the length of the working day. Workers were also given official permission to petition against the regulations of the owners. The government reserved the right to dispossess the owner of a "possessional factory," for example, when he discontinued production. And the government threatened to emancipate the workers if the owner employed the workers as domestic servants rather than in production.[91] This public regulation of the employment relationship had the same purpose as the public management of the mountain works: to safeguard the production of goods needed by the government. And it simply reflected the weak position of middle-class entrepreneurs that the government sought to regulate their power over the workers but made no comparable attempt to regulate the landowners' power over their serfs.[92]

To be sure, these regulations were frequently not enforced, and the employers acted as if their powers over the workers were the same as those of the landowners. But the assumption that the government would determine the organization of labor and of production had far-reaching consequences even if opinions concerning this role of the government varied widely. In 1818, officials of the Ministry of the Interior stated that the unrest of workers in the "possessional" enterprises was due to the failure of the government to regulate

> . . . the reciprocal relations and duties of owners and workers. Wages still depend upon the arbitrary decisions of the owner, who naturally proceeds in a selfish manner, since he is not obliged to give an accounting

[91] These details are given in Tugan-Baranowski, *op. cit.*, pp. 130–31. The official sanction of the right to petition was formally revoked in 1767 with reference to aristocratic landowners, but not with regard to middle-class entrepreneurs; however, petitions continued to be submitted regardless of whether they were allowed or prohibited.

[92] *Ibid.*, p. 29. While the entrepreneurs had been permitted in 1736 to discipline the ascribed workers by corporal punishment, all further penalties were to be administered by governmental authorities to whom "delinquent" workers were to be handed over by their employers.

to the government. . . . By the same token the workers are lazy, which in turn leads to penalties and corporal punishment, and that gives them the excuse to address wailing protests to the government.

Only a thoroughgoing regulation of all the "possessional" enterprises would put an end to this. Yet, the same Ministry was of a different opinion eight years later (1826). By then the regulation of the largest "possessional" enterprises had been attempted in view of the interminable complaints by owners about workers and by workers about owners. This had not solved the problem, however, for aside from the specific problems involved there was this basic difficulty:

> The factory regulations set down how the owner should use his workers; hence the latter have an excuse to think of themselves as independent and to resist their master as soon as he undertakes anything at all. . . . The workers imagine that they are not obliged to produce for their master unless this is stipulated in the regulation. Hence, the authority of the owner is held by them in little esteem.[93]

Thus, the officials would vacillate between the attempt to regulate everything and the recognition that regulations produced more problems than they solved. And this vacillation was necessarily increased by employers who wanted the government to aid their exploitation of the work force and by aristocratic spokesmen who would criticize the conduct of these employers and represent themselves (on these occasions) as paternalistic protectors of the serfs.[94]

Such varied opinions were necessarily reflected in the actual regulation of the employment relationship. Officials of the central government tended to favor the middle-class entrepreneur, since deliveries to the government depended upon the continuity of production. Local administrators, on the other hand, were concerned with maintaining peace and order, aside from their general antagonism to middle-class employers, and they would at times placate the workers by listening to their complaints.[95] Thus, self-interest and expediency governed the actions of those concerned with the relations between employers and workers. Yet such considerations led to consequences which transcended expediency. Employers, officials, and landowners were unanimous in the belief that "it is necessary to break the spirit [of the workers] and to humiliate them." But the conflict of interest among them prevented a clear-cut approach to factory regulation, which alternated rather between attempts to supervise the employers as well as the workers in

---

[93] Quoted in Tugan-Baranowski, *op. cit.*, pp. 137–40.
[94] The details of this controversy are given in *ibid.*, pp. 190–95, 198–201.
[95] *Ibid.*, p. 194.

response to the complaints from both sides and efforts to ensure the complete subordination of the workers to their employers. The resulting uncertainty of the masters encouraged among the workers the familiar idea, compounded of expediency and sincere conviction, that their cruel suffering was the work of officials who abused their authority. The workers believed above all that the supreme authority of the Tsar gave the government the power and the responsibility to right their wrongs, while it gave the people the right to petition the Tsar. Thus, the ideologies of the masters not only committed the government to certain lines of action, but also gave rise to expectations among the masses. It will be useful to examine the resulting interaction of officials, employers, and workers, for their conflicting beliefs established the basic pattern of labor management in the more developed industry of the later nineteenth century.

On the basis of files in the Ministry of Finance Tugan-Baranowski surveyed the history of unrest in twenty-three "possessional" enterprises, and his findings, which cover the period from the 1790's to the 1840's, give an insight into the practical implications of the ideologies I have discussed. Low wages were the most frequent source of unrest, especially where free workers were employed also, since the latter earned often twice as much as the "possessional" workers. Complaints were frequent also with reference to the penalties and deductions which were imposed by the employers. In other cases unrest was occasioned by the work conditions imposed on children or on the aged and infirm, such as a fifteen- to seventeen-hour day in the winter. Again, some of the very old workers were simply deprived of all wages. There were complaints about cruel mistreatment, complaints against the military recruitment of workers in lieu of the serfs belonging to the employer, against the sale of workers' families to estate owners, against the use of land belonging to the workers in the interest of the employers, against the employment of workers on other tasks than factory labor, against the refusal to issue passports [96] to workers, against prohibiting women to marry persons outside the factory's work force, and so on. The long list reflects typical complaints of workers in the early phases of industrialization as well as the peculiar problems arising from the use of forced labor in the Russian factories of the late eighteenth and early nineteenth centuries.[97]

It is of interest to see how the Tsarist government handled these recurrent complaints, and in the case of several factories Tugan-Baranow-

[96] Instituted by the Tsarist government in an effort to regulate internal migration and to ensure the collection of taxes.

[97] Ibid., pp. 159–62.

ski presents case histories of "labor relations" for a fifty-year period. One of these concerns the "possessional" enterprise of Osokin in Kazan, in which a total of 1,400 ascribed workers were employed. A schematic tabulation of this case history provides us with a summary view of the interaction among officials, employers, and workers, even though the case involved "possessional" workers only.[98] In the overwhelming majority of instances the authorities sided with the employers, and met the protest of the workers with dire warnings and severe punishments. In a few cases the government recognized the justice of a complaint against the employer. But more important than the partiality of the officials was the *assumption of employers and workers alike that the government and even the Tsar personally would determine their rights and obligations.* Hence, employers looked to the authorities for support in their dealings with recalcitrant workers, while the workers appealed to the same authorities to hear their grievances and protect them against abuse and exploitation.

Efforts by the authorities to stabilize the relations between employers and workers by comprehensive regulations (e.g., the rules established in 1818) were of no avail. By these rules the authorities sought to secure for the employer his absolute power over the workers. And since they identified his power with the security of the established order, they would consistently refuse the petitions of the workers and indeed deny them the right of petition. Yet, this position of the government was inherently unstable. By its comprehensive regulation of the relations between employers and workers the government asserted its ultimate authority over both groups, and then it proceeded to use this authority to grant complete powers to the employers and deny all rights to the workers. Both of these actions had their rationale. The Tsarist government was in the hands of aristocrats, who could never consent to grant to a middle-class employer the same absolute power which they regarded as an exclusive prerogative of the aristocracy; hence, the employer's actions had to be regulated. The same officials were also concerned with safeguarding the established order: hence, the employer must have complete authority over his workers and all peti-

---

[98] I treat this case history as representative for these reasons. It is one of several contained in Tugan-Baranowski, and all of these tell the same story. Also, it gives the same picture as the material on privately owned mountain works, to which reference has been made, if allowance is made for the difference of rural and urban location and the consequent differences in the labor problem. It is further in keeping with the logic of the situation arising from the relations among officials, employers, aristocratic landowners, and workers, which have been analyzed.

TABLE 3.   SCHEMATIC HISTORY OF LABOR RELATIONS IN A KAZAN FACTORY, 1796–1849 *

Year	Workers Petition Against	Petition of Employer	Addressed to	Action of Government and Result
1796	Low wages.		Senator Mavrin (on local inspection)	Senator accepts petition; wages increased.
1798	Low wages, cruelty of employer		Tsar Paul	Dismissed as groundless by government officials.
1800	Low wages, cruelty of employer		Minister of Justice	Rejected; workers threatened with dire penalties, commanded to vouch for future obedience in writing; workers refuse
1806		For more ample authority over the workers, employment of women.	Senate	Employer authorized to punish workers for refusal to work and misdemeanors; workers resist employment of women.
1813	Punishment of fellow-workers by the *knut* and transportation to Siberia.		Senate	Petition called officially the result of "cantankerous self-deception"; petitioning workers indicted for bringing false charges; provincial governor instructed to ensure obedience of workers.
1817	Employers' illegal exercise of authority over them, on the basis that they were descendants of free-men and had not been purchased.		Count Pavlovic	Petition declared to be without foundation; workers are ordered to declare their obedience to their masters in writing.

1817–1818	Same as above.	Tsar	Never reached the Tsar; workers' two emissaries imprisoned and tortured; one died as a result. Government official sent to investigate the affair insists on the need to enforce obedience to the master and to destroy workers' false ideas of freedom. *He also lays down rules for the factory.*
1818	Cruel treatment leading to violent death of fellow workers; owner's disregard of several edicts.	Minister of Interior and President of the Council of the State	Senate instructs Governor to seek out those who had incited the workers and send them for life to the cloth factory at Irkutsk.
1819	Mistreatment.	Two senators	Senators demand that the government put an end to the arbitrary actions of the workers by severe measures. Workers refuse to work.
1820	Mistreatment.	Governor	Governor demands written promise to obey masters. Government confirms the 1818 regulations which are read by Governor. Workers protest. Ten of them are arrested, 8 of whom were sent to Irkutsk.
1820–1823	Similar petitions repeated.	Minister of Interior	Government investigation of secret agreement among workers not to yield. Eleven workers are severely whipped. At least one of them dies during whipping.
1829 and 1832	Cruel treatment and disregard of petitions by Kazan Governor.	Tsar Nicholas	Workers are told that they were deluded by fantastic demands and are guilty of rebellious moods.
1834	Cruel treatment and unjust conscription to Army.	Tsar Nicholas	Investigation Commission appointed to convince workers that they were legally bound to the factory. But workers continue demands for emancipation and complaints of cruelty.
1836	Old charges reiterated.	Tsar Nicholas	Large numbers of workers whipped cruelly; 51 workers sent to military service or Siberia. Employer given right to force wives and children to work in factory. Workers continue resistance.
1849			Emancipation of workers.

* Based on Tugan-Baranowski, *op. cit.*, pp. 167–76.

tions against him must be denied. It is not surprising that the workers in effect utilized this inherent contradiction. They would accept the autocratic supremacy of the Tsar and seek to enlist it on behalf of a control over the employers. The government could not explicitly reject this demand; it could only declare that it was the Tsar's arbitrary will to give absolute power to the employer. But by their astonishing perseverance in the face of all methods of oppression, the workers helped to establish, albeit unwittingly and in the long run, that it was impossible for the Tsar to assert his absolute authority and to divest himself of it at one and the same time.[99] This "limitation" of autocratic power had a profound impact upon the relations between employers and workers, for eventually it compelled the Tsarist government to extend rather than restrict its regulation of manufacturing enterprises.

e. The Management of Industry in an Autocratic Regime

During the years preceding and following the emancipation of the serfs (1861), the Russian economy began to develop more rapidly than before. The number of industrial enterprises in the towns increased, the creation of an industrial work force was accelerated, and employers became more insistent in their demands for freedom from governmental regulation. These changes posed a basic problem for the Tsarist regime, because they offered new opportunities for freedom for individuals and groups, while the Tsar and his officials were unwilling or unable to relinquish the principle of autocratic rule. According to this principle, the position of each social class and the relations among them are regulated by the government. The fact is that emancipation even led to an extension of governmental regulations rather than the reverse. In the past, the government had granted the landowners complete power over the serfs, but with emancipation it became neces-

---

[99] In the case of aristocratic landowners the Tsarist government had declared that their powers over the serfs were absolute, and it had *not* attempted to regulate the relations between them. When such regulation proved necessary for reasons of state, as in the privately owned mountain works, the government would resume their operation rather than attempt to regulate that operation under private ownership. Cf. pp. 165–67 for a discussion of this point. Yet even this favored treatment of the aristocracy did not constitute a basic abrogation of power on the part of the Tsars. Although the landowners' power over their serfs was absolute, they could be divested of that power and of their land at will; that is, their privileges were contingent upon good behavior and the pleasure of the Tsar. And the serfs continued to be liable to the state for the payment of taxes, even though their masters were charged with the responsibility for tax collection.

sary for the government to regulate the relations between the free peasants and their former masters. As Alexander II stated in an interview with Bismarck: "God only knows what might be the ultimate outcome of the current transactions between peasants and landowners, if the power of the Tsar were not strong enough to give an unconditional guarantee of leadership." [100]

At first, a similar extension of governmental regulation did not apply to industry. From the 1840's onward, the government proceeded to act toward the employers as it had earlier toward the landowners: allowing them virtually complete freedom to manage their enterprise as they saw fit. Yet, intensified regulation of agriculture also intensified the demand for the regulation of industry. And indeed the mere centralization of industrial problems in the cities made it difficult, and eventually impossible, for the government to pursue the same hands-off policy as it had earlier in the case of landowners and serfs. For a time, governmental control of factory conditions was held in abeyance owing to the prevailing reluctance to curtail the power of employers. But this dominant trend was accompanied by an unremitting concern of some officials with plans for regulating the relations between employers and workers; and, in the 1880's, these plans were put into effect.

A brief statistical account of the industrial development during the nineteenth century will indicate the relative magnitude of the problems with which the Tsarist government had to deal. Various estimates had placed the number of industrial workers by the early 1800's at approximately 100,000. By 1860 that figure had increased to a little over half a million. In the following 37 years the number of industrial workers grew to about 2.1 millions (1897), the increase being especially rapid in the early 1870's and in the 1890's.[101] Another index of economic growth during this period was the increase in railroad construction, which is illustrated by the table on the following page.

During the 1890's the number of enterprises increased by 26 per cent, while the value of production rose by 113 per cent. The acceleration of economic growth in the last decades of the nineteenth century is indicated clearly by the fact that the annual rate at which the value of production increased was 26.1 million rubles in 1878–1887, 41.6 million rubles in 1888–1892, and 161.2 million rubles during 1893–1897.[102]

[100] Cited in Karl Staehlin, *Geschichte Russlands* (Königsberg: Ost-Europa Verlag, 1939), IV:1, p. 81.

[101] See Rashin, *op. cit.*, p. 23, and Lyashchenko, *op. cit.*, pp. 487, 526.

[102] *Ibid.*, pp. 526–27.

TABLE 4.   MILES OF RAILROAD TRACK IN SELECTED YEARS *

1857	1,000
1865	3,500
1871	10,200
1881	21,100
1885–1889	24,900
1890–1894	27,900
1895–1898	34,100

* Lyashchenko, *op. cit.*, pp. 491, 515.   It should be added, however, that development was retarded by the economic crises of 1873–1875 and 1881–1882 and that metal- and machine-production did not keep pace with railroad construction.   Hence, the market expansion due to railroad construction resulted in an unbalanced development of the Russian economy.

The development of an industrial work force, which accompanied these economic changes, was characterized by high labor mobility between town and country.   Prior to the emancipation of 1861, the employers of "possessional workers" had complained about the unreliability of their labor supply; for the serfs who worked in the factory to earn their *obrok* were frequently recalled by their masters.   Yet, emancipation and the greater availability of free labor did not reduce labor mobility and turnover.   Although high taxes, an increasing population and insufficient land allotments gradually compelled more and more peasants to seek employment in the industrial enterprises of the towns, the rural ties of the industrial workers remained strong.   And in its effort to regularize the supply of labor and to stabilize its system of internal revenue, the government adopted methods which actually strengthened these rural ties and hence perpetuated labor mobility.   In many instances emancipation had done away with the practice of having the landowners act as the local tax-collectors of the government.   Henceforth, responsibility for the collection of the souls-tax was imposed upon the village community as a whole.   And those communities as well as the government wanted to stabilize each person's legal residence so as to ensure his payment of the tax.   The villages would use the periodic redistribution of the land to equalize the tax burden among the members of the community; and they would use their control of passports as a means of forestalling tax evasion.   Moreover, the government made it difficult for the individual to sell, or waive his claim to his share of the land, for this would enable him to leave the community and hence jeopardize the payment of taxes.[103]   Unlike the enclosures of the

[103] Boris Brutzkus, "The Historical Peculiarities of the Social and Economic Development of Russia," in Bendix and Lipset, eds., *Class, Status and Power*, p. 524.

eighteenth and early nineteenth centuries in England, the emancipation of serfs and the system of passports tended to retard the creation of a landless industrial work force.

There is some scattered statistical evidence for the semirural character of Russian factory labor in the second half of the nineteenth century. From the 1860's to the 1890's the number of passports issued annually in 50 territories (*gubernii*) increased from 13.9 to 53.1 per thousand. While migration as a whole increased, workers continued to go back and forth between the towns and their native village. Figures for the Moscow district during 1879–1885 show that two-thirds of the workers were recent recruits to the industrial labor force. About one-third of them had been employed in factories for not more than six years, while the other third had been in such employment from seven to fifteen years.[104] Studies of other areas indicate a somewhat higher proportion of workers who had become members of the industrial work force by the 1880's. In one such study 55 per cent of the factory workers were found to be sons of factory workers, while studies for the 1890's show again a somewhat lower proportion (ca. 41 per cent) of workers with "factory antecedents." [105] It is also interesting that, in 1869, 34 per cent of the inhabitants of Petersburg were registered as residents in village communities; in 1872 the corresponding proportion for Moscow was 44 per cent.[106] While average figures may be misleading, it is instructive that in the last two decades of the nineteenth century approximately 90 per cent of the industrial workers were the sons of peasants, but that only 45 to 60 per cent of these peasant fathers had *not* worked in the factories themselves.[107] These figures certainly suggest that for many workers the village had become the place where their relatives lived and their passports would be renewed. But for a large number of workers the tie to their village must have remained strong if one may judge from the high labor turnover in Russian industry. According to one report on the factories in Petersburg for 1904, the whole work force had to be replaced about once a year on the average; and it was regarded as favorable if 10 per cent of the work force was permanent.[108]

This semirural character of the industrial work force became a promi-

---

[104] See Rashin, *op. cit.*, pp. 104, 292, 368.

[105] *Ibid.*, p. 393. See also Tugan-Baranowski, *op. cit.*, pp. 519–23.

[106] Alphons Thun, *Landwirtschaft und Gewerbe in Mittelrussland seit Aufhebung der Leibeigenschaft* (Vol. II of Staats- und sozialwissenschaftliche Forschungen, ed. by Gustav Schmoller; Leipzig: Duncker and Humblot, 1880), p. 173.

[107] Lyashchenko, *op. cit.*, p. 544.

[108] Otto Goebel, *Entwicklungsgang der russischen Industriearbeiter bis zur ersten Revolution* (Leipzig: B. G. Teubner, 1920), p. 13.

nent element in the intellectual controversies of the time. Prior to the emancipation it had been fashionable to denounce the evils of the factory system and to make invidious contrasts between the idyllic life of the peasants and the lurid fate of industrial workers.[109] Among Tsarist officials this anti-industrialism was reinforced especially by such disturbing events as the French Revolution of 1830, the street-fighting of the Lyon proletariat, and the wave of popular uprisings in 1848. This concern may be illustrated by the suggestion of one official who recommended that in every city the number of factories should simply be limited by governmental decree.

> In order to maintain the peace and welfare which Russia alone possesses at the present time, the government cannot permit that people without home and morals [i.e., industrial workers] congregate in one place, for such people will readily join any movement which disturbs the peace and order of public and private life.[110]

And yet, other officials were less apprehensive because they believed that the peculiar conditions of the Russian industrial development would safeguard her against these dangerous tendencies of western Europe. The Napoleonic invasion had destroyed many enterprises, especially in Moscow; moreover, many previously subsidized enterprises went bankrupt. As a result large numbers of industrial workers drifted back to the land and into the household industries (*kustar*).[111] And this development of the *kustar* industry by former factory workers, as well as the continued mobility of workers between town and country, were phenomena which government officials and other spokesmen used to point up the unique characteristics of Russian industrialization.

In 1834, and again in 1845, the Minister of Finance pointed out that in Russia the development of factories was more advantageous, since the industrial workers were in reality peasants who returned to their land as soon as they left factory employment; hence, the employers could

[109] Examples of these arguments from the 1810's to the 1840's are cited in detail in Tugan-Baranowski, *op. cit.,* pp. 319–36. It may be added that even the advocates of Westernization were highly critical of the factory system and sought out redeeming features in the Russian economy. Cf. the denunciation of industrialism in such Westernizers as Belinsky and Herzen, quoted in Richard Hare, *Pioneers of Russian Social Thought* (New York: Oxford University Press, 1951), pp. 48, 246–47.

[110] This argument is contained in a memorandum of 1848 which was regarded as "very important" by Tsar Nicholas himself. Cited in Tugan-Baranowski, *op. cit.,* p. 211.

[111] Thun, *op. cit.,* pp. 160–61 states that in Moscow alone 600 enterprises were destroyed.

not have too great an influence upon them, and the workers themselves were not likely to congregate in a dangerous way. For during slack periods the worker returned to his home, where he had shelter and a meagre subsistence. As a result, there existed at most a small urban proletariat and the grave consequences of factory labor, such as immorality, stupidity, degradation, disturbances, and demands for higher wages, were avoided.[112] By the middle of the nineteenth century industrialization had as yet made little progress and such official praise of its absence is perhaps not surprising. But the point is that these views remained in vogue throughout the century. For example, at an All-Russian Congress of Manufacturers in 1870 a spokesman declared that in Russia a working class did not exist. Factory workers and all other workers who engaged in productive activities came into being only when their agricultural work allowed them the necessary leisure.[113] Even after the railroad boom of the 1880's such views were expressed by high officials of the Tsarist government, who would eulogize the superior attributes of Russian industry by pointing to the semirural character of its work force.

> . . . workmen in Russian factories are at the same time landowners, who are not factory workmen by profession; the wages they earn in factories . . . are only accessory to what they get by their agricultural labours. The workman loves his land, and does not like to leave it permanently for the factory; he has, therefore, continual intercourse with his village, and goes there yearly to see his relatives and neighbors, and still more to cultivate his own little farm . . . In making a contract with the manufacturer, he always has in view that, in case of failure, he can always return to his village, where he will get board and lodging.[114]

To some extent such an argument was used to justify what the government found itself unable to prevent. Yet, it also reflected an acceptance of high labor turnover and its consequences as a peculiar condition of Russian society, for Mikhailovski went on to point out that in the manufacturing towns of central Russia the wages changed regularly twice a year. Since many workers returned to their villages during the spring in order to work in the fields, wages were from 10 to 20 per

[112] Tugan-Baranowski, *op. cit.*, pp. 210, 362–64. For a model description of patriarchal labor relations which were highly commended by the government see *ibid.*, pp. 365–66.

[113] *Ibid.*, p. 614.

[114] J. T. Mikhailovski, "Wages and Working Hours in Factories," in John M. Crawford, ed., *The Industries of Russia* (Prepared by the Department of Trade and Manufactures for the World's Columbia Exposition in Chicago; St. Petersburg, 1893), Vol. II, p. 515. The author was Chief Inspector of Factories.

cent higher during the spring and summer for at that time factory hands became scarce.[115]

The acceptance of labor turnover and the ideological endorsement of a semirural, industrial work force over a period of almost a century gives a spurious impression of agreement, for these government spokesmen, like the employers themselves, were very directly concerned with the problems arising from a high labor turnover. And their efforts to stabilize the relations between employers and workers vacillated between a nearly unqualified endorsement of the employer's authority and occasional attempts by the government to subject employers and workers alike to a system of detailed and officially supervised regulations. Both policies had strong advocates throughout the nineteenth century, among manufacturers as well as among government officials. The employers who paid low wages and whose methods of production were backward technologically, opposed all government interference and demanded time and again that their own absolute authority over the workers should receive official sanction. This position was strongly defended in the Ministry of Finance, which was responsible for the collection of taxes and hence disposed toward supporting the employers upon whose success the revenue of the state depended. Other employers, however, favored governmental regulation because their machines were modern and they paid relatively high wages. And in the interest of maintaining their own standards they advocated regulations which would eliminate the marginal producer and reduce cutthroat competition made possible by low wages, excessively long hours, and shoddy products.[116] These advocates of governmental regulation found supporters among the officials in the Ministry of the Interior, whose responsibility for maintaining law and order disposed them toward limiting the power of employers, though they would act only when too many disturbances of the workers indicated the necessity for official intervention. It is apparent that in each case entrepreneurial ideology in nineteenth-century Russia was formulated through the interaction between groups of employers and of government officials.

[115] *Ibid.* This Tsarist official also pointed out that a large number of these semi-industrial workers were unskilled, because they had remained peasants; they shifted readily from one factory to another, and their wages were very low since they merely supplemented their agricultural earnings.

[116] See Tugan-Baranowski, *op. cit.*, pp. 460–63 where the persistent conflict between the manufacturers in Petersburg and in Moscow is explained in these terms. Similar conflicts among manufacturers occurred in the course of Western industrialization.

The conflict between the spokesmen for employer supremacy and the spokesmen for governmental regulation was never evenly balanced. The record of factory legislation during the nineteenth century clearly indicates that on balance the Tsarist regime was more reluctant to interfere with the employers than to suppress disturbances among workers. Attempts by the government to regulate the relations between employers and workers were made as early as 1845, but the limitation of child labor which this decree envisaged was re-enacted and actually enforced only in 1882. In that year the government also organized a factory inspectorate which provided the first effective means of enforcement. By 1886 the government proceeded to issue really comprehensive regulations of labor relations, a step which was prompted by extensive disturbances among the workers. Yet, as the disturbances subsided and the protest of the manufacturers increased many of these regulations were relaxed, although by then the principle of governmental regulation was more firmly established.[117] Thus, the government repeatedly shrank from interfering with the managerial practices of employers, since it was predisposed to rely upon the absolute authority of the masters in order to control the work force. Only prolonged unrest among the workers led to limitations upon the power of employers.

Since a high labor turnover prevailed throughout the period of employer supremacy, the penalties and facilities administered by the employers themselves reveal their various efforts to stabilize the supply of labor and control the conduct of the workers. It was common practice for employers to build barracks for their workers and to provide facilities for the purchase of necessities on the premises of the factory. Efforts were made to curb labor mobility by long-term wage contracts and by penalizing workers who left before the expiration of such contracts.[118] The employers sought to control the conduct of workers by the imposition of fines or other penalties in case they violated the standard rules against shortages, defective production, or being late to work. In addition, however, the employers attempted to control every detail of the worker's life, partly because he lived on the premises of the factory and partly because necessity and tradition gave to labor relations the character of a household discipline. Fines were imposed in case of absence from the factory barracks at certain prohibited hours. Visitors could not be received if their stay exceeded the "length of an ordi-

---

[117] See *ibid.*, pp. 206–7, 459, 468–75, 479–80.

[118] Cf. Gerhard von Schulze-Gaevernitz, *Volkswirtschaftliche Studien aus Russland* (Leipzig: Duncker and Humblot, 1899), pp. 141–44.

nary visit." Workers were forbidden to put pictures on the walls of their rooms.

> During the working hours it is forbidden to sing or to dance. At night it is forbidden to use the samovar. The workers must always assume a humble and courteous attitude and treat the women decently without insulting them either by action or in words. After ten o'clock at night every worker must remain in his room. Except in case of necessity, he may not enter other rooms or walk around the hall.[119]

These rules imposed a quasi-military pattern of conduct in the barracks which hardly differed from the management of serfs, although now the workers were nominally free.

The same pattern was enforced in the factory itself. Laborers and craftsmen were not allowed to leave the shop carrying candles; they could not smoke during working hours even in the dining halls or in the factory yard.

> Furthermore it is forbidden to set up boxing matches or to have any kind of game or play a joke which is harmful to others, to toss coins for money or other articles, to bring wine into the shop, or use abusive or indecent words. Laborers and craftsmen of both sexes and all ages must go to church on Sundays and holidays.

Those found guilty of violating these rules were subject to punishment by the judicial authorities, or they were subject to a fine, part of which was paid "for the benefit of the accuser." [120] The conditions under which workers were allowed to lodge complaints against the administration of these and other rules placed the entire burden of proof on those least able to obtain it. And the complaints had to be brought before administrative and judicial authorities which were sympathetic with the employer, since complaints as such were evidence of rebellion and thereby came within the jurisdiction of these authorities automatically.

Since these outside authorities would protect the employers against the protests of their own workers, many employers acted as arbitrarily as the landowners had in an analogous situation. For example, some

---

[119] These regulations are contained in a collection of original documents by A. M. Pankratova, ed., *Rabochee Dvizhenie v Rossii v XIX Veke* (Moscow: Government Publications of Political Literature, 1950), Vol. II, Part 2, pp. 596–97. I am indebted to my assistant, Mr. Gaston Rimlinger, for his survey of these materials and several translations.

[120] The foregoing rules were issued for the workers of the Danilov factories in Moscow, in 1870. See Pankratova, *op. cit.*, Vol. II, Part 1, pp. 543–45. It may be added that these rules were officially approved by the Moscow Chief of Police.

employers would pay a worker only when he "needed" it—in their judgment. Whether the worker had to pay his tax in the village or pay for work done on his land or meet a family emergency, the employer would make inquiries in order to confirm the information given by the worker. This system of wage payments was justified, according to one report, because regular payments would lead to undesirable consequences.

> If paid every month, the majority of the workers would receive such a small amount of money that they would not be in a position to derive any benefit from it. They would spend the money foolishly, as they usually do, and upon returning home at the end of the year without their earnings, they would invent various tales as excuses, and thus undermine the confidence in the factory. But now, as they receive a more important sum, from 30 to 130 rubles at one time, they naturally take it home almost in its entirety.[121]

While this justification of low wages appears transparent and naive to us, it may well be that both the low level of wages and the traditional tutelage which resulted were taken for granted; but it is clear, at the same time, that the employers utilized these methods to make the workers as completely dependent as possible. According to one report for 1884, employers would arbitrarily reduce wages during the duration of the contract or by means of the fines they imposed, and thus increase the indebtedness of the workers to factory stores from which some employers derived the largest part of their profits. Indeed, workers often had to appeal to their employers in the most abject manner to be paid the wages which they had earned.[122] There is no need to extend this record of abuses, which is familiar enough from the industrial history of other countries. The Russian case differs only in the sense that the semirural character of the work force prompted employers to use methods which resembled the landowner's exploitation of his serfs more closely than a Western manufacturer's exploitation of his workers.[123]

These practices of the employers provoked disturbances and interfered with production. In the past, enterprises had been closely supervised or even taken over by the government, when it appeared that

---

[121] *Ibid.*, Vol. II, Part 1, pp. 589–90. This quotation and the rules concerning wage payments are taken from a report of the Troitsky cloth factory of 1876.

[122] See Tugan-Baranowski, *op. cit.*, pp. 463–66.

[123] Even then parallels can be found in other areas in which the workers retained their rural ties, as in the system of contract labor in some colonial dependencies, or wherever company towns were established to attract and settle a floating labor force.

private management led to uncontrollable unrest. It may be asked why the government failed to act in this manner during the nineteenth century. The question is pertinent since governmental supervision of "possessional factories" belonging to middle-class employers had been quite extensive, especially in the case of enterprises which produced primarily for the government. Yet despite this earlier record of governmental management or supervision, employers were left in complete command of their enterprises until the 1880's. One reason for the decline of most governmental control over economic enterprises was that the importance of the government as an economic agent declined along with the expansion of industry. The major reason for governmental management of the mountain works or for the close supervision of "possessional factories" had been that the government depended upon these enterprises for supplies, but this dependence on particular enterprises declined with the expansion of industry as a whole. Hence, proposals to institute governmental regulations of the factories were frequently defeated or sidetracked by Tsarist officials and also by employers who opposed governmental control and exercised considerable influence inside the government. Another reason for the declining regulation of industrial enterprises was that even the officials who favored the governmental control of employers were concerned lest such control undermine the authority relationships essential to an autocratic regime. They were fully aware of the danger that the workers would interpret the regulation of labor relations as tantamount to an official recognition of grievances. Hence, every step of the government had to be guarded against the danger of insubordination and against the risk of provoking "unjustified" demands.[124]

It should be remembered, however, that interest in the regulation of labor relations was kept alive throughout the period during which the employers' authority went virtually unchecked (approximately, 1840–1882). There were several reasons for this continued interest. Some prominent Tsarist officials favored regulations, because they agreed with certain manufacturers, as we have seen. Others did so simply because they opposed the employers, or because they felt responsible for maintaining peace and order. This last consideration was perhaps most important, for disturbances among workers recurred, and the expression of their grievances alternated erratically and dangerously between demonstrations of abject humility and direct threats to the life and property of employers. Moreover, the government's unwillingness

[124] *Ibid.*, pp. 204–6 and *passim*.

or reluctance to interfere could not be acted upon consistently, because the employers of factory labor were obliged to act in a quasi-administrative capacity with regard to the passports of their employees. Therefore, some intervention with the employers was inevitable as long as the government sought to ensure the collection of taxes and the internal security of the country by stabilizing and controlling the residence of all persons.

All these latent tendencies toward the regulation of labor relations came to a head in the 1870's. At that time, frequent disturbances among the workers led to an increasing intervention of police officers and inspectors in the management of the factories. Their efforts reveal the characteristic problems of labor management under an autocratic regime.[125] To prevent further unrest, certain duties were now stipulated for the employers (in addition to the duties of workers). Now, as before, the major purpose was to safeguard the authority of employers, but to do so it became necessary to prevent their abuses as well as lend support to their power. Given the heavy bias in favor of the employers, it is obvious that this supervision increased only gradually. For example, the Chancellory records of 1872 for the Moscow Territory contain a document which listed the "obligations and rights of the master" as well as the "obligations of factory workers." [126] The employer's "just and kind" treatment of the workers was demanded. The payment of wages in kind was expressly prohibited. Masters were forbidden to reduce wages arbitrarily during the life of a contract, while formerly only the workers were denied the right to demand an increase of wages. Moreover, employers were obligated to keep workbooks, in which the employment conditions of each worker were stipulated. The regulations of the factory were to be posted where they could be seen by all. And in addition to various rules pertaining to the handling of passports, the master "for his part was obligated to see to it that factory workers and craftsmen are by no means left to their wilfulness and allowed to quarrel and fight," a rule which presumably covered the employer's obligation to supervise the moral life of the workers.[127]

Mild as these regulations were, they were apparently ignored by the employers, and disturbances among the workers continued. The fol-

---

[125] It should be remembered that the Tsarist police was concerned with labor management even in the absence of any governmental regulations. Employers would call upon the police for support, and the police regarded the maintenance of order in the factories as part of its responsibility for internal security.

[126] The "rights" of the workers are omitted, significantly enough.

[127] See Pankratova, *op. cit.*, Vol. II, Part 1, pp. 547–49.

lowing report of the Moscow Chief of Police in 1875 may be regarded as typical.

> Upon examining these books, the assistant public prosecutor found that they recorded no fixed contracts for other than year-long workers. Contracts were, therefore, considered open, and the master could act as he pleased on every occasion. Moreover, the books did not record the time at which work was to stop on the eves of holidays, which constitutes an important and fundamental stipulation. The laborers work until 8 or 9 o'clock and actually have no opportunity to go to church. They reported this to the master already before Easter, but it received no attention. The master himself is rarely at the factory. He leaves the direction of his business to his representatives and the factory office, which often fails to forward to the master the complaints it receives.[128]

The result of this investigation was a policeman's answer to a problem of policing. In a city with many factories, it was thought important to introduce uniform conditions in all of them, to stipulate these conditions formally, to have agreement among all manufacturers concerning these common arrangements, and to subject all the factories to the inspection of special police officials.

> It would then be possible through the surveillance of the factories by a police officer to have always an opportunity to investigate everything on the spot, with the assistance of a designated government official. This same official would examine the master's announcement of employment conditions at the time the workers are hired by the factory, and in given cases explain the stipulations to the workers.[129]

Let everything be written down: then the authorities can inspect on the spot and explain these written rules to the workers.

It is apparent from these reports that the police officials, who were responsible for the maintenance of peace and order, looked upon the problems of labor management as primarily a question of detailed supervision. From their viewpoint such supervision was quite consistent with support for the authority of employers. Police officials simply had to concern themselves with the employment conditions in the factories wherever the power of employers was insufficient to cope with the unrest which occurred. Yet this approach by the police unwittingly encouraged the continuation of disturbances, for the beliefs which inspired the protest of the workers were an exact counterpart of this supervision of labor management by government officials. Implicitly this surveillance acknowledged that the Tsarist government had ultimate responsibility for the conditions in the factories. And every

[128] Pankratova, *op. cit.*, Vol. II, Part 2, p. 83.
[129] *Ibid.*, p. 84.

intervention with the employers tended to invalidate the demand for the *unconditional* subordination of the workers; the workers would use this intervention as evidence that justified their protest against the employers. Every protest of the workers, however, was countered by further assertions of unconditional authority on the part of the employers, who could rely upon the police to suppress disturbances even as they vigorously opposed the efforts of the police to supervise their managerial practices.[130] Given the fact that police supervision did not succeed in preventing either unrest or abuses, it was logical that eventually the government would attempt to regulate the relations between employers and workers comprehensively by matching the severe penalties for the workers by an increased control of the employers.[131] In the present context it is of importance to examine the manner in which responsible Tsarist officials approached the comprehensive supervision of labor management.

A report of 1884 for the Petersburg District, written by a police captain, is especially illuminating in this respect, since it contained observations on the "state of mind of the working population" as well as policy recommendations to the authorities. The report stated that the working class consisted of two strata, the permanent and the temporary factory workers. The permanent workers were less backward than the others, but "very wicked." They had had "a substantial amount of undesirable experience," which consisted in reading half-understood books of doubtful content, in placing absurd interpretations on newspaper articles and in discussing problems with agents of the anarchist party. These workers would explain their misery and helplessness by the "so-called social injustice" rather than by their own conduct.

Given time, the majority of the remaining workers will follow exactly the same route. The temporary workers, having been torn from the

[130] The record of the employers' opposition to governmental regulation is traced in Tugan-Baranowski, *op. cit.*, pp. 200–3, 209, 213–17, 442–44, 450–54, 475–80, and *passim*. The arguments of these Russian employers consisted of the same apologetic mixture of justification and denial which I have described for the English manufacturers in the early nineteenth century. See above pp. 86–89.

[131] Details concerning the law of 1886 are given in *ibid.*, pp. 473–75, and by Jacob Walkin, "The Attitude of the Tsarist Government toward the Labor Problem," *The American Slavic and East European Review,* Vol. XIII (April, 1954), pp. 172–73 and *passim*. It is misleading, however, to treat the comprehensive legislation of 1886 without relating it to the record of government inaction in the preceding period, as Walkin seems to do.

land against their will on account of the smallness of their holdings constitute a group which is politically and morally more reliable. But some of these workers, although not many, have been corrupted by the permanent workers through drinking, debauchery and all kinds of false doctrine. The corrupted workers may in time spread this infection even among the agricultural population.

And this diagnosis of the evil was followed by the suggestion that *"it would now be desirable to organize a reaction against this evil"* [my italics]. To do so it was suggested that books on political economy be published and supplied to the workers, adding the characteristic remark that this could be financed by the manufacturers since the government had established protective tariffs for the benefit of the employers. The report concluded with this summary evaluation:

> The relationship between manufacturers and workers leaves much to be desired. In most cases the masters try to pay the workers as little as possible, and have no other concern. And the workers have absolutely no respect for the masters. The question of wages often leads to discontent. It would be desirable to have a special organization carefully watching over the relationship between these two classes.[132]

These suggestions illustrate the dilemma of an autocratic regime which attempted to regulate the relations between employers and workers. The police insisted on the absolute authority of the employer, though it would interfere with him when this was deemed necessary. Yet such intervention could not go far, for it would undermine the authority the government endeavored to protect. And when it was found that the ruthless suppression of disturbances did not prevent the spread of "anarchism," it was logical to suggest that the government itself "organize a reaction against this evil." Consequently, some Tsarist officials conceived the idea that police officials should keep the workers under control by becoming their leaders in trade unions and benefit societies which would be supervised closely by the police. This system of "police socialism" was actually tried under the leadership of Zubatov, the Moscow Chief of Police. Zubatov made a vigorous attack upon the abuses which had made the employers generally detested by the population. Since the workers had lost all confidence in the authorities, it had become the responsibility of the police to restore that confidence. The police would "widen the rights of workers" by obtaining concessions from the manufacturers, but in a manner which safeguarded the established order against disturbances. In this way Zubatov proposed to convince the workingmen "that every humbled and

[132] Pankratova, *op. cit.,* Vol. II, Part 2, pp. 635–36.

insulted person finds in the Political Police Department paternal attention, advice, support and assistance by word and deed." The employers countered this attack upon them by maintaining that the government was sacrificing their interests in order to protect itself against the
unrest of the people. And they contended that political rather than
economic concessions were needed to accomplish this end.[133] Of course,
the government could not for long encourage the collective actions of
the workers and undermine the authority of the employers. Hence,
police socialism was a short-lived expedient, albeit one which helped to
precipitate the revolution of 1905.[134]

But this expedient is of interest not as an event but as a symptom.
Autocratic regimes confront a basic dilemma. By making enemies of
their subjects they forego the benefits of a more or less willing cooperation. To be sure, reliance on servility and coercion can accomplish a
great deal. But where cooperation is lacking, the tasks to be accomplished by coercion and hence the methods of coercion tend to multiply. In nineteenth-century Russia employers and government officials
found that the limits of effective coercion had been reached. Further
measures of suppression increased rather than decreased the disturbances among workers, and this consequence made it imperative to resort to other methods. In order to control their hostile workers, employers would rely on, and reward, informers in order to detect transgressions and ensure the observance of rules. And since disturbances
continued despite all efforts to suppress them, some Tsarist officials
proposed that the police prevent further unrest by joining and leading
the organizations of workers so that they could be controlled from
within rather than from above. This approach involved basic ambiguities. Too timid a representation of the workers was bound to be
ineffective, since the police had to compete with dedicated revolutionaries in winning the loyalty of the workers. But if the police won the
confidence of the workers by a forceful representation of their interests,
its demands would quickly exceed the concessions which the authorities
were willing to tolerate.[135]

[133] See R. von Ungern-Sternberg, *Über die wirtschaftliche und rechtliche Lage
der St. Petersburger Arbeiterschaft* (Berlin: Puttkammer and Mühlbrecht, 1909),
pp. 80–81.

[134] It may be added that Zubatov was penalized by the authorities when his
attempt failed, though previously the same authorities had endorsed his efforts.
The elaboration of this practice as a principle of rule by a Soviet regime is
traced in Chapter 6.

[135] Mavor, *op. cit.*, Vol. II, pp. 204–5.

These ambiguities are significant beyond the fact that they help to explain why "police socialism" failed to preserve the Tsarist regime. For this whole attempt implied that an autocratic regime can win public acceptance by organizing consent from a position of authority and from among the masses, at one and the same time. This idea was an outgrowth of Russian autocracy and it has proved to be an important legacy for the management of labor in a revolutionary era. So far I have considered the ideologies of industrialism and of labor management in the Russia of the Tsars. Before concluding this discussion, I want to consider the problem of labor management as it was envisaged in the writings of Lenin.

f. The Problem of Labor Management in a Revolutionary Era

The revolution of 1905 signalized the failure of Tsarist autocracy. When the people marched to the Winter Palace to present their petition to the Tsar in person, they were still prompted by the traditional and quasi-religious belief in the Tsar as the stern but just father of his subjects. Lesser men had committed abuses in his name, but without his knowledge and against his will. When this peaceful demonstration was dispersed by rifle fire which killed or wounded hundreds of people, beliefs that had helped to sustain the Tsarist regime for over two hundred years were destroyed. And it was symbolic of this regime that Gapon, the leader of the procession to the Winter Palace, who had been an agent of the police, had endeavored to contain the protest which had now overwhelmed him. The Tsarist government had been unable to control the exercise of power by landowners and employers even though the Tsar's personal supremacy had prevented the development of these classes into relatively autonomous groups. The revolution of 1905 indicated that the government was also unable to control the resulting protest of the people.

Nevertheless, Tsarist autocracy had aspired to a principle of rule which was not to be abandoned, even after the Russian Revolution of 1917. According to this principle, all relations among men in society are an outgrowth of a sovereign will, that of the Tsar or that of the people as "represented" by the Communist party. In this sense "police socialism" had been a consistent, albeit self-defeating, end result of the Tsarist regime. If the actions of all men, as well as the relations among them, were subject to the Tsar's sovereign will, then it was consistent for government officials to control the actions of employers as well as of workers, and to do so from "within" as well as from above. It was simply a part of that control to play one group against the other: to increase the authority of employers in order to curb disturbances among workers, to supervise the practices of employers, and also curb their abuses by increasing the "rights of workers" under proper supervision. My purpose is to show that fundamentally the same principle of rule is contained in the writings of Lenin, albeit in a different ideological framework.

Since the Tsar and his officials had forfeited their trust, the authority of government must be restored to the people. Under the old regime the masses of the people were oppressed by a minority; hence, large numbers were needed for the coercive and administrative apparatus of the state. After the revolution, however, the vast majority of the people would rule over their former oppressors. Therefore, there would be no need for the special institutions of a ruling minority, such as a privileged officialdom or the higher echelons of a standing army. Instead, "the majority can itself directly fulfill all these functions; and the more the discharge of the functions of state power devolves upon the people generally, the less need is there for the existence of this power." [136] Accordingly, Lenin speculated that "*all* will take a turn in management," [137] whether it was the management of the government or of industry.

This ideology of direct management by the people has never been abandoned, even though in practice it was gradually discarded after the Russian Revolution of 1917. Lenin was soon aware of the fact that this compelling symbol of the revolution did not provide a guide to action. But instead of abandoning it, he simply reiterated it along with the demand that the Soviet government utilize "all that is best in capitalism" such as labor discipline, the Taylor system, piecework, and competition.[138]

> For the first time after centuries of working for others, of working in subjection for the exploiter, it has become possible to *work for oneself* . . . [but] now that a Socialist government is in power our task is to organize competition. . . .[139]

[136] Lenin, *State and Revolution* (New York: International Publishers, 1932), p. 37. A more detailed discussion is contained in Reinhard Bendix, "Socialism and the Theory of Bureaucracy," *Canadian Journal of Economics and Political Science*, Vol. XVI (1950), pp. 501–14.

[137] Lenin, *op. cit.*, p. 98.

[138] Lenin, *Selected Works* (New York: International Publishers, n.d.), Vol. VII, pp. 322–33. Cf. pp. 206–7 below.

[139] Lenin, *Selected Works*, Vol. IX, pp. 413–14.

That is, Lenin subscribed to the traditions of social protest in Russia with the first sentence. He generalized the age-old demand of the peasants for land of their own by making it a demand of the "masses" and by simply identifying the individual's management of his property with the idea of an individual's participation in collective ownership and management. And his demand in the second sentence meant that the government organize the conditions under which everyone would work. The apparent contradiction between "working for oneself" and working under conditions prescribed by the government was resolved by the contention that the workers now controlled the government and everything done by *their* government was in their interest by definition.

The logic of this position was similar to the logic of Tsarist autocracy, even though the explicit ideologies of the two differed fundamentally. Tsarist autocracy had been defended by the claim that all were alike as servants of the Tsar, but that it was the Tsar's arbitrary will to make the many subject to the power of the few. Now, it was contended that all were alike in owning the means of production and in working for themselves, but that it was the will of all (expressed through "their" socialist government) to make each subject to working conditions prescribed collectively. In the one case the ideal of equal subordination to the highest authority was used to effect the greatest inequality of subordination. And in the other, the ideal of freedom by virtue of equal claim to ownership and managerial function was used to effect the greatest subordination to the control of the party. In both cases the ideal was made to appear compatible with conflicting practice, because the sovereign will had so declared itself.

In theory the Tsarist officials had regarded employers and workers as equally subject to the will of the Tsar and loyal submission to that will was the mark of good citizenship. In practice they had maintained that the employer's power was absolute, except on those occasions when the disruptive consequences of that power forced the government to supervise the relations between employers and workers in all details. In theory Lenin believed that all workers were equal participants in the management of industry and government and that loyal submission to the Communist party represented their best interests and expressed their sovereign will. Therefore, he maintained that managers and workers should manage as well as obey, much as officials and employers under the Tsars were called upon to manage *and* to obey. Lenin's practical proposals in these respects may be summarized as follows:

    (1) All former managers (e.g., capitalists, bureaucrats, etc.) must be subordinated and strictly controlled by representatives of the workers

and peasants, who must learn all they can from the "bourgeois experts" in order to make their control of them the more effective and in order to replace them eventually;

(2) The masses of the people must participate actively in planning the policies which should govern production and distribution, but during the workday they must observe iron discipline and subordinate themselves unconditionally to the dictatorial will of one man, the Soviet manager;

(3) The Courts must be used to inculcate labor-discipline. Anyone who violated the demands of labor-discipline must be discovered, brought before the Courts, and punished mercilessly. The most class-conscious members of the proletariat must do all they can to facilitate this function of the Courts.[140]

Clearly, the purpose of these and similar proposals was to combine the technical efficiency of hierarchical organization with the creative initiative and the uninhibited flow of suggestions which Lenin expected to emerge from the masses. "Our aim is to draw *the whole of the poor* into the practical work of administration . . . our aim is to ensure that *every* toiler, after having finished his eight hours' 'lesson' in productive labour, shall perform state duties *gratis*." [141] To accomplish this purpose Lenin wanted to endow the Soviet manager with dictatorial authority within the context of his assigned task, and then subject the managerial policies which defined that task to absolute popular control. The basic contradiction of this position may be illustrated by reference to the 1920 debates over the position of trade-unions in Soviet society.

The issues of this debate were defined by the opposing viewpoints of Trotsky and Tomsky. One represented a logically consistent revolutionary position while the other represented an equally consistent "trade-unionist" position. To Trotsky there could be no conflict of interests under a proletarian dictatorship between trade-unions and the managers of industry, since both represented the government of the victorious proletariat. He believed that the trade-unions should create an "atmosphere of productivity" and that they should manage the national economy in cooperation with the political representatives of the workers' state. On the other hand, Tomsky believed that trade unionists were the representatives of the workers' economic interests. They should, therefore, be sole managers of industry: as such they would defend the interests of the workers against the remnants of the bour-

---

[140] These three proposals have been summarized from Lenin's essay "Immediate Tasks of the Soviet Government," published in April, 1918, and from " 'Left-Wing' Childishness and Petty-Bourgeois Mentality," published in May, 1918. See his *Selected Works*, Vol. VII, pp. 322, 373–76; 344–45; 339–40. Cf. also pp. 421–22 of the same volume.

[141] *Ibid.*, p. 346.

geoisie as well as against the possible abuses of Soviet officials. According to Tomsky, a majority of administrative positions should be filled by workers. And every member of the Communist party should be required to perform at least three months of manual labor every year, presumably as an annual test of fidelity to the cause.[142]

Lenin's position in this debate combined both viewpoints. In a resolution submitted to the Ninth Congress of the Communist party he proposed that the managers of industry should be selected on the basis of their technical proficiency, their character, and their business ability; but while he stressed the need for technical knowledge and the importance of a single managerial authority within the plant, he assigned to the trade-unions a series of quasi-managerial functions.[143]   The Fifth All-Russian Conference of Trade Unions (1920) issued a series of resolutions in which the "Tasks of the Trade Unions in Production" were defined. Lenin endorsed these resolutions, according to which it was the particular province of the trade-unions to "organize labor for the tasks of production."   To be able to do so efficiently the trade-unions were called upon to cooperate directly with the Council of the National Economy in drawing up the general production program.   But in addition the trade-unions were assigned the special task of educating the workers.   According to Resolution 6:

> The introduction of genuine labor discipline, the successful combating of labor desertion, etc., are conceivable only if the whole mass of participants in production take a *conscious part* in the fulfillment of these tasks. This cannot be achieved by *bureaucratic methods and orders from above;* every participant in production must understand the need for and expediency of the production tasks he is carrying out; every participant in production must not only take part in the fulfillment of tasks given from above, but also take an intelligent part in remedying all technical and organizational defects in the sphere of production.
>
> The task of the trade unions in this sphere is enormous.   They must teach *their members in every shop,* in every factory, *to note and take into account all defects in the utilization of labor power that result from the*

[142] See Manya Gordon, *Workers before and after Lenin* (New York: E. P. Dutton and Company, Inc., 1941), pp. 81–83, 252–53, for a discussion of this debate.   Cf. also Isaac Deutscher, *Soviet Trade Unions* (London: Royal Institute of International Affairs, 1950), Chap. 2.

[143] It should be added that in theory there was to be a division of labor between the manager's responsibility for the organization of production, the trade-union's responsibility for the management of labor, and the party's responsibility for political agitation.   This agitation, however, has always included production and management and hence has manipulated the different groups in terms of their "political" responsibility for practical success, to the detriment of the division of labor between them.

improper utilization of technical resources or from unsatisfactory administration. *The sum total of the experience of the individual enterprises* and of every industry must be utilized in a determined struggle against red tape, laxity and bureaucracy.[144]

According to these resolutions, the trade-unions would seem to have functions which are superior to those of the manager of industry. They are charged with partial responsibility for drawing up the plans of production which the manager is then obliged to execute. They are charged also with the education of the working masses to the end that the workers will show labor discipline and take a critically intelligent part in the organization of production. This end was not to be accomplished by "bureaucratic methods and orders from above": the trade-unions must educate the workers and organize their initiative. At the same time, the trade-unions themselves were totally subordinated to the directives of the Communist party; yet, according to Lenin, this did not mean that they no longer served to protect the interests of the workers.

> . . . our state is a workers' state with bureaucratic distortions. . . .
> Does that mean that the trade unions have nothing to protect, that we
> can dispense with them in the protection of the material and spiritual
> interests of the entirely organized proletariat? No . . . Our present
> state is such that the entirely organized proletariat must protect itself, and
> we must utilize these workers' organizations for the purpose of protecting
> the workers from their own state and in order that the workers may pro-
> tect our state.[145]

Lenin's idea was that the trade-unions as representatives of the workers should participate in the management of industry and at the same time criticize that management and defend the workers' interests against it. Since the trade-unions are directed by the dictatorial party, this is not different basically from the other idea that an agency of the state should participate in the workers' movement to direct its protest into officially approved channels. It is true, of course, that the trade-unions and the police are different organizations which were here called upon to perform such "extremely peculiar"[146] functions. And it is also true that Lenin made the most of the fact that the trade-unions were the representatives of the workers' interest, while his invectives knew no limit with regard to the Tsarist police. Yet the difference is perhaps more apparent than real. For Lenin insisted with extraordinary forcefulness that all policies, including the policies of the trade-unions,

---

[144] Quoted in Lenin, *Selected Works,* Vol. IX, pp. 24–25.
[145] *Ibid.,* IX, pp. 9–10.
[146] This is Lenin's candid characterization of trade-unions.

should be directed by the central organs of the Communist party in much the same way that the Tsarist police was subject to the Minister of the Interior and to the Tsar himself. Thus, autocratic as well as Communist rulers on occasion call upon the people to make their demands or to participate in the formulation of policies, while the police as well as the trade-unions see to it that these demands and this participation remained within "proper" bounds.[147]

The underlying logic of this position is that under a sovereign will the same person or organization can be made to perform both subordinate and superordinate functions. By their participation in the management of industry the trade-unions would represent the workers and thereby approach the ideal of workers' control of industry. By their inculcation of labor discipline the trade-unions would function in a managerial capacity in the interest of the workers as this interest is authoritatively defined by the party. According to Lenin, the "most advanced" workers recognized that the party formulated the "real" interests of their class, though this "knowledge" had to be taught to their less class-conscious fellows.[148] But the trade-unions were also to defend the workers against the "bureaucratic distortions of the Soviet apparatus."[149]

The same dual function was assigned to the trade-unions in industry itself. There the absolute will of the manager and the promotion of labor discipline were in the interest of technical efficiency and thereby in the interest of the workers themselves. Hence, the trade-union should

[147] There is this difference, however, between Lenin and Zubatov. Lenin denied the existence of political authority by maintaining that the central bodies of the Communist party represented the "true" interests of the proletariat, while those who differed were either dupes or traitors. Zubatov, on the other hand, never claimed that his men were anything but agents of the police; he wanted to have it accrue to the benefit of the authorities, if these acknowledged police agents really supported the demands of the workers. Hence, he would have admitted that he followed orders from above, while Lenin wanted to have it both ways: that everybody participated in policy-making, that the power of the party was absolute, and that this absolute power represented the participation of every man. The consequence of this "democratic centralism" for the Soviet pattern of industrial management will be discussed in Chapter 6.

[148] The sophistry of this argument is obvious. Though the trade-unions did not have power of coercion, they organized disciplinary "courts" before which the cases of "labor deserters" were heard. In this action the trade-unions were said to defend the interests of the overwhelming majority of the workers against individual violators. Yet the will or the interests of this majority was interpreted authoritatively by the small number of the "most advanced" workers, namely the activists of the trade-unions and the party.

[149] *Ibid.*, Vol. IX, p. 73.

support both. Yet it should also defend the workers against "bureaucratic orders from above" and encourage them to criticize the insufficient utilization of resources. To comply with these directives the trade-unions would have to support the authority of the manager and at the same time be able to criticize him. They would have to promote labor discipline and productivity, not bureaucratically, however, but by encouraging the right attitudes and the right men within the ranks of labor. Thus, the trade-unions would follow directives from "above" and support "spontaneous initiative from below" at one and the same time.[150] I shall attempt to show in Chapter 6 that Soviet policies and practices of industrial management have been interpreted in the light of these initial ideological commitments.

[150] Lenin's view of trade-unions under a Soviet regime illustrates a principle of rule which has had very general application in Soviet theory and practice. Leopold Haimson has pointed out that administration from above and personalized leadership of individuals and groups are concepts which have been traditionally distinguished in Russian (*upravleniye* and *rukovodstvo*). See Leopold Haimson, "Decision-Making and Communications in Russian Industry," *Studies in Soviet Communication* (Cambridge: Center for International Studies, Massachusetts Institute of Technology, 1952), Vol. II, Part 5, pp. 357–59.

PART TWO

CHAPTER 4

The Bureaucratization
of Economic Enterprises

*The man who did most work with his
arms could think least what he was doing,
reflect least what might come of the common action, and so command least. The
man who commanded most could obviously, from his greater verbal activity, act
less vigorously with his arms. In a larger
assembly of men, combining their energies
to one end, the class of those persons who
take the less direct share in the common
work the more their energy is turned to
command, is still more sharply defined.—*
Leo Tolstoy, *War and Peace.*

a. Ideologies of Management in Retrospect

The preceding discussion has surveyed in some detail the ideological
controversies which have accompanied the rise of industry in England
and in Russia. The social and ideological developments in these two
countries have left legacies of liberalism and of autocracy, which have
had decisive influence in the modern world, each in its own way. The
early development of these legacies has been traced in the specific context of the master-servant relationship in industry. I have examined
the legitimation of authority in economic enterprises as well as the

ideologies of protest on the part of the emerging industrial work force. In Part III of this book I shall turn to the self-legitimation of industrial managers in the contemporary world. At this point, however, it is advisable to stand back and survey the larger implications of the detailed picture which I have presented.

A study of the ideologies of management is not concerned with the origin of the capitalist spirit; it is concerned rather with the ideological weapons employed in the struggle for or against industrialization. Wherever modern industry is first introduced, entrepreneurial activity is accorded little social prestige: the contempt of the landowning aristocracy for the enterprising merchant was vigorous in England and in Russia, as we have seen. Also craftsmen and peasants are frequently reluctant to offer their services to manufacturers. That reluctance is reflected both in their "inadequate" response to the incentives offered and in their antagonism to the discipline required in factory production. Employers and their spokesmen will defend industry and attack its opponents by using political influence and economic pressures. They will explain and justify their practices by ideologies which are closely related to their economic interests. When ideologies are formulated to defend a set of economic interests, it is more illuminating to examine the strategy of argument than to insist that the argument is selfish. In the present case an important part of that strategy consists in the persuasion of the employers themselves.

Every class is more or less heterogeneous in its social composition.[1] Ideologies often help to create a cohesive group out of more or less diverse elements. In the case of employers, such cohesion may arise because the conflicts of interest among employers give way to an overriding unity by virtue of their common encounter with a hostile social environment. Under these conditions ideologies help to define and to advance certain core interests of the group. And this on-going definition of material interests helps to persuade and unite the members of the group in the process of defending their interests against opposing groups. Without such continual ideological reinforcement the class consciousness of a solidary group cannot persist.[2]

---

[1] T. H. Marshall has consequently suggested that *class* should be defined as any social group which achieves unity of thought and action despite the antagonisms which divide its members. See his essay on "The Nature of Class Conflict," in Bendix and Lipset, *Class, Status and Power*, pp. 81–83.

[2] Cf. Reinhard Bendix and S. M. Lipset, "Karl Marx' Theory of Social Classes," in *ibid.*, pp. 26–35.

It may be useful to relate this aspect of the ideologies of management to an earlier study of legitimation.   More than a generation ago Max Weber analyzed the religious doctrines which made the pursuit of economic gain legitimate as over against older religious doctrines which condemned it.

> Religion has psychologically met a very general need.   The fortunate is seldom satisfied with the fact of being fortunate.   Beyond this, he needs to know that he has a *right* to his good fortune.   He wants to be convinced that he "deserved" it, and above all, that he deserves it in comparison with others.   He wishes to be allowed the belief that the less fortunate also merely experiences his due.   Good fortune thus wants to be "legitimate" fortune.[3]

Weber showed how the doctrines of the Puritan divines made the fortunes of their parishioners seem legitimate.   These doctrines helped to buttress the self-esteem of a rising entrepreneurial class: Weber's intention was to explain the emergence of a new code of conduct, which he called "innerworldly asceticism."   Religious beliefs, which in part accounted for this change in conduct, were used to justify the economic success to which it led.

In the preceding two chapters I have tried to show the range of ideas which have been used since the inception of capitalism to justify or to accommodate the managerial activities of employers and their agents. In England the quest for legitimation continued during the latter half of the eighteenth century, even though Puritanism already provided a higher justification for a more or less unrestrained economic activity.   But there was need to justify the rejection of government interference in economic affairs in an age when such "interference" was generally accepted as in the national interest.   It was necessary to justify the means used to create a docile and readily available labor force in an age when labor was neither docile nor readily available where and when it was needed.   And the entrepreneurial class had to fight for social recognition when the ruling aristocracy regarded the trader and manufacturer with contempt and ill-concealed derision.   In its attack upon these and other obstacles, the English entrepreneurial class developed a social and ideological cohesion which went beyond the Puritan ethic, and which accomplished that break with traditionalism in economic life which industrialization required.

In Russia most of the factors that had facilitated the industrialization of the West were absent.   Handicraft production and urban development were retarded; science and technology were imported rather than in-

---

[3] H. H. Gerth and C. W. Mills, *From Max Weber*, p. 271.

digenous; the entrepreneurial class was weakened by its dependence upon government, by competition with foreign merchants and with economic enterprises on landed estates; beliefs favoring industrialization such as an interest in technology or the doctrines of Puritanism were nonexistent. In this setting, entrepreneurial activity was largely initiated by the reforms of Peter the Great, and hence subject to the requirements of national defense and the needs of government. The ideological significance of Peter's reforms is attested by the fact that for two and a half centuries thereafter it was debated whether the industrial development of Russia should follow Western "precedents" or remain in keeping with the unique character of Russian institutions. While Peter's idea of an industrial development initiated and directed by the government was strongly opposed and quickly abandoned, the principle of autocracy which had inspired Peter's reforms remained the ideology that dominated industry. Even though this principle was far less effective in practice than at the level of ideology, its long-run result was that the relations between social classes and particularly the exercise of authority by the employers were believed to be subject to the will of the highest power. Hence the grounds of legitimation consisted throughout in references to goals of the community as these were defined by the highest political bodies.[4] In their affirmations of autocratic power the Tsars would express their solicitude for the welfare of their people, and the dictatorship of the proletariat is justified on the ground that it has terminated the exploitation of man by man.

Ideologies of management have been considered so far in the context of two divergent historical traditions. In England they were regarded as class ideologies in the broad sense, i.e., ideas which were formulated to express and promote the ideal and material interests of specific social groups. In Russia the ideologies of social groups were affected throughout by considerations of state, since all group formations and relationships were subject to the Tsar's will, theoretically, and to a more or less sporadic supervision by the police and by the bureaucracy. These ideologies have a particular bearing on the employment relationship, and in the preceding discussion attention was focused upon

---

[4] It is symptomatic that entrepreneurial activities of the individualist type familiar in the West occurred primarily among the lowest social groups, such as peasant serfs and religious dissenters. The dependence of these serfs upon their masters has been discussed above. It is also of interest that the sect of the "old believers," which was very active economically and frequently successful, was primarily recruited from among the peasants. For comments on the economic activities of this sect, see Schulze-Gaevernitz, *op. cit.*, pp. 28–29 and *passim.*

the social position of employers and workers in the beginning phase of industrialization. I turn now to a consideration of ideologies in terms of their immediate relevance to the performance of work.

b. Ideologies and the Ethics of Work Performance

In his work on the Protestant Ethic Max Weber attempted to show that religious beliefs had a direct influence upon the economic activities of a social group. Theological doctrines had created an acute sense of uncertainty concerning salvation which intensified the work habits and the asceticism of the parishioners, and consequently gave great impetus to the development of entrepreneurial activity. This Puritan credo became seculiarized as the concern with uncertainty decreased and as men became more confident in the foreordained coincidence between virtue and success. Secularization advanced further as failure in the world was attributed to a lack of foresight even in such matters as marriage, and later on to the absence of those individual qualities which "manifestly" had led to success in the case of the great men of affairs. This process of secularization suggests an increasingly complacent satisfaction with things as they are and a decreasing concern with the driving uncertainties of a religious conscience. But it suggests also that secular beliefs had an increasing influence upon the economic conduct of employers and workers alike. To be sure, many of the early entrepreneurs continued to order their lives in accordance with the severe precepts of the Puritan credo. As time went on, however, entrepreneurs turned to the secular ideology of individual striving and success at the same time that modern industry made increasing demands upon the exertions and the self-discipline of industrial workers.

The ideology of the English entrepreneurial class involved arguments of defense and attack which served to define the position of industry and of those who promoted industry. Whether the workers were regarded as "depraved" or whether they were admonished to exert themselves, it is unlikely that employers and their spokesmen expected their ideas to affect the standards of work performance, one way or the other. Given the relative abundance of labor, they were content to rely on the pressure of necessity to ensure the work performance they needed. Moreover, the relatively simple methods of production and a lack of organizational know-how probably contributed to this lack of concern with the worker in any other terms.

In the household industry, for example, the merchant employer furnished the raw materials to each of a number of domestic workers in separate households, and their performance could be supervised with accuracy when the finished product was delivered and the piece rate paid. Under these conditions, there was no "need" for an ethic of work performance, because this organization of production imposed the whole burden of substandard work performance upon the worker himself and, hence, did not present a managerial problem. In the textile manufactories the labor supply was frequently abundant enough to exert a similar pressure upon the labor force. Labor management was a significant problem only where labor was scarce, as in the Scottish mills of Robert Owen or in the famous Lowell Mills of New England. In these exceptional enterprises, reliance was placed upon the moralistic upbringing of the operatives, as well as upon the effects of education and of welfare measures.[5] Generally speaking, however, the operation of industry did not depend upon a conscious managerial concern with the attitudes of workers. The early industrialists became concerned only when in their opinion the workers became antagonistic. Then their indignation at the impertinence of the "lower orders" would frequently prompt them to use every means to stem the tide of rebellion. In the early phases of industrialization, the entrepreneurial concern with the workers was not managerial at all, if by "managerial" we mean the deliberate use of means to organize and control the work force of an enterprise.

Yet even in the early industrial enterprises of England, it was insufficient to rely exclusively upon the pressures of the market and the use of coercion to control the work force. In practice, the workers were managed by a reliance upon the traditions of craftsmanship and of the master-servant relationship. However important these traditions were for industrialization,[6] they were not always compatible with the requirements of industrial production. Traditionally, skilled work was performed at a leisurely pace or in spurts of great intensity, but always at the discretion of the individual worker. In modern industry work must be performed above all with regular intensity. Traditionally, the skilled worker was trained to work accurately on individual designs; in modern industry he must adapt his sense of accuracy to the requirements

[5] See Hannah Josephson, *The Golden Threads* (New York: Duell, Sloan and Pearce, Inc., 1949), pp. 22–23. Mrs. Josephson has emphasized that both Owen and Lowell relied for their labor supply upon workers who had to be attracted from a distance, whose upbringing was moralistic and strict, at any rate in many cases, and for whom adequate housing had to be provided which facilitated both education and supervision.

[6] Cf. the discussion on pp. 51–56.

of standardization. In handicraft production, each individual owned his own tools and was responsible for their care; by and large this is not true in modern industry, so that the care of tools and machinery is divorced from the pride of ownership. Traditionally, skills were handed down from generation to generation and, consequently, were subject to individual variations. In industry the effort has been to a standardize the steps of work performance as much as possible. It is probable that entrepreneurs could ignore this relative incompatibility of traditional work methods with industrial production as long as managerial responsibility as well as all risks of managerial failure fell to the lot of the subcontractors.

The problems of labor management have come to the fore, wherever the organization of production involved the concentration of all work operations within the enterprise and depended to some extent upon an *internalized* ethic of work performance on the part of unskilled as well as of skilled workers. Under the conditions of factory production, such an ethic involves a number of variables. Workers must be willing to do the work assigned with a degree of steady intensity. They must have a positive interest in accuracy and exercise reasonable care in the treatment of tools and machinery. And they must be willing to comply with general rules as well as with specific orders in a manner which strikes some reasonable balance between the extremes of blind obedience and capricious unpredictability. And it is this last qualification which brings the general attributes of an ethic of work performance within the framework of an industrial organization; for under conditions of factory production the intensity of work, its accuracy, and the careful treatment of tools and machinery cannot remain the attributes of an individual's performance. Rather these qualities of work must be coordinated with the production schedule, and that coordination depends to some extent on the good judgment of each worker in his every act of complying with rules and orders.[7]

---

[7] The importance of such "good judgment" is naturally much greater in the case of the skilled worker than in the case of the unskilled, but it is neither absent nor negligible in the case of the latter. What can be "accomplished" by ordinary workers if they decide to withhold their good judgment is well illustrated by the case of inmates of Nazi concentration camps, who were employed in factories during the war and who sabotaged the production effort by consistently asking for detailed instructions on what to do next. According to Eugen Kogon, they managed to reduce production in this manner up to 80 per cent. See Eugen Kogon, *Der SS Staat* (Stockholm: Bermann-Fischer, 1947), pp. 341–43.

It is probable that in England this ethic of work performance developed among the masses of workers out of the combined legacies of craftsmanship, the Puritan ethic, and the rising ideology of individual striving and success. But it is important to add that these legacies had become effective among industrial workers (and that to a certain extent the workers had become adapted to the disciplines of factory work) *prior* to the growth of modern, large-scale industry. It is easiest to appreciate the significance of timing in this respect by considering the contrast with the Russian development.

The doctrines of autocratic rule assumed the total depravity of workers and serfs. An ethic of work performance was not expected of the laboring masses; it was assumed rather that they owed the utmost exertions to their masters and that they needed to be punished severely if they failed in their obligations. Autocratic rule relied upon the omnipresence of fear and coercion to make workers and serfs act as they ought to act, and its ideological appeals exclusively stressed the sacred duty of submission.

> . . . in their instruction to the people [the clergy] should remind them how sacred is the duty of submitting to the authorities, and above all to the Highest authority; how necessary is a trusting and united respect for the government, which of course knows better than private persons what is the good of all, and cannot but wish the well-being of its subjects; and how dangerous is credulous acceptance of injudicious or ill-intentioned advice, from which proceed folly and disorders. . . .[8]

The distinctive feature of this and many similar appeals was the emphasis upon submission to the government as the principal rule of conduct. Subordination to the master was but a token of the worker's submission to the highest authority. And this political interpretation of obedience precluded ideological appeals concerned with the inculcation of work habits, just as the rank consciousness of Russian employers found expression in the expectation that coercion and fear rather than conscience would prompt the worker to exert himself.

It is instructive to consider the comparison with England. There also the assumption was widespread in the late eighteenth and early nineteenth centuries that the laboring poor were depraved. Complete submission to the higher classes and the government was demanded without equivocation. A real concern with the attitudes of workers only arose (as it did in Russia) when the people showed signs of rebelliousness. Yet these similarities were superficial. In England, the depravity

---

[8] Statement of the Metropolitan Filaret of Moscow in 1839, advising the police on how the peasants could be quieted, cited in John S. Curtiss, *Church and State in Russia* (New York: Columbia University Press, 1940), p. 30.

of the poor was rarely mentioned without reference to the good qualities which every self-respecting man can develop, and the demands for submission were couched in terms which made submission synonymous with ideal qualities of work and conduct.[9] There was little distinction between the work performance expected of the ideal laborer and the submission expected of the laborer as a citizen to the authority of government. In Russia, this distinction was fundamental. Employers failed to appeal to the conscience or self-esteem of the workers; and the reliance on fear and coercion effectively precluded the development of an internalized ethic of work performance. The demand for submission, on the other hand, was only related to civil obedience and religious orthodoxy, but not to any other aspect of personal conduct. It may be suggested that the employers acted as they did because their own self-esteem depended upon an exercise of authority patterned after that of the landowners and the Tsar. And the officials of the Tsarist government were concerned with the conduct of the people only in so far as the maintenance of public order made that concern necessary. To have gone beyond the suppression of disturbances would have been outside the established routine of officials, for whom an unconditional submission to the Tsar's supreme power was an unquestioned axiom.

Under these circumstances, an ethic of work performance did not become a managerial problem in Russia until after the revolution of 1917 and hence until industrialization had become synonymous with the development of large-scale enterprises. It is instructive to read Lenin's reflections on this problem, written in 1918.

> The Russian is a bad worker compared with workers of the advanced countries. Nor could it be otherwise under the Tsarist regime and in view of the tenacity of the remnants of serfdom. The task that the Soviet government must set the people in all its scope is—learn to work. The Taylor system, the last word of capitalism in this respect, like all capitalist progress, is a combination of subtle brutality of bourgeois exploitation and a number of its greatest scientific achievements in the field of analyzing mechanical motions during work, the elimination of superfluous and awkward motions, the working out of correct methods of work, the introduction of the best systems of accounting and control, etc. The Soviet Republic must at all costs adopt all that is valuable in the achieve-

---

[9] The polemical literature initiated by Marx always reserved its most caustic invectives for the hypocrisy of employers, who admonished starving workers to work hard, live frugally, and be content with their lot. Yet the contrast with Russia suggests that this moralizing approach differed significantly from a demand for submission as such. The selfish interests which no doubt dominated both approaches cannot explain the difference between them, nor is the repeated "discovery" of these interests very illuminating in itself.

ments of science and technology in this field. The possibility of building socialism will be determined precisely by our success in combining the Soviet government and the Soviet organization of administration with the modern achievements of capitalism.[10]

In the years following the revolution this program was acted upon, and many of these efforts were uncoordinated as well as controversial. In the literature of the 1920's there is abundant evidence of an apotheosis of technology; the poets of the revolution vied with one another in their efforts to celebrate the thundering machines, the world-shaking power of man, and the vision of an industrialized Russian nation emerging from the empty steppes.[11] There were virulent debates about the "new collective man" as contrasted with the "soul-encumbered individual man," whose image suggested decadence, capitalist heresy, and an idealistic interpretation of history. Nearly all spokesmen of the revolution believed fervently in the creative initiative of the masses, presumably because they were acutely aware of Russian backwardness.

These views were by no means confined to the poets and theorists of the revolution; they were applied directly to the problems of productivity and labor discipline in economic enterprises. In accordance with a resolution of the Central Trade Union Council of 1920, A. K. Gastev, who was a poet as well as an industrial engineer, founded a Central Labor Institute, which was to promote the scientific study of factory organization and of industrial psychology. The purpose of this institute was stated in these characteristic terms:

> The cultural level of the masses is low, yet they believe themselves close to a turning-point in history. Their spirit is growth, they await great determining gestures, they dream of great men, who are leaders, they anticipate the advent of gigantic technical powers. Europe and America are guarding established traditions, while Eastern Europe witnesses a spring-flood of an incomparable love of life, an unlimited belief in progress. The land of tremendous rivers, unruly hurricanes, steppes without limit, which is peopled by pilgrims and pioneers, will give birth to an unusual

[10] Lenin, *Selected Works*, Vol. VII, pp. 332–33. It may be added that Lenin inveighed against the " 'Left-Wing' Childishness and Petty-Bourgeois Mentality" (in *ibid.*, pp. 351–78) of those who feared that labor discipline would restore capitalism, alienate the workers, diminish their initiative, and thereby jeopardize productivity. Lenin's praise of work habits may be found in *ibid.*, Vol. VIII, pp. 238–46, and Vol. IX, pp. 447 and *passim*. The Taylor system, mentioned by Lenin, is discussed below on pp. 274–81.

[11] See, for example, Herbert Marshall, ed., *Mayakovsky and his Poetry* (London: The Pilot Press, 1945), pp. 49, 52–53, and *passim;* C. M. Bowra, *A Second Book of Russian Verse* (London: The Macmillan Company, 1948), pp. 75 and *passim;* René Fülöp-Miller, *The Mind and Face of Bolshevism* (London: G. P. Putnam's Sons, 1927), pp. 127–249.

patriotism and will call into life courageous men of daring deeds and accomplishments. . . .

We shall participate in these new battalions, and our Institute should become their first banner.[12]

Gastev's Labor Institute was to develop a new science of work. All bodily movements of the worker were to be analyzed in terms of the basic elements of striking and pushing. On the basis of such knowledge the workers would be trained to improve their discipline and increase their productivity. The goal was to make the greater part of all work automatic and to accept the mechanization of life as fearlessly as one accepted the growth of trees or the expansion of the railway.[13]

Gastev's methods were attacked vigorously, but the scientific study of management and of industrial psychology were officially endorsed and promoted. Many different approaches were tried and technical as well as political controversies developed along with scientific experimentation. But this concern of the technicians and the authorities with the problems of management and productivity was paralleled also by an organized popular movement to promote "scientific labor organization." In June, 1923, first in the ranks of the Red Army and then in offices and factories, small groups were formed which resolved to fight for the "proper use and economy of time." Soon, similar groups were constituted in many parts of the country. It is probable that the formation of these groups was entrusted to the "activists" of the trade-union and the party, a device which Communist ideology explains as the leadership of the masses by the most advanced segment of the working class. These groups were formally organized in the *Time League,* whose members were obliged to keep a timecard on which they would record their daily activities. Each member was further obligated to protest against, and to report, every waste of time he encountered. Here is the text of a leaflet with which the *Time League* sought to eliminate the "organizational illiteracy" of the Russian people:

Time!   System!   Energy!
What do these words mean?
Time:
  Measure your time, control it!
  Do everything on time! exactly, on the minute!
  Save time, make time count, work fast!
  Divide your time correctly, time for work and time for leisure!
  Utilize your leisure so as to work better afterwards!

[12] Quoted in Franziska Baumgarten, *Arbeitswissenschaft und Psychotechnik in Russland* (München: R. Oldenbourg, 1924), p. 13.
[13] *Ibid.,* p. 16.

System:
Everything according to plan, according to system!
A notebook for the system. Order in your place of work!
Each must work according to plan.
Energy:
Pursue your goal stubbornly!
Try hard. Don't retreat after failures!
Always finish what you have started!
Communist Americanism, realism and vigilance! [14]

Again a comparison with the Western industrial development is instructive. To "make time count," to use leisure "so as to work better afterwards," to be orderly and work according to plan, to show perseverance in the face of reverses: these were the familiar admonitions of the Puritan divines in late seventeenth-century England. Two centuries were to elapse before in the late nineteenth century men like Frederick W. Taylor turned their attention to problems of industrial organization and labor management.[15] Another way of making the same observation is to state that in the West two hundred years of moral and religious education preceded the rise of modern large-scale industry, in which the technical and administrative organization of the enterprise make unprecedented demands upon the discipline of the individual worker. In Russia, on the other hand, both developments coincided, mass education of the workers and the technical and administrative organization of large-scale industry occurring at one and the same time.[16] Thus, in the West mass education of the people was the result of unplanned growth which "scientific management" could take for granted. In Russia the development of labor discipline and of "scientific manage-

---

[14] Quoted in *ibid.*, pp. 111–12. The phrase "Communist Americanism" reflects the enthusiasm for technology in the early 1920's, when "America" was the symbol of technological advance. To emulate and surpass the West was a popular goal before it was claimed that Russia was in every way superior to the West. This shift became known at the end of World War II, but it probably began during the first years of Hitler's regime in Germany. See Klaus Mehnert, *Stalin vs. Marx* (London: G. Allen and Unwin, 1952).

[15] Taylor's name is the most famous, but efforts similar to his were made in a number of countries. Some British pioneers are discussed in Urwick and Brech, *The Making of Scientific Management*, Vols. I and II, while French and German work in this field is reviewed in L. H. A. Geck, *Die sozialen Arbeitsverhältnisse im Wandel der Zeit* (Berlin: Julius Springer, 1931).

[16] Likewise, a widespread enthusiasm for technology developed in Russia at the same time that the most advanced techniques of production were introduced, while in England these two phases were separated by two or three generations. In this respect Russia is, however, rather typical, since broadly the same contrast may be made between England and Germany or Japan.

ment" were attempted at the same time under the leadership of the dictatorial party and subject to its supervision.

As we have seen, Tsarist officials had at one point attempted to implement autocratic rule by supervising the employer's power over the workers and by supervising the workers' reactions to the employers. Lenin had transformed this tendency into a principle of government under the dictatorship of the proletariat. And it was in keeping with his precepts if in the early 1920's the Soviet government sponsored "scientific management" as well as a mass movement for greater labor discipline, thus illustrating the twin demands for authoritative directives within the enterprise and the correction and better implementation of these directives by the organization of mass initiative.[17] The relations between managers and workers, however, were imbued with political significance, not merely because of this dual intrusion of government, but because this intrusion was legitimized by references to the backwardness of Russia and to her encirclement by capitalist enemies. That backwardness had to be overcome; the country had to become independent of foreign aid; it had to be in possession of the most advanced industry of the world, to preserve its independence and secure the final victory of socialism. The exercise of authority in economic enterprises and the agitation among the people for labor discipline and productivity were both means to these political ends.[18] Among the masses of the people an ethic was propagated according to which every work performance was to be a test of allegiance to a national cause and a world mission.

I have considered the ideologies of management in their relation to an ethic of work performance at the beginning of industrialization. It is apparent that the contrast between ideologies in England and Russia was accentuated by the discrepancy in timing between mass education and the organization of large-scale economic enterprises. However, both the belief in individual striving and success and the belief in work as an act of political allegiance have had to cope with the

---

[17] In the West, "scientific management" was introduced on the tacit assumption that labor discipline existed already but needed to be redirected. Moreover, employers and their agents act from positions of authority and are in no position to supplement their efforts by the "organization of mass initiative."

[18] These are the arguments with which Stalin justified the necessity of forced industrialization. Cf. his speech, "The Right Deviation of the CPSU," cited in K. A. Petrossjan, *Die sowjetische Methode der Industrialisierung* (Berlin: Verlag Die Wirtschaft, 1953), p. 202. For a summary of the official position of the party see *ibid.*, pp. 58–92, 199–216.

problems posed by the internal bureaucratization of industry.[19] I shall consider the factual evidence for this bureaucratization before I turn to an examination of its organizational and ideological implications.

c. Indexes of Bureaucratization

The most useful, single index of the internal bureaucratization of economic enterprises is the proportion of salaried employees in the occupational structure of a country. With industrialization the proportion of independent individual proprietors declines and that of economically dependent employees increases. Among dependent employees the proportion of salaried workers increases more rapidly than that of manual workers wherever the number of large-scale economic enterprises increases rapidly. In the United States, for instance, the total gainfully occupied population increased by 49 per cent from 1910 to 1940. During this period individual proprietors increased by 17 per cent, manual workers by 49 per cent, and salaried employees by 127 per cent.[20] These illustrative figures point to significant changes in the occupational structure, which are relatively recent. The bureaucratization of economic enterprises, however, began with the Industrial Revolution.

At one time individual entrepreneurs performed a large variety of routine administrative tasks in addition to their "distinct economic function of undertaking new things," which Schumpeter has singled out for special emphasis.[21] Seen historically, bureaucratization may be interpreted as the increasing subdivision of the functions which the owner-managers of the early enterprises had performed personally in

[19] "Bureaucracy" is used here in its descriptive sense, which *Webster's New Collegiate Dictionary* defines as "routine procedure in administration," as "a system of carrying on the business of government by means of bureaus, each controlled by a chief." The government under consideration here is, of course, the government of industry. I prefer the term "bureaucratization" to the term "bureaucracy," because the first term indicates that an on-going process is under consideration, which the terms "bureaucracy" or "administration" do not. The process I have in mind is the gradual substitution of "routine procedures" for traditional practices. The implications of this use of terms are discussed in Sections *d* and *e* of this chapter.

[20] The absolute figures for the period are: gainfully occupied from 34.7 to 51.6 millions; individual proprietors from 3.2 to 3.8 millions; manual workers from 19.7 to 29.5 millions; and salaried employees from 5.6 to 12.7 millions. See Lewis Corey, "The Middle Class," in Bendix and Lipset, *Class, Status and Power*, p. 372.

[21] Cf. Schumpeter, *Capitalism, Socialism, and Democracy*, p. 132.

the course of their daily routine.   These functions may be divided into labor management, technical staff work, administrative management, and mercantile functions of purchasing, sales, and finance.   As the work involved became more extensive and complex with the development of economic enterprises, it came to be delegated to subordinates both with regard to routine work and with regard to selected aspects of the entrepreneurial function proper.[22]   During the initial period of growth, the most important subordinates were likely to be relatives of the founder or persons who had earned his confidence and who frequently married into his family.   The administrative and managerial work of early entrepreneurs, the importance of family ties, and the rather gradual increase of salaried employees in the early period (compared with the increase of workers) are reflected in the following record of a Swedish firm: [23]

TABLE 5. NUMBER OF SALARIED EMPLOYEES AND WORKERS IN A SWEDISH FIRM, 1845–1873

Year	Plant Managers and Draftsmen	Bookkeeper and Correspondent	Total Salaried	Total Number of Workers
1845	2	1	3 *	30
1855	4	3	7 †	210
1865	6	6	12	288
1873	9	6	15	435

* All members of the family.
† Includes four members of the family.

This increase in the number of salaried employees was coterminous with changes in the organization of economic enterprises.   These changes can be understood most clearly by contrasting the system of subcontracting with the position of the foreman in modern industry. Subcontracting typically involved a contract between a merchant enterpriser and one or several subcontractors, in which the latter obliged themselves to deliver a given quantity of goods at a stipulated quality and price.   The organization of labor and sometimes also of production

[22] Fritz Croner has made the interesting suggestion that the relatively high social status even of salaried employees who are poorly paid may be attributed to the fact that their work was at one time a part of the entrepreneur's daily task. See Fritz Croner, *Die Angestellten in der Modernen Gesellschaft* (Frankfurt: Humboldt Verlag, 1954), pp. 34–38.

[23] Cf. the interesting historical illustrations of these tendencies in *ibid.*, pp. 34–56 and *passim*. The table is taken, in abbreviated form, from p. 103 of the same work.

was left to the subcontractors.[24] Today, subcontracting in this sense has disappeared completely from industries which require heavy capital investments, the concentration of operations in single plants and highly technical as well as long-run planning of production. Most of the functions which the subcontractors performed have been assigned to separate departments, and the immediate foreman of the workers has retained only the function of direct supervision. It may be useful to summarize the changes which have occurred in a highly developed branch of production such as the English metal industries, by comparing the functions of the early subcontractors with those of the modern foremen.[25]

Rights and Duties	Subcontractors	Foremen
Makes employment contract with workers	x	...
Makes production contract with employer	x	...
Recruits and selects workers	x	only in part
Trains and inducts workers	x	only in part
Supervises and disciplines workers	x	only in part
Pays workers on a time- or piece-basis	x	...
Has a legal right to a share in the profits	x	...
His wage is paid on a time-basis	...	x

This transformation in the management of labor has made the foreman of today into an executive agent of various departments which specialize in one or another of the separate functions of contract nego-

[24] Whether the subcontractors only organized the labor force, or whether they also organized the process of production, depended upon how much the subcontracting system of a given industry was removed from the domestic industry. In some instances subcontractors were merely another link between scattered domestic workers and the merchant-entrepreneur. In other cases, such as the metal industries, the entrepreneur had built the plant and the subcontractor served primarily as an organizer and supervisor of labor at the blast furnace. What form the subcontracting system took depended upon the technology and the consequent degree of concentration in the different industries.

[25] I am indebted to William T. Delaney for his survey of these materials. The summary list is taken from William T. Delaney, *The Spirit and Structure of Labor-Management in England, 1840–1940* (M.A. Thesis, Department of Sociology and Social Institutions, University of California, Berkley, 1952), p. 66. It may be added that this confrontation omits important intermediate steps in the development from "subcontracting" to modern foremanship.

TABLE 6. Number of Administrative and Production Employees in Industry for Selected Countries and Selected Years *

Year	(A) Administrative Employees †	(P) Production Employees	A/P
	I. *United States*		
1899	348,000	4,496,000	7.7%
1909	750,000	6,256,000	12.0
1923	1,280,000	8,187,000	15.6
1929	1,496,000	8,361,000	17.9
1937	1,518,000	8,553,000	17.7
1947	2,578,000	11,916,000	21.6
	II. *France*		
1901	425,000	3,609,000	11.8
1906	392,000	3,772,000	10.4
1921	671,000	4,650,000	14.7
1926	699,000	5,458,000	12.8
1931	762,000	5,496,000	13.9
1936	635,000	4,355,000	14.6
	III. *Great Britain*		
1907	408,000	4,755,000	8.6
1924	627,000	4,708,000	13.0
1930	589,000	4,286,000	13.7
1935	676,000	4,482,000	15.0
1948	1,126,000	5,651,000	20.0
	IV. *Germany* ‡		
1895	266,000	5,530,000	4.8
1907	606,000	7,922,000	7.6
1925	1,122,000	9,463,000	11.9
1933	802,000	5,718,000	14.0
	V. *Sweden*		
1915	25,000	374,000	6.6
1920	37,000	417,000	8.9
1925	34,000	392,000	8.7
1930	45,000	455,000	9.9
1935	54,000	471,000	11.5
1940	76,000	555,000	13.7
1945	111,000	639,000	17.3
1950	140,000	663,000	21.0

* Figures in this table have been obtained from the following sources:

United States: Recomputed from Seymour Melman, "The Rise of Administrative Overhead in the Manufacturing Industries of the United States, 1899–1947," *Oxford Economic Papers* (1951), Vol. III, p. 66.

France: Ministère du Travail et de la Prévoyance Sociale, *Résultats du Recensement Général de la Population 1906*, Vol. I, 2nd section, p. 187, Table IV

214

tiation, personnel recruitment, training, and so on. Increasingly, it has become a matter of discretion whether or not these departments consult the foreman. The following summary, based on a study of one hundred American companies which were sampled for the purpose of analyzing the *best* practices in American industry, illustrates this point clearly.

Hiring. In two-thirds of the companies replying, the personnel department interviews and selects new employees, while the foreman has final say; but in one-third the foreman has no voice in hiring.

Discharge. Foremen have some say in discharge, but only in one-tenth of all cases can they discharge without any consultation.

Pay Increases and Promotion. These must almost always be approved by other authorities.

Discipline. In only one-tenth of all cases do foremen have complete charge of discipline.

Grievances. Discussion with the foreman is generally the first step in the grievance procedure, but the extent to which he settles grievances is not clear. A small sample in the automotive-aircraft industries shows that this may range from 45 per cent to 80 per cent.

Policy-making. Only 20 per cent of the companies replying held policy-meetings with foremen.[26]

These findings illustrate the process of internal bureaucratization in the most advanced industries with regard to the management of labor. That process consists in the subdivision of this (as of other) entre-

---

(for 1901 and 1906); *ibid.*, (1927), Vol. XLVII, pp. 11, 13 (for 1921). Sous-secretariat d'état et d'Economie Nationale, Bureau de la Statistique Générale, *Recensement Général de la Population* (1931), Vol. I, 3rd section, p. 95 (data for 1926), p. 94 (data for 1931); Institut National de la Statistique et des Etudes Economiques, Statistique Générale de la France, *Annuaire Statistique* (1946), Vol. LVI, pp. 17, 19 (for 1936).

Great Britain: Seymour Melman, *Dynamics of Industrial Productivity* (Chapter 11, Table 1), unpublished manuscript, by permission of the author.

Germany: Statistik des Deutschen Reichs, Berlin, 1937, Vol. 466, Table 7, p. 194. *Sweden:* Croner, *op. cit.*, pp. 120–21.

Great care has been taken to make the figures for each country internally consistent and to make them as comparable as possible for all five countries. Success in this respect, however, can only be proximate, and it is best to think of comparisons among several countries in terms of orders of magnitude and over-all trends.

† The figures for administrative employees *exclude* owners and top executives.

‡ The German and French series were not extended beyond the 1930's because the more recent figures cannot be put on a basis comparable with the earlier figures. Taken independently, however, the more recent data also show an increasing bureaucratization.

[26] Ernest Dale, *The Development of Foremen in Management* (Research Report No. 7; New York: American Management Association, 1945), p. 9.

preneurial functions with the result that each phase, such as recruitment, pay administration, etc., becomes the task of a separate administrative staff consisting of technical and administrative specialists as well as of a number of salaried employees performing routine work.

Historically, the clearest index of bureaucratization is the over-all increase in the number of salaried employees. While it is clear that bureaucratization in this sense is a characteristic trend in all industrialized countries, it is noteworthy that there exist marked differences between them. A very general, quantitative measure of this trend may be obtained, at any rate, for a recent period by comparing the number of administrative (or salaried) employees with the number of production workers in the manufacturing industries of several countries. In Table 6 figures are given for the United States, France, Great Britain, Germany, and Sweden in selected years.

For each country an A/P ratio has been added, which indicates the number of administrative employees as a per cent of the number of production employees. This ratio is a useful measure of the composition of employees in industrial enterprises in each of the several years, and it is instructive to observe the striking differences between countries (Chart I). While the A/P ratio has increased in all of them, that in-

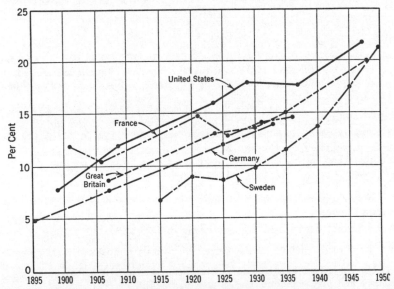

CHART I. Ratios of administrative and production employees for five countries in selected years.

crease has been most marked in the United States and Sweden, while it has been more moderate in Great Britain and Germany. In the case of France, it is noteworthy that in the early years of the twentieth century the level of bureaucratization of French industry (as measured by this index) was considerably higher than in any of the other countries. During subsequent years, however, the French index remained at roughly the same level, while the corresponding index of the other countries increased markedly, though at different rates.

As an index of bureaucratization the A/P ratio reflects cumulative changes in the proportionate composition of employees in industry, but it does not represent the rates of change in the total numbers over time. While both the proportion and the numbers of administrative employees have increased, it may be noted that these increases have occurred at varying rates in the several countries. These rates may be compared with the corresponding rate of change in the number of production employees. To facilitate this comparison, the two trends have been plotted for each country on separate, semilogarithmic charts so that the increasing numbers of administrative and of production employees can be seen together with their respective rates of change over time. (Charts II to VI.) By this method of representation, several other similarities and differences among these five countries become apparent.[27] Except in the case of France, the most rapid increase of administrative employees occurred in the earliest period covered by our data. In the case of Sweden, the United States, and Great Britain, the slope of the curve representing administrative employees decreases after this initial period and then increases again. In the case of Germany, our data do not extend beyond this period of decrease.[28] These diminishing increases or absolute decreases in the number of administrative employees seem to coincide with the depression in the several countries. But it is striking that in France the slope of the declining curve is nearly the same for both administrative and production employees, while in Germany production employees declined much faster than administrative employees.

Another pattern emerges if the charts are examined in terms of the relation between the two curves over the whole period. In the case of the United States and Sweden, there is a notable and rather steady increase in the number of production employees as well as an almost

[27] The curves are interpolations between the years for which the data were available and may, therefore, hide certain fluctuations.

[28] For Sweden the period of decrease is 1920–1925, for Great Britain, 1924–1930, for the United States, 1929–1937, for Germany, 1925–1933.

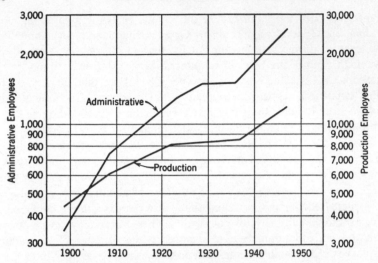

CHART II.   Increase in the number of administrative and production employees in industry, the United States, 1899–1947 (in thousands).

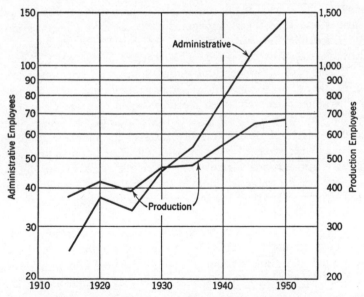

CHART III.   Increase in the number of administrative and production employees in industry, Sweden, 1915–1950 (in thousands).

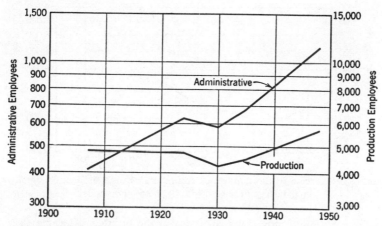

CHART IV.   Increase in the number of administrative and production employees
in industry, Great Britain, 1907–1948 (in thousands).

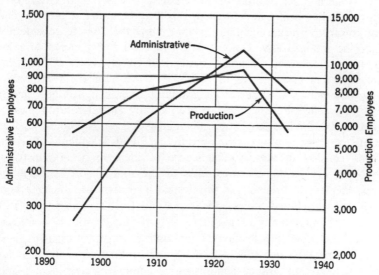

CHART V.   Increase in the number of administrative and production employees
in industry, Germany, 1895–1933 (in thousands).

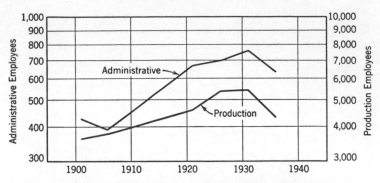

CHART VI. Increase in the number of administrative and production employees in industry, France, 1901–1936 (in thousands).

equally steady and more rapid increase in the number of administrative employees. In Great Britain the number of production employees remained the same or decreased from 1907 to 1930 and increased slowly thereafter, while during the entire period except for the interval 1924 to 1930 the number of administrative employees increased. Compared with the United States and Sweden, this may be called a greater tendency toward bureaucratization in the sense that for a considerable period the administrative employees in English industry increased, while production employees did not. France and Germany are distinguished from the other countries in the sense that the number of production employees increased rather more gradually and then declined sharply during the depression, in the case of Germany almost returning to the level of 1895. While this pattern distinguishes these two countries from the others, there is also a striking difference between them. This difference consists in the very high rate of increase of administrative employees in Germany compared with the much more gradual and erratic increase in France. In this respect Germany was, in fact, comparable to the United States and Sweden, at least for the period 1895 to 1925, when Germany's rapid increase in both categories of employees reflected the rapid introduction of rationalization measures in industry. In this respect France differs from the other three countries as does Great Britain. In France administrative employees started at a relatively high level and increased rather gradually. It is at least plausible to suggest that a relatively large number and/or a rapid increase of administrative employees points to a bureaucratization in the negative sense if it is not accompanied by a fairly steady (though not equally rapid) increase in the number of production employees.

The purpose of these figures and charts has been to present a comparative inventory of bureaucratization in the manufacturing enterprises of several highly industrialized countries. The data presented point to an interesting field of comparative investigation,[29] but their function in the present study is to highlight the rather dramatic change in the organizational structure of economic enterprises. How dramatic this change has been in some instances may be illustrated by some figures for the American meat-packing firm, Swift and Company. In 1923 this firm employed 50,000 workers, who were managed by 500 executives; in 1950 the firm employed 75,000 workers who were managed by 2,150 executives. Thus, during a twenty-seven-year period the ratio changed from one executive for every 100 workers to one executive for every 35 workers.[30] Changes such as this have altered the setting of managerial activities and ideologies to such an extent that it appeared advisable to separate the analysis of the early from the modern phase of industrialization.

So far I have considered the bureaucratization of industry in overall historical terms; however, it is interesting to examine the differential incidence of the process as well, for within any one economy the increase in the number and proportion of administrative employees will differ by size of establishment and by industry. The following data for Germany give a breakdown by size of establishment. The data are interesting for several reasons. They show that during this twenty-six-year period the proportion of administrators in German industry increased somewhat more than that of technicians, but the technicians increased proportionately with size while the administrators did not. A high proportion of administrative employees occurred already in enterprises employing from 6 to 50 workers, but this proportion declined somewhat with the size of the enterprise. For example, in 1933 the proportion of administrators was lower in the enterprises employing 1,000+ (7 per cent) than in those employing between 51 and 200 workers (9.9 per cent). Since the German Census (unlike the American) distinguishes between administrative employees and technicians, it enables us to qualify Seymour Melman's conclusion from the American data that bureaucratization varies inversely with the size of establishment.[31] In Germany, this is true only with regard to administrative employees,

[29] Cf. the study by Seymour Melman, *Dynamics of Industrial Productivity*, cited previously, and the work by P. Sargant Florence. See p. 240, n. 65.

[30] "Bringing up the Boss," *Fortune Magazine* (June, 1951), p. 119.

[31] Cf. Melman, "The Rise of Administrative Overhead," *op. cit.*, p. 90.

TABLE 7. PER CENT DISTRIBUTION OF EMPLOYEES IN GERMAN INDUSTRY BY SIZE OF ESTABLISHMENT AND EMPLOYMENT STATUS, 1907–1933 *

Year and Size of Establishment	Salary Earners (Administrative)	Salary Earners (Technicians)	Wage Earners	Participating Family Members
1907:				
1–5	0.7	1.6	80.1	17.6
6–50	4.6	3.6	90.0	1.8
51–200	4.8	3.7	91.5	0.05
201–1000	3.6	3.5	92.9	0.008
1000+	3.1	3.9	93.0	...
1925:				
1–5	2.0	1.0	74.6	22.4
6–50	7.8	2.8	87.0	2.4
51–200	7.7	3.9	88.3	0.1
201–1000	6.7	4.6	88.7	0.005
1000+	5.8	5.9	88.3	...
1933:				
1–5	3.0	0.5	65.7	30.8
6–50	10.3	2.5	82.1	5.1
51–200	9.9	4.2	85.8	0.06
201–1000	8.2	4.8	87.0	0.006
1000+	7.0	6.0	87.0	...

* The data for 1907 are taken from Kaiserliches Statistisches Amt, *Statistik des Deutschen Reichs*, 1910, Vol. 213, pp. 71–77, Table 3; the data for 1925 are taken from Statistisches Reichsamt, *Statistik des Deutschen Reichs*, 1929, Vol. 413, pp. 14–29, Table 3; the data for 1933 are taken from Statistisches Reichsamt, *Statistik des Deutschen Reichs*, 1935, Vol. 462, Part 3, Table 5, pp. 3/24–3/25.

but false with regard to technicians. Because administrative employees are always more numerous than technicians, however, the over-all tendency remains for bureaucratization to be highest in the smaller firms. A detailed examination of the German Census for 1933 revealed that for 21 industries the maximum concentration of administrative employees was found in enterprises employing 11 to 50 workers, whereas the maximum concentration of technicians was found in enterprises employing 1,000+ workers.[32] It seems probable that this finding will prove to be valid for many, if not for all highly industrialized countries. Finally, these data show clearly that the proportion of family members

[32] This conclusion is based on computations from *Statistik des Deutschen Reichs*, Vol. 462, No. 3, Volks, Berufs, und Betriebszählung vom 16. Juni, 1933, pp. 3/7, 3/8.

who participate in the enterprise is largest in the smallest firms and declines rapidly as the size of the firm increases. The official commentary of the *Statistik des Deutschen Reichs*, 1935, adds the explanation that the participation of family members is primarily found in handicraft shops, domestic industry, and in commerce. In addition, it may be noted that in the small firms the participation of family members increased rapidly as economic conditions declined in the 1920's and 1930's. This suggests that such participation has become in part a response to economic emergency.

As mentioned previously, bureaucratization varies with the type of industry. Hence, the over-all increase in the proportion of administrative employees over time and with size may be examined also in terms of the factors which account for the striking differences among industries. In this connection it is of interest to cite the explanatory comments of the German Census (1933), which refer particularly to the relative concentration of salaried employees in different industries.

> The administrative apparatus is especially extensive in those industries in which the process of production is largely mechanized, and in which a relatively small number of workers are required to service the machines. The highest proportion of administrative employees in relation to the entire work force is to be found in the chemical industry (16.2%) and in public utilities providing water, gas and electricity (14.3%). There are also some branches of the food industry, such as cooking oil, margarine, wine and liquor, which have an extensive administrative apparatus. Industries, on the other hand, which are of the handicraft type, or in which human labor plays a significant role in production, have a relatively small administrative staff. For example, relatively few commercial (and administrative) employees are employed in the mining industry, where they constitute 1.5% of the work force in iron ore mining, 1.7% in coal mining, etc.[33]

Although cross-national comparisons along these lines are rather hazardous, it may be suggested that these considerations apply generally. Thus, a high proportion of administrative and technical employees will be found in most capital intensive industries, especially in those which process raw materials in large vats, tanks, or blast furnaces and also in those which manufacture complicated machines or equipment requiring close supervision and considerable technical staff. Such comparisons may be made, for example, between the chemical industries and the public utilities of Germany and Sweden, petroleum refining and flour milling in Germany and the United States: in these industries the proportion of administrative and technical employees is

[33] *Statistik des Deutschen Reichs*, Vol. 462–463, p. 3/8.

uniformly high. This is also true of industries which require much supervision and technical work, like the German optical industry and the American photoengraving and business machine industry. At the other end, one may compare the hat and the boots and shoe industries of both Germany and the United States, in which the proportion of administrative and technical employees is low.[34]

This discussion of the indexes of bureaucratization has been confined so far to a consideration of manufacturing enterprises. Although this is the major concern of the present study, it is necessary to see the bureaucratization of these enterprises in relation to similar processes occurring in other branches of an industrialized economy. Such an over-all perspective can be obtained by considering the increase in the number of salaried employees in manufacturing enterprises in relation to the shift of the working population between the primary, secondary, and tertiary branches of production, which Colin Clark's work has made familiar. The occupational census of 1950 for the Federal Republic of Germany gives a breakdown of the gainfully employed population, which highlights the differential incidence of bureaucratization in this respect.

These figures give an interesting profile of the occupational structure of a highly industrialized economy. The number of self-employed constitutes about one-seventh of the work force. Broadly speaking, self-employment may be interpreted as a token of small enterprises in which relatively few salaried workers are employed. The small, independent farmer, the owner of a machine shop, an independent professional, and a grocery store managed by its owner are examples in the several branches of production. It is of interest that in Germany the

---

[34] I have confined these examples to those comparisons which seem feasible between data from the German Census, data for the United States contained in Melman's study and data for Sweden contained in the study by Croner. Such comparisons are difficult because of differences in the technological development of the same industries in different countries and because of differences in the labor supply and the training of administrative personnel. Cf. the forthcoming studies of Frederick Harbison and his associates on the management of steel companies in several countries. In a preliminary memorandum, Harbison has reported that an American steel company employed ten times as many technicians as a comparable German steel company, more than three times as many general foremen and foremen, one-fifth as many junior technical and clerical employees. While such cross-cultural comparisons of similar enterprises in the same industry are illuminating, it may be suggested that a comparison of parallel contrasts, say, between the steel and the boot and shoe industry in two or more countries, may also be rewarding.

TABLE 8. Number and Per Cent of Gainfully Employed Population in the Federal Republic of Germany, by Principal Branches of Production and Occupational Status, 1950 *

Occupational Status	Primary		Secondary		Tertiary		Total Number
	Number	Per Cent	Number	Per Cent	Number	Per Cent	
I. Independents, workers on own account	1,252,395	24.5	938,083	10.0	1,066,990	15.0	3,257,468
II. Participating family members	2,732,743	53.4	164,542	1.8	287,105	4.0	3,184,390
III. Civil servants	7,395	0.1	2,930	...†	868,206	12.2	878,531
IV. Salaried employees	32,388	0.6	1,106,120	11.8	2,339,730	32.5	3,478,238
V. Workers	1,088,731	21.3	7,127,871	76.3	2,574,943	36.1	10,791,545
Total	5,113,652	99.9	9,339,546	99.9	7,136,974	99.8	21,590,172

* The table includes all gainfully occupied persons, excluding the unemployed and those for whom no definite occupation could be ascertained. The German Census distinguishes among (a) agriculture, animal husbandry, forestry, gardening, and fishing (primary); (b) mining, quarries, utilities, iron and metal manufacturing, manufacturing (other than iron or metal), building and construction (secondary); (c) commerce, banking and insurance, service, transportation, public service (tertiary). *Source: Statistisches Jahrbuch für die Bundesrepublik Deutschland*, 1953, pp. 110–11.
† Below one-tenth of 1 per cent.

self-employed are rather evenly distributed among primary, secondary, and tertiary production, while four-fifths of all family members who help the principal wage-earner are in primary production. If these figures indicate the distribution of the small, nonbureaucratic enterprises, the relative development of internal bureaucratization is apparent from the figures on salaried employees. Somewhat over two-thirds of all salaried employees work in tertiary production, where they constitute about one-third of the work force employed. In terms of this single criterion it is obvious that commerce, transportation, and the service industries are most bureaucratized, since in this branch of production the number of salaried employees is almost equal to the number of workers. Manufacturing, mining, and construction rank second in this respect: almost one-third of all salaried employees work in this secondary branch, but they constitute only 11.8 per cent of the work force in view of the high concentration of production workers. It is apparent, then, that the shift of the working population into tertiary production is principally responsible for the rapid bureaucratization of economic enterprises in highly industrialized countries.

The preceding consideration of indexes of internal bureaucratization does not include data on the Russian development, inasmuch as comparable figures could not be obtained.[35] It may be assumed that with regard to salaried employees changes have taken place in the course of Russian industrialization broadly similar to those we have traced.[36] A like assumption cannot be made with regard to the entrepreneur or manager, whose position has been transformed along with the internal bureaucratization of economic enterprises. In the next section I shall discuss this transformation in terms of the changing career pattern of the "business elite" in the United States. And I shall attempt to relate this development to the Russian scene by making certain comparisons regarding the position of management in the two countries.

d. The Bureaucratization of Management

The proportion of administrative employees varies over time as well as between enterprises of different types and sizes today. These variations have been paralleled by changes in the task and the careers of "business leaders," which in turn reflect changes in the management of economic enterprises. It will be useful to examine the internal bureaucratization of contemporary enterprises before turning to a study of the changing career patterns of entrepreneurs and managers.

The increasing size of industrial enterprises entails certain administrative problems which in each case require for their solution the addition of salaried personnel.[37] Dale points out that in the smallest enterprise the major problem involves the division of work among the owner-manager, perhaps some member of his family, and a few employees. As the enterprise increases in size, it becomes necessary for the owner-manager to delegate to subordinates responsibility for many functions, which he has performed personally in the past. Subsequently, it becomes necessary to delegate further managerial functions, and the problem arises how to do this without overburdening the chief executive officer of the company (span of control). With further increases in

[35] The frequent reclassification and discontinuance of published series makes it impossible to obtain trend figures for administrative and production employees, quite aside from problems of classification. For example, figures for "large-scale industry" in 1923 and 1936 give an A/P ratio of 15.3 and 15.8, respectively, but the classification of "administrative employees" is too unclear for purposes of comparison aside from the shortness of the period. See *Trud v SSSR* (Tsentral'-noe upravlenie narodnokhoziaistvennogo ucheta Gosplana; Moskva, 1936), p. 91.

[36] The organizational structure of Russian industry is discussed in the official handbook by A. Arakelian, *Industrial Management in the USSR* (Washington, D. C.: Public Affairs Press, 1950), pp. 84–100, 122–36.

[37] Ernest Dale, *Planning and Developing the Company Organization Structure* (Research Report No. 20; New York: American Management Association, 1952).

size this problem is solved in part by making one or several staff assistants available to the executive so that his energies can be concentrated on the essential tasks of his position. In still larger enterprises, it may become necessary to hire staff specialists, who will be charged with responsibility for developing plans in several departments of the enterprise. A further increase in size is likely to bring to the fore the problem of decision-making, since the complexity of the enterprise makes it impossible for any one person to have sufficient information for intelligent decision-making; hence, the different management functions become coordinated through group decision-making. And finally it becomes necessary to increase the degree to which responsibility is delegated to subordinates by decentralizing the operations of the enterprise so that each of its branches can be operated efficiently.[38]

This list of managerial devices is a useful guide to an understanding of bureaucratization. According to Dale, these devices are employed as an enterprise passes through different stages of growth to solve the problems of organization that arise as a result of this growth. Of course, these problems of organization continue to demand attention even after the "stage" at which they had to be dealt with initially. Both the addition of administrative staff and changes in the functions of management are concomitants of the managerial devices which Dale has listed. I turn now to a consideration of the career patterns among the business elite as another index of internal bureaucratization.[39]

[38] *Ibid.*, pp. 23–119. I have purposely omitted from this account Dale's estimate of the size of the enterprise at which each of these problems is likely to arise. It seems to me safer to treat this sequence of managerial problems in the sense that the logic of organization will give rise to these problems as the complexity of organization increases. Some small enterprises can be very complex, even if no large enterprises are simple.

[39] Since the following data on the changing career patterns of the American business elite are based on independent study, it is necessary to indicate briefly the procedures used to obtain these results. The basic source of information was the *National Cyclopedia of American Biography,* from which 887 usable biographies of businessmen were obtained. This number represents a sample consisting of every ninth businessman who was born between 1771 and 1920. The Cyclopedia did not, however, contain a sufficient number of cases in the earliest and the most recent periods. Hence, the original sample was supplemented by obtaining 100 biographies of *all* businessmen born between 1771 and 1800, which were contained in the *Dictionary of American Biography* and did not duplicate those already chosen from the Cyclopedia. An additional 110 biographies of businessmen were obtained from *Current Biography,* by choosing *all* businessmen contained in the editions from 1945 to 1952, provided the subject was born after 1890 and not already contained in the original sample from the Cyclopedia. For a more detailed comparison of this with other studies of the American busi-

Since the beginning of the nineteenth century the organization of industry has been transformed.   In order to analyze the effect of bureaucratization on the career patterns of the business and industrial elite, it has been necessary to devise a typology of careers that would facilitate such an analysis.[40]   The career types of business and industrial leaders may be designated by the terms: heirs, entrepreneurs, and bureaucrats.   The career pattern of heirs is most easily characterized. Their outstanding trait is that they have inherited considerable wealth and, hence, have come to control a firm either through direct legacy or through purchase.   Neither entrepreneurs nor bureaucrats are "heirs" in this sense, although this does not preclude their having received assistance from their families at the start of their careers.   But if entrepreneurs and bureaucrats are clearly distinguished from heirs, the distinction between entrepreneurs and bureaucrats is not equally simple. Entrepreneurs start firms of their own at some point in their careers; bureaucrats do not.   At the climax of their careers entrepreneurs are substantial owners of a firm, while bureaucrats are typically salaried executives.   Entrepreneurs sometimes spend a part of their careers as salaried employees; bureaucrats do so invariably and for a major portion of their careers.   These are important distinctions, but in some cases they are distinctions of degree.   Thus, the careers of bureaucrats tend to show a succession of salaried jobs, which lead to an executive position; but then the man may buy into an old firm or may be hired as an executive and become a part-owner.   Entrepreneurs, on the other hand, may hold several salaried jobs before they assume a proprietary position.   In such cases it is a matter of judgment how the careers are to be classified; in this instance, that judgment depends upon the length of time the individual has held a salaried position.[41]

ness elite, cf. the forthcoming publication by S. M. Lipset, Reinhard Bendix, *et al., Studies in Social Mobility.*

[40] Other purposes may require other typologies.   As yet there is little work on the methodological problems involved in the typology of career patterns. The typology discussed in the text was formulated initially on the basis of inspecting some of the 1,097 biographical entries used in the sample, and its utility has been confirmed by the degree to which it reveals significant differences between careers.   Of course, this procedure does not constitute the confirmation of a hypothesis; it merely attests to the utility of a classificatory scheme.

[41] In doubtful cases we have attempted to make a judgment in terms of the dominant characteristics of a career.   This has not been possible, however, in all cases, especially when the individual concerned had, in fact, two careers.   An example of such an unclassifiable case is the bureaucratic career of a salaried executive, who upon reaching this position retires and makes a fortune as a

TABLE 9. PERCENTAGE DISTRIBUTION OF THE AMERICAN BUSINESS ELITE, BY CAREER TYPE AND BY DATE OF BIRTH *

Career-Type	1771–1800 (N = 121)	1801–1830 (N = 75)	1831–1860 (N = 332)	1861–1890 (N = 344)	1891–1920 (N = 131)
Entrepreneurs	76	68	56	36	18
Bureaucrats	5	16	21	29	48
Heirs	19	16	23	35	34
Total	100	100	100	100	100
Not Classifiable	1 (1%)	12 (14%)	21 (6%)	34 (9%)	11 (7%)
Total Subjects	122	87	353	378	142

* Subjects have been classified by the time-period into which their year of birth fell.

Table 9 shows the major results of our study. It presents the classification of a little over 1,000 biographies of prominent businessmen and industrialists by career type. It shows clearly that the proportion of entrepreneurs has sharply declined in the course of American industrialization at the same time that the proportion of "industrial bureaucrats" has increased.[42]

Table 9 shows that the proportion of heirs in the business elite of each generation has gradually increased.[43] This increase of heirs may indicate a proportionate increase in the success with which prominent families of industrialists have managed to facilitate the careers of their descendants. It is difficult to regard this result with confidence until it is confirmed by an independent check. But on the face of it, the study seems to indicate that in spite of the increasing capital requirements of giant firms, there were enough investment opportunities in smaller firms, where a wealthy individual could still acquire a substantial interest.[44] And it should be remembered that the *National Cyclopedia*

realtor. We have not tried to force such cases into our categories. By listing them as "not classifiable" we have some assurance that the majority of the classifications are relatively unambiguous. A fuller description of the career types used in this study is contained in a note at the end of this chapter.

[42] These results are corroborated by William Miller, "The Business Elite in Business Bureaucracies," in William Miller, ed., *Men in Business* (Cambridge: Harvard University Press, 1952), pp. 286–305. Subsequent tables report results primarily for the period since 1831, because this is sufficient to show the contrast of career types, which is of interest here.

[43] This finding coincides with other data which show that the proportion of all business leaders who have received assistance throughout their careers has increased from 18 per cent to 31 per cent.

[44] Heirs come exclusively from such families, by definition.

of American Biography contains profiles of all business leaders judged prominent enough by rather general criteria.[45]

It should be obvious that this differentiation of career patterns is based on over-all judgments of each career. The differences between career patterns are not likely to be evident with the same clarity in any single index that may be devised. For one thing, entrepreneurs, bureaucrats, and heirs alike have participated in the on-going changes of American society; hence, there are no significant differences between them in some respects, while in others the differences may be small. Thus, detailed compilations show that all three types of businessmen and industrialists have predominantly come from families which already occupied a privileged economic position. Likewise, all three types have participated more than the average in the rising educational level of the general population.

One important difference in educational attainment is to be noted. Of the prominent businessmen born between 1831 and 1875 who became entrepreneurs and bureaucrats about two-thirds attained at most a high-school education, while about one-third went to college or beyond. (The heirs divide evenly in this respect.) Yet, for those businessmen born between 1876 and 1920 the educational picture changes: two-thirds or more of the bureaucrats and the heirs attended college, while the educational attainment of the entrepreneurs remained the same.

TABLE 10. PERCENTAGE OF AMERICAN BUSINESS LEADERS ATTAINING DIFFERENT LEVELS OF EDUCATION, BY CAREER TYPE AND DATE OF BIRTH

Period and Educational Attainment	Entrepreneurs	Bureaucrats	Heirs
1831–1875	(N = 234)	(N = 115)	(N = 143)
High school or less	66	62	50
College or more	34	38	50
	100	100	100
1876–1920	(N = 117)	(N = 145)	(N = 165)
High school or less	62	35	28
College or more	38	65	72
	100	100	100

One can infer from these data that the higher level of educational attainment which both the bureaucrats and the heirs show in the second

[45] Hence, our sample is likely to include many individuals which would be excluded in studies which define the term *business leader* more narrowly. Cf. Lipset, Bendix, *et al.*, *Studies of Social Mobility.*

period was the result of very different conditions. For men who depend in part upon education for success in their careers, higher education is a means to career advancement; but for the heirs who are secure in their career chances, higher educational attainment simply reflects their high status and the increasing importance of education in the population generally. It is significant in this respect that the decline of entrepreneurs is reflected in their failure to increase their educational "preparedness." For the increasing educational requirements of modern industry are likely to militate against individuals without educational background. Although this factor is probably a secondary one, it shows clearly that the anti-educational bias of the self-made man has taken its toll.

Another bias of the self-made man is the belief that the young man must start to work early in his life if he wants to get ahead. By tabulating our three career types in terms of the age at the time of the first job, we find that the entrepreneurs were most reluctant to part with this tradition. While the proportion of bureaucrats and heirs who had been born between 1831 and 1875 and who started work before they were twenty years old had already dropped to less than one-third (26 per cent and 30 per cent, respectively), the corresponding proportion of entrepreneurs was still 45 per cent. Of the subjects born after 1876, however, over three-quarters in each career type started work at age twenty-one or over,[46] a finding which suggests that by the last decade of the nineteenth century the age at the start of the work career no longer distinguished between career types.

The bureaucrats among business leaders seem to have participated more than heirs and entrepreneurs in another secular change. The first job an individual takes may not be a good predictor of his subsequent career, especially in the case of future business leaders whose careers are by definition mobile and unpredictable; but the first job is an index of the prevailing outlook on economic activities, for it has been part of the "ideological equalitarianism" in American society to esteem an eminent man if in his youth he also did lowly jobs like everyone else.[47]

[46] The start of an individual's work career is closely related to a low level of educational attainment; however, by selecting age twenty as our criterion, it became apparent that the two variables are not identical. For those born between 1876 and 1920, only 38 per cent of the entrepreneurs went to college, but 77 per cent took their first job at age twenty-one or over.

[47] A fuller discussion is contained in S. M. Lipset and Reinhard Bendix, "Ideological Equalitarianism and Social Mobility in the United States," *Transactions of the Second World Congress of Sociology* (London: International Sociological Association, 1954), Vol. II, pp. 34–54.

It seems that his rise to fame is more praiseworthy if he began his career in a humble position. And it might be added that the strength of this value is not notably diminished by the fact that many of those who started so humbly did not really have to do so, inasmuch as their families were quite well off. It is, therefore, of interest that business and industrial leaders seem to be on the way toward abandoning this tradition, while it seems to have remained strongest among the heirs.[48]

TABLE 11. PERCENTAGE DISTRIBUTION OF FIRST JOBS OF THE AMERICAN BUSINESS ELITE, BY STATUS LEVEL AND DATE OF BIRTH

Period and Status Level of First Job	Entrepreneurs	Bureaucrats	Heirs
1831–1875	(N = 219)	(N = 110)	(N = 125)
High Status *	31	24	33
Low Status †	69	76	67
	100	100	100
1876–1920	(N = 51)	(N = 103)	(N = 79)
High Status	43	43	39
Low Status	57	57	61
	100	100	100

* Includes first jobs as proprietors, firm members, executives, government officials, and professionals.

† Includes first jobs as white-collar workers, salesmen, and manual laborers.

Of course, this distinction between the high or the low status of a first job is quite crude, and the interpretation of these figures is inevitably speculative. Yet a comparison between the two periods shows a clear trend in the same direction for each type of career: an increasing proportion of business leaders begin their work careers in a job of relatively high status. To be sure, a majority still start their careers in the traditional manner. And it is improbable that this practice will be abandoned, since it is an important experience for the future executive to have worked in the lower rungs of the enterprise hierarchy (quite apart from the symbolic meaning attached to the idea of "working from the ground up"). But it may well become even less common than it is in the modern generation of business leaders to start their careers in this manner, since few of them really need to take first jobs of low status and since there are many training substitutes for the experience

[48] It is conceivable that in American society heirs must prove more than others that they accept the premise of equalitarianism.

itself. The men we have classified as "bureaucrats" have so far gone most rapidly in the direction of beginning their careers in positions involving considerable skill and responsibility. If their precedent presages a more general development in the future, then we may see a further impairment of the "rags to riches" myth. As we shall see later, there are signs already that the myth itself is superseded gradually by alternative beliefs, even in the United States, where that myth has swayed the popular imagination more than in any other country.[49]

The bureaucratization of economic enterprises is reflected in the career patterns of business leaders in still another way. As we have seen, bureaucratization involves a detailed subdivision of administrative organization in the enterprise, and such subdivision involves by definition a considerable increase in the number of jobs between the top and the bottom of the administrative hierarchy. This increase means two things: a larger number of ranks and an increase in the number of positions at each rank. These facts should have a decisive influence upon the careers of industrialists. The entrepreneurs, whose careers frequently develop with the enterprise they have helped to initiate, need not spend their time in moving up an administrative hierarchy, and they may, therefore, achieve success at a relatively early age. The industrial bureaucrat, on the other hand, is characterized by a career which involves his gradual advancement from job to job within an administrative hierarchy. Hence, he can be expected to achieve economic success relatively late. For the heirs it is not possible to hypothesize a typical "age of first success." [50]

It would follow from these findings that the careers of entrepreneurs and bureaucrats especially should also show significant differences with reference to the number of positions which each has held during the whole course of his career. In part, this is simply a correlative of age. If entrepreneurs achieve their economic success early, they cannot have held as many positions as the industrial bureaucrats who achieve their success relatively late. The two variables, however, are not synonymous. "First success" at an early age is theoretically quite compatible with a large number of positions held throughout a career, unless it is characteristic for the man who achieves success early to have subse-

---

[49] To avoid misunderstanding I should add that these remarks refer to ideologies, not to "opportunity trends" in American society.

[50] In the case of heirs success depends to a considerable extent upon relations within the family of entrepreneurs, and this factor cannot have a determinate effect upon the age at which an heir may be said to be successful.

TABLE 12. PERCENTAGE DISTRIBUTION OF ENTREPRENEURS, BUREAUCRATS
AND HEIRS, BY AGE AT THE TIME OF "FIRST SUCCESS" AND BY DATE OF BIRTH

Period and Age at Time of "First Success" *	Entrepreneurs	Bureaucrats	Heirs
1831–1875	(N = 137)	(N = 107)	(N = 143)
30 years or under	72	25	56
31 years or over	28	75	44
	100	100	100
1876–1920	(N = 59)	(N = 108)	(N = 84)
30 years or under	76	24	48
31 years or over	24	76	52
	100	100	100

* We have classified our subjects by the age at which they achieved their
"first success," since no other dividing point within the careers of different men
is equally comparable.

quently a relatively stable career in which he changes his jobs rather
infrequently. Of course, the converse is not true, since the man who
achieves success relatively late is likely to have held a rather large
number of positions. While the figures bear out these considerations,
it is of interest that the career pattern of entrepreneurs shows the effects
of bureaucratization, even though entrepreneurs tend to hold fewer
positions during their work history than do bureaucrats. Of the entrepreneurs born between 1771 and 1830 (N = 143), 28 per cent held
five positions or more throughout their careers, a percentage which rose
to 44 per cent for the period 1831–1875 and fell slightly to 39 per cent
for the period 1876–1920. But if an increasing proportion of entrepreneurs held a relatively large number of jobs, a majority of them
(72, 56, and 61 per cent, respectively) has continued to hold four positions or less. By way of contrast it should be mentioned that the proportion of bureaucrats who held five or more positions during their
careers increased from 62 per cent (1831–1875) to 82 per cent (1876–
1920).[51]

Similar contrasts between career patterns are obtained, if they are
compared with regard to two other criteria: transfers between firms and

[51] Recent studies of the job mobility of executives show that the average number of positions held by "industrial bureaucrats" is likely to increase still further.
See Booz, Allen and Hamilton, Management Consultants, *The Growing Problem
of Executive Turnover* (privately printed, 1953).

TABLE 13. Percentage Distribution of Interfirm and Interindustry Transfers of Entrepreneurs and Bureaucrats, by Frequency of Transfer and by Date of Birth

Period and Number of Interfirm and Interindustry Transfers *	Entrepreneurs	Bureaucrats	Per Cent Difference Between Career Types
1831–1875			
Interfirm Transfers	(N = 277)	(N = 99)	
2 or less	66	51⎫	
3 or more	34	49⎭	±15
	——	——	
	100	100	
Interindustry Transfers	(N = 277)	(N = 120)	
1 or none	63	75⎫	
2 or more	37	25⎭	±12
	——	——	
	100	100	
1876–1920			
Interfirm Transfers	(N = 59)	(N = 110)	
2 or less	68	55⎫	
3 or more	32	45⎭	±13
	——	——	
	100	100	
Interindustry Transfers	(N = 60)	(N = 108)	
1 or none	58	71⎫	
2 or more	42	29⎭	±13
	——	——	
	100	100	

* Transfers between firms occur more readily than between industries. Hence, a different measure of mobility had to be used for the two types of transfers.

between industries. As can be expected, the heirs among the business elite showed the least mobility: about 90 per cent of them made two or less transfers between firms and one or no transfer between industries, in each of the periods. Entrepreneurs as well as bureaucrats show more mobility than that. There is no significant change in the mobility pattern of entrepreneurs between these two periods, except possibly a slight increase in the number of interindustry transfers in the recent past. Likewise, there is no significant change over time in the mobility pattern of the bureaucrats, but there is a rather striking difference between them: entrepreneurs show more mobility between industries, while bureaucrats show more mobility between firms. The difference reflects the major characteristics of each type. As Schumpeter has emphasized, the entrepreneur is characterized primarily by his innovating function in the economy. Consequently, he shows a tendency to work in several industries, presumably prompted by the demands of his innovating activity. The bureaucrat, on the other hand, has a primary interest in regular advancement up the administrative hierarchy, and detailed knowledge of the problems of one industry will facilitate his career. This experience can be gained in many firms, and indeed his chances for promotion increase the more he is "in demand" by other firms. Hence, bureaucrats show a greater mobility between firms compared with their entrepreneurial colleagues, but a lesser mobility between industries.

Taken together, these changes in career patterns of the American "business elite" may be regarded as an outgrowth of internal bureaucratization in economic enterprises. Comparable data for the "business elite" in Soviet Russia are not available. Nevertheless, it is possible to consider certain parallels and contrasts, especially with regard to the internal and external bureaucratization of economic enterprises. The preceding survey of American data suggests the increasing importance of "business leaders" who tend to advance more or less slowly through promotion from job to job. This increase in the proportion of "bureaucrats" among the business elite reflects the general increase of salaried employees in economic enterprises and certain parallels to these changes have occurred in Soviet Russia as well.[52] Both the proportion and the number of managers and technicians increased in Russia considerably faster than it ever did in the United States, since rapid economic expansion coincided not only with the destruction of the old elite but also with repeated purges of the new.

> . . . while the total number of workers and employees more than doubled in roughly the first decade of the Plans, the size of the intelligensia increased at the striking rate of 3.8 times between 1926 and 1937. In the same period the number of responsible managers of large and small scale enterprises increased by 4.6 times, and other categories showed even more

[52] The following comparison between factory directors in the United States and in Soviet Russia omits a consideration of Russia in the period between 1917 and the Seventeenth Party Congress in 1934, when major administrative changes were instituted as a result of experiences during the first few years of intensified industrialization. The policies of the earlier period and the changes of 1934 are sketched in Gregory Bienstock, S. M. Schwarz, and Aaron Yugow, *Management in Russian Industry and Agriculture* (New York: Oxford University Press, 1944), pp. 3–16 and *passim*. While these changes were very important, they did not disrupt the continuity of the Russian legacies discussed on pp. 190–97, 209–10. Cf. Haimson, *op. cit.*, pp. 369–76.

marked expansion—the number of engineers and architects being 7.9 times and the number of scientific workers being 5.9 times greater in 1937 than in 1926.[53]

This precipitous expansion of the managerial elite was achieved by centralized direction of education and recruitment. The process is reflected in the results of some sample studies. In 1934, half of a sample of factory directors under the Commissariat of Heavy Industry had only primary school education; two years later, that proportion was still 40 per cent. During the same two-year interval, the proportion of factory directors with higher education rose from 26 per cent to 46 per cent, but this increase was in part due to brief and inferior training courses taken by those who already had extensive experience in industry. It appears probable that the proportion of factory directors with higher education subsequently increased, constituting in 1939 between 82 per cent and 87 per cent of the directors of defense industry and of ferrous metallurgy.[54] The emphasis, however, on higher education as a prerequisite for top managerial positions was checked by the tendency to entrust these positions to members of the Communist party. It is significant in this respect that in the sample studies cited, the overwhelming majority of the factory directors were party members but had little education compared with the Chief Engineers, all of whom had had technical training, while only one-third were members of the party.[55] Thus, in 1939 only 27.6 per cent of all directors of economic establishments were found to have academic training.[56] These findings, however, are compatible with the rapid increase of education among the administrative employees in Soviet industry as a whole. According to Arakelian, 1,045,000 new "specialists" were graduated from the colleges between 1928 and 1940, and the Census for 1939 indicated that 90 per cent of all "specialists" with college education had "completed college during the years of Soviet power." [57] It should be added that persistent efforts have been made to increase the educational level of party officials

[53] Alex Inkeles, "Social Stratification and Mobility in the Soviet Union," in Bendix and Lipset, *Class, Status and Power*, p. 612. In the United States the total number of salaried technicians and managers only doubled between 1910 and 1940, while the total number of workers and clerical employees increased by one-half.

[54] These sample studies by Soviet authorities are reported in David Granick, *Management of the Industrial Firm in the USSR* (New York: Columbia University Press, 1954), pp. 43, 290–91.

[55] *Ibid.*, pp. 48–49.

[56] See Alexander Vucinich, *Soviet Economic Institutions* (Hoover Institute Studies; Stanford: Stanford University Press, 1952), p. 27.

[57] Arakelian, *op. cit.*, p. 89.

which in the long run will also effect an increase in the educational level of factory directors.[58]

This planned creation of a new managerial elite differs strikingly from the inadvertent development of the American "business elite" which I have traced. One aspect of this contrast is obviously the social origin of the two groups. A high proportion of Russian factory directors has come from families of workers and peasants.[59] In the United States, on the other hand, the number of business leaders coming from families of farmers has declined and that coming from worker families has been low throughout.[60] Although this contrast is undeniable, it is also easy to exaggerate. In 1936, Stalin declared that 80 to 90 per cent of the "intelligentsia" had come from the peasantry and the working class. Yet this statement should be considered together with Malenkov's statement of 1941, according to which a large percentage of leading factory positions were held by incompetent men.[61] Presumably, Malenkov referred in part to the managers who had been recruited because of their party work and their social origin—despite their lack of training. While this practice may continue as long as the demand for trained personnel exceeds the supply, there are very significant tendencies pointing toward an increasing self-recruitment of the elite.[62] Clearly, it will remain an open question for some time to come whether on balance these tendencies will lead to more or less status differentiation and status "inheritance" than has been characteristic of the much more gradual recruitment of farmers and workers into the managerial elite of the older industrialized countries.

[58] Vucinich, *op. cit.,* p. 26

[59] Cf. Granick, *op. cit.,* p. 56 and *passim,* with Bienstock, Schwarz, and Yugow, *op. cit.,* pp. 121–22, for conflicting interpretations on this point. While Schwarz seems to have overstated his case, the question of the continued upward mobility of workers cannot be answered on the basis of sample studies up to 1941, as Granick seems to believe. Cf. the article by Inkeles cited above.

[60] Three recent studies are William Miller, "The Business Elite in Business Bureaucracies," in Miller, ed., *op. cit.,* pp. 286–307; Mabel Newcomer, "The Chief Executive of Large Business Corporations," *Explorations in Entrepreneurial History,* Vol. V (October, 1952), pp. 1–34; and Suzanne Keller, *The Social Origins and Career Lines of Three Generations of American Business Leaders* (Ph.D. Dissertation, Columbia University, 1953). Cf. the forthcoming publication by Lipset, Bendix, *et al., Studies in Social Mobility* for a comparison of these studies.

[61] Vucinich, *op. cit.,* p. 24.

[62] The relevant evidence on this point is summarized in Inkeles, *op. cit.,* pp. 613–22. An interesting analysis of increasing status awareness among the new Soviet elite is contained in *Ost-Probleme,* Vol. VI (December 10, 1954), pp. 1980–83.

The great short-run contrast between the social origin of the managerial elite in Russia and the United States is bound up entirely with the existence or absence of centralized planning. It will be useful to compare and contrast the internal and external bureaucratization of economic enterprises in the two systems, especially in terms of the respective positions of the directors or managers. In this respect there are a number of similar developments in Soviet Russia and the United States (as well as in other Western countries). Reference has been made to the increasing educational level among Soviet factory directors and among American business leaders, which reflects the common imperatives of large-scale organization and complex technology. Likewise there is evidence in both countries of the growing importance of step-by-step advancement, so characteristic of bureaucratic careers and so necessary, apparently, in terms of the cumulative experience which such careers facilitate.[63] Among American business leaders the bureaucrats were also distinguished from the entrepreneurs by the fact that a majority of the former held large numbers of jobs during their careers and that this majority was increasing significantly over time. There is evidence that the job mobility of Russian factory directors was high indeed, roughly three-quarters of the factory directors sampled heading their firms on the average less than three years.[64]

Finally, economic enterprises have been organized increasingly in both countries on the basis of the so-called line-and-staff system, which is an organizational index of bureaucratization. The term "line" refers to the hierarchical system of an organization in which one individual issues all commands to subordinates; the term "staff" refers to a division of labor in management in the sense that technical and administrative experts perform fact-finding and advisory functions and that specialized aspects of managerial direction are delegated to submanagers. A combination of these two organizational arrangements poses certain inherent problems which must be solved from case to case.

[63] Cf. the increasing proportion of "bureaucrats" among American business leaders with Granick's finding of a sharp *decrease* in the proportion of factory directors who made their mark outside industry before being appointed to leading positions in industry. See Granick, *op. cit.*, p. 52.

[64] *Ibid.*, p. 51. Though no comparable measure is available, it is quite probable that the job mobility of Soviet managers was much higher than that of managers in Western countries, partly because of political manipulation, especially during the period of the Purges in the late 1930's, and partly because of the great speed of Russian industrialization. Another reason for mobility has been the party's effort to prevent or disrupt the formation of illicit alliances. See Hain:son, *op. cit.*, pp. 457–58.

The hierarchical structure, so well suited for the efficient communication of commands, limits the use of expert management and advice; the functional [staff] system, allowing the use of expert managers and advisers, divides up the execution of commands too much for effective large-scale operation. A system is thus sought which will relieve top government by striking an efficient balance in the division and concentration of rule and work.[65]

The achievement of such balance has posed difficult problems wherever it has been attempted. Too great a proliferation of staff work unnecessarily increases overhead as well as the work load of top management. Also the difficulties of managerial coordination increase markedly wherever the centralized system of a command hierarchy is modified by the introduction of staff specialists for advisory and executive functions. But the similarities between the staff-and-line organization of economic enterprises in the two systems end with this statement of the problems involved.

One major contrast between Russian and American managers consists in the respective relation between the agencies of decision-making and the management of the enterprise. Florence has described the core of "top government" in British and American industry.

> Men at the top level of authority . . . are those making the final decisions on general policy. In industry this policy deals with the question of the kinds of products, and amounts of those kinds, to make . . . , with the related question of the prices to charge; and in modern mechanized industry with the question of the amount and kind of equipment in which to invest. . . . With these questions of policy may go questions of general strategy; especially the attitude to competitors or potential competitors: whether to combine or associate with them, follow their lead, or engage in genuine competition.[66]

Once these decisions are made, their execution devolves upon management proper; and while the recruitment of the managers and the organizational structure of the enterprise are determined by "top government," the details of execution and control are entrusted to management. As a consequence, authority *within* management is delegated to a considerable extent, and a major task of the director and his immediate associates consists in the coordination of submanagers, who

[65] P. Sargant Florence, *The Logic of British and American Industry* (London: Routledge and Kegan Paul Ltd., 1953), p. 157. A Soviet discussion of the same problem is contained in Arakelian, *op. cit.,* pp. 122–27, and in S. E. Kamenizer, *Organisation und Planung des sozialistischen Industriebetriebes* (Berlin: Verlag Die Wirtschaft, 1953), pp. 111–38. The latter work was published in Moscow in 1950 and is an officially licensed textbook.

[66] Florence, *op. cit.,* p. 163.

have considerable authority in their own right. Emphasis is placed therefore upon organizational arrangements that will facilitate this coordination on the tacit assumption that within the limits set by the "top government" the director has supreme authority over the enterprise. Indeed, this authority is largely taken for granted; interference with it by superordinated bodies is not anticipated; hence, the delegation of authority within enterprises is encouraged.

In Soviet Russia the "top government" over economic enterprises is vested in the Commissariat or Ministry for a branch of production, and operative control is exercised by the subdivisions (*glavki*) of these governmental agencies.[67] These superordinated planning bodies issue directives and control their execution in a manner which combines general policy directives with detailed instructions. They impose exact controls over execution by requiring reports at short intervals, but they also regard violations with studied laxity if such violations prove successful. They engage in sudden campaigns for major changes of plan and of technical and administrative organization, but they also insist upon the absolute authority of the director over the enterprise.[68] Thus, the pressure for plan fulfillment under conditions of changing plan strategy often leads the various governmental agencies to insist both upon strict compliance with their directives of the moment and upon a display of initiative which will lead to a vigorous execution of all directives issued. The same pressure leads also to the growth of an administrative apparatus as an ever-ready instrument of planning and control. In Soviet literature, nothing is said concerning the institutionalized uncertainty and inconsistency of planning and control policies, since each policy is justified in turn as an indispensable means for the fulfillment of the plan, which is sanctioned by the highest party authorities. The external bureaucratization of governmental agencies is sharply criticized, however. The great centralization of administration, the petty supervision, and the vice of extremely detailed planning are said to restrict the opportunities of the director for displaying "great initiative, enterprise, and maneuverability." Such restrictions are said to occur despite his "great rights and duties" and despite the fact that he enjoys "the enormous confidence of the Party and the government." [69] Such centralization is criticized further because "neither local resources

[67] Cf. Granick, *op. cit.,* pp. 14–27.

[68] Granick has analyzed these conflicting tendencies in some detail and has shown the different organizational levels at which the several tendencies are likely to occur. Cf. *ibid.,* Ch. VI and *passim.*

[69] Arakelian, *op. cit.,* pp. 140–41.

nor local requirements can be fully calculated from the center," [70] and because it leads to a very wasteful growth of the administrative staff.[71]

This external bureaucratization of economic enterprises and the principle of detailed directives and controls are an indispensable part of Soviet planning, however much its administrative excesses are deplored and on occasion checked by more or less drastic measures. It should be clearly stated, of course, that increased governmental regulation has occurred in all highly industrialized countries with the result that administrative staffs have increased both in the enterprises and in the governmental agencies concerned with them. The broad objective of this bureaucratization has not been the detailed direction of the economy, but the proximate equalization of bargaining strength among groups with conflicting interests, an objective that includes the prohibition of "unfair or fraudulent practices," since these remain unchecked when there are great inequalities of bargaining strength. This endeavor to stipulate the limits of permissible actions has led everywhere to a gradual extension of governmental regulations. In the field of labor relations, for example, the original object of regulation in the United States was the equalization of bargaining strength between capital and labor. Subsequently, the object became to contain the impact of bargaining upon the public with the result that the procedure and scope of bargaining were regulated also. As a consequence, employers and trade-unions have come to supplement their bargaining by efforts to influence governmental policies that set the bench marks of bargaining. The limits of bargaining are, therefore, in dispute. And the shifting political resolutions of that dispute lead to a gradual increase of external bureaucratization at the same time that managers and trade-union leaders test their respective power and skills in the bargaining process. Under Soviet planning, however, bargaining itself is eliminated, since wages, working conditions, and welfare measures are incorporated in the economic plan. Hence, the initiative and enterprise of the factory director and the trade-union become a matter of official concern because the plan can only be fulfilled by the use of methods and of resources which cannot be fully "calculated from the center." [72]

[70] *Ibid.*, p. 138.

[71] *Ibid.*, p. 145: ". . . on January 1, 1946, of the total number of specialists with a college education employed by industrial ministries and offices, only 25.6 per cent worked directly in production, 23.1 per cent in factory administrations, and the remaining mass (51.3 per cent) in medium and high administrative sections."

[72] As a result, a factory's production potential is officially regarded as having no fixed limits and factory directors are consequently evaluated in terms of the

As a consequence, the absolute authority of the director over the enterprise is emphasized a good bit more in the Soviet Union than in the United States.

The director of an enterprise is its full empowered manager. He has at his disposal all the material and monetary resources of the enterprise, and directly manages the drafting of workshop tasks (technical, industrial and financial plans), and of the plans for technical progress and capital construction. The director selects all the basic personnel, establishes the procedure for the work of the entire collective, verifies the results and the progress of the work of the personnel, and maintains labor, planning and financial discipline. The orders from a director of an enterprise have unconditionally obligatory force for all workers. The director bears full responsibility for the work of the enterprise as a whole, for the fulfilment of the quantitative and qualitative indices of the state planned task, for the correct and economical expenditure of resources, and for the correct organization of labor.[73]

This formulation by a Soviet writer is suggestive, because it makes clear that the planning authorities look upon the director's "great rights" of command as merely the necessary means for the fulfillment of his "great duty." Hence, it is a "right" which is not enjoyed by the individual but conferred upon him as a privilege, the exercise of which is obligatory and must be controlled.[74]

This continued control is not at all incompatible with the grant of very extensive powers to the director. His right to hire and fire is absolute, though in particular cases it may be subject to control by the party organization. He has a "director's fund" from which he can give special rewards in return for cooperation and efficient production and indeed his power to do so increases with the economic success of the enterprise. Success also strengthens his position with the party and with the ministries. Under these conditions his power over his sub-

activitism or partisanship which they display in overcoming "merely" technical or administrative bottlenecks. Cf. Haimson, *op. cit.,* pp. 437–43.

[73] Arakelian, *op. cit.,* p. 123. As a consequence, the director finds himself forced to interfere directly in the production process, and this practice is officially encouraged as a principle of Soviet leadership. See Haimson, *op. cit.,* pp. 378–79.

[74] It is of interest that this approach is nearly identical with Tsarist practice. "According to an edict of Catherine II each aristocratic assembly had the right to discuss all public affairs touching upon its interests and to petition the government accordingly. Yet the government had viewed the matter from the beginning as if this clearly formulated law meant nothing and as if in every instance [the discussion of public affairs] required a separate prescription by the government." Engelmann, *op. cit.,* p. 283. Here also a "right" is not granted to be enjoyed but conferred piecemeal to be exercised under supervision.

ordinates is indeed absolute, and he will use it to place upon them as much pressure and responsibility for results as are placed upon himself. Rather than delegate executive authority and discretion to subordinates, he will charge them with responsibilities whose fulfillment he is likely to superintend at frequent intervals, just as the Commissariat and its subdivision superintend his own. Cooperation within the managerial ranks depends, then, upon the absolute power of the director and the absolute dependence of his assistants upon him as long as the enterprise is successful. But when there are signs of failure, this mutual dependence and support disintegrate quickly into a precarious collaboration of men, all of whom are more or less forced to use illegal means to attain or simulate plan fulfillment.[75]   The consequence of these conditions is that in Soviet enterprises the director seeks to achieve a maximum concentration of commands and controls in his own person, while the functional division of managerial tasks tends to be confined to staff work. This method of internal bureaucratization differs strikingly from those developed in the large-scale enterprises of the West, where efforts are made to organize and to coordinate responsible sub- and sub-substructures in order

> to relieve the load on the men in top government of a large organization, so that they may be free to concentrate their thought on high policy and the means to plan, command and check that policy efficiently with expert management and advice.[76]

e. Managerial Problems and Alternatives

The bureaucratization of economic enterprises has been considered so far in terms of the ethic of work performance which such enterprises require, the absolute and proportionate increase of salaried employees, the career patterns of the "business elite," and the organizational position of managers. Before resuming the analysis of ideologies of management, it will be useful to consider the managerial problems which typically result from the growing size and complexity of organizations. These problems consist principally in the development and administration of regulations which together constitute the criteria of bureaucracy as Max Weber has enumerated them. This regulation of administrative employees *tends* to be characterized by:

[75] Merle Fainsod, *How Russia is Ruled* (Cambridge: Harvard University Press, 1953), pp. 427–29. See also Haimson, *op. cit.,* pp. 403–6.

[76] Florence, *op. cit.,* p. 148. For evidence on the variety of these efforts, cf. the work of Ernest Dale, *Planning and Developing the Company Organization Structure,* cited above.

(a) Defined rights and duties, which are prescribed in written regulations;

(b) Authority relations between positions which are ordered systematically;

(c) Appointment and promotion which are regulated and are based on contractual agreement;

(d) Technical training (or experience) as a formal condition of employment;

(e) Fixed monetary salaries;

(f) A strict separation of office and incumbent in the sense that the employee does not own the "means of administration" and cannot appropriate the position;

(g) Administrative work as a full-time occupation.[77]

Each of these characteristics stands for a condition of employment in modern economic enterprises as well as in governmental administration. And the internal bureaucratization of enterprises may be interpreted as the manifold, cumulative, and more or less successful imposition of these employment conditions since the Industrial Revolution. Bureaucratization is an on-going process in the sense that these employment conditions must be instituted and administered under ever changing conditions.

The problems of management arising from this process of bureaucratization can be characterized in a general way by contrasting each bureaucratic condition of employment with its nonbureaucratic or antibureaucratic counterpart.

The endeavor to define rights and duties in accordance with formal (impersonal) criteria will encounter persistent attempts to interpret them in a manner the individual concerned regards as advantageous to himself.

The systematic ordering of authority relationships will be opposed— though often quite unwittingly—by attempts to subject these relationships to informal bargaining by using favors of various kinds.

[77] Gerth and Mills, *From Max Weber,* pp. 196–98. It should be added that Weber's analysis dealt with the development of governmental institutions in the context of a comparative analysis in which the organizational and ideological rationale of bureaucracy was contrasted with that of patrimonial and charismatic rule. To use Weber's concepts outside this context requires a reinterpretation; otherwise Weber's intentions as well as his contribution to knowledge are distorted and easy to criticize, as, for example, in Alvin W. Gouldner, "On Weber's Analysis of Bureaucratic Rules," in Robert K. Merton, *et al.,* eds., *Reader in Bureaucracy* (Glencoe: The Free Press, 1952), pp. 48–51. Cf. Reinhard Bendix, "Bureaucracy: The Problem and its Setting," *American Sociological Review,* Vol. XII (1947), pp. 493–507.

Similar personal considerations may also affect the appointment and promotion of employees, even when there is outward compliance with the rules.

Technical training as a condition of employment is perhaps least subject to such practices, though even here personal relationships and subjective interpretations may modify what would otherwise be a purely formal adherence to this condition. I think of such factors as the preference of hiring officials for applicants who have certain personal characteristics as well as the required technical competence. Subjective evaluation also enters into the weighting of a candidate's experience, professional standing, and so on.

Similar considerations apply to fixed monetary salaries. Although salary scales can be readily fixed and administered, appointment and promotion are subject to bargaining and personal influence, as is the whole system of job classification without which a salary scale is meaningless. In addition, there are continual efforts at supplementing any given salary scale by various fringe benefits which are not as readily systematized as the scale itself, and hence permit the maneuvering which the scale seeks to eliminate.

The strict separation between office and incumbent, between the position and the employee, is an ideal condition which is rarely achieved in practice, especially with regard to salaried employees and skilled workers. Incumbents endow their work performance with personal qualities that range from dispensable idiosyncrasies to untransferable and often indispensable skills, so that some measure of identification of the employee with his position is unavoidable. To be sure, under modern conditions of employment the individual cannot appropriate his position in the sense in which, say, in the British government during the eighteenth century administrative offices were a form of private property a family could pass on from one generation to the next. The safeguards against dismissal established in modern government and industry under the slogan of "job security" have endowed employment with a quasi-proprietary character which is more or less incompatible with the strict separation between the job and the employee.

While the idea of work as a full-time occupation is generally accepted, the intensity of work is subject to disputes and interpretations. "Full-time" is unambiguous as contrasted with part-time or avocational work. But the amount of work done in a full-time occupation continues to be a most controversial condition of employment, which employers seek to regularize by the use of incentives and penalties and which workers interpret in their own way by the practice of output restriction.

Thus, the internal bureaucratization of economic enterprises is an on-going process in which management subjects the conditions of employment to an impersonal systematization, while the employees seek to modify the implementation of the rules in a manner they regard as advantageous to themselves. In this way, employees continue to "bargain" silently over the rules governing their employment, long after they have signed the contract which stipulates these rules in a seemingly unambiguous manner. And managers endeavor to minimize or eliminate this "silent bargaining" (and thereby to maximize the predictable performance of employees) by the strategic use of penalties, incentives, and ideological appeals. But the execution of these and other managerial tasks is beset by certain persistent, logical incompatibilities that seem to be inherent in the structure of hierarchical organizations.

The problem of communication is a case in point. The hierarchy of ranks indispensable in large organizations involves a formally unambiguous order of authority. All subordinates receive their orders from superiors, who by definition know more about the policy of the organization and its "proper" execution than those whom they command. Yet their superior knowledge is limited or circumscribed by the fact that their high rank within the organization removes them automatically from day-to-day experience with its operational problems. In the parlance of organizational theory, this is called the problem of two-way communication. But, as Florence has pointed out, the information which should come up the line of authority from those who are in daily touch with operational problems "tends to be neglected for the very reason that it comes from a subordinate." [78] It should be emphasized that the reason for such neglect is not necessarily the ill-will of superiors or the ineptitude of subordinates. It is rather that the hierarchy of ranks involves different levels of information so that subordinates are not in a good position to judge what aspects of day-to-day operation are of special interest to their superiors. Nor is it possible for superiors to spell this out in too much detail, for this would interfere with the very delegation of responsibility which large-scale organizations make necessary. Hence, subordinates are left to judge in some measure what their superiors want or ought to know. Since the subordinate's performance is evaluated in part by his manner of keeping the superior informed, the information he supplies is likely to be an amalgam of the necessary, the frivolous, and the self-serving.

It would certainly be wrong to assume that this dilemma leaves the managers of industry in a state of suspended animation. Superiors and

[78] Florence, *op. cit.*, p. 153.

subordinates deal with this and similar problems daily and find varying solutions for them, which circumstances and organizational skill may suggest. But the point is that dilemmas of this kind are endemic in hierarchical organizations. Herbert Simon has shown how such dilemmas have led to administrative theories, which are as contradictory as proverbs. Administrative efficiency is said to require specialization. But it also requires a unity of command often incompatible with specialization. Efficiency makes it mandatory that each superior have a limited number of subordinates (span of control) in keeping with his ability to supervise them. This principle, however, implies that new levels of organization must be set up whenever the number of subordinates has increased beyond their superiors' ability to control them effectively. Hence, the principle conflicts with one that is equally valid: before being acted upon, matters should pass through as few levels of organization as possible. Again, the efficiency of organizations is thought to be maximized by organizing workers into groups according to the function they perform, the public they serve, the area they administer, or the procedures they employ. Yet these criteria of specialization often conflict with one another. Hence, the manager has not only the task of reconciling such organizational specialization with the other principles mentioned, but also of weighing the merits of conflicting criteria and choosing among them.[79]

These problems of large-scale organizations have been brought to the fore with the increasing size and complexity of modern industry. They were of concern to industrial managers long before the theorists of modern administration formulated principles. And while the bureaucratization of industry has brought to prominence specialists of organizational management, the managers themselves have had to find day-to-day solutions for the problems these dilemmas pose. In this endeavor managers have typically resorted to ideological appeals, not as a substitute for material incentives and organizational improvements, but as a means by which to increase, if possible, the cooperation of employees, given the organizational environment in which they had to work. These common managerial problems have been approached in two fundamentally different ways.

Under the conditions of Western civilization the appeals of management have presupposed, albeit tacitly, that workers, salaried employees,

[79] The preceding paragraph is based on Herbert Simon, *Administrative Behavior* (New York: The Macmillan Company, 1948), pp. 20–44. However, I regard these dilemmas as endemic in organizations, while Simon regards them as unnecessary shortcomings of administrative theory.

and managers share a universe of discourse despite the many barriers of interest and belief which exist between them. For example, managers appeal to the good faith of their subordinates in order to enlist their cooperation. Time and again they find that these appeals are received with indifference or suspicion and hostility. Yet, the appeals continue to be made, presumably because managers and their spokesmen believe that they have a chance to be heard *some* of the time, in part because their appeals are often directed to their own group and serve more to express their feelings than to change the ideas and feelings of employees, and also because they more or less accept a high level of frustration as part of the managerial job. On the other hand, workers in western Europe and in the United States accept the general idea that they owe a "fair day's work for a fair day's wage." True, this maxim does not mean to the worker what it means to his boss, but it does imply a conception of minimum effort acknowledged as obligatory by the worker. Like their opposite numbers, workers and their representatives continue to appeal for the acceptance of their position by the public and by management, presumably also in the hope of winning partial assent, of strengthening the self-persuasion of their own group, and in the expectation of meeting considerable indifference or hostility.

When all allowances have been made for the ambiguity of ideas and the ambivalence of feelings, there remains a vague residue of understanding between workers and managers as members of the same community. These shared beliefs probably consist on both sides in tolerance for the existence of conflicting ideas and interests ("If I were in his position, I'd argue the same way . . .") as well as in the *partial* acceptance of the claims made by the opposing group.[80] Yet, such common understandings are compatible with the belief, more or less mutually accepted, that the authority of employers over their subordinates not only reflects the imperatives of industrial organization but also the existence of class differences. When managers make their appeals for cooperation, they automatically identify themselves as persons in authority who formulate and who speak for the interests of the organization they lead. Although the distribution of rewards is in dispute and conflicts of interest are intense, the difference of status and power between managers and workers is by and large accepted.[81]

[80] For the United States this partial recognition of the claims made by the opposing group is described in E. Wight Bakke, *Mutual Survival* (New Haven: Labor and Management Center, Yale University, 1946).

[81] Among the industrialized nations of the West this pattern of "antagonistic cooperation" varies considerably. In the Federal Republic of Germany the

Yet industrialization and the bureaucratization of economic enterprises have occurred in countries where these rudimentary assumptions do not apply.   And Lenin's as well as Stalin's recommendations concerning the principles of industrial organization are an interesting commentary on their absence.   "The Russian is a bad worker," according to Lenin, and he must be taught to work by combining the most developed techniques of capitalism with Soviet government and administration.   This can be accomplished only if managers have absolute, dictatorial authority within the enterprises under their direction.   Yet managers (especially those inherited from the Tsarist regime) cannot be trusted: they must be "subordinated and strictly controlled by the representatives of the workers and peasants," and their administrative and technical work must be discussed in party meetings.

> We must learn to combine the "meeting" democracy of the toiling masses—turbulent, surging, overflowing its banks like a spring flood— with *iron* discipline while at work, with *unquestioning obedience* to the will of a single person, the Soviet leader, while at work.[82]

This conception of managerial authority within the enterprise and control from without was *not* merely a response to revolutionary emergencies.   Rather it reflected the legacies of Tsarist rule under which employers and workers and the relations between them had been subjected to authoritative control.

Under Soviet rule this control is exercised by a dictatorial party, which does not rely upon the existence of common understandings but seeks to create them by political means.   While the absolute authority of the factory director is strongly emphasized, its exercise is to be controlled by governmental agencies.   Moreover, correct decision-making, proper execution and control are impossible without considering the experience and obtaining the support of the masses, according to Stalin.[83]   Indeed, every work performance in economic enterprises should be controlled from above as well as from below.

> Verification by managers from above is combined with verification by the masses from below.   This also assures the correct direction of production. Comrade Stalin says that the range of view of a manager is more or less

American pattern is almost reversed in the sense that status and power differences are in dispute between management and the trade-unions, while by and large the distribution of rewards is not.   See Clark Kerr, "The Trade Union Movement and the Redistribution of Power in Postwar Germany," *The Quarterly Journal of Economics,* Vol. LXVIII (November, 1954), pp. 535–64.

[82] Lenin, *Selected Works,* Vol. VII, p. 345.

[83] Cf. Kamenizer, *op. cit.,* p. 114.

limited: He sees people, things and events only from one side, from above and from the managerial summit. The masses, after all, see them from the other side—from below. Therefore the field of vision of the masses is also limited to a certain extent. "In order to obtain a correct solution of a problem, these two experiences must be united. Only in this case will management be correct." [84]

This, then, defines the distinguishing mark of management-labor relations in a totalitarian society: that the decision-making authority of managers is not only controlled from above but must be in line with the "experience of the masses," as this "experience" is represented and manipulated by the party. It is likewise characteristic that the workers are not only subordinated to the managers, but are also called upon—under the guidance of the party, of course—to criticize and help correct the administrative and technical work of management. Thus, the social differences between managers and workers are obliterated in the sense that superiors are subordinated and subordinates are made superiors. This simultaneous super- and subordination of all ranks in society arises from their total subordination to the political controls of the party. Under this system differences of power, of status, and of rewards are at least as great as in any "class society," but the conflicts among organized groups over these differences are totally suppressed.[85]

*   *   *

In modern industry the cooperation needed involves the spirit in which subordinates exercise their judgment. Beyond what commands can effect and supervision can control, beyond what incentives can induce and penalties prevent, there exists an exercise of discretion important even in relatively menial jobs, which managers of economic enterprises seek to enlist for the achievement of managerial ends. This is a shorthand way of describing the managerial problems solved today in two, diametrically opposed ways. I now turn to a consideration of these alternatives.

Note on career patterns of American business leaders (see p. 228)

Biographical entries in the *National Cyclopedia of American Biography* were classified into three types of career patterns in accordance with the following criteria:

[84] Arakelian, *op. cit.*, p. 160.

[85] Cf. Chapter 6, where this position is examined in detail. It may be useful to add that the suppression of class conflict under totalitarian rule is not synonymous with the elimination of conflicts between persons and cliques in the various bureaucratic hierarchies.

1. *Heir:*
   (*a*) Inherited control of firm.
   (*b*) Inherited wealth used to buy control of firm or to incorporate a new firm.
2. *Entrepreneur:*
   (*a*) Started own firm.
   (*b*) Worked up from a white-collar job to become the owner or part-owner of a firm.
   (*c*) Utilized specialized education or experience to start a new firm of his own or to become a part-owner of an established firm.
   (*d*) Started own firm with assistance from his family.
3. *Bureaucrat:*
   (*a*) Worked up to an executive position within a given firm
     (1) from a white-collar job;
     (2) from a technical or professional job.
   (*b*) Transferred to an established firm at the executive level
     (1) after having worked his way up in another firm;
     (2) after having worked in government.
   (*c*) Got important job in middle management after receiving special training in management.
   (*d*) Got important job in middle management through family or other connections.

As indicated in the text, heirs are distinguished from the other two types—entrepreneurs and bureaucrats—by virtue of the fact that their entire career is based on inherited wealth. Compared with this, the assistance which entrepreneurs and bureaucrats received from their families was facilitating rather than determining.

The overlap between the entrepreneurs and bureaucrats is greater, and it should be noted that cases in which a man had both types of careers were listed as "not classifiable." In the other cases an attempt was made to classify careers in terms of their dominant characteristics. Vague as that sounds, it did not prove unmanageable in practice. The following examples refer to the white-collar work of an entrepreneur and the executive position of a bureaucrat to illustrate how these distinctions were employed.

Examples of 2*b:* Typical cases are those of boys who start as office boys or clerks or perhaps bookkeepers in a commercial or financial firm and after a time are given a partnership in the firm. This was a common pattern especially in the pre-Civil War period, when entrepreneurs still performed a good bit of the menial work themselves.

Example of 3*b:* A typical case would be that of an individual who advances steadily from position to position for a twenty-year period and then buys a part-ownership in another established firm. This pattern was common in wholesale trade during the second half of the nineteenth century.

Thus, if the white-collar phase of a career was relatively short and its "ownership phase" appeared to involve considerable risk-taking, the career was classified as entrepreneurial; but if the first of these phases was prolonged while the second appeared to involve little more than a top-administrative position, the career was classified as bureaucratic.

PART THREE

CHAPTER 5

The American Experience

I believe that ambitious men in democracies . . . care much more for success than for fame. What they most ask of men is obedience, what they most covet is empire. . . . I confess that I apprehend much less for democratic society from the boldness than from the mediocrity of desires. What appears to me most to be dreaded is that in the midst of the small, incessant occupations of private life, ambition should lose its vigor and its greatness . . . so that the march of society should every day become more tranquil and less aspiring.—
Alexis de Tocqueville, *Democracy in America.*

a. Economic Expansion, Survival, and the Power of Thought

In the period from 1880 to 1910 the United States underwent the most rapid economic expansion of any industrialized country for a comparable period of time. A country may be said to enter an advanced stage of industrialization once less than 50 per cent of its population is engaged in primary production (agriculture, forestry, and fishing). Judged by this index alone, America was an industrial late-comer, for England had reached this halfway mark before 1841, France before 1866, Germany about 1870, and the United States shortly before 1880.

TABLE 14. Percentage Distribution of the Gainfully Occupied Population in the United States by Major Industrial Subdivisions, 1870–1910

	Per Cent of Gainfully Occupied Population in		
Year	Primary	Secondary	Tertiary
1870	53.5	21.9	24.6
1880	49.9	23.7	26.4
1890	43.4	25.6	31.0
1900	38.2	27.2	34.6
1910	31.6	31.1	37.3

In 1870 more than twice as many people were engaged in primary production than in either of the other two branches. By 1910 the gainfully occupied population was almost evenly divided among them. If it is remembered that during this same period the population of the United States increased from 39.8 million to 91.1 million people, it is apparent that its economic development after the Civil War was one of unprecedented rapidity.[1]

This speed of economic expansion was reflected in the ruthless practices of American business leaders and in the strident ideologies espoused during this time. In England measures of social reform and the organization of workers in trade-unions were well under way in the 1860's and 1870's. In the United States, workers began to organize on a mass basis only in the 1890's, hampered as they were by the willingness of immigrants to work at lower wages. Social reform with regard to factory conditions did not begin in earnest until after the turn of the century. It is not surprising, therefore, that the Gospel of Work and Hope that Samuel Smiles had begun to preach in England from the 1850's on gained its greatest popularity in the United States. That popularity was much enhanced by a fusion of the ideas of Smiles with those of Herbert Spencer. In a letter to Spencer, written in 1860, Henry Ward Beecher had written that "the peculiar condition of American society has made [Spencer's ideas] . . . far more fruitful and quickening here than in Europe."[2] That peculiar condition of American society after the Civil War was not only the speed of its economic de-

[1] The data on the changing occupational distribution are taken from Colin Clark, *The Conditions of Economic Progress* (London: The Macmillan Company, Inc., 1951), pp. 404, 408–9, 413. Secondary production includes manufacture, mining and building; tertiary production includes trade, transportation, communication, domestic, personal and professional service.

[2] Quoted in Richard Hofstadter, *Social Darwinism in American Thought, 1860–1915* (Philadelphia: University of Pennsylvania Press, 1945), p. 18.

velopment, but the widespread awareness of "unlimited" possibilities. The American popularizers understood Spencer's ideas to be a combination of Malthus' emphasis on the struggle for existence, Smiles's elaboration of the virtues needed for success, and Darwin's theory of evolution. But in this combination the pessimism of a Malthus had been superseded by a totally unqualified optimism which believed itself doubly reinforced by the certainty of biological laws. The ideas which Smiles had propounded as a matter of personal conviction and experience were interpreted by Spencer's American followers as certain facts, grounded in the laws of evolution and confirmed by science. Accordingly, success and riches were regarded as signs of progress and as the reward of those who had proved themselves in the struggle for survival. In that struggle no quarters were given, and the success and well-being of the "fittest" was inevitably accompanied by the grinding poverty of those who had failed. Moreover, the success of the few and powerful was not necessarily believed to indicate personal virtue and cultural achievement, for the popularizers of Spencer readily admitted the selfishness, the materialism, and even the political corruption that were by-products of the struggle for existence. They merely claimed that these evils were an outgrowth of human nature and that given this "fact" civilization would not advance at all if such evils were to be avoided. To the ideological spokesmen of the Gilded Age these doctrines contained the scientific explanation of the facts of economic life, and they gave vivid descriptions of how well these ideas fit in with the experience of American business leaders.

> It would be strange if the "captain of the industry" did not sometimes manifest a militant spirit, for he has risen from the ranks largely because he was a better fighter than most of us. Competitive commercial life is not a flowery bed of ease, but a battlefield where the "struggle for existence" is defining the industrially "fittest to survive." In this country the great prizes are not found in Congress, in literature, in law, in medicine, but in industry. The successful man is praised and honored for his success. The social rewards of business prosperity, in power, in praise, and luxury, are so great as to entice men of the greatest intellectual faculties. Men of splendid abilities find in the career of a manufacturer or merchant an opportunity for the most intense energy. The very perils of the situation have a fascination for adventurous and inventive spirits. In this fierce, though voiceless, contest, a peculiar type of manhood is developed, characterized by vitality, energy, concentration, skill in combining numerous forces for an end, and great foresight into the consequences of social events.[3]

[3] C. R. Henderson, "Business Men and Social Theorists," *American Journal of Sociology*, Vol. I (1896), pp. 385–86.

But the business leaders themselves, as well as the writers of self-help tracts who celebrated their careers, tended to emphasize the virtues of character and the Christian mission of business enterprise, whereas the ideas of "social Darwinism" were developed by journalists and academicians.[4] This difference in emphasis should not be overstated of course; it merely illustrated that business leaders were more at home in the language of religion than in the language of science. Certainly, writers of every kind were at one in paying homage to the men who stood as the champions and symbols of their age.

A journalist writing in 1892 about Jay Gould, the financier, declared his life to be "a thrilling tale, full of romance, and fraught with importance for generations." A memorial speaker declared in 1913 that Morgan had made society his debtor, for he ranked with the great men of the past who have enabled society to pass through wars and revolutions and to ward off the perils to life and property. A railroad president stated in 1901 that the love of money was bad, but the desire to get money was the foundation of all commercial and social advance. College presidents spoke of the increasing opportunities for young men which business success had brought about, one of them declaring that "there are more successful men in every calling today than ever before." In 1900 the Rev. M. D. Babcock declared that "Business is religion, and religion is business. The man who does not make a business of his religion has a business life of no character. . . . If God gives us the possibilities and power to get wealth, to acquire influence, to be forces in the world, what is the true conception of life but divine ownership and human administration?" "The lowest passions of mankind," wrote a professor at Yale University, "ostentation and ambition, petty rivalry, the love of saving and the love of gain, while they bring their own penalty upon the individual who unduly indulges them, are still overruled for good in their operation upon the interests of society." Even *The Nation,* a liberal journal, maintained in 1888 that the capitalists of today are the workingmen of yesterday, just as the workingmen of today are the capitalists of tomorrow. Many public spokesmen, it seems, agreed with the editors of one journal who declared that wealth was "a sociological blessing, not a sociological danger." "Everywhere,"

[4] See Irvin G. Wyllie, *The Self-Made Man in America* (New Brunswick: Rutgers University Press, 1954), pp. 83–87. Cf. also Robert S. McClosky, *American Conservatism in the Age of Enterprise* (Cambridge: Harvard University Press, 1951), pp. 134–67, where Andrew Carnegie's ambivalent avowal of ethical values is analyzed in the context of his adherence to Spencer's doctrine.

states A. W. Griswold, from whose study these quotations have been selected, "honor was being done to the captains of industry and kings of enterprise." [5]

In the United States this celebration of the businessman as hero went further than in England at the time of Samuel Smiles. Smiles's work had emphasized the hope for success, to which everyone was entitled who cultivated the virtues of self-help, thrift, character, and duty. In the United States that same optimism received a powerful impetus from the ideas of Herbert Spencer. In the public mind the preoccupation of many writers with the grim struggle for survival was modified markedly by the confidence with which every bitter cost of that struggle was regarded as a cornerstone of ever increasing progress. Probably the most uncompromising expression of this creed is contained in the writings of William Graham Sumner. In his view:

> All institutions are to be tested by the degree to which they guarantee liberty. . . . A human being has a life to live, a career to run. He is a centre of powers to work, and of capacities to suffer. What his powers may be—whether they can carry him far or not; what his chances may be, whether wide or restricted; what his fortune may be, whether to suffer much or little—are questions of his personal destiny which he must work out and endure as he can. . . .[6]

The function of institutions was merely to guarantee to man the use of all his powers to enhance his own welfare. In this view democracy cannot admit claims for favor on any ground whatever; poverty does not constitute a ground for claiming assistance, and riches do not entitle men to privilege. Every man is as sovereign as every other man; each desires independence and equality with others. And each must accept the full consequences of his status. "He is," concluded Sumner, "in a certain sense, an isolated man." [7]

On this basis the employer's authority was justified by oft-repeated references to his success, which was a sign both of his virtue and of his superior abilities. Those who failed were believed to lack the requisite qualities, and they were enjoined to obey the men whose success entitled them to command. This division of mankind was reiterated on all sides, not merely in general terms as a consequence of the struggle for survival but with specific application to the authority relationship in industry.

[5] Cf. A. W. Griswold, *The American Gospel of Success* (M.A. Dissertation, Yale University, 1933), pp. 89–95.

[6] William Graham Sumner, *What Social Classes Owe Each Other* (New York: Harper and Brothers, 1883), pp. 34–35.

[7] *Ibid.*, p. 39.

The power to generate great ideas, the power to command great armies, the power to make great discoveries in the fields of science, the power to move the world with tongue or pen, the power to originate and conduct great industrial enterprises and accumulate great fortunes,—always has been and always will be the inheritance of the few.[8]

And as leaders of industry were here likened to the great of the world in all fields of endeavor, so their employees were assigned in perpetuity to the humble position to which their modest talents entitled them.

Many a man is entirely incapable of assuming responsibility. He is a success as the led, but not as the leader. He lacks the courage of will-ingness to assume responsibility and the ability of handling others. He was born for a salaried man, and a salaried man he had better remain. If he goes into business for himself, the chances are that he will fail, or live close to impending disaster.[9]

This division between employers and their men was held to illustrate the survival of the fittest and most virtuous, since the one possessed the power to originate and conduct great enterprises and the other "obvi-ously" did not. Indeed, the workers would live in squalor and want without the beneficial guidance of capital and brains.

This was a harsh doctrine, whether it was couched in the language of religious virtue or of the struggle for survival. The public at large very probably shared the conviction of the spokesmen who celebrated the tycoons of American industry and their achievements. Yet the pop-ularity of this harsh doctrine posed a dilemma for the many people who were neither tycoons nor yet lived in squalor and want. And for these people the fashionable answer was that "the problem of success comes back now as it always has come to individual qualities." [10] This theme had had its origin in the Puritan credo, whose secularization may be said to have reached its climax in the "New Thought" movement of the late nineteenth and early twentieth century. This movement was in-spired by the belief that certain thoughts in themselves were sufficient to lead to wealth and success. To the teachers of this movement "suc-cess . . . meaning the attaining of financial reward . . . must depend largely upon the Personal Magnetism of the seeker after success." [11]

The "New Thought" movement had its greatest popularity in the United States from 1895 to 1915. It did not lack religious overtones,

[8] F. O. Willey, *The Laborer and the Capitalist* (New York: National Economic League, 1896), p. 42.

[9] N. C. Fowler, *The Boy, How to Help Him Succeed* (New York: Moffat, Yard and Company, 1902), pp. 56–57.

[10] Quoted from the *World's Work* in Griswold, *op. cit.,* p. 92.

[11] Quoted in *ibid.,* p. 101.

for it deified the individual, made his mental capacities an emanation of God, and conceived of the universe as a manifestation of a vague, spiritualistic and omnipresent essence. Yet in a thriving business civilization which celebrated the businessman as hero, the movement rapidly gained a large following by virtue of a secular belief in "mental power." With their banishment of the devil and of luck from the roster of forces governing human life, the spokesmen of this movement fused their belief in "mind is power" with the standard interpretation of economic success as the outcome of energy, ambition, determination, perseverance, patience, prudence, and the rest. "Business success is due to certain qualities of mind," declared one of them. "Anything is yours if you only want it hard enough. Just think of that. *Anything!* Try it. Try it in earnest and you will succeed. It is the operation of a mighty law." [12]

The number of publications in which hack writers expounded this theme was very large. In *The Conquest of Poverty* Helen Wilmans maintained that a man can "actually create wealth by the character of the thoughts he entertains." Men's failure to develop the forces dormant within them is the reason why they are not rich. In *Your Forces and How to Use Them* a writer declared that a steady job and good wages were not the road to success; a man must not be content to be managed by others, he must instead use his skills to get his product and himself before the public. A "New Thought" tract, *Mastery of Fate,* saw a genius slumbering in the subconscious of every mind. In *Practical Methods for Self-Development* Elizabeth Towne wrote that money flows through the world like blood, it is as free as air, and men can obtain plenty of money if they will rid themselves of fear and cultivate "the *wealthy* attitude of mind." The "Power Book Library" by Frank C. Haddock contained such works as *The Power of Success, Business Power, The Culture of Courage, Practical Psychology,* and others, whose purpose was to teach "Exactly what to do and How to do Exactly That." If the content of these books failed to be as "exact" as this statement of purpose promised, the purchasers were not apparently discouraged by this deficiency: The *Power of Will* sold 600,000 copies from 1907 to 1923 at a price of $3.00 to $4.00. By 1925 the books of Orison Swett Marden had sold some 3 million copies, and their inspirational content is indicated with sufficient clarity in such titles as *Pushing to the Front, or Success Under Difficulties* (1894), *Architects of Fate, The Secret of*

<hr>

[12] Quoted from Atkinson, *Thought Force in Business* (Chicago, 1901) in Griswold, *op. cit.,* pp. 101–2.

Achievement, Economy, The Victorious Attitude, Success Fundamentals, and *Prosperity: How to Attract It.* President McKinley and the industrialist Charles M. Schwab publicly endorsed Marden's work, and American mothers named their children after him.[13]

It would be too simple to dismiss this celebration of mental power as a means to success by calling it an illusory promise which would induce workers and employees to exert themselves. Although it may be true that many a person was deluded by these messages of hope, it is equally true that the delusion was not confined to any one class. Probably, a majority of readers and publicists were sincerely persuaded that adherence to these beliefs was a stepping-stone to a better future. The coincidence of rapid economic expansion in the latter decades of the nineteenth century with the spread of Spencer's doctrines of the struggle for survival had imparted new vigor to the doctrines of Samuel Smiles. And this amalgam of ideas was now reduced for the many to the simple formula that the fittest survived by virtue of their character. Hence, any individual's failure could in principle be remedied by a sincere effort at "taking thought" and at developing the required character.

This apotheosis of individual effort was seen as the key to all problems of the age. Business leaders who had the power to "conduct great industrial enterprises and accumulate large fortunes" were ranked with the illustrious few in other fields of endeavor. Yet illustrious as their abilities were, and great as the gulf was between the children of light and the children of darkness, it was steadfastly asserted that only a man's deliberate failure to do his utmost could account for his lack of success. There certainly were differences in inherited ability; some were born leaders and others were not. But only the ability or endowment of the individual, not the circumstances of his life, were believed to be responsible for his success or his failure. And nothing but striving to the utmost was apparently regarded as a satisfactory test of an individual's endowment or ability. Thus, Andrew Carnegie vigorously denied that chance or luck had had any influence upon his own promotion.[14] A real estate agent in New York declared that those who lived in poor tenements did so as a matter of choice.[15] And in an opinion poll among 319 Americans of "marked accomplishment" only 22 out of the 287 who answered this question attributed the "majority of failures"

[13] For this description of the "New Thought" movement I have relied on A. W. Griswold's account of it. See *ibid.,* pp. 96–117.

[14] Quoted in Orison Swett Marden, *How They Succeeded* (Boston: Lothrop Publishing Company, 1901), pp. 261–62.

[15] Willey, *The Laborer and the Capitalist,* p. 305.

to such factors as adverse circumstances or bad luck. The remaining 265 "compiled" a long list of weaknesses of character or of ability which leaves no doubt that they thought the individual at fault for his failure to make good in the world.[16]

Apparently, everyone agreed that effort was the high road to success; yet this idea was undergoing subtle transformations, nonetheless. Many writers were now dwelling strongly on the *personal qualities* which would prompt a man to exert himself and achieve success. In attempting to spell out what these qualities were, accepted traits such as duty, thrift, perseverance, loyalty, and others, which Smiles had already found serviceable, were reiterated. But the same theme could be varied slightly by a quasi-religious celebration which submerged all specific personal traits in one vague, all-embracing upsurge of the "power of thought." No one questioned this new emphasis, since writers and readers alike could readily bring to mind the close connection between the "new thought" and the "old effort." Still, the panegyrics on the mysterious powers of the mind often left little room for the more conventional praise of character and effort. The theme was minor, if it is considered against the background of a thriving and confident business civilization; but it was important nonetheless. In a society in which success and the successful received unstinted and unremitting praise, there were bound to be many believers who joined in that praise, whose exertions were beyond question, but who did not succeed. The "New Thought" movement enabled them to gather up new courage for the endless quest by the hopes which they could pin on "taking thought" as well as on "taking action." This belief in success among the unsuccessful continues as an undercurrent which has helped to sustain the major themes of American managerial ideology.

> It is not enough simply to believe in your work . . . or even be stimulated by it . . . you have to be so completely inspired by and in love with your work that success cannot evade you. . . .

[16] Nathaniel C. Fowler, *op. cit.*, pp. 156–57. The strength of this faith is perhaps indicated by the fact that in their answer to another question 151 out of 294 thought that ability without experience would accomplish success, while another 37 thought this would happen occasionally. Only 70 declared that ability alone was not sufficient. *Ibid.*, p. 146. Another expression of the same faith is the fact that many prominent business leaders opposed college education as unnecessary or positively harmful for a business career. Cf. Marden, *op. cit.*, pp. 27–28, 112–13, for the testimony of Marshall Field and Andrew Carnegie. There were others, however, who were less negative. See Marden, *op. cit.*, pp. 79–80 for a statement of Philip D. Armour.

Striving to attain right mental attitude has contributed to the success of many who hold top spots in business today. And those who reap the greater rewards are they who realize that cultivating the right mental attitude begins anew with each day. . . .[17]

Such statements are readily included in the publicity releases of American managers, for the "right mental attitude" consists—as far as they are concerned—in personal qualities such as cooperation, determination, loyalty, which are in the accepted tradition of Samuel Smiles. These statements show also that the traditional doctrine of strenuous effort has been modified; it has become amalgamated with a mystique of personal and mental magnetism which has made a hard-boiled tradition congenial to every man.

And a similar modification has occurred in another respect. Smiles had extolled personal qualities to the end that their cultivation would enable the individual to help himself rise in the world of business; his intention and that of his many successors was to help people help themselves—to use a modern phrasing of this major tenet. Yet in a world of large-scale economic enterprises the individual worker and employee had become increasingly dependent. Their advancement, such as it was, resulted from promotion rather than from the market value of their work performance. These two are certainly related. But the bureaucratization of industry made it increasingly difficult to see the relevance of admonitions which had been fashioned after the independent entrepreneur who had to prove himself in competing with others like him on an impersonal market. Self-help has remained a favorite slogan, nevertheless. It could be readily accommodated to a bureaucratic environment by re-christening it "initiative": managers could certainly use initiative in their employees, even if they did not quite know what to do with "self-help."[18] Such modifications of American managerial ideology were

---

[17] The source of these statements is a leaflet series published by *Attitudes Unlimited,* Oakland, California, and distributed to firms and religious groups which subscribe to the series. Date of publication is 1949.

[18] It is an interesting corollary of this accommodation that Smiles's idea of "self-help" has come into fashion entirely outside the economic context in which it originated. In the public mind it has become synonymous with "Howtoism," as one writer has called it, i.e., with the idea that a man should be able to do things by himself, from building a house to fixing the kitchen sink, from learning how to relax to bringing up Junior. See the perceptive survey of this literature by Dwight Macdonald, "Howtoism," *The New Yorker* (May 22, 1954), pp. 74–99, as well as the editorial comment on *Time's* survey of the booming "Do-it-yourself" business: "As mass-production techniques have broken jobs into smaller and smaller parts, the average American worker has often lost sight of the end product he is helping to build; his feeling of accomplishment has been

foreshadowed as early as the first decade of the twentieth century, when the great vogue of Spencer's "survival of the fittest" simply ignored the emerging managerial problems and seemed to condemn the unsuccessful. The "New Thought" movement did not challenge Spencer. But it helped to accommodate his ideas to the management of large-scale enterprises and it helped to sustain the faith of many who otherwise might have felt condemned by the ideas in which they believed. And since these ideological mollifications of the struggle for survival have persisted from the turn of the century to the present day, it is probable that they have helped to reconcile the American dream of struggle and success with the humdrum realities of economic life.

But in the decades preceding World War I the celebration of effort and ruthless competition was so immensely popular that many writers saw little reason to embellish its harshness. Indeed, some of them emphasized that the idea of cooperation between groups of opposing interests, such as capital and labor, was clearly inconsistent with the facts of economic life.[19] Such insistence on logic could hardly appeal to the employers. They interpreted their own success in the struggle as ample justification of their absolute authority in the enterprise, and all those who had not been successful had to submit to that authority without qualifications. Hence, they would attribute conflicts between employers and workers to the latter's unwillingness to exert themselves, not to the workers' own participation in the competitive struggle. Indeed, it was easy enough to interpret the competitive striving of the individual so that it would be in line with the needs of employers for work performance and discipline.

> We have recently been hearing much maudlin sympathy expressed for the "down-trodden denizen of the sweatshop" and the "homeless wanderer searching for honest employment," and with it all often go many hard words for the men in power.
> Nothing is said about the employer who grows old before his time in a vain attempt to get frowsy ne'er-do-wells to do intelligent work; and

whittled away. . . . In the same way, the meaning of the tasks performed by white-collar employees and executives often becomes lost in the complexities of giant corporations. . . . But in his home workshop, anyone from president down to file clerk can take satisfaction from the fine table, chair, or cabinet taking shape under his own hands—and bulge with pride again as he shows them off to friends." (*Time*, August 2, 1954, p. 63.)

[19] A man like Sumner strongly disagreed with those who held that employers and employees were partners in a common enterprise. Instead he believed that their interests were antagonistic, for the employer wanted to have labor plentiful but capital scarce and well rewarded, while the worker wanted to have capital plentiful but labor scare and highly paid. See Sumner, *op. cit.*, pp. 84–85.

his long, patient striving with "help" that does nothing but loaf when his back is turned. In every store and factory there is a constant weeding-out process going on. No matter how good times are, this sorting continues, only if times are hard and work is scarce, the sorting is done finer—but out, and forever out, the incompetent and unworthy go. It is the survival of the fittest. Self-interest prompts every employer to keep the best—those who can carry a message to Garcia.[20]

Hubbard's book was full of strong language and derisive wit about the ne'er-do-wells whose incapacity for independent action, whose moral stupidity, whose infirmity of will were a never-ending source of vexation for employers and the ever-ready cause of failure among employees. It is apparent that Hubbard, and presumably the many employers who found his diatribes entertaining, were not concerned with the willingness of workers to cooperate. If they did not, so much the worse for them.

Clearly, this approach did not disguise the employer's assertion of his interests. And it is hardly surprising that the workers reacted in kind. In 1897 American trade-unions had 447,000 members; seven years later, they had 2,072,700 members. That fivefold increase was accompanied by considerable violence on both sides; for in a world which subscribed to the struggle for survival with such single-minded vigor, it was likely that each group would assert itself with all the means at its disposal and would not count the social and human cost of the struggle.

The workers' response to the harsh practices and doctrines of their employers should have been widely accepted, if logic decided such issues. Nothing in the Spencerian decalogue said that only the businessmen's methods in the struggle for survival were acceptable to progressive evolution. And indeed, Sumner was consistent enough to endorse properly conducted strikes and trade-unions as necessary weapons in the worker's struggle for existence. In his view of the social world success in that struggle was the ultimate arbiter of right and wrong, and this standard could be applied to strikes as well.

. . . a strike for wages is a clear case of a strife in which ultimate success is a complete test of the justifiability of the course of those who

[20] Elbert Hubbard, *A Message to Garcia*, ed. by R. W. G. Vail (New York: New York Public Library, 1930), p. 14. The book was published originally in 1899. Its title refers to a Lt. A. S. Rowan who delivered an important message to General Calixto Garcia after crossing enemy lines and the disease-infested Cuban jungle. The book was very popular and its title became a symbol of competitive striving.

made the strife.   If the men win the advance, it proves that they ought to have had it.   If they do not win, it proves that they were wrong to strike.[21]

Given his premises, Sumner's logic was sound, but it is doubtful that it was widely appreciated.   Instead, American employers insisted vigorously that they would do as they pleased with their own and that they would not yield to the pressure of trade-unions.   In countering the rising tide of trade-unionism they showed none of Sumner's willingness to allow the workers the use of the strike and of trade-unions in the struggle for existence.

> Organized labor knows but one law and that is the law of physical force—the law of the Huns and Vandals, the law of the savage.   All its purposes are accomplished either by actual force or by the threat of force. . . . It is, in all essential features, a mob power knowing no master except its own will.   Its history is stained with blood and ruin. . . . It extends its tactics of coercion and intimidation over all classes, dictating to the press and to the politicians and strangling independence of thought and American manhood.[22]

Such violent words were in keeping with the violent actions on both sides.   Words and actions were often fanned to white heat, not only by the abuses of the other side, but also by cumulative frustrations.   Widespread discontent had been stirring among workers long before 1897, but it had been and continued to be checked by the immigration of new ethnic groups which tended to undermine efforts at organizing the workers.   Under the circumstances violent actions were sometimes the only way in which the opposition to the trade-unions on the part of employers *and* of workers could be overcome.   In their way employers had been responding sporadically to the demands of their workers with schemes of employee representation, by improving methods of wage payments, by organizing cooperative stores or accident and sickness benefits, by instituting schemes of profit-sharing, and by the construction of company towns in which they would exhibit varying degrees of benevolence.[23]   By such measures American employers hoped to undermine the appeal of the trade-unions, and they reacted vigorously and with hurt indignation when they did not succeed.   By the first decade of the twentieth century the decision had apparently been reached: that

[21] Sumner, *op. cit.*, pp. 91–92.

[22] David M. Perry, President of the National Association of Manufacturers, in *Proceedings of the N.A.M.* (1903), p. 17.

[23] See Ida M. Tarbell, *The Nationalizing of Business, 1878–1898* (New York: The Macmillan Company, Inc., 1936), pp. 168–78.

employers could not fight trade-unions individually. Various associations such as the NAM or the National Metal Trades Association prepared a collective counterattack.

b. The Ideology of the Open Shop

The "Open Shop Campaign" appeared to consist of little else than the employers' ever more vigorous assertion of their authority and strength. But the employers' endorsement of the need for collective action was a clear-cut departure from established ideas and practices. To be sure, employers had organized in the past in order to have their common interests represented more effectively. But never before had they organized in order to solve problems of management within the enterprise. To engage in a collective approach to this problem implied that the employer's vaunted authority within his plant was not as absolute as he had claimed. The rising tide of trade-unionism forced American employers to acknowledge, however implicitly, that their own individual authority in the enterprise no longer sufficed. It is necessary to appreciate the novelty of this theme. American businessmen and industrialists were the recognized elite of society.[24] Their great wealth was accepted as a well-earned reward for their outstanding fitness in the struggle for survival. And when these ideas were applied to the relations between capital and labor, the workers were merely admonished to struggle for survival on the terms acceptable to their employers. Yet at this pinnacle of their social recognition American businessmen were challenged by the trade-unions. And they were challenged in the employer's central activity, the management of his "own" plant, where his authority was supposedly absolute. It is not surprising that the ideology of the open shop, the employers' response to this challenge, came to embody all the sacred symbols by which their own fortunes could be identified with the foundation of the social order.

The outlook of American employers changed also in other respects during the open-shop campaign, but these changes are less obvious because the old language of struggle and success and the actions exemplifying that language seemed to be merely intensified. One of these changes consisted in the fact that the employers were being forced to concern themselves with labor as a problem rather than "solve" it by simply dismissing the worker who would not do. That is, the employers

---

[24] Cf. the editorial comment that prominent foreign visitors came to see the men of wealth rather than the statesmen and soldiers as formerly, cited in Griswold, *op. cit.*, p. 93.

found it necessary to do more than weed out the "unfit," reward the "good" workers, and denounce generally the incapacity, moral stupidity, and infirmity of those who did not respond "adequately." Even if the employers' response to the challenge of unionism consisted of little else than an insistence upon their own authority and participation in campaigns against the unions, this still implied that the employers were giving their single-minded attention to the labor *problem* as they had not done previously.[25] And in so doing the employers tended to meet the trade-union challenge head-on by stressing the worker's absolute duty of obedience. The righteous vigor with which they adhered to their own beliefs in a society which extolled their accomplishments apparently made any other approach unthinkable. Yet too vigorous a demand for obedience tended to militate against the praise of competitive drive and individual success and thus emasculate the very ideal employers consciously upheld.

At the convention of the National Association of Manufacturers in 1903 it was clearly recognized that a collective approach to the labor problem constituted a new departure. In the past, the employers' associations had concerned themselves with the promotion of trade, leaving the handling of the labor problem to the discretion of each employer.[26] Now a departure from this traditional policy was justified by the challenge of the trade-unions. Presumably, the speakers had in mind not only the change in NAM policy, but the fact that it gave to an

[25] In focussing attention upon organizations like the National Founders Association and the National Metal Trades Association and publications like *The Review* I have deliberately chosen the "bastions" of conservative opinion among employers. If it is true that opinion among employers was veering away from an unadulterated espousal of the struggle for survival, then evidence to this effect should be adduced from among those who had held these views most firmly. It should be mentioned, however, that a number of prominent employers were willing to go considerably further in their revision of the Spencerian view. Specifically, they were prepared to recognize trade-union organizations as a legitimate form of collective action if they were "properly" conducted. And they acknowledged the difference of interest between capital and labor but believed them to be reconcilable; to this end they advocated the adoption of procedures for conciliation and arbitration. Spokesmen of these views were represented in *The National Civic Federation,* which was organized in 1900. Cf. the formulation of principles in The National Civic Federation, *Industrial Conciliation* (New York: G. P. Putnam's Sons, 1902), pp. viii–x, 269–73, and the presidential address of Seth Low in *Proceedings of the National Civic Federation* (12th Annual Meeting; New York: The National Civic Federation, 1912), pp. 9–25.

[26] Cf. Olive Chace, "The Open Shop Campaign," in E. Wight Bakke and Clark Kerr, eds., *Unions, Management, and the Public* (New York: Harcourt, Brace and Company, 1949), p. 276.

association of employers the right to advise its members on questions of labor policy. Whereas Social Darwinism had encouraged the view that the employer's authority was assured and that his management of labor posed no problem, the open-shop campaign prompted employers as a group for the first time to formulate principles of managerial policy. And the various attempts to do that made it apparent that the management of labor required more refined techniques than polemics against workers and the instant dismissal of the "unfit." These larger implications of the open-shop campaign are evident to some extent from its coincidence with the rise of scientific management and of industrial psychology, which will be discussed subsequently. But they emerge also from the concerted efforts of dealing with the labor problem.

Emphasis upon the absolute authority of the employer was perhaps the most prominent theme of the open-shop campaign as it developed during the early twentieth century. The National Metal Trade Association issued a declaration of principles which clearly made the authority of the employer the cardinal issue.

> Since we, as employers, are responsible for the work turned out by our workmen, we must have full discretion to designate the men we consider competent to perform the work and to determine the conditions under which that work shall be prosecuted, the question of the competency of the men being determined solely by us. While disavowing any intention to interfere with the proper functions of labor organizations, we will not admit of any interference with the management of our business.[27]

Vigorous action was taken in line with this declaration of principles. American employers' associations used every means at their disposal to enforce the absolute authority of each employer in his plant. In his assessment of these methods in 1921 Robert F. Hoxie presented a detailed list which makes it clear that the campaign was conducted prin-

[27] It should be added that *The Review*, and from 1918 on *The Open Shop Review*, was the official publication of the National Metal Trade Association, which was issued monthly until 1931. This journal contains for the most part reprints of articles or addresses by employers and their spokesmen. The publication was intended and has generally been accepted as the mouthpiece of conservative opinion among American employers. In addition to the "principle" quoted above it may be useful to cite two other "principles" of the NMTA: (1) "Freedom of Employment: It is the privilege of the employee to leave our employ whenever he sees fit, and it is the privilege of the employer to discharge any workman when he sees fit. (2) Relations of Employees: Every workman who elects to work in a foundry of a member of this Association will be required to work peacefully and harmoniously with his fellow employees, and to work loyally for the interests of his employer." These principles were frequently reprinted on the inside cover of *The Review*.

cipally on three fronts. The most important of these was an effort to undermine the basis of trade-union organization. Employers established counter-organizations which paralleled the different levels of trade-union organizations. They used their power to hire and fire in order to discriminate in favor of cooperative and against uncooperative employees. Various inducements were used to lure trade-union leaders away from their organizations, in this way depriving the unions of their most effective men. If such leaders could not be won over, they were accused publicly of horrendous crimes and rank radicalism. Blacklists were used against "agitators" and unwanted workers. Labor spies were employed to obtain knowledge of union plans. Strikebreakers were organized; the militia and the police were called upon to forestall union action or undermine its effectiveness. Still, the employers also organized trade schools and agitated for vocational training facilities, so that the worker would have an opportunity to improve his skills and to imbibe the "proper" philosophy of labor-management relations. In addition, the employers' associations engaged in vigorous publicity campaigns in which they attacked trade-unions and defended their own practices. Large-scale appeals were made to the public, systematic use was made of the courts, political support was given to men sympathetic to the employers, and labor legislation regarded as detrimental was opposed by all means, fair and foul. Thirdly, efforts were made to ensure the solidarity of the employers themselves. Financial and other aid was extended to employers who were having labor trouble and measures were taken against employers who cooperated with the unions.[28]

Coercion and physical violence were widely used in the pursuit of these policies. Little trouble was taken to disguise this fact, though the employers did not feel quite confident enough to justify it publicly. The arguments put forth to justify the absolute authority of the employer were primarily negative: a plethora of words expounding the evils of unions and of workers who did not cooperate with their employers. The language was that of combat, not of peace. In *The Review* of 1910 only one article expressed the hope for a peaceful outcome of the battle between capital and labor.[29] For the rest workers were invited to cooperate on the ground that trade-unionists engaged in physical violence. Picketing was said to be a demoralizing and waste-

[28] See Robert F. Hoxie, *Trade Unionism in the United States* (New York: D. Appleton-Century Company, 1921), pp. 190–96.

[29] The following discussion presents a summary of the views expressed in this publication of the National Metal Trades Association.

ful policy by which trade-unions supported strikers in idleness and drunkenness. The President of Harvard University declared that labor-unions degraded human character because they encouraged restriction of output. Details were given on the cost of strikes and of membership fees; only union officials were said to profit from the unions. Also, workers were reminded repeatedly that the unions interfered with their right to work for whom they pleased, while employers protected that right. Hence, it was in the workers' interest to have an "open shop." The great goal of employers was to have a cooperative enterprise of mutual benefit to both capital and labor, but that cooperation was vitiated by the trade-unions. The unions restricted output, opposed labor-saving machines, and interfered with production by fomenting discontent and by invading managerial prerogatives. Against all this the employers must defend their just interests, but, on the whole, the references to action were very tame compared with the full scope of union-busting activities taking place.

This vigorous and collective approach to the labor problem was designed to defend the absolute authority of management within the enterprise. Ideologically, this approach was justified by the responsibilities of management and by its contributions to the workers' well-being. The relations between employers and employees were regarded as purely economic.

> The employer is willing to pay for results, and in fact results are the only thing upon which the value of labor can be based.[30]

No employer can do otherwise; yet to pay for the results of labor, and indeed to maximize what labor will receive, is by no means simple.

> When we engage the services of a "human machine" we always have certain duties laid out which the newcomer is expected to undertake, and we try to get the best man for the place. . . .
> Now when we purchase a machine tool and find it slightly unfitted for requirements, we can usually make a change in construction, which will correct the difficulty in it. Why? Because the machine tool is never supersensitive; it is never obstinate, perverse, discouraged.
> If the human machine could be controlled by the set rules that govern machine tool operation, the world would be a much different place. . . .
> There will be hardly a dissenting voice if we make the statement that *to get the best results from men, offer inducements commensurate with the cost to them of maximum labor.*[31]

[30] *The Review* (October, 1910), p. 35.
[31] *Ibid.* (August, 1910), pp. 39–40.

A certain note of regret entered into this contrast of man and machine; much as the difference was emphasized, the connotation remained that the man must be paid for his labor in proportion to his input—if not of oil, then of muscle. In addition management had the task of making the men feel that their employers had their "general comfort and ease of mind at heart." It was stated that the "man problem" is as important as the "machine problem" and the "sales problem." Employers were personally concerned with the welfare of their workers, but their opportunity of improving their own condition and that of their workers depended upon the "elimination of the union intrigue, its demoralizing influence, its presentation of ridiculous proposals." [32] For upon that elimination hinged the increased efficiency and profitability of the enterprise.

Only one article of *The Review* in 1910 dealt directly with the functions of management and explained why absolute authority as well as the willing cooperation of the workers was essential for the success of the enterprise. Workers could accomplish nothing without the cooperation of management. Before a worker could give undivided attention to his particular job, for which he was especially fitted and for which the manager had employed him, he would have to do many things foreign to his job and better done by others. He would waste time getting materials or the right drawings or the proper tools; and his foreman might be too busy to get these things when they were needed. His machine might be out of adjustment, or its speed wrong for the work to be done; or again the man might not know how to do a particular job most efficiently, even if he were skilled.

> . . . there is no end to the things that you [the manager] may thus find which, if you think about them rightly, you will conclude that it is really your part of the business as a true manager to have looked after in a careful and systematic manner, in order to get the most out of your machines and their attendants.[33]

Hence, the employer was as much of a worker as his employee. But unlike the employee, he was not particular about his hours or about doing too much. In fact, management was the work of a small group of men with ability and capital which made the labor of thousands productive, and it was this labor "of highest capacity and greatest ability" without which all productive effort would be precarious.

In 1910 this positive evaluation of the role of employers and managers was a minor theme; primary emphasis was placed upon the need of managers to concern themselves with the "man problem." Methods

[32] *Ibid.* (January, 1910), p. 7.   [33] *Ibid.* (July, 1910), p. 15.

were recommended on how to increase labor productivity, and considerable attention was given to the assertion that management does not
abuse its absolute authority within the enterprise and could not do so
even if it wanted to. Evidence was cited that wages had been increased
rather than decreased under conditions of an open shop; not the ill
will of the employer but the condition of the market was responsible
for a reduction of wages, when that occurred. Moreover, many employers had instituted welfare measures which, according to *The Review,*
gave the lie to the claim of union leaders that employers were the
enemies of the workingman. Employers expected to benefit by these
actions—in the form of faithful, efficient service; but the fact remained
that they benefited the employees as well. The possibility of introducing such measures depended, however, upon productivity and profits.
Hence, if the worker would benefit from such plans, it was in his interest
to cooperate with management and to seek advancement for himself
within the enterprise by improving his workmanship and by increasing
his output. He could not hope to profit from his exertions by joining
a trade-union, for that would oblige him to help carry the burden of
those who did not exert themselves.

Labor had become a problem to American employers, and their
emphatic concern with anti-union agitation tended, inadvertently, to eat
the heart out of the glorification of success.

> No man can ever hope to reach a very high position or to advance
> very far on the road to success through the efforts of some other man,
> or organization, and the man who depends upon his union to get him a
> position, and to set his wages, will never get very far in his trade. He
> may hold his job, . . . but he can never hope to be more than he is—
> a mere drudge. But if he is awakened to the fact that it is within himself
> to "make good," to better his condition by bettering his workmanship, to
> make more money, *to have the confidence, respect, and cooperation of his*
> *employer by showing that he is worthy of these things,* and that all this
> can be had only by the expenditure of a little energy and ambition, and
> by mastering the trade which he has heretofore only partially understood,
> and which his indifference has prevented him from thoroughly acquiring,
> then there is a chance for even the unskillful man to perfect himself, and
> to advance his own interests, which can never be done under the present
> system.[34]

The virtue of hard work and the goal of success are still there. But in
their eagerness to fight the trade-unions, employers not merely encouraged the worker to advance his own interests as an individual. They
made it quite clear that he would be a "mere drudge," that he would

[34] *Ibid.* (October, 1910), pp. 38–39. My italics.

not better his condition and make more money, unless he gained the "confidence, respect, and cooperation of his employer." In the course of the open-shop campaign the apotheosis of success was thus undermined by its apostles. For in their continued preaching to the workers, the employers were saying in effect that it was they who prescribed the conditions of success or failure. Hard work was not enough; the worker must show himself worthy. And in substituting their judgment for the impersonal decisions of the market, the employers intimated that the myth was for them alone.

c. Scientific Management and Managerial Ideology

1. The contribution of Frederick W. Taylor

The open-shop campaign went hand in hand with the rise of the scientific management movement. In their attack upon the trade-unions, American employers came to make their own absolute authority within the plant so central a tenet that the compliance of the worker became ideologically a far more important value than his independence and initiative. Scientific management went a step further in the same direction. It proposed to study each work performance in order to ascertain scientifically the "one best way" of doing each task. And it made the results of such inquiry into a set of rules which each worker had to follow to the letter if he was to earn the premium offered for increased output.

> It becomes the duty of those on the management's side to deliberately study the character, the nature and the performance of each workman with a view to finding out his limitations on the one hand, but even more important, his possibilities for development on the other hand; and then, as deliberately and as systematically to train and help and teach this workman, giving him, wherever it is possible, those opportunities for advancement which will finally enable him to do the highest and most interesting and most profitable class of work for which his natural abilities fit him, and which are open to him in the particular company in which he is employed.[35]

And by maximizing the productive efficiency of each worker, scientific management would also maximize the earnings of workers and em-

[35] This statement of the duties of management is contained in Frederick W. Taylor's testimony before the *Special House Committee to Investigate the Taylor and Other Systems of Shop Management,* reprinted in Frederick W. Taylor, *Scientific Management* (New York: Harper and Brothers, 1947), p. 42. These hearings were held in 1912. I have primarily relied upon them for this exposition of Taylor's ideas, since under cross-examination their major outline is more readily apparent.

ployers. Hence, all conflicts between capital and labor would be resolved by the findings of science.

The open-shop campaign had been designed primarily to safeguard the absolute authority of the employer. Scientific management and, somewhat later on, industrial psychology sought to provide a guide on what to do with that authority in the face of the increasing complexity of industrial organizations. I shall attempt to show that the ideology of the open shop and of scientific management taken together prepared the ground for a changed image of employers and workers. Inadvertently, both helped to undermine the Spencerian struggle for survival as the dominant symbol of an industrial society.

Scientific management was believed to hold great promise for the nation as a whole, since it claimed to promote material wealth and social harmony at the same time. The aim was to use all available resources and knowledge of the universe in order to realize definite ideals, declared H. L. Gantt in 1912. A year later, M. L. Cooke stated that the visions of Christianity and the dreams of democracy could not be fully realized until "the principles of scientific management have permeated every nook and cranny of the working world." [36] And Hugo Muensterberg gave this early appraisal of the promise of "industrial psychology":

> . . . still more important than the naked commercial profit on both sides is the cultural gain which will come to the total economic life of the nation, as soon as every one can be brought to the place where his best energies may be unfolded and his greatest personal satisfaction secured. The economic experimental psychology offers no more inspiring idea than this adjustment of work and psyche by which mental dissatisfaction in the work, mental depression and discouragement, may be replaced in our social community by overflowing joy and perfect inner harmony.[37]

Such expectations differed little from those of the "New Thought" movement. The pioneers of scientific management also believed that ever increasing wealth would become available to those who took sufficient thought; however, they proposed to accomplish this common end by the application of scientific methods, not by "mental power" or "a wealthy attitude of mind."

The original impetus for Taylor's work came from the traditional complaint of employers that their workers were both inefficient and un-

---

[36] Quoted in Dwight Waldo, *The Administrative State* (New York: The Ronald Press, 1948), p. 52.

[37] Hugo Muensterberg, *Psychology and Industrial Efficiency* (Boston: Houghton Mifflin Company, 1913), p. 308.

willing to exert themselves. To remove inefficiency and prevent indolence Taylor proposed a series of new duties, which management must assume, if it is to obtain the initiative of the workers ("their hard work, their good will, their ingenuity") with absolute regularity.

> First, the development of the science, i.e., the gathering in on the part of those on the management's side of all knowledge which in the past has been kept in the heads of the workmen; second, the scientific selection and the progressive development of the workmen; third, the bringing of the science and the scientifically selected and trained men together; and, fourth, the constant and intimate cooperation which always occurs between the men on the management's side and the workmen.[38]

And that cooperation was assured, because the performance of these new duties would enable employers to achieve higher profits and pay higher wages.

In his testimony before the House Committee Taylor declared that his "whole object was to remove the cause for antagonism between the boss and the men who were under him." Under the old system that antagonism had arisen because increases in output had led to a reduction of wages, because the boss "was trying to drive [the workers] and they were not going to be driven." [39] The causes of this condition in industrial relations could *not* be removed by any of the devices of scientific management, however useful these were in themselves.

> Scientific management is not any efficiency device . . . not a system of figuring costs, . . . not a piecework system, . . . not a bonus system, . . . not a premium system, . . . it is not holding a stop watch on a man and writing things down about him, . . . it is not time-study, it is not motion study . . . ; it is not any of the devices which the average man calls to mind when scientific management is spoken of. . . .
>   . . . in its essence scientific management involves a complete mental revolution on the part of the workingmen. . . . And it involves an equally complete mental revolution on the part of those on the management's side. . . .
>   The great revolution that takes place in the mental attitude of the two parties under scientific management is that both sides take their eyes off of the division of the surplus as the all-important matter, and together turn their attention toward increasing the size of the surplus until this surplus becomes so large . . . that there is ample room for a large increase in wages for the workmen and an equally large increase in profits for the manufacturer.[40]

38 Taylor, *Testimony* . . . , *op. cit.*, p. 48.
39 *Ibid.*, pp. 128–29.
40 *Ibid.*, pp. 26, 27, 29–30.

Once this mental revolution had occurred on both sides, the devices of scientific management would be adopted with the willing cooperation of managers and workers alike. As a consequence, the increased output and surplus would be so large that all frictions between employers and workers would be eliminated. Thus, the harmony between them was both the cause and the consequence of that increase in output at which all of Taylor's efforts were directed.

The basic change in outlook, which the adoption of scientific management required, had several important consequences, according to Taylor. Under scientific management trade-unions would not exist, because workers would be free to present their complaints and would receive high wages in any case.[41] Hence, the reasons for collective bargaining were removed: the grievance of one man would be listened to as carefully as the grievance of a hundred.

> And what I want to emphasize is that the kind of attention which any protest from the men receives under scientific management is not that which is subject to the personal prejudice or to the personal judgment of the employer, but it is the type of attention which immediately starts a careful scientific investigation as to all of the facts in the case, and this investigation is pursued until results have been obtained which satisfy both sides of the justice of the conclusion. Under these circumstances, then, collective bargaining becomes a matter of trifling importance.[42]

Through the use of scientific methods, cooperation between employers and workers not only increases wealth and makes collective bargaining unnecessary. Their use is also the best way of settling grievances,[43] because scientific analysis will remove them from the realm of personal prejudice and arbitrary judgment.

By the same token science removes the old-fashioned, dictatorial methods from the employer's exercise of authority. Taylor denied that he envisaged a cooperation which depended upon the worker's compliance with the policies and judgments of the head manager.[44]

[41] *Ibid.*, pp. 150, 182–83. Taylor emphasized that his only objection to unions was their practice of output restriction. In all other respects, such as higher wages and shorter hours, he favored the same goals, which of course could be realized more effectively by scientific management than by trade-union agitation.

[42] *Ibid.*, p. 151.

[43] *Ibid.*, p .151: ". . . all that is necessary under the true scientific management is for the attention of management to be called to the fact that a bad condition exists to have a scientific investigation started, the results of which should be satisfactory to both sides."

[44] Under scientific management the need for discipline would be at a minimum. See *ibid.*, pp. 215–17.

> Under scientific management arbitrary power, arbitrary dictation, ceases; and every single subject, large and small, becomes the question for scientific investigation, for reduction to law. . . .
>
> The man at the head of the business under scientific management is governed by rules and laws which have been developed through hundreds of experiments just as much as the workman is, and the standards which have been developed are equitable. . . . Those questions which are under other systems subject to arbitrary judgment and are therefore open to disagreement have under scientific management been the subject of the most minute and careful study in which both the workman and the management have taken part, and they have been settled to the satisfaction of both sides.[45]

Thus, Taylor "eliminated" the personal exercise of authority altogether. Once his methods had been introduced, the managers would be as much subject to rules and discipline as the workers themselves. And these rules would not be arbitrary, for they would be determined by impartial inquiry, not by the judgment of those who exercised authority. Thus cooperation resulted from the fact that workers and managers complied with the results of scientific investigations, though it also depended upon a prior mental revolution which made the wholehearted acceptance of these results possible.

Although the personal exercise of authority was diminished or eliminated in Taylor's view, its "scientific" exercise was at a maximum. The new tasks of management required it to gather in "all of the great mass of traditional knowledge, which in the past has been in the heads of the workmen, and in the physical skill and knack of the workman, which he has acquired through years of experience." [46]   Once this was accomplished, and the workers were scientifically selected, management would have the job of bringing "science and the workman together."   To do so it was necessary to promote "the training and development of each individual in the establishment so that he can do (at his fastest pace and with the maximum of efficiency) the highest class of work for which his natural abilities fit him." [47]   This approach to labor management implied two principal ideas: first, that abilities differ among people, and, secondly, that there are certain types of work in which a given individual could excel in pace and efficiency.   It was the task of management to place the right worker in any given job.   Here, too, scientific management would remove from job placement of employees the arbitrary judgments of workers and managers alike.

[45] *Ibid.,* pp. 211, 189.
[46] *Ibid.,* p. 40.
[47] Taylor, *Principles of Scientific Management, op..cit.,* p. 12.

With this elimination of guesswork there would be only two kinds of failures: those for whom the proper niche had not been found and those who would not work. Since it was only a question of time and of the necessary adjustments to find the "highest class of work" for men of the first kind, Taylor believed that

> the only man who does not come under "first class," as I have defined it, is the man who can work and won't work. I have tried to make it clear that for each type of workman some job can be found at which he is "first class," with the exception of those men who are perfectly well able to do the job, but won't do it.[48]

This view of the masses of workingmen imposed an enormous responsibility upon the managers of industry. It became their task to assess the natural abilities of each man (and the requirements of each job), in order to place the man in a position in which he would do his best work and, if possible, develop further his native abilities.

Taylor's approach to the relations between employers and workers involved a complete overhauling of traditional managerial ideologies, even though he did not change the basic assumption of employers that men pursue their self-interest and attempt to maximize their prosperity. In the past this view had implied that the industrial worker like everyone else would enjoy his success or suffer from his failures in the struggle for existence—a solitary being. Now Taylor maintained that the prosperity of all was diminished if the individual worker failed to reach his highest state of efficiency. In the past, the worker who was caught "soldiering" was fired. Now Taylor made a resolute attack upon all methods of output restriction by introducing labor-saving devices and prescribing more efficient work methods. In his attempts to do this, he encountered the strong hostility of the workingman, which he sought to overcome by paying incentive wages in return for compliance with his instructions. Conventional employers had *penalized* workers who failed to produce, but Taylor proposed that the employers *prevent* the worker from doing less than "turning out his largest daily output."

In this reorientation of managerial ideology the old image of the worker and of the employer became obsolete. The worth of the workingman was no longer self-evident from his success in the struggle for survival, or even from his compliance with the wishes of his employer. It was determined, instead, by tests which ascertained his present and potential abilities, in order to place him where he would do the "highest class of work" of which he was capable. For if the tests had

[48] Taylor, *Testimony* . . . , *op. cit.,* p. 176.

"spoken" and he did not turn out "first class" work, then he was—according to Taylor—one of those who can work but won't. That is to say, the worth of a man would be judged *apart from* the struggle in which he had to give evidence of his abilities; henceforth, his fitness would be tested by scientific studies. As a consequence, the image of the employer became transformed as well. From a man whose success in the world made him the natural leader of the industrial order he had become a leader of men whose success depended in part upon a science which would place each man in "the highest class of work for which his natural abilities fit him." The man's wages, the employer's profit, the public's welfare due to increased production, and the harmonious cooperation between capital and labor: all this came to depend in Taylor's view upon developing the science of each trade and upon the employer's willingness to abide by the laws which these sciences established.

It is not surprising that American employers did not readily accept this new conception of their role. In his testimony before the House Committee Taylor stated that

> nine-tenths of our trouble has been to "bring" those on the management's side to do their fair share of the work and only one-tenth of our trouble has come on the workman's side. Invariably we find very great opposition on the part of those on the management's side to do their new duties and comparatively little opposition on the part of the workmen to cooperate in doing their new duties.[49]

Of course, this difference in the reaction of workers and employers resulted directly from their different positions of authority. The employers could accept scientific management or leave it alone; workers could merely resist in a clandestine way when their employer had decided to adopt it. But the employers resisted Taylor's approach in many cases, because they opposed this substitution of techniques for judgment and discretion. After all, Taylor had questioned their good judgment and superior ability which had been the subject of public celebration for many years. Hence, many employers regarded his methods as an unwarranted interference with managerial prerogatives.[50]

---

[49] Taylor, *Testimony* . . . , *op. cit.,* p. 43. See also pp. 153, 212.

[50] Specific examples of this opposition of the employers are given in Copley's biography of Taylor. It is of interest that Taylor included in his contracts the stipulation that "the company must do as I tell them," which he sought to enforce by reserving the right to withdraw from the work at any time, "in case they refuse to follow my directions." Quoted from a letter by Taylor in F. B. Copley, *Frederick W. Taylor* (New York: Harper and Brothers, 1923), Vol. I, p. 417.

The major objectives of scientific management were identical with those of most employers. Taylor denounced "soldiering" as much as employers did; he opposed the bad practices of trade-unions; in setting work standards he would deal only with individual workers, much as he insisted that he was not opposed to collective bargaining. And although he denied repeatedly that the employer would be arbitrary and dictatorial, he insisted that his science of work performance should have absolute authority. Friction between Taylor and many employers may have occurred most frequently whenever it became apparent that in the face of an uncertain outcome his methods required initial increases in cost. But the major point is that American employers did not regard Taylor's methods as an effective answer to the challenge of trade-unionism, even when they decided to adopt these methods to solve some of their managerial problems. In their struggle against trade-unions employers made use of weapons which differed strikingly from the tests and measurements that were the hallmark of scientific management. Yet the principal ideas in Taylor's work were widely accepted: the social philosophy rather than the techniques of scientific management became a part of prevailing managerial ideology.[51]

2. Changes in emphasis after World War I

Cooperation between employers and workers had been the explicit objective of scientific management. American employers adopted "cooperation" as a slogan in their attempts to stem the rising tide of trade-unionism, even as they were engaged in violent industrial conflict. "Cooperation" sounded less harsh than "absolute authority" exercised by those who had succeeded in the struggle for survival. To employers, however, cooperation did not mean "adoption of scientific methods," as it had to Taylor. To them it meant the organization of committees representing the workers of an enterprise—under the sponsorship and surveillance of the employer. Such committees or company unions were often instituted in connection with the introduction of various welfare

[51] One may question the candor of Taylor's statements before the House Committee, since his life's work was challenged and he was certainly attempting to make the best case he could. Yet this scepticism is not relevant in this case. He had always made it clear that he was on the side of management. On two points, however, he had to be "at war" with the employers: his system required that they comply with the results of his studies and that they pay their workers higher wages for increased output. In testifying on these points he certainly tried to make a good case against the abuse of his system by the employers. His natural bias in favor of the employers, however, made him often insensitive to the existence of such abuses. Cf. *Testimony* . . . , *op. cit.*, pp. 191–92.

measures, which could be jointly administered by the employer and the "representatives" of his workers.[52]

Such schemes were said to demonstrate the harmony of interests between employers and workers. Industrial partnership was declared to be the proper way—the American way—to overcome industrial unrest, and on occasion during the 1920's the idea of partnership in industry appeared to supersede the individualism of Spencer's struggle for survival. Important though this emphasis on cooperation was, however, it came about subtly and under the guise of old ideas endlessly reiterated. In line with earlier panegyrics to cooperation, this desired state was declared to be absent from the industrial scene because of trade-union agitation and bolshevism. Labor's demands were the work of agitators, of politicians who catered to organized labor, and—more important than either—the result of a growing desire to escape work altogether. Taylor's preoccupation with "soldiering" had become a major theme of managerial ideology in 1920.

> . . . the breakdown of morale in workers . . . is full of peril for America. Few seem to want to work any more than is absolutely necessary. Many want something for nothing, do not care how they do their work and constantly seek to "pass the buck." . . .
> There is a certain determination to live without work, or with as little work as possible, in thousands of American workers, which is a greater peril to our country than the Reds can ever be.[53]

This reluctance to work, together with the reduction of hours and the abolition of piecework, had led to a decrease in output per man. Indeed, throughout the issues of *The Open Shop Review* in 1920 facts and figures were cited to show that wages went up while production declined. Bolshevist agitators and labor's desire to live without work were held responsible for such evidence of industrial "unrest." And employers declared repeatedly that the country needed "industrial peace and freedom from unrest."

Thus, the managerial ideologies of the 1920's had lost none of their old "bite." Workers still wanted something for nothing, and the remedies suggested to cure this "old evil" were not essentially different from the incentives and threats and union-busting activities American

[52] By 1922, there were 385 companies maintaining 725 plans of employee representation, which together involved 690,000 workers. See National Industrial Conference Board, *Collective Bargaining through Employee Representation* (New York: 1933), p. 16.

[53] "Bolshevism—How to Counteract It," *The Open Shop Review* (July, 1920), pp. 265–66.

employers had used for some years past. The language employed after World War I, however, was not that of combat and struggle, which had prevailed in 1910. There was now a marked emphasis on the value of cooperation and industrial peace prompted no doubt by the recent experience in the war. And in line with this emphasis the writers of *The Open Shop Review* in 1920 developed a somewhat altered imagery of the three "partners" in the economic enterprise: capital, managers, and labor.

The conception of capital remained the same. Without capital men would be in a primitive state. Capital is indispensable, and nothing should be done to discourage it. Agitators proposed to reduce profits and to increase wages; but such a policy would merely retard industrial progress.[54] Capital and labor should cooperate, they should understand each other better; for capital is an outgrowth of virtues such as diligence, frugality, and honesty which are within the reach of everyone. And every worker is, in fact, a potential capitalist, since everyone should be so regarded who earns a dollar but does not spend it.

Less conventional was the increased attention devoted to the role of the manager. As the size and the complexity of industry increased, the "need for men of brains . . . becomes obvious. There must be men to organize and direct the operation of our enterprises, for without them civilization would come crashing down about our ears—as in Bolshevist Russia." [55] The skill of these men was needed much like the body needs a central nervous system. In business central control was needed, for without it poverty and hardship would prevail as in the countries of Asia. Indeed, these men of brains were responsible for the economic progress we have made—together with capital and labor. Their role in the industrial plant must be to plan the organization of production and to insist upon disciplined execution. The questions having to do with the hours of labor, the rate of output, the price of labor and of material, questions of investment, of management, and of discipline must be answered by those competent to deal with them. Because the management of an enterprise required more ability than does manual labor, it followed that the managers held their positions because of their special endowment. Since their work required superior ability, it was only right that they were paid accordingly. They worked harder and carried greater responsibilities than the employees.

In this assessment of the managers of industry there was as before a

---

[54] Note here the different emphasis of Taylor who favored high profits *and* high wages.

[55] *Ibid.* (October, 1920), p. 400.

notable emphasis on the gulf which divides them from the common laborer. Nothing but ruin would result if managerial tasks were undertaken by the average worker. It was not reasonable to expect that workers who did not have the requisite experience could advise on the management of industry, just as it was unreasonable to entrust a government to the rule of the people instead of their representatives. Indeed, if those would-be leaders of the world were men of marked ability, they would not be mere laborers and agitators, for there is a great demand in industry for men of superior ability.

The praise of business leaders for their achievements and the denunciation of workers for their failure had been a familiar theme. The businessman as hero had been held up as the model the worker was invited to admire and to emulate. Before 1920 this rhetoric of the believers and the hacks had not been curbed by the patent fact that the aggressive qualities of the business hero were out of place in the office and the factory. After World War I, however, there were signs that the image of the worker would be transported from this abstract landscape of the struggle for existence to the concrete surroundings of economic enterprises.

> The one great demand of the world is that you be useful. If you are not useful, there is no place for you. You may be able to qualify for a big job or a small job, but whatever it is, take hold of the job that fits you best. That is the place where you will be the most useful and the most successful.[56]

This statement did not beckon a man to exert himself in the hope of limitless horizons. Labor was an essential member of the industrial partnership; but if it was to rank as a partner, it must act as one. Without work a man has no right to live. Each man must work with enthusiasm in his job; he must not mind the clock; he must make it known that he desires to make good. Such a man is well spoken of by his employer; he is promoted because of his good habits; his neighbors will praise him. But instead of living up to these expectations, "we covet our neighbor's possessions without emulating his push, and then complain at seeming inequality in distribution of the world's goods."[57] To counteract such dangerous tendencies the law of Nature and of God was invoked to extol the blessings of labor and condemn the sin of idleness.[58] Work itself was praised for the satisfactions arising from

[56] *Ibid.* (April, 1919), p. 134.
[57] *Ibid.* (September, 1919), p. 357.
[58] *Ibid.* (April, 1920), pp. 134–35.

it rather than for the success to which it might lead. The ideal of success tended to be treated as an eternal verity that could safely be left to inference, whenever the virtues of labor were eulogized.

> It matters not whether one's job be to stoke a furnace, pound a typewriter, handle tools, tend looms, dig coal, run an engine, answer correspondence, teach children, sweep the streets, preach, plow, sell goods or edit a publication, the work can be done in a way that ennobles character or in a way that degrades it.
> Not the nature of the work, but the nature of the spirit in which the work is done, counts.
> . . . work which takes the full creative effort of a man is the greatest of all pleasures. And the humblest of tasks can be so shaped as to absorb a deal of creative energy.[59]

I have suggested that after World War I representative spokesmen of American employers developed a somewhat altered managerial ideology. Instead of the struggle for survival, they emphasized cooperation; instead of regarding success as self-explanatory, they began to consider the duties of managers; and instead of exhorting workers to emulate their employers and achieve success, they emphasized the modest rewards and inherent satisfactions of good work. Of course these changes were not as abrupt or clear-cut as this summary makes them appear; but gradual and vague though they were, they reflected the same orientation which had inspired the work of Frederick Taylor. In the wake of the scientific management movement employers were generally assigned important managerial functions whose performance had been taken for granted more readily in previous years. Also, scientific management was both a cause and a consequence of a changing image of the ideal industrial worker, and by the 1920's this was beginning to tell in the growing emphasis of representative statements upon the virtues of work and compliance rather than of initiative and competitive drive. It is quite probable that American businessmen in 1920 would have vigorously rejected the suggestion that they were about to abandon the American dream, that they had begun to extol the virtue of work as an alternative to the promise of success—as far as the masses of workers were concerned. In support of that rejection they might have said that nothing at all had changed in their outlook upon the industrial scene. The virtue of labor had always been a mainstay of managerial ideology; after all, they had always said that the worker's attitude toward work "compels success." They had always declared that part of that desired attitude was an eagerness to cooperate with the employer, to

[59] *Ibid.* (November, 1920), p. 447, and (July, 1920), p. 266.

comply with his wishes.   No doubt, they had always said these things.

But the point is that the open-shop ideology together with the scientific management movement was gradually giving a new meaning to the old phrases.   The principal tenet of both movements was the assertion of the employer's absolute authority and the verbal acceptance but actual rejection of trade-unions and of collective bargaining.[60]   This assertion of the employer's authority could not remain confined to anti-unionism, when the exercise of that authority had become a problem.   Confronted with a rising trade-union movement and with the increasing complexity of managerial problems, American employers found time and again that the old formulas had lost some of their magic certainty.   The mere investigation of managerial practices implied that the activities identified with success were no longer taken for granted.   While the celebration of the businessman continued unabated, increasing attention was being devoted to the specific qualities and practices which had made him successful.   A similar change of meaning occurred with regard to the image of the worker.   The radicalism, indolence, and assorted vices of the worker continued to be a popular object of moral indignation.   But the denunciation of workers or the praise of success was not enough when American managers were devoting their attention increasingly to the problems of labor management.

Clearly, Taylor's work provided technical answers and a social philosophy in the face of these uncertainties.   While some aspect of his approach was accepted by many American employers, relatively few accepted all of it.   In fact, employers looked upon scientific management exactly as Taylor had insisted that they should not: as an arsenal of devices designed to simplify and improve the management of labor. They might adopt the piecework and bonus system, but neglect time-and-motion studies.   They might conduct such studies, but neglect Taylor's ideas on foremanship.   Or they might emphasize primarily the need for an improved system of cost accounting.   But all these were mere adjuncts of scientific management, according to Taylor, for they could be adopted without the mental revolution he regarded as

[60] It is true that both the NAM and the Chamber of Commerce declared themselves in favor of collective bargaining in principle.   Taylor and his followers took a somewhat similar position.   But such declarations were always accompanied by stipulations which made it clear that the bargaining acceptable to employers was confined to company unions which they controlled.   And Taylor had made it clear that scientific management would make collective bargaining unnecessary.   The policies of the NAM and of the Chamber of Commerce are discussed in Rev. Jerome L. Toner, *The Closed Shop* (Washington: American Council on Public Affairs, 1944), 115–47.

mandatory. And this is precisely what made scientific management popular among American employers. They could adopt any or all of Taylor's devices, and they could advocate cooperation between capital and labor, without accepting the idea that they must submit the management of their enterprises to the results of scientific study. Still, employers who rejected the "mental revolution" which Taylor had demanded of them, could no longer rely upon the struggle for survival as the arbiter of work performance and success within their own enterprises. Henceforth, they would have to solve the problems of management in a deliberate manner.

d. Changing Images of Man in Industry in the 1920's and 1930's

The increasing complexity of industrial organizations, the ideas of scientific management, the assertion of the employer's absolute authority in his fight against trade-unions, and in particular his preference for dealing with, and appealing to, the *individual* worker rather than the trade-unions: these tendencies taken together had the effect of changing the prevailing images of workers and managers in industry. In the eyes of American employers the industrial worker was being transformed from a person whose striving after success was only limited by his inherent abilities into one whose position in industry and whose success in that position must be ascertained systematically, if not scientifically. And the manager or executive was being transformed from a person whose success made his superiority self-evident into one whose success was due to managerial abilities which (unlike the self-evident fitness in the struggle for survival) required analysis and specialized training. It will be helpful to consider the changing image of the worker and then the changing image of the manager or executive.[61]

[61] The following discussion is based in part on a reading of *The Management Review* and its antecedent publications. These were: *The National Association of Corporation Schools Bulletin* (or N.A.C.S. Bulletin), March, 1914–August, 1920; *The National Association of Corporation Training Bulletin* (or N.A.C.T. Bulletin), September, 1920–January, 1922; *Corporation Training,* February–April, 1922; *Personnel Administration,* May, 1922–March, 1923; *American Management Review* (or AMR), April, 1923–December, 1925; *The Management Review* since January, 1926. It should be added that these publications contain, for the most part, reprints and reviews of articles or speeches published elsewhere, though original articles were published occasionally.

All of these journals were published under the auspices of the American Management Association and its predecessors. While the emphasis up to 1923 when the present name AMA was adopted was primarily on the formal education of future executives, since that time it has been on "human relations." The official

By the 1920's American employers were confronted with an unprecedented situation. The idea that incentive wages, threats, and instant dismissal were not sufficient to manage a work force, that it was necessary to select and train workers on the basis of scientific findings, helped to undermine the employers' previous ideological certainty. In the past employers had been concerned with ideas only insofar as these helped to explain and justify the pursuit of their interests. Now, in their attempts to solve their increasingly complex managerial problems, employers found that they could not rely upon the supposedly unequivocal answers of science, as Taylor had insisted. As labor management began to rely upon industrial psychologists and other personnel specialists, it became apparent that these experts were not of one mind, but expressed conflicting doctrines in psychology and its allied human sciences. When Taylor and his followers proposed that the selection and training of workers be put on a scientific basis, they opened the way not to the promotion of industrial harmony on the basis of scientific findings, but to the involvement of industrialists in intellectual debates for which their training and interests had not prepared them.[62]

1. Managerial conceptions of "The Worker"

Throughout the course of modern industrialization the conventional ideas about workers had been exceedingly simple. They had been in bad repute. According to the Puritans, they were idle and dissolute and, hence, lacking in virtue. Malthus had added to the conventional catalogue of their vices the lack of foresight that prompted them to raise families before they could afford it. In the following generation,

statement of purpose in 1923 read in part: "The day when American management can afford to treat the human factor as 'taken for granted' has gone by and today emphasis must be laid on the human factor in commerce and industry and we must apply to it the same careful study that has been given during the last few decades to materials and machinery." See *AMR*, Vol. XII (April, 1923), p. 5. Considering the date of this statement, it is apparent that the publication of the AMA can be accepted as reflecting the views of "progressive" managers.

[62] Related to this is the fact that in the past the social and intellectual distance between employers and men of ideas had been very great. This distance had made it possible for men of action to be unconcerned with the niceties and complexities of intellectual trends, while men of ideas were unconcerned with the relations between ideas and the promotion of material interests. But that distance diminished as men of ideas became directly useful for the management of economic enterprises. Then employers became involved in the complexities of intellectual history, and men of ideas found their every thought given an unaccustomed finality by the mere association with material interests.

Bright and Smiles shifted the emphasis from a denunciation of vices to a commendation of virtues. Spencer and his followers took up this theme, celebrating the virtues of success in the struggle for survival, though also denouncing the vice of failure. Even Taylor was still heir to this tradition, for he could only distinguish between "first class" workers and those who would not work. For two centuries and more the worker had not "posed" an intellectual problem for the rich. Endless reiteration had confirmed the belief that workers were poor out of the evil purpose of their hearts; hence, poverty was a moral problem and a proper subject of moral exhortation. But in the course of the 1920's and 1930's the worker was to become the subject of scientific tests, whose attitudes and aptitudes had to be taken into account by management. Uncertainty with regard to the traditional views of the worker increased gradually as employers became concerned with *proper* methods of labor management. While it has been assumed from the days of Adam Smith to the present that the masses of men were motivated by economic self-interest, Taylor had made it clear that workers did not really know enough to maximize their prosperity; they might be expert in their trade, but they were unable to understand the "science" of it. Hence, they had to be taught and guided by management to achieve their maximum efficiency.[63] Similarly, industrial psychologists could not rely upon the universal desire for betterment to see to it that job applicants would get the positions for which they were best qualified; classification of jobs and tests of aptitude would accomplish what the unaided pursuit of self-interest could not. It had become necessary to interpret the meaning of self-interest as far as the worker was concerned. Although American employers continued to believe that failure and poverty resulted from defects of character, in practice they were undertaking to forestall the old vices of idleness by the new methods of human engineering. These methods required them to diagnose the aptitude of each worker, to plan proper job placements, and to provide the material as well as the social incentives which would prompt the worker to maximize his output. And to do these things it became more important to explain what was on the worker's mind than to engage in moral condemnation.

[63] Cf. Taylor, *Testimony* . . . , *op. cit.*, p. 49: ". . . the man who is fit to work at any particular trade is unable to understand the science of that trade without the kindly help and cooperation of men of a totally different type of education, men whose education is not necessarily higher but a different type from his own."

In the early 1920's behaviorism led to conclusions that lent themselves readily to managerial use. In the first volume of the *Journal of
Applied Psychology,* E. H. Fish wrote under the title "Human Engineering":

> It seems to be very largely a question of knowing or judging what given
> individuals or groups of individuals will do under a given set of conditions,
> and knowing from experience, which seems to be our only guide as yet,
> what people have done under such circumstances; provide suitable means
> so that the circumstances and what follows from them may go along
> the line which will bring the greatest profit to the company employing
> the men.[64]

Such a statement was appropriate to the management of labor, for it
suggested that the worker's behavior could be controlled by means of
changing the environmental stimuli to which he responded. This view
was obviously suggested by the traditional practices of employers who
sought to control the work performance of their employees by the alternate use of penalties and incentives.[65] Yet other psychological doctrines
of the day were equally compatible with the interests of employers.
Among these instinct psychology was of special importance. Industrial
psychologists pointed to the importance of innate feelings which in
their view were part of a common human nature, and which could be
ignored by employers only at their peril.

> . . . old mother nature has loaded us down with a bunch of feelings
> that we lug around with us through life, and it is the tramping on these
> feelings that causes most of the misunderstandings of the shop, and drives
> men into unions and Bolshevik gatherings, where they are received with
> "false sympathy" and allowed to cuss the foreman and damn capital or do
> any other act of self-expression from heaving a brick at the loyal em-
> ployees entering the plant to killing a cop or two.
> If I had men working for me I would not make a mistake by thinking
> that all a man works for is money. He works for money to live, but his
> greatest desire is for "Self-Expression," and an overwhelming desire to
> count among his fellow-men to be somebody other than an unidentified
> human unit in an industrial organization.[66]

Thus, a recognition of the basic desire for self-expression could be
readily linked with the conventional denunciation of unions, of Bolshe-

[64] E. H. Fish, "Human Engineering," *Journal of Applied Psychology,* Vol. I
(1917), p. 174.

[65] A detailed exposition of this view that managers might control and direct
the conduct of their workers through the manipulation of their industrial environment is found in H. E. Burtt, *Psychology and Industrial Efficiency* (New York:
D. Appleton and Company, 1929).

[66] N.A.C.S. *Bulletin,* Vol. VII (February, 1920), p. 92.

viks, and of criminal tendencies. But the satisfaction of such instinctual tendencies also provided the employer with an opportunity of
meeting the demands of labor by means and methods of his own choosing. Hence, the employment of industrial psychologists might do no
more than to flavor the conventional arguments of employers with the
jargon of conflicting schools of thought and to empty the "pursuit of
self-interest" of such simple meanings as it had had in the past. This
use of psychological doctrines did nothing to solve the practical problems of management.

To that end a type of vocational psychology came into fashion which
was readily compatible with behaviorism *and* with instinct psychology.
Beginning with the well-known program of intelligence tests in the
army during World War I, the individual worker came to be considered
as a conglomerate of traits that could be measured by tests. It did not
matter whether these traits were regarded as innate or acquired. What
mattered, from the point of view of the employers, was that the tests
could be utilized in the selection and job placement of employees. The
introduction of these testing techniques was, therefore, welcomed with
the highest expectations.

> The new developments in the science of psychology indicate that in the
> not distant future the individual will be able to determine, to a fairly
> accurate degree, his actual value as a worker. In other words, authorities
> on psychology are now in agreement that through the use of psychological
> tests the degree of intelligence of an individual may be accurately deter-
> mined. It is possible, also, through recently devised tests, to determine in a
> measure at least whether or not the individual possesses mechanical skill,
> salesmanship, or other special talents. This branch of the science is just
> being developed. The business world will be amazed when the final story
> of the development and usefulness of the personnel division of the war
> department is known.[67]

These high expectations did not last. Soon managers declared that
personnel matters would never be wholly determined by science and
"cold-blooded" facts. While some traits could be tested—and it would
be foolish not to do so—tests were merely experiments in which certain qualities could *not* be measured.[68] Apparently, there were no clear
dividing lines between different "grades of men" and the choice between men of equal quality had to be made frequently in terms of "the
simple fundamental things of a man's personality." [69] In 1925 a spokes-

---

[67] N.A.C.S. *Bulletin,* Vol. VI (March, 1919), p. 103.
[68] *AMR,* Vol. XII (November, 1923), pp. 3–4.
[69] N.A.C.T. *Bulletin,* Vol. VIII (September, 1921), pp. 423–24.

man for the American Management Association declared that vocational psychology was not an exact science and that no one approach applied to all industries.[70]

Reservations such as these did not alter the fact that employers were confronted with a managerial problem for which the use of tests was admirably suited. That problem was "to interpret the traits of the individual, classify the characteristics of the job, and then guide the individual into the job for which he is supremely fitted." [71] To accomplish these ends employers found it necessary to look upon job applicants as a reservoir of needed skills, which had to be assessed in order to put the management of labor on a systematic basis.

> Employment practice demands that we know in intimate detail the nature and causes of these variations [between individuals]. The fundamental problem in employment becomes the measurement of the amounts of the traits in each applicant or worker.[72]

Such practical imperatives easily won out over the uncertainties and shortcomings of psychology.

Tests of aptitudes and skills had repercussions of their own which quickly led from the measurement of work performance to a concern with the worker's attitudes. Early in the development of vocational tests it was asserted that the abilities of individuals could not be investigated apart from the interests which "energized" them.[73] Hence, most vocational tests included a probing of attitudes together with the assessment of aptitudes and skills. In support of this practice the sophisticated could cite the authority of William James, according to whom "a man is what he thinks, and what he thinks is based largely on the philosophy he accepts." [74] And if that was too highbrow, he could say more bluntly: "What a man thinks he ought to be—that's what he is. No one gets along whose thoughts are not right." [75] Looking backward upon the development I have traced, it appears that this emphasis upon the attitudes of individual workers was one more variation on the major theme of the "New Thought" movement. A man's thoughts or attitudes must be of the right kind, if he is to succeed. But subsequent developments made it clear that the same idea was capable of

---

70 *AMR*, Vol. XIV (May, 1925), p. 147.

71 N.A.C.S. *Bulletin*, Vol. IV (May, 1917), p. 26.

72 *AMR*, Vol. XIII (March, 1924), p. 9.

73 Frank Watts, "The Construction of Tests for the Discovery of Vocational Fitness," *Journal of Applied Psychology*, Vol. V (1921), p. 250.

74 N.A.C.S. *Bulletin*, Vol. VI (September, 1919), p. 389.

75 *Ibid.*, Vol. II (May, 1915), p. 14.

other applications. Employers found that tests of performance or of aptitude were not enough; it was necessary to ascertain the interests and beliefs of the individual. Hence, industrial psychology "must embrace in its scope consideration of the influence of stimuli outside industry on industrial behavior, and of stimuli within industry on behavior in wider social relations." [76] That is, it was necessary to concern oneself with the factors that determined the industrial worker as a whole man rather than merely as a bundle of skills and aptitudes.

This growing concern with the attitudes of workers was a striking departure from the image of the struggle for survival, in which only the actions of a man counted, not his feelings. Managers and their personnel specialists began to engage in speculations concerning the "real" desires of their employees. Some said that workers demanded recognition for themselves in terms of an equality of worth with their employers; they wanted to take pride in their work. Hence, the whole union movement was evidence of the workers' struggle "to obtain a recognized place in society." [77] Workers wanted to have a recognized status within industry; they needed to feel that they contributed significantly to its success and that their jobs involved a constructive career.[78] One manager admonished his colleagues to remember their own history, for they had been encouraged or discouraged, angered or pleased by the same experiences as their workers. And he suggested that management should explain company policy and fundamental economics to its workers, simply and clearly, just as a parent explained the family program to the children: that would win their cooperation.[79] Another manager protested against the habit of patronizing workers and against a mere reliance on mechanical devices.[80] Also, the workers lacked one factor necessary for their fullest efficiency, even if they had high wages and steady employment: they needed a sense of ownership.[81] Attempts were made to satisfy this "instinct of ownership" by advancing schemes of profit-sharing or stock ownership among workers.[82]

[76] *AMR*, Vol. XIII (October, 1924), p. 18.

[77] N.A.C.T. *Bulletin*, Vol. VIII (August, 1921), p. 345.

[78] *The Management Review*, Vol. XV (February, 1926), p. 51.

[79] *AMR*, Vol. XII (April, 1923), pp. 11–14.

[80] *AMR*, Vol. XII (November, 1923), pp. 7–8.

[81] *The Management Review*, Vol. XVII (February, 1923), p. 48. It is interesting that by 1940 this sense of ownership was linked to job security. Cf., *Ibid.*, Vol. XXIX (June, 1940), p. 202.

[82] Cf. Burtt, *op. cit.*, p. 286, and Ordway Tead, *Instincts in Industry* (New York: Houghton Mifflin Company, 1918), pp. 67–85. It may be added that some companies like the American Telephone and Telegraph Company have run large

Very frequently this concern with the attitudes of workers took the form of criticizing existing practices or conditions, which contributed to the frustration of the workers' feelings and desires. As early as 1921 spokesmen for the employers gave critical attention to the increase of specialization and of repetitive work, tendencies which had been a major complaint of the critics of capitalism during the nineteenth century. These developments had led to a sacrifice of individuality and had

> resulted in a loss of creative interest on the part of the worker. . . . It is quite impossible to restore the direct personal contact of former days. . . . There must be found . . . a way of . . . reawakening interest in creation, in craftsmanship, and contribution of labor's intelligence to management. We must enlist the interest and confidence of the employee in the business and business processes. . . .[83]

If that seems a far-fetched aspiration, the statement is still significant as an indication of awareness. And since it was difficult at best to do much to encourage the workers' creative interest in their jobs, employers frequently were reminded to create a sense of satisfaction among their employees. "Treat workers as human beings. Show your interest in their personal success and welfare." [84] That is, if the work holds no interest, show your interest in the worker.

By the 1930's this awareness of workers as "human beings" was widespread among American employers. Failure to treat workers as human beings came to be regarded as the cause of low morale, poor craftsmanship, unresponsiveness, and confusion. Management was accused by its own spokesmen of neglecting to give to the employee "what every human being asks of life: respect for his personality, his human dignity, an environment that he comprehends, and an assurance that he is progressing." [85] Workers wanted to be treated "not as servants, but as cooperators, which is indeed their true status." [86]

ads indicating both the large number of people who own A T & T shares and the humble jobs which these "owners" hold, often in the company itself. Yet this is more of an argument with regard to the wide distribution of dividends than with regard to the idea of ownership itself. The latter seems to have taken hold primarily among workers who have, or hope to have, a chance of owning a small business themselves. For a judicious appraisal of both fact and fancy cf. Kurt Mayer, "Business Enterprise: Traditional Symbol of Opportunity," *British Journal of Sociology*, Vol. IV (1953), pp. 160–80.

[83] N.A.C.T. *Bulletin*, Vol. VIII (October, 1921), p. 436.

[84] *The Management Review*, Vol. XVII (February, 1928), p. 59.

[85] *Ibid.*, Vol. XXVI (October, 1937), p. 340.

[86] *Ibid.*, Vol. XXVII (February, 1938), p. 39.

The recognition of the worker as a "cooperator" whose personality and dignity, whose attitudes and inner feelings must be respected, certainly constituted a major change in the prevailing climate of opinion among American employers. In the past, the worker had been regarded as a source of labor services or as a participant in the competitive struggle, and this image had not contained any human features other than those which corresponded to his subordinate position in the enterprise and in the scheme of things entire. This image was undergoing a change, but it is also important to recognize that the new ideas were frequently a mere rephrasing of the old "stand-bys" of managerial ideology. Or else, the new and the old ideas were expressed side by side, as if there were no difference between them. Managers were admonished that they should do all in their power to give an outlet to each employee's creative spirit, for nothing was as satisfying to a man as to create something worth while.[87] But managers were also told that "nothing will take the place of proper wage incentives," however much they might do along other lines.[88] American employers were criticized by one of their number for ignoring the personality of the laborer; yet another spokesman would declare that workers preferred cash to welfare, though the editors of *The Management Review* called this a "reactionary view." [89] If some spokesmen declared that workers demanded an outlet for their creative drive, others referred to scientific studies which had shown repetitive work to be "challenging and absorbing." [90] While management was admonished to recognize the worker's human dignity, it was also reminded that failure in this respect would prompt the workers to seek "solace in the unions." Though a writer might demand that the worker be given a sense of pride in his performance, he would add that the humanizing of personnel relations in industry would pay larger dividends than any other improvement of managerial practices.[91] And if management was urged to recognize the demands of workers for a social recognition of their status in industry, these demands were disparaged to make them palatable.

The form that this inner feeling takes often seems trivial: a desire for toilets as clean as the boss's, a decent period for eating lunch; foremen

[87] N.A.C.S. *Bulletin,* Vol. VII (February, 1920), p. 93.
[88] *AMR,* Vol. XII (April, 1923), p. 13.
[89] Cf. *The Management Review,* Vol. XV (September, 1926), p. 288, and *Ibid.,* Vol. XVI (February, 1927), p. 55.
[90] *Ibid.,* Vol. XXV (June, 1936), p. 188.
[91] *Ibid.,* Vol. XXVI (January, 1937), p. 22.

who don't swear at their men; a friendliness at the plant that preserves
the identity of Jim or Charley and doesn't turn him into number 3098 on a
cold-blooded payroll.[92]

This writer added significantly that a neglect of these "trivial" demands
would only give rise to others which would be more disagreeable to
employers.

Thus, the recognition of the attitudes and feelings of workers has
never been far removed from a now hidden, now open acknowledgment
of material interests. The ambiguity of these formulations made it
easy for employers to feel with equal sincerity either that the old symbols of the struggle for survival were as valid as ever or that the new
emphasis upon the attitudes of workers constituted a major change
which redeemed the sins of the past. Both of these interpretations are
correct—in part. It is true that the vocabulary of motives by which
the spokesmen of management describe their image of the industrial
worker has changed significantly since the days when it was fashionable to denounce him as selfish, short-sighted, and incapable; but the
increasing emphasis upon the attitudes and feelings of workers by
itself did not necessarily mitigate or humanize the managerial view.

> People are tractable, docile, gullible, uncritical—and wanting to be led.
> But far more than this is deeply true of them. They want to feel united,
> tied, bound to something, some cause, bigger than they, commanding
> them yet worthy of them, summoning them to significance in living.[93]

Such a statement certainly takes the attitudes and feelings of workers
into account, but it still is merely a "psychological" characterization of
the "great unwashed," who are unreasonable, sentimental, emotional,
ignorant, intellectually incapable, and destined to follow the leadership
of their betters.

Such antithetical views of the worker reflected the conflicting demands to which a manager in modern industry must respond. The
growth of industry had brought to the fore a concern with the effect
of attitudes and feelings upon the work performance of the employee.
But this concern could not reduce the pressure that prompted managers
to regard workers as a factor of production.

> Employee counselors have the problem of trying to help reconcile in
> the conduct of the day's work the employee's rightful search for personal
> expression and growth, and the company's search for productivity of
> reasonable quantity and quality.[94]

[92] *Ibid.*, Vol. XXXIII (March, 1944), p. 75.
[93] *Ibid.*, Vol. XXIV (June, 1935), p. 172.
[94] *Ibid.*, Vol. XXXIII (February, 1944), p. 42.

There is certainly too much judicious balance in this statement, for while the bulk of the verbal imagery deals with the "search for expression and growth," the bulk of managerial effort is no doubt directed toward the more or less efficient operation of economic enterprises. Hierarchical organizations involve relations of authority, in which the managers are responsible for securing "productivity of reasonable quantity and quality," and it is in their discretion to decide how much this objective can be reconciled with the "employee's rightful search." Still it appears that by the late 1930's and 1940's the managerial image of the worker differed sharply from the idea that he was motivated by short-sighted greed and that his failure demonstrated his incapacity to succeed. While it has remained easy to slide from a professed concern with the attitudes of workers into the traditional denunciations of the "poor," such a concern is itself *one* of the ways in which the exercise of authority in industry as well as the emotional burdens of routine work may be made more humane. To assess that possibility it is necessary to consider the changing image of the manager as well.

2. Managerial conceptions of "The Manager"

Taylor's work in scientific management, the work of industrial psychologists in selection and job placement, and the entire open-shop campaign had for their common denominator the endeavor to enlist the cooperation of workers in a manner that would combat unions and increase efficiency. While these immediate responses to the threat of trade-unions were each in its way a reassertion of the employer's or manager's absolute authority, they also modified the exercise of that authority significantly and thereby prompted a reassessment of its ideological rationale. As we have seen, other factors pointed in the same direction. The bureaucratization of economic institutions had affected the career patterns of industrial and business leaders. Presumably, this process had put a premium on qualities of conduct which differed in important respects from the aggressive individualism of the early entrepreneurs or the "robber barons." Bureaucratization had made the exercise of authority in modern enterprises into a task, for which staff work and committee work, the elaboration of rules, the delegation of authority, and the specialization of administrative functions were indispensable tools. The use of these tools inevitably raised questions concerning the traditional justification of authority, according to which each man had the right to do with his own as he pleased. These managerial practices were visible evidence of that impersonality in modern

enterprises which arises from the subdivision and technical refinement
of administrative organizations and from the consequent interposition
of many links in the chain of command. Thus, trade-unionism and
bureaucratization have had the same effect in one respect. They have
pressed upon managers the task of achieving efficient cooperation in
the face of increased resistance from the workers and in the face of the
increased need for deliberately organizing the cooperation among the
administrative and managerial employees. What was the ideological
response?

I have shown that by the 1920's American employers and managers
had turned their attention to the attitudes and feelings of employees.
By so doing they were inadvertently questioning the basis of their own
authority. As long as they had regarded success itself as the sign of
virtue and of superior qualities, no further justification of industrial
leadership had been necessary. The counterpart of this belief had
been that failure was the sign of vice and incapacity. And since success
and failure resulted from the struggle for survival, it was beyond the
reach of human interference. Now employers and managers proposed
to do something about workers who failed to produce efficiently and to
cooperate fully. Apparently they were no longer satisfied to regard such
failure as the unavoidable outcome of the competitive struggle. Instead they would investigate the causes of failure and prevent their
recurrence by the development of appropriate managerial policies. The
qualities of leadership needed for this purpose were necessarily different
from, and less self-evident than, those required for success in the struggle for survival. Among American employers the superiority of industrial leaders was as unquestioned as ever, but it had become the subject
of discussion as well as of celebration.

Scientific investigations of industrial problems had been initiated in
order to substitute reliable, impersonal methods for the dependence of
work performance and job placement upon traditions, personal whims,
and rule-of-thumb experience. Industrial psychologists and management experts were hired to do this job. They were pioneers and regarded themselves as such, and the logic of their situation demanded that
they extend the application of their techniques wherever "merely"
traditional practices prevailed. And as Taylor had insisted throughout
his career, this was the case among managers even more than among
workers. Hence, the "mind of management" called for exploration.

Now that the American worker's mind has been explored—and in some
cases staked out—by investigators in laboratory and overalls, one

might be led to expect a similar exploration of the mind of management, insofar as it affects employee relations. . . .

Our thinking about the human side of industry is frequently ineffective, because we assume a gulf between the interests of management and employees; not only the gulf of antagonism, but most frequently that of dissimilarity. We think, for instance, of management's interest in profits as entirely differing from, though not necessarily opposed to, the employee's interest in wages. We leave the two groups of interests on different planes and continue to wonder why divergence continues. The study of the employee's mind alone will not solve, and often confuses, the problem. The mind of management is also an integral part of human relationships in industry.[95]

But to explore this "integral part" posed problems for a managerial ideology for which the old stand-bys no longer sufficed.

During the 1920's and 1930's the problems of efficient, managerial organization received increasing attention. As it became apparent that the tasks of management were indeed complex and required uncommon skills, it also became necessary to see to the training of future managers which implied, of course, that these skills could be taught and learned. To be sure, one of Taylor's followers had noted the paradox that the science of management could not produce managers, that great leaders were born and not made.[96] But Taylor himself had maintained that the adoption of his methods presupposed a mental revolution on the side of management, as well as of labor. Hence, it became more generally accepted that "a leader is both born and made"[97] and that it was consequently possible and indeed necessary to make a critical evaluation of managers and their practices.

As a matter of fact, we all know that the great majority of executives have "fallen down" in the human organization of their plants. . . . There has been in some cases, it is true, lack of tact, lack of good sense and lack of an understanding of modern democratic tendencies. The real difficulty, however, has been one of neglect—the fact that in spite of our capacity for handling human beings when we put our mind to it, we executives have treated the question of human organization in our plants as a minor instead of as a major problem.[98]

To remedy such shortcomings, countless improvements could be made, according to a spokesman writing in 1926. There were good and bad employers, intelligent and unintelligent managers, which was inevitable

[95] *AMR*, Vol. XIII (May, 1924), pp. 6–7.

[96] A. H. Church, *The Science and Practice of Management* (New York: Engineering Magazine Company, 1914), pp. 283–84.

[97] *The Management Review*, Vol. XVII (January, 1928), p. 48.

[98] *AMR*, Vol. XII (April, 1923), pp. 7–8.

in a large group. But management was giving "more serious, enlightened thought to its many problems than ever before." [99]

This was largely wishful thinking in 1926, but the distinction between good and bad managers and the suggestion that managerial practices could be improved pointed nevertheless to a gradual change of managerial ideologies. The superiority of the successful man was no longer taken for granted by some people, who apparently felt that success in one respect might well coincide with failure in others. Thus, questions had been posed and distinctions had been made which imparted uncertainty to the ready equation of virtue with success and which would lead eventually to inquiries into the "mind of management." For the time being they led to speculations concerning the qualities of successful employers and managers, which consisted of little more than psychologically worded descriptions of qualities which were the telltale signs of leadership. Although the industrial psychologists of the 1920's often enumerated qualities much as, say, Elbert Hubbard had at the turn of the century, the two differed, nevertheless, as discussion differs from moral exhortation.

The eulogistic or descriptive enumeration of the qualities which distinguished the successful man had been a constant refrain of the "success" literature. In the 1840's the "habits of business" were said to include "industry, arrangement, calculation, prudence, punctuality, and perseverance." [100] In the preface to the second edition of his major work, *Self-Help with Illustrations of Character, Conduct and Perseverance,* Samuel Smiles had restated his major purpose in very similar terms. He had endeavored

> . . . to re-inculcate these old-fashioned but wholesome lessons, . . . that youth must work in order to enjoy—that nothing creditable can be accomplished without application and diligence—that the student must not be daunted by difficulties, but conquer them by patience and preseverance—and that, above all, he must seek elevation of character, without which capacity is worthless and wordly success is naught.[101]

All these qualities related to the work performance of an individual and did not seem to envisage that the task required the cooperation of others. Almost the opposite is true of the many lists of personal

---

[99] *The Management Review,* Vol. XV (November, 1926), p. 332.

[100] Quoted in Harvey J. Wexler, "How to Succeed in Business, 1840–1860," *Explorations in Entrepreneurial History,* Vol. I (January, 1949), p. 27.

[101] Smiles, *Self-Help,* p. vii. Many of the same qualities were also celebrated in the American self-help literature of the second half of the nineteenth century. See Wyllie, *The Self-Made Man,* pp. 40–54.

qualities which were published in *The Management Review* in the period from 1918 to 1938.

Now as then the purpose of these lists was to define the successful man. In 1918, intelligence, ability, enthusiasm, honesty, and fairness were the qualities listed.[102] Ten years later, the "leader" was characterized in these terms: he should be worthy of his authority, eager to acquire new information, willing to learn from subordinates, anxious to see them develop, able to take criticism and acknowledge mistakes, and so on. And it was pointed out that such qualities "are not necessarily inherited, but . . . can be developed by training." [103] And in 1938 a questionnaire was circularized among managers themselves, who listed personal appearance, intelligence, willingness to assume responsibility, self-control, broadmindedness, and decisiveness as the first six of a dozen "executive traits." [104] These three lists as well as many related enumerations included most of the admirable traits commonly attributed to ideal images of man. But despite this diversity, some traits recurred: fairness, enthusiasm, intelligence, ability, and honesty. Vague as these qualities were, they differed strikingly from some of the ideological traditions I have considered. For the conception of "the manager" which emerged during the 1920's was that of a man who did his work extremely well, but "half" of whose work consisted in the skillful handling of others. Fairness and enthusiasm were qualities of special importance in interpersonal relations, and other terms such as intelligence and ability were used increasingly to refer to human organization rather than to work performance. This orientation might still be expressed in the typically blunt language of the old-fashioned, tough-minded businessman:

> Not only one's knowledge of the world and men must be utilized, but other men's brains, their hands and their money, for no one ever succeeded in a large way who did not make use of the abilities and possessions of others. The man who, because he studies, thinks, and understands, is capable of such utilization owes it to himself, to those others, and to the world to go forward, for thereby are all benefited.[105]

But while the idea of success as a reward of virtue was as much in evidence in this as in many subsequent statements, the point is that the virtues of the successful man had gradually changed. The managerial conception of "the manager" was accommodated more or less slowly

---

[102] N.A.C.S. *Bulletin,* Vol. V (December, 1918), pp. 549–50.
[103] *The Management Review,* Vol. XVII (February, 1928), p. 48.
[104] *Ibid.,* Vol. XXVII (September, 1938), p. 303.
[105] N.A.C.T. *Bulletin,* Vol. XVIII (July, 1921), pp. 297–98.

to the demands which the increasing size and bureaucratization of modern enterprises made upon their leading personnel.[106]

Like the entrepreneurs of old a manager was judged to be "good" only if he produced. Hence, the ideal qualities required in managing men were related to production. As a writer pointed out in 1924, managers were mistaken who failed to see the value of personality and of the ability to deal with people *as a factor of production*. He argued for "sympathetic supervision" on the ground that it would result in better production and hence made "sound business sense."[107] Though industrial psychologists might struggle with the task of defining the traits required for executive leadership,[108] managers and their spokesmen had no difficulty in defining the personal qualities leadership required. The authority of the manager was said to be a position of trust, not of personal power, and its exercise required

> . . . that kind of mental equipment that enables a person to take full and discriminating account of the human factors in a business problem. The better industrial day of the future, if it comes, must, I believe, be made up of concrete situations wisely handled by people who are mentally and emotionally capable of giving human facts their proper weight in business analysis and action.[109]

The question now facing management was how this emerging conception of the ideal manager could be used to stimulate the ambition of the people at large to try and do likewise. The classic text of the success literature in this, its modern version, was *Public Speaking and Influencing Men in Business,* written by Dale Carnegie in 1926 and used as the "official text" by organizations such as the New York Telephone Company, the American Institute of Banking, the Y.M.C.A. Schools, the National Institute of Credit, and others.[110]

---

[106] Of the 12 qualities which managers themselves were invited to rank, only 4 could be said to relate to work at all, while the remaining 8 qualities had a bearing primarily upon the individual's capacity to get along with others. It would be tedious to multiply the examples from *The Management Review,* but it is worth adding that the same emphasis is evident in other publications. Cf. for example B. C. Forbes, ed., *America's Fifty Foremost Business Leaders* (New York: B. C. Forbes and Sons Publishing Company, Inc., 1948), p. x.

[107] *AMR,* Vol. XIII (May, 1924), p. 4.

[108] Cf., for example, the pessimistic conclusion of Edward K. Strong, "Vocational Guidance for the Executive," *Journal of Applied Psychology,* Vol. XI (1927), p. 347.

[109] *The Management Review,* Vol. XVI (March, 1927), p. 77.

[110] A new version of this book was published in 1936 under the title *How to Win Friends and Influence People.* It has sold a total of 4 million copies.

In his foreword to this book Lowell Thomas wrote a testimonial to Dale Carnegie, which gave the gist of this and many similar books with admirable clarity.

> Carnegie started at first to conduct merely a course in public speaking; but the students who came were businessmen. Many of them hadn't seen the inside of a classroom in thirty years. Most of them were paying their tuition on the installment plan. They wanted results; and they wanted them quick—results that they could use the next day in business interviews and in speaking before groups.
>
> So he was forced to be swift and practical. Consequently, he has developed a system of training that is unique—a striking combination of Public Speaking, Salesmanship, Human Relationships, Personality Development and Applied Psychology. . . . Dale Carnegie . . . has created one of the most significant movements in adult education.[111]

This ideology of "personality salesmanship" appeared to put within reach of the average person the means by which to climb the ladder to success; yet its widespread public acceptance implied a prior disillusion with the more old-fashioned methods of achieving success such as "industry, arrangement, calculation, prudence, punctuality, and perseverance." The bureaucratization of economic enterprises had obviously increased the number of steps from the bottom to the top at the same time that it had made the Puritan virtues more or less obsolete.

Carnegie pointed out that we have only four contacts with people, and, hence, that our success or failure depended upon how we handled these contacts. "We are evaluated and classified by four things: by what we do, by how we look, by what we say, and how we say it." [112] To instruct his students on how to influence people by the arts of "tact, praise, modesty, and a little hypocrisy," [113] Carnegie told his tales about how one man had succeeded and how another had failed. He felt that people did not want to be lectured at, nor did they want to listen to praises of the homely virtues. They wanted to be entertained by one of the most interesting things in the world: "glorified gossip" about "How to Succeed." [114] By thus elaborating upon the skills of "personality

[111] Lowell Thomas, "Introduction" to Dale Carnegie, *Public Speaking and Influencing Men of Business* (New York: Association Press, 1938), p. x.

[112] Dale Carnegie, *op. cit.*, p. 509. It is interesting to contrast this emphasis on talk with the emphasis on reticence of an earlier day: "On the way up, reticence is important; once one is there, it is obligatory. Speech is alive with the germ of commitment. The less you say, the less vulnerable you are." This descriptive statement refers to the tycoons of the early twentieth century. See S. N. Behrman, "The Silent Men," *The New Yorker* (November 3, 1951), p. 52.

[113] Carnegie, *op. cit.*, p. 99.   [114] *Ibid.*, p. 429.

salesmanship," he helped to replace the independent entrepreneur who would achieve success in the competitive struggle with the image of a man whose success depended upon the art of "winning friends and influencing people" in a career consisting of promotions from lower to higher positions. From the standpoint of the individual salaried employee, these techniques appeared to be a means of career advancement. From the standpoint of management, they seemed to facilitate the coordination of a growing and increasingly specialized administrative staff.

But from the standpoint of the average worker in industry or business, the message of Dale Carnegie was not nearly as relevant as the old-fashioned symbols had been, which admonished him to work hard, live frugally, and strive toward economic independence. If it was true, as Carnegie maintained, that "we are evaluated . . . by what we do, by how we look, by what we say, and how we say it," then it is clear that only the first of these criteria could be applied to the worker in the shop. How he looked or what he said had little importance for the worker, but it was of great significance for the salaried employee, since

> There is a positive and definite relation between leadership and personality; the more personality the individual has, the more likely he is to be called to positions of leadership.[115]

Although this statement was made in a different context, it reflected an opinion widespread among managers, and its classic simplicity makes it clear that this approach did not apply to workers at all. For workers are not active participants in the bureaucratic apparatus of economic enterprises. Rather that apparatus is set up to organize and regulate their day-to-day work performance.[116]

A success ideology applicable to managers and salaried employees rather than to workers was likely to be reflected in a major difference between the managerial conceptions of "the manager" and "the worker." While the spokesmen of American employers have continued to "spell out" what qualities characterize a "successful leader," they have also continued to concern themselves—under the influence of industrial psychology and of the day-to-day problems of personnel relations—with the attitudes and feelings of workers. Thus, qualities such as fairness, enthusiasm, intelligence, and ability were considered alongside com-

[115] Edward G. Flemming, "A Factor Analysis of the Personality of High School Leaders," *Journal of Applied Psychology*, XIX (1935), p. 599.

[116] This apparatus has of course other functions, but these are irrelevant in the present context.

pilations of "what the worker wants." In 16 lists published in *The Management Review* from 1922 to 1937, the "wants of workers" appearing most often [aside from adequate wages (10)] were: self-respect (8), good working conditions (7), security (7), special benefits (6), and self-expression, opportunity to get ahead, and democratic participation in labor management in at least 5 of the lists.[117] The contrast between these *real* wants of workers and the *ideal* qualities of the successful leader must obviously be great.[118] But the development of managerial ideology had led to this result by applying the techniques of personnel management to workers while continuing the traditional celebration of the successful man (albeit in terms borrowed from various schools of psychology). While inquiries into the attitudes and feelings of workers had gone forward, the inquiries into the "mind of management" had lagged behind.

This contrast between the "real" worker and the "ideal" manager was readily interpreted in the sense that the gulf dividing the two was unbridgeable. As in the case of the earlier arguments derived from the struggle for survival, reasons were found for the view that the successful man was quite unlike his less able fellow.

> The number of people of relatively low intelligence is vastly greater than is generally appreciated and . . . this mass of low-level intelligence is an enormous menace to democracy unless it is recognized and properly treated. . . .
> The intelligent group must do the planning and organizing for the mass, . . . our whole attitude toward lower grades of intelligence must be . . . based upon an intelligent understanding of the mental capacity of each individual. . . .[119]

[117] The numbers in parenthesis indicate the number of lists in which the "want" appeared.

[118] This difference between wants and qualities is illustrated by the "arguments" in which the writers in *The Management Review* engaged from time to time. Conventionally, they will comment on the absence or presence of ambition among workers. For example, a writer declared in 1937 that "in general, workers have surprisingly little of the desire to share the responsibilities of running the establishment." But he was contradicted two years later by the statement that "nearly every working person has his eye on some kind of managerial job." See *The Management Review,* Vol. XXVI (March, 1937), p. 92, and *ibid.,* Vol. XXVIII (September, 1939), p. 290. Earlier writers might have called the first lazy while applauding the second as imbued with ambition. Instead, the "analysis" of wants has superseded the praise or blame of qualities.

[119] H. H. Goddard, "The Levels of Intelligence," in Lionel D. Edie, ed., *Practical Psychology for Business Executives* (New York: H. W. Wilson Company, 1922), p. 48.

Thus, arguments from industrial psychology would support the traditional belief that the authority and success of employers and managers resulted inevitably from their superior endowment. But arguments derived from psychology could also be used to emphasize the basic similarity between workers and managers. By referring to their motivation rather than to their endowment, it was plausible to conclude that managers and workers were made of common human stuff and, hence, to deny any basic distinction between them.

> Neither the laborer nor his boss "checks" his human nature at the plant door. He does not "park" his inmost desires and become merely a pay envelope or profit-hunter. Each man is motivated in his work by the same five impulses that motivate his leisure, and the capitalist, the supervisor, and the employee do not differ materially in their motives.[120]

Apparently, it was just as easy to use psychology in order to "prove" the innate superiority of employers as it was to "prove" the basic similarity between employers and employees. In this respect, little if anything had changed from the time when references to the struggle for survival had been used to demonstrate the superiority of the successful as well as the "equal opportunity" of each to achieve success, that is, if he were "equal" to the challenge.

It would be easy to argue that managerial ideologies had not changed at all by the 1920's or 1930's, that they had merely undergone a change in vocabulary which left their major tenets intact. The argument would be deceiving, nevertheless.[121] For while it is true that the justifi-

---

[120] *Corporation Training*, X (June, 1922), p. 4. The five impulses listed in the article are: the desire for activity "at which he can succeed;" the desire to attain mastery over something or someone; the desire of "being mastered in turn by brainy likable people;" the desire for congenial company and surroundings; and the desire for approval by others.

[121] A test of this argument is readily available in the last volume of *The Open Shop Review*, published in 1931. In order to examine the changing conceptions of workers and managers I have made use of the publications of the American Management Association, because the conscious purpose of the AMA was to reform managerial beliefs and practices. The conscious purpose of *The Open Shop Review* was to hold fast to the traditional approach. Yet, by 1931 the promise of success had become attenuated even in that publication. While the old virtues were still commended, hard work would only lead to a better job and more money. Arguments concerning the "struggle for survival" were used primarily to fight "socialism," not to exalt the leaders and denounce the led. Although the problems of labor management are not discussed in detail and the tough manager is still praised, it is admitted that the handling of men requires more thought than the mastery of machines, and it is also stated that real grievances must be remedied immediately. The tough talk is still in evidence, but it

cations of authority in economic enterprises have much in common regardless of the changing vocabularies in which they are expressed, it is true also that the ideology of a rising managerial elite had inadvertently emptied the hallowed promise of success of its old and clear cut meaning. In the past every man had been said to "look forward and hope to be a hired labourer this year and the next, work for himself afterwards, and finally hire men to work for him." [122] Now, the bureaucratization of economic enterprises had greatly modified the career opportunities of ordinary employees. Though it is true that the old ideal of economic independence has survived, perhaps more among workers than among salaried employees and managers, it is important to note here the new and different managerial interpretation of success with regard to ordinary workers. "Any man can have a measure of success . . . , if he can find out what he is adapted to," or, it may be added, if the management can find it out for him.[123] In keeping with *this* conception of success, B. C. Forbes has stated that most people have the qualities which lead to success in moderate degree. If these qualities are "wisely cultivated and exercised, [they] may be depended upon to earn at least a moderate measure of success." [124]

The notable moderation of such statements does not mean that exceptionally successful men are no longer held up as symbols of inspiration and emulation. It means rather that the celebration of the industrial leader can no longer suffice. When A. P. Sloan writes that "the corporation [is] a pyramid of opportunities from the bottom toward the top with thousands of chances for advancement," he refers to the promise of a bureaucratic career, not to the earlier image of the individual enterpriser.[125] The qualities which are useful in a bureaucratic career, have become the leitmotiv of managerial appeals.

*   *   *

During the 1920's and 1930's the managerial conception of "the worker" and of "the manager" underwent significant changes. The worker had been regarded as a more or less short-sighted and incapable

shows a gradual accommodation to the changing images of workers and managers, which I have traced.

[122] Abraham Lincoln, *Complete Works,* ed. by John G. Nicolay and John Hay (New York: The Century Company, 1920), Vol. V, p. 361.

[123] N.A.C.S. *Bulletin,* Vol. II (May, 1915), p. 23.

[124] B. C. Forbes, ed., *op. cit.* (1948), p. x.

[125] A. P. Sloan, *Adventures of a White-Collar Man* (New York: Doubleday, Doran and Company, 1941), p. 153.

person who had failed in the struggle for survival, and who had to be left to enjoy or endure his lot as best he could. Gradually, the worker came to be viewed as an embodiment of aptitudes and feelings, which had to be assessed so that his job assignment would be advantageous to him and profitable to the enterprise. From a person whose chances for success were vague but unlimited as long as he had not yet proved himself, the worker had become a person whose chances for success had become specific and restricted, depending as they did upon discretionary evaluations and promotions by management. From a person to whom hope and virtue had been preached, he had become a person whose aptitudes and attitudes had to be tested. The managerial conception of "the manager" had changed also, but perhaps not so drastically. The leaders of economic enterprises had been regarded as men whose success in the struggle for survival testified to their superior abilities, and these abilities consisted of such qualities as perseverance, capacity for work, prudence as well as daring, and others. Success and self-evident superiority were sufficient justification of authority. Gradually, however, these leaders became more consciously preoccupied with the complex tasks of management. The imagery of 'their superior virtues changed accordingly from the praise of qualities ideally suited to the competitive struggle to a praise of qualities ideally suited to the management of men and to the advancement of careers in a bureaucratic environment. Under the impact of bureaucratization the virtues ideally embodied in the successful man of business had become incongruous with the job the worker had to do. It is this ideological dilemma which has been "resolved" by a new synthesis of old ideas in the work of Elton Mayo.

e. The Contribution of Elton Mayo to Managerial Ideology

In commenting at this point on the work of Elton Mayo, I propose to single out that aspect of his work which, in my judgment, constitutes his special contribution to American managerial ideology.[126] We have seen that during the 1920's and 1930's, adaptability and skill in

---

[126] For many years prior to his retirement and death in 1949, Mayo was Professor of Industrial Research at the School of Business Administration, Harvard University. His influence on the academic profession and especially upon the disciplines of sociology, psychology, and their various applied fields has been extensive. It has likewise been extensive with regard to the education of businessmen. I do not propose to assess the extent of these influences of Mayo's work. Nor do I propose to offer another comprehensive summary and critical evaluation of his work such as have appeared frequently in recent years.

human relations were praised rather than effort and competitive drive in the struggle for survival. Managerial thinking underwent a significant change as this new set of virtues was commended to the ambitious. Yet the new virtues were not applied to the worker, as the old virtues had been. Employers and their spokesmen tended to discuss the worker in terms of his "real" wants rather than in terms of an ideal image. This is the ideological dilemma Mayo resolved. He reinterpreted the nature of man so that workers, salaried employees, and managers could once again be discussed in terms of the same basic human qualities. By this reinterpretation he succeeded in eliminating the praise of "virtue" from the perspective of managerial ideology. Henceforth, managers as well as workers were to be the subject of scientific analysis, for Mayo based his image of both upon a series of scientific studies.

The sequence of his research studies in industrial problems reads like a rehearsal of past opinions among managers and industrial psychologists, as Mayo himself has pointed out. His first study was concerned with the problem of labor turnover in the spinning department of a Philadelphia textile mill. In this study an attempt was made to examine the relation between differently arranged rest periods and productivity, for it was widely assumed that "proper" rest periods would lead to increased output. The results were interpreted by Mayo at the time in terms of the physiological and psychological effect of rest upon fatigue and "pessimistic reverie."

The next study was the famous, prolonged observation of six girls making telephone assemblies. This demonstrated that productivity increased, and markedly so, almost regardless of the experimental changes which were introduced. Certainly the most striking finding of these researches was not that the girls responded to positive incentives with higher productivity but that they continued to increase their output when the original working conditions were reintroduced and all the positive incentives were withdrawn. The studies also showed increased productivity in successive test periods, even though the working conditions remained the same. In looking back upon these findings Mayo has summarized their significance in these terms:

> . . . the major experimental change was introduced when those in charge sought to hold the situation humanly steady . . . by getting the cooperation of the workers. What actually happened was that six individuals became a team and the team gave itself wholeheartedly and spontaneously to cooperation in the experiment. The consequence was that they felt themselves to be participating, freely and without afterthought, and were happy in the knowledge that they were working without coercion

from above or limitation from below. They were themselves astonished at the consequence, for they felt they were working under less pressure than ever before. . . .[127]

This conclusion was written after many years of reflection. The researchers themselves arrived at it painstakingly after the cumulative evidence of the "Relay Assembly Test Room" refuted one after another of the many variables which had commonly been associated in the minds of managers and industrial psychologists with increases in productivity.[128]

It is of interest that the further researches of Elton Mayo and his group again reflected established tendencies in managerial thinking. One study, which was suggested by the experimental investigation of the six girls, consisted of an extensive interviewing program, in which 21,000 employees were interviewed over a three-year period. The purpose of this program was to discover the personal and social factors which were related to the dissatisfactions of employees and to the variations in their output. And this inquiry into personal factors as well as into the social demands impinging upon the worker both outside and inside the plant led in turn to a more intensive inquiry into the "informal" relations among the members of a work group. The latter study led to the conclusion that social demands within the group resulted in the more or less tacit agreement of workers on standards of work performance. This agreement was used by the work group to render managerial directives ineffective and to maximize the advantages to the group as the workers conceived of them.

[127] Elton Mayo, *The Social Problems of an Industrial Civilization* (Boston: Graduate School of Business Administration, Harvard University, 1945), pp. 72–73. Cf. also the remark of Fritz Roethlisberger that for the purpose of this experiment all the conditions prevailing in the shop were altered. See his *Management and Morale* (Cambridge: Harvard University Press, 1943), p. 14. It may be added that originally two operators were selected for the experiment who were known to be friendly, and these two were invited to select four other girls with whom they would like to work. One of these girls worked as a layout operator, while the other five were the assemblers whose productivity was studied. This is the "human situation" to which the first sentence of Mayo's statement refers.

[128] The work of T. N. Whitehead, *The Industrial Worker* (Cambridge: Harvard University Press, 1938), 2 vols., consists of elaborate statistical checks on the relation between productivity and such variables as temperature of the workroom, hours of sleep, fluctuations in the weather, results of physical examinations, and many others. None of the environmental and physiological factors, which were so tested, proved to be significant statistically.

Major contributions in the history of ideas often consist in an author's striking summary of old ideas. I believe this is true of Mayo's work. There are traces of the "New Thought" movement in his emphasis upon the strategic importance of mental and emotional factors in the make-up of managers and workers. The promise of success is rather lacking in Mayo in keeping with the changing images of man in industry, which I have traced. Cooperation in industry is identified by Mayo with society's capacity to survive; and this belief is akin to, if not identical with, the ideal of cooperation which inspired the employee-representation plans and the open-shop campaign of the 1920's. Mayo's neglect of trade-unions and of their role in industry is well in line with the open-shop campaign also, for in this campaign employers were not only fighting unions, but also introducing many measures designed to forestall them by satisfying the demands of workers in line with managerial objectives.[129]

Some managers had also anticipated Mayo with regard to a reassessment of the motivation of workers. During the 1920's, several writers had pointed out that it was wrong to think workers were interested only in money. Instead workers wanted to feel they were doing something worth while and that they had the respect of others. They wanted "to be somebody other than an unidentified human unit in an industrial organization." [130] Failure to take this into account would wreck even the best intentioned welfare plans. "I know of one plant in particular," wrote a manager in 1923,

> where everything conceivable seems to have been provided for the workman, but which fails as an example of maximum achievement, because of a taint of patronization. This makes it lose whatever significance it might otherwise have. . . . We must remember that we are living in a democratic community. Managerial achievement in human organization is not dependent on mechanical devices nor routine methods. . . . We are leading men, not handling robots.[131]

In comments such as these there was an awareness of the human problems in labor management that had not been apparent before. Nevertheless, these were incidental remarks which could not make inroads upon the settled conviction that workers were wage-pursuing automata or at any rate that employers could consider them only as factors of

[129] Mayo proposed methods in this connection which differed from those in vogue during the open-shop campaign. His proposals were an outgrowth of the changing conceptions traced in Section *d*, above.

[130] N.A.C.S. *Bulletin,* Vol. VII (February, 1920), p. 92.

[131] *AMR*, Vol. XII (November, 1923), pp. 7–8.

production. Even the managerial emphasis upon the attitudes and feelings of workers was often little more than a reference to another cost factor, which had to be taken into account. Views like these were mere intimations of Mayo's contribution. For Mayo used scientific investigations to prove workers were not self-interested individuals but persons with attitudes and feelings which had to be considered in terms other than a test of their aptitudes for better job placement.

A comparison and contrast between Mayo and Taylor is most illuminating in this connection. Mayo certainly shared Taylor's belief in science as the foundation upon which an enlightened management should base its approach. Taylor had advanced the idea of a managerial elite, which by means of a "mental revolution" could increase wages as well as profits. To do so it had only to base its shop management and the selection and training of workers upon the results of scientific studies. Though Mayo did not accept Taylor's techniques, his conception of a managerial or administrative elite which would bring about industrial harmony and increased production had much in common with Taylor's idea of a managerial elite. Both men were concerned with discovering the causes of low productivity or of output restriction; both insisted that industrial conflicts were harmful and that the cooperation of employers and workers should be increased; and both attributed the output restrictions of workers to the mistaken views of labor *and* management.

Nevertheless, Taylor differed from Mayo on certain major points. He thought workers were justified to restrict their output as long as their increased productivity was *not* reflected in higher earnings.[132]   In this respect Taylor was certainly not typical of the managers, whose ideas and practices he sought to influence. Yet he and they were at one in their endeavor to test each worker *as an individual,* since in their judgment it was his aptitude for work which counted, not his relations to his fellow-workers. As a group, workers were regarded as intrinsically hostile to management, since they tended to promote both the organization of trade-unions and the output restriction which trade-unions encouraged.[133]   In these respects Taylor and his followers con-

[132] In his testimony before the House Committee Taylor criticized employers repeatedly for their practice of revising downward their standards of calculating wages when the productivity of their workers increased. Cf. Taylor, *Testimony . . . , op. cit.,* p. 133.

[133] Taylor accepted these views of management, but he probably differed somewhat from the average manager by his insistence that the individual worker's

tinued the tradition of regarding each worker as a wage-maximizing individual in isolation.

Elton Mayo broke with that tradition. His research confirmed his belief that workers acted in natural solidarity with their fellows, not as isolated individuals. As a result of Mayo's work, there was a marked increase in the existing tendency of managers and their spokesmen to concern themselves with the attitudes and feelings of workers. Moreover, Mayo extended his analysis to the qualities and practices of management, and he reinterpreted the meaning of managerial authority in industry.

During the 1920's and 1930's, industrial psychologists had attempted to put the selection, training, and job placement of workers on a scientific basis. This concern with relative aptitudes for different work operations had led to speculations concerning the motivation of workers, but this had never gone much beyond a commonplace reflection of currently fashionable psychological theories. Mayo brought these trends together into a new and striking synthesis which he contrasted with the "rabble hypothesis" of economic theory. According to that hypothesis, (1) society consists of unorganized individuals, (2) every individual acts in a manner calculated to secure his self-interest, and (3) every individual thinks logically. In opposing these received opinions Mayo concluded that:

> It is at least evident that the economists' presupposition of individual self-preservation as motive and logic as instrument is not characteristic of the industrial facts ordinarily encountered. The desire to stand well with one's fellows, the so-called human instinct of association, easily outweighs the merely individual interest and the logic of reasoning upon which so many spurious principles of management are based.

Mayo pointed out that most people do not think logically or systematically most of the time. They do so rather when they meet a personal crisis, which they seek to meet by logical thinking only because they can no longer rely upon social routine. Thus, both logical thinking and the pursuit of self-interest appeared to Mayo as a measure of last resort "when social association has failed," for such association makes logical thinking unnecessary and imparts to the individual socially

cooperation with the tests of scientific management should be enlisted with the definite assurance of higher earnings, if productivity was increased as a result. According to Taylor's own testimony, there were many managers who were willing enough to systematize job placement through aptitude tests and training programs, but who were unwilling to reward higher output with higher earnings.

sanctioned standards in lieu of his personally defined self-interest.[134] In this view economic self-interest appears as the exception rather than the rule; and the willingness of the worker to cooperate with management and increase his output is *no longer* conceived as a response to appropriate incentives. Instead the worker is seen as the product of personal sentiments and emotional involvements; his thinking is non-logical, and his conduct on the job is determined by his "desire to stand well with [his] fellows." [135] It is apparent that this approach tended to intensify the managerial concern with the attitudes and feelings of workers at the same time that it de-emphasized the importance of their economic self-interest.[136]

Mayo's second contribution consisted in providing a new vocabulary of motivation for the managerial interpretation of managers and workers. In the 1920's the ideal image of the salaried employee and manager had been contrasted with real wants of the worker, a contrast of images which seemed to exclude the worker from the promise of striving and success as he had never been excluded before. In lieu of the calculated pursuit of self-interest and the struggle for survival, and also in lieu of a career of "winning friends and influencing people," Mayo developed an image of man as a creature of sentiments and nonlogical thinking, whose one overriding motive was the desire to stand well with his fellows. This image was applied to employers and workers alike.

Nevertheless, the significance of these common human traits differed between these two groups, according to Mayo. In his critique of economic reasoning Mayo had pointed out that only individuals "who have failed to develop the ordinary skills of human association" attempt to solve their personal problems by a recourse to logical thinking rather than to social routines. It is their lack of social skills which transforms a social situation into an emergency, from which they must then extricate themselves by the calculated pursuit of self-interest by logical

[134] Mayo, *Social Problems,* pp. 40–44. Cf. also Mayo's own summary, *ibid.,* pp. 111–12.

[135] It may be remarked that Mayo's view of the worker extends past tendencies of managerial thinking in so far as it sees him both as a product of his social environment and of his instinctual equipment. In Mayo's view human instincts are satisfied primarily in man's social environment, and he assigns to management the task of manipulating "human relations" in this environment so as to satisfy these instincts and obtain increased production. Cf. Mayo, *Social Problems,* p. 122, and *The Human Problems of an Industrial Civilization* (Boston: Division of Research, Harvard Business School, 1946), p. 185.

[136] The impact of Mayo's ideas on the ideas and practices of the managers themselves will be considered in the next section.

reasoning.[137]   Although "social routines" suffice for the most part in the life of the worker and "logical reasoning" comes into play only when he is conspicuously lacking in "human skill" or when he confronts an emergency, it *ought to be* the other way around as far as the administrative or managerial elite is concerned.   Mayo was emphatic in demanding that the elite control its sentiments, develop logical thinking, and, hence, master the "human-social facts."

> We have failed to train students in the study of social situations; we have thought that first-class technical training was sufficient in a modern and mechanical age.   As a consequence we are technically competent as no other age in history has been; and we combine this with utter social incompetence.   This defect of education and administration has of recent years become a menace to the whole future of civilization. . . .

And he follows this indictment with his vision of the future:

> The administrator of the future must be able to understand the human-social facts for what they actually are, unfettered by his own emotion or prejudice.   He cannot achieve this ability except by careful training—a training that must include knowledge of relevant technical skills, of the systematic ordering of operations, and of the organization of cooperation.[138]

The test of success in this view is the ability of a man to develop unemotional control over himself in order to master the technical operations and organize the human cooperation indispensable to the success of an enterprise.   Mayo identified "success," which is not mentioned explicitly in his work, with the "effective organization of sustained cooperation." [139]

This approach to human nature and industrial organization terminated the change from a praise of virtues to an analysis of qualities.   Mayo made short shrift of the invidious distinction between the real wants of workers and the ideal qualities of employers.   Unlike Taylor, he resolutely advocated an analysis of the wants and qualities of employers as well as of workers.   He saw the individuals in both groups as creatures of sentiment and nonlogical thinking.   The difference between them consisted simply in the capacity of an administrative elite to engage in logical thinking, to be independent from social routines, to free themselves from emotional involvement in order to "assess and handle the concrete

[137] Mayo, *Social Problems*, p. 43.
[138] *Ibid.*, pp. 120, 122.
[139] I leave out of account at this point that for Mayo the ideal of economic prosperity had been superseded by the ideal of effective cooperation, which he identified with the survival of civilization.

difficulties of human collaboration." [140]   These were exceptional attainments by definition.   Indeed, it may be noted that Mayo did not speak altogether of the same kind of "logical reasoning" when referring to the two groups of workers and managers.   For in his critique of economics he speaks of logical thinking in terms of the calculated pursuit of self-interest, and this refers clearly to the masses of the people.   But in his critical appraisal of the administrative elite he refers to a "logic of understanding" that is needed in order to "organize sustained cooperation."   The implication is of course that the elite can understand the "nonlogic" of the masses, while the masses resort to logic only in emergencies and because of their lack of social skills.   Yet, despite this dissimilarity between managers and men, Mayo looked upon both groups with the same scientific detachment.   Different as the abilities are between managers and workers, both groups are properly the subject of scientific analysis which will ensure cooperation in economic enterprises.   Henceforth, the managerial elite would no longer be the subject of moral exhortation, for its "virtues" were no longer the self-evident synonyms of success.   Rather success and virtue had become synonymous with the "human-social skills" which, according to Mayo, would result from the systematic training of the managerial elite of the future.

Mayo's third contribution involved a reinterpretation of managerial authority.   The guiding consideration of his research had been to work toward a society in which it is "possible for the individual to feel, as he works, that his work is socially necessary; he must be able to see beyond his group to the society."   Already in 1919 he had concluded that failure in this respect would make the disintegration of society inevitable.[141]   Such rather portentous statements have recurred frequently in Mayo's work, and his researches make clear what they mean.   In his earliest study of a Philadelphia textile mill the productivity of the spinning department increased most strikingly, not simply when various rest-pause arrangements were introduced, but when one of them was introduced in response to the particular wishes of the workers themselves.   In the case of the Relay Assembly Test Room productivity

---

[140] Cf. Mayo, *Human Problems,* p. 185, and *Social Problems,* p. 122.   To have *one* vocabulary of motives for employers and workers did not mean of course that there was no fundamental difference between them.   It meant only that the individuals in both groups had the same basic desires.   It meant also that logical thinking, independence from social routines, and lack of emotional involvement are as accessible to the worker as success in the struggle for survival.

[141] Elton Mayo, *Democracy and Freedom, An Essay in Social Logic* (Melbourne: The Macmillan Company, Inc., 1919), p. 37.

increased, according to Mayo, because the cooperation of the workers had been obtained. They had had an opportunity to choose their fellow-workers and therefore constituted a team that worked without "coercion from above or limitation from below." These are positive instances of cooperation. But in his search for the factors which account for cooperation Mayo also came upon instances of noncooperation. In the analysis of a work group (the Bank Wiring Observation Room) he and his associates discovered conclusive evidence of informal group control over the work performance of individual group members.

Critics of Mayo and his school have pointed out that both the willing teamwork of the six relay assemblers and the output restriction of 14 workers in the Bank Wiring Room were instances of cooperation. But in a managerial context this objection is beside the point. As T. N. Whitehead has said:

> What is feared of integration within a small group is that it may organize itself in opposition to the larger whole—and this it certainly will do if its existence be threatened; but equally, a protected group will endeavor to satisfy its wider interests by collaborating with the organization of which it is a logical part. In this way, its loyalty will extend to the firm as a whole.[142]

What can managers do so that their work groups feel protected in their interests, what can they do so that individual workers will reassess their personal and social involvements inside and outside the enterprise in such a way as to increase their productivity? Whitehead's answer to this question is, I think, representative of the "Mayo School."

> Change, to be acceptable to a group, must come from within, and must appear as the visible need of its present activities. . . . So management in industry can lead its groups to just that extent to which it is itself accepted by those groups, and it can lead no further; anything beyond that will be resisted as compulsive interruption to social living.[143]

And what Whitehead says of the work group applies to the individual as well. The change from output restriction to willing cooperation depends in both instances upon an indirect inducement. Hence, Mayo's view of the managerial task may be defined as the endeavor to provide an organizational environment in which employees can fulfill their "eager human desire for cooperative activity."[144] The major objective of management is to foster cooperative teamwork among its employees.

---

[142] T. N. Whitehead, *Leadership in a Free Society* (Cambridge: Harvard University Press, 1936), pp. 98–99.

[143] *Ibid.*, p. 110.

[144] Mayo, *Social Problems*, p. 112.

An important means to this end is personnel counseling or interviewing. At the conclusion of the first study at Hawthorne, Mayo and his associates developed an extensive interviewing program of 21,000 employees, in order to examine more broadly than before the personal and social factors responsible for the failure or success of the individual's work performance. It is true that the interviewer in industry has no authority and takes no action. Mayo believed, however, that the interview with employees was a principal, if indirect, method by which management could obtain the cooperation of the individual worker; for, according to Mayo, the interview

(1) Aids the individual to get rid of useless emotional complications.
. . . He is thus enabled to give himself good advice—a procedure far more effective than advice accepted from another. . . .
(2) Has demonstrated its capacity to aid the individual to associate more easily, more satisfactorily with other persons. . . .
(3) Develops [the individual's] desire and capacity to work better with management. . . . Someone, the interviewer, representing (for the worker) the plant organization outside his own group, has aided him to work better with his own group. This is the beginning of the necessary double loyalty—to his own group and to the larger organization. . . .[145]

While change in the conduct of the individual or the group must come from within, the interview is the means by which this inner change is brought about. This same view is advanced in the work of Chester Barnard, who maintains that all orders from above must receive the tacit consent of those to whom they are issued before they can be executed properly and efficiently.[146]

To deny that in modern enterprises authority can be exercised against the will of subordinates is tantamount to the assertion that authority is ineffective without "spontaneous cooperation." [147] In this

[145] Mayo, *Social Problems,* pp. 84–85. In addition to these three points, Mayo mentions also that interviewing provides important training for administrators and constitutes a very valuable source of information for management.
[146] Chester Barnard, *The Functions of the Executive* (Cambridge: Harvard University Press, 1938), pp. 163–65.
[147] The meaning of this term in the writings of Mayo and others is suggestive but obscure. *Spontaneous* seems to be a synonym for *willing,* but this willingness of the individual does *not* preclude the intrusion of managerial inducements. It is not a synonym for *voluntary.* It implies rather that "the eager human desire for cooperative activity still persists in the ordinary person and can be utilized by intelligent and straightforward management. . . ." Mayo, *Social Problems,* p. 112. Cf. also the quotation from *ibid.,* pp. 72–73, cited above, in which the cooperation of the six girls is called *spontaneous* despite the fact that it was based on the deliberate planning of the research staff.

view the demand for willing cooperation with management stands at least on a par with the efforts to enlist this cooperation through financial incentives. Such incentives are not excluded, of course, but under progressive management, work should be done out of an inner persuasion, according to Mayo and his many followers. They seem to say that by working an employee manifests his allegiance as much as he earns a living. And they seem to be in no doubt that the satisfaction derived from such allegiance outweighs the satisfaction derived from material benefits.

In the following section I shall consider Mayo's contribution in terms of its broader implications for American managerial ideology.

f. Managerial Appeals and the Limitations of Managerial Power

The changing images of American managerial ideology have reflected the increasing bureaucratization of economic enterprises. But this very general "correspondence" between the managerial interpretation and the managerial organization of the industrial order fails to reveal the disparities between what is said and what is done and the diversities in practice and ideology which underlie the major trends. These disparities and diversities are important for a full understanding of American managerial ideologies. In this concluding section I propose to examine the relations between ideology and action, in order to assess the assets and liabilities of "the American experience." My conclusion will be that Mayo's ideological synthesis has found only limited acceptance in managerial *practice,* but that its contribution to managerial *ideology* has been pervasive. In the first part of this section, I shall examine some characteristic examples of the relation between practice and ideology, and, in the second, I shall analyze the on-going reconsideration of American managerial ideology in terms of its sociological significance.

I. Mayo presented his contribution to managerial ideology as a proposal for a comprehensive reassessment of managerial practices. The philosophy of his human relations approach has been adopted by management in some instances, and it is instructive to observe how it is made to work. General Electric spends roughly $5 million annually on an extensive training program, in which some 1,000 college graduates are given instruction by GE employees and opportunities for a variety of on-the-job experiences for periods from one and one-half years upward. This program comprises a number of alternative curricula in the different aspects of the company's operations, and the trainee has the option to elect one or another "major" under the guidance of his super-

visor much as he did in college. Training consists in specific job skills,
in the first instance. But throughout heavy emphasis is placed on a
variety of broad subjects (such as personnel, labor, management, etc.),
and there is little doubt that the company seeks to encourage the development of professional managers. Thus, the company may be said
to realize Mayo's demand for the deliberate training of a managerial
elite, a fact which is highlighted by its need to fill over 1,500 executive
positions within the next decade.

This training program also illustrates Mayo's approach in another
respect. Throughout its course the trainees are under the closest surveillance through successive ratings of their performance by means of
tests, interviews, and more informal methods. And this surveillance, the
content of the courses, as well as the informal relations among the
trainees are so organized that each receives both instruction and practical experience in the arts of "human relations."

> If the task of the manager is not work so much as the managing of
> other people's work, it follows that getting along with people is far and
> away the most important skill of all. . . . The critical importance of get-
> ting along with people is driven home to the trainee by the sheer mechanics
> of the program. He learns human relations by doing as well as by precept.
> . . . In Schenectady [the Company's country club for its supervisory per-
> sonnel] the trainee enjoys what is essentially a continuation of fraternity
> life, and when he goes out to the branches he will find that there as well
> his social needs can be filled within the company orbit.
>
> Getting along with one's peers is as important in class as in after-
> hours camaraderie. A trainee takes his schooling as a member of a group,
> not as a lone individual, and the give-and-take in the "case-study" group
> discussions is itself a practical lesson in group dynamics. . . .
>
> Even heavier is the premium put on skilled communication with one's
> superiors. Somewhere along the line trainees must get themselves hired
> into a regular job; deliberately, the company program has been so set up
> that this rests in great measure on the way in which trainees take advantage
> of the many contacts that rotation from place to place affords.[148]

As a result of this experience during their training period, the candidates
see themselves as future managers who "will not drive their subordinates . . . [but] motivate them."

This goal is clearly in line with official company policy. Management
at General Electric feels that improved working conditions and the
many welfare measures have fallen short "of achieving the loyalty, teamwork, and cooperation necessary for maximum productivity, minimum
cost, and highest efficiency." But the techniques of "intensive communi-

---

[148] "The Crown Princes of Business," *Fortune* Magazine (October, 1953), p. 153.
The preceding description of the GE training program is based on this article.

cation" are believed to succeed, where these other measures have failed.[149] The methods used are those of oral communication: weekend meetings for middle management and supervisors, evening dinner meetings, regular staff meetings at all levels, closer individual contacts. Analogous methods are proposed for the man-to-man contacts between supervisors and workers in the shop. The goal of these and other methods is to facilitate the flow of essential information from management downward and to provide opportunities for participation and self-expression on the part of subordinates. There must be evidence that suggestions receive careful consideration. Close personal relationship between each subordinate and his immediate superior must be facilitated. Subordinates should get quick decisions, prompt advice and answers to their questions. The objective of such methods of supervision is to motivate the work team. But even good supervision is not enough, for the "employee will always sense the presence of 'The Company'" behind the supervisor. Top management must show its sincere interest in him as an individual by establishing its own direct contacts with the employees. The purpose of these contacts is "to endow this mythical personality which the employee calls 'The Company' with the qualities of friendliness, consideration, fairness, and competence." [150]

Much in this program of "intensive communication" corresponds to the changed outlook which Elton Mayo commended to American business leaders, although the methods employed are more varied perhaps than those Mayo proposed. There is evidence here of a concern with the attitudes and feelings of workers *and* of managers. There is a very concerted effort to educate the managerial elite. And there is an awareness of the "emotional tensions and pressures" which lead to loss of interest and efficiency, though the emphasis here is not as strong as it was in Mayo's work. Above all there is a wholehearted acceptance of Mayo's major point. Men are not isolated individuals who seek to maximize their economic self-interest; they are group members who seek to maximize the satisfactions derived from the social prestige they enjoy among their fellows. Clearly, the management of the General Electric Company has sought to implement this synthesis of American managerial ideology.

But there are indications that such a comprehensive adoption of Mayo's approach gives rise to problems and difficulties, which limit its general acceptance, quite aside from its occasional success in some

---

[149] General Electric Company, *Employee Communication: Executive Summary* (New York: n.d.), pp. 3–5. Published in 1952.
[150] *Ibid.*, p. 23.

enterprises. For example, a number of enterprises instituted special training programs for future executives but subsequently decided to abandon them. Other companies have resolutely rejected such experiments and have limited their training to a brief orientation course; they have relied instead upon job experience and regular promotions as the most suitable preparation of their future executives. Spokesmen for management have stated that special training programs for future executives have a disruptive effect on the rest of the organization by singling out a group of men as the executives of the future. They also have a bad effect on trainees by giving them an exaggerated sense of their own importance. Training programs involve considerable investment and the possibility of a vested interest in the trainees. Moreover, it is difficult to test performance effectively during the training period. All this militates against a rigorous screening of trainees. Also, trainees are not productive. Despite their trial periods on different job assignments, they show a tendency to talk about management rather than about production.[151]

Other considerations have probably reinforced these reservations. Increasing attention is being given to the training of executives. But such training presupposes that the skills of management are known. Mayo had denied this when he criticized management for its "social incompetence." Naturally managers find it difficult to accept this open condemnation of their past performance, even though current managerial practices come in for a great deal of intramural criticism. As a result various compromises are found. The problems of management are considered to be so complex that they demand expert guidance, specialized training, and so on. If the training of future executives in the enterprise poses too many difficulties, managers are frequently given leaves of absence to take special training courses at the universities.[152] Again, special problems of management are approached on an *ad hoc* basis by calling in management consultants or by instituting various forms of "agonizing reappraisals" by the members of the managerial team. This reluctance to accept sweeping reforms is not unlike the earlier resistance to Taylor's demand for a "mental revolution." For

---

[151] This summary of critical judgments is based on "The Crown Princes of Business," *op. cit.*, pp. 262–64.

[152] Since 1943 some 1,690 executives have taken the Harvard course on advanced management, and similar courses are offered at other universities. No doubt, such training has been very influential, but to assess this influence it would be useful to examine the reception these executives receive in their home offices after completing the course.

training programs, management consultants, tests of executive personnel, and other devices which rely upon the aid of outsiders involve, for the most part, a reliance upon scientific findings and, hence, a subordination to the authority of scientists. And that conflicts with the imperatives of managerial authority and with the need to assert the superiority of managerial performance. While praise of virtues has declined in favor of a more analytical attention to managerial shortcomings and to the need for improvements, managers can be expected to temper their critical analysis by pointing with pride to some superior performance right there on the premises.

Such reservations have arisen also with regard to Mayo's novel approach to the motivation of workers. He had sought to enlist their "wholehearted cooperation" not by an appeal to their self-interest, but by various measures designed to satisfy their desire for meaningful activity and for prestige among their fellows. The policy of "intensive communication" at General Electric was conceived as a means to this end. That such a policy may lead to very problematic results is evident from the human-relations program at the Hawthorne plants of the Western Electric Company, which is of special interest because the famous experiments were conducted in this plant.[153]

The management of this company is clearly progressive in Mayo's sense. The human-relations program, which was developed on the basis of the Hawthorne studies, has been continued for many years. It should be noted that this program which in 1949 required an expenditure of $326,000 is only one of a large number of facilities provided for 20,000 employees. Nevertheless, despite the relatively small part of the counseling service in the total human-relations program of the company, it is of special significance since it embodies Mayo's specific proposals for an interviewing program as a means of labor management. In 1950, the service employed thirty full-time interviewers, whose principal job was to provide employees with the opportunity for informal, confidential interviews. According to Mayo, the purpose of the interviews was to enable employees to rid themselves of "useless emotional complications," associate more easily with others, and work better with management.[154]

In practice, the program did not appear nearly so simple to any of the persons directly concerned with it. The Wilenskys report that each

[153] The following summary is based on the detailed survey by Jeanne L. and Harold L. Wilensky, "Personnel Counselling: The Hawthorne Case," *American Journal of Sociology*, Vol. LVII (November, 1951), pp. 265–80.

[154] Cf. Mayo, *Social Problems*, pp. 84–85, cited on p. 318, n. 145.

group exhibited a wide range of responses. Among the counselors themselves they found "sincere missionaries" who believed that counseling helped employees solve problems, which they could not handle unaided. Some counselors, at the other extreme, felt that they were in effect cheating the employees who came to them for interviews, since they could do nothing to help them with their problems. Perhaps the majority of the counselors felt keenly at some time or another the real limitation of dealing merely with the attitudes toward problems rather than with the problems themselves. Apparently, many sensed that the employee might have little to gain and much to lose if he needed real help rather than emotional release. Among supervisors a similar range of responses was noted. There were the old-timers who longed for the days when employees could be told what to do, and there were others who had more or less absorbed the ideas which inspired the counseling program. But the pressure for performance often limited the understanding of the human-relations approach even among the latter. For the most part, supervisors seemed to tolerate the approach on the ground that there must be some good in a program for which a company spends money— and they were likely to use counseling most when they had a supervisory problem they found tough to handle.

A similar range of views seemed to exist among managers. While the program itself was based on the good will of some executives, others apparently questioned its benefits. And these reservations prompted those responsible for the counseling program to attempt "selling" it to management. The arguments used for this purpose give an insight into the human-relations approach under conditions of critical appraisal by management rather than in the more familiar context of theoretical exposition. Spokesmen for counseling at Hawthorne pointed to its usefulness during periods of stress, when an employee is down-graded or when layoffs occur. They emphasized their own neutral position and that counseling merely afforded employees an opportunity to express their ideas and feelings. They emphasized also that this opportunity itself will usually result in a modification of attitudes. An employee who can talk it over will view his negative experience from other angles; and he may evaluate it more positively than he had initially. "Talking it over" has a "calming effect" upon the individual employee, and leads not only to a reassessment of the individual's situation, but often also to a "better" understanding of company policies. Though it was denied that the program forestalled trade-union activity by draining off grievances, it was asserted that counseling "serves to modify excessive demands" and "dissipates many complaints and grievances before they develop into serious disturbances." [155] Probably this argument was primarily intended to mitigate management's opposition to counseling. But it also carried weight with those executives who looked upon the program in a favorable light.

> We can never achieve industrial harmony merely by dealing with the demands of organized labor. We must go beyond this and find ways of building up the human organization within our plants so as to satisfy needs which otherwise result in frustration and irrational demands. The encouraging note to me is that if we state the problem this way, we have a goal toward which we all can work from day to day as we go about our jobs. It doesn't call for a new plan or a new policy or for the expenditure of money. Rather it calls for a skill in human relations. . . .[156]

Thus, even an executive who favors the Mayo approach bestows his most telling praise by emphasizing that really everyone can and should develop "skill in human relations" and that no special organizational arrangements are needed to accomplish this goal. He believes apparently that Mayo's demand for an elite of the future can be met here and now.

The experience at Hawthorne is significant, because it illustrates the problems that arise when management becomes concerned with the emotional life of workers. To be sure, managers may find it congenial to regard workers as "victims of emotional complications and obsessive thinking." They may find it useful to implement this view through a counseling service, which seeks to remove or neutralize emotional difficulties that interfere with the work situation. Managers, however, are not likely to think of this as more than one among many devices. And they are not likely to expect the "eager human desire for cooperative activity" to be acted out once the "emotional complications" are removed. Indeed, they could not act upon these premises, even if they believed in them; for too great an emphasis upon counseling as a means

---

[155] Quoted from a training manual of the Personnel Service Branch in Wilensky, op. cit., p. 277. It may be added that in one three-month period 599 cases were referred to the counselors, of which 80 per cent involved company problems and 20 per cent personal situations. This preponderance of job-oriented interviews does not indicate that the counseling service concerns itself primarily with the "useless emotional complications" and the "obsessive thinking" upon which Mayo had put such emphasis.

[156] David Levinger, "Supervisory and Leadership Problems" [presented at a Western Electric Staff conference, May 23, 1950] quoted in Wilensky, op. cit., p. 280.

of control would seriously curtail the other and more tangible methods of labor management, which have been traditionally employed. The interest in economic gain is likely to appear as a more manageable motive than "emotional complications" and social prestige. Hence, a reinterpretation of worker motivation which emphasizes the latter at the expense of the former may appear unsound, because it would seem to militate against the effective managerial control of the work force.

It is apparent that Mayo's demand for a new managerial elite as well as his reinterpretation of worker motivation have encountered many unforeseen difficulties. These practical difficulties, however, are not a true measure of the influence of Mayo's ideas, for these ideas have helped to reorient managerial practice *and* ideology. Some managers who employ the methods of human relations have little taste for Mayo's social philosophy. And others who do not care for human-relations methods have found some aspect of Mayo's social philosophy much to their liking. There are indications that many American managers have adopted the *language* of the human-relations approach, whether or not they have adopted its practices or its ideas.

An organization such as the National Association of Manufacturers is the voice of unreconstructed conservatism and well known as such among the public at large as well as among a substantial portion of the business community. But even the NAM has come to employ the new terminology. In its declaration of principles the Association demands that American employers should encourage

> full consideration of the human personality and the need for individual recognition, opportunity, and development. Such consideration includes the provision of working conditions which protect the health, well-being, dignity, and self-respect of the individual employee.[157]

And the declaration goes on to commend "two-way channels of communication between employers and employees" as the method best suited to cultivate "teamwork through better understanding." But the teamwork which the Association envisages is a one-sided affair, even though it enjoins employers to seek an understanding of the hopes and aspirations of their workers. What workers say is called *information* which management can use to "eliminate misunderstandings." But what employers tell their employees are the *facts* (a free and steady flow of them at that), which "will promote teamwork, cooperation, and har-

[157] National Association of Manufacturers, *Industry Believes* (New York, 1953), pp. 7–8. Since 1953 this statement has been modified slightly.

mony." [158] Thus, in the words used to describe "two-way" communication, subordinates are expected to listen so they may learn, while managers merely receive information which they can use. To be sure, other spokesmen of management might betray less readily than the NAM that the communication of which they speak is merely a new verbal dress for the traditional authority relationship between employers and employees. But I think it would be wrong to discount this acceptance of a new language even by those who are almost entirely opposed to its implications. The fact is that Mayo's synthesis has been capable of making widely divergent managerial approaches sound alike, and this capacity is one of the tests of a successful ideology. His contribution may well be to have brought about a change of outlook among American managers as a whole, a possibility which is obscured by the appearance of hypocrisy which a mere use of his language implies. For it may not be inconsequential that even those who remain hostile to the human-relations approach adopt some of its language. In the long run, the use of a terminology may exert a cumulative pressure toward the acceptance of new practices which differ from those previously regarded as inviolate, even if they also differ from the words used to describe them. It is of interest to examine this blending of a traditional approach to the management of the work force with the acceptance of some of the terminology which the human-relations approach has made fashionable.

General Motors Corporation is a case in point. The principal tenet of the GM management is the belief in providing "more and better things for more people," a goal which "can only be achieved when the organization works as a team." [159] The symbol of the "team" alternates with that of the "business family" in the releases of the company. And it should be noted that this symbol emphasizes not only cooperation in general, but the constructive role each worker plays in the enterprise as a whole. As such it is certainly intended as an answer to the many management spokesmen who have called upon management to provide their workers with a sense of worth-while achievement, with the feeling that their work is "socially necessary" (Mayo). But in GM this theme is interpreted in the traditional manner. It is stressed continually that the welfare of all members of the "team" depends upon the continued

[158] *Ibid.*, p. 10. Along the same lines, Whyte cites a company handbook on employee communication in which "listening to employees" is treated in 60 lines, but "telling employees" takes up 240. See William H. Whyte, Jr., *Is Anybody Listening?* (New York: Simon and Schuster, Inc., 1952), p. 29.

[159] General Motors Corporation, *Third Conference for College and University Educators* (June 16, 1947), p. 18.

success of the enterprise. The principal consideration is, therefore, the stability and continued success of the company, which are secured and judged by "sound management." Accordingly, there is an unequivocal order of authority in the company, which is communicated in handbooks prepared for employees. The management decides upon what constitutes fair pay, fair treatment, and the right job for each employee, and it provides the opportunities for his advancement.[160] Clearly, there is no suggestion here that orders will be executed only if employees give their tacit consent. The implication is rather that they will be executed because management has unquestioned authority.

Workers and salaried employees are reminded frequently that their well-being as well as that of the company and of the nation depends upon increased productivity per man-hour. Their job requires their undivided attention, and they act against their own interests when they concern themselves with the policies of the Company. This concern is the exclusive prerogative and responsibility of management. Only those individuals who possess an innate thirst for knowledge and a will to advance can attain managerial positions. They must work hard and long, undiscouraged and uncomplaining. In a pamphlet addressed to college graduates, it is stated that

> General Motors executives are all men who have been promoted from the ranks. . . . Any employee who has ability, patience and willingness to cooperate and learn from the experience of others and who realizes that his educational background is primarily a foundation on which he can build experience, has the right attitude to progress.[161]

Thus, the college graduate is enjoined to follow the example of men who have already shown their patience and willingness to cooperate, qualities obviously necessary and useful in a large, bureaucratic enterprise. But while there is stress on adaptability in this approach to the prospective employee, there is emphasis upon the know-how of the accomplished manager, which embraces such solid virtues as technical knowledge, leadership ability, insight, social poise, and wisdom.[162]

[160] General Motors Corporation, *Working with General Motors* (A Handbook for Salaried Men and Women), p. 54.

[161] General Motors Corporation, *The College Graduate and General Motors*, p. 19.

[162] General Motors Corporation, *Man to Man on the Job*, pp. 62–70. All this, it may be added, is not left to chance since the company has organized a General Motors Institute, at which executives and supervisors are trained "to meet the requirements of their positions more effectively and to prepare for promotion." The Institute also provides the "education and training required for the induc-

It is in keeping with this approach that the management of GM regards trade-unions as a source of disruptive influence. Union leaders habitually invade managerial prerogatives, make fantastic demands which ignore the "economic facts of life," and the whole range of union activities tends to harm employee relations by further separating the manager from the workers. It also interferes with production to the detriment of workers and the nation. In view of this estimate spokesmen for GM state it as management's task to deal with the trade-union at arm's length and in strictly legal terms while at the same time working toward greater employee-cooperation and counteracting the depersonalization of human relations in industry.

> When the employer and employee worked side by side, human relations in industry were almost altogether personal. In the development of American industry, several things have happened to pull these two further and further apart. First, as more people were employed, the employer learned to know the individual worker less well. . . . The creation of the corporation marked the second step in impersonalizing human relations in industry. Instead of the employee having a single employer, he has a body of persons. . . . The organization and recognition of the union marked the third break in satisfactory relations between worker and employers. . . . Humanistic considerations would be unnatural and unreal between these two legal institutions [the union and the company]. Broad human sympathies and a charitable understanding of human frailties can exist between human beings only. . . .
>
> I do not believe in making the union contact the only one between our employees and ourselves. . . . I am hopeful that . . . we as a staff can deal with it in such a manner that the union aspect will be only one little segment, or whatever segment it cares to be. . . . I think we can find a way in which we can get the employee cooperation in our plants . . . , because it is a better place to work than if we went the other way and concentrate all our efforts in making union-management committees successful.[163]

Consequently, it is the policy of GM management to re-establish a personal relationship between the worker and management through the foreman as an intermediary, and thereby to revive a personal loyalty of the worker to the "team" of which he is a member. The man-to-man relationship between the foreman and the worker is said to be

tion of young men of potential into the ranks of General Motors with sound foundations both technical and practical for development into future leadership positions." Cf. General Motors Institute, *Co-operative Programs*, Vol. XVIII (1946–47), p. 3.

[163] Statement of Mr. Coen, Vice-President in charge of employee relations at the Third Conference, *op. cit.*, pp. 47–49.

"not greatly different from the employer and his employee who worked side by side and whose relationships were warm and personal." [164]

Considerable attention has, therefore, been given to the training of foremen, who were urged to become well acquainted with the men under them in order to gain their respect and loyalty. If the publicity on this point can be taken at face value, foremen are given a sort of human-relations course in miniature, which is designed to sensitize them to the personal and social problems that affect the worker's behavior on the job.[165] Similarly, various policies have been initiated which are designed to emphasize the good things about jobs at General Motors rather than the bad, "which have been magnified to the point where people are dwelling on them." [166] To prevent employees from doing that, General Motors eliminated their opportunity for lodging complaints (the so-called gripe-sheets); and the Company adopted policies designed to increase worker satisfaction. Among these the most important were the establishment of new manufacturing units in small communities which provided workers with a more congenial environment, and the spreading of work throughout the year so as to minimize the effect of seasonal fluctuations upon the hourly worker. GM has also engaged in a major effort on the "ideological front" in its "My Job and Why I Like It" contest, which according to C. E. Wilson "caused the 175,000 General Motors men and women who wrote letters to stop and think about what was good about their jobs." [167]

The management of General Motors is aware of the fact that workers have personal and social involvements which affect their behavior on the job. The qualities for which executives are praised are in accord with Mayo's stress on the "human-social skills." Further, the impersonality of industrial work is recognized explicitly and ostensible steps are taken to counteract it and improve cooperation at the place of work by a training program for foremen. In this sense one may speak of the pervasive influence of Elton Mayo's contribution to managerial ideology. But it is clear that this adoption of fashionable ideas has failed to modify the strongly old-fashioned outlook of General Motors executives. Workers

[164] *Ibid.*, p. 47.

[165] General Motors Corporation, *Man to Man on the Job,* pp. 23–24, 52–53, 79–80.

[166] Third Conference, *op. cit.,* p. 118. Note the striking contrast here with the view prevailing at Hawthorne, where the worker is regarded in Mayo's terms as a "victim of emotional complications and obsessive thinking."

[167] General Motors Corporation, *My Job and Why I Like It* (Winning Entries; 1947), p. 175. The company also engaged in other publicity campaigns, but these are not relevant in the present context.

are treated as individuals who must take care of their own interests. Hence, the company "protects" them against the union. And the publicity emphasizes that its various insurance schemes are not intended to provide full protection, which is an individual responsibility; the Company merely lends a helping hand.[168] While the "human-social skills" of its executives are stressed, major emphasis is placed on their hard work and technical know-how both as the prime reason for their success and as ample justification for their absolute authority in the enterprise. And the cooperation of the workers is "secured" by ignoring their emotional complications, by discouraging the union as much as possible, by stressing the positive aspects of their jobs and by encouraging them to cooperate under the "personalized" guidance of the foremen.

II. The human-relations approach has been only partially accepted in American managerial practice, since it gives rise to many problems even as it solves others. What, then, accounts for its increasing popularity as an ideology? The explicit purpose of managerial appeals had always been to enlist the cooperation of the many with the few. And until the 1920's at least there had been no ideological recognition of any group which stood between the leaders and the led. Hence, the many were called upon for their own good to emulate, and to cooperate with, the successful few who had proved their worth. But this simple conception of industrial society was questioned implicitly by the mere existence of large numbers who believed in spectacular success but who attained only moderate comfort themselves. The desires and beliefs of these people were articulated in the secular mystique of "mental power," which on the whole remained outside the mainstream of American managerial ideology. Yet the people to whom the "New Thought" appealed *did not* remain outside the economic enterprises of the nation.[169] As they became employed, they had to accommodate their desires and beliefs to the imperatives of bureaucratic organizations. Increasingly they were confronted with problems of management and with opportunities for advancement, for which the "New Thought" was not an adequate ideological response. It was no longer a matter of making the doctrine of hard work and success in the struggle for survival palatable

---

[168] Third Conference, *op. cit.*, p. 97.

[169] Between 1910 and 1940 the proportion of self-employed businessmen and professionals declined from 9.4 to 7.5 per cent of the gainfully occupied population, while the proportion of salaried employees rose during the same period from 16.1 to 24.7 per cent. The total number of the gainfully occupied increased from 34.7 million to 51.6 million at the same time. See Lewis Corey, "The Middle Class," in Bendix and Lipset, *Class, Status and Power*, p. 372.

to those who believed in it but did not succeed.   Instead, a rationale was needed for those whose own careers put a premium on the strategies of bureaucratic advancement.   This vacuum was filled by the human-relations approach which combined the traditions of "New Thought," personality-salesmanship, and industrial psychology.

This approach differs from the traditional managerial appeals in the sense that it idealizes not the leaders of industry but their lieutenants, and in the sense that it enlists the cooperation of workers, not with employers but with industrial bureaucrats.   In this vision of the industrial world a new elite stands at the top of the hierarchy, an elite which performs its tasks successfully here and now, not in some distant future as Mayo implied when he proposed to train a new "administrative elite."   And the successful man is no longer believed to be the one who survives in the competitive struggle, but the one who has the ability to lead a complex organization.   Many superior qualities contribute to his make-up, of course.   But the increasing concern with the attitudes and feelings seems to have simplified Mayo's demand for "human-social skills" to the point where the successful manager is the man who can control his emotions, whereas workers and employees are those who cannot.

> He [the leader] knows that the master of men has physical energies and skills and intellectual abilities, vision and integrity, and he knows that above all, the leader must have emotional balance and control. The great leader is even-tempered when others rage, brave when others fear, calm when others are excited, self-controlled when others indulge.[170]

In this image of the "leader" his superior abilities are still mentioned. But the accent has shifted from the competitive struggle to the tasks of organizational leadership.   Clearly, these tasks will be greatly facilitated if employees and managers also learn to be even-tempered, full of initiative and self-control.   Indeed, on their way up in the bureaucratic hierarchy these are the qualities of personality which must pass the muster of those who are the arbiters of advancement.

[170] Ross Young, *Personnel Manual for Executives* (New York: McGraw-Hill Book Company, Inc., 1947), p. 177.   It may be added that in the 1931 volume of *The Open Shop Review* there is the same tendency to describe the superiority of the employer in terms of his ability to control himself, while others cannot. In fact, writers in this conservative publication had begun to criticize the gruff exterior and aggressive manner, which had once been praised as evidence of the superiority of the successful man.

Yet this abandonment of the old virtues has led to considerable disagreement. Bureaucratic enterprises require management by committees. But while trainees and young executives regard the tedium, the evasive and foolish debates, the suppression of individual decisiveness not only as inevitable, but as a positive good, their superiors often disagree. They certainly admit the importance of good teamwork, but they deplore its cost—the time spent with others rather than on the job itself, the need for clearance, the discouragement of individual initiative and aggression. And they insist that the old-fashioned qualities are as important in the large-scale corporation as they were at an earlier time. The same contrast of views is found on other issues. Younger executives endorse an unqualified commitment to the organization which encompasses all phases of their life with benefits they "cannot afford to miss." But others question this view; they may be just as eager and sincere to express their loyalty, but they will expect a *quid pro quo,* and they will see nothing incompatible in looking for better opportunities elsewhere. Some think that "creative leadership" can be made into a specialized staff job while top executives act as well-balanced regulators of the initiative of their subordinates; but others deplore this tendency toward the well-rounded personality and believe that the nonconformity of the ambitious individualist remains as indispensable as ever.[171]

This controversy between the old view and the new does not get much publicity. If one were to judge only from the speeches and publications in which American managers address their fellows, it would appear that the proponents of the human-relations approach have won the day already. There is certainly considerable evidence to show that the popularity of this approach is a consequence, in the first instance, of the changing managerial problems in large-scale economic enterprises. And the spokesmen of management who hold out for the more old-fashioned virtues and who see many drawbacks in this popularity of the bureaucratic arts may well be in the minority, as the *Fortune* survey indicated. But this minority consists of those who advance to positions of top management. They will continue to find "imagination," "initiative," "vigor," and the other traditional virtues more serviceable than the tempered qualities of the human-relations

---

[171] The above summary is based on a survey of executive opinion reported by *Fortune* Magazine. See "The Crown Princes of Business," *op. cit.,* pp. 264–68 and William H. Whyte, Jr., "How Hard Do Executives Work?", *Fortune* Magazine (January, 1954), pp. 108–11, 148–52. These reports are based on two surveys of a cross-section of American business executives.

approach, even though they also admit that the latter is indispensable in the large-scale economic enterprises of today. What then are the limitations, if any, of this envelopment of the individual by the exigencies of the corporate life? Or must we conclude that the individualism of Smiles and Sumner has been abandoned altogether in favor of a new corporate collectivism, in which capable, out-going, well-rounded, but not brilliant men handle others like them and act not upon decisions, but upon agreements reached after discussion and consultation? [172] While an answer to these questions must be tentative, there are several indications that the great popularity of the human-relations approach gives a distorted picture of its real influence.

The trainees and young executives, who favor this approach, are necessarily more numerous than their older superiors, who look upon it with skepticism. The minority of top executives who tend to emphasize these drawbacks are too busy and disinterested to care much about "all this talk," but they often hold the reins of power and have much to say about the promotion of the eager advocates of human relations. On the other hand, the younger executives number among them the personnel men and public-relations experts whose jobs make them into vociferous spokesmen, naturally inclined to generalize from the present realities of their bureaucratic careers.

Another distortion arises from the inevitable disparity between ideology and practice. Throughout the century and more when individualistic beliefs were the most popular, there was little or no relationship between these beliefs and managerial practice. While business leaders were celebrated for their personal achievements, they insisted upon strictly autocratic relationships within their own enterprises.[173] And just as there was little tolerance of individualism in the enterprises of old, so there is probably in the management of economic enterprises today much less group-mindedness than the publicists would have us believe. The very fact that the most energetic spokesmen of the human-relations approach are themselves subordinates rather than top executives would suggest that they have a strong interest in advocating a view of management which maximizes their own importance in the scheme

[172] The group-mindedness of middle management inside the corporation and in "private" life has been analyzed with great perception by William H. Whyte, Jr., in a series of articles in *Fortune* Magazine. See his *Is Anybody Listening?*, pp. 109–205, and his forthcoming volume on social life in the suburbs and on the group prejudices of personnel managers and other human-relations experts.

[173] For those inclined to overestimate the individualism of the earlier period it should be added that the qualities celebrated in the late nineteenth century were those of "successful mediocrity." See Wyllie, *The Self-Made Man*, pp. 35 ff.

of things entire.[174] Moreover, it is to be remembered that the human-relations ideology consists of prescription as much as of description, which would suggest that actual human relations in bureaucratic organizations are highly problematic and call for constant attention and remedial action.

In this respect it may be instructive to consider this approach as analogous to the rules of polite manners which came into vogue with the rise of royal absolutism in the fifteenth and sixteenth centuries. As the king concentrated power and wealth in his hands, the nobility had to forego gradually the social life and the aggressive piracy of the provinces and to adapt itself to the outwardly peaceable manners of a society at Court.[175] Some nobles began to pursue by intrigue and polite manners the same ends of personal aggrandizement which others had pursued before by frequent recourse to physical violence. But this change in conduct was an adaptation to a change in power relationships which did *not* signify an automatic change in attitude and purpose. I suggest that the changeover from the idealization of the "strenuous life" to the idealization of "human relations" may be an adaptation of a similar kind. The manners commended by the personnel experts of modern American industry certainly facilitate the cooperation which management requires, much as the commendation of polite manners facilitated peace at the Royal Court. But neither the one nor the other necessarily means what it appears to mean. For the calm eyes which never stray from the other's gaze, the easy control in which laughter is natural but never forced, the attentive and receptive manner, the well-rounded good-fellowship, the ability to elicit participation and to accomplish change without upsetting relationships—may be so many devices for personal advancement while the man is on his way up.[176] Though his

---

[174] In a characteristic passage of a textbook on personnel administration the future personnel manager is advised to act and talk like a vice-president in his relations with top management, even if this is not his actual rank. See Paul Pigors and Charles A. Myers, *Personnel Administration* (New York: McGraw-Hill Book Company, Inc., 1947), pp. 308–9. For a generally critical assessment of personnel management see Peter Drucker, *The Practice of Management* (New York: Harper and Brothers, 1954), pp. 273–88.

[175] Cf. the striking analysis of this process in Norbert Elias, *Über den Prozess der Zivilisation* (Basel: Haus zum Falken, 1939), Vol. II, *passim*. See also Reinhard Bendix, "Compliant Behavior and Individual Personality," *American Journal of Sociology*, Vol. LVIII (November, 1952), pp. 302–3.

[176] I owe this characterization of the ideal manager to William H. Whyte, Jr. It should be noted that an adroit man can use the symbols of personal adjustment and of teamwork for his own advance as well as for better human relations. The literature on human relations in industry simply ignores this possibility.

manner also facilitates teamwork at the managerial level, it is well to remember that successful teamwork is a tool in the internal politics of an enterprise as well as a requirement for efficient operations.

The rules of conduct which are appropriate to teamwork and the ideology which idealizes the values of human relations are attempts to standardize and facilitate the internal operation of bureaucratic enterprises. It is often overlooked, however, that such enterprises are governed by two antithetical principles which result from the division of labor. As organizations increase in size and complexity efforts are made to routinize their operations by job classifications, product standardization, budgetary regulations, and other measures designed to simplify procedures and simultaneously increase central control. The tendency of these efforts is to reduce the exercise of discretion by subordinates. There is an equally important tendency in the opposite direction, however; for the use of standardized procedures which accompanies bureaucratization also leads to a lengthening of the chain of command and, hence, to an increased subdivision and delegation of authority. While an effort is made to centralize top decision-making along with this delegation of authority, it is probably inevitable that the discretionary exercise of authority increases at the intermediate levels. The human-relations approach seeks to ensure the "right" use of discretion at these intermediate levels, but too much emphasis on group decisions and teamwork runs the danger of eliminating discretionary judgments altogether. Clearly, these are problems of managerial practice which vary from one enterprise to another, and this very diversity of approaches points to continued, pragmatic experimentation in this field.

Standardized routines and teamwork are indispensable in large-scale organizations. It is improbable that they can operate efficiently without initiative and imagination, though in a bureaucratic environment these are likely to differ in kind from the qualities ascribed to an individual entrepreneur.[177] It may be objected that teamwork and initia-

---

[177] If the initiative of the "classical" entrepreneur is defined, with Schumpeter, as "undertaking new things [which] lie outside of the routine tasks which everybody understands," then it can be made compatible with a bureaucratized industry only if it is exercised in the context of its routinized environment, but not if the individual ignores the "routine tasks" and the "hostile environment" to which Schumpeter refers. I believe the incompatibilities between initiative and bureaucratic organization are relative rather than absolute, as Schumpeter seems to suggest. That is to say, there are forms of initiative, e.g., creative imagination in the field of organizational management, which are an important element in

tive, conformity and imagination make incompatible demands upon the individual manager, that no one can "be an individualist privately and a conformist publicly." [178]   Certainly these are conflicting pressures which impose a real burden upon the individual, and it is not surprising that the ideology of human relations has evaded these burdens in its projection of the out-going, well-rounded member of the managerial team.   It would be misleading, however, to take this image any more literally than the earlier one of the industrial tycoon whose single-minded pursuit of success in the struggle for survival knew of no inner conflicts.[179]   I would suggest rather that no more than a few individuals are likely to become true replicas of these ideal images.   Hence, it is all the more important that the ideological resolution of the conflicting demands for teamwork and initiative may seem to relieve the pressures which are a concomitant of the managerial job.   But such resolution and relief can only be partially successful.   Even if the rising generation of young executives should be able to conform to the ideal image of "the manager" which the human relations approach has propagated, that is not likely to eliminate the conflicting pressures to which their actual work will be exposed, nor for that matter the psychological burdens to which these pressures give rise.

These considerations point to certain limitations of the human-relations approach.   But they do not deny that there is increasing evidence of a managerial collectivism in large-scale economic enterprises, in the United States and elsewhere.[180]   There are those who see

modern industry but quite incompatible with Schumpeter's image of the entrepreneur.

[178] Statement by the president of a corporation quoted in Whyte, "How Hard Do Executives Work?" *op. cit.,* p. 152.

[179] This literal interpretation of managerial ideologies is evident in David Riesman's suggestive remarks on the major change in character from the "inner-directed" personality of the "captain of industry" to the "other-directed" personality of the industrial bureaucrat. See his *The Lonely Crowd* (New Haven: Yale University Press, 1950), pp. 166–74. Riesman's psychological interpretation may be contrasted with the study by Sigmund Diamond who has interpreted the change from entrepreneurial individualism in the nineteenth century to the modern conception of the business leader as an ideological response to the growing attacks upon the entrepreneur and upon the economic system. Diamond's study is based on an analysis of editorial obituaries which reflect the changing conceptions of the business leader as the cultural hero of American society. See Sigmund Diamond, *The Reputation of the American Businessman* (Cambridge: Harvard University Press, 1955), pp. 176–82.

[180] There is no space here to explore similar developments elsewhere. For related evidence in Germany see Carl Dreyfuss, *Occupation and Ideology of the*

in this evidence the threat of totalitarianism. This is indeed the crucial issue which the study of managerial ideologies poses in our time. The management of large-scale enterprises will be greatly facilitated if workers as well as managers regard their daily work as a token of their allegiance. Since noncooperation in any form presents a problem to management, it is reasonable to expect a constant and perhaps an increasing concern with inducing a cooperative attitude among the employees. This concern is certainly the momentum behind the popularity of the human-relations approach. And the danger is real that salaried employees and managers will become committed with their every attitude and action to the large-scale enterprises of today, although this danger is mitigated by the somewhat tenuous limitations to which I have referred.

But the appeal for work as a token of allegiance encounters competing appeals outside the range of managerial power, especially at the lower levels of the managerial hierarchy. Foremost among these are the appeals of the trade-unions. Less articulate but perhaps of equal significance are the so-called informal relations among workers, which have been brought to prominence by the Hawthorne studies. These relations are significant aside from their effect on productivity, to which primary attention has been given. For the exchange of ideas, the leadership patterns and the consensus on standards of work performance and of conduct generally which emerge from these relations represent a range of activity, by which workers engage in strategies of independence [181] inside the organization of which they are a part. That these strategies of output restriction, cooperative teamwork, or indifferent neutralism as over against managerial directives (to name three typical variants) result from group action rather than individual action, does not only indicate the social nature of man, as Mayo and his followers maintain. It also points to the effect of large-scale organizations upon the individual employee. In such organizations it may be of no avail to the worker to engage in individual strategies of independence so that he

---

Salaried Employee (No. 14–15 of Translation into English of Foreign Social Science Monographs; New York: Department of Social Science, Columbia University, 1938). Cf. also the ready acceptance of the spirit of Mayo's work by British socialists in R. H. S. Crossman, ed., *New Fabian Essays* (London: Turnstile Press, 1952), pp. 129–32.

[181] This phrase "strategies of independence" refers to the same types of activities as Thorstein Veblen's "conscientious withdrawal of efficiency," but I prefer it to Veblen's since it encompasses all activities which manifest the worker's desire for independence from managerial control.

will seek passive and active support for his actions. And his ability to limit his allegiance to management is enhanced by the extent to which his competing allegiance to other groups of organizations makes available to him opportunities for deviant action which management cannot or does not prevent.[182] Hence, the managerial appeals to the loyalty of the worker must compete with the concomitant and partially conflicting appeals of the trade-unions. Also, managerial power is limited by the many opportunities in the work situation and outside the plant, which enable the worker to discount or dismiss these appeals if he so desires. Under these circumstances managerial appeals will often be effective only to the extent that material services or benefits help to bear them out.

In this assessment of managerial ideologies in present-day United States I have expressed several cautions which should guard us against an overestimation of the trend I have described. But there is no doubt about the trend itself. The celebration of individual character and effort has in some measure been superseded by a belief in individual adaptability just as the image of the struggle for survival and the pursuit of self-interest has been superseded by the image of cooperative teamwork. The change has been gradual and ambiguous, for the old ideas have been rephrased rather than abandoned. But there are many factors which may be expected to give a cumulative reinforcement to this ideological change, from the operational imperatives of large organizations to the increasingly intimate tie-in between nationwide economic enterprises and national interests both at home and abroad.[183] Under these conditions it is pertinent to ask whether the collectivism of large-scale enterprises may give "rise to a general monstrosity that bosses not only our working hours but invades our homes and dictates our thoughts

[182] It does not follow that he always avails himself of the opportunities that are open to him or that he admits the existence of conflict between his actions and his contractual obligations to the company. Hence, my point is not to contradict the findings of several studies which report that workers express their loyalty to the union *and* to management, even where the two are in conflict. Cf. Lois R. Dean, "Union Activity and Dual Loyalty," *Industrial and Labor Relations Review,* Vol. VII (July, 1954), pp. 526–36.

[183] In this respect, Diamond has shown that today the success of American business leaders is attributed to the strength of the economic system rather than to the virtues of individual character, though the latter are not ignored. See Diamond, *op. cit.,* Chapter VI. This change in the reputation of business leaders is paralleled by their own increasing concern with their national responsibilities. Though these shifts in reputation and ideology do not have a direct bearing on the authority relationship analyzed in this study, they corroborate its results.

and dreams." [184]   My answer is: Not by itself.   The danger of totalitarianism does not consist in ideological appeals as such, even though these appeals may closely resemble the ideologies of some totalitarian regime.   That danger becomes acute only when these appeals become one of the means for the centralized manipulation of interactions among managers and workers, as well as of the conflicts between them.

Specifically, a totalitarian control of industry is established when the leaders of management *and* of the workers are forced to become the agents of the *same* political organization.   It is true that this end is achieved even in countries with democratic institutions, when national emergencies force a suspension of unregulated interaction within the ranks of management and labor.   And there is reason for concern that a semblance of this result may come about at the ideological level, when the continuation of the cold war places a premium on conformity and thus intensifies the celebration of cooperative teamwork at the expense of the individual.   But before attempting to assess these possibilities it will be helpful to analyze the managerial practices and ideologies which characterize the totalitarian organization of industry.   The following chapter examines a society that is deliberately organized on the principle of perpetual emergency.

[184] Eric Hoffer, *The Passionate State of Mind* (New York: Harper and Brothers, 1955), p. 91.

CHAPTER 6

Managerial Ideologies
in the Russian Orbit

> *The enthusiastic apologists of the factory*
> *system have nothing more damning to*
> *urge against a general organization of the*
> *labour of society than that it would turn*
> *all society into one immense factory.—*
> Karl Marx, *Capital*.

a. Dominant Class and Ruling Party

Ideologies affect and reflect action without necessarily involving the personal convictions of the actors or their spokesmen. It is probable that among the American employers who reiterate arguments about their own superiority and the various deficiencies of workers, there are a few cynics, a few "true believers" (Eric Hoffer), and a majority who do not give it much thought. Most employers and managers engage in this ideological defense and attack almost as a matter of course. Though they affect no interest in ideas, they are probably imbued with those currently in fashion among their fellows.   Indeed, the strength of a managerial ideology does not depend upon the glibness of its articulate spokesmen, but upon the readiness with which given practical problems can be phrased by employers and managers themselves in terms of the "arguments" which tradition and continued publicity bring to mind.[1] The popularity of such ideologies depends upon their appropriateness to the experience of employers and managers as well as upon the "waves" of fashion occurring among them.   Among men of action who read little, ideas are likely to spread as a consequence of their practical experience and personal associations.   Although the pressure for conformity among these men should not be underestimated, it is a sporadic and haphazard pressure which gives way when it conflicts with interest and experience.

At several points the preceding discussion of the American experience has suggested that ideologies are reiterated endlessly and are essentially ambiguous.   I suggest here that they tend to spread and change more or less as fashions change, and that they do not necessarily involve the private convictions of those who espouse them.   They are the opinions which given groups of men have "on public display."[2]   Both the ambiguity of ideologies and the lack of personal involvement often provide an opening wedge for new ideas, or at least for new emphases. In the case of managerial ideologies in the United States such new emphases have been introduced, as we have seen, under the guise of reiterating opinions in "good standing"; and even the more traditional ideologies have been formulated anew in the terminology which had become currently fashionable.   Thus, it is difficult to discern the changing trends of managerial ideologies, for the "new" and the "old" themes often blend as if they were one and the same, and opposing views have been formulated by equally prominent spokesmen of American employers and managers.

There exists, then, considerable leeway for ideological diversity even as the ambiguous and noncommittal character of managerial ideologies

[1] This probably distinguishes the modern specialists in personnel and public relations from many of their managerial colleagues.   What is a matter of conviction for the former is merely a way of talking for the latter.

[2] This distinction between public statements and private convictions does not necessarily mean that those who espouse the ideologies of management do not believe in them (always excepting the minority of "true believers").   But the conventional opinions which are reiterated in casual conversation among fellow-managers are not, for the most part, sustained by a private or personal commitment (somewhat in the same sense in which we customarily use the words of our language without reflecting upon their meaning).

facilitate a superficial agreement among the "members" of this dominant social class. The formal organizations of American employers and managers reveal somewhat parallel characteristics. Their purpose is to promote the interests of "industry" or "business" collectively. But these organizations are frequently in the hands of public-relations specialists, and policies are often directed by a minority of powerful industrialists. This concentration of publicity and policy determination in the hands of a few gives a spurious impression of unanimity. In fact, it frequently happens that the majority of the members act as independently from the stated policies of the organization as the actions of the organization are uninfluenced by them.[3] This lack of commitment to their own interest organizations exists side by side with the very considerable ideological and political influence which some employers and managers do, in fact, exert.

These considerations are relevant here because they indicate a basic limitation of the power to dominate on the part of dominant classes. Such classes have a pervasive tendency to rationalize their position and to exert considerable pressure on the individual "member" to comply with the conventions of that position both ideologically and in the conduct of his everyday affairs. But this pressure can induce compliance only through the force of convention and of the expectations of others. This pressure often is considerable; sometimes it is very great. But even dominant social classes cannot add to it the power of coercion over their own "members," largely because they do not possess the power of exclusion. Employers are "members" of a dominant class because of their position in the production process, not because they have joined; and even if they join an organization to promote their interests, they will never be expelled if their beliefs and practices deviate from those of the rest. Of course, my point is not to deny the existence of a more or less uniform outlook among employers; it is rather to assert that such uniformity exists side by side with the opportunity to espouse diverse beliefs and practices and that in a social class and its formal organizations the means to eradicate such diversity are unavailable.

In turning now to an examination of managerial ideologies within the Russian orbit, the problems I have been dealing with will appear in

[3] Cf. the unpublished study by Alfred S. Cleveland, *Some Aspects of Organized Industry* (Ph.D. Dissertation, Harvard University, 1928). An assessment of this diversity of opinion for the years following World War II is contained in Clark Kerr, "Employer Policies in Industrial Relations," in C. E. Warne, ed., *Labor in Post-War America* (New York: Remsen Press, 1949), pp. 43–76. See also the critical appraisal of NAM publicity by prominent business executives in Whyte, *Is Anybody Listening?*, pp. 17–20.

a new light.   Instead of a *dominant class* I shall be dealing with a *ruling party*.   It is characteristic of such a party that it.creates a new dominant class after its conquest of power.   To analyze the managerial ideologies of this ruling party, it is necessary first to characterize the party in its relation to the factors of social class.

A central tenet of Marxism is the edict that a labor movement (or party) will become the organized, political arm of the working class. This movement was thought to stand in the vanguard of the class in the sense that the leaders of the movement have a better and more "scientific" understanding of the historical situation than the average worker. For Marx the relation between the movement and the workers was primarily a question of intellectual leadership based upon his own "correct" interpretation of history.   Although this idea implied an inevitable distance, especially between the leaders of the labor movement and the workers, Marx believed that this distance would eventually disappear.   The changes in the capitalist economy which he predicted would compel the masses to join the labor movement and to act in accordance with the laws of historical development, so that the political and propagandistic efforts of winning the masses for the movement merely accelerated an on-going development.   The accent of Marx's work was upon an intellectual mastery of historical laws, and this approach seemed to make it unnecessary to deal with the perennial problem of the rule of the few over the many.   By making the few *and* the many part of an on-going movement of history, Marx believed that the few were merely ahead of the many, but not above them.   Through their better understanding, the few were clearing the way for the masses and, hence, were speeding up a development in which all must participate sooner or later.[4]

[4] This interpretation of Marx deals with a question which he never addressed directly.   I have sought to combine his emphasis upon the "scientific theory of socialism" as the indispensable weapon of the labor movement with his emphasis upon the social and economic conditions which made the political awakening and the eventual success of the workers inevitable.   Cf. the following comments on the French "petty bourgeoisie": ". . . one must not form the narrow-minded notion that the petty bourgeoisie, on principle, wishes to enforce an egoistic class interest. . . . Just as little must one imagine that the democratic representatives are all shopkeepers or enthusiastic champions of shopkeepers.   According to their education and their individual position, they may be separated from them as widely as heaven from earth.   What makes them representatives of the petty bourgeoisie is the fact that in their minds they do not go beyond the limits which the latter do not go beyond in life, that they are consequently driven theoretically to the same tasks and solutions to which material interest and social position practically drive the latter.   This is in general the relationship of the *political*

While Marx differentiated between the leaders and the masses primarily on intellectual grounds, Lenin provided an organizational rationale. For Lenin the members of the party constituted the vanguard of the proletariat, whose "correct" understanding of history was vouchsafed by their adherence to Marxist theory. Since he assumed the validity of the theory (and of his own interpretation), the success of the party which adhered to that theory depended upon the enforcement of "iron discipline" within its ranks. The logic of this position was that all those belonged to the vanguard of the working class who adhered to the "correct" Marxist doctrine and strictly abided by the rules of party discipline in their every thought and action. Hence, discipline and orthodoxy rather than position within the production process were made the criteria of membership, and collective action came to depend upon the loyalty rather than upon the economic interests of the members. The party was, therefore, a principle of organization which—in Lenin's formulation—superseded that of "social class" even prior to the conquest of power. It is of interest to restate Lenin's views of the party in the terms in which Stalin reiterated them after the conquest of power—in the year of Lenin's death.

According to Stalin, the party constituted the vanguard of the proletariat; it was the organized section of the proletariat; it was the highest form among the class organizations of the proletariat; it was the instrument of the dictatorship of the proletariat; the party's unity of will was incompatible with factions; and it was always strengthened by being purged of "opportunistic elements." Each of these turgid phrases characterizes an aspect of the power which the few can wield over the many; each of them gives expression to the distance between the party and the class it claims to lead.

The party is a *vanguard* in Stalin's sense in that it incorporates the "best elements" of the working class, who possess a knowledge of the "laws of development" and are consequently "ahead" of the working class. This is the kind of party which is capable of "lifting the masses to the level of the class interests of the proletariat." Yet the vanguard party must also be a part of the working class; it cannot lead the class if it lacks close ties with the masses. The party is the *organized section* of the proletariat. As such it represents the epitome of discipline and organization. According to Stalin, this means that there is a strict hierarchy of upper and lower echelons of leadership, that within the

and literary representatives of a class to the class that they represent." Karl Marx, *The 18th Brumaire of Louis Bonaparte* (New York: International Publishers, n.d.), pp. 43–44.

party the subordination of the minority to the majority is complete, and that the resolutions of the party are binding on all its members. The working class has many organizations, such as trade-unions, cooperatives, women's clubs, youth organizations, and others. Of these *"class" organizations* the party is the highest form, and all other organizations must adhere to one policy in order to serve the working class. This does not mean that these other organizations are subordinate to the party, but that some party members are also members of these diverse organizations and as such assume a leading role in "coordinating" their activities. The party is an *instrument of the dictatorship of the proletariat* in the sense that it inspires the millions of the proletarian mass with the spirit of discipline and organization, thereby creating in the masses a bulwark against the corrosive influences of petty-bourgeois habits. To accomplish this a disciplined and united party is indispensable, and such a party cannot be created without preventing factions and purging dissident ("opportunistic") elements.[5]

These principles of organization make it apparent that the party of Lenin and Stalin differs fundamentally from the social classes whose struggle Marx had regarded as the major content of human history. A party of this type can deliberately create unity and discipline among its members, while the pursuit of economic interests permits and sometimes encourages diversity of belief and practice among those whose class position is identical. Marx's and Lenin's careers in exile frequently consisted of a long series of polemics which they pursued until the opponent had declared his agreement or until the irreconcilable ideological differences had led to a personal or organizational separation. Their attitude implied that ideological purity was far more important than the number of political allies; this enforcement of ideological unity has been developed into an elaborate system since their day.

The absolute commitment of the individual to the party as an organization is a condition of his membership. First as a candidate for membership, and then as a member of the party, the individual is subject to repeated tests of his loyalty. These tests are those of action, in the first instance, since the whole purpose of unity and discipline is the single-minded coordination of all party activities. To accomplish this coordination, however, it is necessary to have ideological unity as well, which is again tested in the repeated avowals of commitment to party principles by each member. The test of a member's commitment consists

[5] Joseph Stalin, *Foundations of Leninism* (New York: International Publishers, 1932), pp. 104–20. This volume is based on a series of lectures which Stalin gave at Sverdlov University in April, 1924.

in his implementation of momentary decisions by the highest party authority, whatever they are and however frequently they change.

The demand that the party completely dominate the life of its members imparts unique importance to its ideology. The function of the ideology is to provide a universal rationale for each decision and activity so that the members have a ready vocabulary of private motives and public reasons which differs radically from every common universe of discourse. What matters here is not the personal persuasion of the individual member, but the alacrity with which he responds appropriately—i.e., with the current slogans and the fashionable turns of phrases—to the clues emanating from the central organs of the party. But to do so promptly he must have available the basic tenets of an all-embracing ideology. Ideally, such an ideology will enable the party to rely upon a core of shared understanding among its members; actually, it more often involves a catechismic recital of standard phrases. Moreover, the ideology imposes upon the party the continual obligation to bring within its purview not merely all new policies, but all views concerning society and nature.

The most obvious reason for this universalism of Communist ideology is the danger of schism as in all sects. It would be impossible to distinguish between adherence to or deviation from the party line, unless a party line was authoritatively formulated in all fields. And since policies change in response to changing circumstances, mutually incompatible but equally authoritative party lines are issued at irregular intervals. This often leads to dilemmas and purges, but that is a price which must be paid. All policies of the highest party authority are justified in terms of doctrinal orthodoxy as interpreted by that authority and the universal ideology justifies each successive party line in absolute terms. Without this ideology it would be impossible to test the continued commitment of party members and to hold them responsible for any failure to implement the directives. And without this test it would in turn be impossible to be absolutely sure of the unity and iron discipline indispensable for a party organized on the same basis as a combat unit.

Yet the more disciplined and united such a combat party is, the more problematic is its relation to the masses of the people who are not party members. Declarations that the party is the vanguard of the proletariat alternate with demands that the party strengthen its contact with the masses. The two declarations are mutually exclusive, strictly speaking. For the more united and disciplined the party is within, the more it is ahead of the people. The more the party seeks to lift the masses to a class consciousness they do not possess, the greater the distance between them is likely to be.[6] It is this ever open gap which *each* present party line is designed to "negotiate." And the principal ideological weapon in this respect is the theory that "explains" the rule of the party as merely the leadership of the masses by their own vanguard and in their own interests.

The principal end achieved by these devices is the absolute control of party authorities over functionaries and members. The purpose of that control is presumably a more effective implementation of policies in the society at large, i.e., the direction of persons who are not themselves members of the party. Ordinarily, these "private" persons would be expected to think and act in accordance with the interests which their personal desires and social position suggest. In the case of industry these interests would be expected to lead to collective thoughts and actions among workers and among managers, resulting in more or less in-group solidarity and intergroup conflict. But such group formation presupposes the freedom of interaction among workers and among managers, including the freedom of interaction between group members and group leaders.[7] A totalitarian party seeks to prevent this more

---

[6] Communist leaders have always been aware of this dilemma. In their terminology this is the problem of the "right" and the "left" deviation. "Right deviationists" in the official view are those who advocate that the party should be closer to the masses and should not move too rapidly and too far ahead. "Left deviationists" are those who want the party to assert its leadership more vigorously and increase its demands on the masses still further. Yet the official view of the correct relationship between the party and the masses is never known until it is announced, which makes reciprocal recriminations, recantations, and purges an indispensable part of the system. Hence, the system ensures maximum flexibility and centralization at the top and maximum rigidity and dependence below, while the uncertainty of *every* present party line is an instrument both for the retention of power at the top and for the implementation of policies below. In the latter respect it can always be "shown" that the present implementation of the party line by the lower echelons is either too far ahead or too far behind the "masses."

[7] This freedom of interaction among members of a group is an indispensable condition of social-class formation. It is not a sufficient condition, however, since the fact that a number of individuals share a common social and economic position only means that they will tend to respond more or less uniformly to their common social situation. Whether this tendency will lead to collective action still depends upon favorable situational factors *and* upon the availability of leaders who are capable of organizing such action. The effect of a totalitarian regime upon the formation of social classes may be described briefly as the successful elimination of the "favorable situational factors" and of the leaders who could utilize these factors. In the absence of these sufficient conditions for the formation of social classes, interaction still takes place among individuals who share a common

or less spontaneous group formation in industry by superimposing its own hierarchy of authority over the rank-order of authority within economic enterprises.

This development implies that the different positions within the production process are subordinated to a new principle of organization which functions not in terms of a pursuit of economic interests, but in terms of political decisions made from on high. The party's principal task of management is, therefore, to use its control of party functionaries to control the management of economic enterprises. The details of this external bureaucratization cannot be suggested in a brief statement; they form a substantial part of the subsequent discussion. But it is important to emphasize at the outset that this superimposition of controls by party members over all ranks of the hierarchy of economic enterprises seeks to establish the party organization as the single source of ideological unity and concerted action.[8] Schematically put, the party functionaries at the managerial level check on the managers as well as the workers, just as the functionaries at the level of the workers check on them as well as on the managers. The party insists repeatedly that its functionaries should not interfere with the operation of economic enterprises, though subsequently they are held responsible for the success of that operation. This "inconsistency" is made inevitable by the party's own principle of organization, which calls for the superordination of the party over every rank-order within the society which arises from the division of labor and its attendant social and economic differences.

Hence, there are striking differences between a dominant class and a ruling party, and the functions of their respective managerial ideologies hinge upon these differences. In the case of a dominant class,

social and economic position. Such interaction is the concomitant of *social differentiation* (by occupation, income, style of life, etc.), a concept which should be distinguished from "social class." For a discussion of the factors which are "favorable" to the formation of a class see Bendix and Lipset, "Karl Marx' Theory of Social Classes," in Bendix and Lipset, *Class, Status and Power*, p. 30.

[8] This is perhaps the major difference between a modern party dictatorship and the bureaucratic absolutism of, say, eighteenth-century France or of the Chinese dynasties. Within the ministries of a regime of bureaucratic absolutism various interest groups can still find it possible to safeguard and even to enhance their social and economic position. Totalitarian parties, on the other hand, often succeed in eliminating this intrusion of social-class groupings; instead interest groupings arise *de novo* within the apparatus of the party. Of course, such groupings within the party may be initiated through social and economic ties outside the organization; but the party is clearly jeopardized when such ties become more significant factors in group formation than position within the party's rank-order of authority.

the employers and managers of economic enterprises occupy positions entailing very considerable power within these enterprises and in the nation at large. But these positions do *not* entail either an identity of interests or an ideological unanimity. These can be won through voluntary organizations; in the United States there are *many* organizations designed for this purpose. Each of these represents some common ideas and interests of employers and managers. The common ideology of all employers will be a rather vague amalgam such as I have described with regard to the relations between employers and workers. A certain identity of beliefs does emerge from a common class position and from varied responses to problems commonly encountered in the day-to-day operation of economic enterprises. Still, these shared opinions allow each employer to interpret the facts in a manner suitable to his own experiences and interests; and out of this interplay between the individual's response and his tendency to think like his fellows there arises a drift of collective opinion which will tend to change gradually in response to changing conditions. The power of such a class can be very great, but it will tend to be a composite of divided powers; and the managerial ideology of such a class will be an amalgam of many views and, hence, compatible with the coherence as well as with the diversity of that class.

A ruling party is distinguished from a dominant class by the fact that its interests and ideology are authoritatively defined by a central governing body. A common *class* position entails a predisposition toward an identity of interests or ideological unanimity, which may or may not be given organizational implementation. A ruling party, on the other hand, utilizes existing social differences, or creates new ones, as one of the many ways in which it exercises authority. As a consequence of its monopoly of power it establishes and enforces its own criteria, by which those who satisfy party directives or enhance the interests of the organization are benefited at the discretion of its central committee. Since the beneficiaries of the regime exercise power and receive benefits at the discretion of the governing body, their power and benefits are always contingent upon further decisions favorable to them. This is, indeed, a classless society in which a common social and economic position does not enable a group of individuals to organize in order to implement their common interests. It is a society of one-party rule that seeks to destroy all possibilities of independent group formation. While that rule cannot directly control the interactions within a social group, it seeks to accomplish that end by separating individuals from the group and by enlisting them within the party's ranks. In particular the party makes every effort to separate the individuals capable of leadership from the group which might engage in collective action under their guidance. The following sections will examine the organizational and ideological weapons with which these aims are pursued in the field of industrial relations.

In what follows I shall consider managerial ideologies in the East Zone of Germany.[9] The zone has been subjected to an extensive process of sovietization, and the "Soviet experience" is officially propounded as the model to be emulated in all aspects of social, economic, and intellectual life. In the field of industrial organizations, specifically, most of the institutional arrangements and, indeed, many of the written materials employed are direct translations from official Russian texts. Moreover, my personal knowledge of German conditions as well as the desire to study Communist managerial ideologies in a restricted and relatively accessible area suggested the choice of East Germany.

This case study involves an analysis which differs somewhat from the approach employed so far. In Chapters 2, 3, and 5 I have treated the development of industrial organizations and of managerial ideologies over time. This treatment assumed that ideas become widely accepted and then again less popular in response to shared experiences and as a result of a spread of fashion. An example of this kind was the growing attention to the worker in American managerial ideology. In part this development resulted from the increasing institutional importance of industrial psychologists and from the problems of labor management arising in a bureaucratized industry. But in part the ideas changed because of a psychological contagion among American business leaders who would speak of the worker with a new vocabulary, even if they continued to regard him as they always had.

The study of ideologies in a dictatorial regime involves basically different problems. Neither shared experience nor fashion determines the growth or decline of ideas, when a ruling party has a complete monopoly over all media of communication. Instead ideas are formu-

[9] Designations of the zone vary considerably. References to the "East Zone" stem from the term Soviet Occupation Zone (or *Sowjetische Besatzungszone,* abbreviated as SBZ). Official East German publications refer to the German Democratic Republic (or *Deutsche Demokratische Republik,* abbreviated as DDR), thereby emphasizing the claim to sovereign independence and to political institutions of a democratic character. Of course, the country is neither sovereign nor democratic except in the sense which Soviet propaganda imparts to these words. I shall, therefore, refer to East Germany or to the East or Soviet Zone except in the case of official texts, in which I use the official designation. Cf. also n. 12 below.

lated and disseminated in accordance with political decisions and in an organizational setting which will be examined in the following section. This central direction of ideological developments makes the basic assumptions of the historical perspective inapplicable. When groups of individuals cannot respond publicly to their shared experience except in the prescribed manner, and when the spread of an idea does not depend upon its appeal to the interests and sentiments of individuals, but instead upon their anticipation of repercussions in the bureaucratic echelons above them, then the study of ideologies must be concerned with their use in the implementation of dictatorial rule, while the history of ideologies would be concerned with the changing *policies* of the central body. My purpose in the following analysis is to focus upon the operational use of managerial ideologies in a Communist dictatorship rather than upon the changes of policy to which everyone must conform. In this respect, the choice of East Germany commends itself, because Soviet Russia's supremacy over the zone at the end of World War II favored the rapid adoption of ready-made managerial practices and ideologies, whose pattern had developed in Russia herself over a thirty-year period. This pattern is more easily observed, where we can neglect its historical evolution without undue distortion.

I shall turn first to a consideration of the controls by which economic enterprises in the East Zone are directed.

b. The Structure of Controls over Economic Enterprises

In modern capitalist economies the firm is "the governing organization exercising control over production and distribution. The management of labor within the firm is not subject to other outside controls." [10] In the planned economy of the East Zone enterprises are not autonomous in this sense, but subject to the specific regulations and the detailed supervision by agencies of the government and of the party. To judge more accurately the institutional setting of managerial ideologies in the East Zone, one needs to have a picture of the structure of these controls as they affect economic enterprises.[11] But since that structure

[10] To be sure, the firm exercises these controls within the limits prescribed by governmental regulations and the general policies of its board of directors and within the terms of a negotiated union contract wherever the latter exists. But within these limits it is appropriate to think of the firm as a self-contained governing organization. The above definition is taken from P. Sargant Florence, *The Logic of British and American Industry*, p. 22.

[11] The following description is based in part on Otto Walther, *Verwaltung, Lenkung und Planung der Wirtschaft in der Sowjetischen Besatzungszone* (Bon-

is complex, it may be helpful to state at the outset the principle of organization on which it is based.

Economic enterprises are controlled by two interlocking hierarchies of authority. One of these extends through successive levels: from the Presidium of the Council of Ministers to the Director and to the workers of the individual enterprise. But at every level of this hierarchy there exists a party organization which itself is part of a different hierarchy of authority and which simultaneously serves the functions of propagandist, executor of special orders, supervisor of plan fulfillment, discoverer of faulty organization, critic of individual performances, and secret police. This is a system of authority in which the duplication of functions is the result neither of confusion (though it may result in confusion) nor of deliberate pitting of one agency against another to the discomfiture of both, though this happens frequently. It is a system rather in which those in authority have instituted two supervisory controls for every directive they issue: one to be exercised by the top manager in command of an administrative unit and the other by the party organization within that unit. Of course, the ultimate authority over both hierarchies is the same. Hence, the party organizations are enjoined to "support" the administrative hierarchy of governmental agencies at the same time that they provide an ever-ready opportunity for the top leaders to intervene with the detailed execution of their own commands, when and where they see fit. This implies that on principle the highest party authorities distrust the reliability of *every* executive agency, including all functionaries of the party itself. Merle Fainsod has aptly called this system the "institutionalization of suspicion." As a consequence, every delegation of authority carries with it the silent reservation that it is imperative to check—and to check repeatedly—on how the orders are carried out in fact. It is a logical outgrowth of this system to have at least two supervisory controls for every command. It is just as logical to check up on the unforeseen consequences of commands either by countermanding the directives issued previously to an executive agency or by instructing another agency to supervise and correct the work of the first. In this fashion it is possible for the Secretariat and the Politbureau of the party to exercise complete authority at the same time that all responsibility falls upon the individuals who must execute the directives coming down the two hierarchies of authority. The whole system seems to be

ner Berichte aus Mittel- und Ostdeutschland; Bonn: Bundesministerium für gesamtdeutsche Fragen, 1953) and pertains to conditions in 1954, unless otherwise noted.

built on the principle that the responsibility of every executive official should exceed his authority.

Supreme authority in East Germany is exercised by the Soviet Control Commission (*Sowjetische Kontroll-Kommission* or SKK), whose administrative unit for the planned economy receives directions from the Supreme Planning Authority (*Gosplan*) in the USSR.[12] Immediately under the Soviet Control Commission is the Central Committee of the Socialist Unity party of Germany (*Zentralkomitee der Sozialistischen Einheitspartei Deutschlands,* abbreviated as ZK of the SED). The permanent decision-making body of this Central Committee is the East German equivalent of the Politbureau. In 1954, the Central Committee consisted of 91 members and 44 candidates, while 14 of the members made up the 9 members and 5 candidates of the Politbureau.[13] All major decisions are made by this smaller body, although they are submitted in the form of resolutions to the Central Committee, which at least nominally makes the final decision, usually by unanimous acclamation. Thus, the Central Committee is merely an important forum for the discussions the Politbureau has decided to publicize, although the Committee is superior to the Politbureau in the statutory sense.

The Secretariat of the Central Committee is the executive agency, which puts into effect the decisions which have been made by the Politbureau and "endorsed" by the Central Committee. As the major executive agency the Secretariat controls the whole apparatus of the party, but it also prepares the resolutions which are then acted on by the Politbureau and the Central Committee.[14]

[12] According to *The New York Times,* June 20, 1954, the USSR withdrew a major part of its staff from the Soviet Control Commission. Both before and since this date there have been several Soviet declarations according full sovereignty to East Germany. According to a report of *The New York Times,* September 21, 1955, Bulganin and Grotewohl signed a treaty "declaring that the East German government was free to settle any questions relating to its domestic and foreign policy." The earlier measure, the recent treaty, and the many public declarations are primarily items for the propaganda analyst and do not affect existing power relations, i.e., the Soviet supremacy in the East Zone. Previously, the German Politbureau would receive its instructions from the Soviet Control Commission; now it may receive more of them from the appropriate authorities in Moscow. I have *not* endeavored to give an up-to-date account of these nominal changes in the relation between the East Zone and Soviet Russia; they have not altered the use of Soviet practices in the management of East German affairs.

[13] Carola Stern, *Die SED, Ein Handbuch über Aufbau, Organisation und Funktion des Parteiapparates* ([Köln]: Verlag für Politik und Wirtschaft, 1954), pp. 49, 62.

[14] Four out of the six members of the Secretariat were simultaneously members (or in one case a candidate) of the Politbureau.

Officially, the Central Committee is always mentioned as the policy-determining body of the party. Hence, the executive agencies of the party, which carry out these policies, are called the subdivisions of the Central Committee, although they are actually controlled by the Secretariat. These subdivisions control corresponding subdivisions of the 15 party headquarters at the district level (*Bezirksleitungen*), and these in turn control the subdivisions of the 237 party headquarters at the county level (*Kreisleitungen*). The subdivisions at each level are under the immediate direction of the party secretary, and each district or county secretary is formally obliged—together with the sub-divisions of his secretariat—to execute the decisions of the respective party headquarters. These secretaries are paid as full-time officials, whereas the members of the district or county headquarters are not. Hence, the secretaries often suggest what these headquarters then "decide"; it is well, therefore, to think of the party secretaries as the key figures in the party hierarchy.[15]

It should be added that this whole hierarchy of Secretariats with their numerous subdivisions checks upon and can interfere with *every* major unit of social and economic life. Every such unit has a party cell [16] among its employees. In each cell the members are called together from time to time in membership meetings (*Betriebsparteiversammlungen*); and activities are directed by a party headquarter (*Betriebspar-*

---

[15] At the national, district, and county level the activities of the party are directed by four interlocking executive agencies. In addition to the Secretariat and the Politbureau (called party headquarters at the district and county levels) there is a party control commission, which combines the functions of intraparty control over the execution of the party line and of an adjudicatory body dealing with the activities of foreign agents, with corruption, the misuse of party or governmental functions, careerism, and with the spread of false rumors in the party. A fourth executive agency is a commission for intraparty audits (*Revisionskommission*), which is also organized at the national, district, and county levels. It should be added that the regular supervision of "party cadres" is not in the hands of the party-control commissions but in those of a subdivision of the Central Party Secretariat, called "Leading Agencies of the Party and the Mass-organizations" (*Leitende Organe der Partei und der Massenorganisationen* or LOPM). The head of LOPM is Karl Schirdewan, who is a member of the Secretariat and the Politbureau. The term "party cadres" in this context refers to the leading party functionaries in each subdivision of the party hierarchy, but the term "cadre" is sometimes used more broadly as a designation for all persons who maintain and strengthen the regime in accordance with the party line.

[16] Cells are formed by workplace or area and they are kept numerically small to increase organizational supervision. See Maurice Duverger, *Political Parties* (New York: John Wiley and Sons, 1954), pp. 27–36 for a general discussion of Communist practice.

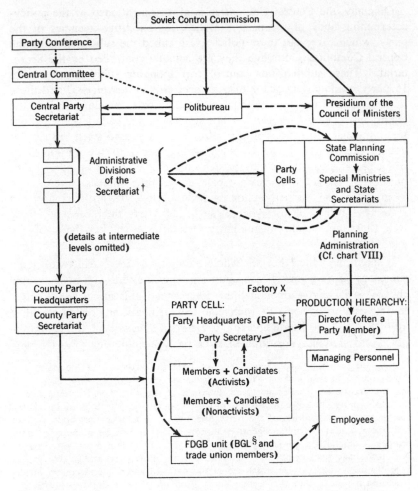

Legend:
⟶ Direct Authority
--- ➤ Effective but informal supervision
----➤ Nominal Authority

CHART VII. The double hierarchy of the party and the government *

* Adapted from Stern, *op. cit.* (Appendix), and Otto Walther, *op. cit.* (Appendix).

† The names of these divisions suggest the range of controls exercised by the Secretariat of the Party:

1. Leading agencies of the Party and Mass Organizations (LOPM)
2. Agitation

(*Legend continued on opposite page*)

teileitung) and a party secretary (*Betriebsparteisekretär*). Such a party cell exists in each major economic enterprise, but it exists also in each governmental agency. For example, not only are there party cells in every coal mine in the East Zone but also in the Central Association of People's Own Enterprises from which each mine receives its directives as well as in the State Secretariat for Coal which is under the State Planning Commission. As a consequence, the Central Party Secretariat has the possibility of sending instructions down the line through its own hierarchy until it reaches the party secretary in Mine X. But the subdivision on, say, planning in the Central Secretariat also has the possibility of giving instructions to the party secretary (or a high official) in the State Secretariat for Coal, who can then send these instructions down the line through the hierarchy of planning agencies until they reach the Director and the party secretary in Mine X.[17]

[17] The direction and supervision of governmental agencies by the party is accomplished in the following manner, according to one source: "Each high government official who belongs to the SED is obliged to work together closely with the division of the SED which has jurisdiction over his field of activity. He receives his instructions from this division, and he must report to it. So-called instructors are sent out by the SED to its own subordinate units, to the mass-organizations as well as to the agencies of governmental administration. Moreover, the party cells (*SED-Betriebsgruppen*) in government agencies, enterprises, and mass organizations have the duty to observe closely the work in their respec-

CHART VII (*continued*)
3. Press and Radio
4. Propaganda
5. Science and Institutions of Higher Learning
6. Elementary Schools
7. Literature and Art
8. Government Administration
9. Labor, Social Welfare, and Health
10. International Cooperation
11. Traffic
12. Protection of People's [i.e., State] property
13. Raw Materials
14. Building Industry
15. Planning and Finance
16. Transportation and Communication
17. Commerce, Consumption, and Light Industry
18. Party Finances and Party Enterprises
19. Internal Administration
20. Archives and Library
There are other divisions, but these appear to be the most important.
‡ BPL = Betriebsparteileitung.
§ BGL = Betriebsgewerkschaftsleitung (Trade-Union headquarters of the Enterprise).

Such links of influence or control exist at many points between the hierarchy of the party and the hierarchy of governmental planning agencies. At all levels below the Central Secretariat and the Politbureau they serve the purpose of checking the performance of executive officials and, if need be, of "facilitating" their fulfillment of the plan. But at the apex of the party hierarchy, some members of the Politbureau and many members of the Central Committee serve in a decision-making and directing capacity, not only for the party but for the government as well. That is to say, these leaders of the SED may be at the same time ministers of the government and as such members of the Council of Ministers (*Ministerrat*). Or they may be ministers with direct responsibility for some phase of economic planning. Several ministers form the Presidium of the Council of Ministers, which is directly subordinate to the Soviet Control Commission and directly superior to the State Planning Commission (*Staatliche Plankommission*).[18]

As far as the direction of economic enterprises is concerned, absolute authority descends directly from the Administration for Planned Economy (*Planökonomische Verwaltung*) in the Soviet Control Commission to the Presidium of the Council of Ministers, the State Planning Commission as well as to the Special Ministries and State Secretariats. The State Planning Commission works out the control figures for production, finance, and manpower, and it watches over the execution of these directives. The Commission is the highest Executive organ, to which all the Special Ministries (*Fachministerien*) and State Secretariats for the different branches of the economy are strictly accountable. Violations of directives issued by the State Planning Commission are classified as "economic crimes" (*Wirtschaftsverbrechen*) and prosecuted accordingly; moreover, no subordinate agency can issue authoritative directives without first obtaining the confirmation of the State Planning

tive units and to report to the leading comrades within these units and under certain circumstances to report directly to the subdivision of the party secretariat which has jurisdiction in the matter." (See *Die SED: Aufbau, Charakter, Situation* (Sonderdruck des SBZ Archiv; Köln: Verlag für Politik und Wirtschaft, 1953), p. 5.

[18] This top hierarchy of the central planning agencies has been reorganized frequently. The effort has been to reduce the number of levels and to make the top planning officials members of the Politbureau or of the Central Committee. As of 1954 the Politbureau had among its members or candidates a minister of Machine Construction, a Minister of the Interior, the Chairman of the State Planning Commission, and the Secretary for Agriculture in the Central Committee. The last is a party position but with obvious responsibility for economic planning.

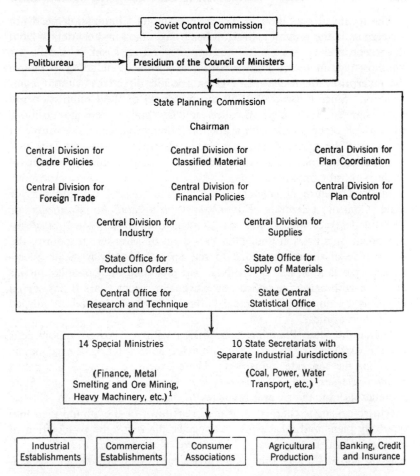

¹Separate associations in each field work out detailed plans for each enterprise or institution.

CHART VIII. The hierarchy of planning agencies, East Germany, 1953.

Commission. No enterprise of the East Zone (with the exception of enterprises directly controlled by Soviet authorities) is entitled to produce without permission of the Commission, which determines both the quantity and quality of what must be produced.[19]

[19] In 1951 Soviet-controlled enterprises produced 32 per cent of the total industrial output of the East Zone. As of January 1, 1954, all these enterprises were returned to East German control with the exception of the Wismut A. G. which has important uranium mines. Details concerning this Soviet sector of the

The technical operation of the State Planning Commission need not concern us in the present context; it has been copied in most details from the Soviet model. Its work is not only beyond criticism, it is done for the most part in secret. All subordinate agencies, including of course the enterprises themselves, are given specific directives without commentary. Since the end of 1950 the personnel of the Commission has been changed drastically, so-called activists have taken the positions from which older people with academic training and generally people of "bourgeois" background had been removed. It is important to add that appointments to positions on the Commission depend upon the approval of the Central Committee of the party.

In the structure of economic controls the Central Commission for State Control (*Zentrale Kommission für Staatliche Kontrolle* or ZKStK) deserves special mention. It was founded in 1948 [20] as an independent organization under the Presidium of Ministers to control the observance of directives issued to the Special Ministries, State Secretariats, associations, and enterprises. At that time the Commission was endowed with extensive police powers, but in recent years it has served primarily as an auxiliary organization in the investigation of alleged "economic crimes."

Under the State Planning Commission with its various subdivisions are the executive agencies responsible for administering the economic plans for the separate industries. These executive agencies are called *Fachministerien* and *Staatssekretariate* (Special Ministries and State Secretariats) for the several branches of the economy.[21] Each of these executive organs is charged with the breakdown of the annual plan into quarterly plans and must work out specific plans for the Association of People's Own Enterprises (*Vereinigung Volkseigener Betriebe*). It may be added that all other enterprises are joined in various associa-

---

East German economy are contained in Anonymous, *Die Sowjetische Hand in der Deutschen Wirtschaft* (Bonner Berichte aus Mittel- und Ostdeutschland; Bonn: Bundesministerium fuer gesamtdeutsche Fragen, 1953), *passim*.

[20] The original designation was Central Control Commission (*Zentrale Kontrollkommission* or ZKK).

[21] In 1953 there were 14 such Ministries and 10 Secretariats. In addition to such conventional departments as finance, health, postal service, there were also others such as mining, machine construction, railroads, etc. The point seems to be that all administrative activities which have in any way to do with the economy have been organized under the State Planning Commission, while the remaining Ministries such as Justice, State Security, Foreign Affairs are directly subject to the Politbureau. However, it should be remembered that leading members of the party also sit on the Presidium of the Council of Ministers.

tions at the zonal or at district, county, or municipal levels. Consequently, for all enterprises there exist three superordinate administrative levels: a division of the State Planning Commission, a Special Ministry or State Secretariat, and the association to which the enterprise itself belongs, and from which, in fact, it receives its detailed and binding directives.[22]

This description of the formal structure is sufficient for our purposes, but one point needs to be elaborated. All planning agencies of the government (down to the individual enterprise) have a personnel link with the party. That is, each organizational unit is under the surveillance of a party member within that unit, who is charged with the responsibility of watching over, and of facilitating, the work performance of individuals in the organization and of the organization as a whole. Frequently, this person will be the secretary of the party cell, who is actually a full-time official of the party; but practice varies considerably in this respect. For example, Heinrich Rau, the Minister of Machine Construction, is a member of the Politbureau, and it is obvious that in that ministry Rau rather than the party secretary will be the decisive figure. Moreover, the party member "in charge" is primarily concerned with political agitation and control, so that technical and managerial decisions are theoretically left to the state official or to the factory director in charge of the organization. But it is difficult to distinguish between political agitation and managerial decisions, since theory and action are considered inseparable as a matter of doctrine and since in practice higher productivity is regarded as the decisive test of successful agitation as well as of successful management.

This aspect of a party dictatorship cannot be understood in terms of the process of bureaucratization discussed above, for it constitutes a deliberate duplication of controls and it also involves a more or less incidental appointment of the same persons at several levels of these

[22] In sketching this structure of the controls which impinges on each economic enterprise in the East Zone I have deviated from the official, legal description in only two respects. I have neglected the "legislatures" at the district, provincial (Laender) and zonal levels, and the President of the "German Democratic Republic," to whom the legislatures refer their enactments and who has nominal responsibility for their execution. Below the President the controls are exercised at the various levels I have described: the Presidium of the Council of Ministers, the State Planning Commission, etc. However, parliamentary control of executive action is simulated when the legislature of the East Zone unanimously endorses the enactments previously prepared by the Politbureau and the Secretariat of the party and endorsed by the party's Central Committee.

interlocking hierarchies of authority.[23]   As such it is not an outgrowth of
the division of labor necessitated by the growing complexity of organizations.   Authoritarian rule means presumably that each individual and
level of organization is strictly accountable to those above, and by the
same token that each has complete authority over those below.   Such
an organizational structure is ideally characteristic of an army, not of a
political dictatorship.   In the latter each level of organization is strictly
accountable to those above *and* at the same time subject to the arbitrary
(though not unregulated) surveillance by a party cadre of the same
organizational unit.   Likewise, each individual's authority over the individuals on the next lower level is limited by the arbitrary (though not
unregulated) surveillance exercised by the party cadre at that lower
level.[24]   We may, therefore, expect that a principal tool of Communist
rule consists in simultaneously manipulating the governmental controls
from above and the party controls, which are organizationally outside
the governmental hierarchy and which are ideologically represented as
expressing the "will of the people," from "below."

This organization of the planning economy in a Communist party
dictatorship reflects today the twin impulses which characterized Lenin's
thinking on this problem during the first years after the Revolution of
1917.   In Lenin's view the central direction of an enterprise by qualified
personnel and political agitation among the masses were both indispensable for increasing the productivity of the workers and for improving the
organization of production.   Throughout the recent history of Russian
industrialization this approach has led to an emphasis now on the importance of "one-man management" and then on the importance of
mass initiative, depending on the shifting exigencies of the regime.   At
the level of the party line one may trace in the changing directives of the
top leaders their response to these exigencies, one of which consists
no doubt in the cumulative exaggerations by the lower echelons of one
or the other emphasis which previous party directives had endorsed.[25]

[23] Of the 135 members and candidates in the party's Central Committee 61
occupied leading positions in the government and the economy. See Stern,
op. cit., pp. 47–48.

[24] It is difficult to find adjectives which describe this "surveillance" accurately.
It is "arbitrary" in the sense that it results from decisions by higher party authorities which have no logic and continuity at the local level. But it is neither
unregulated nor unpredictable. It consists in the more or less prompt response
of the higher echelons to defects of performance below, but it also reflects shifting
power alignments within the higher echelons themselves.

[25] See the discussion in Bienstock, Schwarz, and Yugow, *Management in Russian Industry,* pp. 17–31 and *passim* for an analysis of the shift from "worker

This double emphasis has, therefore, gone through a history of doctrinal as well as practical accommodations to the changing requirements of the drive for productivity, though it should be added that these accommodations are also exploited for the internecine struggles between groups and individuals within the party. While the tie between a leader's political ascendancy and his "productivity performance" has at times been close, the two are by no means synonymous. For the most part, productivity is evaluated as a sign of political loyalty or reliability; it is not a token of power. Political ascendancy within the party is far more dependent upon personal and organizational ties than upon productivity performance, though the latter may weaken or strengthen these ties. Relatively independent as the struggle for power may be from the drive for productivity, there is no doubt that both may involve the strategic alternations of policies favoring "one-man management" or the economic responsibilities of the party. Hence, it is not surprising that this "double-edged formula" is regarded officially as the distinctive characteristic of industrial enterprises under socialism.

The meaning of this approach is illustrated by a Russian textbook on industrial organization, which was published under the auspices of the State Planning Commission of the USSR (*Gosplan*) in 1950, and has been made available in a German translation in the East Zone. The role of the director or manager of an enterprise is described in the following terms:

control" to "one-man management." While this shift reflected a major change in administrative organization, the party line continues to alternate between these poles. "In the period from 1939 to the end of 1940, the party press clearly demanded that party organizations refrain from usurping the administrative functions of management and that higher party instances keep from 'depersonalizing' lower party organs. Beginning approximately in November, 1940, the party line shifted to an emphasis on the economic responsibilities of lower and higher party organizations alike. . . . With the end of the war emergency, the party line veered to the other side of these double-edged formulas. After the publication in *Pravda*, in 1944 and 1945, of a number of letters in which factory directors 'complained' of their lack of authority, the Soviet press began to call for a clearcut differentiation between the activities of party organizers and management—i.e., for greater managerial autonomy—and for nonusurpation of the functions of primary organizations by higher party instances. . . . Approximately in August, 1948, the party line shifted once again, this time toward more active economic work and tighter economic control by party organizations. . . . Since approximately the end of 1949 the official line has been calling once again for managerial *yedinonachaliye* (one-man management) and for a 'political,' rather than 'economic,' emphasis in the activities of party organizations in industry." See Haimson, "Decision-making and Communications in Russian Industry," *op. cit.*, pp. 492–94.

The Director of a factory or an enterprise is the agent [*Beauftragte*] of the Soviet State. He determines the ways and means by which the enterprise can fulfill the tasks set for it by the economic plan; he secures for the enterprise the supply of the necessary material and technical means; he organizes the work of production; he ensures the manufacture of high-grade products, takes care of their distribution, and is responsible for the success of all work in the enterprise. Standing at the head of the enterprise-collective he takes all necessary measures in order to develop the collective, Stachanovite labor in all respects.[26]

The authority of the Director is absolute within the enterprise. He is charged with responsibility for the fulfillment of the plan and he is given the powers necessary to accomplish this end. It is, therefore, of interest how this textbook deals with the activities of the party organization in the enterprise since the Director's absolute authority does *not* include authority over the party

Kamenizer explains that the entire economic life of the country is governed by the Communist party. The party "sends" the best workers, who are devoted to the working class and to the socialist state, into the main positions of the state apparatus. It controls the work of all administrative bodies and "secures for them the support of broad strata of the working people." The party also issues directives which determine the nature and direction of the work done by these administrative bodies. And these functions of the party are also and in every respect the guiding considerations for the party cells in the individual enterprises.[27] The role of the party in "socialist industrial enterprises" is one which emphasizes simultaneously the support the party gives to the authority of the Director *and* the help it can give him by way of critiques and suggestions to improve his work. Likewise, the party mobilizes the masses for the fulfillment of production plans *and* it is active in the protection of their interests. These mutually conflicting functions are made to appear harmonious at the verbal level.

> The basic units of the party organizations control the administrative activity and give active support to the directives initiated by the management, by posing in turn the pressing problems which concern the plant or factory. The party organization improves the quality of work in the enterprise by using its authority to strengthen the position of the Director who is the independent leader of the enterprise, and by getting the entire party collective * to participate in the solution of technical and economic tasks.

[26] See Kamenizer, *Organisation und Planung des Sozialistischen Industriebetriebes,* p. 119.
[27] *Ibid.,* p. 134.

The party organizations mobilize the masses for the fulfillment of the production plans, for the strengthening of labor discipline and for the development of socialist competition. They fight against mismanagement, lead the work of the collective for the improvement of work in the enterprise, care for the lifting of the cultural level and of the economic position of all workers, and develop the collective, Stachanovite labor in the sections and divisions and in the entire enterprise.[28]

Kamenizer points out that Stalin emphasized these responsibilities of the party organizations already in 1923. According to this and many subsequent directives, party organizations were entitled to control the administrative work of the enterprise.

Yet the author maintains that this does not limit or interfere with the absolute authority of the Director over the enterprise. Instead, the Director as well as each subordinate section chief and foreman is able to rely in his work on the support of the party.

The party's right to control gives it the possibility of mobilizing the masses in overcoming difficulties by the better utilization of the experience in production which the best parts of the working class, the Communists, have acquired. It also makes it possible for the party to strengthen the masses in the struggle against bureaucratism and against conduct inimical to the state, evils which are still to be found in isolated sections of the administrative apparatus.[29]

That is to say, the party organization lends its support to the authority of the Director by making his control over the work force more effective; it does so by mobilizing the masses to emulate the work methods of the best workers. Hence, what the Director is attempting to achieve through authoritative directives, namely an increase in productivity, is in part accomplished for him by the organizing activities of the party among the workers of the enterprise. But the party also "strengthens the masses in the struggle against bureaucratism and against conduct inimical to the state," which means of course that the party itself proposes to detect and fight against these evils.

It is an easy matter of dialectical agility to "prove" that this latter activity of the party also strengthens the authority of the Director. It is said to free his administrative apparatus from the remaining evils which beset it, though the party rather than the Director accomplishes

[28] Ibid. * The reference is here presumably to the members of the party cell. But the jargon also refers frequently to nonparty Bolsheviks or Communists, i.e., activists who do not belong to the party but who are coopted terminologically, so to speak. These activists are probably included also in the above reference to the "entire party collective."

[29] Ibid., p. 135.

this end. These conflicting assertions concerning the Director's absolute authority and the party's managerial functions are compatible ideologically, because all activities of the enterprise are an outgrowth of the party's dictatorial rule. In directing the enterprise the Director is following orders which result from the policy decisions of the highest party body. Hence, in supporting his authority the party cell in the enterprise is likewise following these decisions. On the other hand, the party also follows directives in struggling against bureaucratism in industrial management. In doing so the party formulates and represents the interests of the best parts of the working class, which are in turn identified with the party. By the same token, the Director acts against these interests and counter to the decisions of the party in so far as he tolerates bureaucratism in the managerial ranks.

The outstanding characteristic of this organizational structure is the complete absorption of the relation between management and labor in the omniscient and omnipresent dictatorship of the party. Since both the authority of the Director and the compliance of the work force are construed as outgrowths of party directives, it is obvious that neither "authority" nor "compliance" retain their ordinary meaning. Indeed, the relation between management and labor takes on the form of a declaration of fealty to the dictatorial party, in which each group is obliged to exert itself to the utmost and to be eternally vigilant against transgressions of one and all. It is understood, of course, that both exertions and vigilance are under the central direction of all levels of the party organization. This conception of industrial relations is given an apt expression in the institution of the collective agreement. In Russia, this term had been originally applied to contracts between the representatives of management and labor, which actually stipulated the conditions of work and were legally binding as such. But with the advance of centralized planning, working conditions came to be regulated by law or administrative enactment. Consequently, collective agreements were transformed into mere commentaries on the law, and these in turn were eventually abandoned as obsolete.[30] However, collective agreements were reintroduced in Russia in 1947 at the suggestion of Stalin, and by 1952 their standardized content had been adopted almost verbatim throughout the East Zone. These agreements primarily contain pledges by management, trade-union representatives, and individual workers concerning the detailed duties each obliges himself to fulfill

[30] See N. G. Alexandrov, ed., *Lehrbuch des Sowjetischen Arbeitsrechts* (18. Beiheft zur Sowjetwissenschaft; Berlin: Verlag Kultur und Fortschritt, 1952), pp. 159–60.

during the ensuing year.   The agreements merely recapitulate the statutory regulations pertaining to the wage structure and the working conditions of the enterprise.   Hence, their major purpose is presumably to buttress the production goals of the Plan by enjoining upon management and workers a politically or legally enforceable obligation to "fulfill and overfulfill" these goals.   Accordingly, this institution is defined

> as an agreement between the management of an enterprise on the one hand, and the trade union committee acting in the name of workers and employees on the other, in which the *reciprocal obligations* of the participants are set down with regard to the fulfillment and overfulfillment of the production plan, the improvement of the organization of work and of labor safety as well as the improvement of the material and cultural living conditions of workers and employees.[31]

It is logical that the foundation of a dictatorially planned economy consists in the mutual pledge of management and labor to perform the task which the party has assigned to them.   And this pledge is further reinforced by the assertion that in a socialist society conflicts cannot exist between planning officials and workers, between managers and trade-union functionaries, because "all have the common goal of increasing labor productivity, of improving the material well-being and the cultural level of the workers. . . ."[32]

I have surveyed the structure of controls over economic enterprises in East Germany.   The question is: How are these controls actually manipulated in this system?   For the uses of managerial ideologics depend upon that manipulation.

c. The Manipulation of Controls over Economic Enterprises

The Socialist Unity party manipulates the structure of controls which I have outlined.   It is important to understand how the party views

[31] *Ibid.*, p. 161.   My italics.   These collective agreements represent the culmination of a thirty-year development in Soviet Russia, but were introduced in East Germany during a three-year period.   The reference in the text to "politically enforceable obligations" refers to the Soviet distinction between legal and political moral obligations; it goes without saying that the latter can be enforced by all manner of pressures which the party can bring to bear upon the individual.   These political moral obligations are "voluntarily assumed" (*Selbstverpflichtungen*), according to the official interpretation.   Cf. the discussion below in Section *f.*

[32] *Ibid.*, p. 157.   It may be added that in accordance with this definition the relations between management and workers have the character of "comradely cooperation and mutual help" and, hence, are free of exploitation.   Therefore, labor conflicts in a socialist society do not result from class antagonism, but from the "capitalist remnants" in the consciousness of individuals, which on occasion produce bureaucratic distortions, egoistic demands, etc.   See *ibid.*, p. 283.

this manipulation of the controls it has set up. In order to see these views in the perspective of the present study it is useful to consider the contrast between managerial ideologies in a democratic and in a totalitarian setting.

In the analysis of the American case I could confine myself to a broad discussion of bureaucratization within the organization of economic enterprises. For the leaders of these enterprises managerial appeals constitute an amalgam of what they believe, what they believe to be in their interest, and what they think will appeal to the audience they have in mind. For most of them managerial ideologies do not involve policy considerations which are more or less secret, but appeals which may create a favorable climate of opinion. In an economy in which accountants appraise "good will" in dollars and cents, it is certainly plausible for economic enterprises to spend considerable sums in creating "good will"—especially if they can deduct such expenses for tax purposes and if advertisers and public-relations men "prove" time and again how worth-while these appeals are. But there is much uncertainty concerning the relation of fact and fancy in this ideological creation of "good will." In so far as these appeals relate to industrial practices at all, they are justifications of that which is done or which is proposed. As such these managerial ideologies may make a given action more effective. But they do not provide a comprehensive vocabulary of aims and motives in which *all* managerial and technical directives are presented. They are not formulated in the expectation that they will guide a course of action.

In a Communist dictatorship the party constitutes a second bureaucracy which is intended to "facilitate" and control the operation of all economic enterprises. In this system managerial ideologies are a means of manipulation in the interlocking hierarchies of the party and the planned economy. In particular, all planning directives are bound up officially with the doctrine of the party. A central tenet of this doctrine is that theory and action are inextricably linked; "mere" ideology or propaganda is officially condemned. Any statement of an idea or a belief is treated as a personal commitment to a course of action. Hence, ideas are propagated in the expectation that they will prompt men to act in the desired manner, and the whole apparatus of the party is, indeed, set up to implement this expectation by organizational means. And because ideas are treated as indicating a line of action, so all actions, however trivial, are reported in the press by relating them to the policies and doctrines of the party as instances of fulfillment or deviation. It becomes difficult, then, to distinguish between ideology and action, because all words have become "action-oriented" by an officially sanctioned custom.[33]

It is important to see that this use or misuse of the language is itself an instrument of rule. The practice by which all words are related to action makes it indispensable to prescribe not only all actions, but all words as well. And since all courses of action are defined ideologically, a major task of the party authorities consists in evaluating the words and actions of their subordinates in terms of their conformity with the ideological orientation of the moment, the party line. For themselves these authorities claim that their words and actions are as one, that they excel both in doctrinal orthodoxy and in militant action. Even the mistakes of the Politbureau can only be admitted in the form of spontaneous self-criticism by the Politbureau itself. Such self-criticism is one of the officially sanctioned devices which brings actions into line with the directives of the party, but for the most part it occurs only after a given course of action has been criticized publicly. The Politbureau reserves for itself the highest form of self-criticism, which arises supposedly from an ever vigilant self-appraisal and does not depend upon a prior critical evaluation by others.[34]

All lower echelons of the party and, of course, all other organizational units fall short of such perfection. Party publications are filled with militantly worded criticism which shows up one functionary after another whose actions fall short of the goals set for them. The highest party authority uses this criticism as a tool to bolster its own position and improve the implementation of its directives. Nevertheless, this criticism is an important source of information about a dictatorship, for it reveals the strains to which the internal organization of the regime is subject as well as some of the methods the party uses to relieve them. I make use of this information in the following discussion, but I should

---

[33] Cf. Ernst Otto Maetzke, "Die Parteisprache in der Sowjetzone," *Vierteljahrshefte für Zeitgeschichte,* Vol. I (1953), pp. 339–46, and Walter Richter, "Zur Entwicklung der deutschen Sprache in der sowjetischen Besatzungszone," *Europa Archiv,* Vol. VIII (1953), pp. 6053–56.

[34] It is interesting in this respect that in responding to the spontaneous uprisings of June 17, 1953, the spokesmen of the party frequently insisted that the resolutions changing the policy of the party had been passed already on June 9. The implication is not only that the uprising was unnecessary, aside from being criminal and the result of Western agents, but also that the highest party authorities are the first to recognize and acknowledge a mistake, once it has been made. Of course, the occasions are rare indeed, when the Politbureau admits a mistake, since it has an effective monopoly of criticizing everybody and everything without being the object of criticism itself.

make it clear that such public criticism of officials and functionaries reveals nothing of the actual discussions of policy within the party. These are barred from public view by the principle of hierarchical discipline.

> If there are differences in the Politburo, its decision by majority vote is binding on all members and they are not allowed by Bolshevik precepts to discuss their point of difference even in the Central Committee. Dissidents in the Central Committee must defend the committee's point of view even in the party; party decisions have to be defended outside the party even by members who disagree with them. Thus at every level disagreement is kept to the group of minimum size, and at each step down the hierarchical scale the next larger body is presented with a unanimous mandate. The secrecy of each body's deliberations in sacred; for a member of a committee to discuss them with someone in a lower hierarchical unit is the Communist equivalent of a serious misdemeanor.[35]

Accordingly, every public statement by a party official expresses the decisions of the corresponding headquarters (*Leitung*) at his level of the hierarchy. The deliberations of that body and especially differences of opinion within it are kept secret. Hence, the several headquarters of the party hierarchy constitute a secret society within the larger society even after the party has acquired a monopoly of power.[36]

Most agencies of the government and the economy are not permitted to adhere to this principle of organization. The party derives a major source of its power from shrouding its own deliberations in secrecy while insisting that the deliberations and actions of all other organizations should be open to inspection. This policy is implemented by establishing a party cell in each nonparty organization. On the basis of reports received from the leaders of these cells the party authorities are in a position to control the planning agencies of the government as well as each economic enterprise. And one of the methods by which this control is exercised consists in publicly staged discussions of high party functionaries, in which a few merits and many deficiencies of executive officials at various levels are held up for public notice. A good example of this was the Tenth Conference of the Central Committee of the Socialist Unity party, held on November 20–22, 1952. The problems discussed at the Conference had to do with the party's management of controls over the economy. Since I shall analyze only

[35] Ruth Fischer, *Stalin and German Communism* (Cambridge: Harvard University Press, 1948), pp. 451–52.

[36] And the Party Control Commissions at the zonal, district, and county levels of the party may be said to constitute another secret society.

the deficiencies which the various speakers discussed specifically, I should make it clear that in each case the mention of defects was followed immediately by a kind of pep talk for greater effort along the lines decreed by the party. No speaker left any doubt that in his opinion the problems would be solved, the "guilty" punished, and the plan "fulfilled and overfulfilled." The fact is that a Communist regime operates with a double bureaucracy in which problems that arise and are solved in one form and soon turn up in other forms. Official party doctrine sees these difficulties overcome by the invincible strength of the party. It is true that they are overcome. But this is accomplished at the expense of those who must suffer degradation, imprisonment, or death.[37]

Deficiencies of industrial managers. At the Tenth Conference of the Central Committee (1952) industrial managers were denounced for their deliberate evasion of the Five-Year Plan. For instance, out of 140 positions of great economic significance, 88 positions had not been filled by the third quarter of 1952. Some enterprises had "fulfilled" their planned production quota, but they had done so by increasing the output of some secondary items in little demand while failing to fulfill the production quota for important commodities. Enterprises in the textile industry had produced stockings and wearing apparel which were not in demand, but had ignored the directives of the Ministry to produce other commodities. In some cases quantities of raw materials had been demanded far in excess of what was needed. For instance, the state secretariat for the food industry had requested ten times as much coal as was needed, according to the control division of the State Planning Commission. Also many enterprises had incurred great losses because they had utilized allocated raw material uneconomically; they had exceeded the stipulated wage fund and employed superfluous

[37] Unless indicated otherwise the following discussion is based on Walter Ulbricht, *Lehren des XIX Parteitages der KPdSU für den Aufbau des Sozialismus in der Deutschen Demokratischen Republik,* Referat und Diskussionsreden auf der 10. Tagung des Zentralkomitees der SED. (Berlin: Dietz Verlag, 1952.) Ulbricht is the secretary of the Central Committee and the most powerful political figure in the East Zone. All other speakers are members of the Central Committee, some are also members of the Politbureau, and all occupy important positions in the party and in the government. I shall refer to them by name only where the context requires it, since all speak as functionaries of the party. All speak on behalf of improving the actions and effective controls of the party, though in doing so they may also defend one and attack another faction within the party. In what follows I am concerned with the first, not with the second, function of public debate in a dictatorial regime.

workers.[38]   Finally, a majority of enterprises had failed to introduce "technical work-norms"; the norms used were outmoded, were easily "overfulfilled," and, consequently, were no incentive to increased productivity.[39]   At the conference Ulbricht concluded this enumeration of deficiencies with the declaration that managers who failed to fulfill the plan must stand aside and be replaced by men who fulfill the tasks assigned to them and therefy justify the confidence which the party and the people place in them.

It should be added that the recital of such failures is a standard item on the agenda of party conferences.   As often as not these "failures" probably consist of maneuvers which enable managers to fulfill the plan in a nominal sense, of simple evasions of one rule in order to comply with another, or of attempts to avoid the unforeseen repercussions of directives for which the party would hold the individual responsible. Undoubtedly in many cases failures arise from the bureaucratic complications of the planning apparatus, from material shortages, from the issuance of incompatible directives and from other similar causes, quite aside from actual mistakes or blunders of the managers themselves. The detailed reasons, however, are officially ignored.   All speeches at the Tenth Conference attribute failures of performance to acts of sabotage.   In this respect the keynote was sounded by Otto Grotewohl, the Prime Minister.

> We are now frequently confronted with the question: are we dealing here with stupidity or with crime? . . . We have found repeatedly that in the economy and the state apparatus even comrades of good will have tolerated occurrences where one can no longer believe in stupidity.   In this connection it must be stated that the period has begun for us now in which we must be clear about the fact that stupidity can go only up to a certain limit.   From this limit on stupidity must be regarded by us as a crime.[40]

But the doctrine which maintains the unity of theory and action cannot distinguish between stupidity and crime and we may be sure that Grotewohl is not really concerned with that distinction.   Managers who have

---

[38] *Ibid.,* p. 32.   It must be understood that "superfluous" refers here to the number of workers in excess of the planned figure.   Thus, Ulbricht refers to the Ministry for Machine Construction as employing 9,700 service personnel above the number allowed by the plan.

[39] *Ibid.,* pp. 32–33.   "Technical work-norms" (*Technisch begründete Arbeitsnormen* or TAN) have been characterized as essential for the success of the plan. Details on this point are discussed in Section *f* of this chapter.

[40] *Ibid.,* pp. 176–77.

failed are inevitably suspected of a potential or actual deviation from the theoretical position of the party line.   Failure to fulfill the plan or the frequent occurrence of bottlenecks in production and distribution becomes, therefore, the subject of detailed investigations by party and government authorities whose aim is the detection of "sabotage." In such investigations the burden of proof is on the manager to show that the failure was not caused by himself.   He may endeavor to shift the responsibility to objective difficulties, though if he is prudent he will add a bit of "public self-criticism" to his defense.   The authorities will endeavor to prevent such evasions and find the "guilty" individuals.   Their investigations start with the assumption that the failure or breakdown was caused by the deliberate action of individuals. This assumption is necessary, partly because it is inadmissible that the highest authorities could be responsible for the specific difficulties of the planned economy in operation and partly also because these authorities reserve for themselves the exclusive right to decide when circumstances rather than individuals are responsible for the difficulties which have arisen.[41]   If it permitted stupidity to rank high among the causes of failure, the party would diminish its effective control of officials and functionaries, and it would relax its drive for performance.

That drive could not be maintained if the leaders of a dictatorial regime considered stupidity among the pardonable failings of man. The fact is that the lapses of industrial managers and other officials are endemic in this regime, not merely because they fail as weak men will, but because the party in its unremitting drive to achieve the possible continually demands the impossible.   To take a simple example: the East Zone authorities are aware that safety measures are necessary to avoid losses of man-hours, if not of manpower, and hence of productivity.   Administrative enactments as well as "voluntary obligations" of managers in the collective agreements see to the observation and improvement of safety regulations—on paper.   But the party's drive for productivity takes precedence over all other concerns in the eyes of management, for the penalties may be severe if the production quotas are not met.   Of course, no party authority declares that safety measures may be neglected; on the contrary, they insist that they must be fully observed *and* that production quotas must be fulfilled and over-

[41] That is to say, the authorities reserve for themselves the right to explain their very rare mistakes by reference to objective difficulties, but they do not permit individual executives to use the same argument.   The individuals who do so anyway are accused of tolerance toward "adverse conditions" or of a lack of the proper party spirit.   Cf. the discussion at the end of this section.

fulfilled. But the fulfillment of the quotas is checked periodically during the year, and the disastrous consequences of neglecting safety measures are intangible for a time and may be avoided altogether, if luck
holds out. Hence, production is increased and safety is neglected.[42]
The point of this is not only that individual managers are held criminally
liable if disaster strikes after all. It is rather that the regime does not
permit such partly incompatible goals as productivity and safety to be
balanced by anyone but the highest planning authorities. The party
continually presses for production as well as safety, and managers and
engineers are suspected of sabotage and boycott if they do not achieve
a maximum of both. If the stupidity of these executives were a recognized cause of failure, the capacity of the party to exert pressure on
them would be considerably diminished. As it is, party authorities
reiterate incompatible directives and hunt for the "guilty" when a
disaster is the result.

In his concluding remarks at the Tenth Conference Walter Ulbricht
illustrated this approach. He referred to the remarks of a miner, according to whom the disaster at the Martin Hoop pit could have been
avoided if the authorities had initiated the investigation of sabotage
three years earlier.[43] The matter was not that simple, however, because the danger was, according to Ulbricht, that earlier proceedings
against one or two guilty individuals would have enabled the rest to
escape to the West. This meant that 48 men died in a mine disaster
while the party waited in order to catch all the "saboteurs." What
mattered in the eyes of party authorities was that the party's pressure
for higher productivity and maximum safety would continue undimin-
ished and the hunt for all the "saboteurs" was simply another means to
that end. That it was up to the executives to make out as best they
could in complying with the party's drive for productivity is well illustrated by a comment of one of the accused at the trial which followed
the disaster: "I took the position that the production quota had to be
met first. In doing this I forgot about the men." But, of course, the
party had always insisted that proper attention should be paid to safety,
although it had also insisted on higher productivity. Indeed, on the
day when the Supreme Court convicted the men "responsible" for the
disaster to from 4 to 12 years of hard labor, Ulbricht publicly com-

[42] Cf. the survey by E. Lonny, "Arbeitsschutz-Erfahrungen im 'Arbeiter-Staat,' "
Ost-Probleme, Vol. VII (April, 1955), pp. 681–89.

[43] Note, incidentally, that the top man of the party initiates his defense of
official actions by this (probably fictitious) reference to the voice of the people.

mended one of the work brigades in the same mine for having over-fulfilled the plan by 222 per cent.[44]

Clearly, unremitting pressure is a principle of rule. In concluding his reference to the Martin Hoop disaster, Ulbricht assured his listeners that the Politbureau had undertaken a thoroughgoing investigation. In addition, the case had been investigated by several agencies which worked independently of one another.[45] Consequently, all the guilty individuals had now been caught. But in saying this, Ulbricht immediately added that generally there were people in the government and in various public institutions who were somehow connected with this sabotage, although the party was unable to prove in detail who these people were and where they worked. Thus, no case of "sabotage" is permitted to be closed. Even the claim by the most powerful man in the East Zone that all the "saboteurs" had been found is accompanied by the insinuation that other unknown and unnamed enemies are lurking in the "higher state apparatus and various institutions." [46]

Deficiencies of government officials. The suspicion of sabotage is not acted upon nearly as often as it is used in order to exert pressure. In practice, it would be difficult to treat all the deficiencies of managers and engineers as "economic crimes," simply because these men must be relied upon to get the work of production done, and a political interpretation of their deficiencies tends to reduce the trained personnel that is available. This limitation is probably less relevant in the case of government officials, whose work is less technical. It may be, therefore, that government officials are more subject to the detailed controls of the party than are managers and technicians, though the officials

[44] See Gerhard Haas and Alfred Leutwein, *Die rechtliche und soziale Lage der Arbeitnehmer in der Sowjetzone und in Ostberlin* (Bonner Berichte aus Mittel- und Ostdeutschland; Bonn: Bundesministerium für gesamtdeutsche Fragen, 1953), p. 32.

[45] The use of several independent agencies to accomplish a given task is a technique of dictatorial regimes as old as tyranny itself. While it represents an attempt of the authorities to test the performance of these various competing agencies, it represents at the same time an opportunity for each of the agencies to excel the others in thoroughly exposing the suspected saboteurs and thereby diverting attention from itself. It is also of interest that Ulbricht diagnoses the Martin-Hoop disaster as corresponding to a stage in the history of Soviet purges: the Shakhty case of 1927–28 against a group of leading industrial engineers. This reference to the Soviet model is only one of many at the Conference: all of them are designed to legitimate official actions and interpretations of the party.

[46] *Lehren des XIX Parteitages . . . ,* pp. 214–15.

may, on the other hand, have more of an opportunity to protect themselves politically.

The goal of the party is to fill all positions of the state apparatus with people who identify themselves with the tasks of socialist construction. Until this can be accomplished the party is admonished to face up to an intensification of the class struggle.[47] This is illustrated by frequent comments which express a concern with the efficacy of the planning agencies. Officials of the Special Ministries and State Secretariats are said to make excessive demands for supplies which threaten to "transform our plans into a hodgepodge of fantastic figures." [48] These officials are also accused of deliberately decreasing production plans and of failing to utilize fully existing productive capacities. Such actions are a crime against the party and the state, which points to the continuing danger from capitalists and saboteurs. To fight these shortcomings the State Planning Commission is called upon to appoint persons whose exclusive task it is to detect unused reserves and to fight "decisively" against the tendency of officials to scale down production plans. The remedy is symptomatic: just as every failure is regarded as an act of sabotage, so every action to counteract it consists in special campaigns and/or the appointment of special officials to deal with it.

To understand the impetus that prompts the government constantly to increase the number and variety of controls, one must also be aware of the many defects of which government officials are accused. For instance, Bruno Leuschner, the Chairman of the State Planning Commission, accuses some of the leading economic administrators of indifference toward the preparation and fulfillment of the plan with the result that the required forecasts are seriously delayed. Indeed, some ministries avoid making forecasts altogether; they even delay the confirmation of projects and thereby also the planning of prospective investments. Moreover, planning commissions of districts and counties have neglected to search for unused reserves and to check on the plan fulfillment of enterprises and production associations within their areas.

Officials in the Special Ministries and State Secretariats also should work hand in hand with the enterprises within their jurisdiction; otherwise their plans remain "formal," and a merely formal approach to planning leads to difficulties of execution, especially to an insufficient utilization of resources. But close cooperation between the Ministries and the enterprises does not exist. And where it does exist, as when government officials together with the industrial managers exceeded the

[47] *Ibid.,* pp. 46–47.
[48] *Ibid.,* p. 31.

control figures for the wage fund by approximately 2 billion Deutsche Mark (East German currency), it amounts to a clear violation of directives issued by the Politbureau. Likewise, local administrative agencies are accused of not being "sufficiently familiar" with the resolutions of the party and the government. Leuschner cites the example of agencies which continue to demand state aid for cultural activities in industrial enterprises, although a directive had been issued that these activities should be financed out of the savings accumulating in each enterprise.[49]

The fact that these two violations are mentioned merely in a reproving manner and without the cry of sabotage probably indicates that the party was not prepared to correct these defects too vigorously, for the time being. According to Leuschner, these instances show that the Directors of economic enterprises and the leading officials of the Special Ministries and State Secretariats do not abide by the resolutions of the party, do not concentrate on the utilization of existing resources, do not show "state discipline," and ignore the figures given out by the party and by the government. To correct these deficiencies the State Planning Commission sent out for the first time its entire personnel to re-examine every investment in about 80 enterprises. The result of this special investigation was that in 60 enterprises a saving of 170 million DM could be effected, and Leuschner contends that this was accomplished without diminishing either the production or the social services of these enterprises.[50]

The use of special investigating commissions of one kind or another is only one of the means by which the regime seeks to control and correct the actions of its government officials. Another is illustrated at the Tenth Conference by a remark of Heinrich Rau, a member of the Politbureau and a high official in one of the central planning agen-

[49] It is probable that such demands for continued state aid constitute a silent protest against the use of local savings for "cultural activities." The point is that these activities are organized by and for the party. And all too often they are used to promote the productivity drives, which lead to the savings from which they are to be financed.

[50] *Ibid.*, pp. 161–64. The finding points to the effective collusion of ministries and enterprises in their maneuvers to make the pressures on them more tolerable. It also points to the difficulties which superordinate agencies encounter in effectively controlling the execution of the plan, since the State Planning Commission has a special division of control which presumably would make it unnecessary to use the personnel of the head office for such extraordinary assignments. However, this unusual procedure may also have been a means of exerting additional pressure in view of the difficulties of plan fulfillment during 1952.

cies. Rau states that the Central Committee had passed a resolution, according to which the Directors of enterprises had full personal responsibility for their operation. Yet the Special Ministries and State Secretariats interfered constantly with the management and the work schedule of the enterprises by issuing directives, though their knowledge of these enterprises was quite insufficient. In Rau's opinion it was the job of the party secretary to support the Director in his rejection of such interference, and not to tolerate the illegitimate intrusion of government officials in the operation of the plant.[51]

Considerable light is thrown on the functioning of the double hierarchy of government and party authorities, if one contrasts Rau's suggestion with the case cited by Leuschner. There the entire office staff of the State Planning Commission was used to control on the spot the execution of its own directives, to detect unused resources, and to prevent excessive demands for supplies. In the case mentioned by Rau it is the party secretary within the enterprise who should defend the Director against the undue interference of the higher governmental authorities. That is to say, the actions of industrial managers may be controlled and corrected by his own superiors within the government hierarchy. But these superior officials may be controlled in turn by a party secretary who works in an enterprise that is subject to their authority. The point is that the party secretary is outside the governmental hierarchy of authority and that he can be called into action wherever bottlenecks develop and regardless of formal lines of authority. Leading party spokesmen recognize that this disjunction between the two hierarchies leads to great complications. Yet their criticism of managers and officials invariably ends by calling upon the party for better and still more vigorous action.

Deficiencies of party functionaries. Just as the party is supposed to be omnipotent, so its responsibilities are regarded as all-encompassing. Yet the performance of party functionaries falls far short of such perfection. To be sure, the deficiencies of party work were attributed in the first place to the work of saboteurs. Terrorists had attacked leading functionaries of agricultural production associations; functionaries of the SED had been murdered; and the "bandits had been shielded" by a number of mayors who had remained "neutral." Also reactionary peasants had obeyed the instructions of West Berlin agents and had organized in order to beat up "progressive workers" under the guise of getting drunk.[52]

[51] *Ibid.*, pp. 168–69.
[52] *Ibid.*, pp. 51–52.

Admittedly, improvement was urgently needed if the party was to meet its self-imposed responsibilities. This task had been made more difficult, because many party functionaries had been appointed in various administrative positions in the government. According to Ulbricht, this had been an indispensable step even though it had inevitably weakened the party in its own work.[53] Even so, still more party workers are needed in administrative positions, and it is necessary to "develop" party functionaries accordingly, especially by increasing their technical knowledge.

It is further necessary to improve the work of the party cadres. There were still some functionaries who apparently believed that all was going well when mistakes and weaknesses remained hidden, and this bad tradition must be eliminated from the party. Functionaries who are about to make a mistake must be warned openly and honestly; and they must be punished if they make the mistake anyhow, otherwise they will repeat the mistake. And this approach should be applied to everyone regardless of rank. Those leading party functionaries were mistaken who apparently believed that the statutes and directives of the party applied to the average member but not to themselves.[54]

But even training, close supervision, and "iron discipline" are not enough. In employing its functionaries as an omnipresent and ever-ready means to correct and control the work of managers, government officials, and, in fact, everyone else, the party gets involved in perennial dilemmas. And the manipulation of its controls over the economy as well as the uses of its managerial ideologies are revealed by the manner in which these dilemmas are handled. For example, local units of the party had been directed not to interfere with the internal affairs of the collective farms (*Landwirtschaftliche Produktionsgenossenschaften*). And some party functionaries had concluded that they need not concern themselves with these associations. But this was entirely wrong. They had the duty to consult with, and to help, the officials of these associations. In fact, party workers had not only to concern themselves with the difficulties of these officials, but also must actively help to overcome them. Characteristically, it is left open how the

---

[53] Cf. Otto Grotewohl's comment that 160,000 party workers had filled administrative positions at all levels of the government. This statement is contained in *Der Neue Kurs und die Aufgaben der Partei* (15. Tagung des Zentralkomitees der SED; Berlin: Dietz Verlag, 1953), p. 24.

[54] *Ibid.*, pp. 68–69. Apparently, Ulbricht takes it for granted that all party functionaries are subject to a system of constant and omnipresent supervision. Otherwise, it would be hard to know of mistakes which "are about to be made."

political agitation of party functionaries can help without leading to interference.[55]

A similar dilemma arises in the relations between the party and Ministries of the government which are located in Berlin. Each Ministry has a party cell, and all of these cells are subject to the leadership of the party headquarters in Berlin. At the Tenth Conference the Berlin headquarters was seriously called to account, because it had issued directives to the party cells in the Ministries, but had failed to supervise the execution of these directives.

> This does not mean that the Party leadership of the Berlin district itself should interfere with the work of the Ministries. But the district leadership must guarantee the correct organization of party work in the Ministries, and the Ministers must take an active part in the life of their own basic organization [i.e., the party cell within the Ministry] and in the Berlin organization.[56]

In this case, the party cadres in the Ministries are accused of inaction which is in turn attributed to a failure of the district headquarters to impose party discipline. But it is immediately added that the headquarters should not interfere with the work of the Ministry. To remedy both the inactivity of the cell and the slackness of the headquarters the ministers are pointedly reminded that they should participate in the activities of both organizational units.

The point of these arrangements is that the party insists simultaneously upon the authority of both hierarchies, and that it emphasizes the one or the other as the occasion demands. Thus, party spokesmen emphasize time and again that the Directors of economic enterprises and the top officials of the government have absolute authority over their respective organizations, because they must see to it that the work gets done. But the spokesmen also emphasize that the party as a whole is responsible for correcting mistakes, defeating the "enemy," and safeguarding the unity of its ranks. And since both lines of authority should be coordinated, executive officials and party functionaries are constantly reminded of a double responsibility. That is, officials are told not only that they are responsible for the success of their organization and have complete authority over it, but also that they must cooperate with the party cadre in their organization at every step. Likewise, party functionaries are told to be vigilant, to discover errors, to remove bottlenecks, to help in the fulfillment of the plan, but *not* to

[55] *Ibid.*, p. 53.
[56] *Ibid.*, pp. 69–70.

interfere with the work of the organization in which they execute these manifold duties.

The party makes these conflicting demands upon its functionaries and all executive officials in the same manner in which it urges them to maximize safety as well as production. The burden of reconciling such conflicting directives lies in both cases upon the individual responsible for their execution. The party even specifies how the coordination between the two hierarchies is to be put into practice. In commenting upon the "leading role of the party organization in the enterprises" Walter Ulbricht has stated:

> Here and there the party headquarters in the enterprise has the tendency, so to speak, to take over the functions of management and to become a kind of *Ersatz* management. It would be more correct, however, if a leading member of management would belong to the party secretariat of the enterprise: the manager or his deputy, a leading trade-union functionary, comrades who are responsible for the economic operation of the plant, for the struggle over the interests of the workers, etc. In this way all decisive questions could be discussed within the party headquarters of the enterprise.[57]

The ideal organizational arrangement is, therefore, to ensure both the authority of the management *and* of the party, by making a leading executive a member of the party headquarters in the organization. This has a double advantage. On the one hand, it facilitates the control of executives by the party, for, as members of the party, they are subject to its discipline; but, on the other hand, it also reinforces the executive's authority in the enterprise, because his management is fully supported by the leaders of the party cell. Thus, the conflicting directives of the party are to be worked out in joint consultation between party functionaries and executive officials, and, since they are held collectively responsible for their execution, party authorities are free to press them for the maximum fulfillment of *all* directives.[58]

---

[57] See *Die Organisationsarbeit der SED* (Schriftenreihe für den Parteiarbeiter, Heft 1; Berlin: Dietz Verlag, 1949), p. 46.

[58] It should be added that this joint consultation of functionaries and executives is a counterpart to the "mutual obligation" of management and labor which is incorporated in the collective agreements. The idea in both cases is to force every participant to make his every action public and to implant in him as much suspicion toward his collaborator as the party authorities have toward both of them. A revealing characterization of collective leadership along these lines comes from a Chinese Communist source: "By collective leadership we understand a system in which all principal questions must be decided by all leading personalities on the basis of careful examination and collective discussion. . . . No one should presume to decide principal questions by himself. . . . It goes

It is doubtful whether the built-in difficulties of this double hierarchy could be removed by the principle of collective leadership,[59] even if all executive officials were party members and participated in the activities of the basic party organization. To be sure, theoretically there should be no such difficulty, for the duties to be performed within each hierarchy are quite distinct. Executives will be judged by the tangible results of their organization; they will be condemned for all failures of execution, for they are the people responsible for getting things done. Party functionaries, on the other hand, are responsible for errors, negligence, deviation, opportunism, etc., in their agitational and organizational work. Strictly speaking, they can be guilty only of having failed to get others to do things. But in practice there is considerable overlap, for the deficient production record of an executive is frequently judged politically, whether he is a party member or not, and the success of a party secretary's agitational work is frequently judged in terms of the production record of the plant to which he is assigned. As Leopold Haimson has observed:

> . . . the Party organizer is made responsible for the success of plan fulfillment. Since he carries this responsibility, it is to his interest, as much as to the director's, to get reasonable targets and adequate resources and personnel for plan fulfillment. For this reason, the *Partorg* may appeal through Party channels when the plan targets assigned are *neobosnovanniye* [without foundation]. He may also request greater allocations or

without saying that collective leadership is the most important means to secure the unity and strength of the party. Collective leadership improves criticism and self-criticism at all levels of the party, the development of the party spirit and consciousness of the members, *and it facilitates the control of each functionary regardless of his position.* Moreover, collective leadership means collective study and mutual control . . . for the system enables each member of the party committee to impart his wisdom and experience to his comrades and to make up for his own weaknesses and shortcomings by learning to accept their wisdom and experience." Quoted from a Peking paper of November, 1953, in *Ost-Probleme,* Vol. VI (May, 1954), p. 731. My italics. Cf. also the comment of Karl Schirdewan in his discussion of "Collectivity—Highest Principle of Leadership in the Party": "In the future the control of the activities of a functionary should not merely concern itself with the fulfillment of his task, but with the manner in which he has fulfilled it. This method of control will be strengthened by the principle of collective leadership." See his *Die Vorbereitung des IV. Parteitages und die Wahl der leitenden Organe der Partei* (Speech at the Sixteenth Conference of the Central Committee of the SED; Berlin: Dietz Verlag, 1953), pp. 42–46.

[59] It should be added that at the level of ideology this principle is primarily applied to the party rather than to the collaboration between managers and party cadres, though it is instructive that, according to Ulbricht, the difficulties of this collaboration are supposed to be resolved by the same device.

resources and manpower, . . . but after the yearly plan targets and alloca-
tions have been set, the relationship between the *Partorg* and the "production chiefs" of the enterprise will tend to become considerably more
charged. The *Partorg* will usually press the management, and press them
very hard, to fulfill the assigned production targets and even to raise them,
for upon the fulfillment—and overfulfillment—of these targets will depend his own security and prospects of advancement. In this process, he
may use cajolements and threats, he may insist that the manager draw on
the "reserves" that they are keeping for emergencies, he may advocate
"shock" methods of organization of production and intensive exploitation
of machinery and men to a degree that even the more politically-minded
managers would not consider practical.[60]

This conflict is likely to come to the fore wherever the *Partorg* finds
himself compelled to use agitational methods to overcome technical or administrative obstacles. Because of his distance from the
actual performance of the work he seeks to maximize, it is relatively
easy for him to ignore these obstacles. And it is imperative that he
do so if his agitational methods of dealing with recurring bottlenecks
are to be effective. Those with direct responsibility for performance
will emphasize the practical limitations, while the *Partorg* views them
with studied neglect, and this makes for conflict between himself and
the executive officials.

Such conflict is welcome to the leaders of the party—despite Ulbricht's demand for collaboration between managers and party headquarters in the enterprise.[61] But the tension between party functionaries and executive officials also presents the party with managerial
problems of its own. By controlling everything without having any
operational functions, the leaders of the party have the advantage of
great flexibility. This advantage of the leaders, however, presents

[60] Haimson, *op. cit.,* pp. 462–63.

[61] For collaboration can turn into collusion and conflict is an effective antidote
to that real danger. That executive officials and party functionaries frequently
attempt to form collusive alliances which would protect them against the pressure
of the party and the planning agencies is suggested by Section I, 2(*k*) of the
Party Statute, adopted at the Fourth Party Congress in April, 1954. The section
reads: "The Party member is obligated unerringly to abide by the directive of
the Party concerning the correct selection of cadres in terms of their political and
technical qualifications. Whoever violates the Party's principles of cadre-policy,
whoever fails to exercise the necessary vigilance, *whoever selects fellow-workers
on the basis of friendship or personal loyalty because they are relatives or come
from the same area, must be called to account severely in accordance with the
spirit of the Party, and may be expelled from the Party.*" See Informationsbüro
West, *Das Statut der SED von 1946 bis 1954* (mimeographed), p. 4. Emphasis
in the original.

considerable difficulties to the functionaries. At the Tenth Conference, Ulbricht stated that the tolerance of mistakes and adverse conditions must be done away with and more exacting demands must be made of each party member. "Even some experienced colleagues and faithful comrades disregard the laws of social development and do not understand that *what was correct yesterday is already outdated and incorrect today.*" [62] Since the only correct and authoritative interpretation of these "laws" is rendered by the highest party authorities, it follows that every party functionary must develop the ability of changing his ideas and actions from one day to the next in line with party directives, or even of anticipating impending changes in these directives in order not to be caught off guard. Yet the flexibility which is demanded as a token of loyalty must be combined with the unbending determination not to tolerate mistakes and adverse conditions. For the party the danger of achieving complete flexibility is that of creating a corps of functionaries who are devoted yes-men, capable of following *every* directive and incapable of initiating anything.

Under this relentless pressure party functionaries typically resort to various expedients. Ulbricht complains that resolutions are adopted without immediately seeing to the details of implementing them. Even resolutions of the Central Committee are not acted upon for months at the lower levels of the party hierarchy, and then only by passing "formal" resolutions in turn. To prevent this evasion the Central Committee frequently dispatches special control commissions (*Instrukteurbrigaden*) into the local districts to examine the work of the local party organizations, and thus to check up on the regular reports which the Secretariat of the Central Committee receives from the party secretaries at the lower levels of the hierarchy.[63] Yet Ulbricht points out that these control commissions run the danger not only of checking up on the performance of local party organizations, but of doing their work over again. The implication is that the party cannot do its work, if it must correct the execution of its directives at the lower levels. For no hierarchical organization can function even inefficiently, if its superior authorities must spend a major part of their time in doing

[62] *Lehren des XIX Parteitages* . . . , p. 56. My italics. On another occasion Ulbricht opposed the "organizational dogmatism" of some comrades who "are of the opinion that what was correct one or two years ago must also be still correct today." And he added significantly: "Other comrades say, since something must be changed today, it was also wrong in times past." This is a significant commentary both on the flexibility desired and on the efforts of the comrades to be orthodox. Cf. *Organisationsarbeit der SED*, p. 28.

[63] *Lehren des XIX Parteitages* . . . , pp. 63–65.

better what its subordinates have done inadequately. Yet a dictatorial party cannot rid itself of the basic distrust with which it regards its own functionaries. Hence, its leaders demand the "fulfilment and over-fulfilment" of every directive, and they continue to suspect that the cadres act too little and too late.

Both this demand and this suspicion are reflected in the official ideology of the Socialist Unity party. The fact that the party has absolute power prompts its leading officials to act and speak as if the party were omnipotent. This belief was stated explicitly at the Tenth Conference of the Central Committee.

> . . . all party-comrades must be conscious of the fact not only that the party has the general task of agitation, but that it has the main responsibility for the interpretation of the laws and resolutions of the party and the government, as well as for their accurate execution.[64]

Or to cite a statement by one of the lesser functionaries:

> . . . as members of the Central Committee we must remember that in the end we are responsible for everything that is done in the ministries, main administrative units, and in the management of associations.[65]

Yet these assertions of the party's omnipotence stand in awkward contrast to the fact that party authorities are officially concerned with an apparently unending series of mistakes and shortcomings. How can the claim be reconciled with this spotty record of achievement? This question was answered by Ulbricht, who criticized the widespread belief that the government could do everything. People failed to understand that the laws of political economy are objective laws that cannot be changed arbitrarily.

> Men can discover the basic economic law of a given socio-economic formation [such as capitalism or feudalism], they can utilize this law, they can clear the way for other tendencies which are trying to break through, but they cannot cancel the economic laws or simply create new ones.[66]

For example, the government cannot lower the prices of consumer goods unless the costs of production have been decreased and produc-

[64] Statement of Walter Ulbricht in *ibid.*, p. 66.

[65] Statement by Herta Bergmann in *ibid.*, p. 145. The associations referred to are presumably the organizations in which the different enterprises in one branch of production are coordinated.

[66] *Ibid.*, p. 22. Ulbricht speaks of "anderen *Gesetzen*, die zum Durchbruch drängen," which is ungrammatical as well as obscurantist, but my translation renders the meaning. Ulbricht bases his statement on J. W. Stalin, *Ökonomische Probleme des Sozialismus in der UdSSR* (Berlin: Dietz Verlag, 1953), pp. 3–11.

tion increased. Also an increase in wages is not a mere matter of governmental decree; it can occur only to the extent that productivity has increased first.[67]

It is apparent that this theory and the specific statements about the limitations of government are immediately serviceable to a dictatorial regime. At the time (1952), the theory and its application explained both the omnipotence of the dictatorial party and its inability to improve living conditions; for the party purports to utilize basic economic laws when it issues directives, but declares itself unable to "cancel existing laws or create new ones" when it decides not to issue directives. However, for party functionaries, government officials, and industrial managers this latitude of interpretation is inadmissible. They must bear in mind that "the word *impossible* is to be banned once and for all from the vocabulary of the German language." [68] They must follow party directives and they cannot presume to say that certain directives are contrary to economic laws. In other words, party functionaries must display a passionate intolerance toward "adverse conditions" and leave it to the Politbureau to have the necessary insight into the limitations of bureaucratic planning.

It may be useful to outline the principles of manipulation which have been discussed in this section.

(*a*) The party operates the two hierarchies of authority so that all decision-making within the party is secret while all decision-making within the executive agencies of the government is subject to surveillance by a party organizer.

(*b*) The party employs the suspicion of sabotage as a principal means of ensuring the subordination of executive officials, and it seeks to maximize their performance by demanding the impossible. Obviously, the suspicion is perpetuated because performance falls short of the goal, and excessive goals continue to be set because collusion and withdrawal of efficiency are suspected.

(*c*) The party's felt need to maximize subordination as well as the pressure for performance also leads to a multiplication of controls. The two hierarchies enable the party to supplement the usual controls from the top down by charging its functionaries at various levels with supervisory responsibilities in addition to their agitational and organizational work. Hence, there is a tendency to conclude every critical

[67] Ulbricht in *Lehren des XIX Parteitages* . . . , pp. 19–24, 34–36.

[68] Statement of Walter Ulbricht in *Der Fünfjahrplan und die Perspektiven der Volkswirtschaft* (Berlin: Dietz Verlag, 1951), p. 91.

appraisal of executive officials with a demand for remedial action by
the party.

(d) The official call for action by party functionaries consists typically of the demand to help, but not to interfere with, the executive
officials. This demand leads to conflicts between functionaries and
executives, which are denied in theory but encouraged in practice. The
burden of responsibility for the reconciliation of conflicting demands
is imposed upon executive officials and party functionaries, which again
maximizes the control over both as well as the pressure for performance. That pressure is maintained specifically by the agitational and
organizational work of the party functionaries; hence, the manipulation
by the party leaders depends ultimately upon their control of the party
cadres. This control is examined in the next section.

d. Party and Trade-union in Response to a Crisis

In manipulating the economy the Politbureau seeks to concentrate
the power of decision-making and control entirely in its hands, while
it imposes the burden of implementing the excessive goals and the incompatible directives of the shifting party line upon the functionaries of
the party. Under these circumstances it is to be expected that the
conflict between functionaries and executive officials is paralleled by a
kind of tacit struggle between the party leaders and its functionaries.
Lest the party be compelled to spend too much of its effort on the supervision of its functionaries, it must get them to exercise some initiative.
Thus, party spokesmen complain with heavy irony that functionaries
must have a head on their shoulders; they should not say every time
that they are still waiting for specific instructions.[69] And on occasion
the Politbureau will ostentatiously refuse the request for a decision but
insist instead that the basic organization of the party make its own
decision first, which may then be scrutinized by the authorities.[70] The
party, however, can never go far in this direction without declaring that
it is imperative to control the execution of directives in every detail.
The initiative of lower functionaries contains the twin dangers of evasion and deviation, and it is necessary to be on vigilant guard against
both.

> . . . frequently one finds remarks to the effect that the control [over
> the execution of] resolutions should be put into effect after a certain amount
> of time has elapsed. . . . But we believe that this is an incorrect ap-

[69] Cf. *Die Organisationsarbeit der SED*, p. 35 (see also n. 62).

[70] *Ibid.*, p. 19. "Basic organization" (*Grundorganisation*) is party jargon for
"party cell."

proach; for the control over the execution of resolutions should begin *already the day after* the resolution was passed.[71]

But these ubiquitous controls virtually envelop each functionary, and they help to create the lack of initiative which is officially deplored. For the functionaries of the party will endeavor to act according to instructions in a more or less literal sense,[72] and without instructions they will try to avoid action altogether since the slightest deviation can have grave consequences. The party seeks to overcome these tendencies among functionaries by insisting that they stay in continuous contact with the organization and, hence, by exerting unrelenting pressure upon them. The resulting cooperation between the party and its subordinate organizations may be illustrated by the recent history of the relations between the party and the East German trade-union federation (*Freier Deutscher Gewerkschaftsbund* or FDGB).

The Socialist Unity party had engaged in a program of rapid economic development since its "election" in October, 1950. This program was incorporated in a Five-Year Plan after the Soviet model which placed a disproportionate emphasis on heavy industry and a corresponding de-emphasis on the production of consumer goods. The plan also involved an intensified drive for greater productivity, which rapidly deprived the workers of the East Zone of the right to strike or to influence the determination of wages and working conditions, and which subjected them to a carefully elaborated system of norm increases that rewarded the best workers lavishly and decreased the take-home pay for the majority.

The functionaries of the FDGB were charged with primary responsibility for enlisting the support of the workers for the party's Five-Year Plan and specifically for the repeated increases in productivity which the Plan demanded. Specifically, in 1951, the FDGB used all methods of agitation and ill-disguised extortion to introduce the new "collective agreements" which involved important additional advantages for the management of industry—and, hence, for the party and the government—but equally important disadvantages for the workers. As a result, the FDGB became identified in the eyes of East German workers as an executive agent of the party and the government, not as an organization representing their interests.[73] The methods used by the

[71] *Ibid.,* pp. 80–81. My italics.
[72] Hence, there are frequent admonitions to the effect that resolutions must be written so that they can be acted upon.
[73] Details on this point are contained in Alfred Leutwein, *Der Betriebskollektivvertrag in der sowjetischen Besatzungszone* (Bonner Berichte aus Mittel- und

functionaries of the party and the trade-union readily explain the antagonism of the workers quite aside from the material deprivations which this agitation imposed upon them. For instance, the term "extortion" was used by a construction worker in East Berlin who was requested by a party functionary to give his consent to a norm increase on the ground that certain other work groups had already given theirs. The fact was that they had not. Another, and perhaps one of the most favored methods, is to hold public meetings at which the spokesmen of the party and the trade-union advance the party line of the moment and at which strategically placed "activists" among the workers speak up "spontaneously" in support of it. Under the eyes of the activists, the functionaries, and the secret police, no one is likely to stand up and "be counted" as opposing the officially sponsored resolution.

Toward the end of 1951 the antagonism of the workers against the FDGB and its employed or coopted functionaries had become sufficiently pronounced to receive official notice. In an article by Rudolf Herrnstadt, the editor of *Neues Deutschland,* the official publication of the SED, a campaign was launched to restore the FDGB to its function of representing the interests of the workers. Union functionaries were denounced as "heartless bureaucrats" who would not even listen to the requests and complaints of the members, let alone deal with them. They were denounced officially for their deliberate neglect or extenuation of real hardships. And their commandeering manner was now vilified, although shortly before just that manner had been indispensable to push through collective agreements, norm increases, and like measures in the face of the workers' passive resistance. At the same time, leading spokesmen of the FDGB attacked the practice of union-shop committees to work hand in hand with management, although the same men had previously encouraged just that practice. The representation of the workers' interests by the trade-union was soon concentrated primarily on the remaining private enterprises, where it served the SED as an additional weapon in its effort to nationalize or liquidate these enterprises. The FDGB was relieved of certain tasks, on the other hand, which had previously deepened the cleavage between the trade-union and the workers. The FDGB had been the spearhead in the liquidation of the legal provisions protecting the workers' rights. Now that the determination of labor conditions had become a matter of state regulation, the task of the FDGB was eased, especially since the rul-

Ostdeutschland; Bonn: Bundesministerium für gesamtdeutsche Fragen, 1954), and in Haas and Leutwein, *op. cit.,* pp. 14–23.

ings announced in May, 1952, constituted an improvement of working conditions compared with those of 1951.

Toward the end of 1952, this change in the position of the FDGB was modified in turn when it became clear that the Plan was not being fulfilled for that year, and especially that the wage fund stipulated in the Plan was exceeded to a considerable extent.[74] Hence, the decision was made by the leaders of the SED to withdraw the previous concessions to the workers and once more to issue the demand for increased productivity. The resumption of the production drive by the party simply meant that once again the trade-unions would spearhead it, although they had not recovered from their last loss of popularity. This change of the party line was reflected in a press release of January 15, 1953, in which the SED scored the ideological carelessness of the *Tribüne,* the official publication of the FDGB. In this release everything was again condemned that had been commended previously (in the editorial of Herrnstadt). The *Tribüne* was rebuked for its emphasis upon the representational function of the trade-union, when the important thing was ideological clarity, the correct attitude toward work, toward work-norms, and toward the principle of pay according to output (*Leistungslohn*). The release also criticized the slogans of the paper which tended to emphasize the differences of interest between management and the trade-union shop committees, and it attacked the practice of the FDGB of criticizing managers rather than trade-union functionaries, although that practice had been initiated by the party only a year before.[75]

In other words, the change of the party line in the first months of 1953, which eventually provoked the widespread uprisings of June 17, meant simply that the party employed the FDGB in pursuit of the new task, as the party had formerly employed it in pursuit of the old. From the viewpoint of organizational efficiency, this emphasizes the crucial importance of Ulbricht's reminder "that what was correct yesterday is already outdated and incorrect today." The crisis of June 17 provides us with a striking illustration of the importance of this dictum. The crisis was intensive enough to provide a critical test for the regime and to help bring to the fore problems and relationships which are more readily disguised in normal times. I shall briefly review the events

[74] Cf. the similar remark by Bruno Leuschner in the meeting of the Central Committee in 1952, cited above, pp. 376–77

[75] The preceding account of the development from 1951 to 1953 is based in part on Gerhard Haas, *Der FDGB im Jahre 1954* (Bonn: Bundesministerium fuer gesamtdeutsche Fragen, 1954).

leading to the uprising and then examine the relations between the party and the FDGB as these stand revealed in the official declarations both before and after June 17.

During the winter of 1952 and during the first months of 1953, dissatisfaction rose rapidly. One index of growing dissatisfaction was the sudden increase in the number of refugees from the Soviet Zone. In the period from 1949 to 1952 that number had fluctuated between 51 and 76 thousand during the first half of these years, and between 74 and 96 thousand during the second half. From January to May of 1953, 184,793 refugees were counted, or about 1,230 per day on the average.[76] Another index of growing dissatisfaction during early 1953 was repeated instances of more or less open protest on the part of workers, and the increasing frequency with which the East Zone press reported instances in which party or trade-union functionaries were afraid to agitate for higher productivity.[77]

In April and May several measures of the government increased these general dissatisfactions. On April 9, the Council of Ministers decided to withdraw rationing cards from several groups of the population, a measure which apparently aroused such protest that it was reversed in a meeting on May 28. In this same meeting the famous decision was reached to increase by 10 per cent the average work-norms in the "decisive" branches of production, a step which was officially characterized as designed for the "maximum satisfaction of the material and cultural needs of the toilers." [78] By June 9, the Central Committee of the SED,

[76] It is of interest that the social composition of these refugees was almost representative of the population in the Soviet Zone, although salaried employees were somewhat over-represented as compared with workers and independent entrepreneurs. The 1946 Census of the Soviet Zone indicates 18 per cent independents, 20 per cent salaried employees, and 62 per cent workers, while a 1952 sample study of 1,074 refugees to the West shows 13 per cent independents, 34 per cent salaried employees, and 53 per cent workers. (Subsequent Census reports did not contain a break between salaried employees and workers.) See Stephanie Muenke, *Symptomatische Aussagen über wirtschaftliche und soziale Verhältnisse in der Sowjetzone 1952* (Sonderheft 19, Deutsches Institut für Wirtschaftsforschung; Berlin: Duncker and Humblot, n.d.), p. 16.

[77] Cf. the first thirteen documents reprinted in *Der Volksaufstand vom 17. Juni, 1953* (Denkschrift über den Juni-Aufstand in der Sowjetischen Besatzungszone und in Ostberlin; Bonn: Bundesministerium für gesamtdeutsche Fragen, 1953), pp. 17–29.

[78] *Ibid.,* p. 32. It may be added that this was the first case in which norm increases were issued by government decree. Previously, they had been "organized from below" by means of trade-union and party agitation in favor of "voluntarily assumed obligations" in the collective agreements.

and on subsequent days the Council of Ministers and the municipal council of East Berlin, declared that the party and the government had committed a number of errors, which these authorities were prepared to acknowledge and correct publicly. The errors specifically mentioned were the new regulation of rationing cards, certain measures affecting agriculture and private commerce, and severe methods of tax collection, errors which had prompted "numerous persons" to leave the Republic (Soviet Zone).[79]

It must be emphasized that these pronouncements contained *no* mention of the norm increases which had just been decreed, and it is clear that they were addressed primarily to the large numbers of businessmen, technicians, and salaried employees who were leaving East Germany. In fact, the agitation among the workers, which had been in evidence for months, continued unabated. During these weeks, certain construction workers in the Stalin Allee (Berlin) had specifically protested against the methods by which functionaries of the party sought to induce workers to increase their norms "voluntarily." [80] Nevertheless, on June 16, the official publication of the FDGB brought a statement which "acknowledged" that some workers had protested against the norm increases of May 28.[81] According to the *Tribüne,* this protest

[79] *Ibid.,* p. 35. Reference to the documentary evidence probably makes the changes prior to June 17 appear as more abrupt than they were in fact. Rumors concerning changes in Soviet policy were widespread, and there was a noticeable uncertainty among party officials following the death of Stalin and the subsequent changes of the party line. Apparently many workers were encouraged to act more openly as long as they believed that the regime faced a serious crisis and might not survive it. Cf. "Der Aufstand im Juni," *Der Monat,* V (September, 1953), p. 597, and Stefan Brant, *Der Aufstand* (Stuttgart: Steingrüben Verlag, 1954), pp. 40–81.

[80] *Der Volksaufstand . . . ,* pp. 41–43. This report on the relation between East Berlin construction workers and party functionaries was published in *Neues Deutschland* (June 14, 1953) under the title "Es wird Zeit den Holzhammer beiseite zu legen."

[81] Here and elsewhere in this section I am treating the relations between party leaders and subordinate functionaries as a problem of organizational management in a dictatorial regime. The same facts can be interpreted differently: instead of the word *acknowledge* I might have said that the leaders of the FDGB *supported* the protest of the workers and thereby expressed the policy of a faction which opposed the party leaders in the only way open to them under the circumstances. In certain instances opposition groups form within the party or its subordinate organizations and their existence must be inferred from differences in policy or personal position which are brought to light in more or less subtle ways (e.g., guarded statements in the press, significant changes in the order of precedence at official functions, etc.). But it is misleading indeed to think that every evidence

took the form of asking whether the decrees concerning increases in work-norms were still correct and valid in the light of the declarations of the Politbureau and the Council of Ministers of June 9 and 11. The point is (though the *Tribüne* did not mention this) that the declarations had made no reference to this question; apparently the workers were using the official admission of mistakes as a means to obtain concessions in the question of work-norms. At any rate, in officially responding to this protest the *Tribüne* declared that the resolutions concerning the increase of work-norms were absolutely correct. Moreover, it was now imperative to act upon the resolution concerning the 10 per cent increase in work-norms, since the declarations of June 9 and 11 were designed to improve the living conditions of the population. On June 16, the day of this editorial in the FDGB paper, there were work stoppages, demonstrations, and uprisings which spread to 295 localities throughout the East Zone on the following days.[82]

The Politbureau issued a declaration on June 16 which reiterated the need for norm increases on a voluntary basis, but which stated that it was entirely mistaken to effect a 10 per cent increase of work-norms by administrative fiat. By inviting the government and the trade-unions to reconsider the decision of May 28, the declaration made it obvious that this decision was still in force on June 16.

It is of interest to follow the same series of events as they are reflected in successive official statements by the spokesman of the trade-unions and of the party. The November, 1952, Conference of the Central Committee, which I have examined in the previous section,

of conflict between higher and lower echelons of the hierarchy of party organizations points to the existence of opposition groups. These conflicts may give rise to the formation of a faction, but they recur regularly even without that result— as a response to the logic of the organizational tasks at different levels of the hierarchy. In the case under discussion there is no indication that Warnke, the leader of the FDGB, was a member of the opposition group of Herrnstadt and Zaisser, who were expelled from the Central Committee in July, 1953, and from the SED in January, 1954.

[82] According to reports available to the Bundesministerium für gesamtdeutsche Fragen, work stoppages occurred in 138 communities; work stoppages and demonstrations in 83; work stoppages, demonstrations, and uprisings (such as attacks on the police, etc.) in 51; and all three forms of protest together with successful or attempted release of political prisoners in 23. It may be added that 328 towns were placed under martial law, while Soviet military forces were employed in 153 communities. The disturbances were in all likelihood spontaneous. Their simultaneous spread throughout the zone, however, may be attributed to the news reporting of the events in East Berlin by RIAS, the American-sponsored radio station in West Berlin.

occurred at a time of widespread dissatisfactions among the workers and other segments of the population. Nevertheless, the party reversed its previous leniency and insisted once again upon an intensified drive for greater productivity. Since the functionaries of the FDGB were called upon to spearhead this new productivity drive, it is obvious that they had to bear the brunt of dissatisfaction among the workers. In the light of these circumstances there is special significance in the declaration of Herbert Warnke, the head of the FDGB, at the November, 1952, Conference that "it is impossible to improve the work of the trade-unions without the help of the party and in particular of the party cadres in the enterprises." [83] The statement suggests that in periods of crisis trade-unionists will seek active help from the party since its directives force them to incur an extra measure of unpopularity among the workers.

The drive for productivity, however, did not let up during the early months of 1953 and led, as we have seen, to a rapid increase in the number of persons leaving the East Zone. Nevertheless, the party decided to answer these difficulties with still more stringent measures in April and May and consequently the difficulties in the work of the trade-unions increased still further. An article by Warnke published in May, 1953, indicates that the functionaries of the FDGB had become very reluctant to cope with these mounting difficulties. [84] Many trade-union shop committees (*Betriebsgewerkschaftsleitungen* or BGL) had been preparing the forthcoming collective agreements without having any information concerning the discussions on this topic at the preceding FDGB Convention. For instance, a county secretary in Dresden had reported on this Convention for exactly five minutes, and then he had violated its clear instructions enjoining upon all units the urgent need for savings, by demanding increased contributions from headquarters. In Magdeburg, seminars concerning the new collective agreements had been conducted by people who had not read the relevant speeches at the Convention. It was no wonder they believed that this year's agreements should be copied from last year's. But this would mean that the new agreements would not contain either increased worknorms or more voluntarily assumed obligations (*Selbstverpflichtungen*). Another example: Stalin had demanded a close tie between workers and peasants. To implement this the FDGB was urging enterprises to act

---

[83] *Lehren des XIX Parteitages* . . . , p. 109.

[84] The following discussion is a brief synopsis of Herbert Warnke, "Grössere Sorge um die Erziehung und Schulung unserer Kader," *Die Arbeit*, Vol. VII (May, 1953), pp. 333–36.

as sponsors of collective farms and to incorporate such a sponsorship in their collective agreements. But in the publishing house of the FDGB itself the work force had refused to accept such a sponsorship! Comrade Malenkov had called such a disregard of resolutions "the worst form of bureaucratism." The functionaries of the Railroad Union had even ignored a resolution of the Central Committee, according to which the Director of the enterprise has sole responsibility for its operation. It had been necessary to discuss with them at great length that they had no right to alter the administrative structure of the state railroad.

> It is apparent that some functionaries have not yet understood that the [workers'] right of codetermination does not consist in interference with the management of the enterprise or in signing all sorts of papers. Rather it is necessary to elevate this right to codetermination to the level of co-responsibility, which is to be made manifest in the fulfillment of all obligations arising from the collective agreement, i.e., in the fulfillment of the plan for the enterprise especially through the organization of production contests, through conferences on production problems, and through the realization of the social and cultural measures envisaged by the plan.[85]

This recital of woes by the head of the FDGB is noteworthy precisely because it is identical with literally hundreds of other declarations despite the fact that at the same time high party authorities were actively considering the mounting crisis facing the regime. The remedies suggested for the improvement of trade-union work are also identical with those suggested many times before: functionaries should study Lenin and Stalin, they should comprehend the resolutions, every functionary should be given a study program which would be controlled to insure that he does his lessons properly, students in the trade-union schools should be selected more carefully, and so on and on. In the face of an impending revolt trade-unionists are told that they should study more at the risk of doing less so that what they do will at least be right. It must be assumed that a man as highly placed as Warnke would have had some intimation that a crisis was approaching; or, if not, that the mere accumulation of difficulties would have prompted him to resort to special measures in order to overcome them. But the characteristic fact is that Warnke said exactly the same thing he had been saying for years, and the inference certainly suggests itself that he was not free to say anything else. It is in keeping with this

---

[85] *Ibid.*, pp. 334–35. The term "Wettbewerbe" cannot be translated by competitions, although the plural is used occasionally. But, by making the plural a standard phrase, the East Zone party jargon has changed the meaning of the term so that "production contests" is the nearest English equivalent.

interpretation that the writers of the FDGB still declared on June 16 in the *Tribüne* that the 10 per cent increase in work-norms would continue to be in effect.[86] Apparently, the pressure on the FDGB to agitate for increased work-norms was unrelieved up to the day the Politbureau decided to call it off for the time being.

It will also be of interest to observe how the relationship of the party and the FDGB was handled by the official spokesmen *after* June 17. The Central Committee of the SED held a meeting on July 24–26, in which the events of June 17 were discussed at some length. In his address to the Committee Ulbricht criticized the trade-union shop committees in the enterprises among other things. As I review this criticism, it is well to bear in mind that this is the response of the most powerful leader of a dictatorial party to a widespread rebellion as well as the justification for one more change in the party line.

On June 17 the "Fascist agents" had aimed especially at the trade-unions, according to Ulbricht. These agents had been discrediting the unions by making them responsible for the norm increases which the decision to construct a socialist society had entailed. But neither the heads of the FDGB nor the leaders of the industrial unions had, in fact, participated in working out the decrees which had aroused the opposition of the workers. It would seem that this statement was intended to safeguard the unions from unjustified attack; however, it was immediately followed by the official criticism of the FDGB, whose mistaken policy had provided an opportunity for the "Fascist agents."

> The mistake of the trade-union leadership was that in its effort to put into effect the slogan "Produce more so as to live better" it had become the elongated arm of management. The unions did not represent the daily interests of the workers sufficiently.[87]

A short six months before, the party had condemned the FDGB journal for its mistaken talk about "representing the interests of the workers." As a consequence, the FDGB had concentrated on increasing production and had neglected the interests of the workers. And now, just

---

[86] In a radio interview on June 17, Otto Nuschke, the Deputy Prime Minister of the East Zone government, declared that the uprisings had been precipitated by this statement in *Die Tribüne*. He also stated, as many other spokesmen did after him, that the whole thing was unnecessary because the increase in work-norms had long since been rescinded. This contention was simply false, but, after the uprising, various spokesmen wanted to make it appear as if the declarations of June 9 and 11 had contained a revocation of the increase in work-norms. The interview with Nuschke is reprinted in *Der Volksaufstand . . .* , pp. 44–45.

[87] Ulbricht in *Der Neue Kurs . . .* , pp. 91–92.

after the uprising against this drive for greater productivity, the spokesman of the party was "protecting" the FDGB by exempting it from responsibility for this drive while accusing it of having neglected the interests of the workers. This, indeed, illustrates the characteristic relationship between a dictatorial party and all subordinate organizations, for the latter are held responsible for the consequences of high policy decisions at the same time that they are exempted from having participated in them. The point is that the highest party authorities change their policy from time to time, but on the day after the change they will steadfastly hold the subordinate organizations responsible for having failed to act in the past in accordance with the new party line.

It is of interest to compare this position of the party leader with a major article by Herbert Warnke, "The Trade Unions and the New Party Line," in which the head of the FDGB commented in turn on the events of June 17 and their aftermath. Like Ulbricht, he begins with a recital of the major successes achieved by trade-unions. In turning to the mistakes of trade-union work, Warnke copies Ulbricht directly by declaring that the unions had helped to increase production, but had not seen to the improvement of living conditions. He repeats the standard enumeration of failings: trade-union functionaries work bureaucratically; they violate intra-union democracy; everything is done by hired secretaries, not by unpaid unionists; collective agreements are imposed without the active consent of the workers and they fail to remove bad working conditions; the union functionaries do not see to the fulfillment of obligations, and so on and on. But in addition to these standard phrases an attempt is made to rehabilitate the badly damaged position of the FDGB. The FDGB had favored the increase of work-norms because it favored the increase of productivity. But the Federation had not agreed with the ministries, secretariats, and managers, which had maintained that an increase in work-norms had inevitably to be accompanied by an indirect decrease in total wages.[88]

---

[88] Warnke makes this accusation against "Wirtschaftsorgane" and the context makes it clear that he refers to the agencies which regulate work-norms under the State Planning Commission. The term is deliberately vague, however, presumably just in case someone should take exception to this statement; but despite this vagueness it is clear that *no* reference is made to the party. Naturally, it is the party which is responsible for the policy of increasing norms and holding the "wage fund" constant, although this is nowhere stated explicitly. However, Otto Grotewohl's speech before the Fifteenth Conference of the Central Committee at least intimates that this is, in fact, a general opinion in the ruling circles of the SED. In announcing the "new course," Grotewohl points out that the reduction of work-norms to their previous level, the withdrawal of previous reclassifications

This is clearly an answer to the accusation that the FDGB had neglected the interests of the workers by engaging in a drive for increased productivity in collusion with management. The claim is made that the "Wirtschaftsorgane" were at fault. They had introduced higher work-norms bureaucratically, i.e., without consulting the trade-unions and without simultaneously improving the organization of production, which would have made it possible at least to maintain wages at the same nominal level. Of course, Warnke throws in a proper measure of public self-criticism by admitting that the unions had not represented their views forcefully enough. But the burden of the argument is "to pass the buck." The ministries and the managers had ignored the trade-union's "right to codetermination" and had decreed the notorious norm increases unilaterally.[89] And after attributing the major blame for the events of June 17 to the "Wirtschaftsorgane," the head of the FDGB expressed his satisfaction with a resolution of the party's Central Committee (passed after June 17), in which the party blamed its own functionaries in the approved manner for some of the deficiencies of trade-union work.

> Party-functionaries have frequently kept the trade unions in leading-strings instead of helping them, and they have violated intra-union democracy by administrative intervention. These methods of party work must forever belong to the past. . . .

of workers in lower wage groups, the restoration of previous low railroad fares, etc., were costing the state enormous sums. While this is mentioned in the context of admitting that the planned economic development had been set at too rapid a rate and had led to hardships, it is pretty clear that with another change in the party line these hardships may again appear as indispensable for the building of socialism and the destruction of class enemies. The point is that for these reasons both maximum productivity and maximum savings have been advocated simultaneously so that an increase of work-norms and the reduction of the wage bill go hand in hand. For Grotewohl's statement see Der Neue Kurs . . . , pp. 15–16.

[89] Herbert Warnke, "Die Gewerkschaften und der neue Kurs," Die Arbeit, Vol. VII (September, 1953), p. 606. This "right to codetermination" is incorporated in the statutes of the FDGB, but it is interpreted to mean "co-responsibility" in implementing managerial directives in 9 cases out of 10. On occasion, it can be used, however, in effecting an adaptation to a change of the party line, as in the present instance. Also, Warnke maintains that the wage increases, the withdrawal of wage reductions, and other measures favorable to the workers which were initiated after June 17, had been decided upon at the suggestion of the FDGB, although Ulbricht had publicly excluded the FDGB from participation in policy decisions only in July. Such verbal defenses, however, are apparently standard devices of Communist functionaries, and they seem to be quite safe as long as they employ the proper party jargon and follow the party line of the moment; it is quite immaterial that they may be contrary to fact.

The Party can give decisive aid to the trade unions in changing their work by eliminating once and for all its commandeering of trade union functionaries. . . .[90]

I have surveyed the official responses of the party and the FDGB to the uprisings of June 17, in order to interpret the frequent demand that the functionaries who have been criticized publicly should maintain "contact with the party." It is apparent that this demand is not easy to follow. If the consequences of this system were not so deadly serious, affecting as they do the very lives of guilty and innocent alike, one would be tempted to think of this network of interlocking hierarchies as a kind of charade. Every level of organization in this regime is accused at one time or another of interfering with the work of some other. Party functionaries should not interfere with the work of ministries, managers, or trade-unions, but they are instructed to "aid" the work of each. Trade-unions should not interfere with the work of management, but they should not permit the managers to increase work-norms without consulting them. Government officials should not interfere with the management of the enterprises, which are formally subordinate to them. But they have exclusive responsibility for seeing to the execution of the plan and should, therefore, explain their decrees as well as mobilize managers and workers in the enterprise in order to put the decrees into effect.[91] Hence, properly speaking, every functionary is instructed not to interfere with the work of another but to "aid" him in the appropriate way. In every case the party reserves for itself the right to judge and to distinguish "aid" from "interference." Naturally, that distinction changes with the exigencies of the party line and of each situation, so that every subordinate functionary is necessarily uncertain whether he is "interfering" or "aiding" in the approved manner. The party will judge him only after he has committed himself to a course of action so that its absolute authority and his absolute uncertainty condition one another.

But the uncertainties of functionaries do not arise only from their "contacts with the party." They arise also from their "contacts with the masses." The regime seeks to use its absolute control of functionaries and executive officials to direct the vast majority of people who do not

[90] Quoted in *ibid.*, p. 609. Cf. the similar remarks of Walter Ulbricht in *Der Neue Kurs* . . . , pp. 92–93 (see n. 88), in which some of these commandeering methods are specified. Ulbricht emphasizes especially that party leaders were in the habit of transferring trade-union functionaries from one position to another and that the party cadres would often simply take over the work of the trade-unions in the enterprises instead of helping them to do their work better.

[91] Statement by Ulbricht in *Der Neue Kurs* . . . , pp. 81–82.

belong to the party or work for the government. The managerial ideologies of the party are revealed especially in its attempts at manipulating this contact between the functionaries and the masses.

e. The "Contact with the Masses"

Spokesmen of the party constantly repeat in well-publicized critiques that the functionaries and officials lack "contact with the masses." The admonition to establish this contact, to strengthen it, to make it "still closer" is offered as the standard remedy that will correct mistakes, overcome weakness, prevent opportunism, help to overfulfill the plan and generally strengthen "Bolshevik partisanship." But the admonition has two quite different meanings: contact with the party and contact with the people who belong to no organization. A statement by Otto Grotewohl is a case in point.

> Comrades begin to believe in the omnipotence of administration, in the omnipotence of the bureaucratic apparatus, from the moment they enter the state apparatus; and they act accordingly. They forget too soon that the confidence of the working masses is our most envigorating element, that administrative work can be developed successfully only through the closest cooperation with the laboring people [werktätige Menschen].
> This question of confidence in our workers is also conditioned naturally by the deficient cooperation of leading government officials with our organizations [i.e., the party].
> Some comrades say, for example, that they have no time to meet their obligations as comrades in our basic organizations. This idea is false and very harmful. We must demand with all emphasis that our administrative employees in the state apparatus comply with their obligations to the party. Otherwise, there is the great danger of a separation from the party and in the end a separation from the working masses.[92]

Grotewohl's emphasis is clearly on "cooperation with the party," and on "cooperation with the laboring people" only "in the end" and through the party. This is in keeping with the official doctrine, according to which the party as the "most progressive" section represents the interests of the working class as a whole. Still, the weight of doctrine and the exigencies of rule make it unavoidable time and again to acknowledge the existence of the "laboring people" as distinct from the party. To speak of the party as the "most progressive" section implies that there are many workers who are "not yet progressive," who "still" retain remnants of a "capitalist consciousness." And even the members of the party, who constitute the vanguard of the working class, require

[92] *Lehren des XIX Parteitages* . . . , pp. 180–81.

constant efforts of inculcating that partisanship which is supposed to distinguish them from the workers who are not party members.

The *direct* contact between the party and the masses becomes an acute problem wherever the regime comes face to face with the task of influencing workers. This problem is avoided as long as possible. Functionaries much prefer to deal with other functionaries and, if not with them, then at least with those people whose membership in the party or one of its affiliated organizations makes them especially susceptible to the thousand and one pressures the party can bring to bear. This preference and the party's constant efforts to counteract it reflect a high degree of hostility to the regime, especially among the industrial workers of the zone, and it *may be* that this strong, albeit for the most part passive, resistance distinguishes the satellite countries from Russia herself.

Many factors account for this condition of the regime, which found dramatic expression in the uprisings of June 17. The country is occupied by a foreign power, and this is not disguised by the fact that all authority is ostensibly exercised by the German leaders of a dictatorial party.[93] At least of equal importance are the traditions of the German labor movement, which were built up over a fifty-year period and which are very much alive despite the destruction of that movement by the Nazi regime. A majority of the *older* workers were organized before 1933 in trade-unions and many of the younger workers come from families in which a trade-union tradition is still strong. As a result, workers continually assess the performance of the Communist regime in terms of a very damaging, critical standard. Hostility toward the regime is high also because the SED includes many people with anti-Communist leanings, and its purges of the rank and file as well as its systematic training of selected party members have not gone very far

[93] It may be mentioned that leading functionaries of the SED, such as Ulbricht, Pieck, Zaisser, and others, acquired Soviet citizenship while in Russian exile during the Nazi period. In 1953 there were 12 out of 81 members and candidates of the Central Committee and 8 out of 13 members and candidates of the Politbureau who were Soviet citizens at the same time that they were leading officials of a supposedly sovereign regime. Spokesmen of the party have declared repeatedly that "unconditional friendship to the Soviet Union" was regarded as the touchstone of political reliability. See, for example, Ulbricht's statement in *Die Organisationsarbeit der SED*, p. 21. This friendship is not reciprocated, however. According to one report, 30 leading Soviet employees of the Soviet-directed uranium enterprise, SAG Wismut, were ordered back to Russia in January, 1953, because they had violated existing regulations, according to which Soviet citizens "were strictly forbidden to engage in any personal contacts with the residents of the enemy-country."

as yet, even though there have been extensive efforts in these directions.[94] And despite the importance of authoritarianism in her cultural tradition, it should be added that in Germany a Communist regime cannot rely on a deep-seated tolerance for personal abuse and public self-abasement, especially if these are publicly identified with Soviet domination.[95] But if these factors distinguish the East Zone from Soviet Russia, they also make it apparent that such a regime can function, and function successfully, even if the "toiling masses," to whom Communist orators make such frequent and possessive references, are almost wholly opposed to it.

The functionaries of the party are separated by fear and hostility from the rank and file of party members and from the "laboring people." Evidence on this score may be gleaned again from the public discussions of the party. At the Tenth Conference of the Central Committee, speaker after speaker had insisted that the bureaucratic manner of officials can and must be checked through closer and constant "contact with the masses." For instance, leading officials in the mining industry and in the Ministry of Mines are accused of having failed to base

[94] According to *The New York Times,* March 15, 1954, Ulbricht stated in September, 1953, that 400,000 out of 1,230,000 members of the SED were former Social Democrats. This is a substantial number, though it represents a decline from 52.3 to 32.5 per cent in the period from 1946 to 1953. In its efforts to purge its ranks, the party lost over 500,000 members between 1949 and 1953. See *Die ideologische und organisatorische Entwicklung der SED* (Sopade Informationsdienst, Denkschrift 40; Bonn: Vorstand der Sozialdemokratischen Partei Deutschlands, n.d.), p. 12. Yet despite this purge, Ulbricht speaks of only 150,000 to 200,000 party members who have been separately organized within the party because they are regarded as reliable. At the Fourth Party Congress (1954) Schirdewan put the number of activists even lower, at 90,000. See Stern, *op. cit.,* p. 150.

[95] The close imitation of the Russian model extends to matters of personal conduct: functionaries of the SED are judged by Soviet standards, and their subservience to Soviet stereotypes is another reason for the hostility of workers. For example, their public self-criticism must contain fulsome praise of leaders such as Lenin, Stalin, Pieck, and others, equally fulsome thanks to "our Soviet friends," ringing declarations concerning the unfaltering leadership of the party, and personally humiliating recantations. There are other touches of Sovietization. For example, Gerhard Eisler, lecturer in the party's subdivision for agitation, was publicly accused of dictatorial methods and an unwillingness to acknowledge his mistakes. In his public recantation Eisler admitted his mistakes not only in his present work but also in his deviation from the line of the German Communist party in 1928. Incidents of this kind are the subject of many jokes which circulate in the East Zone, a form of "public protest" well known in Germany from the Hitler period.

their work upon the support of the masses. And their deliberate reduction of planning figures is said to stem from their "lack of confidence
in the creative abilities of our laboring people." [96] But "creative abilities" is simply another phrase for the movement of activists, which is
directly organized by the party.[97] By the constant reiteration of this
and similar phrases party spokesmen edge closer, so to speak, to a concern with the people, who are not as yet within the fold. Thus,
Ulbricht stated at the same conference that workers, activists, and
engineers were ten times smarter than the best technical experts in the
Ministry. Hence, a ministry which has no contact with the engineers
in the factories and which does not conduct conferences with activists is
really incapable of fulfilling its tasks adequately.

> We have come to the conclusion that one can solve these tasks [bureau-
> cratic actions, sabotage, etc.] only by means of a broad mobilization of the
> progressive forces. That is . . . one has to raise the questions openly,
> not only before comrades of the SED, but before a meeting of party-mem-
> bers, engineers, activists as well as non-party people, in which everyone
> has a right to say what he thinks.[98]

The reference is still to a "mobilization" of party members and activists.
But this is to have a "broad" character which suggests both that some
members and activists have not yet been mobilized and that, as Ulbricht
adds, nonparty people should be included.

The uprisings of June 17 indicated clearly that the party had not
succeeded in this mobilization and in his evaluation of these events
the First Secretary devoted a whole section of his speech to "the winning
over of the entire working-class." The main task of the party was to
develop political work among the masses, especially in the working class.
Those nonparty workers who did not participate in the demonstrations
of June 17 (Ulbricht calls this "who fought courageously against the
provocateurs") were to be invited to the meetings of the party cell,
because their opinions and criticisms were of special value. The party
needed workers and, according to Ulbricht, these men had given evidence of their sympathies by holding themselves aloof from the agitation of June 17. They should be given special attention. Experienced

[96] *Lehren des XIX Parteitages* . . . , p. 126.

[97] "Activist" is party jargon for all workers who exceed previously established
work-norms, usually with the help of party organizations, whether they are party
members or not. As we shall see, the party makes every effort to recruit the
activist as a member and to make party members into activists.

[98] *Ibid.*, pp. 214–15. The significance of organized meetings in which "everyone
has a right to say what he thinks" is discussed on pp. 412–17.

functionaries should hold discussions with workers in their homes, in factories and offices, with regard to the lessons of June 17. Greater attention should be given to telltale signs and especially to complaints from the workers. The secretaries of county and district headquarters should spend half of their time with the basic organizations of the party in factories and offices and help them in their work. Propaganda should not be separate from the daily political work among the masses. In the membership meetings of the party it should be guaranteed that a discussion of the policies and operations of the party takes place. There was a conspicuous failure of "criticism from below," from among the rank and file.[99]

All this seems to indicate that the party had not succeeded in enlisting the nonparty workers it needed, that they had not been given attention, that their complaints had been ignored, that secretaries had not spoken before meetings and had failed to take a hand in the party work at the grass-roots level, and that the meetings of party cells had taken place among the functionaries, for the most part, with the members sitting in silence or at best speaking according to instructions because they had to. Spokesmen of the party made it clear that these shortcomings arise from the reluctance of its functionaries to go among the "laboring people," from their inclination to associate with one another and to agitate among those who are already tied to the party in some way.

> There are functionaries who are afraid when 50% of the delegates are unaffiliated with any party as for example at the county-conference in Mühlhausen. These functionaries were terrified by the fact that at the county-conference of the Society [for German-Soviet Friendship] entirely new people rather than party-orators participated in the discussion. These functionaries break out in a sweat instead of working with these new people and welcoming the fact that they have come.[100]

[99] Ulbricht, *Der Neue Kurs . . .* , pp. 69–78. That such comments are symptomatic rather than accidental is indicated by two statements of Ulbricht in another context. At a SED conference on organizational questions he assured his listeners that "the comrades who speak at this Conference today speak on the basis of specific instructions as these have been laid down in a resolution of the Politbureau." And later in the same speech he introduced a reference to a specific mistake in the work of a party unit with the words: "If I were convinced that this example was an exception, I would not mention it here." See *Die Organisationsarbeit der SED,* pp. 13, 46.

[100] *Lehren des XIX Parteitages . . .* , p. 187. "Party orators" is a free but fairly accurate translation of "routinierte Diskussionsredner," which literally means "routinized discussants" and has a derogatory implication.

Apparently, the functionaries do not welcome the "new people," and the official discussions of this problem help to explain their reluctance, at least in one respect.

According to Ulbricht, salaried employees rather than workers made up from 70 to 80 per cent of the personnel in the party headquarters of certain enterprises. It was imperative that the proportion of workers be increased.[101] The proportion of salaried employees who implement the directives of the party must obviously be high, since all full-time functionaries who were workers formerly are now salaried employees.[102] Yet the proportion of manual workers among the *membership* has also been strikingly low for a party which claims to represent the working class; indeed, it has been declining.[103] Taken together, these figures suggest that a career as a party functionary offers many workers an important avenue of social mobility, but that the average worker shows considerable reluctance to join the party.

Reports concerning the actual contacts of functionaries and "the masses" bear out what these figures suggest, that the reasons for hostility and fear are on both sides tangible and immediate. For instance, in several enterprises of the East Zone the distribution of a Christmas bonus was made dependent upon membership in the FDGB, a measure which was likely to increase both the antagonism between members and nonmembers as well as between the leaders of the trade-union shop committees and the rest of the work force.[104] Such favoritism has not

---

[101] Cf. *Der Neue Kurs* . . . , p. 88. The frequent reiteration of this demand indicates that the party is meeting with considerable difficulties in this respect.

[102] At the Fourth Party Congress in 1954 it was stated that 89.8 per cent of the 1,780 *voting delegates* were workers and 3 per cent salaried employees *by social origin*, while in terms of their present occupation 43.9 per cent were workers and 34.6 per cent were salaried employees.

[103] See Schirdewan, *Die Vorbereitung des IV Parteitages* . . . , pp. 15–16, according to whom the proportion of the *membership* which is made up of persons *currently employed* as manual laborers varies from 23.6 to 44.5 per cent in different localities. Official statements of the party also disclose the proportion of workers among the total membership, as follows: 1947, 47.9 per cent; 1949, 44.5 per cent; 1950, 41.3 per cent; and 1954, 39.1 per cent, i.e., a decline of 8.8 per cent. These figures are rather striking in view of the party's ability to doctor them. The sources for the figures are given in Stern, *Die SED* . . . , pp. 154–55.

[104] References to reports which are not otherwise identified are based upon the files of the Archiv Friesdorf, Bad Godesberg, mentioned in the Acknowledgments. These reports consist primarily of detailed interviews with refugees from the East Zone or of reports on specific occurrences which have been received through contact with local informants.

remained sporadic. To strengthen the work of party cells in the enterprises the Politbureau passed a resolution in April, 1953, according to which members and candidates of the party may not be dismissed or shifted to another job without permission of the party's county headquarters.[105] On the other hand, functionaries of the party and its affiliated organizations "enjoy" special legal protection. For instance, a night watchman, who was also a habitual drunkard, had been appointed as Deputy Mayor in a village. To celebrate the occasion he went on a binge, whereupon some local firemen put him—slightly incapacitated—on a cart and paraded with him through the town. They were promptly arrested and accused of incitement to boycott. An acquittal of the men on the ground that they had played a practical joke was appealed to a higher court at the insistence of the District Attorney who argued that "this contemptuous treatment of a political functionary was no joke at a time of an intensified class-struggle." This illustration is not frivolous. For according to a decision of the German Supreme Court, it is not admissible to interpret *any* assault or other act of physical violence against members of "democratic organizations" as a mere disturbance of the peace, if such an act is intended to prevent them from pursuing their political activities. And since every act against the functionaries of the regime would prevent them from pursuing their political activities, whether by intention or not, it appears that the Supreme Court would judge all such acts as evidence of "incitement to boycott against democratic institutions and organizations" according to Article 6 of the Constitution.[106]

However, the functionaries of the party and of its various affiliated organizations fear the "contact with the masses" for more specific reasons than the favored treatment they receive. The party forces them to engage in a relentless drive for its momentary goals, and their functions are whatever the party decides them to be. But the party also prescribes the methods to be used. The functionaries have not only the task to obtain compliance with party directives, but to do so by "democratic methods." After all, the principal tenet of the party is that it represents the working class. The specific actions, which the party seeks to put into effect, are interpreted as representing the de-

105 Quoted in Stern, *op. cit.*, p. 145.

106 "Acts of violence against members of democratic organizations, which are intended to prevent a continuation of their political activity, are to be punished exclusively according to Article 6 of the Constitution, *even though they give the external appearance of constituting a disturbance of the peace.*" Cf. decision quoted in Ministerium der Justiz, ed., *Neue Justiz* (·Berlin: Deutscher Zentralverlag, 1952), Vol. VI, pp. 129–30. My italics.

cisions of the people themselves. And to do that it becomes necessary to avoid commandeering methods and all formal, bureaucratic actions, as the functionaries are constantly reminded.· To quote from the letter of an apparently devoted functionary, which Ulbricht used at an organizational Conference in order to show where the cadres needed to be improved:

> I would like to ask you to discuss this question at the Conference, since this is the vital question for us. How do we induce the laboring masses to go with us voluntarily? This gives me grave concern. We isolate ourselves, do not pay attention to their opinion, do not enlist their collaboration. We sun ourselves in the success of a well-attended demonstration, for which the factories have provided a two-hour leave. But we are not able to have them [the laboring masses] engage in an activity voluntarily; contests and Hennecke-shifts can hardly be organized; meetings after quitting-time are empty. This is true down to the basic party-organizations.[107]

Thus, the "contact with the masses" remains elusive even as the demand for it is reiterated, and as a result the functionaries of the party and its affiliated organizations use a variety of methods by which the consent of the masses is "organized."

Evidence concerning these methods is fragmentary. Enough incidents are known, however, to piece together the logic of the situation which the functionaries confront. Their maneuvers in the engineering of consent are predetermined in their end result. Although the directives of the party do not prescribe the methods to be used, except in general terms, they place exclusive responsibility for their implementation on the functionaries, who know from experience that they will be penalized if they do not "deliver."[108] For example, at the time the

---

[107] Quoted in Ulbricht, *Die Organisationsarbeit der SED,* p. 57. "Hennecke-shifts" are the German equivalent of "Stachanovite-shifts." As in Russia, the so-called Hennecke movement was started by a miner, an old Communist functionary, who exceeded his norm in 1948 by 380 per cent, albeit on the basis of preparations facilitating his work and altering most of the ordinary conditions of work. "Hennecke-shifts" refers to the pledge of work brigades to increase their output during a special shift by a certain percentage, usually to commemorate some festive occasion such as Stalin's or Pieck's birthday, etc.

[108] The duties of the Central Party Control Commission and its subordinate organizations are officially defined as follows: "(a) It [the Commission] examines how the resolutions of the Party Congress and of the Central Committee are executed by the party-organization, and it leads the struggle for the unity and the purity of the party. (b) It holds those party members accountable, who are guilty of violating party resolutions and party discipline." The penalties at the disposal of the Commission range from a warning to a reprimand, a severe reprimand and exclusion from the party. The Commission can also have guilty

Politbureau had decided to introduce collective agreements in all enterprises of the East Zone, major responsibility for their "voluntary" adoption by the workers was placed on the functionaries of the FDGB. In issuing its directives, the Politbureau clearly assumed that the adoption of these agreements was a foregone conclusion. Hence, the difficulties which the FDGB encountered would be overcome, according to party spokesmen, if the FDGB intensified its agitational work, particularly by repeated *public meetings,* in which all the issues would be discussed and all oppositional arguments overcome.[109] Indeed, functionaries are officially reminded time and again that they should not give merely formal reports to the membership meeting, but should encourage "open" discussions of the issues presented and invite "criticism from below."

Given this pressure from above and the tacit, but unmistakable resistance from below, functionaries typically resort to a mixture of evasions and threats to obtain the formal endorsement they need. There is one report according to which all workers of an enterprise "signed" a resolution for "peace," a result which the functionaries accomplished by rapidly going through the shop at the beginning of the shift and shouting that everybody favored the resolution, they would sign the names, and anyone who did not want to sign should let them know. Other reports tell of meetings held after hours, so that only the party members who have often been compelled to do so will attend; or of meetings in which the discussion of the official report is taken up by party

party members shifted to other jobs, or removed from their positions, and it can turn them over to the Security Police (*Staatssicherheitsdienst*), which is the East German equivalent of the Gestapo or the MVD. Cf. Stern, *op. cit.*, pp. 85–88.

[109] Collective agreements were initiated by the Labor Law of April 19, 1950, and implemented by an administrative enactment of February 15, 1951. During 1951 the resistance of the workers delayed the adoption of collective agreements in many enterprises until the end of the plan year, while in 1952 their adoption was delayed until the middle of the year. At the 1954 Fourth Party Congress it was stated that by the beginning of April only 40 per cent of the collective agreements had been concluded, although all of them should have been concluded by the fifteenth of that month. Secretary Ziller of the Central Committee reiterated once again that the matter had been handled in a "formal manner" and that the resistance of the enemy had found expression in the refusal to assume "voluntary obligations," to accept production contests, and especially in the rejection of the proposal that the FDGB headquarters control the fulfillment of the obligations which had been assumed. See *Löhne, Arbeitsnormen und unbezahlte Arbeit in der Sowjetzone* (Sopade Informationsdienst, Denkschrift 48; Bonn: Vorstand der Sozialdemokratischen Partei Deutschlands, n.d.), p. 49; Haas and Leutwein, *op. cit.*, pp. 18–19; and K. C. Thalheim, ed., *Die wirtschaftliche und soziale Entwicklung in Ostberlin und der sowjetischen Besatzungszone* (mimeographed; Berlin, April 1–15, 1954), p. 10.

members who have been designated previously and whose remarks have been "organized" beforehand. Such prearranged "discussions" are perhaps the favored method, because they give a semblance of that "inner-party democracy" which is so frequently demanded. And it goes without saying that the functionaries use all kinds of pressure to get party members to attend and participate in these meetings, for their "right" to speak is construed as a duty and their failure to perform appropriately is a cause for suspicion.[110] Still other methods are used when it comes to voting on the resolutions which have been submitted. Sometimes voice votes are preferred, because the secretary can readily ignore the "No's" that he hears. At other times, when the vote goes against the official resolution, the meeting is simply postponed to another, and presumably better prepared, day. Again, the presence of a silent majority is ignored and the secretary will declare a resolution unanimously adopted, if 20 out of 200 vote for it, and no one votes against it. And when the pressure is on to detect the "enemy," preventive actions of the Security Police increase in lieu of the more usual reliance on the omnipresent threat of such actions.

These and other methods go far to explain the hostility of the workers.[111] Since open opposition is impossible for the most part, the

[110] By implication much of this is admitted in the statement by Schirdewan that the functionaries had let the political and educational preparation of membership meetings take care of itself, while spending all their time with the organizational preparation. See Schirdewan, *op. cit.*, pp. 38–39. It may be added that the methods actually used become even more blatant as the pressure on the functionaries increases. During the aftermath of June 17, functionaries of the party and the trade-unions were officially obliged to hold public meetings, at which the experience of June 17 was to be discussed, often with the aid of some leading official of the party or the government. Thus, in one case a member of the Politbureau spoke in a factory and invited the free discussion of the workers, promising immunity to anyone who spoke up. Only a fraction of those volunteering to speak could be heard for reasons of time, but a considerable number of these speakers were arrested later. In another case, members of the SED and the FDGB were instructed to place themselves throughout the large hall and report to the party secretary any conversations which were critical of the regime. Reports from the factories of the East Zone eight months after the uprising indicate that a systematic campaign continues which seeks to ferret out and hand over to the Security Police all those who took part in, or spoke up during or after, the uprisings of June 17. Agents of the Security Police have apparently been stationed in all the major enterprises.

[111] It is pertinent to add here that conditions in the East Zone probably differ significantly in this respect from those obtaining in Russia herself. Russian workers may have a greater tolerance for boredom and may take it for granted that the meetings which they must attend will move from a prearranged beginning through prearranged steps to a prearranged conclusion. This psychological atmos-

workers attempt to get by with as little compliance as possible. If they have joined the SED for one reason or another, they will often evade the duties stipulated for party members as long as they can. Thus, in a report on attendance at party meetings in July, 1952, it was stated that in 20 counties an average of less than 65 per cent of the members attended the meetings. And in the meetings of the fall of 1953, which were designed to "evaluate" the events of June 17, the average attendance in a number of large enterprises had dropped to from 25 to 50 per cent.[112] Frequently, they manage to avoid joining the party by joining one of its affiliated organizations, such as the FDGB or the Society for German-Soviet Friendship. And having joined these organizations, they will avoid meetings or go in arrears on their dues, if they can do so without too much risk.[113] In other instances again, opposition takes the form of production slowdowns, momentary but demonstrative work stoppages, rejection of "voluntary obligations" or of proposed speed-ups, and many others. All these methods have in common that they afford the individual worker a high degree of anonymity and thereby minimize the danger of detection by the Secret Police.

It would be far-fetched to assume that the party authorities are unaware either of the methods which their functionaries use or of the hostility which they help to generate. Indeed, if they had had any illusions on this score, it is clear that the uprisings of June 17 would have dispelled them. It is, therefore, of interest to observe the manner in which

phere is graphically described in Gregory Klimov, *Berlin Kreml* (Köln: Kiepenheuer und Witsch, 1953), pp. 337–38, though Klimov has reference to a meeting in which candidates are nominated and endorsed for a forthcoming election. Where only boredom is generated, it is also probable that the functionaries are merely thought to do a job they have to do. The result is that everyone concerned wants to get the whole thing over with in the proper way because that cannot be avoided, but with as little difficulty and as quickly as possible. Speculative as these remarks are, it should not be forgotten that the Soviet regime has not only a thirty-five-year record of brutality but also a record of successful industrialization in a backward country. Tolerance for police methods among those not directly affected is likely to be considerable, when there is a record of accomplishment on the other side. Such considerations, however, are clearly inapplicable in some of the satellite countries.

[112] See Stern, *op. cit.*, p. 147, where the sources for these figures are cited.

[113] By no means are all workers organized in the FDGB. One eyewitness reports, for example, that in an enterprise employing 650 workers, examination disclosed that only 45 per cent were members of the FDGB. Such investigations, however, are not as frequent as may be, since the FDGB functionaries have no interest in publicizing such incriminating evidence. It is not surprising that their record-keeping is often subjected to official criticism, but it is doubtful that this defect is primarily the result of inefficiency or ineptitude.

party officials responded to that evident failure of the party's contact with the masses. In his assessment of these events Ulbricht placed heavy emphasis upon the functionaries who had failed—aside from attributing the whole affair to the conspiratorial activities of Western agents. In one case, a prominent party official had not understood how to distinguish between workers who were properly dissatisfied with certain conditions and those who had organized demonstrations. In a certain factory, the party secretary had actually participated in the demonstrations and had promised strike pay to the workers. In the face of that, the leaders of the party cell had failed to state their own position publicly, and they had accepted a declaration of the rank and file which expressed continued confidence in this secretary. There had even been a case in which the enemies of the people had come out into the open with slogans against the Oder-Neisse border.[114] But not one member of the party, not even a comrade from the county headquarters who was present, defended the peace policy of the party and the government.

These are serious phenomena which are due to political mistakes in the work of quite a few county-headquarters. In these enterprises there is an apparent lack of leadership by the county headquarters with regard to political work among the masses. There have been discussions of the economic questions of the day, but one has evaded the basic questions of taking a position in favor of our policy of peace and against the policy of revenge on the part of West German tycoons, bankers and their minions.
The enemies were aided in their evil work through the formal bureaucratic methods of many party headquarters. The fact is that the secretaries of quite a few party cells had little contact with the workers, that they were leading from their desk and did not have their ear to the ground among the work-force. The elected leaders of the party-cell participated little in the actual solution of problems and in the actual leadership [of the party members]. This was one of the major reasons why in a number of large enterprises the workers had no confidence in the party leadership.[115]

[114] This is the new Soviet-sponsored eastern border between Germany and Poland, which in effect cedes extensive German territories to Poland. While the Western Powers attempted to make this border a temporary, administrative arrangement until the peace conference, the indefinite postponement of the latter has established it *de facto,* and the SED has endorsed it unconditionally.

[115] *Der Neue Kurs . . . ,* pp. 86–87. The phrase "quite a few" is my rendition of "manche" or "einige," although "some" is the more literal translation. However, the polemic and defensive context of these official declarations changes the meaning of "manche" in the sense that the agencies and functionaries which are criticized publicly cannot be admitted to be "many," while the criticism itself is provoked because there are "quite a few." Other phrases reflect the same effort to combine the necessity to criticize with the obligation to express confidence in the party's leadership and success, e.g., the statement that a given

Thus, the answer of this leader of the party is exactly the same in every crisis and with regard to every problem, for his criticism of party functionaries covers the whole range of their possible activities. The functionaries are condemned for their failure to defend and agitate for the party line; and they are condemned for their "formal bureaucratic methods" and for their failure to concern themselves with the grievances and personal interests of the workers (*Sorge um den Menschen* is the official party slogan).

But these directives of the party are incompatible one with the other. For the required "success" in the propagation of the party line can only be achieved by neglecting the awkward question whether this propaganda has carried conviction. And conversely any real attention to the grievances of the workers would militate against the agitation among them for the shifting directives of the party. This dilemma of party functionaries reflects once more the tendency of the regime to maximize the pressure put upon its officials and functionaries. It is moreover a conscious application of the doctrine that the party and its functionaries lead the working class. Hence, the very conflict between the interests of the workers and the demands and directives of the party is officially regarded as an opportunity for a still better and more intensified education of the people. Time and again the implementation of directives is said to depend upon the "successful persuasion of the work force," upon membership meetings which are the most important "school of party education." [116] Indeed "the exchange of opinions in the meetings of the party activists or of the members constitutes the most important means for an exchange of experience, for the clarification of problems and for the eradication of mistakes and false lines of thought among the comrades." [117]

course of action should be pursued "still more successfully" in the future. The standardization of such phrases in all party publications and pronouncements is facilitated by the way in which meetings are conducted. They begin regularly with a lengthy report of the secretary and proceed through a succession of speeches, called "discussion" officially, which consist of comments and elaborations on the major themes of the secretary's report. In this way the speakers can use both the clues and language of that report.

[116] See Ulbricht in *Die Organisationsarbeit der SED,* p. 46 and Schirdewan, *op. cit.,* pp. 37–42.

[117] *Die Organisationsarbeit der SED,* p. 37. The use of such meetings for the detection of potential enemies is only a by-product of the belief that everyone should give a public accounting of his responsibilities to the "collective" and hence be subject to "criticism." This organized use of the "collective" as a means of controlling individual behavior was developed by A. S. Makarenko in his settlements for juvenile delinquents. Characteristically enough, Makarenko has discussed his

The repeated demands for such meetings suggest that they do not occur, and indeed the party's own directives do not permit them. For just as the party does not allow executives or functionaries to use their judgment in striking a balance between conflicting directives or in bringing that conflict to the notice of their superiors, so the party only allows meetings to take place in which this most important "exchange of opinions and experiences" is prearranged. To be sure, this is not admitted in so many words, but it may be inferred from the remedy which party spokesmen offer for the improvement of membership meetings. At the meetings of the Central Committee in 1952, Ulbricht suggested that the formal bureaucratic methods of officials and party functionaries could only be combated by developing "criticism from below." He had harsh words for those officials who had shown themselves impervious to the criticism of their actions. But he also stated that this desired "criticism from below" would not develop unless those who exercised a "healthy critique," were convinced that they would be supported by the party and that the evils laid bare would actually be eliminated.[118] Apparently, Ulbricht mentions "criticism from below" only to distinguish immediately between a "healthy critique" and one that is by implication "unhealthy." Therefore, anyone who might offer such "criticism from below" has no assurance whatever that he will be supported by the party, that his criticism will be interpreted as "healthy" rather than as an act of sabotage. Consequently, he will make doubly sure beforehand, if he desires to speak at all, that the party will approve of what he proposes to say. And this demand for prior clearance virtually necessitates that prior organization of all meetings, which effectively prevents the "criticism from below" that is officially advocated. Although party spokesmen ostensibly regard this criticism as a necessary corrective for the ancient sins of bureaucracy—buck-passing, self-protective alliances among functionaries, formal adherence to rules, falsification of reports— they do not permit the criticism they demand. Consequently, party functionaries continue to organize "criticism from below" in order to keep criticism "healthy." [119]

methods as providing a model for the collective education of man in Soviet society, in which personal and collective goals are in harmony. Cf. A. S. Makarenko, *Ausgewählte Pädagogische Schriften* (Berlin: Volk und Wissen, 1953), pp. 77–78 and *passim*.

[118] *Lehren des XIX Parteitages* . . . , p. 60.

[119] It is useful to add a caveat at this point. The central organization of "criticism from below" is an important weapon of the party, but one should not think of this manipulation as more monolithic than it probably is. To voice any criticism without prior clearance through proper channels is dangerous

The development of criticism and self-criticism in membership meetings as well as among officials and functionaries in the government and the party is always advocated on the ground that it will improve the vaunted "contact with the masses." But since the party retains absolute control over this device of "inner-party democracy," it is, in fact, still another way of checking up on the performance of functionaries whom the party authorities do not trust.[120] That is, campaigns of "criticism and self-criticism" are planned less for the purpose of obtaining information than on the basis of information already obtained. The campaigns are designed to remove strategic bottlenecks and publicly to correct the mistakes of functionaries in a manner which imposes the burden of responsibility upon a designated individual. They are another method of controlling the functionaries of the party and its affiliated organizations, but they do not facilitate "contact with the masses." On the contrary, these campaigns help to increase still further the distance between the "laboring people" and the functionaries and activists of the party. For it is obvious from the setting and the stereotyped language of these "discussions" that they merely simulate the exchange of experience which this planning has made impossible.[121]

business, but it probably happens anyway, often through a skillful blurring of the party line with heterodox opinions. Given the official encouragement of "criticism and self-criticism," such occurrences are hard to avoid. On occasion they may even be employed by one or another of the factions among the higher echelons of the party, either to test out the strategic opportunities of a given situation with relatively little risk to the higher functionaries or to gain an advantage over others by a correct anticipation of a change in party line. It also happens probably that some unanticipated criticism is utilized by higher party authorities to ferret out and correct the "mistakes" of lower functionaries, though the same end can also be achieved by "planting" such a criticism without the knowledge of the functionary who is to be disciplined. Too much manipulation from the top also dries up a source of grass-roots information, though it is hard to know how important this consideration is. An outsider cannot hope to comprehend all the uses to which "criticism and self-criticism" can be put in a dictatorial regime, but he should try to arrive at a balanced judgment of the possibilities of manipulation. The functionaries themselves seek to offest that manipulation by ostensibly engaging in "criticism and self-criticism," but in a formal, routinized manner. This is officially criticized as "bureaucratic" and as lacking in partisanship.

[120] Cf. the statement by Martin Drath concerning the assumption of disloyalty even with regard to the functionaries of the SED in his *Verfassungsrecht und Verfassungswirklichkeit in der Sowjetischen Besatzungszone* (Bonn: Bundesministerium für gesamtdeutsche Fragen, 1954), pp. 42–47.

[121] Moreover, official statements make it clear that the party organizes this "contact with the masses." "Criticism and self-criticism are not an automatic and

Why then does a dictatorial party which has successfully destroyed all organized resistance engage in this elaborate pretense of "inner-party democracy"? I think it far-fetched to assume that the officials of the party expect to get more "contact with the masses" and more exchange of experience by the development of criticism and self-criticism, although this expectation belongs to the standard repertoire of their public statements. On the contrary, criticism and self-criticism are above all a device by which the distance between functionaries and the "laboring people" is deliberately enlarged, and by which the involvement of the functionaries in the activities of the party is rendered still more irrevocable. Like all totalitarian parties, the SED is a militant sect which must enforce "iron discipline" on its functionaries so that they will constitute an ever-ready instrument of organized action. But the enforcement of that discipline must not remain an intraparty affair, lest an individual functionary be allowed to walk among the "laboring people" as a man among men. A militant sect cannot be satisfied with that; it must stigmatize all its officials, and if possible all its members, so that their identity cannot be obscured by the individual or mistaken by the public. For only then can the party be sure that its hold over the functionaries has not been weakened, that they have not been corrupted by their "contact with the [nonparty] masses."

The principal goal of the party is, therefore, to have absolute control over its own apparatus and all other objectives are subordinated to this.

spontaneous driving force in the development of our society; they unfold rather under the leadership and through the directives of the party. The party is in a position to recognize mistakes and shortcomings in time and to lead the Soviet people in eradicating these mistakes and shortcomings." See M. A. Leonov, *Kritik und Selbstkritik* (Berlin: Verlag Kultur und Fortschritt, n.d.), pp. 34–35. A more practical comment to the same effect is contained in another pamphlet. "The agitators can greatly aid the party-organizations in the preparation of meetings. The agitators, who are in continuous and direct contact with the workers, and who know their ideas and moods, can in many cases give pointers to the party organization as to the questions which should be dealt with in the general meeting. Once the agenda of the meeting has been determined, the agitators must then aid all those who want to step forward in the discussion, propose to them the outline and the major points of the speech, and must give them all possible assistance with regard to the manner in which the basic ideas, the conclusions and the proposals can best be formulated." See O. Kremnyova, *Die Erfahrungen der politischen Agitation in den Betrieben* (Bibliothek des Agitators; Berlin, Dietz Verlag, 1951), pp. 46–47. This is one of a series of publications, which corresponds to a similar series published under the auspices of the Russian Central Committee.

> It must become proverbial that no political activist may be left alone; one must be concerned with him; one must help him and guide him; for only in this way can one enhance the responsibility of the activists, strengthen their authority and develop new and capable cadres.[122]

But the functionaries constitute only the advance-guard of the party. If it is a principal task of their superiors in the party "not to leave them alone," it is in turn a major task of the functionaries to be actively concerned with the party members.

> We are obliged to do battle for each member of the party, to subject him firmly to the rules governing the education of party members. *A party member who is not subject to the control of his elected leaders can of course become the victim or the tool of the enemy.*[123]

To bring the members as well as the functionaries within its fold the party must have a method of testing the conduct of each member, at the same time that the test itself helps to erect a barrier between the member and the nonparty masses. To achieve this the party must accomplish two things. It must prevent the individual member from keeping things to himself, and it must prevent him from hiding before his fellows all the opinions and actions which would betray his identification with the party. If he kept things to himself, the party would run the danger of thoughts and potential actions subversive to its rule. And if he could hide his identity as a party member, he could have a private life among his fellows because they would not be put on their guard against him; but then he would be beyond the grasp of the party and, hence, a potential threat to its absolute authority. The party can more or less avoid both of these eventualities, if the individual member and functionary is made to participate in the criticism and self-criticism of "inner-party democracy." For in that case he will not be left alone, the chances are diminished that he can keep things to himself, and he will become stigmatized in the eyes of the "laboring masses." To be sure, his participation in the ritual of criticism and self-criticism may become entirely routine, but it will show nonetheless whether or not he defends the policies of the party in all situations, in public, and in the face of the latent hostility which his open identification with the party has helped to create. Hence, criticism and self-criticism are devices that help the party to manipulate the "contact with the masses" so that its function-

---

[122] Statement of Paul Verner in *Die Organisationsarbeit der SED,* p. 73. Verner was the head of the Central Committee's division for party organization and control (*Organisations-Instrukteurabteilung*) in 1949; this division has since been reorganized and is now headed by Karl Schirdewan.

[123] Schirdewan, *op. cit.,* p. 53. My italics.

aries become alien missionaries among their own people. The loyalty of these "missionaries" to the party may well be tested, then, by their attitude toward criticism and self-criticism, which has been called "the touchstone of socialist consciousness in our people, because it is an indication of their capacity to put the interests of society above their own peace of mind." [124]

f. The Isolation of the Activists

The methods nominally employed to establish "contact with the masses" facilitate the party's control of the functionaries and help to isolate them. Although the jargon obscures these facts, it is not really intended to hide them.[125] For the doctrine of the party emphasizes the division of the "laboring people" into the workers and the vanguard, and indeed the doctrinal and practical elaboration of that division is essential for its exercise of power.

Totalitarian parties confront a paradox. Their functionaries must be isolated from the people so that party discipline is maximized and the danger of political deviation is kept at a minimum. But such parties must also extend their influence to the people who do the day's work so that they will do it better than before. Prior to the Bolshevik conquest of power, Lenin had acknowledged this distinction by his division of the working class into a majority which was only concerned with better wages and working conditions and a minority of professional revolutionaries who were privy to a "knowledge" of the laws of society and history. In the countries within the Soviet orbit that distinction has since been elaborated. There the party as a whole is called the vanguard of the working class, but its ranks are subdivided into candidates for membership, members, activists, and functionaries. That is to say, those who have applied for membership must pass through a probationary period during which their conduct will be carefully observed. Once they have become full-fledged members they do not necessarily measure up to expectations, if one may judge from the admonition that the party

---

124 Leonov, *op. cit.,* p. 34.

125 This double meaning of party slogans is part of the manipulation of the language, which I noted earlier. For example, "inner-party democracy" is said to entitle every member to speak up in party meetings. If someone were to say that this right is a duty and that the content of what is said is prescribed, a Communist doctrinaire would answer that a member with the proper class consciousness sees no distinction between his rights and duties as a member and that he agrees with the party line and, hence, expresses both party policy and his own opinions.

should "do battle for each party member." Hence, members are subdivided into those who are activists and those who fail in some way to do
their duty as party members. Activist members are divided in turn from
the functionaries proper by the fact that the latter have been officially
appointed to a position in the party hierarchy. And finally, functionaries
are judged and consequently divided in terms of the degree to which they
come up to the expectations of higher party authorities, and of course
in terms of their relative rank within the party hierarchy. The masses of
nonparty people are subdivided into workers, peasants, and intelligentsia,
and each of these subdivisions is divided in turn in terms of the party's
political criteria. There are the conscious or unconscious "victims or
tools of the enemy." Others lag behind, they retain "remnants of capitalist consciousness," they have "not yet" awakened to their "real" interests. And finally there are nonparty activists, people of whose conduct the party approves, but who have not yet been persuaded to apply
for membership in the party.[126]

It is apparent that the SED, like other Communist parties, systematically attempts to create a class structure of its own, which is superimposed upon the solidarity and the conflicts of interest which would otherwise arise from the organization of production. The party does not
obliterate the distinctive status of different socio-economic groups (except of course in the case of the "capitalists"); indeed, it accentuates
existing differences by giving high economic rewards to those individuals in every social group who "fulfill and overfulfill" the plan. But
the status discrimination which arises from striking differences in income is not sufficient from the viewpoint of the party. Rather the party
seeks to bring into its own or affiliated organizations all those who are
highly rewarded for their work performance and conversely it attempts
to get those who are party members to excel also in the drive for productivity.[127] To accomplish these twin goals the party typically resorts

126 On special occasions these subdivisions are refined further, as when
Ulbricht declared that the workers who had not participated in the demonstrations of June 17 had "fought courageously against the provocateurs" and should
be given special attention, even though they were not members of the party.

127 In view of the large-scale emigration from the East Zone, the SED has
had to compromise on this point, especially with regard to experienced industrial
managers and members of the technical intelligentsia. In the first years after
the war, discrimination against these groups ran high, in line with the prejudices of
Communist functionaries from before 1933. Since then official spokesmen have
not only justified publicly the very high economic rewards offered to managers
and technicians; they have also emphasized that these "intellectuals" were not
expected to join the party or espouse its doctrines as long as they re-

to all devices which will help to increase the distinctions between the groups which are positively and negatively privileged. And indeed, this is the device by which the party establishes "contact with the masses"— after all. By a combination of incentives, penalties, and psychological devices the party rewards those who cooperate in its drive for production, and in so doing it erects a barrier of hostility between these activists and the majority of workers. In every Communist regime there is a struggle between those more or less committed to the party and the nonparty masses. While the functionaries seek to increase and to drive the first group with all the means at the disposal of a dictatorial regime, the people at large can "resist" only in silence and withdrawal. For the party eliminates all potential leaders by cooptation, suppression, or persecution, and, hence, it deprives the workers of the leadership necessary for concerted action.

Party officials regard the increase in productivity and the development of the activist movement as second in importance only to their absolute control over the party functionaries. The exercise of rule is much the same in both cases. It consists in the first instance in ample material rewards for all—functionaries or activists—who do the party's bidding. It consists secondly in making the "social visibility" of the group as conspicuous as possible so that the included as well as the excluded cannot mistake or disguise who belongs to what. Thirdly, attractions and deterrents are added in the sense that the functionaries and activists are made to feel not merely conspicuous but important at the same time that they are subject to detailed supervision and must consequently continue to "perform" in order to retain their status and their rewards. These and related "measures" are noteworthy because they help to create a social collective, in which individuals with similar economic interests are joined, but without much solidarity of belief or action, for the party seeks to prevent all cooperative actions which are based on an uncontrolled coalescence of interests. A brief review of these measures will exemplify the managerial practices and ideologies of a Communist dictatorship, where these finally come in "contact with the masses."

The first and principal means of managing the work force is the

frained from "boycotting" the "democratic" institutions of the Zone and were successful in their economic performance. For details see Alfred Leutwein, *Die "Technische Intelligenz" in der Sowjetischen Besatzungszone* (Bonner Berichte aus Mittel- und Ostdeutschland; Bonn: Bundesministerium für gesamtdeutsche Fragen, 1953), especially pp. 7–26, and M. G. Lange, Ernst Richert, and Otto Stammer, "Das Problem der 'Neuen Intelligenz' in der Sowjetischen Besatzungszone," in *Veritas, Justitia, Libertas* (*Festschrift* for the Bicentennial Celebrations of Columbia University; Berlin: Colloquium Verlag, 1954), pp. 191–246.

strategic use of wage incentives. Since 1950 wage rates in the Soviet Zone have been set not by agreement between management and trade-union representatives, but by administrative enactment of the State Planning Commission and its subordinate Ministries and State Secretariats. Officially, wages are determined according to the principle "equal wages for equal work." In practice this principle has meant that all differences between workers in terms of age, sex, and seniority have been disregarded in the interest of maximum productivity.[128]

The planning authorities determine the wage groups for the respective industries down to the individual enterprise. The differences between each of the wage groups, and, hence, between the total earnings of workers in the lowest and highest wage group, are made deliberately large—in the interest of maximizing the incentives for productivity and improvement of skills. Compared with the wage rates of the West, these differences are very great: in the machine-construction industry of the East Zone the wage rate in wage group 8 is 3.11 times that of wage group 1; while in the metal industry of West Berlin, the highest wage rate is 1.78 times the lowest.[129] These differences are even greater in the industries to which the planning authorities attach special importance, as Table 15 shows. Moreover, the planning authorities stipulate the proportion of workers in a given industry which may be assigned to

TABLE 15. HOURLY WAGES IN EAST MARK FOR ACTIVISTS, SKILLED WORKERS, AND AUXILIARY WORKERS, IN SELECTED INDUSTRIES, 1952

	Activists (Piece Rate) Wage Group 8	Skilled Workers (Time Rate) Wage Group 5	Auxiliary Workers Wage Group 1
Coal Mining	4.50	1.91	1.10
Lignite Mining	3.14	1.58	0.94
Metallurgy	3.10	1.47	0.87
Basic Chemicals	2.44	1.41	0.76
Machine Construction	1.91	1.24	0.87
Textiles	1.59	1.27	0.68

Source: Sopade Informationsdienst, *Löhne, Arbeitsnormen und unbezahlte Arbeit in der Sowjetzone*, p. 20.

[128] Hence, safeguards against the exploitation of women and youths have been systematically reduced and older workers are not protected by seniority. As a consequence, earnings have been sharply reduced for all those who are naturally handicapped in the competition with physically stronger fellow-workers.

[129] Anonymous, *Die Ausbeutung der menschlichen Arbeitskraft* (Bonner Berichte aus Mittel- und Ostdeutschland; Bonn: Bundesministerium für gesamtdeutsche Fragen, 1953), pp. 19–20. The comparison does *not* include forced labor and, hence, fails to reveal the full extent of the contrast.

each of the wage groups, so that their changing emphasis on one or another branch of production may be reflected by the increasing or decreasing proportion of workers in the high or the low wage groups, as the case may be. The importance of different industries is also reflected by corresponding differences in the spread of the entire wage scale.[130]

Considered merely in terms of earnings it is clear that the party or nonparty activists who are assigned to wage group 8 are singled out in their own eyes as well as in the eyes of their fellow-workers. Moreover, activists receive—in addition to their regular earnings—a 10 per cent premium for having fulfilled their quota and up to 25 per cent if they overfulfill it.[131] If they are foremen of a work group, or if their shop as a whole receives a premium, or if they are singled out for special awards, they receive still other additions to their base pay. Also, the wages of shop foremen (*Meister*) were increased in July, 1952, by about 80 per cent with the result that for them the range of the lowest wage group was 310–490 DM while the range of the highest was 580–920 DM.[132] According to one estimate, these activists constitute about 5 per cent of the work force in the East Zone, or roughly 180,000 persons. The composition of this group fluctuates, since few are able to keep up the required performance for long. But it is clear that the incentives to become an activist are very great.

[130] For example, about one-half of the workers in the metallurgical industries, one-fifth of the quarry and affiliated workers (*Steine und Erden*), but seven-tenths of the workers in mining were assigned to the four highest wage groups in December, 1951. However, 62.1 per cent of all workers in the Soviet Zone were assigned to the four lowest wage groups. *Ibid.*, pp. 16–17.

[131] Ordinary workers do not receive a premium for fulfilling their quota.

[132] This compares with an average net monthly income of 341 DM for the most highly paid workers (mining, underground). See Dorothea Faber, *Einkommenstruktur und Lebenshaltung in der sowjetischen Besatzungszone* (Bonner Berichte aus Mittel- und Ostdeutschland; Bonn: Bundesministerium für gesamtdeutsche Fragen, 1953), pp. 28, 82, 88. It should be added that the differentiation between the eight wage groups for workers was further increased when the first four wage groups received *no* increases, while wage groups 5 to 8 were increased by 13, 32.9, 62, and 97.4 per cent, respectively. In the most favored industries, such as mining and machine construction, these increases have led to a 1:3.5 and 1:3.1 difference between the lowest and highest wage group. See Haas and Leutwein, *op. cit.*, pp. 85–86. The separate and very favorable treatment of the so-called "technical intelligentsia" is analyzed separately in Alfred Leutwein, *Die 'Technische Intelligenz'.* . . . I mention merely that it provides in addition to high salaries a large number of special privileges and premiums, which have been the object of considerable resentment and, consequently, of much propaganda against egalitarianism (*Gleichmacherei*).

Material incentives are, however, only one of the methods which the planning authorities of the zone employ to manage the work force. The *pièce de résistance* of their efforts is the handling of work-norms, as the events of June 17 suggest. Immediately after World War II, the authorities had instituted the principle of "progressive piece rates" (*progressiver Leistungslohn*) as the means to increase labor productivity. Output in excess of a stipulated norm was rewarded by wage increases, and although these increases were set at a low rate, they led to a substantial increase of the total wage bill. At the end of 1948, Soviet spokesmen subjected this approach to a scathing critique and demanded the introduction of "correct" norms and the promotion of the movement of activists. These spokesmen pointed out that the workers were producing above the stipulated norm simply because the norm was too low. To establish "correct" norms it was necessary to encourage activists— the "progressive section" of the working class—and to use their work performance rather than the calculated averages between the best and the worst workers as the basis for reassessing the "outmoded" norms.[133]

In response to this Soviet critique the East Zone authorities immediately dropped the principle of "progressive piece rates" and ever since then they have launched repeated campaigns designed to promote activists in the different industries. In each of these the objective was the same: to use the outstanding performance of an activist (however achieved) as the basis for reassessing work-norms with the result that the good as well as the average workers must increase their output in

[133] This standard is officially designated as "work-norms based on technical considerations" (*technisch begründete Arbeitsnormen*) in contrast to the norms based on conventional time studies (*erfahrungsstatistische Normen*). The difference between these two types of norms is essentially that the "technical work-norms" are computed on the basis of the work performance of activists. According to the official Russian interpretation, the old norms were computed as an arithmetic mean between the best and the poorest workers, while the "technical work-norms" are computed as the mean between the activist or Stachanovite and the *previously established* work-norm. Since the performance of the activist is frequently facilitated by special preparations and therefore exceeds that of the best ordinary workers, it follows that "technical work-norms" prescribe the performance of these best workers (under ordinary conditions) as the new norm. As a consequence, the new norms lead to substantial wage reductions unless the average worker comes at least close to the performance of the best ordinary workers, while the latter must become activists if they want to maintain their previous earnings. For details see *Ausbeutung* . . . , pp. 32–40, and the official Soviet interpretation in J. Punsky and A. Galtsov, *Die technische Arbeitsnormung in der sozialistischen Industrie* (37. Beiheft zur "Sowjetwissenschaft"; Berlin: Verlag Kultur und Fortschritt, 1953, pp. 7–25).

order to avoid a pay cut.[134] Each of these campaigns for the upgrading of work-norms is publicly identified with the name of one or another activist, and for each German activist there is a Soviet model which he has "followed."

Main Characteristic of Production Effort	Soviet Initiator	East German Imitator
Saving of materials, further specialization and education of slow workers.	Matrossov, Moscow shoe factory	Shoe factory Weissenfeld
Improved job placement, "voluntary obligation" to improve work methods and train unskilled workers.	Rossisky, Moscow instrument factory	Mischel, VVB SANAR, Altenburg Lange, VVB FENA Colditz
Obligation to disseminate Stachanovite work methods on a mass basis.	F. Kovalyov, Moscow textile factory	Mueller and Chemnitz, VVB SANAR
Organization of "brigades of excellent quality."	Alexander Chutkikh, Krasnokhol textile factory	Striemann, VEB TUFA, Cottbus
Improvement of machines outside working hours; increase of work speed. Organization of "complex brigades" involving cooperation of workers and "intelligentsia."	Bykov, Moscow lathe operator	Wirth, lathe operator, Sachsenwerk Radeberg (SAG)
Personal responsibility for the care of tools and machinery.	Nina Nasarova, Ural automobile works	Frieda Hoffman Sachsenwerk Radeberg
Shortened accounting methods.	Prof. Lozinsky	G. Opitz, VVB Energie und Kraftmaschinenbau
Servicing a large number of looms.	Maria Shidirova	Berta Schulz ("Deserving Activist"), Goerlitz
Obligation to drive cars for very long distances without major overhaul.	Titov and Maltsev	Schneider ("Hero of Labor")

Source: Aus der Fabrik des Sowjetmenschen (Bonn: Bundesministerium für gesamtdeutsche Fragen, n.d.).

[134] Official commentary in the East Zone has never effectively hidden that the activist movement aims not merely at an increase of productivity, but also at lower average earnings for those who cannot keep up the increased pace. In April, 1952, the Central Committee acknowledged that "not only many workers but planning officials and trade-union functionaries" believed that technical work-

The source from which these nine examples are chosen lists an admittedly incomplete total of 64 more or less different methods for the increase and/or rationalization of production, each of them identified by the name of an individual or an enterprise, and each of them modeled after some Soviet precedent.

The campaigns staged by the party cell, the FDGB, and the management in "encouraging" one or another of these activists are, of course, only one of a large number of ways in which the authorities support the movement of activists, and the objectives of this movement involve all possible aspects of production. Thus, factory magazines, trade-union publications, newspapers, the publications for party functionaries, for agitators, for teachers, for the members of youth organizations, for students, as well as the movies, plays, and radio programs contain a never-ending stream of demands, commendations, and cautionary tales that deal with such topics as:

(a) The further training of workers

(b) The further substitution of "technical work-norms" (TAN) for simple statistical norms

(c) The utilization of inventions, production conferences, and the development of new work methods

(d) The mechanization and intensification of the production process

(e) The improvement of work discipline involving promptness, cleanliness, orderliness, care for tools and machinery and state property generally, full utilization of the workday, etc.

(f) The systematic saving of raw materials, electricity, etc.

(g) The improvement of quality and of product assortment

norms were introduced to lower wages. The Committee called this a "mistaken opinion," but it admitted that higher work-norms would lead to "temporary repercussions" and even to the "danger of lower wages." To avoid this possibility (sic!) it suggested the retention of the previous wage level for a three-month period after the norms had been increased "in the expectation that after this period of transition the previous level of earnings will be achieved with the new norms." See Löhne, Arbeitsnormen . . . , pp. 32–33. In other words, in three months every worker will have increased his output sufficiently to avoid a pay cut. Also revealing in this connection is the fact that after June 17, the Politbureau decided to revamp the assignment of workers to the different wage groups, declaring that workers who wanted to remain in their present wage group must improve their qualifications. The purpose was to increase the difference between lowest and highest wage groups from 1:3.5 to 1:5. Thus, the Politbureau attempted to do through a re-examination of "qualifications" what it could not do through the work-norms: decrease the wage bill. It may be added that the doctrinaire interprets such increased production as evidence of the workers' "progressive attitude towards work" in contrast to "capitalist exploitation."

The list is endless and it includes on occasion objectives which caricature the very drive of which they form a part, as in the case of premiums which were to be paid for "increased output" of revenue agents who discovered additional sources of revenue especially in privately owned enterprises.[135]

But activists are made conspicuous in the eyes of their fellow-workers not only by their high earnings and by the multifarious publicity campaigns with which their names become associated, but also by the fact that the details of these productivity drives are incorporated in the text of the collective agreements between management and the trade-union. The trade-union headquarters of an enterprise (*Betriebsgewerkschaftsleitung* or BGL) will obligate itself, for example, to support management in the more widespread adoption of "technical work-norms" by means of intensive publicity campaigns. The BGL will promise to start a new "socialist contest" by a certain date, or it will declare to do "persistent work of persuasion" (*beharrliche Überzeugungsarbeit*) in order to ensure the fulfillment of accepted obligations to produce a certain output. Literally hundreds of such general obligations as well as many specific obligations are incorporated in the collective agreements. Now standard procedure calls for meetings of the FDGB membership in which the proposals of the BGL for the collective agreement will be "discussed." These meetings illustrate the persistent fiction of the regime that the FDGB and the party represent the interests of the workers, as well as the persistent need to obtain the "cooperation" of some workers, who have become activists. Individual workers stand up in such meetings and suggest or "discuss" or advocate and endorse one or another of these proposals. Since no one dares openly to contradict these supposed spokesmen of the workers (it makes no difference whether they have been coopted or have volunteered), it is obvious that they will become the object of a smoldering hostility and that their identity as rate-busters on behalf of the party's production drives will not soon be forgotten.

This isolation of the activists is enhanced still further, because the party and its affiliated organizations make very sure that their "activism" is not allowed to stand as a mere interest in higher earnings. Instead it is intimately tied up with the entire political ideology of the regime. The text of a *Selbstverpflichtung* is a case in point:

[135] These premiums were abolished in October, 1953, because they were said to be incompatible with the present development of the DDR. Stripped of its jargon, this probably means that the authorities decided to call a halt for the time being to the continuous harassing of the remaining private enterprises in the zone.

OBLIGATION

The loss of our comrade Stalin moves me very deeply. I would like to give expression to my close tie [*Verbundenheit*] with our party and my friendship towards the Soviet Union by devoting all my energy [to the preservation of] peace. For this reason I assume herewith the following obligation. . . .[136]

The same intimate relation between production drives and the entire political orientation of the party is manifest in the preamble of the standard collective agreements. Such a preamble will contain a reference to the resolutions of the last SED Conference, to their significance for peace, national unification, and a better life for laboring people, to the picneering doctrines of Marx, Engels, Lenin, and Stalin, to the significance of the collective agreement, to the help received from Soviet innovators, scientists, and technicians, to the importance of "socialist competition." It will also contain references to the "voluntary" obligations of the agreement as evidence of a rising socialist consciousness and to the will of all concerned to realize within the enterprise the economic laws of socialism discovered by Comrade Stalin.

The legacy of the great Stalin gives us strength for greater achievements, for the implacable struggle against all enemies of our constructive undertaking, it enhances the vigilance against saboteurs and the ideologies of the class-enemy, it enhances the readiness to defend our homeland. Based on the confidence in our government and in the vanguard of the German people, the proud Socialist Unity Party of Germany, we, the management and the workers of our public enterprise, Bau-Union Dresden, do hereby conclude this collective agreement for 1953 as a mutual pledge for the fulfillment of our plan.[137]

[136] Quoted in Leutwein, *Der Betriebskollektivvertrag* . . . , p. 37. The phrase "by devoting all my energy for peace . . ." does not properly render the quasi-military connotation of "durch den Einsatz meiner ganzen Kraft für den Frieden. . . ."

[137] Translated from an unpublished manuscript. It may be added that Soviet interpreters and their counterpart in the East Zone distinguish between obligations which are legally enforceable and those which are of a moral-political character. Thus, the obligation to further develop "socialist competition" is not legally enforceable, while, say, the obligation of management to build additional housing for workers should be. The distinction is of doubtful importance, however, since the pressure exerted by the party and its organizations does not necessarily correspond to it. Management's obligation to build may not be enforced, while the FDGB's pledge to promote contests may be enforced. Moreover, the introduction of the "dispatcher system" (the term is borrowed from American railroading practice) also helps to blur this distinction, since in all the important enterprises a dispatcher controls the fulfillment of the plan and of the specific obligations which have been assumed, regardless of whether or not the latter are legally enforceable. Cf. the discussion in Leutwein, *Der Betriebskollektivvertrag* . . . , pp. 29–34, 38–41.

The deliberate isolation of the activists goes even further than the combination of high earnings, publicity, and the campaigns for collective agreements and voluntary obligations might indicate, for the party and its affiliated organizations face a serious dilemma in their attempts to recruit activists. Given the tremendous emphasis on increasing productivity one would think that all those who offer innovations or at least increase output would be counted as activists and rewarded accordingly. But skill or physical strength do not carry a party card; there is at least an even chance that politically unreliable workers, the "victims and tools of the enemy" will be as amply endowed in this respect as the party-faithful. Indeed, they might well have a better than even chance, since the entirely reliable party-followers are a minority by definition, which is bound to include a number of careerists, whose only stock-in-trade is party loyalty. At any rate, it is clear that the party cannot afford to tolerate among the activists men and women on whose political loyalty it cannot count, even though their work performance be outstanding. And since political considerations enter into the recruitment of activists, it is apparent that the rewards will frequently go to the loyal rather than to the efficient. Hence, it is necessary to examine briefly the political manipulation of the activist movement.

The manager of an enterprise has the official responsibility to assign each worker to that wage group to which his qualifications entitle him. This procedure involves discretionary judgments of many kinds. The manager is in a position to assign "politically deserving" workers to a higher wage group than their qualifications justify, and he may want to do so in the interest of getting along with the party cell in "his" enterprise, whether or not he is a member himself. He could do so legally enough as in the case of a production contest between two enterprises, in which "work performance" was evaluated in terms of a point system. The rules provided for 5 points to be credited for attendance of meetings, 1 to 10 points for special accomplishments outside of working hours, 5 to 20 points for small improvements, and 5 to 15 points for cleanliness at the place of work. All of these can be readily interpreted in line with political criteria.[138] In addition to such manipulation of wage-group assignments, it is often admitted that the "political attitude" of the worker must be taken into consideration. In the case of skilled workers assignment to one of the eight wage groups is preceded by a political examination in addition to the examination of their technical

---

[138] For details see *Kommunistische Gewerkschaftspolitik* (Sopade Informationsdienst, Denkschrift 26; Hannover: Vorstand der Sozialdemokratischen Partei Deutschlands, n.d.), pp. 14–16.

qualifications. Such workers are questioned concerning "the meaning of competition, the Five-Year Plan, the methods of Soviet and German innovators to increase labor productivity, a clear understanding with regard to the significance of the Soviet Union, and the necessity of creating a national army in the DDR." [139] And after June 17, discussions of the Politbureau emphasized that the determination of the minimum qualification for each wage group should not occur without due consideration being given to the political attitude of the worker.

Such political manipulation of labor management frequently leads to a silent tug of war. For the assignments to wage groups or the distribution of premiums provide the functionaries of the party and the FDGB with the opportunity of recruiting workers as activists by the use of incentives rather than by propaganda. Naturally, they have a strong interest in rewarding those who have proved cooperative. In one factory only the party-faithful received the premiums, and then only 20 actual production workers as against 48 salaried employees. In another, a meeting was called to celebrate the founding of the DDR, and at the meeting the workers were asked to nominate candidates for the distribution of premiums. That request was met first with silence and later on with shouted denunciations like: "We don't need any sweat-shop premium; stick it on your hat." Finally, members of the party proposed some names which were "accepted unanimously" with four or six hands lifted. In still a third case the "Day of Activists" was celebrated with speeches and the distribution of awards. One of the recipients responded by announcing that she would increase her norm by 10 per cent; rumor had it that the premium was a bribe to get a voluntary norm increase, and this activist was ostracized from that day on.[140] Given the pressure

[139] Quoted from an article in *Die Wirtschaft* of September 12, 1952, in *Löhne, Arbeitsnormen . . .* , p. 23.

[140] Obviously, the methods are many, crude as well as subtle, and it is impossible to characterize them all, even if the information were available. It should be added, however, that one of the standard methods is to appeal to the young, as well as the newly employed, since from the viewpoint of the party they have in their favor strength as well as a lack of integration with the established work force. Thus, in one of the uranium mines present norms were exceeded by organizing newly employed workers in separate work brigades and preventing their contact with the workers who had more seniority in the enterprise, presumably because the latter would "corrupt" them. Also, the Youth Law of February 8, 1950, granted the Free German Youth (*Freie Deutsche Jugend* or FDJ) wide powers of agitation in factories and business concerns "to promote production and suppress bureaucratic tendencies and sabotage." See also the remark of Walter Ulbricht that one should put members of the FDJ into the positions of people who are incapable of changing their bureaucratic methods, in *Der Fünfjahrplan . . .* , p. 94. Aside from such dec-

under which they are forced to operate, it is not surprising that the functionaries of the party and the trade-union favor those workers who do their bidding and disregard, if need be, questions of qualification or work performance.

The reaction of the workers is not difficult to guess. They are bound to have a keen sense for the distinction between work and loyalty. On the other hand, they cannot simply oppose the movement of activists as such. For the incentives to produce more are very high, and the wage rates for the average worker are set too low to make slowdown practices very inviting. In addition, personal circumstances probably account for a great deal in their judgment: a man with a large family will simply be forced to cooperate in order to be assigned to a high wage group and earn some of the awards which are periodically distributed to activists. And it is probable that fine distinctions are made between such a worker and another who is single, let us say, and whose enthusiasm for the cause exceeds his capacity for, or interest in, work performance. But given the antagonism of the workers toward the norm increases whose adoption the exceptional output of activists facilitates, the burden of proof is on the activist to show that he is a "regular fellow" and not a rate-buster. The tenseness of the situation is well illustrated by a directive issued by the FDGB to all subordinate affiliates. Activists were to be given official titles like "best worker," "activist," "meritorious activist," or "hero of labor"; they were entitled to receive such a distinction (and the corresponding premium) twice, and the official communications of all FDGB units were obliged to use these designations. Moreover, all FDGB units are instructed to see to it that the official emblems of the activists are worn and easily visible at all official functions. It is obvious from this directive that the FDGB was far more intent than the activists to make sure that everyone would be able to see who they are.

The preceding discussion indicates that the party and its organizations do everything in order to make the activists as conspicuous as possible. The "contact with the masses," which the leaders keep demanding and from which the functionaries repeatedly recoil, turns out in the end to

larations, the accent on youth is evident from the fact that of the 2,201 delegates to the Third Party Congress almost one-half were less than thirty years old. See *Die ideologische und organisatorische Entwicklung der SED*, p. 20. It is uncertain though how far the party has carried this emphasis, since we have data only for 1950. At that time, 38.5 per cent of the party members were under forty years of age, as contrasted with 56.1 per cent under forty years of age for the population as a whole. See Stern, *op. cit.*, p. 158, for data on membership composition.

consist in the attempt to drive a wedge between the "masses" and all those who are brought by one means or another to cooperate with the party. And yet, all spokesmen of the regime continue to insist that the new work-norms are not ordered "from above," that instead they are suggested "from below," that they are the spontaneous contribution of the activists who have a new attitude toward work. Hence, every innovation and every increase in output is identified with the name of an individual worker (or at most of an enterprise). Reports in the press never fail to identify the individual activists by name and place of work, even though the methods of rationalization are well known only to the engineers, are officially publicized after their Soviet "inventor," and could not possibly be put into effect without detailed guidance from above.

But the organization of activists under the pretence that this constitutes a spontaneous movement of the people is more than merely another argument for the legitimacy of the regime. Here again the conflict of interests between the activists and the "laboring people" is never really denied, and it is not fanciful to suggest that it is encouraged. The hostility between activists and workers helps to cement the ties of the activists with the regime, and the workers who oppose, or withdraw from, the movement of activists are officially regarded as retaining remnants of "capitalist consciousness" and as potential or actual saboteurs. It is of interest to see how an official spokesman applies this orientation to the specific problem of work-norms.

> The changing consciousness of the workers, the emergence of a new ideological relationship to work itself, indeed to the machine, provides us with one of the most decisive opportunities for an unexpectedly quick development of our industry, our technology, and our economy as a whole.
> The relationship of the workers to their work has already been changed significantly. The Hennecke movement is a vivid expression of this. Was it not true that the worker was always intent on pulling the wool over the eyes of the time-keeper and the time-study engineer? But can we ascertain our new technical work-norms and at the same time retain that old relationship between the worker and the time-study engineer? That would mean that we fail to utilize the experience of our activists, of the most progressive, the most qualified workers.[141]

---

[141] Statement of Fritz Selbmann (April, 1949) at a conference on managerial techniques quoted in *Kommunistische Gewerkschaftspolitik*, p. 23. At the time Selbmann was Vice-Chairman of the German Economic Commission (*Deutsche Wirtschaftskommission*), which was the top administrative body in the Soviet Zone prior to the proclamation of the German Democratic Republic in October, 1949. Selbmann is a veteran Communist functionary, who has served as Minister for Heavy Industry since 1953.

The statement makes a simple but revealing point. The antagonism of the workers to the methods of time-study (and the methods of rationalizing production which grow out of them) is incompatible with the need of the regime to increase productivity and decrease the total wage bill. As the "progressive" part of the working class, the activists represent the "real" or "historic" interests of that class. They introduce the new attitude toward work in which the worker identifies himself with the increase of productivity demanded by the party and the planning authorities. By singling out the deceit which workers in "capitalist industry" had practiced on time-study engineers, Selbmann reveals the crucial point of attack. If the regime introduced new work-norms "from above," if it failed to organize their "acceptance from below," it would also run the risk of being deceived.[142] Consequently, the industrial relations of the East Zone are organized on the principle that this risk of deception must be avoided in a manner which leaves nothing to chance.

To prevent such deception it is necessary to undermine the natural solidarity of work groups,[143] as well as all tendencies toward collusion between workers, functionaries, and managers. The first line of approach consists in the material incentives I have described briefly. These incentives are supplemented, as we have seen, by constant publicity campaigns in which activists are personally eulogized while others are singled out for a detailed and equally public discussion of their failings. The isolation of the activists is buttressed further by their public identification with the party in the collective agreements, in the meetings of the

[142] It is instructive in this connection that the Politbureau utilized this distinction in its declaration concerning the "false" introduction of work-norms on June 17. "The increase of work-norms should not and cannot be carried out by administrative methods, but solely and entirely on the basis of conviction and voluntary action." See Der Volksaufstand vom 17. Juni, p. 46. The facts belie this declaration; they reveal as in other dictatorships that "conviction and voluntary action" on the part of the workers develop as a result of what Goebbels called "organized spontaneity," although genuine conviction may grow as a result of interaction among functionaries and activists.

[143] By "natural solidarity" I have reference to the development of shared understandings among the members of a work group, especially with regard to "becoming" or "unbecoming" conduct in the work situation. As the famous Hawthorne studies have shown, such understandings may lead to increased or to restricted output. In the present context such solidarity is especially important in connection with attempts to deceive time-study engineers, in order to avoid high work-norms. A number of studies have shown that these practices are widespread in American industry. The Communist "line" is to commend these practices as appropriate for the worker's struggle against the capitalist, but to condemn them and suppress them in the nationalized industries of the Soviet orbit.

work force, and in addition by the display of their portraits, by flags at their place of work as well as by the bestowal of honorary titles, documents, pins, medals, and prizes. Obviously, all these inducements are accompanied by a whole catalogue of penalties: public censure before an assembly of workers or on the bulletin board, reprimand, serious reprimand, notice to the family (presumably to induce pressure on the worker from his family), withdrawal of 50 per cent of the premium for three months, withdrawal of the entire premium for the same period, permanent reassignment to another job at lower pay, dismissal after proper notice, instant dismissal.[144]

Taken together, all these measures create a new class of activists, and one can only speculate about the consequences. It is probable that they help to impart a sense of thorough insecurity to all interpersonal relations. Functionaries and activists know that their every action is being watched by agents of the party, and they are likely to feel conspicuously identified in the face of a more or less hostile audience. In this environment of suspicion and hostility their actions are prompted alternately by their fear of the few and their fear of the many, by evasive maneuvers which enable them to abide by the letter but not by the spirit of party directives, and also by occasional attempts to "demonstrate" to fellow-workers that they are "regular guys"—when this can be done safely. Beyond that they are likely to fear each other which will keep some check on their evasions and quite an effective check on any efforts to develop solidarity, rather than "contact," with the masses. This manipulated imprisonment without bars is an essential element of the party's rule, for the party forces its functionaries and activists to come to terms with their permanent alienation from the work force at the same time that it urges them with unremitting insistence to strengthen their "contact with the masses." By so doing the party maximizes its managerial control over its functionaries at the same time that it obtains the cooperation of *individual* activists under conditions which ensure that they will remain as isolated from each other as they are isolated from their fellow-workers. Activists constitute a collective of individuals, who are all equally dependent upon the party for the satisfaction of their economic interests, but these interests do not result in a common understanding among them. In this way the party is able to

---

[144] And "instant dismissal" is often followed by an investigation of the case by the Security Police which may result in still greater penalties. The introduction of Soviet labor legislation would make these penalties applicable to all workers. To what extent they are already applied administratively and in the absence of enabling legislation it is difficult to say.

avoid that deception of the few by the many, which is a frequent by-product of the division of labor in economic enterprises; for it offers a premium to the rate-buster under conditions where all tacit discrimination of his fellow-workers against him only enhances the control of the party over him. Since the incentives for increased productivity are very high at the same time that all overt hostility against activists is effectively suppressed, it is apparent that the party's management of the work force rests upon the destruction of its potential leadership. This destruction is defended as the inevitable conflict between the "progressive section" of the working class and the large number of those workers who still retain remnants of a "capitalist consciousness," who have not yet developed the new "progressive" attitude toward human labor. It is essential to an understanding of Communist rule to see that this creation and manipulation of hostility between activists and workers is the fulcrum of its managerial practice and ideology.[145]

This hostility results from the pressure which the Politbureau and the Secretariat of the Central Committee exert upon all subordinate party functionaries, who in turn use all the means at their disposal in effecting a separation of the activists from the workers at large. This manipulation of pressures is officially related to the position of the socialist homeland, which is encircled by capitalist enemies, harassed by an economic blockade through which these enemies seek to destroy socialism, and endangered by the ever present threat of imperialist wars. The speed of the industrial development was, therefore, interpreted as the cornerstone of socialist construction and of the preservation of national independence. Hence, the actions of the Politbureau, which impose deprivations upon every citizen and crush all internal enemies, are explained as the only correct response to the dictates of the historical development. And the Communist interpretation of that development serves to simulate by ideological appeals the conditions of a permanent national emergency.

[145] It is tempting to speculate about the long-run effects of this approach in the case of Soviet Russia. Presumably, the activists become identified with the system which has provided them with their opportunities, and the syphoning off of the most active workers into an upper class tends to leave the remaining majority of workers an amorphous collective of individuals. Thus, the long-run effect of Communist rule almost reverses its short-run effect. Initially, the drive for productivity tends to create an amorphous collective of activists, while the remaining majority of workers retain their identification with each other. In the long run, however, the quest for the classless society ends in the destruction of the working class in whose name it was undertaken and in the creation of a new ruling "collective" in which the relations among individuals can no longer take place in privacy.

CHAPTER 7

Conclusion: Industrialization, Ideologies, and Social Structure

Since World War II American social scientists have become pre-occupied with the industrialization of underdeveloped areas. Considering the recent history of our disciplines, this is a relatively novel undertaking insofar as it involves the study of social change in complex social structures on a comparative basis. One approach to such a study consists in the selection of a social problem encountered in several societies but resolved differently in each. In this study I have used this approach by examining the authority relationship between employers and workers and the ideologies of management which justify that authority. This concluding chapter considers some implications of this analysis.

The first part summarizes the changes of ideology that have occurred in Anglo-American and in Russian civilization over a two-hundred year period. The second part deals with the historical significance of ideol-

[1] Revised text of the MacIver Lecture delivered before the District of Columbia Sociological Society, February 3, 1959. Reprinted from *American Sociological Review*, Vol. 24, No. 5, October, 1959.

ogies of management, and the third part with the theoretical implications of a study that treats such ideologies as an index of social structure. In the fourth part I turn to the problem of bureaucratization and to the difference between totalitarian and non-totalitarian forms of subordination in industry.

Changes in Ideology

At the inception of industrialization in England an ideology of traditionalism prevailed; John Stuart Mill called it the "theory of dependence." According to this view the laboring poor are children, who must be governed, who should not be allowed to think for themselves, who must perform their assigned tasks obediently and with alacrity, who must show deference to their superiors, and who—if they only conduct themselves virtuously—will be protected by their betters against the vicissitudes of life. This interpretation of authority is self-confirming and self-serving.[2] But it sets up the presumption that the dependence of the poor and the responsibility of the rich are the valid moral rules of the social order. In the course of industrial development these ideas were gradually modified. As the responsibility of the rich was increasingly rejected by the advocates of laissez-faire, the dependence of the poor was turned from an inevitable into a self-imposed fate. As it was "demonstrated" that the rich cannot care for the poor without decreasing the national wealth, it was also asserted that by abstinence and exertion the poor can better their lot. The same virtues which in the 18th century were extolled so that the lowly would not aspire above their station were praised by the middle of the 19th century because they enabled a man to raise himself by his own efforts.

In England, and even more in America, this praise of effort led toward the end of the 19th century to an apotheosis of the struggle for existence. The militant language of an ethics of the jungle was applied to the relations between employers and workers. Riches and poverty merely reflect differences of ability and effort. The employer's success is evidence of his fitness for survival, and as such justifies his absolute authority over the enterprise. This assertion of authority has a clear-cut meaning only as long as most managerial functions are in the hands of one man. The idea becomes ambiguous as the use of expertise in the management of enterprises increases and the managerial function be-

---

[2] The laboring poor are asked to prove their virtue by their obedience, but they are also told that their dependence results from a natural inferiority. Similarly, the ruling classes are said to be responsible for the deserving poor, and if they do not meet this responsibility, it is only, they say, because the poor who suffer are not deserving.

comes subdivided and specialized. Yet the idea of the employer's absolute authority over his enterprise coincided with the "scientific management" movement which sought to give him expert advice on what to do with that authority. It may be suggested, therefore, that the doctrines of Social Darwinism gradually lost their appeal, in part because changes in industrial organization gave rise to a changing imagery of men in industry. From the Gilded Age to the 1920's workers and managers were self-evident failures or successes in a struggle for survival in which they were the recalcitrant objects or the exasperated originators of managerial commands. Today they have become individuals—ingroups whose skills must be improved and allocated systematically and whose productivity must be maximized by appropriate attention to their psychological makeup. Thus, over the past two hundred years, managerial ideologies in Anglo-American civilization have changed from the "theory of dependence" to laissez-faire, to Social Darwinism, and finally to the "human relations" approach.

In the Russian development we also find the assertion of paternal authority and of child-like dependence, and in much the same terms as in England. But in Russia this ideology of traditionalism was a very different thing from what it was in England because of the Tsar's assertion of supreme authority over all the people. This authority remained intact regardless of how many privileges the Tsar granted to the landlords and regardless of how rarely he interfered in fact with the use and abuse of these privileges. Ideologically the Tsar maintained his preeminence through repeated assertions concerning his paternal care and responsibility for all of "his" people. Through repeated petitions and sporadic revolts the people used this Tsarist claim in order to obtain redress for their grievances against landlords and employers. Finally, because of the early centralization of authority under the Muscovite rulers, the whole distribution of wealth and rank among the aristocracy turned upon the competition for favors at the Court and hence reinforced the Tsar's supremacy.[3]

During the second half of the 19th century this pattern of Tsarist autocracy had far-reaching consequences. The dislocations incident to the emancipation of the serfs (1861) and the development of industry

[3] In Russia the landed aristocracy never succeeded in making itself the unavoidable intermediary between the ruler and the people in contrast with Western Europe, where the ruler's administrative and juridical authority in effect ended at the boundaries of the estate, though this contrast merely states the end-result of protracted struggles over the division of authority. Cf. Max Weber, *Wirtschaft und Gesellschaft*, Tuebingen: Mohr, 1925, II Chapter 7 and esp. pp. 720–723.

brought in their train assertions of absolute authority by the employers, efforts of the workers to organize themselves, and sporadic attempts of the government to regulate the relationship between them. Although ostensibly acting on an equitable basis, the government in fact supported the employers against the workers. Much of this is again broadly familiar from the English experience; but Russia's historical legacies prevented the shift in ideology which has been described for England. As long as Tsarist autocracy remained intact neither the rejection of responsibility by the Tsar and the ruling strata nor the demand for the self-dependence of the workers developed. Instead, the Tsar and his officials continued to espouse the ideology of traditionalism. Quite consistently, Tsarist officials sought to superintend both employers and workers in order to mitigate or suppress the struggles between them. That is, the officials aided *and* curbed the employers' exercise of authority as well as the workers' efforts to formulate grievances and organize protest movements.

Tsarist autocracy was overthrown in the Russian revolutions of 1905 and 1917. Although vast differences were brought about by the revolution, the managerial ideology of Tsarism lived on in a modified form. In theory, Tsarist officials had regarded employers and workers as equally subject to the will of the Tsar; loyal submission to that will was the mark of good citizenship. In theory, Lenin believed that all workers were equal participants in the management of industry and government; their loyal submission to the Communist party represented their best interest and expressed their sovereign will. The logic of Lenin's, as of the Tsarist position, is that under a sovereign authority the same person or organization can and should perform both subordinate and superordinate functions. For example, Soviet labor unions approach the ideal of workers' control of industry when they are called upon to participate in the management of industry. But they also function in a managerial capacity when they inculcate labor discipline among their members under the authoritative direction of the Communist Party.

Ideologically this position is defended on the ground that the party represents the historical interests of the proletariat against the short-run interests of individuals and factions. In this orientation one can still see survivals of Tsarist autocracy since all wisdom and responsibility reside in a small group or indeed in one man who, like the Tsar, knows better than private persons what is the good of all, and cannot but wish the well-being of the people. But there is also an important difference. The leaders of the Russian revolution were faced with the task of developing self-discipline and initiative among workers if a suitable industrial

work-force was to become available.[4]   They proceeded to inculcate these
qualities by the direct or indirect subordination of everyone to the discipline of the Communist party.   This policy continued the Tsarist tradition by making all matters the object of organizational manipulation
rather than of personal striving; but it also represented a break with the
past in that it was no longer restricted to personal submission.

Historical Significance of Ideological Change

What are the historical implications of this analysis of managerial
ideologies?   Ruling groups everywhere, including the rulers of developing industrial societies, justify their good fortune as well as the ill fortune of those subject to their authority.   Their self-serving arguments
may not appear as a promising field of research; in fact, the whole
development of industrialization has been accompanied by an intellectual
rejection of such ideologies as unworthy of consideration. Yet the fact
is that all industrialization involves the organization of enterprises in
which a few command and many obey; and the ideas developed by the
few and the many, I believe, may be considered a symptom of changing
class relations and hence as a clue to an understanding of industrial
societies.[5]

Historically, ideologies of management became significant in the transition from a pre-industrial to an industrial society.   The authority
exercised by employers was recognized as distinct from the authority of
government.   This was a novel experience even in Western Europe
where there was precedent for such autonomy in other institutions, because the industrial entrepreneurs were "new men" rather than a ruling
class buttressed by tradition.   This was also the period during which
the discipline of sociology originated.   Under the impact of the French
revolution society came to be conceived in terms of forces that are independent from, as well as antagonistic to, the formal institutions of the
body politic.   Some early elaborations of this key idea enable us to
see the historical significance of ideologies of management.

The authority of employers rests on the contractual acquisition of
property, which the 18th century philosophers made the conceptual
basis of the social order.   In Rousseau's view that order can be and
ought to be based on a general will which presupposes that the individual
acts for the whole community.   In such a society, as George Herbert
Mead has pointed out, ". . . the citizen can give laws only to the extent

---

[4] Lenin's statement that "the Russian is a bad worker" and his advocacy of the
Taylor system and of electrification as the road to socialism are indicative of the
fact that the problems of complex industrial organizations came to the fore at once.

[5] See above, pp. vii–viii, 1–2.

that his volitions are an expression of the rights which he recognizes in others, . . . [and] which the others recognize in him. . . ."⁶ This approach provides a model for a society based on consent so that the power of rule-making is exercised by all and for all. This foundation of society upon a "general will" was directly related to the institution of property. As Mead has stated,

> If one wills to possess that which is his own so that he has absolute control over it as property, he does so on the assumption that everyone else will possess his own property and exercise absolute control over it. That is, the individual wills his control over his property only in so far as he wills the same sort of control for everyone else over property.⁷

Thus, the idea of a reciprocal recognition of rights specifically presupposed the equality of citizens as property-owners.

This implication gave pause to some 18th and 19th century philosophers. They noted that the reciprocity of rights among property owners based on freedom of contract does not apply to the relations between employers and workers. As early as 1807 the German philosopher Hegel formulated the problematic nature of this relationship in a manner which anticipates the modern psychology of the self, just as Rousseau's "general will" anticipates the sociological analysis of interaction. Hegel maintains that men come to a recognition of themselves through a process whereby each accepts the self-recognition of the other and is in turn accepted by him. That is, each man's sense of identity depends upon his acceptance of the identity of others and upon their acceptance of himself. In Hegel's view this reciprocity is lacking in the relation between master and servant. The master does not act towards himself as he acts towards the servant; and the servant does not do towards others what his servitude makes him do against himself. In this way the mutuality of recognition is destroyed and the relations between master and servant become one-sided and unequal.⁸

In Western Europe this inequality of the employment-relationship coincided with the ideological and institutional decline of traditional subordination. Yet while the old justifications of subordination crumbled and new aspirations were awakened among the masses of the people,

---

⁶ George Herbert Mead, *Movements of Thought in the Nineteenth Century*, Chicago: University of Chicago Press, 1936, p. 21.

⁷ *Ibid*, p. 17.

⁸ Georg Friedrich Wilhelm Hegel, *Phänomenologie des Geistes*, Leipzig: Felix Mainer, 1928, pp. 143, 147. My paraphrasing attempts to convey Hegel's meaning without use of his language. The relevant passages are readily accessible in C. J. Friedrich, editor, *The Philosophy of Hegel*, New York: Modern Library, 1953, pp. 399–410.

their experience of inequality continued. According to Tocqueville this problem had a differential impact upon masters and servants. In the secret persuasion of his mind the master continues to think of himself as superior; but he no longer recognizes any paternal responsibilities toward the servant. Still, he wants his servants to be content with their servile condition. In effect, the master wishes to enjoy the age-old privileges without acknowledging their concomitant obligations; and the servant rebels against his subordination, which is no longer a divine obligation and is not yet perceived as a contractual obligation.

> Then it is that [in] the dwelling of every citizen . . . a secret and internal warfare is going on between powers ever rivals and suspicious of each other: the master is ill-natured and weak, the servant ill-natured and intractable; the one constantly attempts to evade by unfair restrictions his obligation to protect and to remunerate, the other his obligation to obey. The reins of domestic government dangle between them, to be snatched at by one or the other. The lines that divide authority from oppression, liberty from license, and right from might are to their eyes so jumbled together and confused that no one knows exactly what he is or what he may be or what he ought to be. Such a condition is not democracy, but revolution.[9]

In the 19th century men like Hegel, Tocqueville, and Lorenz von Stein pointed out that the spread of equalitarian ideas was causing a transition in the relations between masters and servants. This transition may be called a crisis of aspirations. In Tocqueville's words the servants "consent to serve and they blush to obey. . . . [They] rebel in their hearts against a subordination to which they have subjected themselves. . . . They are inclined to consider him who orders them as an unjust usurper of their own rights."[10] As a consequence most European countries witnessed the rise of a "fourth estate" which struggled against existing legal liabilities and for basic civil rights, above all the right to suffrage. In a parliamentary debate on Chartism, Disraeli remarked that this struggle was invested with a degree of sentiment usually absent from merely economic or political contests. To the extent that such complex movements can be characterized by a common denominator this sentiment referred, I think, to the workers' quest for a public recognition of their equal status as citizens.[11] Where this and

[9] Alexis de Tocqueville, *Democracy in America*, New York: Vintage Books, 1945, II, p. 195. Some phrases in the preceding paragraph are also taken from this chapter of Tocqueville's work.

[10] *Ibid.*

[11] See above, pp. 34–46, 150–162. I deal with this aspect in more detail in "The Lower Classes in the Age of Democratic Revolution." *Industrial Relations* (forthcoming).

other civil rights became accepted, such recognition compensated for the continued social and economic subordination of the workers and thus assuaged the crisis of aspirations. Moreover, the political utilization of these civil rights could lead to a recognition of basic social rights which today is embodied in the institutions of social welfare characteristic of many Western democracies.[12] The initial crisis of aspirations continued, on the other hand, where civil rights were rejected or where their acceptance was postponed for too long, leading either to an eventual revolutionary upheaval as in Tsarist Russia, or to a more or less damaging exacerbation of class-relations as in Italy and France.

My hypothesis is that the break with the traditional subordination of the people gave rise to a generic problem of many industrial societies.[13] The question of 19th century Europe concerned the terms on which a society undergoing industrialization will incorporate its newly recruited industrial work force within the economic and political community of the nation. Ideologies of management are significant because they contribute to each country's answer to this question. In England the workers were invited to become their own masters, if they did not wish to obey; in Russia they were told that their subordination was less onerous than it seemed, because their own superiors were also servants of the almighty Tsar.

Theoretical Significance of Ideologies

What are the theoretical implications of this approach? Ideologies of management may be considered indexes of the flexibility or rigidity with which the dominant groups in the two countries were prepared to meet the challenge from below. This "preparedness" or collective tendency to act is analogous to the concept of character-structure in the individual: it may be defined as an "inner capacity" for recreating similar lines of action under more or less identical conditions.[14] The ideol-

[12] For a perceptive analysis of this development see T. H. Marshall, *Citizenship and Social Class,* Cambridge: At the University Press, 1950, Chapter 1. The statement in the text refers specifically to England. Social rights have been instituted in other ways, sometimes in order to withhold the establishment of civil rights as in Imperial Germany.

[13] An expanded statement of this point will be found in my article "A Study of Managerial Ideologies," *Economic Development and Cultural Change,* 5 (January, 1957), pp. 118–128.

[14] The quoted phrase occurs in Burckhardt's definition of the objective of culture-history, which "goes to the heart of past mankind [because] it declares what mankind *was, wanted, thought, perceived,* and *was able to do.* In this way culture-history deals with what is constant, and in the end this constant appears greater and more important than the momentary, a quality appears to be greater and more instructive than an action. For actions are only the individual expressions of a

ogies of management, which reflect this "inner capacity," naturally provoke new challenges and these in turn lead to new managerial responses, so that at the societal level there is a replication of the action-reaction process so typical of interaction among individuals.

An analysis of this process must deal with those explicitly formulated ideas that are as close as possible to the collective experience of employers and workers. This social philosophizing of and for the ordinary man as a participant occurs at a level somewhere between his attitudes as an individual and the sophisticated formulations of the social theorist. Such philosophizing is exemplified by what Andrew Ure wrote in his *Philosophy of Manufacturers* or by what the publicity-men for General Motors say in their pamphlet *Man to Man on the Job*. However, the serious analysis of such documents is at variance with the prevailing tendency to dismiss them as obviously biased and hence unworthy of consideration on their own terms. Marx, it may be recalled, reserved some of his choicest invective for his characterization of Ure's book, and in this respect Marx was a forerunner of the intellectuals born in the 1850's and 1860's. Freud, Durkheim, Pareto, and others shared with Marx the search for some underlying principle or force that could explain the manifest beliefs and actions making up the external record of individual and collective behavior.[15] Many writers of this generation were less interested in what a man said, than in why he said it. Accordingly, ideologies of management might be dismissed because they *merely* express a class-interest, or because they do not reveal the *real* attitudes of the employers, or because they disguise *actual* exploitative practices, or because all this talk tells us nothing about man's behavior or about his personality structure. These various objections have in common an intellectual preoccupation with covert forces that can explain the manifest content of the social world.

Modern social science owes to this intellectual tradition many important insights, but also many of its aberrations. Where the phenomena of the social world are treated merely as the reflection of "hidden forces," speculation easily becomes uncontrolled, with the result that observable evidence is dismissed from consideration as being "irrelevant" or "uninteresting" on theoretical grounds. The difficulty is familiar in Marx's theory of history which encouraged him to treat whole series of facts as epiphenomena, such as the "false consciousness" of the workers

---

certain inner capacity, which is always able to recreate these same actions. Goals and presuppositions are, therefore, as important as events." See Jacob Burckhardt, *Griechische Kulturgeschichte*, Stuttgart: Kroener, 1952, Vol. I, p. 6.

[15] Cf. H. Stuart Hughes, *Consciousness and Society*, New York: Knopf, 1958, which gives a perceptive analysis of this "generation."

that was bound to be superseded in the course of history. Similarly, the Freudian approach tends to devalue a behavioristic study of social life because it deals with the appearance rather than the underlying motivations of social action. Again, the use of organic analogies in the study of society treats all actions as dependent adjustments to other actions (or environmental conditions); consequently this approach devalues all deliberate and all innovative activity, since upon analysis such activity will be revealed as yet another dependent adjustment. In in-expert hands all of these approaches lead to a cavalier construction of the evidence which can always be more easily imputed to the "underlying determinants" than analyzed in detail on its own ground.

Yet human experience occurs at this phenomenological level—and the study of ideologies of management illustrates that it can also provide an approach to our understanding of the social structure.[16] The managerial interpretations of the authority relationship in economic enterprises together with the workers' contrast-conception concerning their collective position in an emerging industrial society constitute a composite image of class relations which has changed over time and which also differs from country to country. This aspect of the changing social structure may be studied by examining each ideological position in terms of its logical corollaries as these relate to the authority of the employers and in a wider sense to the class position of employers and workers in the society. Where these corollaries create major problems for the complacent self-interest of the group, one may expect the development of tensions, and perhaps of change, ideologically and institutionally.[17]

Such ideologies, and this is a second level of analysis, are in part expediential rationalizations for the problems confronting the entrepreneur, and in part the result of historically cumulative response-patterns among social groups. In this way ideologies are formulated through the constant interplay between current contingencies and historical legacies.

[16] By "ideologies" I do not refer to attitudes of the type that can be elicited in a questionnaire study, but to the "constant process of formulation and reformulation by which spokesmen identified with a social group seek to articulate what they sense to be its shared understandings." See above, p. xii. I call these articulations "ideologies" in the specific sense of "ideas considered in the context of group-action." All ideas may be analyzed from this viewpoint; hence I depart from the identification of "ideologies" with false or misleading ideas.

[17] For example, at the turn of the century American employers asserted their absolute authority over the workers but this assertion lacked content until the bureaucratization of industry brought to the fore experts who worked out methods for the exercise of authority. Again, the Tsar's assertion of authority over all the people inadvertently encouraged the peasants to appeal to the Tsar for redress of grievances. This procedure is adapted from that used by Max Weber in his sociology of religion.

As Marx put it, "men make their own history," but they do so "under circumstances directly given and transmitted from the past." (Marxian dogmatism consistently sacrificed the first to the second part of this generalization.[18]) Accordingly, ideologies of management can be explained only in part as rationalizations of self-interest; they also result from the legacy of institutions and ideas which is "adopted" by each generation much as a child "adopts" the grammar of his native language. Historical legacies are thus a part of the social structure: they should not be excluded from a discipline that focusses attention upon the persistence of group-structures. In the following section an attempt is made to show the link between historical legacies and the structure of industrial societies by relating ideologies of management to the bureaucratization of industry.

Ideologies, Industrial Bureaucracy, and Totalitarianism

Since the 18th century Anglo-American and Russian civilizations have witnessed a growing managerial concern with the attitudes as well as the productivity of workers. It is possible to relate this change of ideology to a large number of the developments which comprise the transition from an early to a mature industrial society. The changing structure of industrial organizations was only one of these developments. Yet the bureaucratization of economic enterprises is of special importance for any attempt to "interpret the difference of fact and ideology between a totalitarian and nontotalitarian form of subordination in economic enterprises."[19] Bureaucratization is also especially suitable for a comparative study of authority relations in industry, since it involves processes that are directly comparable in two such different civilizations as England and Russia. This choice of focus deliberately eschews a

---

[18] The sentence immediately following this quotation reads: "The tradition of all the dead generations weighs like a nightmare on the brain of the living." See Karl Marx, *The 18th Brumaire of Louis Bonaparte,* New York: International Publishers, n.d., p. 13. I do not accept this polemical exaggeration, since traditions are enabling as well as disabling, but the emphasis upon the impact of cultural tradition on current ideologies is more in line with the facts than the effort to explain the latter solely in terms of the problems the businessman encounters in his work. Such an interpretation leads to an elimination of ideological changes, and of differences between ideologies, since all ideologies are in this sense responses to the strains endemic in modern society. Cf. Francis X. Sutton et al., *The American Business Creed,* Cambridge: Harvard University Press, 1956, *passim,* where the change of business ideologies over time is denied and where these ideologies are explained in exactly the same terms as nationalism and anti-capitalism. See also the comments of Leland Jenks, "Business Ideologies," *Explorations of Entrepreneurial History,* 10 (October, 1957), pp. 1–7.

[19] See above, p. x.

comprehensive theory of society in favor of selecting a problem which, if suitable for comparative analysis, will also lead to an analysis of social structures. For, if comparable groups in different societies confront and over time resolve a common problem, then a comparative analysis of their divergent resolutions will reveal the divergence of social structures in a process of change.[20]

Problems of a systematic management of labor come to the fore where the increasing complexity of economic enterprises makes their operation more and more dependent upon an *ethic of work performance.* This ethic involves a degree of steady intensity of work, reasonable accuracy, and a compliance with general rules and specific orders that falls somewhere between blind obedience and unpredictable caprice. Where personal supervision is replaced by impersonal rules the efficiency of an organization will vary with the degree to which these attributes of work-performance are realized, and this realization is part of the on-going bureaucratization of economic enterprises. That is to say, management subjects the conditions of employment to an impersonal systematization, while the employees seek to modify the implementation of the rules as their personal interests and their commitment (or lack of commitment) to the goals of the organization dictate. As everyone knows, there is no more effective means of organizational sabotage than a letter-perfect compliance with all the rules and a consistent refusal of the employees to use their own judgment. "Beyond what commands can effect and supervision can control, beyond what incentives can induce and penalties prevent, there exists an exercise of discretion important even in relatively menial jobs, which managers of economic enterprises seek to enlist for the achievement of managerial ends."[21] In the literature on organizations this exercise of discretion by subordinates is known by a number of terms: Veblen called it the "withdrawal of efficiency;" Max Weber referred to it as the bureaucratic tendency towards secrecy; Herbert

---

[20] Here again I am indebted to the work of Max Weber, although more to what he did in his own studies than to what he wrote about them in his methodology. See my *Max Weber, An Intellectual Portrait,* New York: Doubleday, 1960, Chapter 8.

[21] See above, p. 251. To avoid a possible misunderstanding I add that this assertion, which is elaborated in *ibid.,* pp. 244–251, is in my judgment compatible with the endeavor to put managerial decision-making on a more scientific basis. The substitution of machine methods for manual operations is obviously an ongoing process that has greatly curtailed the areas of possible discretion, although machine methods also create new opportunities for discretionary judgments. But while these methods and organizational manipulations may curtail and reallocate the areas in which discretion is possible or desired, and may in this way achieve greater efficiency, they cannot, I believe, eliminate discretion.

Simon might call it the "zone of non-acceptance." I have suggested the phrase "strategies of independence" so as to get away from the negative connotations of the other terms, since the exercise of discretion may serve to achieve, as well as to subvert, the goals of an organization.

Now, the great difference between totalitarian and nontotalitarian forms of subordination consists in the managerial handling of this generic attribute of all authority relations. The historical legacies of some Western countries have encouraged management to presuppose the existence of a common universe of discourse between superiors and subordinates, and this presupposition is related to the successful resolution of the crisis of aspirations. From the evangelism and the tough-minded laissez-faire approach of 18th century England to the latest refinement of the "human relations" approach, managerial appeals have been addressed to the good faith of subordinates in order to enlist their cooperation. Whether such good faith existed is less important than that such appeals were made, though it is probable that in England and the United States large masses of workers in one way or another accepted managerial authority as legitimate even if they were indifferent to, or rejected, the managerial appeals themselves.[22] In Russia, on the other hand, historical legacies did *not* encourage management (under the Tsars) to presuppose the existence of a common universe of discourse between superiors and subordinates. From the time of Peter the Great to the period of rapid industrial growth in the last decades preceding World War I managerial appeals were addressed to the workers' duty of obedience towards all those in positions of authority. Whether or not the workers actually developed a sense of duty, the appeals presupposed that they had not. Accordingly, officials and managers did not rely on the good faith among their subordinates, but attempted instead to eliminate the subordinates' strategies of independence.

This managerial refusal to accept the tacit evasion of rules and norms or the uncontrolled exercise of judgment is related to a specific type of bureaucratization which constitutes the fundamental principle of totalitarian government. In such a regime the will of the highest party authorities is absolute in the interest of their substantive objectives. The party may disregard not only all formal procedures by which laws are validated but also its own previous rulings; and where norms may be changed at a moment's notice, the rule of law is destroyed. Totalitarianism also does away with the principle of a single line of authority. Instead of relying on an enactment of laws and on the supervision of

[22] Cf. above, pp. 248–249, for a fuller statement.

their execution from the top, totalitarian regimes use the hierarchy of the party in order to expedite and control at each step the execution of orders through the regular administrative channels. This may be seen as the major device by which such regimes seek to prevent officials from escaping inspection while compelling them to use their expertise in an intensified effort to implement the orders of the regime. A totalitarian government is based, therefore, on two interlocking hierarchies of authority. The work of every factory, of every governmental office, of every unit of the army or the secret police, as well as every cultural or social organization, is programmed, coordinated, and supervised by some agency of government. But it is also propagandized, expedited, criticized, spied upon, and incorporated in special campaigns by an agency of the totalitarian party, which is separately responsible to the higher party authorities.

The rationale of this principle of a double government can be stated within the framework of Max Weber's analysis of bureaucracy. An ideally functioning bureaucracy in his sense is the most efficient method of solving large-scale organizational tasks. But this is true only *if* these tasks involve a more or less stable orientation towards norms which seek to maintain the rule of law and to achieve an equitable administration of affairs. These conditions are absent where tasks are assigned by an omnipotent *and* revolutionary authority. Under the simulated combat conditions of a totalitarian regime the norms that govern conduct do not stay put for any length of time, although each norm in turn will be the basis of an unremitting drive for prodigies of achievement. In response, subordinates will tend to use their devices of concealment for the sake of systematic, if tacit, strategies of independence. They will do so not only for reasons of convenience, but because the demands made upon them by the regime are "irrational" from the viewpoint of expert knowledge and systematic procedure.[23] The party, on the other hand, seeks to prevent the types of concealment that make such collective strategies possible by putting every worker and official under maximum pressure to utilize their expertise to the fullest extent. This is the rationale of a double hierarchy of government, which places a party

[23] Hence they will do so even for the purpose of achieving the objectives of the party itself. Cf. Joseph Berliner, *Factory and Manager in the USSR,* Cambridge: Harvard University Press, 1957, which documents that the most successful Soviet managers use the systematic subversion of authoritative commands for the purpose of realizing the ends of these commands as well as for their personal convenience. This fact suggests that "good faith" can be inculcated in many ways, even by the systematic distrust of all subordinates, provided of course that the distrust has a higher rationale, such as the utopian and nationalist ideology of Russian Communism.

functionary at the side of every work unit in order to prevent concealment and to apply pressure. The two hierarchies would be required, even if all key positions in government and industry were filled by party functionaries. For a functionary turned worker or official would still be responsible for "overfulfilling" the plan, while the new party functionary would still be charged with keeping that official under pressure and surveillance.[24]

In this way totalitarianism replaces the old system of stratification by a new one based on criteria of activism and party orthodoxy. The ethic of work performance on which this regime relies is not the product of century-long growth as in the West, but of material incentives and of a political supervision that seeks to prevent evasion from below as well as from above. For example, the collective "bargaining" agreements of Soviet industry are in fact declarations of loyalty in which individuals and groups pledge themselves publicly to an overfulfillment of the plan, while the subsequent organization of public confessionals, the manipulation of status differences between activists and others, the principle of collective leadership, and further devices seek to maximize performance and prevent the "withdrawal of efficiency." The individual subordinate is surrounded almost literally. Aside from ordinary incentives he is controlled by his superior and by the party agitator who stands at the side of his superior, but he is also controlled "from below" in the sense that the social pressures of his peer group are manipulated by party agitators and their agents. This institutionalization of suspicion and the consequent elimination of privacy are justified on the ground that the party "represents" the masses, spearheads the drive for Russian industrialization, and leads the cause of world communism.

Summary

The purpose of this conclusion has been to state the case for a comparative analysis of social structures, which pays attention to the historical continuity of societies as well as to the concatenation of group structures and deliberate, self-interested action in the process of social change. In lieu of abstract considerations I have tried to make this case by analyzing some implications of ideologies of management in the course of industrialization.

The change of ideologies of management during the last two centuries

---

[24] For a more generalized treatment of this approach to totalitarianism, cf. Bendix, "The Cultural and Political Setting of Economic Rationality in Western and Eastern Europe," in Gregory Grossman, editor, *Value and Plan: Economic Calculation and Organization in Eastern Europe,* Berkeley: University of California Press, 1960.

in Anglo-American and in Russian civilization was similar in so far as it can be characterized as an increased managerial concern with the attitudes of workers that presumably account for their differential productivity. This overall similarity coincides, however, with a fundamental divergence. In Western civilization the authority relations between employers and workers remained a more or less autonomous realm of group activity even where the "human relations" approach has replaced the earlier individualism. In Russia, the employment relationship has been subjected throughout to a superordinate authority which regulated the conduct of employers and workers and which could transform superiors into subordinates or (more rarely subordinates into superiors, when governmental policies seemed to warrant such action.

This comparison of ideologies of management is significant for specific historical reasons in addition to the fact that authority relations in economic enterprises are a universal attribute of industrialization and hence lend themselves to a comparative analysis. Ideologies of management became significant when the equalitarianism of property owners, brought to the fore by the French revolution and by the legal codifications which followed, was contrasted with the inequality of the employment relationship. A heightened awareness of this inequality coincided with the decline of a traditional subordination of the lower classes and hence with a rise of aspirations for social and political as well as for legal equality. In England these demands for equal rights of citizenship on the part of the lower classes eventuated in a painful but peaceful reconstitution of class relations; in Russia, the same demands were rejected and finally led to the revolutions of 1905 and 1917.

The comparative study of ideologies of management is of theoretical as well as of historical interest. Such ideologies may be considered indexes of a readiness to act which together with the ideological responses of other groups, can provide us with a clue to the class relations of a society. Ideologies, it is assumed, are an integral part of culture, which should be analyzed on its own terms as an index of the social structure, much as the neurotic symptoms of an individual are analyzed as an index of his personality. It is further assumed that such ideologies are expediential rationalizations of what are taken to be the material interests of a group, but that such rationalizations tend to be circumscribed by the historical legacies which are a part of a country's developing social structure.

Although ideologies of management can be treated as a clue to class relations, it is also worthwhile to relate them to other aspects of the social structure. One such aspect, which is especially suitable for a comparison of totalitarian and non-totalitarian regimes, is the fact that all industrial enterprises undergo a process of bureaucratization and all bureaucracy involves the use of discretion in the execution of commands. Comparison between the Anglo-American and the Russian tradition reveals that in the two cases managerial appeals have differed in terms of whether or not they have presupposed the good faith of subordinates. Where that supposition has not been made, the drive for industrialization takes the specific form of a double hierarchy of government which is designed to apply maximum pressure on subordinates and to forestall their evasion of commands by supplementing executive with political controls at every point in the chain of command.

Both English and American and Russian industrialization have been marked by bureaucratization, and bureaucratization certainly threatens the development of initiative.[25] But the Soviet case also illustrates that this threat may provoke counter measures. One might speak of an institutionalization of initiative in the totalitarian party and one can speculate that the dynamic drive of the Soviet regime might be jeopardized by too much relaxation of a Cold War which appears to justify that drive. This is, I submit, the new context in which the comparative study of ideologies of management will continue to be an intellectual challenge.

[25] Cf. Joseph Schumpeter, *Capitalism, Socialism and Democracy*, New York: Harper, 1950 (Torchbook edition, 1962), where this theme is elaborated.

Credits

Below are listed the several publishing firms from whom permission has been received to reprint passages from their publications. Permission to use these materials in the present work is gratefully acknowledged.

Publisher	Author	Title	Pages
George Allen & Unwin, Ltd.	G. C. Allen	The Industrial Development of Birmingham and the Black Country (1929)	146
	Marian Bowley	Nassau Senior and Classical Economics (1937)	290–292
American Management Assoc.	American Management Review	Vol. XII, April, 1923 November, 1923 Vol. XIII, March, 1924 October, 1924 May, 1924	7–8 7–8 9 18 6–7
	Ernest Dale	The Development of Foremen in Management	9
	American Management Review	Vol. XVI, March, 1927 Vol. XXIV, June, 1935 Vol. XXVI, October, 1937 Vol. XXXIII, February, 1944 March, 1944	77 172 340 42 75
American Psychological Assoc.	E. H. Fish	"Human Engineering" in Journal of Applied Psychology, Vol. I (1917)	174
Association Press	Lowell Thomas	In the Introduction to Dale Carnegie, Public Speaking and Influencing Men of Business (1938)	x
University of Birmingham	Erich Roll	An Early Experiment in Industrial Organization, Being a History of the Firm of Boulton & Watt, 1775–1805 (1930)	221–222 250–251
	E. Lipson	The History of the Woolen and Worsted Industries (1921)	176
Adams & Charles Black, Ltd.	M. G. Jones	The Charity School Movement (1938)	36, 74, and 74–75
Cambridge University Press	John S. Curtiss	Church and State in Russia (1940)	30
Columbia University Press	G. M. Trevelyan	The Life of John Bright (1913)	17, 90–91, 113–114, 184
Constable & Co., Ltd.	V. O. Kluchevsky	A History of Russia (1912), Vols. III, IV	148–149, 132, 143, 224, 227, and 236
J. M. Dent & Sons, Ltd. E. P. Dutton & Co., Inc.	James Mavor	An Economic History of Russia (1914), Vols. I, II	25, 454–455
Drake Son & Parton	Sidney and Beatrice Webb	English Poor Law History, Part II: The Last Hundred Years (1929)	14–15
Fortune Magazine	—	"The Crown Princes of Business" (October 1953)	153

451

Publisher	Author	Title	Pages
Harper & Brothers	Joseph Schumpeter	Capitalism, Socialism and Democracy (1950)	132
Harvard University Press	Frederick W. Taylor	Scientific Management (1947)	42
	Elton Mayo	The Social Problems of an Industrial Civilization (1945)	72–73, 40–44, 120, 122, 84–85, and 112
	T. N. Whitehead	Leadership in a Free Society (1936)	98–99, 110
	Ruth Fischer	Stalin and German Communism (1948)	451–452
Houghton, Mifflin & Co.	Hugo Muensterberg	Psychology and Industrial Efficiency (1913)	308
International Publishers	V. I. Lenin	State and Revolution (1932)	37
		Selected Works, (n.d.), Vol. IX	9–10, 24–25, 413–414
		Vol. VII	332–333, 345
Alfred A. Knopf	A. de Tocqueville	Democracy in America (1954), Vol. II	168–171, 261, 194–195
The Macmillan Company	Witt Bowden	Industrial Society in England Towards the End of the 18th Century (1925)	40, 42–43, 155, 156–157
Manchester University Press	George Unwin, Arthur Hulme and George Taylor	Samuel Oldknow and the Arkwrights (1924)	205
	T. S. Ashton	An Eighteenth Century Industrialist: Peter Stubs of Warrington, 1756–1806 (1939)	28–29
	T. S. Ashton	Iron and Steel in the Industrial Revolution (1951)	209–210
	Arthur Redford	Labour Migration in England, 1800–50 (1926)	15, 157
McGraw-Hill Book Co.	Ross Young	Personnel Manual for Executives (1947)	177
National Association of Mfg.	—	Industry Believes (1953)	7–8
University of North Carolina Press	P. Sargent Florence	The Logic of British and American Industry (1953)	148, 157, 163
R. Oldenburg	Franziska Baumgarten	Arbeitswissenschaft und Psychotechnik in Russland (1924)	13, 111–112
Oxford University Press	James Boswell	The Life of Samuel Johnson (1952)	182
	H. H. Gerth and C. Wright Mills, eds.	From Max Weber: Essays in Sociology (1946)	271
Princeton University Press	John Perry	"The State of Russia" in Peter Putnam, ed., Seven Britons in Imperial Russia (1952)	61
Public Affairs Press	A. Arakelian	Industrial Management in the USSR (1950)	123, 145, 160
Rinehart & Co.	Karl Polanyi	The Great Transformation (1944)	79
St. Martin's Press	Colin Clark	Conditions of Economic Progress (1951)	404, 408–409, 413
Humboldt Verlag	Fritz Croner	Die Angestellten in der Modernen Gesellschaft (1954)	103, 120–121
Yale University Press	George Vernadsky	The Mongols and Russia (Vol. III of A History of Russia, 1953)	389–390

Author Index *

* Italicized numbers indicate pages on which full publication references appear for the works cited.

Subject Index